THE SPECTRE OF WAR

The Spectre
of War

INTERNATIONAL COMMUNISM AND
THE ORIGINS OF WORLD WAR II

JONATHAN HASLAM

PRINCETON UNIVERSITY PRESS

PRINCETON & OXFORD

Published by Princeton University Press
41 William Street, Princeton, New Jersey 08540
6 Oxford Street, Woodstock, Oxfordshire OX20 1TR

press.princeton.edu

All Rights Reserved

Library of Congress Cataloging-in-Publication Data

Names: Haslam, Jonathan, author.
Title: The spectre of war : international communism and the origins of
    World War II / Jonathan Haslam.
Description: Princeton : Princeton University Press, 2021. | Series: Princeton
    studies in international history and politics | Includes bibliographical
    references and index.
Identifiers: LCCN 2020035229 | ISBN 9780691182650 (hardback) |
    ISBN 9780691219110 (ebook)
Subjects: LCSH: Communism—Europe—History—20th century. |
    Social stratification—Europe—History—20th century. | Propaganda,
    Communist—Europe—History—20th century. | Europe—Politics and
    government—20th century. | Europe—Foreign relations—20th century. |
    Europe—History—20th century.
Classification: LCC HX238 .H37 2021 | DDC 940.53/112–dc23
LC record available at https://lccn.loc.gov/2020035229

British Library Cataloging-in-Publication Data is available

Editorial: Bridget Flannery-McCoy and Alena Chekhanov
Production Editorial: Kathleen Cioffi
Text and Jacket Design: Karl Spurzem
Production: Danielle Amatucci
Publicity: Maria Whelan and Kate Farquhar-Thomsen

Jacket image: Alfonso Sánchez Portela, *Proclamation of the Second Spanish Republic, April 14, 1931*. Courtesy of Museo Nacional Centro de Arte, Reina Sofía, Madrid, Spain

This book has been composed in Arno

Printed on acid-free paper. ∞

Printed in the United States of America

10 9 8 7 6 5 4 3 2 1

CONTENTS

     Conclusions   380

                              Notes   387
                        Bibliography   449
                          Index   465

PREFACE

The world we live in was shaped by the Second World War. Understanding what happened and why still matters. The lessons have still to be learned.

   None of us turns to history with an entirely open mind, however. For those of us who were children in the Britain of the early 1950s, the war was still very much a part of our lives and our consciousness. London was still in part a bombed-out city. The massive concrete anti-tank blocks scattered along stretches of the south coast were still visible. Every so often beaches had to be closed because unexploded bombs had been uncovered by the tide. Our aged neighbours still had an air-raid shelter under the garden rockery. The lead-lined windows in my bedroom had been partially blown in by a blast of spare ordnance dropped by the Luftwaffe to lighten the load before its bombers made the sea-crossing to occupied Europe. Teachers at school carried their military rank; one was absent for days on end from bouts of malaria. We read war comics in black and white; the Germans were our enemies. Granny, who had worked as a volunteer in the London auxiliary fire brigade (1916–18), refused to discuss the last war, or the one before that or, indeed, the South African War, where she had lost a brother. Grandpa's hearing was bad from the big guns and he had been blinded for nearly a year from mustard gas in the Great War. Yet somehow he hated only the French. My great aunt at Belsize Park regularly rehearsed for us what had happened when a V-1 rocket appeared out of nowhere and the buzz suddenly stopped, everyone waiting for the inevitable explosion. An uncle remembered trying to stop Belgian peasants from taking pot-shots at German paratroopers in 1940 as though out hunting game on the flats; later, as a member of the Royal Army Medical Corps in the Pacific, he recalled the horror of re-entering hospitals with patients disembowelled in their beds by the Japanese when they overran allied positions. I remember a father who fell curiously silent, with memories he could not share; a mother who had broken down and fled the Blitz to join the land army in the countryside.

As children, our thoughts, while vastly expanding in extent and depth, are rapidly taken up and developed within family and society, as we are not just educated in facts, but also indoctrinated into every kind of myth. The idea that we can objectively learn lessons from history must therefore be taken with a pinch of salt, though we should never be deterred from trying.

The story of the origins of the Second World War has long been used by politicians as a dramatic allegory for the international crises of the present. The stark lesson drummed into the immediate postwar generation—certainly in Britain, where the consequences of naïveté were the most severe, but also in France, which suffered so much from the failure of Britain to lead in the right direction, and in the United States, which at first stood aside but eventually had to carry the burden—was that appeasing dictators only whets their appetite.

Subsequently the lesson was successfully applied in the Cold War against the Soviet Union, where the command economy ultimately collapsed, squeezed by competition with the United States. But—and this too should not be forgotten—it was equally disastrously misapplied, most notably against Nasser of Egypt by Sir Anthony Eden in 1956. No doubt both the use and the abuse of history will continue.

There is, however, another crucial lesson from the story that has all too frequently been overlooked. Our understanding of international relations in the twentieth century cannot be reduced to the simplicity of traditional balance-of-power politics without doing serious damage to the truth. The indifferent application of our understanding of inter-state relations in one epoch to an entirely different time is not a sound recipe for success, as historian A.J.P. Taylor discovered when he moved from analysing the nineteenth century to explaining a very different twentieth century.[1]

The Bolshevik revolution of 1917 changed the conduct of international relations. It shook the foundations of the European states system. It was assumed that although the allied war of intervention had failed to strangle the rebellious infant in its cradle, Soviet Russia would, under sustained pressure to conform from its more powerful neighbours, sooner or later miraculously transform into a "normal" country. This assumption grew out of the determinism of the classical economics which lay at the roots of nineteenth-century liberalism in Britain. It gave the predominantly liberal officials in the Foreign Office a comforting rationale for the much favoured policy of doing nothing—or "watchful waiting", as they preferred to call it.

Thus the exile of Trotsky in 1929 after the triumph of Stalin was completely misunderstood. The only real difference between the two in terms of international relations was that whereas, on the whole, Trotsky believed that foreigners had the capacity to make their own revolutions, because the capitalist order was inherently unstable, Stalin equally firmly believed that foreigners were generally too incompetent to manage it without direct military assistance from the Soviet Union, because the underlying conditions were by no means as propitious as Trotsky supposed. Germany was not the only instance of this.

Though the importance of such world shattering events as the Bolshevik revolution has never been in question, historians of international relations have since the 1960s found themselves under attack. Social historians—far removed from scenes of battle—casually dismissed the value of military history, diplomatic history and the history of political thought as old hat. Instead they advanced the untested proposition that social history was "the most important area of research in history" and that all future historical study should be centred on it.[2] That never happened, however, because it is inherently preposterous to claim that one branch of history, in this case the social, holds all the answers. And even to say that it is primary is merely bold assertion, nothing more.[3] On the other hand, it was justifiable to challenge the complacency predominant among notable historians of international relations.

Buttressed by knights of the realm—the type who were usually chosen to write elegant official histories or edit Foreign Office documents with due diligence, such as Sir Llewellyn Woodward or Sir Charles Webster—diplomatic history certainly offered tempting targets to snipers from opposing camps. Reviewing a meticulous account of the Manchurian crisis (1931)—Japan's assault on China—that was based almost entirely on British and American diplomatic archives, the Sinologist John Gittings took its author to task for ignoring Chinese sources available even in English. The target of his attack, Christopher Thorne, whose scholarship had delivered a penetrating critique of Britain's appeasement of Hitler's Germany, was accused of bending over backwards to excuse the British and the Americans for not standing up to Japan. "Diplomacy is often said to be the art of the possible", Gittings wrote. "It is perhaps less that than it is the art of asserting one's country has done all that is possible when it has done nothing at all." Having thus censured Thorne, Gittings walloped a very hard ball into an open goal. He caustically alluded to "one of those rare passages where the diplomatic historian allows the fundamental assumptions on which he operates to become explicit, too often illustrating his essential subservience to the myth-making of the official diplomats".[4] Ouch! But was Thorne an exception to the rule or was he fairly typical?

Zara Steiner's massive second volume in her Oxford history of Europe, *The Triumph of the Dark: European International History 1933–1939*, came under fire more recently. One assertive reviewer excoriated it as "old-fashioned international history, barely discussing the ideological and social forces lying behind diplomacy".[5] Yet Steiner did deliberately call attention to the fact that "ideological assumptions affected the way statesmen and their advisers saw the world about them. It mattered that Neville Chamberlain hated war and believed that wasteful arms races led to conflict. He assumed that others shared his views."[6]

But there is more to add. Important though he was, Chamberlain as prime minister was not alone in his beliefs, and they went much further than an instinctive aversion to war. Steiner, however, offered no broader consideration of the attitudes and prejudices prevailing at the top of society: not just among ministers, but also in the assumptions, written and unwritten, of the Foreign Office clerks whose minutes and despatches are so frequently cited. This was, after all, a society run by a homogeneous caste who had, with very few exceptions, attended the leading private schools and university at Oxford or Cambridge. Steiner herself was as a novice researcher the awkward target of no doubt well-meant but patronising remarks from those such as Sir Orme Sargent, who agreed to an interview: "A woman, an American, a Jew? Studying the Foreign Office?" But she never let personal experience of blimpish officials colour the text. No less a figure than Britain's best-dressed ambassador to Berlin, Sir Nevile Henderson, was surely not so wide of the mark when he told the Germans that "Great Britain should not be rated as a democracy but as an aristocracy" and that the "aristocratic ruling class was at present on the defensive against the broad mass of the popular front".[7]

This study has been written in the recognition that as a consequence of these factors a discernible bias is built into those state documents that we usually rely upon so heavily for our accounts. Thus the history of international relations has to be scrutinised on more than one level and in more than one dimension. Omitting China's side of the story—the victim's side—from his account of the Manchurian crisis was not a deliberate act on the part of Thorne. But it was also not entirely accidental, in that it followed directly from the sources chosen. The values inherent in relying on those sources, cultural and political, subconsciously shaped the result, and those values were too embedded to be challenged. The prevailing notion of what is "normal" tends to go untested, and this underlines the fact that unguarded empiricism is never a sensible way of proceeding. A suite of diplomatic documents alone never provides all the answers, however closely they are examined—and, remember, not all of those for the interwar period are declassified, even now. For instance, annual reports written by British diplomats stationed in foreign capitals such as Paris are still unaccountably closed. In the 1990s I had to go to Moscow to find the minutes of the Committee of Imperial Defence for 20 December 1936. And when I complained to an official from the Cabinet Office, her blunt retort was, "Why should we be dictated to by the Russians?" We still have no access to the files of Britain's secret service, MI6, for the interwar period, let alone those of the Soviet equivalent. To a greater or lesser extent, historians are thus held hostage to government censorship. This being so, how are they to break out?

To offset bias, official papers have therefore to be transcended. It is a serious error to scrutinise them in isolation (that is to say, exclusively from within the confines of one's own language and one's own culture), which is unfortunately too often the norm in the English-speaking world. The diplomatic sources have to be triangulated (from various foreign archives reflecting distinctive national perspectives); contextualised (within the domestic realm, where beliefs originate and are reinforced); and, of no lesser importance, interrogated for what is not always made explicit—the unwritten assumptions of those who in haste composed the texts for purely operational purposes—as well as for what the documents say directly. That requires heightened consciousness of the mindset prevailing at the time of their composition, as well as active imaginative insight.

Ideas and assumptions matter just as much as do more elaborate ideologies that make explicit the purposes of power. Raw power alone goes only so far in ensuring that the behaviour of governments is identical in differing circumstances. For this reason statesmen who lapse into the reassuring predictability of balance-of-power politics tend to come unstuck. The international situation never looks the same from every perspective. The interwar period is a case in point. Not everyone subscribed to "the comity of nations". Rivalry between the great powers after 1917 was acutely affected by a battle of ideas that reached above and beyond the normal preoccupations of diplomatic practitioners accustomed to the European states system from 1815 to 1914. In this sense, the twentieth century more closely resembled the era of the wars of religion of early modern Europe or of the French Revolution than that of the nineteenth-century Concert of Europe upon which eminent diplomatic historians traditionally cut their teeth.

Seen through the lens of classical realism or the opaque windows of a department of state, the international relations of the interwar period actually make little sense. It soon becomes evident that divergent and contested purposes drove foreign policy which cannot be explained along traditional lines. Indeed, politicians and diplomats came to fear more the insidious power of ideas than the measurable components of military capabilities. So, on the one hand, a country with demonstrably weak offensive military capabilities—Soviet Russia—could seem all-threatening because of the power of its ideology. Yet a state armed to the teeth and bellicose in rhetoric—Nazi Germany—could appear acceptable as an idiosyncratic member of the club because it was assumed to share core beliefs. Its ideology was seen by those ruling a country like Britain as none too pleasant, perhaps, but complementary rather than menacing. So instead of worrying about fascism, the British élite worried more about what would likely as not replace it—Communism—were fascism to be destabilised and overthrown. Silent complicity, as witnessed during the Spanish Civil War, can thus be observed among those who would not have advocated openly an alignment with fascist states. The roots of anxiety lay well beyond the confines of ministries of state: in society at large, where, since the First World War, traditional loyalties could no longer be taken for granted.

It therefore does not make sense to reduce intention in foreign affairs to *ragion di stato* or *raison d'état*: to the interests of the state that override every other interest. After all, who exactly ran the state? Who were the custodians of diplomacy? They may not all have been the sons of "gentlemen of independent means" with a lot to lose. But more than a few undoubtedly were, certainly in London and Paris. Could these men (and they were inevitably only men) define the interests of the state without reflecting their own sectional interest? One does not have to be a Marxist to suppose that those ruling the state are likely, if unchecked, to serve the interests of their own class, whether aristocracy or bourgeoisie. The Renaissance idea of *ragion di stato* was developed precisely to offset such distortions. It was not suggested that governments invariably further the interests of the state, so much as that they *should* do so in the interests of society as a whole rather than furthering sectional or ideological interests. The historian, like the political scientist, is entirely wrong to read this back to front and simply assume that *ragion di stato* corresponds to what states actually do and have always done.[8]

The bias is one not only of class, moreover, but also of nation. One need only research in a number of foreign archives to become exceptionally aware of entire societies whose practices are centuries old and are not at all easily captured in neat formulations by those who blandly assume that the makers and executors of policy are "rational actors". This is a highly misleading notion borrowed from political science which in turn took it from economics, at the very time that discerning economists such as Kenneth Arrow were abandoning it.[9] And whose rationality are we referring to? It is a form of imperial provincialism strikingly apparent across the social sciences in Britain and the United States, particularly in the study of international relations, that takes it for granted we all reason alike regardless of social and national provenance. Thus examining the conduct of foreign policy within a vacuum inevitably makes for misleading assumptions, not perhaps about what has been happening but certainly about why.

So are we left with an impossible task? How are we to get into the minds of those taking and executing decisions in ministries of foreign affairs? Declassified despatches and policy memoranda obviously count for a great deal, but not for everything. In the modern era, busy bureaucrats write elliptical telegrams that have to be enciphered at one end and deciphered at the other, before being reviewed or minuted speedily upon receipt. They are not about to waste valuable time telling each other what they already know, nor do so in position papers directed at the secretary of state, who is, after all, even busier than they are and a politician wedded to particular insights or prejudices. Personal papers such as diaries help, though some are written with an eye to becoming the arbiter of past events. But without them we would be lost—where, indeed, would we be without the indiscretions of Harold Nicolson, or Neville Chamberlain's letters to his sisters? Access is, however, not infrequently problematic. As historians of the interwar period have found, the great houses of the British aristocracy—such as the Devonshires and the Bedfords—who were highly influential at certain points in foreign affairs, have in notable instances not given access to relevant primary sources that could embarrass the family. Some former ministers, such as Richard (R.A.B.) Butler, destroyed crucial papers, such as those touching on peace feelers to Germany in the summer of 1940, that contradicted the dissembling memoirs they had put into print. And in Britain, oppressive libel laws enabled culprits such as Sir Joseph Ball and Lord Rothschild to threaten court action in order to prevent the truth from being outed—in Ball's instance, secret overtures to Mussolini; in Rothschild's, hidden complicity with the Cambridge Five.[10] For these various reasons, foreign observers are, generally speaking, far more likely to be able to identify an implicit consensus of thought prevalent among those ruling another state than are those safely on the inside.

The aim of this study is to bring together the history of international relations from the outside and the history of ideas from the inside: ideas projected to conscious purpose in international relations.

I do not normally use research assistance, because to do so automatically rules out unexpected finds that the specialist alone will recognise for what they are. Granted, not everyone who sets out in the wrong direction discovers America. But ordering the wrong file in haste can have a back-handed advantage, in that what turns up may be a document more useful than what was requested. Similarly, ransacking library stacks for a book that has been taken out may lead to works whose existence was unknown to the researcher. Serendipity is everything to the alert historian.

So all mistakes are most definitely my own. I have several people to thank. The diligent readers for Princeton University Press rescued me from verbal infelicities in the first draft. And Kathleen Cioffi and Bridget Flannery-McCoy at the Press have seen this project onto paper. Several colleagues helped me to locate secondary sources I might have overlooked, including Paul Hoser, on Germany, and John Pollard, on the Vatican. Vladimir Pechatnov obtained for me a new volume of documents that saved me a great deal of time. And Julián Casanova kindly reviewed my Spanish chapter. The list of archives I wish to thank can be found at the end of the work—but does not include the Vatican Secret Archive, unfortunately, which lived up to its name. Its overseers granted permission to see an array of formally declassified documents that were then denied to me on arrival. The cynical response to my exasperation—*is anything open?*—was, "Yes, relations with Switzerland from 1945 to 1955." But special gratitude should go, on the other hand, to the archivists at Churchill College, Cambridge, a splendid institution, and to the tireless staff at the Historical and Social Sciences Library at the Institute for Advanced Study in Princeton, especially Marcia Tucker and Kirstie Venanzi. Though much of the archival research dates back to my years at Birmingham University in the 1970s, at Stanford and Berkeley in the 1980s and in Cambridge through the 1990s, it is at the Institute that I researched and wrote under ideal conditions since election to the Kennan Chair in 2015. Lastly, I am forever grateful to be sharing my life, my ideas and my mistakes with Karina Urbach, a dedicated historian of distinction, who challenges my writing and gives meaning to everything I do; as does too my beloved son, Timothy.

Princeton, NJ, May 2021

THE SPECTRE OF WAR

Introduction

It is, sometimes, these changes which are going on around us of which we are least aware.

—MAYNARD KEYNES[1]

Why should anyone believe that Communism played a crucial role in the origins of World War II? The word scarcely appears in the index of standard works on the subject.

Yet the threat of revolution posed by the Bolsheviks, as the Communists were once better known, proved critical to the emergence of fascism. It was also a central consideration in the failure of states menaced by Hitler's Germany to unite against the immediate and very tangible threat he posed to their survival. Although brooding along the margins of Europe for more than two decades after the revolution with military power insufficient for offensive operations to endanger Central Europe, the Soviet Union nevertheless incarnated an impending threat to capitalism worldwide. Entire countries, including Poland, Romania and Czechoslovakia, were all the more easily isolated, picked off one by one and then wiped off the map by Hitler because for each of them the dread of Communist rule ultimately proved greater than their fear of the Nazis. This makes more sense when it is borne in mind that whereas the menace from Eastern Europe—the Soviet Union—was well established by the mid-1930s, the scale and depth of that looming from Central Europe—Nazi Germany—had yet to reveal itself in full.

The story therefore does not begin where it is usually assumed to, in the 1930s, though this is when it reaches its climax. It is also essential to understand its genesis from the 1920s. Indeed, the First World War (1914–18) had barely ended before the dangers pending for the postwar era became apparent. Delegates were already en route to Paris in January 1919 for the primary purpose of redrawing the maps of Europe and the Near East, when from London *The Times* issued an electrifying call to confront the "[d]anger of Bolshevist imperialism". "Of all problems before the Peace Conference", the leader page thundered, "none is quite so urgent as that of our relations with the new Imperialism of the Russian Bolshevists. And in none is delay so dangerous or so injurious to the well-being of our friends. The idea is very prevalent in this country that however pestilent Bolshevism may be, only Russians are the sufferers, and we should be well advised not to meet its troubles. Whatever truth there may ever have been in that view has evaporated. The present Russian government—and an appreciation of this fact is crucial to an understanding of our problem—is the most Imperialistically minded in Europe."[2]

But how was it that the triumph of the Bolshevik revolution in Russia could so rapidly threaten to undercut plans for postwar Europe? The answer was not hard to see. The Bolshevik creed—or Marxism-Leninism, as we would call it today—offered the most immediate, drastic solution to the social and economic deprivation not just of the working classes of the world, but also of the impoverished peasant. Conditions were ripe by 1918 when revolutionary propaganda spread like wildfire across the globe. In Europe, as the Swiss ambassador to France reported, "Everywhere there are disturbances, riots and convulsions."[3] And wherever one looked, popular discontent varied only in the degree of severity. The scale and intensity of modern conflict accelerated by industrialisation had imposed an immense and, in places, intolerable strain on the societies caught up in the First World War. Contiguous, multinational Leviathans—the Russian, the Austro-Hungarian and the Ottoman empires—imploded under relentless bombardment and the economic and social strain of total war.

By comparison the democracies were far better off in their capacity to forge a national consensus. Yet they too found it possible to sustain a titanic struggle for survival only through making extravagant empty promises of social reform—in Britain "homes fit for heroes" that were never built—and of more egalitarian income distribution, delaying the inevitable moment when these promissory notes would fall due in the likelihood that the means for delivering on them would be insufficient to meet pressing demand. Liberals were rapidly transforming themselves into socialists while socialists were rapidly abandoning reformist socialism for Marxism; and Marxism was being appropriated by the fanatical "Vladimir Ilyich" (Lenin). The prewar European states system that had emerged unscathed from the French revolutionary wars of the previous century now tottered and threatened to collapse as its central components succumbed to revolt.

First came the tumultuous "October Revolution" in which Lenin took the Russian Empire by surprise in November 1917. Then came Benito Mussolini's triumphal "March on Rome" in October 1922. Though in principle a victor, Italy had suffered an unresolved political crisis for decades that was exacerbated rather than alleviated by joining Britain and France (the Entente) in war. On the right, deprived of territorial gains at the expense of fallen empires, pent-up nationalist sentiment amplified by dubious colonial conquest was never satiated. On the left, meanwhile, widespread social unrest—culminating in the occupation of the factories in 1920 and widespread disorder—was inspired by the inflammatory example of the October Revolution. Yet fascism rather than Communism triumphed. And by 1923 the fascists of the NSDAP (Nazi Party) had also gained a hold in Germany. Under the spell of the hitherto entirely unknown aspirant architect Adolf Hitler, they seized centre stage to the south, in Bavaria. From the outset in Munich, its capital, Hitler fixed upon the revolutionary menace of international Bolshevism as the central danger to the nation and indissolubly interconnected with Jews at home and abroad. Whatever Hitler's other goals, his ultimate aim was to liquidate the Jews in Germany; his devoted followers, brutalised by war and humiliated by unexpected defeat, eagerly inhaled the intoxicating rhetoric. Simultaneously, far beyond the boundaries of Europe, as hopes for revolution faded in Moscow, revolution in China became the order of the day—and its primary victim was Britain, the country's financial overlord.

When from 1937 to 1939 the threat of yet another war appeared on the horizon, the lingering menace of revolution from Bolshevism explained in large part why Britain rejected co-operation with the Soviet Union to deter German aggression. The reasoning was simple, but for the most part concealed in the form of an unwritten assumption, certainly never fully articulated to the population at large: far rather buy off Hitler with timely territorial concessions, even at the cost of dismembering dependent states in Central and Eastern Europe, than risk ushering Communist power into the heart of the continent. Insufficiently understood is the undoubted fact that throughout the 1930s leading conservative politicians within the democracies not only welcomed fascism into power but thereafter also feared that, were fascism overthrown in Italy or Germany—and fascism was seen as only an interim solution—Communism would be almost certain to take its place. The events immediately following the Second World War certainly suggest that such fears were not entirely misplaced. Confidence in the sturdiness of the underlying capitalist system and its democratic legacy was at its nadir. The Great Depression had seen to that.

Thus beyond the spectre of war loomed the more menacing spectre of revolution; a spectre that in the end hastened the advent of a war that from being a distant possibility grew into an immediate certainty. And this grim vision haunted the known world: from San Francisco to Shanghai, from Vladivostok through Berlin to London. Its persistence infinitely complicated the search for peace through collective security as envisaged in the Covenant of the League of Nations, which itself ultimately foundered on unrealistic liberal and socialist expectations. Rearmament was consistently rejected by the left. Pacifism predominated. Yet liberals and socialists sincerely believed in collective security, even though it could not be ensured without force of arms. This fundamental paradox was never resolved, ultimately rendering the reformist left utterly impotent and therefore to be discarded as irrelevant.

Revolution in the form of Communism/Bolshevism—"Workers of the world unite"—was not merely a Marxist idea or even merely a Leninist platform for the fundamental economic and social reconstruction of Soviet Russia. For the existing capitalist system it was also a lethal international contagion, as Lenin openly boasted; one for which no known antidote or vaccine then existed. It was People's Commissar for Foreign Affairs Georgii Chicherin who, dapper in dress shirt and frockcoat, as late as August 1921 described Soviet Russia unequivocally as "the citadel of world revolution".[4] But it fell to the Communist International (Comintern) to subvert the restoration of the established diplomatic values and practices of the prewar order. As "the headquarters of the world revolution" in Moscow, Comintern drew upon and gave purpose to the forces of blind frustration that had accumulated within Europe and the colonial world beyond.[5] Anticipating an uprising in Germany that eventually had to be aborted, in November 1923 a secretary of the Bolshevik Party's Central Committee, Vyacheslav Molotov, reminded all Communists that "the October revolution in Russia is the first blow against capitalism. The victorious proletarian revolution in Germany is a yet more powerful blow against it." It followed that "the workers of all countries must help the German proletariat".[6] This was, Lenin bragged, "a completely different kind of international relations".[7] And Comintern was central to that purpose, whereas the People's Commissariat for Foreign Affairs (Narkomindel) was free to act without regard to any principle, Communist or otherwise. "Principles!" a senior Russian diplomat said to the startled Chinese ambassador, when asked what the general principles underlying Soviet diplomacy were. "In diplomacy there are no principles, only experience."[8]

Lenin was a genius at improvisation in relentless pursuit of world revolution. From the outset Communist parties were established across the globe and financed with vast sums of Russian money. Infiltration and subversion of the capitalist camp were the order of the day. "Comintern has dozens of ties and agents in every country," Lenin boasted.[9] Trotsky, briefly people's commissar for foreign affairs before building the Red Army, commented by letter in 1923 that "until the war . . . the political lines were far more defined. All international relations were

more stable and every ambassador worked within the framework of de-
lineated treaties, relationships and traditions. If you like, diplomacy was
one of position. These days every situation . . . has fundamentally altered. Diplomacy is a consummate war of movement, of which one
flank is London, the other Beijing or Tokyo."[10]

The customary forms of international relations were thus systematically overturned by Moscow's messianic commitment to overturning
the established international order at all costs and as soon as practicable.
At the receiving end throughout Europe, the bureaucratic élite, dressed
for the day in detachable collars and morning suits, sitting down to work
despatching and receiving ciphered telegrams to and from the embassies of Europe, found their customary conduct of diplomacy repeatedly
frustrated by Comintern subversion across the globe. The new régime
in Moscow obviously had no respect for its bourgeois counterparts. The
reaction was predictable: extravagant rhetoric and threats of war or economic blockade. Facing down retaliation required strong nerves in the
Kremlin. And for men like Lenin and Stalin this was par for the course.
The resulting indignation merely confirmed them in the belief that the
threat they posed was effective. The British foreign secretary, a stickler
for tradition, put the matter plaintively in 1927: "What we ask of them
is not that they shall change their domestic institutions . . . but that they
shall henceforth make their policy conform to the ordinary comity of
nations, and abstain from the effort to promote world revolution and
from all interference in our internal affairs."[11]

The Bolsheviks, however, were not about to change their practices,
especially their pursuit of world revolution, since that would require a
change in their very nature. Nor were they about to miss any opportunity that arose from cultivating friction between the victor powers and
the defeated: what they called "inter-imperialist contradictions". Was
this not how they had managed to slip through the cracks and seize
power in the first place? For Lenin and those who succeeded him, gam-
bling on potential revolutions was not merely a matter of belief but an
urgent priority for survival. The initial advantage lay in the fact that the
economies of Europe were prostrated by the wholesale destruction of
capital infrastructure across the entire continent. War had impoverished

the leading trading states of Europe, a situation made all the worse as newly emergent, not least xenophobic and protectionist nation states—victors and vanquished alike—emerged from the wreck of the Russian and Austro-Hungarian empires. These countries through no fault of their own found themselves faced with an insoluble dilemma. They were from the outset torn from within between the observation of two mutually exclusive principles: the search for ethnically homogeneous state boundaries on the one hand, and strategically defensible frontiers on the other. When confronted by the need to choose between the two at any given moment, they invariably decided upon whatever offered the greater amount of territory—a recipe for international conflict, and, of course, a godsend to a master tactician like Hitler, seeking to exacerbate relations between those whose lands he coveted.

War had also unstitched the seams that held society together. This was not just a matter of alienation from government. The state had always maintained its supremacy through the monopoly of force. But as a result of the 1914–18 war, millions of men aged eighteen or over had been brutalised in order to win against the enemy. Ex-combatants knew how to shoot and to use the bayonet to deadly effect. A gun was never hard to find, even in countries like Britain, where domestic possession was still legal. Immediately after the war, indeed for some years thereafter, Germany was not unique in multiple examples of random political assassination and violent public disorder. In Italy the demobilised were the main object of concern on the part of nervous liberal governments anxious for public order. Soldiers returning from war soon fell ready prey in 1919 as likely recruits to Mussolini's *fasci di combattimento*. And acute social dislocation presented a unique opportunity for the expansion of Communism not just in Europe, but across the globe—a critical objective for those who believed that the traditional state was a thing of the past.

In spite of what has been asserted, the revolutionary objectives set by Lenin were sustained, albeit more cautiously, even under Stalin, as they were under his successors (whether they pursued them purposefully or not; some were manifestly indifferent). The system to which they answered was such that the only issue differentiating them was that of degree and opportunity, not one of principle. The weight of the past was overwhelming. It towered over them. The priority given to international revolution thus varied from one leader to another, but was itself never extinguished even in the worst of times. It was in this sense an integral part of the structure; an inescapable legacy. Indeed, it was precisely these subversive ambitions that inspired Hitler's vision of *Götterdäm-merung* and critically undermined the trust of Britain and France in the Soviet Union as a potential ally in confronting Nazi Germany during the late 1930s.

Britain was, indeed, a case in point. By virtue of economic weight alone, it had to form the cornerstone of any alliance intended against the threat from Nazi Germany. Historians of British foreign policy, however, have tended to see everything with too much hindsight, through the eyes of post-imperial Britain. They have neglected the critical fact that interwar London also presided over a massive global empire, and that this empire had visibly begun disintegrating from its zenith in 1919. As a consequence, Britain was necessarily a distracted power, not only inclined to give way in Europe to meet more urgent, far-flung needs, but also shaping its European purposes with an eye fixed not only on domestic economic needs but also on pressing imperial priorities. When, for instance, it was reported that Prince Bismarck of the German embassy in London had told Hitler that "a very influential section of British public opinion strongly favours non-interference in European affairs", the general reaction expressed in the Foreign Office was one of indignant surprise. Yet the wily and cynical realist Orme Sargent retorted, "But is not Bismarck unfortunately right?"[12] Absolutely.

Foreign policy was first and foremost about imperial interests: defence, imperial defence. It was no accident that at the top of the armed forces sat the Committee of Imperial Defence. During this era of unparalleled colonial unrest, when even schoolboys in Cairo came out on strike against the British, overseas policy represented a desperate attempt to hold back the incoming tidal wave of change that inevitably exacerbated the intensity of domestic political debate. Thus to many, certainly in the British Conservative Party, the security of Western Europe was of course significant, but a commitment of only secondary importance; while that of Eastern Europe was of no importance at all.[13] It was almost as though, with the First World War over, Britain had finished with Europe, and now was the time to return to purely domestic or imperial concerns.

In the end it all came down to money. Democratic governments rose and fell on the back of successful or failing economies, and increases in taxation were always unpopular. Empires had never appeared for any reason other than the accumulation of wealth and its secure protection. India was the largest market for British goods, including a very high proportion of manufactures.[14] China came second. Conservative minister Neville Chamberlain, former lord mayor of Birmingham, was one who highlighted the fact that the evacuation of Shanghai and Hong Kong would destroy one of the greatest sources from which Britain drew trade.[15] Here the clash with Communism, in the form of the first Chinese revolution (1925–27), was never a matter of doubt. Sir Cecil Clementi, governor of Hong Kong, announced in no uncertain terms that "[w]e are quite determined to have no Bolshevism in the Colony".[16]

The interwar era must be seen as one whole. By focusing almost exclusively on European developments, historians have overlooked the direct link between Comintern's subversion of the empire in the 1920s and attitudes to Russia in Europe through the 1930s. This oversight is encouraged by reading too much into Trotsky's expulsion from the Soviet Union and the ascendancy of Stalin from 1929. Many, certainly in the Foreign Office, believed that world revolution had been dropped entirely—indeed some historians unfortunately still do; an assumption made plausible by the fact that Comintern's offensive ceased to be as effective as it had once been. And Britain's secret intelligence service MI6, on a tight budget that did not allow for setting priorities purely on the basis of sentiment, continued to see the Soviet Union as the main enemy through to the middle of the 1930s.[17]

It was not for lack of effort from below that Comintern was relatively ineffective. Successful pursuit of the class war crucially depended upon more than the painful contraction of living standards. Ironically the collapse of the US stock market on Wall Street in 1929, the long-awaited catalyst to revolution in the West, lent credence to the assumption that revolution was dead, because it failed to accelerate the revolutionary tide. In key parts of Europe, and to the surprise of many, reformist Social Democracy stepped in to prop up the existing socio-economic order. Where were the Communists, the sections of Comintern? They were, indeed, instructed to fight the social democrats at every turn, although—and this was critical—not to the point of seizing power. Meanwhile the Kremlin, urgently in need of respite, reined in Communist hotheads prematurely eager for revolutionary action as it bought time for the hasty modernisation of Russia from top to bottom. Yet this pause was not meant as anything more than an enforced tactical retreat. It was never intended as surrender and abandonment of the cause. The forces that drove Comintern from below within the Soviet Communist Party were marking time only reluctantly and not without complaint, as was evident in challenges to Stalin's ascendancy during the year of crisis, 1932. Those who ruled Britain and had the most to lose fully understood that the relatively calm sea might prove to be only an ebb tide.

With over eight million Germans out of work, the Great Depression was enough to hand Hitler an unparalleled opportunity. In Germany as in Britain, Social Democracy dominated the working-class vote sufficiently to neutralise through timely palliatives the demands voiced loudly for truly revolutionary change. And those who were inclined to dismiss Hitler's rabble-rousing about the threat from international Bolshevism, even as the Depression undermined living standards and starkly exposed the gulf between rulers and ruled, found to their horror that the tide of revolution unexpectedly rolled in again, engulfing France and Spain during the torrid summer of 1936. Liberal democracy was in peril once more. Mussolini summed up the dilemma of the democracies and their prevailing political beliefs: "Liberalism can be applied to a country where all the parties act within the boundaries of the state, but from the moment one party depends upon or permits itself to be inspired from abroad, liberalism becomes impracticable."[18]

This certainly happened in Spain. Here as in France social turbulence, already apparent in 1934, reached disturbing new heights. The Popular Front, innovated in France and adopted in Moscow primarily to stem the spread of fascism, and duly condemned by Trotsky as a betrayal of the revolution, emerged instead as the revolution's Trojan horse. And whereas in 1928 Comintern amounted to forty parties and 1.6 million members, by 1935 it had grown to sixty-one parties and 3.1 million members.[19] More importantly, it had returned to Western Europe with a dynamic of its own and a broad appeal unseen in the 1920s. Spain was soon riven in two, while France teetered on the edge. All of a sudden Bolshevism re-emerged as a practical proposition in the heart of Europe and at the gateway to empire, decoupling Britain's confidence in France and instantaneously unravelling French confidence in the Soviet Union. It was not long before the road to the East opened for Hitler to march through unimpeded.

Despite all this, the centrality of the role of Communism in the interwar years has taken a long time to be accepted by historians of international relations. The Grand Alliance between Britain, the Soviet Union and the United States in World War II and their falling out in the Cold War that followed had a deadening effect, suppressing within the minds of an entire generation any awareness of the profound conflict over Communism that predated the Second World War and played its own part in generating that war. This suppression, conscious or not, of an awkward truth inadvertently opened a space to the right for polemicists like Ernst Nolte to frame the rise of fascism as the inevitable consequence of the October Revolution.[20] To say the least, this was dangerously simplistic; more importantly, it stifled further historical research as it opened the door to political polemic. For the majority of the academic centre-left, Nolte was sufficient reason to rule out Bolshevism as having played any role at all.

One distortion of history thus prompted another. It was customary in the 1960s to dismiss as of no consequence Hitler's obsessive talk about the dangers from Bolshevism: to assert that it had no real foundations in fact, and to claim that it was entirely disingenuous, being merely a ruse to hoodwink the unsuspecting. A symptom of this approach was reliance upon one diary entry from Italian foreign minister Count Ciano to claim that the Anti-Comintern Pact of 1936 was "really clearly anti-British" (2 November 1937), while ignoring the subsequent entries in which Ciano boasts of "the new, powerful anti-Communist system" (5 November 1937) and "our formidable anti-Russian system" (9 November 1937).[21] And it is perhaps a typical weakness of the diplomatic historian to pay rather more attention to process than to purpose, assuming the motive springs to be known and unchanging as everything inexorably follows its usual geopolitical course. With respect to the interwar era historians and biographers have had no choice but to acknowledge that the personality of Hitler was wholly exceptional: a mind in the grip of an extremely abnormal psychosis. So what more need be said? But one does not have to rationalise Hitler's diplomacy in the manner of A.J.P. Taylor to see that focusing excessively on Hitler's personality can easily obscure perception of other important, underlying explanations for war. One man is not an army.

The larger role of international Communism has thus tended to be cast into the shadows, if no longer entirely discarded, within the traditional narrative explaining the tension between Nazi Germany and the rest of Europe. Moreover, it is of interest to note that this was not a matter of contention between right and left. The loud silence among more conservative historians was, ironically, echoed on the left. Eric Hobsbawm, for example, avoided almost any reference to the Communist International in *The Age of Extremes*. He explicitly rejected the idea that the rise of fascism was in any way a reaction to the Communist movement, no doubt for fear of justifying it: "the Right-wing backlash responded not against Bolshevism as such, but against all movements, and notably the organized working-class, which threatened the existing order of society or could be blamed for its breakdown".[22] Yet there was no way Social Democracy "threatened the existing order of society", as Hobsbawm put it, in the interwar period. On the contrary, socialists notoriously propped it up. The Labour Party in Britain under the famously deferential Ramsay MacDonald was a prime example. The greater fear was of a Communist revolution. That is why Comintern at one notorious stage beginning in 1928 stigmatised social democrats indiscriminately as "social fascists". Only Bolshevism red in tooth and claw actually threatened to overturn capitalism. That was why it appeared in the first place, and why the Third International was created to supplant the Second International; this Hobsbawm surely well understood, as a Communist Party member until the very end.

In depicting the eve of the Second World War, historians have more often than not grudgingly conceded Communism a bit-part only, wandering on and off stage while the audience's attention has been intentionally directed to the familiar interplay between the more reputable actors, as the conventional script of diplomatic history prescribes. Communism deserves, however, to be reinstated in its true role. This is in part what Arno Mayer, writing in 1967, was referring to: "The analytic framework of conventional diplomatic history simply must be enlarged to accommodate the complexities of international relations in an age of mass and crisis politics, in an age of international civil war."[23]

The purpose of this work is thus to reach beyond diplomacy and to return international Communism to where it actually was at the time: never far from centre stage, as an enduring if at times unspoken threat to those in charge of government on both sides of the Rhine; to return it, indeed, to the spotlight in accounting for the drama that unfolded between 1919 and 1941. My larger intention, which connects this work with my history of Russia's Cold War, has been to underscore the intimate connection between the role Bolshevism played before the war and the role it played from 1947, after the brief interval of wartime collaboration had misleadingly suggested that deep ideological differences could be indefinitely suppressed. History has hitherto been excessively compartmentalised, if not chopped into pieces, not least separating the realm of ideas from the world of events. And with respect to periods, the interconnective tissue between the interwar era and the Cold War needs patching back together, to allow us at last to view them as an integral whole.

I

Crossroads to World Revolution, 1917–1920

We are standing at the cross-roads, and a decision has to be come to. Either the world is going down under Bolshevism or the world is going to kill it.

—FIELD-MARSHAL ERICH LUDENDORFF[1]

The First World War demonstrated conclusively that Europe had already lost its way. What Paul Valéry eloquently portrayed as a "disorder of the mind" had taken hold:

> We civilisations now know that we are mortal. We had heard tell of whole worlds vanished, of empires gone to the bottom with all their engines; sunk to the inexplorable bottom of the centuries. . . . And now we see that the abyss of history is large enough for every one. We feel that a civilization is as fragile as a life. . . . An extraordinary tremor has run through the spinal marrow of Europe.[2]

Yet this was not just a tragic and inevitable consequence of so much blood that had been shed in the war. It was also the culmination of a near universal malaise that had preceded its outbreak in 1914.[3] And once Europe's magnetic field had begun to shift violently, the needle lurched from side to side with unnerving fluidity. Extreme ideologies found foothold where social stability proved impossible to sustain, even as drastic measures were inflicted on the mutinous troops and naval ratings of Britain and France. The political temperature soared to new heights as fever took hold.

The entire continent had arrived unexpectedly at a crossroads. But there was no way back. The old certainties of the nineteenth century, dislodged, scattered and pulverised by the unexpectedly destructive conflict of the First World War, lay far behind. Trauma was not confined to the infamous trenches where troops were blinded by mustard gas or deafened by the big guns. On the east coast of England Great Yarmouth's medieval streets were for the first time subject to aerial bombardment from Zeppelins in January 1915. Those living in the way of advancing forces, as in Belgium and northern France, or along the margins of the Russian Empire, on the other hand suffered a great deal more. And those societies least prepared and that themselves fell in battle were the most vulnerable to complete political disintegration. The Russian Empire, backward as it was, became only the first to suffer the consequences, its economy having collapsed under the unsustainable burden of war.

The October Revolution

Russia was thus the first to fall. Anarcho-syndicalist Georges Sorel had eagerly anticipated where the first crack would appear in the wall of Western, capitalist civilisation. "Almost everyone believes today that the war will in no way finish in battle, but in revolution. The question is to know which country will take to the floor. It is more or less generally believed that Russia could well give the signal for great revolutions."[4] Indeed, against all odds, the Bolsheviks under Vladimir Ilyich (Lenin) seized power in Petrograd on 7 November. Though fanatically Marxist, the Russian Communist Party (Bolshevik) had always been totally underestimated. The Bolsheviks were few in number. Yet from then on, under the dynamic leadership of Lenin and Trotsky, their strength of conviction, acute tactical sense and organisational ability proved formidable. The goal of world socialist revolution was universal, their tactics unerringly astute. In some quarters this was much appreciated. Sorel was overtly sympathetic on the grounds that "[t]he Russian events have given the idea of revolution the value of reality that it did not have for a long time in socialist literature".[5]

Thereafter revolutions were no longer merely apparently spontaneous outbursts that rose up from the street as in 1789, 1830 or 1848. And whereas the Paris Commune of 1870 was to some degree orchestrated by anarchists, it had quickly succumbed not only to the vastly superior forces of counter-revolution, but also to the deliberate brutality symbolised to this day in the institution of the Basilica of the Sacré-Coeur de Montmartre, built in large part to "expiate the crimes of the Commune". Lenin was determined that the loss of such an opportunity should never be repeated, certainly not in Russia. Revolutionary terror would see to that. The abortive revolution of 1905 also yielded important lessons, notably in the emergence of workers' councils (soviets). It highlighted as well the critical importance of the international dimension, not only as a Marxist goal but also as the mainstay of counterrevolution. Revolution in Russia would never survive unless it spread beyond national confines. It had to be international or it would be lost. Defeat and the critical financial aid granted by France from 1905 underscored this important lesson.[6] And what happened in Russia reverberated across the borders of empire in Asia: the Russian Revolution was very soon followed by turmoil in the Ottoman Empire, Iran and China. What we have known since 1952 as the Third World was henceforth on the move: "We live now right in the middle of an era of these storms and their blowback on Europe." Lenin welcomed the fact that the millions of Asia were being drawn into "the struggle for the same European ideals".[7]

These other struggles were seen as fraternal to Bolshevism even though they were aimed not at liberating the working class from capitalism but at liberating the colonial world, which meant the local bourgeoisie, from Western imperialism. They were renamed "national liberation fronts", which included, hard as it might be to believe, King Amanullah's tribal Afghanistan. This opportunity carried with it, however, a disadvantage that compounded the problem of seizing power and sustaining the revolution, once attained. This was a fundamental assumption that "the Russian revolution can achieve victory by its own efforts, but it cannot possibly hold and consolidate its gains by its own strength. It cannot do so unless there is a socialist revolution in the West. Without this condition restoration is inevitable." Lenin added that the "Russian revolution has a great international ally both in Europe and in Asia, but, at the same time, and *for that very reason*, it has not only a national, not only a Russian, but also an *international* enemy. Reaction against the mounting proletarian struggle is inevitable in all capitalist countries, and it is uniting the bourgeois governments of the whole world against every popular movement, against every revolution both in Asia and, particularly, in Europe."[8]

Having seized power on 7 November 1917, the Bolsheviks were therefore not surprised to face growing foreign complications. The world war they interrupted had its own dynamic that threatened to overwhelm the revolution. Although they ceased fire unilaterally against the kaiser's Germany, its battle-hardened armies took no notice of Lenin's coup d'état in Petrograd and ploughed on into Russia. They then subjected it to painful territorial amputation and the weight of financial indemnities at the Treaty of Brest-Litovsk in March 1918. As if to confirm the existence of powerful forces in opposition to the revolution, British troops landed in Murmansk, an ice-free port on the Barents Sea, in late July. Ostensibly these forces had been sent to push back the Germans. But their underlying purpose soon became apparent. Instead of marching west to German positions in Finland, they marched south to attack the soldiers of the revolution in Petrograd. This was the first scene in the unfolding allied war of intervention, an undeclared war that for eighteen months was rationalised away by the allies with increasingly implausible, contradictory justifications.

The limits of credibility were reached when in November 1918 the kaiser's régime lost its nerve and unceremoniously imploded. Yet instead of evacuating positions in Russia because their ostensible, original purpose had disappeared, the British promptly reinforced their support for the counter-revolution, even to the point of deploying German troops in the Baltic to push back the Bolsheviks. The open question now was whether the Bolsheviks in turn could manage to save themselves by stimulating and aiding the German socialist revolution within the enemy's camp, or whether they would succumb to the allied invasion. As Lenin leaned in on the globe, the Russian Communist Party newspaper *Pravda* roared that "the World Revolution has begun". In some respects, it did seem so. From Rome, Britain's envoy to the Holy See Count de Salis reported dire warnings from the cardinal secretary of state: "Unless a peace which Germans can accept, and which is not humiliating to them, is shortly reached, Germany will become Bolshevik and the ally and imitator of Russia. In view of the supreme interests of civilisation and of European peace the Holy See considers it its duty to hasten to give warning to Great Britain, and through her to the other Powers of the Entente, urging the conclusion of a speedy and suitable peace."[9]

Those ruling the nascent Weimar Republic obviously shared such sentiments. Foreign Minister Count Brockdorff-Rantzau warned the British "that if the peace terms of the Allies proved so severe as to crush Germany the German Government would refuse to accept them. The Spartacists would then gradually gain control and would attempt to infect enemy and neutral countries with Bolshevik doctrines. The payment of indemnities would thus be avoided, while coercion in the shape of the reimposition of the Blockade would be counteracted by a *rapprochement* with Russia."[10]

The Threat of Revolution in Germany

On 26 March 1919 Britain's Liberal prime minister, David Lloyd George, drew attention to the "greatest danger" looming over the vindictive peace then being negotiated in Paris: the risk "that Germany may throw in her lot with Bolshevism and place her resources, her brains, her vast organizing power at the disposal of the revolutionary fanatics whose dream it is to conquer the world for Bolshevism by force of arms".[11] This was brazen hypocrisy. A demagogue, Lloyd George had fought and won the vengeful "khaki election" in coalition with the Conservatives, promising to squeeze Germany financially "until the pips squeaked".[12] But the fears expressed subsequent to winning the election were widespread, certainly in Britain, where domestic unrest followed speedily on the end of the war and gave rise to momentary panic: policemen on strike, machine-gun nests set up in Glasgow in fear of the militant dockers on the Clyde. The Special Branch of the Metropolitan Police now began to track the enemy within, as did MI5 (counter-intelligence) and, though entirely unauthorised for such purposes, so too did the Secret Intelligence Service, MI6. The cabinet received sometimes alarming weekly summaries of revolutionary activities across the globe through to 1921.

Meanwhile in Catholic Munich, the capital of Bavaria, mass meetings had called for peace at any price. Inspired by pacifist Kurt Eisner, who had just been released from prison and who had propagated documentary revelations about Germany's instigation of the war, rebels installed a revolutionary workers' soviet. The Austrian ex-combatant Adolf Hitler, newly released from war service, bore witness and never forgot it. No opposition rose against the soviet. Indeed, King Ludwig III packed up his dignity with his bags and simply fled. This particular venture collapsed not long afterwards, however, on 21 February 1919. Eisner was assassinated by an avenging monarchist. But others sprung up to take his place. Lenin delighted in the fact that once settled societies were rapidly unravelling across Europe. This was the opportunity of a lifetime for the Bolsheviks, just as it was a mortal threat for the allied leaders, no less than for the vanquished.

Desperately grappling with the immediate consequences of victory and the urgent need to pacify and feed those they had crushed, the British government entertained no illusions. Even before the foundation of Comintern, London acknowledged Bolshevism as "a World Force".[13] While negotiations between the allies proceeded in Paris, Lord President of the council and future foreign secretary, Earl Curzon, circulated a memorandum to cabinet highlighting the Soviet régime's urgent need "to spread its peculiar system through Central and Western Europe before the newly-formed States, such as Poland, are able to build up their own social and political structures and thus act as a barrier to the further advance of Bolshevism".[14] Not surprisingly Field Marshal Sir Henry Wilson, chief of the Imperial General Staff, argued that "conditions in

Germany should be stabilised with a view to keeping the infection as far to the eastward as possible".[15]

Propagating the cause of revolution through Europe and Asia to the Americas had of course begun as soon as the Bolsheviks seized power, though not under any separate, formal institutional auspices. None was required. The task could have been carried out as easily by existing institutions within the Soviet government and Communist Party. Indeed, up to Comintern's foundation the People's Commissariat of Foreign Affairs (Narkomindel) was largely responsible for doing so. At the end of 1918, for instance, Deputy People's Commissar for the East Lev Karakhan wrote to Lenin, "The proposal is to allocate 200,000 [roubles] for the first quarter of the year, January to March 1919, to the Foreign Commissariat for supporting Asian labour organizations and sending agitators to make propaganda in Asia. The cost of each agitator, plus his bonus when he returns, would be as follows: North Korea and Korea—10,000 roubles; South China—20,000 roubles. Similar missions are envisaged for Persia and India."[16] Thus a mechanism for spreading propaganda already existed. But the corpse of the much discredited socialist Second International was undergoing a hasty resurrection in Bern, Switzerland. Lenin urgently needed to upstage this "International of traitors and counter-revolutionaries" with a revolutionary substitute.[17] The eccentric diehard Chicherin, people's commissar, was tasked with making this happen.

Foundation of Comintern

The allied war of intervention and the civil war were still raging when the founders of Comintern gathered on 2 March in great secrecy deep within the Kremlin, now the seat of Soviet power, in the centre of Moscow. This first congress had a more than distinct air of unreality about it. It was to be Soviet Russia's International, a Communist Third International to replace the socialist Second International that had failed to halt the First World War in its tracks as it had promised. The few foreign delegates who made it to Moscow had to run the gauntlet of the allied blockade. "When we convened the first congress in a whole range of countries we had only Communist tendencies and not parties, not even groups," Comintern President Grigorii Zinoviev (Hirsch Apfelbaum) recalled.[18] Once there, these delegates could not reach and directly consult their compatriots. As a consequence, the decisions were effectively imposed upon them by their determined Russian hosts. In all-important Germany, the birthplace of Karl Marx and home to what was nominally the largest 'Marxist' party, the idea of creating a Third, Communist, International was in fact viewed "with great scepticism", because it was not thought that "anything organisationally" could be achieved in the near future.[19] What was not made public was that Spartacist leader Rosa Luxemburg's doubts about Lenin's whole approach to revolution made it anything but predictable that the German thoroughbred would allow itself to be harnessed to the rickety Russian cart. "The essence of socialist society", she had written, "consists in the fact that the great working mass ceases to be a regimented mass, and itself lives and directs in free conscious self-determination the whole political and economic life. . . . The proletarian revolution needs for its purposes no terror, it hates and abominates murder."[20] But when the pliable young Spartacist Hugo Eberlein ("Albrecht") reached Moscow and timidly objected to the immediate establishment of a Third International, he was summarily outvoted by this newly established, unrepresentative body: an unpleasant taste of things to come.

A guest of Nikolai Bukharin, the youngest leading Bolshevik and at that stage far to the left, the writer Arthur Ransome stepped out into the biting cold for some fresh air in the course of the proceedings. There he was surprised to come upon the Finn Yrjö Sirola walking about without hat or coat. "It is March", Sirola insisted in defiance of the temperature. "Spring is coming."[21] This youthful spirit of soaring optimism was everywhere apparent. These were first and foremost inspired militants, indifferent to suffering. Like it or not, the world was going to be changed radically, their own and that of others. When Ransome went to bid farewell to Lenin and tried to persuade the Soviet leader that a revolution in a wealthy and advanced industrialised society like Britain was never on the cards, Lenin unexpectedly retorted that the contagion was like typhoid, for which there was no known cure. "England may seem to you to be untouched, but the microbe is already there." To Lenin it was merely a matter of having the right leadership to bring it about.[22] That, Comintern was expected to provide, and to do so exclusively on the Bolshevik model.

The stark contrast between high-flown expectation and stubborn reality was evident only to those experiencing at first hand the harsh dilemmas the régime faced. Foreign delegates may not have known it but the month of Comintern's foundation was one of acute crisis for the Bolsheviks. Their very survival was at stake, as the Royal Navy bombarded Petrograd. One leading Bolshevik, Leonid Krasin, wrote to his daughters in Scandinavia what amounted to a letter of final farewell in the belief that everything was now over.[23] In that situation Comintern was of little immediate use except as an emblematic beacon from a distant shore.

On 26 March Zinoviev asked the Orgburo of the Party for one million roubles and the requisition of a "big house"—a nickname Comintern soon acquired—for the organisation's executive committee and its operations.[24] They found a large building in Arbat at No. 5 Denezhnyi pereulok, fifteen minutes west of the Kremlin by car. A long and elegant two-floor mansion in pristine stone with tall, broad windows, the building had been deserted by millionaire gold miner Pavel Berg. (Today it is home to the Italian embassy.) Even though Comintern's clandestine services were scattered elsewhere throughout the capital, its main building soon began to attract too much attention. One could see too much just from the street. More space was needed anyway. For some time after its foundation sessions of the executive were not infrequently held in Petrograd, because Zinoviev's most important role was as the city's party secretary. From 1922, after Comintern's branch in Petrograd was closed down, it moved to premises opposite the Kremlin, which were, appropriately, once the site of a church. The four-storey, watery-green structure housing fashionable apartments, built in 1838, still proudly forms the corner of Mokhovaya and Vozdvizhenka and looks onto the Manezh, an elegant exhibition hall used to garage the cars servicing the Kremlin's new occupants.

There the executive committee made the key decisions when Lenin had not already anticipated them with his own. It met twice a month on Sundays, while its smaller bureau, dealing with day-to-day matters, met three times a week at half past ten in the morning. The executive gathered for the first time on 26 March and dealt mainly with housekeeping matters such as gaining secure access to the radio and courier communications systems of Narkomindel. At this early stage Comintern and Narkomindel were not so far apart operationally. Indeed, they were to some extent interchangeable. Narkomindel had the right to representation on Comintern's executive committee. Its first representative was Deputy Commissar for the West Maxim Litvinov, who had spent his years of exile in the leafy suburbs of Hampstead, north London, latterly in the company of a lively Englishwoman, Ivy Lowe, until his sudden, unexpected imprisonment in Brixton.[25]

From the outset Comintern was run more like an army than a debating society. A polyglot from Galicia, Comintern Secretary Karl Radek (Karol Sobelsohn) was proud that the "executive committee of the Third International in contrast to the Second International considers its obligation to intervene very actively and energetically in the affairs of other parties".[26] It was just a matter of putting this into black and white. At the second congress in August 1920 twenty-one conditions for membership were drawn up. The twenty-first condition was proposed by the leading Italian Communist, the Neapolitan engineer Amadeo Bordiga, an extremist though also a hedonist by nature. It was crucial, in that it gave Comintern the right to dictate to member parties. The thrust of this proposal was to shut out reformists who were not true revolutionaries; the ultimate and unintended effect, however, was to reduce Comintern's member parties to not much more than instruments of Soviet control. Even before the conditions had been proposed and debated, at a heated moment early in the first session of the proceedings Radek, in one of the candid outbursts for which he was notorious, exclaimed that "the executive committee of the Communist International is not a federation, but a special organisation that has the right to tell its members what to do".[27]

The Option of Revolutionary War

The second congress took place in public and for that reason could not debate the critical issue of the day: the revolutionary war against expansionist Poland had reached a decisive point. Conscious of weakness, in April both the Communists within Poland and the Bolsheviks in Russia proper sought peace with the Polish government. In mid-May 1920, however, faced with a unique opportunity to restore the imperial borders of the seventeenth century, Poland's president Marshal Józef Piłsudski renewed hostilities with Soviet Russia by attempting to seize Kiev, the historic capital of old Rus, and thus sweep up into Polish arms a population of some four million Ukrainians. Miraculously the Red Army counter-offensive drove his forces back to where they came from. The governments of Europe looked on aghast. The Poles had prodded the bear, which now reared up to strike back. At the point that the Red Army reached the ethnic border of Poland at Brest on 11 July, Foreign Secretary Curzon not unreasonably suggested that the Russians draw to a halt (along what became known as the Curzon Line). But this was revolutionary war, the Napoleonic option for the Bolsheviks, and one that Lenin keenly embraced as an all-or-nothing bid to reach the centre of Europe and spark the Germans into action, taking in the Poles on the way.

At a closed session of a conference of the Russian Communist Party on 22 September Lenin explained what happened next. "We faced the question—should we accept this offer which gave us favourable frontiers and thereby take a stance that was generally speaking simply defensive, or make use of our army's advance and the balance of advantage that we had to assist in the sovietisation of Poland. Here was the fundamental question of a defensive or an offensive war; and we in the Central Committee knew that this was a new question of principle, that we stood at a crossroads with respect to the entire policy of Soviet rule." No one voted against the decision to go on the offensive, though this had not previously been taken with respect to the former imperial territories of Georgia and Estonia. "But in relation to Poland", Lenin continued, "we changed this policy." There was no official resolution placed on the record, "but among ourselves we said that we must probe with bayonets—had the proletariat's social revolution ripened in Poland?" Lenin none the less had to acknowledge that what they were doing was "not completely clear to the best Communist elements of the international community; that is to say, the Communist International". The Germans in particular were disturbed at this abrupt and unilateral change of line. "Such people consider themselves Communists", Lenin jibed, "but some of them remain nationalists and pacificists." The decision "was a critical turning-point not only in the politics of Soviet Russia, but in global politics", Lenin declared. Hitherto they had faced capitalist states alone, "dreaming only of how to find cracks between them so that the adversary could not crush us. And now we said: we are now stronger and to every attempt to attack us we will retaliate with a counter-attack, so that you will know that . . . you will take the risk that for every attack the extent of the Soviet Republic will grow."[28] War had given birth to the Bolshevik revolution. Another conflict on this scale would thus inevitably mean further opportunities. The horrifying shock of "catastrophic defeat" at the gates of Warsaw on 16–19 August 1920 thus meant indefinite postponement of the realisation of the great dream, though certainly not its final abandonment.[29]

The bottom line was that even those Poles who favoured radical change did not want it thrust upon them by the Russians. Meanwhile Radek drafted an article drawing lessons from the Polish setback—to the effect that revolution should not be imposed upon the Poles at the point of a bayonet. Lenin, however, could not have disagreed more:

> Let us take one example: White Poland has not attacked Russia but a proletarian revolution has broken out in Germany. French and British capital attempt to crush Soviet Germany. Would not Soviet Russia be obliged to hurry to the aid of the German proletariat through military and economic measures? Would not White Poland resist with all its forces the Red Army's campaign and the transportation of Russian supplies for the German workers? Should not Soviet Russia extend the hand of support to the German workers over the corpse of White Poland? And should not Polish workers then exert

every effort, however weak they were, to support the Russian and
German workers through the establishment of a Polish Soviet Government on the ruins of White Poland?[30]

In other words, Poland would block the path to Germany. Its needs were
therefore secondary. The Poles would have their revolution thrust down
their throats whether they liked it or not. And revolutionary war would
remain an option open to the Bolsheviks *sine die*. The rest of Europe had
good reason to worry. Poland sat on the front line, uncertain when the
next blow might fall.

An uncomfortable truce between Poland and Soviet Russia signed
on 12 October 1920 was reaffirmed by a peace treaty concluded in Riga
on 18 March 1921. The terms insisted on by Poland left too many Ukrainians and Byelorussians on its side of the frontier to be sustainable over
the long term. This, alongside the Paris Peace, was Poland's Pyrrhic victory, in that one quarter of the country's population was now other than
ethnically Polish and these minorities were consistently hostile to the
régime. The Polish state would thereafter face more than one enemy
within. The obvious question that hung over it was: what would happen
if, or indeed when, the balance of power between Warsaw and Moscow
and Berlin and Warsaw changed?

The same brutal realism that forced this humiliating peace on the
Bolsheviks also dictated a fundamental change in Moscow's tactics.
Revolutionary war was not rejected in principle but postponed as an
option for better times. Zinoviev is reported to have said that "before
Warsaw we had the illusion that capitalism could be taken by frontal
attack. Now it is a war by siege that has to be undertaken."[31] The indirect
approach—Comintern, burrowing away from within—now came into
its own. Conditions remained favourable. Discontent, if not rebellion,
was rife throughout Europe. Lenin poured millions of dollars into the
furthering of unrest worldwide—even while his own population in
the south was driven to cannibalism, prompting the arrival in 1921 of the
American Relief Administration under Republican Herbert Hoover.
Within a matter of months Comintern's impact could be detected everywhere. But Lenin would never live to see the ultimate results in the

decades ahead; an assassin's bullet discharged by the Socialist Revolutionary fanatic Fanny Kaplan in August 1918 eventually saw to that. It was a death postponed—until 1924—but foreordained.

When great powers such as Britain negotiated diplomatic recognition of the Soviet régime in search of the lucrative Russian market, the treaty invariably contained a clause prohibiting revolutionary propaganda. The Soviet government happily signed under its own name while leaving Comintern as a purely Communist Party institution to carry on the devil's work. This sleight of hand greatly amused Lenin: "it shows where the shoe pinches", he chuckled.[32] Not surprisingly, in 1920 British foreign intelligence, MI6, set up its leading station in Berlin, the site chosen by Lenin for Comintern's West European Bureau, in order to focus on revolutionary activity across the length and breadth of Europe.[33]

2

Europe at the Brink

Revolutions are not carried in suitcases.

—KARL RADEK[1]

In the interwar years the threat of revolution lay at the core, not along the periphery, of conflict and conflict resolution in Europe. It is vital to understand that the continent was divided vertically—between classes—as well as horizontally between states. The conduct of international relations could not ignore this awkward and discomforting reality, much as Europe's well-groomed diplomats clearly wished it would go away. And at the centre of the drama lay Germany.

Germany in defeat represented the sum of everyone's hopes and fears. Its future was therefore a matter of universal attention and studied concern from the rest of Europe. But these were purely calculations of power, bereft of psychological insight and foresight. Germany had undoubtedly wrecked the entire prewar order. It could scarcely count on anyone's sympathy among those trying to put the pieces back together. But as a country, it was left stretched on the rack, torn by political extremes. The victorious allies made matters worse by failing to apply to the peace settlement sufficient forbearance to neutralise an acute sense of injustice—however misplaced—that was widespread throughout the country.

To the extent that the allies saw any potential dangers, their attention was directed, wrongly, only to the far left. And even then the much repeated argument that Germany under pressure would explode into a Bolshevik-style revolution failed to convince the sceptics as a plausible reason for an equitable peace settlement. Over a century earlier, in 1815, when Britain and its allies secured the defeat of Napoleon and fears of revolution resurgent were just as real, Foreign Secretary Robert Stewart, the Irish Viscount Castlereagh, had cautiously insisted that the defeated be given their rights so that they would have a vested interest in international stability. But when leading German industrialist Walther Rathenau pleaded that very case in 1919, it came from the mouth of the defeated rather than of the victors. It reeked too much of self-interest and therefore lacked credibility. Rathenau was, after all, not exactly a disinterested party: he was the man who had created the Raw Materials Division of the Ministry of War. He was none the less not altogether wrong. The victorious allies were playing political roulette with the future stability of Europe. Thereafter, in the face of allied demands for reparations, finalised in 1921, the rulers of the Weimar Republic played financial roulette with the future stability of Germany.

In spite of the disastrous economic collapse that followed defeat in Germany, a sustained revolution from indigenous sources persistently failed to materialise: either in 1918–19, before the formation of the Communist Party (KPD), or in March 1921, while the KPD was still very much in its infancy. Yet it was hard for the Bolsheviks to draw the obvious conclusion that the German working class was not inherently revolutionary: though still nominally Marxist, the major party of the left— the Social Democratic Party (SPD)—had long ago evolved from the socialist party it claimed to be into a reformist party. It had, after all, chosen to side with the Junker state rather than risk a leap into the revolutionary abyss. In 1919 the Marxist Rudolf Hilferding, on behalf of the Independent Socialists, remarked that "[i]n Germany they had a Socialist Party which, after the revolution and at the most acute stage of the fight for political power, had not taken its place in the ranks of Labour against the bourgeoisie, but allied itself to the bourgeoisie against a section of the proletariat".[2]

It was not just in Soviet eyes that the revolution had in a fundamental sense been betrayed. The social democrats in charge of the government, most notoriously Gustav Noske, who had enthusiastically supported the war, suppressed with ruthless force the far left that had resolutely opposed it. Noske turned a blind eye as Spartacist leaders Karl Liebknecht and Rosa Luxemburg were assassinated by the right-wing Freikorps. Sir Horace Rumbold, British ambassador in Bern, was correct in reporting to London that effectively Germany was still ruled by the "military and Junker element dominating the Ebert–Scheidemann Government".[3] Thereafter German Social Democracy was toxic as far as the Bolsheviks were concerned. They believed the revolutionary left in Germany had to be recast in the Soviet mould to ensure success, a process known as "Bolshevisation". It meant that what became the largest Communist Party outside Russia, the KPD, was reduced in effect to nothing more than an increasingly wayward and disappointing understudy.

In reconciling themselves to a revolution indefinitely postponed, the Bolsheviks very early on found compensation in close military and commercial collaboration with the Weimar Republic. Weimar Germany was an international outcast at the behest of the French. It was they who insisted on full reparations and on German disarmament. It was they who kept Germany out of the League of Nations and who blocked Lloyd George's attempts to bring Germany into a new political settlement at Genoa in April 1922. The Paris peace settlement with respect to Europe reflected the priorities of France under its vengeful diehard president Henri Poincaré, who had wanted to continue fighting Germany to the bitter end. With Prime Minister Georges Clemenceau at the helm, the Germans were publicly humiliated: they were subjected to massive indemnities; they were disarmed; the left bank of the Rhine was demilitarised; Danzig was amputated from Germany by a corridor passing through Poland; Alsace-Lorraine was returned to France; German Austria was prohibited from unification with Germany proper, while German Bohemia was handed to infant Czechoslovakia; and in the Hall of Mirrors at Versailles, where the Germans were required to agree to terms on penalty of renewed hostilities, they were not even allowed to sit down alongside the other signatory powers. The magnanimity in victory made possible by Castlereagh in 1815 was, in an age of democratic politics, not even seriously considered.

The result was national abasement and military impotence. Germany was abandoned, sandwiched between two insecure and rapidly rearming powers, France and Poland, while the British removed themselves to their island fastness. Yet France did not have everything its own way. Once it was clear that the Americans would not sign up to the League of Nations, the tripartite treaty of security that guaranteed French territorial integrity was defunct; so the French did not even have the certainty of a British alliance. With Russia as a Bolshevik outcast and no longer in play, France sought salvation in a series of military alliances with the new states of Eastern Europe. The French then blocked all measures leading to disarmament that had been provided for under the Versailles Treaty to complement the measures imposed on Germany. Membership of the newly established League of Nations was also denied to Germany. Inevitably Berlin looked elsewhere for compensation. In Moscow they found it.

Soviet–German Soundings

Germany and Russia had long been natural trading partners. Chancellor Otto von Bismarck had counted upon that fact in neutralising potential Russian rivalry during the last quarter of the nineteenth century. As a major producer of raw materials, the Russian economy blended well with its German counterpart, which was primarily industrial. The anecdote that when German circuses first arrived in Russia at the turn of the century the peasants believed that monkeys were made in Hamburg illustrated a larger truth. Germany epitomised the wonders of modern technology. The complementarity in trade and the fact that both were outcasts drew the two régimes into harness, even while the hated social democrats held office in Berlin. The other, less savoury, element of Soviet co-operation with the German right was tolerated rather than welcomed by social democrats. It amounted to German evasion of the Versailles Treaty by means of secret military collaboration between the Reichswehr and the Red Army, between the German military industrial sector and the remnants of the much-depleted armaments industry in Russia.

General Hans von Seeckt, soon chief of Germany's army command, was the first to seek a solution to the strangulating restrictions on the armed forces imposed at Versailles. He did so in firm confidence that close collaboration with the Bolsheviks in Russia could be pursued safely while police enforcement contained the Communists at home.[4] Seeckt's counter-party on the Soviet side, imprisoned in Moabit (Berlin) during August–September 1919, was Radek. Reared in the Austrian section of partitioned Poland and therefore a fluent German speaker, Radek was openly sceptical about the possibilities for revolution beyond Soviet borders, and therefore eager to lock in national security through close collaboration with Germany based on purely geopolitical interests. Unlike almost any other Bolshevik, except Litvinov and Stalin, Radek saw and declared the world revolution to be "a very slow process", and that was as early as 1919.[5]

Seeckt and Radek forged ahead with this shared vision even while the outlook for revolution in Europe still held out hope to Moscow. Eyeing Poland, they readily found common cause in 1920. During the Red Army's march on Warsaw that heady summer, General Seeckt thought a Soviet victory highly likely. "It is very possible", he noted on 26 July, "that the Bolshevik army will advance across the [river] Weichsel to the German frontier. As a result an entirely new political situation will be created. Germany and Russia will be in direct contact with one another. One of the most crucial aims of the Versailles policy, the separation of Germany from Russia by a strong Poland would be thwarted. And Germany would take its position in the power struggle between Russia and the Entente and be forced to grapple with the ideas of the Russian Revolution."[6]

The Russians and the Germans began to lay the ground for intimate collaboration. On 12 August Viktor Kopp, the unofficial Soviet representative in Berlin, acting on behalf of People's Commissar for Military and Naval Affairs Lev Trotsky, told the Germans that the Kremlin was willing to recognise the frontiers of 1914 (returning the territory separating Germany from East Prussia mandated to Poland at Paris in 1919). Should "a Polish Bolshevik government be formed in Warsaw, then this Polish Government will willingly cede to Germany former German territory if it is ethnically German".[7] This was too much for leading Poles in the Soviet régime—not least Felix Dzerzhinsky and Iosif Unshlikht, heading Soviet secret intelligence. Instead, the compromise of plebiscites was suggested. All of this none the less indicated just how far the Bolsheviks were prepared to go in pursuit of tactical advantage along the road to world revolution. The retreat from Warsaw had put an end to discussions about attacking Poland for the time being, however. Reporting from Berlin, Kopp told Chicherin that "the idea of an Eastern orientation, if not quite vanished from the political horizon, has at any event very much faded".[8]

The notion that Russian revolutionary interests and German state interests could so easily be squared was far too radical for most. The German politician Gustav Stresemann, a conservative nationalist not privy to these discussions, had first encountered the Bolsheviks at the Brest-Litovsk negotiations in 1918. He now looked on in horror. As the Red Army was heading for the German frontier two years later, well after Germany's own defeat, Stresemann asked rhetorically, "Do you really think that Lenin, who has continuously preached world revolution, will stop at these borders? What then?"[9] But this did not worry Prussian Junkers focused on the dismemberment of Poland. These calculations were brutally realistic—indeed, pessimistic. Russia as a state was not in any conventional sense a threat to anyone. Although vast in territory, it was confined to the margins of Europe, a predominantly peasant economy; its armed forces numbered no more than three-quarters of a million and were poorly equipped; its limited heavy industry was largely shattered by war. In September 1922 the titan of German heavy industry, Krupp, upon whom tsarist Russia once heavily relied, pulled out of an offer to help rebuild the Russian armaments industry after the revolution. Yet concerted rearmament ultimately turned out to be the great opportunity for both states cast out of the European Concert. A Soviet–German entente also threatened British interests because it aimed to destabilise the peace without which Europe could not once again find economic stability.

Buoyant economic growth in Germany underwrote European prosperity, which greatly enhanced the economy of a major trading state like

Britain, the status-quo power par excellence. The British Empire had reached its peak in 1919, but its population was exhausted by war, so it was primarily interested in peace. The middle classes demanded nothing less. Economic collapse in Europe meant wide-scale political disturbance or, worse still, the prospect of revolution. Thus British and Soviet interests were entirely at odds where Germany was concerned, as were British and French policies. And that conflict of interests expanded as the decade proceeded.

Attempted Revolution in Germany

Germany remained unstable yet tantalisingly out of Comintern's reach, despite its top-heavy presence in Berlin. The Kapp putsch by the German right in March 1920 was overturned by the social democratic trades unions who downed tools, not by the Communist Party. The Communists initially stood aloof because they regarded their socialist rivals, who had stepped in to prop up the status quo in 1918–19, as renegades no different from bourgeois nationalists. Thus when the Communists chose to rise up a year later they, of course, found themselves entirely on their own. And this was the story throughout the decade. A divided left seemed destined to deepen existing antagonisms. Meanwhile the right held firm and gained a magnetic attraction to those alarmed by revolutionary rhetoric and those repelled by the spirit of reconciliation with the Versailles powers holding Germany in a vise. This state of affairs was, however, insufficiently understood anywhere else. Within Germany the sense of it was visceral.

The attempt by the KPD to seize power in March 1921—the *Märzaktion*, as it became known—was always something of a puzzle because it was initiated from Berlin by Comintern emissaries. To the outside world it seemed obvious who was ultimately behind it. But it was actually more complicated than that. The Soviet régime was at this stage in disarray. Lenin and Trotsky, the two leading figures in the Soviet régime, were fatally distracted, entirely taken up with the consequences of a perilous uprising at the Kronstadt naval fortress in the wintry fog of Petrograd by the very sailors who had once signalled the start of the revolution in 1917: "none of us should leave Russia now while we're fighting here for our very lives", Zinoviev told Jules Humbert-Droz, a newly arrived Swiss Communist bewildered at what was going on after witnessing the fighting across the ice of the Neva.[10]

Among German Communists a fatal spirit of intolerance prevailed. KPD leaders Paul Levi and Clara Zetkin tended to side with the right within the international Communist movement. For this they were reprimanded by Zinoviev and ousted from the leadership of the KPD by Mátyás Rákosi, Comintern's representative in Berlin, who was among those who had fled Budapest after the failed revolution of 1919 and then re-established himself as a leading enforcer of Comintern directives. Such men were known as "Turkestanis": a racist epithet stemming from the image of the brutality notoriously associated with warring Turkestan.[11] The KPD had expanded to absorb the Independent Social Democrats in 1920, believing that it would take time before an insurrection could be contemplated with any confidence. But they had also locked out the left, who stood closer to the anarchists in opposing electoral politics. Yet the left had taken with it half of the party's membership in 1919. Those who remained had scores to settle. Now Levi was himself to fall victim to the prevalent sectarian spirit.

The new KPD leadership under Heinrich Brandler stood well to the left and was easily pressed into a premature uprising by Béla Kun, the man who had once been too moderate and believed that this was why he had failed as leader of the abortive Hungarian revolution in 1919.[12] Kun sailed from Petrograd to Stettin as the new Comintern representative in Berlin, operating under the code name "Spanier". In pressing for immediate revolutionary action he was acting on the authority of Zinoviev alone. The motivation for so doing resulted directly from the crisis in Russia caused by the Kronstadt revolt, a personal disaster for Zinoviev as Petrograd party secretary, taking place as it did in his own backyard. "I'll show them how to make a revolution," Kun boasted to Humbert-Droz, Zinoviev's eyes and ears on the incoming team.

Kun insisted to the doubters that the Germans had to take the offensive:

Soviet Russia is in very great danger. Put away any hopes that Russia can survive a decade in isolation. It is apparent that for two years Soviet Russia can hold out without real help from the West European proletariat. You well know what a factor Soviet Russia is for world revolution and what the loss of the Soviet state would mean. If you believe that Soviet Russia will fall within two years without the help of the world revolution, then you must adjust your tactics accordingly to smash the front of the counter-revolution. Don't wait, having taken up a defensive position, while the bourgeoisie chokes the proletariat with the restoration of capitalism.[13]

To this end Comintern disbursed 620,000 gold roubles' worth of currency and valuables through "Comrade Thomas"—Jakob Reich—who turned out not even to be a Communist. No less than 1.22 million was sent to Germany for that year; much of it simply went missing.[14]

In late March the copper miners in Mansfeld, Communist to a man, rose up, rifle in hand, and provided Berlin with the starting point for a more general offensive. This took in the massive chemical factories in Leuna, near Halle in Saxony, and was accompanied by violent incidents elsewhere, including the blowing up of a railway bridge and some banks, disturbances in the Hamburg shipyards and the killing of a security official in Berlin. But none of this amounted to much. The KPD denied it was an uprising and order was easily restored by the authorities, who reinforced the garrison in Berlin. Brandler was arrested and imprisoned.

Subsequently Lenin fully accepted that Kun had made a "stupid" error in initiating an uprising "to help the Russians". Kun was criticised for being "frequently too much to the left".[15] But Kun was, as we have seen, not acting entirely on his own. Zinoviev, as president of Comintern, had sent him for a purpose. Lenin tried and failed to persuade Levi to confine knowledge of the disaster to a small circle, but by the end of the year all of Germany knew about it. It never mattered, within Comintern, who was correct. What counted was strict subordination to discipline from the centre, so the ejection of former leaders from the party was ultimately inevitable.[16] The Russians were more intently focused on shoring up their relationship with the German right.

The Rapallo Relationship

Finally, opportunity beckoned in anticipation of a summit conference in Genoa called by the British to encompass Germany, Russia and the Entente powers in an effort to pacify Europe and re-open newly established barriers to trade. It was scheduled for April 1922. Lenin originally intended to participate but his colleagues insisted that it was too dangerous. Another assassin's bullet was always in the offing: too many people had lost everything in 1917. On 17 January 1922 Radek arrived in Berlin along with Christian Rakovsky and Nikolai Krestinsky, to be joined later by Leonid Krasin, for the primary purpose of negotiating a draft treaty of co-operation with Germany. That draft would soon become the Rapallo Treaty, concluded on 16 April.[17] Arrangements for secret military collaboration, under way in February, picked up speed.

Radek reported from his meetings with Rathenau and Seeckt that the general insisted Germany could escape from its situation "only in rapprochement with Russia", and this sentiment was growing in every direction regardless of party. Throughout the secret talks Seeckt was "very restrained and only at one point did he lose self-control, namely when he spoke about Poland". He did not, however, expect war between the Russians and the Poles in the spring of 1922. But at this point in the discussion "he raised himself up, his eyes began to sparkle like a bear and he said: it [Poland] must be crushed and it will be crushed, just as soon as Russia or Germany get stronger". Any response would have been superfluous. Radek concluded, "It means that the soundings in Germany are over; you can draw the conclusions yourselves; I am doing that on my arrival [in Moscow]."[18]

The German ambassador in Moscow, Ulrich von Brockdorff-Rantzau, was certainly no friend of Bolshevism. On 22 December 1922 he asked what Russia would do should the French cross the frontier into Germany's industrial heartland in order to resolve by force the problem of reparations payments. Trotsky's reply was that this would depend upon how the Germans reacted, as the Russians did not have any great military capability; but "should Poland at France's request invade Silesia, then we will not for one moment stand by; we could not tolerate that, we would go in!"[19] This was, of course, precisely what the Junkers wished to hear.

Only two months before, the US ambassador in Berlin, Alanson Houghton, had argued forcefully that "the time is short . . . Already the conditions are dangerous. Already the Bolshevist tide is beating against the barriers of European civilization. And if once those barriers go down, if the German people in despair, believing that sympathy and help and understanding of their position are denied them, turn for relief to the East, the time is past. That tide will sweep restlessly to the Atlantic."[20] Those in Washington DC needed little reminder. Having opted out of a European settlement that would have tied them down indefinitely, they fretted at the ineptitude of those whom they had so fecklessly deserted for their collective failure to act responsibly. Among American legislators the maverick but highly influential senator from Idaho William Borah warned that "France is adopting the very policy which is going to drive Germany into the hands of the militarists or bolshevists".[21]

Any hope of compromise, however, certainly foundered in Paris. US Ambassador Myron Herrick, a successful businessman, reported that President and Foreign Minister Poincaré "has learned nothing and for-gotten nothing not from lack of intelligence but rather from definite purpose partly because he has staked his political life and reputation on his aggressive policy, perhaps more because of conviction that for France's safety *delenda est Carthago* ['Carthage must be destroyed' (because it was richer than Rome)]".[22] Britain's foreign secretary at the time of the Paris Peace Conference, the cynical realist Sir Arthur Balfour, later as a peer of the realm summed up the conundrum that the French never confronted: France "wanted a Germany rich enough to pay in-demnities, and also a Germany that was ruined".[23]

Britain and the United States could not ignore the plain truth that, as "an essential part of the economic organism of Europe", Germany was in serious trouble. Since 1914 Berlin had been steadily diluting the Reichs-mark by printing too many banknotes rather than taking the unpopular measure of raising taxes to pay its bills. The British understood that bringing finances to order "would break up the present Government and lead to revolution". On 23 May 1922 Lloyd George reminded cabinet that "no one, he presumed, wanted a revolution and if one took place it would be very different from the Russian Revolution. The Russians were among the most incompetent people in Europe whereas in some respects the Germans were the most competent. They would run their revolution in ways which would be much more attractive to our people whereas the Russian methods had revolted our people."[24]

French Forces Invade the Ruhr

As the ruling Liberal–Conservative coalition in London dithered over a solution to the reparations problem, the French decided that the time had come to take matters into their own hands. In January 1923, unable to extract from Germany the full amount of reparations agreed upon in May 1921 and in manifest defiance of the British, French and Belgian forces under General Degoutte invaded the Ruhr basin, ostensibly to extract the industrial raw materials owing to them. The Ruhr contained over 80% of Germany's coal, 80% of pig iron and steel production and 70% of traffic in raw materials and finished products. For Germans, the occupation represented the ultimate humiliation. The British were horrified. Poincaré was out of control.

German resistance was predictable but took an unusual turn, with disastrous consequences as regards the ultimate fate of the Weimar Republic. Chancellor Wilhelm Cuno's government ordered passive resistance and in effect committed national financial suicide by printing money at an even more reckless rate than usual.[25] This inevitably led directly to hyperinflation within months, wiping out at a stroke the hard-earned savings of the middle classes, upon whom the future stability of the new order depended. But, not content with exacting reparations, the French, buoyed up by their apparent success in seizing reparations by force of arms, made a barefaced attempt to dismember the German state. They proclaimed the neighbouring province of the Rhineland a separate republic on 21 October and, having failed there, they tried by force to reconstitute the Bavarian Palatinate as an autonomous state.

These efforts collapsed only when, finally, Curzon stepped in and announced that enough was enough; 147,000 German citizens had been pushed out of the Ruhr, 376 killed and 2,092 wounded by the time the occupation collapsed.[26] The psychological effects on German opinion for the long term were incalculable. The British were effectively thereafter committed against any attempt by the French to take pre-emptive military action anywhere, at any time, against the Germans. And the Germans were bent on revenge.

The Rise of Fascism in Italy

Elsewhere in Europe ideological warfare held sway. Attitudes to fascism, notably on the part of the British, were determined by its potential as a buffer against, if not a counterweight to, the Communist threat. In Moscow Italy was seen as the country most likely to succumb to a Bolshevik revolution. No government commanded any moral authority. Francesco Nitti (1919–20) and Giovanni Giolitti (1920–21), each in turn minister of the interior as well as prime minister, were both badly tainted by financial (Nitti) and political (Giolitti) corruption. Furthermore both administrations were chronically weak. As the hard left pressed upon them, they succumbed bit by bit. As they did so, countervailing resentment grew slowly but resolutely at the local level, inflamed by the right. An ultra-nationalist movement emerged early in 1919, as leagues of ex-combatants reacted violently when socialist anti-militarists blocked the erection of monuments to commemorate the war dead, pouring scorn on those who wore decorations for service to their country. Notwithstanding final victory, the war had been a disaster for all, symbolised above all in the defeat at Caporetto in 1917; the nation, as a nation, commanded no respect. In May 1920, responding in large part to a climate of unremitting intimidation from the far left, a general assembly of the emerging fascist movement met in Milan. The program was vague, and intentionally so. It was said that there was no wish to form a political party or to "feel bound by any specific doctrine". But the movement's opposition to the League of Nations was made clear, and the intention was expressed to free the country from subjugation to

Western financial dominance. Better treatment was proposed for the war-wounded, an eight-hour day for workers, an initial levy on capital and the seizure of church property.[27] But this was just music of the future. Not until their third congress, in Rome on 7–10 November 1921, did the fascists declare themselves a political party.

What the fascists were also reacting to were the waves of strikes in the cities of Rome, Naples, Turin, Milan and Genoa on the trams and railways, among taxi drivers and in the post office and electrical services; matched by those of agricultural labourers in Apulia, Emilia-Romagna and the Veneto. But matters went from bad to worse for capitalism in Italy. The turning-point came after notoriously violent riots in Ancona in June 1920. In Moscow Zinoviev, Bukharin and Lenin believed that now was the moment to spark revolution in Italy.[28] The riots were followed by the occupation of the metal factories in Turin throughout September, which brought the country close to revolution, as it was soon accompanied by other occupations and strikes the length and breadth of the country. Lenin reflected that he would have liked to risk helping Italy, "though, unfortunately, that is now practically impossible".[29]

The government vehemently denied that revolution could represent an immediate danger. It resolutely refused to take any action to protect private property by ending the factory occupations. While the rest of Europe panicked as the Red Army swept across Poland, heading for Warsaw in August, possibly with Berlin to follow, the British expressed amazement that the Italian authorities could affect indifference to the factory occupations: "The Government continued a policy which by themselves is described as neutrality, and by the Employers as an abdication of authority."[30]

"The history of the crisis is really astounding", the British commercial secretary at the embassy in Rome concluded, "with all that it has involved: factories seized, owners and directors driven out and in some cases imprisoned, employers threatened with violence, seizure and sale by the workmen of the owners' material, armed violence in the streets behind sandbag barricades, and firing on the public authorities and the police, assaults on private individuals, seizure of houses. A government taking refuge in silence, twenty days of chaos and almost anarchy."[31] The

British consul-general in Milan, for one, had no doubt that these events "may be compared to a Soviet experience, and that the movement has a political and revolutionary character . . . If the Italian Government still believes that the movement is purely economical and wishes the world to think so too then they are simply playing the part of silly ostrich."[32] . . . The struggle does not involve a fraction of the Italian industries, as the Italian Government would have one believe, but 20,000 works."[33]

Yet what struck the British commercial attaché was less the crisis precipitated by the militants, than their evident failure to reap the harvest they had sown: "The men have missed their opportunity: instead of dominating the situation, they have been mastered by it; bewildered beyond the possibility of revolution, lost in a vortex of conflicting interests, where they might have imposed their will once and for all on a nervous and disorganised country, they have not dared. They have fired, but it was a flash in the pan; they have moved forward, and all the time their world was slipping backward."[34] The aftermath of "the great metallurgical strike" was "not less interesting or important" in the eyes of British diplomats. Giovanni Agnelli, the Machiavellian owner of the gargantuan industrial enterprise Fiat, "declared that it was impossible to continue business under the new conditions created by the workers, and resigned with his colleagues. The workers very soon found themselves in the humiliating position of having to beg him to return."[35]

Communist Antonio Gramsci, a fervent admirer of Georges Sorel, had been the mastermind behind the factory occupations. Gramsci was from the outset a very unorthodox Communist. Although rapidly narrowing, the Communist church was still very broad, broad enough to accommodate those to the left of Leninism who were, even as late as the Spanish Civil War in 1936–39, regarded as errant but fundamentally like-minded souls. Gramsci's idiosyncratic ideological journey was viewed with some suspicion by the more fervent Leninists and his own doubts about it emerged in defeat. He published a post-mortem of events in *L'Ordine Nuovo*, the weekly he edited. "It would be less than frank and sincere", Gramsci acknowledged with evident regret, "to deny that our revolutionary movement has received a heavy blow."[36] And with it the credibility of a revolutionary alternative to Leninism that had been smashed already within Soviet Russia—the Workers' Opposition—was now badly broken. The factory occupations had wounded the capitalist beast but had not killed it. Agnelli was too formidable an opponent. He had skilfully masterminded a tactical retreat with every intention of withdrawing every concession as soon as the time was ripe. The entire economy was faltering. Banks were refusing credit and shareholders were unloading securities; pessimism had taken hold, inhibiting investment. And, as conditions worsened significantly in the course of 1921— the cost of living, already accelerating since the war, rose some 24% between July 1920 and January 1921, while unemployment quadrupled— Agnelli proceeded to meticulously unpick every agreement entered into during his desperate attempt to fend off the revolutionary onslaught.[37]

Factory occupations marked the culmination of the *biennio rosso*— the two "red years" of rampant public disorder and widespread fear for personal safety. In the countryside matters were little better. Farmers and richer peasants whose property was threatened by seizure from revolutionaries reacted by turning to fascists for direct help. Sir George Buchanan, the British ambassador, had previously served as such in Petrograd and had tried to warn the tsar of the dangers ahead, to no avail. It looked as though he was about to repeat the experience. Not only had the government stood aside, but when land was seized in Sicily and other provinces, Prime Minister Giolitti, in conversation with Buchanan, "went so far as to palliate the peasants' action, on the ground that, as uncultivated cornlands were liable to expropriation by the Government, the peasants had but taken the law into their own hands".[38]

What ultimately delivered Italy into the hands of the far right were the divisions deepening on the left that Lenin saw as a necessary purging of reformism. The Italian Socialist Party (PSI) had, like its French counterparts, adhered to Comintern en masse. But it began to split when, at the instigation of the left wing of the Italian party, the second Comintern congress in Petrograd in 1920 imposed the twenty-first condition of membership ensuring absolute obedience. As intended, the reformists under Filippo Turati and the maximalists under Giacinto Serrati were driven off at the Livorno Congress (15–21 January 1921), leaving only the minority to form the Communist Party (PCI). Meanwhile, whereas it was the left who were mainly responsible for the chaos in 1920, the following year found the fascists better organised, backed by financial interests and imposing their own idea of order in the streets, while the government held back from enforcing public safety. Large groups of organised and disciplined fascists swarmed into socialist enclaves like Bologna. And whereas socialists and Communists alike became identified with strikes, the fascists identified themselves with new opportunities for employment, and in the most trying economic conditions. Soon desertion from socialist ranks was matched by mass recruitment by the fascists.

Worse still, eminent intellectuals on the right such as the most respected economists Vilfredo Pareto and Maffeo Pantaleone backed the fascists. Even liberal conservatives such as the celebrated philosopher and historian Benedetto Croce drifted in the direction of fascism as "a temporary, rough-and-ready instrument for the restoration of the State and national authority".[39] This mattered. Throughout Europe, Italy had led the way in the advance of economics, political theory and sociology since the end of the nineteenth century. The status of the intelligentsia in public life was nowhere else so notable.

Rejection of the far left was much greater than fear of the far right. In August the call for a general strike against the fascists—who had been let loose in the cities of northern Italy to wreak havoc, burning down the offices of left-wing newspapers, party headquarters and women's clubs—proved a signal failure. A militant of these years, Mario Montagnana, acknowledged more than two decades later that "fascism was precisely the price of our defeat, the consequence of our mistakes and our weaknesses in the years in which the movement had attained the highest point, in the years in which it appeared—and of this we were convinced—that there was no goal that we would not attain".[40]

At the fascist convention staged in the San Carlo Theatre in Naples on 24 October 1922 Mussolini made a dramatic appearance in a signature black shirt and railed against those in government who had asked what the fascists wanted. "What did they answer?" Mussolini intoned. "Nothing. Worse still, they . . . did a little calculation of our forces; they talked about ministries without portfolio . . . and under-secretaryships.

But all that is a joke . . . we fascists do not intend to be let in by the tradesman's entrance; we fascists do not intend to renounce our formidable, noble birthright to satisfy ourselves with a miserable plate of ministerial beans."[41]

Instead, Mussolini strode to power on 28 October 1922 at the invitation of King Vittorio Emanuele. The government had finally found itself capable of mustering armed resistance to the fascist paramilitaries thronging into Rome and other key cities, only to find the king unwilling to bite the bullet.[42] Mussolini's astute mix of physical intimidation and amiable bonhomie had an extraordinary effect on politicians unaccustomed to his confusing repertoire. Parliament fast became a mere talking shop by agreeing to special powers for the prime minister renewable by the year. Italy was still nominally a democracy, but effectively a fledgling dictatorship. It did not take long for Mussolini to seize the moment and unleash a wave of repression, crushing Communist and socialist alike with unusual efficacy.

In their ignorance the Russians were utterly confused. It was the first time they, or indeed anyone, had seen fascism in operation. "How did Mussolini begin in Italy?" the dominant Comintern secretary Osip Pyatnitsky asked a few years later. "He did not begin by shooting or introducing military courts or adopting a stance favourable to capital. He came out with a demagogic program of improving the position of workers, the petty bourgeoisie and the peasantry. This was his method by which he won over the masses. And when he won them over, when he became strong, then he showed his real face. But he had less strength than the national fascists when he came to power. He had no army; he had only small cadres of fascist militia."[43]

Mussolini's onslaught began with an "unprecedent crusade" against "thousands of Communists and Socialists and the terror grew with every day", Zinoviev stated at the time.[44] The young Communist Umberto Terracini described what happened later, writing to Italian-American comrades:

In the space of a week the police has arrested more than 5000 comrades, among whom are almost all the secretaries of our federations, all the organisers of Communist trades unions, all of our local and county councillors. In addition it has succeeded in appropriating all our financial resources, striking a mortal blow at our press. . . . You cannot imagine what has been happening in our cities and our country-side in the past week: it is a true manhunt that has been organised by the police working with cohorts of fascists.[45]

Unusually, perhaps because they were taken off guard, the Bolsheviks, who were nothing if not disciplined, had difficulty restraining their fury. Another great hope for revolution had been brutally dashed. As recently as 1920 Italy had seemed one of the very few countries ripe for Bolshevism. And although the Communist Party apparatus had been driven underground by the previous régime in March 1921, Mussolini's accession to power none the less came as something of a shock. Indeed, Radek described it as "the most serious defeat that socialism and communism have suffered from the time the period of the world revolution began; a defeat more serious than that of Soviet Hungary because it is a consequence of the spiritual and political failure of Italian socialism and of the entire Italian workers' movement".[46]

It is striking how perilously close the Soviet Politburo came to breaking off diplomatic relations. Vatslav Vorovsky, a Bolshevik though a descendant of the Polish nobility and a man of letters, had begun his experience in international relations at Comintern before Lenin appointed him ambassador to Italy.[47] On 1 November 1922 members of the trade department at the embassy, mainly Italians, were roughed up by Mussolini's *squadristi*. One of them was shot multiple times. "Perhaps we should kick Mussolini and have *everyone* (Vorovsky and the whole delegation) *leave Italy*, and begin *attacking* her over her fascists?" Lenin suggested. "Let us give the Italian *people* some serious help." In this heated atmosphere, on 10 November Vorovsky himself suggested that in retaliation the entire embassy walk out. But on further reflection he withdrew the suggestion.[48]

The danger was that the Soviet state, not just Comintern, would be seen to be acting out of ideological solidarity with the defeated left against the revanchist right. Caution prevailed. A telegram to the ambassador authorised by the Politburo on 8 February 1923 advised him that "our position distinguishing between the Sov[iet] Gov[ernment] and Comintern remains unchangeable".[49] After further agonising, the Kremlin finally decided on 19 February 1923 that breaking off diplomatic relations would be "inexpedient".[50] Vorovsky duly reiterated to the Italians the formal and entirely hollow Soviet stance concerning "the complete absence of any connection whatsoever between my government's activities and the political propaganda of parties active on Russian territory".[51] Recent shocks had none the less left their scars. In a despatch to Moscow that the Italians intercepted and decrypted, Vorovsky exposed his innermost feelings, railing against the "fascist terror" and the régime's isolation from the masses. He predicted on the basis of nothing more solid than emotion that Mussolini would not last very long.[52]

Within months, and to the astonishment and horror of those sharing his dinner table, including Deputy Commissar for Foreign Affairs Maxim Litvinov, the unfortunate Vorovsky was assassinated at the Hotel Cecil in Lausanne on 10 May 1923, not because of who he was but because of the state he represented. His replacement as Soviet ambassador, Konstantin Yurenev, was working-class to the core and built of sterner stuff. Newly arrived in Rome, he decided to invite Mussolini to dinner in mid-July 1924. Instantly a shrill protest rose from Comintern headquarters on the Mokhovaya, directed by Pyatnitsky and Zinoviev to the Politburo. Chicherin, himself sympathetic to Comintern's position, was then told to instruct Yurenev that no such dinners should take place.[53] But Yurenev stubbornly refused to give up. He then decided to invite Mussolini to dine on, of all occasions, the anniversary of the October Revolution—a decision that inevitably provoked further outrage, directed to the Politburo by Zinoviev, Chicherin and Litvinov on 23 October.[54] When Yurenev ignored instructions and pressed on, the Politburo finally stepped in, having been activated by the head of the Latin secretariat of Comintern, Jules Humbert-Droz. On 5 November Stalin, Molotov, Zinoviev, Kamenev and Tomsky voted to remove Yurenev from his post.[55] Evidently even *Realpolitik* had its limits in respect of Moscow's Italian policy.

Meanwhile from Russia Brockdorff-Rantzau advised General Otto Hasse, the chief of staff, against further negotiations with Moscow: Hasse should not forget that "the immediate aim of the Soviet Government is world revolution". For this reason it would be foolish to equip it with armaments only to find those same weapons used against the German government.[56] The ambassador was not far short of the mark. The KPD was in no sense capable of launching an insurrection in the near future. Yet Zinoviev and Bukharin, while taking the waters in Kislovodsk in late July 1923, and with no direct knowledge of Germany, convinced themselves that the time was ripe. Their motives were more complicated than just the will to power. They were also prompted by serious concern lest the KPD lose the initiative to the fascists, as had happened in Italy and Bulgaria.[57] So what they contemplated was pre-emption.

Desperation for relief from the international isolation imposed on the Bolshevik revolution by the absence of similar revolutions elsewhere was expressed by Zinoviev's wife Lilina. She told leading French Communist Marcel Cachin that "[w]ithin five or six years the international proletariat will have to have delivered the revolution, because we could not hold out long term against the hardship and against the invasion of capitalists who are going to make massive efforts to defeat Bolsheviks by their economic infiltration".[58] In mid-August 1923 Zinoviev, who in 1917 had been among the most hesitant, was already blinded by the vision of taking the revolution to the West and forging a "union of Soviet Germany and Soviet Russia" possessing the military capabilities of both. Drunk on his own rhetoric, he demanded "audacity, audacity and more audacity".[59] Radek, a far more intelligent man and dourly sceptical, argued against Zinoviev and sought Trotsky's support. But Trotsky was under sustained attack from his rivals. He had already lost the Commissariat of Military and Naval Affairs and now artfully held aloof on the grounds that he did not have enough information to judge. Stalin, hitherto by nature resolutely the sceptic, initially took the same viewpoint as Radek. "My opinion is that the Germans must be restrained not encouraged", he wrote in his usual unforgiving manner.[60]

By 20 August, however, Stalin, by now the lynchpin of the leadership given Lenin's incapacitation, had unexpectedly reversed his stance on the possibility of revolution in Germany, but not without a caveat. Apart from anything else, Stalin wrote, "[o]ne must in any and every possible way remove any grounds for thinking that the revolution is being 'dictated' or 'inspired' by Russia". He also insisted that any proposals take into account "that the workers' revolution in Germany will probably mean a war on the part of France and Poland (and perhaps also other states) with Germany or—in the best case—a blockade of Germany (no grain supplies from America etc.) against which measures must be immediately taken". He envisaged that considerable mobilisation of Russian resources would be needed. "If we are really to help the Germans—and we will and must help them—then we must also ready ourselves for a war, seriously and on all sides; then in the end the existence of the Soviet federation and the fate of world peace for the near future are at stake."[61] Perhaps Stalin hoped that by stacking the deck in this way he might deter his headstrong comrades from taking a step too far. If this was indeed the case, he failed utterly.

The outlook was fully debated at the Soviet Politburo on 21 August with Radek (as secretary of Comintern's executive committee) and Chicherin (as people's commissar for foreign affairs) also present. Radek expressed fears "that in Germany it would not be Communism that came after Fascism but Fascism after Communism. We cannot contain the masses." He went on to enumerate the differences between Russia and Germany before the revolution, most notably the weight of petty bourgeois farmers in the German countryside and the preponderance of the SPD in the cities. Moscow was overestimating the decline in support for the socialists. Trotsky, in this case eminently practical, was obsessed with the need for a more serious approach to organisation, logistics, preparations, plans and deadlines, the urgency of which had been highlighted by reports he had received from Soviet military advisers on the spot. Trotsky had a low opinion of the KPD leadership "burned" by the *Märzaktion* of 1921, and feared yet another putsch. Stalin instead was typically focused much closer to home, on the survival of Soviet Russia. His vision was reflected in his ordering of likely outcomes: "Either the revolution in Germany comes to grief and wipes us out or the revolution there succeeds and our position is saved."[62] No one else offered anything quite so apocalyptic.

Another Revolutionary Attempt Fails in Germany

So intent were the Bolsheviks on fulfilling their dreams that Zinoviev's extravagant optimism and inflammatory word-spinning blinded everyone. The serious practical defects alluded to by Trotsky, who was by now increasingly isolated and loath to press matters to the point of a breach, were never addressed. Misleading assessments continued to roll in and drown out all sense of caution. By 20 September even Stalin, bent on averting his own imminent isolation, acted entirely out of character by enthusiastically endorsing the premature triumphalism of his deluded colleagues. Not to be outdone, he went one disastrous step further. Hailing the German revolution as an accomplished fact in an uncharacteristically incautious letter to one of the leaders of the KPD, Thalheimer, he declared that the moment was fast approaching when they would be able to transfer "the centre of world revolution from Moscow to Berlin".[63] His theses presented to the Central Committee plenum on 22 September were the final call to arms: "The coming German revolution takes us to the summit of the revolution in Europe and then closer to the world revolution. The chief slogan of the Bolsheviks, that of 'World Revolution', is now for the first time an abstraction taking on flesh and blood."[64] A month later, on the night of 22 October, the abortive uprising began, but only in Hamburg. Someone had bungled, and brave revolutionaries paid for it with their lives.

Radek issued a post-mortem from Berlin on 29 October in a blistering critique aimed at Zinoviev for the Soviet Politburo, copied to Pyatnitsky at Comintern's executive committee. The KPD was, in fact, "undergoing an extreme internal crisis". Party headquarters "gave Moscow a completely unrealistic picture of the Party's preparedness. Everything that Brandler said about armaments is complete and utter nonsense. Had we known that the Party was in no way prepared for an uprising, then we would have talked a hundred times more about getting ready rather than timing."[65]

What exactly happened has long been known. Last-minute advice from Comintern was to hold a general strike before taking up arms. The centre of operations in Saxony had already decided in favour of an uprising and had sent couriers out with instructions across the country. But when a counter-directive to delay was despatched by the KPD, it reached every city but Hamburg, which launched a revolt on its own, not knowing of the change in line.[66] Despite the fact that the Soviet leadership were critical of Radek before and after the uprising, the majority basically accepted his brutal analysis, which was reiterated by Zinoviev in a speech to a plenum of the Central Committee on 15 January 1924.[67] In a search for scapegoats, Brandler was arraigned in the dock. But Zinoviev, true to form, took care to pin the blame on others as well, particularly the usual suspects: the social democrats, whom he described entirely implausibly and irresponsibly as having "become a wing of fascism".[68]

Yet, because none of the Bolshevik leaders understood Germany as well as Radek, they entirely rejected his alternative policy line—to penetrate and fragment fascism—after the failure of the revolution. No one was so far-sighted in respect of what lay ahead and no one was more disregarded than Radek. On 27 December 1923, in a dismissive conclusion worthy of Voltaire's Professor Pangloss, the Politburo argued that "Radek's general view onto the future struggle in Germany stems from an incorrect evaluation of class forces in Germany: an opportunist overevaluation of the disagreements within fascism and an attempt to construct on the bases of these disagreements a policy for the working class of Germany".[69] Radek retaliated: "The Politburo's assertion that my view of the significance of disagreements within the camp of German fascism for the development of the struggle of the working class for power is opportunistic represents an example of an inability to apply Leninism to the German context."[70] But, of course, it made no difference.

Not everyone was convinced by Moscow's elaborate cover-up, certainly in Berlin. The Soviet military adviser to the KPD, Aleksei Shtrodakh, reported that "the mood of the masses is not warlike and not what is necessary for seizing power. And this is not accidental and not a passing occurrence. The population of Germany today is extremely passive politically. A strong belief in revolution does not exist there (such as there was with us)." The more he wrote, the worse it sounded: "everyone asks himself—is it worth risking battle for the sake of a doubtful future; is it worth going from a state of peace to war? A firm and unstated belief cannot even be found amid the broad masses in the Party, let alone the masses of workers."[71]

Heaping the blame on everyone but Moscow was not something that the German Communist Wilhelm Pieck was prepared to accept. Pieck, who had been imprisoned by the kaiser for opposing the war, was in the company of Liebknecht and Luxemburg when the Freikorps came for them, but he had somehow managed to escape. Thereafter he was never easily intimidated. He delivered a withering criticism of Comintern's behaviour. On 8 February 1924 Pieck's speech at the KPD Politburo left no one in doubt. The minutes record that "[t]he basis of his accusation against the IKKI [Comintern executive committee] consisted in the fact that the IKKI incorrectly evaluated the balance of power within Germany in October; it stayed the course for the seizure of power by the proletariat at a time when this was completely illusory and now, instead of openly acknowledging *its* mistakes, dumps everything on the right wing of the party, especially on Iosip [Brandler]". The plan based on "false" premises was "dictated by the IKKI".[72]

It had been a close call. If the attempted revolution had gone ahead the consequences for the Russians would have been far worse. The Red Army was in no condition to fight, but the Poles still were as they had never demobilised. A post-mortem of these events was conducted by Yuri Denike, stationed in Berlin as a member of the short-lived Soviet Diplomatic Information Department. His conclusions supported Radek's call for rethinking Germany. But no one in Moscow was listening.[73] That the fate of the German revolution was critical to the fate of the Russian was still an article of faith. And at Comintern pessimism of any kind was always rebuffed as unwelcome.

Although the Junkers on the far right appeared ready to turn a blind eye to failed Communist uprisings, the newly installed (13 August 1923) chancellor and foreign minister of Germany, Gustav Stresemann, viewed the putsch in Hamburg as an urgent and timely reminder that Moscow simply could not be trusted. Stresemann was now ever more determined to mend fences with the Entente. Even before these events he had, along with President Friedrich Ebert, told Brockdorff-Rantzau, who needed no convincing, that the Reichswehr should no longer conduct talks in Moscow and that the supply of military equipment to Moscow should be purely a matter of business.[74] Stresemann could not contain his revulsion: "Entering a marriage with Communist Russia is like going to bed with someone who has murdered people. In the end one cannot sustain the fiction any longer that the Russian Government is conducting a German-friendly policy while the Third International [Comintern] is doing its utmost to undermine Germany."[75] And when Chicherin disingenuously declared to the press in September 1924 that the Soviet government had no connection with Comintern, Stresemann, by then only foreign minister, was especially incensed. "Such hypocrisy is truly disgusting," he snapped.[76] And Stresemann came to be the central figure in Weimar foreign policy.

Stresemann's push for an understanding with France in the midtwenties is usually presented as a purely pragmatic response to the Ruhr occupation of 1923 and the natural urge to restore German self-respect and become part of the League of Nations, while leaving the eastern border open to peaceful territorial revision. Indeed it was. But missing from this account of his core motivation is the aggravation caused by Moscow's revolutionary zeal.

Fear of revolution did, however, work to Stresemann's advantage in his relations with the creditor nations. Even before the nightmare of the "German October" the United States had been working to restrain France and resolve the reparations problem more to German satisfaction. Herbert Hoover, who presided over the United States from 1929 to 1933, at the peak of isolationism, brooded that after 150 years of separation from Europe, the United States was "dragged by Europe into the War". Consequently, he said, "we had cost the lives of some seventy-five thousand men and disabled over two hundred thousand more. We had spent in loans, or war payments, something like $40,000,000,000; and . . . as a result Europe was now more unstable than it was in 1914."[77]

Although Coolidge's administration was isolationist, for the Republicans money mattered most. Markets had to be stabilised abroad just as at home. Business confidence was critical. Otherwise no one would

t. World War I had for the first time created trade dependence on markets in Europe which, though still slight, was large by historical standards, particularly along the grain belt. Moreover, the massive quantity of debt still owing from the European powers was an issue for financial markets.

Thus the economic stability of Europe remained a priority. In a telegram to the unofficial US delegation to the Reparations Commission on 22 July 1922 the high-minded secretary of state Charles Evans Hughes—nicknamed "Charles the Baptist"—had made plain his concerns. Bolshevism had to be contained in order to stabilise Europe. On no account could Germany be allowed to fall apart.[78] The events of October 1923 underlined the importance of speedy intervention and thus played into Stresemann's hands.

Hitler Emerges

Meanwhile an event of a lower order on the other side of Germany received far less publicity. But it was to have fatal consequences in the years to come, much along the lines that the near-clairvoyant Radek had anticipated. On 9 November an agitator little known outside Bavaria named Adolf Hitler, accompanied by General Erich Ludendorff and some two thousand followers, attempted a coup d'état in Munich as a prelude to taking Berlin.

One year before this fateful move, in mid-November 1922 Hitler had been interviewed by an enterprising officer from the US military attaché's office. At that time the German National Socialist Workers' Party (NSDAP) was, on the officer's view, "less a political party, in the ordinarily accepted meaning of the word than a popular movement . . . as the Bavarian counterpart to the Italian Fascisti". The NSDAP had "recently succeeded in acquiring a political influence in Bavaria quite disproportionate to its actual numerical strength". Indeed, it could count on considerable sympathy within the police, the army and the press. Founded in 1919, what became known as the Nazi Party did not come to the attention of the media until 1921. Hitler was described as "the dominating force in the movement", his personality "undoubtedly . . .

one of the most important factors contributing to its success. . . . His ability to influence a popular assembly is described as uncanny." In private conversation, the officer continued, "he disclosed himself as a forceful and logical speaker, which, when tempered with a fanatical earnestness, made a very deep impression on a neutral listener".

At interview Hitler was surprisingly honest, except in one conspicuous respect. He declared as a basic aim "the overthrow of Marxism, whether in Socialist or Communist garb, and the rewinning [sic] of labor to the Nationalist ideals of state and society. He considers that the present parliamentary form of government in Germany is incapable either of settling Germany's internal or foreign problems. The clash of party interests has proved stronger than love of nation, and the present cabinet crisis in Berlin has effectually demonstrated the impossibility of Germany's rescue from her present difficulties through Democracy." Surprisingly, however, Hitler also played the diplomat, keen to make a good impression. He was realistic about the need to come to terms with France and willing to entertain the idea of paying reparations, albeit at a reduced rate. Hitler said he believed "the 'war of revenge' preached in certain national circles to be an utter absurdity". Then came the glaring omission. Owing, no doubt, to careful calculation to avoid unnecessary antagonism, he skirted the inflammatory issue of anti-Semitism—in contrast to the officer interviewing, who took the view that anti-Semitism throughout Germany, but above all in Bavaria, was "a political factor that cannot be neglected".[79]

On the eve of the Bavarian putsch in early November 1923 two Catalan journalists turned up without notice on Hitler's doorstep at the Nazi newspaper *Völkischer Beobachter* to interview him in the editorial office where they had been told to find him. Briefed that they were from Spain—where Primo de Rivera had just seized power on 13 September in imitation of Mussolini—Hitler enthusiastically opened up to them with astonishing candour, utterly unaware of their true political beliefs, which were the opposite to his own. A thoroughgoing liberal of a kind normally found only in England, Eugenio Xammar wrote up the interview after the putsch, in *La Veu de Catalunya* on 24 November 1923. He had no hesitation in declaring Hitler "a monumental fool". The great value of the interview was that, in contrast to his exchange with the American military officer, Hitler had delivered an entirely uninhibited monologue at a point when he believed he was moments away from seizing power. "The Jewish question is a cancer that is eating away at the national Germanic organism," he ranted. And in a compelling intimation of what lay not so far ahead, he went on to exclaim, "Fortunately political and social cancers are not an incurable disease. There is extermination. If we want Germany to live, we must eliminate the Jews. . . . What do you wish to be done? Do you want them all to be killed in one night? That would be the great solution, evidently, and if this could take place the salvation of Germany would be assured." Unfortunately this would not be possible, he said. He had studied the matter. "The world would overthrow us, instead of thanking us, which is what it should do. The world has not understood the importance of the Jewish question for the simplest reason that the world is dominated by Jews."[80]

In a matter of hours sixteen of Hitler's followers fell under a hail of bullets. Hitler himself, however, was safely spirited away only to be arrested three days later. Yet given the prevalent sympathy for his cause he escaped with a minimal sentence from the court—only five years— with the real prospect of release within a year. Crucially his enforced confinement gave him time to read, reflect, consolidate and write up his creed—not least his by now total commitment to the most extreme anti-Semitism and deeply rooted anti-Bolshevism, and his vaulting ambition to transform Germany into the target and instrument of those beliefs—under the title *Mein Kampf*.[81]

Although exposed to widespread anti-Semitism during his youth in Vienna, Hitler did not formulate his statement on "Rational Anti-Semitism" until 16 June 1919 in a letter to Adolf Gemlich. There he rejected the idea of anti-Semitism driven purely by instinct. This is a crucial statement that clears any misunderstanding as to the provenance of his core beliefs. Indeed, his own family doctor in Linz, Eduard Bloch, was Jewish, and Hitler had a soft spot for him. Once he had become chancellor of Germany, he honoured his debt to Bloch as "a noble Jew" who had done his level best to rescue Hitler's mother from cancer. Bloch was protected in Linz until allowed to leave for the United States.[82]

Hitler's anti-Semitism, like that of the long-standing and popular mayor of Vienna, Karl Lueger, who set a telling example on the eve of World War I, was an artifice that appears to have been designed to appeal to the darkest prejudices of the masses in Central Europe. What *was* instinctive was the acute perception—which Rudolf Hess called Hitler's "rare sensitivity for the public mood"[83]—that this would win as a tactic for mass mobilisation. Almost entirely self-educated politically and grammatically illiterate, Hitler soaked up ideas and impressions from the atmosphere around him—notably his conviction that the state was an organic entity and Bolshevism a virulent bacillus that, unimpeded, represented a mortal threat to it. Much of this was reinforced by extensive conversation with those who early on exerted great influence upon him, most notably Dietrich Eckart, friend and mentor. Strongly anti-Semitic, Eckart was also well-read. From him Hitler became acquainted with the works of Houston Stewart Chamberlain and Paul de Lagarde. The car magnate Henry Ford provided further, contemporary reinforcement. Ford's diatribe against the Jews was issued in German in 1922 as *Der Internationale Jude: Ein Weltproblem*, and Ford's portrait decorated the wall of Hitler's private study.[84] By the beginning of June 1924, the outlines for Hitler's book were already traced, under the draft title "4½ Years Struggling against Lies, Stupidity and Cowardice". And very close to the top of his agenda sat the evil twins, "The Jewish People and Marxism", with "The Bolshevisation of Europe" not much further down.[85] The distinguished French journalist Henri Rollin surely had it right when he described how Hitler and his lieutenants came to their fanaticism: "By the classic phenomenon of auto-suggestion, their conception of the world became an *idée fixe*, a kind of mystical faith so deeply anchored in their minds that nothing, it would seem, could convince them that they were wrong."[86]

It is the custom to assume that on this issue Hitler shared nothing with Mussolini. Not so. A record exists of a conversation between Mussolini and the papal nuncio to Italy, Francesco Borgongini Duca, on 2 February 1930. The subject was the terror inflicted by the Bolsheviks on Roman Catholics during the forced collectivisation of Soviet agriculture, as well as the protests issued by Pope Pius XI.[87] "You have to understand, your

Excellency," Mussolini declared, "that what makes Russia evil are its five million Jews who, with great ability, by placing themselves at the head of Christian renegades from every country—Russians, Lithuanians, Latvians, Poles, Germans, Georgians etc.—make the great mechanism work. They are the connective tissue of an immense bureaucracy that is thus available to the Jews for anti-Christian purposes. The force of this machine lies in its immense power of extermination. One can catch a cat but not an elephant! Napoleon's mistake was that he was unable to see that it could not be caught."[88] But Pius did not need lessons on Bolshevism. He had been the nuncio to Poland during its formative years in the struggle against the Kremlin.

Hitler's anti-Semitism and hostility to Bolshevism made sense only in the context of his conception of the nation state. They formed an indissoluble bond. He was drawn to the view that the state was an organism, a medieval conception revived by Adam Müller in the wake of the Napoleonic wars. He believed that this life force—*lebendige Bewegung*—was revealed in war. Charles Darwin attacked the notion of "man as if he was formed in the air, without ties to the soil". Thomas Malthus had already argued that "the constant tendency in all animated life to increase beyond the nourishment prepared for it" meant that "living space" was vital and in short supply.[89] The Swedish political scientist Rudolf Kjellén then invented the now familiar term *Geopolitik*—geopolitics as distinct from the vague term "political geography". He defined *Geopolitik* as "the study of the state as a geographical organism". He believed that the state was not the product of a contract between rulers and ruled, but something intrinsically organic, self-generating. It could not move, because territory was the "body" of the state, by its nature perishable. "It has a life . . . It is, like a private individual, placed in a struggle for existence which absorbs a greater part of its power and creates an incessant, stronger or weaker, friction with its surroundings." Kjellén's *Staten som lifsform* (The state as a form of life) appeared in 1916 amid the horrors of the First World War. The German Karl Haushofer, a colonel at the front, read the book in translation and immediately identified with it.[90] From Haushofer these ideas reached Rudolf Hess and from Hess they came to Hitler.

Soon after the hostilities ended, Haushofer rapidly turned himself into a successful publicist for these ideas at the University of Munich. He began a journal, the *Zeitschrift für Geopolitik*, for the purpose of educating fellow citizens in *Raumsinn* (or *Raumauffassung*): consciousness of the importance of space. "A great nation", he wrote, "has to break out from a singularly narrow space, crowded with people, without fresh air, a vital space narrowed and mutilated for the past thousand years ... unless either the whole east is opened up for free immigration of the best and most capable people or else the vital spaces still unoccupied are redistributed according to former accomplishments and the ability to create." It was in Munich that Haushofer encountered Rudolf Hess. As Rudiger Hess recalled, "For my father these conversations were the first step leading from an instinctive thought to a conscious political thought."[91] And it was, of course, with his devoted friend and admirer Hess that, in the Landsberg prison, Hitler wrote *Mein Kampf*. "No one else has ever explained and written down what he intends to do more often than I have," Hitler boasted on 30 January 1941.[92]

The view of the nation state as an organism carried with it the requirement of living space (*Lebensraum*) and easily linked to the idea of racial purity, with the Soviet Union as both the main source of contamination and the land for colonisation. Thus not only was it vital for Germany to fight the "Jewish bolshevisation of the world",[93] but "the future goal of our foreign policy does not have a Western or Eastern orientation, but an *Ostpolitik* in the sense of the acquisition of the land needed for our German people."[94] This obsession with living space was thus not a by-product of the perceived need to offset the lack of colonies possessed by Britain and France but a direct extension of Hitler's organicist image of the state. What counted was not territory as such—Hitler was utterly uninterested in recovering Germany's former colonies in Africa, even when the British later tried to thrust them on him—but contiguous territory. Indeed; but the plain truth remains that hardly anyone took him sufficiently seriously.

The year 1924 also saw resolute efforts by the United States and Britain through the Dawes Plan to resurrect Germany's economy and in so doing reduce the chances of war and revolution. Short-term dollar loans became plentiful. However, their availability depended upon demand sustained by US investors and that could be counted on only while the stock market on Wall Street continued to be buoyant.

The collision of interests between Moscow and the West could not have been clearer. "Thanks to the war between capitalist states", People's Commissar Chicherin wrote half a dozen years later, "we seized power and grew stronger, and every exacerbation of antagonisms between Germany and the Entente, France and Italy, Italy and Yugoslavia, England and America, signifies a strengthening of our position; a reduction in all kinds of dangers to us."[95] Although close military co-operation between Moscow and Berlin was strictly secret, rumours of it made the British increasingly anxious to win back German sympathies—at almost any price. The permanent under-secretary at the Foreign Office in London warned of Germany's "violent minority that has learned nothing, and is quite ready to repeat the crime of 1914, provided it possesses the means to do so. The latter cherishes the mirage of a friendly Russia that would promote its aims."[96] The Germans had to be brought back in (at least, the more reasonable among them). Just as the Bolsheviks saw their interest in keeping the Western states at one another's throats, the British saw their opposing interest in harmonising relations between them. And Britain had a score to settle with Soviet Russia along the way.

3

Subverting Great Britain
and Its Empire

Some people forget the years, say 1920–26, when the only danger was
"Bolshevism".

—SIR ALEXANDER CADOGAN, PERMANENT
UNDER-SECRETARY AT THE FOREIGN OFFICE[1]

In Britain, due to the activities of Comintern throughout the 1920s, anti-
Communism evolved into something of a life force of its own, the consequences of which took time to make their full impact. Although the
kingdom was largely safe from the intensity of the class struggle evident
on the continent, the empire most certainly was not. And because Britain led the war of intervention to overthrow the Bolsheviks, it presented
the most important target of Bolshevik propaganda for more than a
decade.

Britain's main rival for world financial supremacy was the United
States. It was mostly through the bank of J. P. Morgan that US credit had
bankrolled Britain's war. Thereafter, however, American isolationism
represented the explicit abdication of direct political involvement in
Europe, though not yet in Asia. Britain emerged by default as the only
truly global power, and thus represented the greatest long-term threat
to the survival of the Soviet régime. No other state was more loathed by

the Bolsheviks. Stalin told the Germans what they wanted to hear some years later: "the Soviet Government never had any sympathy towards England. One only has to glance at the works of Lenin and his pupils to understand that the Bolsheviks always above all railed against and hated England."[2] And that hatred was easily channelled into direct action. Britain was highly vulnerable, far less so for domestic reasons than for the fact that riot and rebellion were already undermining its overstretched and largely indefensible empire that encompassed most of the Caribbean; the greater part of Africa; half of the Middle East; India, Burma, Ceylon and Malaya in their entirety; the treaty ports of China; and the dominions of Canada, New Zealand, Australia and innumerable small islands scattered across the globe at points of strategic interest.

British Vulnerabilities

Britain undoubtedly had serious weaknesses. Not only did the home islands suffer from technological backwardness relative to their major industrial competitors, having industrialised earlier than others, but the British had also significantly under-invested at home, with the exception of housing and transport. Instead they reinvested most of the capital they accrued overseas. The empire had been and remained the major recipient, and the Paris peace settlement of 1919 further expanded British possessions, to their greatest reach in history. The empire thus became recklessly overextended—a step too far that made defence increasingly problematic. Where Britain was richest and weakest was in colonial Asia, notably in India and China, the largest recipients of its investments and the major markets for its declining textile industry, upon which employment in the north-west of England was highly dependent.

The Bolsheviks were quick to identify the colonial world as Britain's Achilles' heel. For although the working class showed stubborn loyalty to crown and country, secured by cheap food, tea and the vote (though not until 1928 for all women), this was most definitely not true of those they had conquered. And when the Hungarian revolution failed in the summer of 1919, the second great figure of the Bolshevik revolution and founder of the Red Army, Trotsky, argued that "the road to Paris and London lies through Afghanistan, Punjab and Bengal".[3] India had become the main target for Bolshevik activity in the East.

This fact was not lost on the British government. In London the most secret Bolshevik intentions were an open book. The Soviet régime had thus far been unable to encrypt their communications in a manner which could not easily be broken, thus inadvertently exposing their plans for revolutionary penetration of the empire.[4] For them this was seen as a matter of life or death.

At Comintern's executive committee on 12 and 14 January 1921 its secretary, Radek,

> indicated that the moment had arrived for the Third International to exert all of its strength to prove its influence not only in Europe but also in the Far and Near East; should this not happen the Third International would have to be declared bankrupt. We must not lose a moment in taking measures to make evident to England, principally England, that our influence is great and that our ideas to fashion a Communist order in the world are founded, not upon dry ground, but on actualities. The past has already taught us to be practical in our work and we have come to the conclusion that if we do not exert an influence upon English Imperialism, English Imperialism will press in upon Soviet Russia and choke the revolution which was brought about with the blood and bodies of our Comrades.[5]

In formulating the Anglo–Soviet trade agreement signed on 16 March 1921 which opened diplomatic relations de facto with Bolshevik Russia, the British believed they had meticulously ensured that the Soviet government would refrain from "any form of hostile action against British interests or the British Empire, especially in India and the Independent State of Afghanistan".[6] But they had severely underestimated Lenin's extraordinary tactical ingenuity. The Russians circumvented this precise stipulation by formally, though implausibly, separating out the identity of Comintern as a cohort of Communist parties from that of the Soviet government proper, even though Comintern had its headquarters in Moscow and was funded, organised and directed by the Soviet authorities. Lenin intended to ensure that the substance of things would remain the same but appear to comply with the wishes of any government signatory to such a treaty. The Anglo–Soviet trade agreement thus provided the model for all future such agreements. "I think we shall ultimately emerge on top as a result of our firm stand that the Communist International is not a governmental institution," Lenin stated, adding that "any attempt to present us with an ultimatum that we get rid of the Communist International is inexcusable. However, the emphasis laid on the matter shows where the shoe pinches and what displeases them in our policy."[7]

This much became apparent as early as 17 September 1921, barely six months after signature of the agreement, when Foreign Secretary Curzon indignantly protested against Soviet breaches, particularly with respect to India, where he had briefly served as viceroy. But matters worsened rather than improved. By April 1923 Curzon was on the verge of breaking off diplomatic relations with the Russians. Only after consulting Ralph Hodgson, the chargé d'affaires in Moscow, did he relent and instead on 8 May issue a broadside that became notorious as the "Curzon Ultimatum". It reiterated the long-standing complaint of Soviet Russia's "anti-British propaganda". On this occasion the foreign secretary— determined to win the argument—set a disastrous precedent and jeopardised the entire cypher-breaking effort by quoting from decrypted communications: Shumiatskii's telegram from the Soviet mission in Teheran to Narkomindel in February itemising funding for anti-British activity; Raskol'nikov's telegram from Kabul of 17 February about aggravating the crisis in Anglo-Afghan relations, also requesting funding to that end; and so on.[8]

The Zinoviev Letter

The ultimatum took the Russians "completely by surprise". Indeed, they fully expected Britain to break off diplomatic relations and possibly resort to war or blockade at any moment.[9] But once it became apparent that the breach was not part of a general strategy, the Russians merely toned down their misbehaviour to a more acceptable degree, which then laid them open to more trouble later when they carried on as they had done before the crisis.[10] The dreaded moment duly came on 21 November 1924 after a new, diehard Conservative government was elected under the premiership of Stanley Baldwin. This time the protest was directed at the so-called Zinoviev Letter: an obvious forgery implicating Comintern in an attempt to subvert the British army.[11]

Though not genuine, the Zinoviev Letter was credible because it was fully consistent with the Comintern program, recently instituted, of subverting the armed forces in all capitalist states. At Comintern such ultra-secret matters were managed by the Orgburo (the organisational bureau). Subversion of the capitalist armed forces had been officially orchestrated on 11 December 1922 with the formation of a standing committee on work in the army, which became known as the standing Military (anti-military or clandestine military) Committee, or "M" Committee for short. Its purpose was threefold: subversion of capitalist armed forces; readiness for revolutionary military warfare; and organisation of proletarian self-defence including the countering of penetration from foreign counter-intelligence. The committee was also involved in providing military training for men from various Communist parties. It was especially active in readying German Communists for the fight in 1923.[12]

Such clandestine operations were further advanced in France under the joint secretary general of the party (1924–26) Jean Cremet, and remained so even after Cremet was publicly exposed in 1927. France was a nation under arms. National military service was still obligatory for all young males, whereas in Britain it had been abolished.[13] But the French took the sanguine view that this was a job for the police. Germany, not Soviet Russia, was the focus of French attention. In Britain, however, the new Conservative cabinet was determined to use the letter to highlight the "whole body of revolutionary propaganda" issued by Comintern; so for them the question of whether it was genuine or fake was redundant. Senior officials either believed in it or lied about it without a second thought. The new foreign secretary, Austen Chamberlain, cautioned Moscow that "the Soviet Government would do well to weigh carefully the consequences of ignoring this [protest]".[14]

Within the Baldwin administration the Ministry of Health lay in the hands of Austen's half-brother, Neville Chamberlain: a dour, provincial figure whose only international concern was at a pinch imperial, rather than European. He readily expressed the same anti-Bolshevik sentiments as fellow ministers. When the governor-general of the Sudan and sirdar of the Egyptian army Sir Lee Stack was assassinated, the British took drastic action in reprisal. Zinoviev immediately announced Comintern's support for the "struggle" of the Egyptian comrades fighting for the independence of their country.[15] For the benefit of his electoral constituency in Birmingham and no doubt to impress fellow ministers, Neville Chamberlain made his mark by expressing his patriotism in the face of Comintern provocation: "nothing is more likely to lead this country into friction and into war with other Powers than to think that we do not mean what we say . . . We are not going to allow the British name to be dragged into the dirt . . . We are not going to allow obligations which are due to us to be flouted."[16] The depth of Chamberlain's antipathy towards the Bolsheviks ensured that once he assumed the office of prime minister in 1937 he and his colleagues were most unlikely to give the Russian régime the benefit of the doubt about anything. And they were by no means the exception in this regard, at home or abroad, particularly within the Conservative Party, and not least because events reinforced rather than allayed well-entrenched suspicion and mistrust established throughout the 1920s.

In all the capitals of Europe the Bolsheviks were regarded as a threat that required a firm hand. The advent to power of diehard Conservatives on the back of the "red scare", not long after Mussolini rounded up Communists in Italy, sparked hopes elsewhere in Europe that the Kremlin would finally be called to account for Comintern interference in the internal affairs of other states. In December 1924 the Yugoslav, Bulgarian and Czech foreign ministers suggested to the British ambassador in Rome "a common European front against the danger. At present the Soviet Government played upon the differences of opinion and policy in the various European capitals. A united front would mean that Bolshevik propaganda in Czecho-Slovakia or Bulgaria would lead to reprisals on the part of Great Britain, France, Italy etc., which would soon bring the Soviet Government to terms."[17] The Spanish ambassador also raised the matter with Austen Chamberlain, saying "under instructions, that his Government was concerned about Communist activities and was quite disposed to join with other Governments in defending society against them". Somewhat disconcerted, the foreign secretary, never quite the diehard his colleagues were, merely responded that he had found similar concerns "amongst many of the representative statesmen" he had recently met in Rome.[18] President Gaston Doumergue also alluded to the fact that France as well as Britain was "affected by the rapidly developing propaganda of Bolshevism among the coloured people".[19] And when Winston Churchill met Pope Pius XI in January 1927 the unease between them passed instantaneously once they "got on to the subject of the Bolsheviks and had a jolly half hour saying what they thought of them".[20]

Austen Chamberlain, however, was not quite the intransigent Tory he pretended to be. He stood close to the centre of British politics. In fact even as late as 1927 he shared Lloyd George's optimism that

Bolshevist Russia is moving, and anyone who watches what is happening there very closely can see a very great difference between the Bolshevist Russia of three or four or five years ago and the Russia of to-day. It will take time, just as Republican France moved at the end of the eighteenth century . . . When you are dealing with revolutionary Governments you are not dealing with anything that is normal, even in diplomatic relations. A revolutionary Government is essentially a propagandist Government. The revolutionary Government at the end of the eighteenth century did its very best, and declared that it was part of its purpose, to overthrow monarchy throughout Europe . . . Unfortunately public opinion in this country got excited by the horrible outrages in France, and we dashed in and we had 23 years of war. You must wait until the fever subsides.[21]

Chamberlain may well have absorbed all this from the complacency prevalent among his more liberal officials. One had suggested that "[a]ll our information goes to show that the process of enforced return to civilized economic methods and points of view is going on slowly but surely, thus still justifying our policy".[22] Another argued there to be "no doubt that a Russian evolution *is* going on in the direction we desire, but of course it is very slow . . . The missionary spirit of the French revolution lasted, I suppose one may say, nearly 15 years, and though it was fostered by war in a degree that does not apply to the Bolshevik revolution, the French had greater clearness of thought, greater similarity of mind and closer contact with the western world to help them in returning to normal standards . . . I do not believe that we can do anything dramatic, whether friendly or unfriendly, to force the pace".[23]

These beliefs had originated with Florus the Epitomist and were elaborated centuries later by the classical economists Adam Smith and David Ricardo. The Foreign Office élite, never lacking self-confidence, had fervent Gladstonian confidence in the political benefits of free trade—that the Communist system would be broken down "not by boycott but by gradually increasing intercourse".[24] That is to say, by expanding trade with Soviet Russia the British expected not only to make a great deal of money but in so doing also to subvert the Communist system. The trouble was that Lenin had read Keynes and sustained a state monopoly of foreign trade precisely to put a stop to the workings of the liberal teleology; and Stalin ended all such dreams by introducing the five-year plan in 1929.

Mindful of the need to appease Conservative opinion, senior officials believed that for the short term a palliative for Soviet misbehaviour would be the imposition of diplomatic isolation. This could be achieved by embracing the Kremlin's only ally, Weimar Germany, and breaking the Rapallo special relationship it had with Moscow by seducing Berlin into a larger settlement that would relegate Russia to the margins of the European states system. Whatever the solution, Britain was the only great power that could lead the pack. Without the United States, which had originally been expected to become co-guarantor of peace in Western Europe, Britain alone was powerful enough to secure France against German attack, albeit at great cost. As tension grew between London and Moscow, the Russians inevitably became anxious lest the British use their leverage over France, which was allied to Russia's immediate neighbours, particularly warlike Poland, to press them into joint action against Russia. The Poles were certainly not to be underestimated as they maintained a standing army of 266,000 and had over 2.5 million trained reservists.[25] The Russians should have saved themselves the worry, however. No such action was ever seriously contemplated.

What saved the Bolsheviks from the worst was the timing. At this stage the French suffered only minimal problems from Bolshevik interference in their empire—rifles and ammunition sent to support the Rif uprising in French Morocco. They were not looking for a quarrel with Moscow. And Britain remained the target par excellence when Comintern crowed about the upsurge in unrest across the colonial and semi-colonial world. On 16 May 1925 the Eastern Department of Comintern's executive committee reported, "Events developing in China, in Egypt, in Morocco, in Anatolia and in the recently suppressed counter-revolutionary uprising of feudal lords in the eastern provinces of Turkey and southern Iran, speak to the hitherto unprecedented progress in the East in favour of the liberation movement directed against the imperialist governments of England, France, Japan, America and others."[26]

Opportunity in China

The massive former empire of China was the unanticipated bone of contention that brought Anglo–Soviet relations to a crisis. It was the country's unique misfortune to be the colony of not one power but several—France, the United States, Japan and Britain. Notoriously, in the park of the international settlement in the industrialised city of Shanghai Chinese were not allowed. The British since 1842 held the lion's share of China. In Shanghai they ran the municipal police force. The British alone milked the lucrative maritime customs service and owned outright the precious island port of Hong Kong. Trouble began very soon after the Bolshevik revolution, when Bolshevik emissaries—"Old Hairy People" (*lao mao-tzu*)—began trekking south through the Siberian hinterland into north-eastern China (Manchuria) and by boat into Shanghai as early as August 1919.[27] Hitherto Chinese radicals had only symbolic leadership and no foreign source of support, financial or otherwise. They now found a ready supply from Moscow. Soviet operations began in China during the spring of 1920.[28] By the autumn the Russians had established an organisational centre in Shanghai—the Eastern secretariat of Comintern—with Chinese, Korean and Japanese sections.[29] On 23 August 1921 fifty-three people gathered in Shanghai at a house within the French section of the International Settlement and then moved to a pleasure boat on a lake outside the city to convene the first congress of the Chinese Communist Party (CCP). Overseeing proceedings were two Comintern representatives, Maring (Sneevliet) and Nikol'skii.[30] But these were only the tentative beginnings.

Within China the Russians worked on two levels. First they based their activities around existing student discussion groups, from which they helped build Communist organisations in Beijing, Shanghai, Tientsin, Canton, Hankow, Nanjing and elsewhere. These Communist circles that came to form the CCP, however, were "isolated from the labour movement, on the one side, and not connected to the national-revolutionary movement on the other". They were therefore "little capable of practical revolutionary work and inclined to satisfy themselves with their own brand of Communism cultivated in a hothouse". They were nevertheless useful in circulating ideas. Soviet propaganda had begun pouring into China. But the party's achievements were minimal until 1925, the beginning of the Chinese revolution, and are reflected in the date which Stalin counted as the birth of the CCP.[31]

The limited short-term return on this effort highlighted the importance of complementary work at the second level.[32] Here the Russians turned to the ready-made Chinese nationalist movement, Guomindang. Formed after the overthrow of the imperial court in 1911, this revolutionary movement had been led by Sun Yat-sen, who was "openly Anglophobe".[33] Conducting policy on these two levels was made all the easier by the fact that Sun did not feel threatened by Comintern's separate role in constructing a new party. He confidently took the view that "at present a Communist state or even the Soviet system cannot be introduced into China".[34] What he wanted most was military assistance with which to hold his own against warlords who had divided China among one another.

China stood at the "hub of international conflicts and the most vulnerable place in international imperialism", and the Soviet ambassador

Adol'f Ioffe, for one, thought that "especially now is the moment, when imperialism is undergoing a crisis in Europe, and revolution is impending, to cast a blow at imperialism at its weakest spot". This spot, he added, "is extremely advantageous to us. The fight against global capitalism has enormous resonance and tremendous opportunities for success. The trends in world politics are strongly felt here, considerably more, than, say, in Central Asia, to which Lenin gave so much significance. China is unquestionably at the juncture of international conflicts and the most vulnerable point of international imperialism."[35]

The task of the Chinese Communists consisted in "playing the role of skirmishers for the national unification of China on a democratic basis".[36] Thus, having helped form the CCP, the Russians proceeded to amalgamate its membership with that of the Guomindang. This tactic had to be "very supple" and "the Communist Party itself had constantly to be borne in mind and therefore one had to know how to exploit the friction between various groups of the bourgeoisie". The decision taken in Moscow, even though open to challenge for "revolutionary opportunism",[37] was none the less "received almost without opposition".[38]

In response to Sun Yat-sen's repeated entreaty, on 8 March 1923 the Soviet Politburo agreed to provide extensive financial support and, more controversially, "a group of political and military advisers".[39] Yet suspicion lingered that Sun was rather more attached to military aid as a solution to his political difficulties than to long-term political reorganisation of the Guomindang. When he came to Moscow in November, Trotsky lectured him in none too tactful a manner: "The Guomindang party must immediately and decisively change the course [rul'] of its policy," he demanded. "At present it has to concentrate all its attention on political work, reducing to a minimum that part of its activity on the military side. Our military effort must not amount to more than five per cent and in no circumstances more than ten per cent of activity on the political side."[40] Almost simultaneously Comintern claimed that the CCP, "formerly a propaganda society for the intelligentsia", had now became closely linked to "broad masses of Chinese workers".[41]

Hitherto Stalin, very much the realist at the fulcrum of the Soviet leadership as they lined up against Trotsky, had been characteristically sceptical about China's possibilities. "Is there *really* a movement and how deep is it?" he asked the deputy commissar for foreign affairs Ambassador Lev Karakhan on 16 June 1924. "Does Sun [Yat-sen] or the Guomindang really have roots, healthy roots? Can one say that the specific gravity of Sun-Guomindang compares to the specific gravity of, say, Kemal [Ataturk of Turkey] and his party?"[42] Stalin's scepticism was not unwarranted. When Soviet political adviser Mikhail Borodin (Mikhail Markovič Gruzenberg) first arrived in China in 1923, he found "Sun Yat-sen with 40 years of revolutionary activity sitting in Canton and he had no power at all. All the power lay in the hands of a few generals. Guomindang as a party properly speaking did not exist." Thereafter the Bolsheviks determined to change all that.[43]

As time went on, however, Stalin became more confident about the Guomindang. In striking contrast, he had doubts about whether the fledgling CCP would ever amount to anything in a country full of peasants. As against the complacent British, who had been a growing presence since the middle of the nineteenth century, the Bolsheviks despaired of ever fully understanding China. Chicherin had indeed complained to Karakhan that "we really know nothing and if we do find out something it is only when some kind of conflict arises which by force of necessity comes to our attention".[44] But lack of information about the CCP was also due to the fact that the reports they relied upon came in from Borodin, who led the military mission to the Guomindang based in Canton, rather than from the CCP leadership itself, based in Shanghai.[45]

The crisis that rescued Soviet policy was triggered by an unintended massacre perpetrated at the centre of British power in semi-colonial China, industrial Shanghai, on 30 May 1925. Chinese workers in textile mills owned by Japanese were beaten when they protested against deteriorating living conditions consequent upon cuts in wages. The Chinese organised and struck, demonstrating under the slogan "Oppose the Beating of People by the Japanese". Fired upon by their employers, they marched into the International Settlement, policed by the British. When a similar event had occurred in 1905 the station had been looted and burned, so this time the police, vastly outnumbered, poorly led and terrified, opened fire on the demonstrators.

Moscow Backs the Revolution in China

This atrocity sparked an uncontrolled blaze that swept through China with alarming rapidity. As in 1900 with the Boxer Rebellion, the tinder of xenophobia was quick to the flame. The anti-Japanese protest turned into a boycott of British goods. Once the conflagration took hold in China, a massive country of some 400 million people, the Russians liberally poured more fuel on the pyre. And the revolution spread rapidly through the main cities. Setting aside all doubts and most certainly aware that any hesitation would make him vulnerable to attack from the opposition, on 9 June 1925 Stalin publicly assailed those of "a nationalist frame of mind" who wanted the Soviet Union to take the "safe" option and abandon the fight in China.[46] Two days later, on 11 June, the Politburo assigned 50,000 roubles ($1.5 million at today's value) from the government's reserve fund to the Chinese on strike in Shanghai.[47] Bear in mind that the British were still intercepting and decrypting Soviet ciphered telegrams and that they were doing so when a major crisis broke.[48] It is notable how important this crisis was for Stalin, because he rarely contacted ambassadors directly; that task was usually delegated to senior diplomats. On this occasion he sent a telegram to Karakhan in Beijing: "Allocations have been made in favour of the strikers; there will be more. Don't worry. We will rigorously sustain the revolutionary movement of the workers."[49]

At Stalin's instigation, on 25 June the Politburo resolved:

1) Absolutely to advance the revolutionary movement in the form of a boycott, partial stoppages and general strikes, especially a general railway strike without fear of exacerbating the crisis; 2) Absolutely abstain from killing and assaults on foreigners, from crudely nationalist outbursts and especially pogroms; warning workers, shop-keepers and the intelligentsia directly not to give provocateurs among the foreigners cause to refer to the movement as something akin to the Boxer rebellion and not to make it easier for the imperialists by this means to intervene by brute force; these precautions must come above all from the Chinese Communist Party. 3) Conduct general

agitation against Chang Tso-lin (an arm of the imperialist powers). . . . 4) (Leave the Chinese government neutral) or, if this does not succeed, rough it up and paralyse the government, while depriving the imperialists of the possibility of concealing their own actions against the Chinese Government . . . (failing this) go so far as to fragment the current government and create a new one drawing in the Guomindang.

One additional, bizarre suggestion was that Karakhan should persuade the Chinese government to propose Soviet arbitration between themselves and the imperialist powers. But whatever was done, no mention should be allowed in public of the role of the Comintern executive committee or the Soviet government. Personnel from the embassy were instructed to take the greatest possible care to conceal their involvement in the unfolding revolution.[50]

Sensitive to Britain's outcry against the eye-catching Soviet role in fomenting these disturbances, the Politburo a little late in the day issued strict instructions to its press agency TASS, on 3 December 1925: "do not exaggerate the eastern danger for West European and American capitalism" and "if possible write less about the active role of the USSR in the eastern events".[51] At Stalin's suggestion the Russians also looked to an insurance policy of seeking "to drive a wedge between Japan, on the one hand, and Anglo-America [sic], on the other" by trying to persuade the Japanese to come to terms with what was going on in China.[52] Ironically, both the British and the Russians looked to the moderate constitutional régime in Japan under Baron Shidehara to help them out.

Not everything went smoothly. Warlord Chang Tso-lin attempted to seize the Chinese Eastern Railway (CER), still owned and run by the Russians, in Manchuria. He was forced to back down as a result of swift armed retribution, but the events did demonstrate the underlying vulnerability of the Soviet Union in a part of the world where they had no effective military capability. That was concentrated in the south of China, where splits between left and right within the Guomindang were inevitable; along with them came growing friction between the Russian military advisers, who were as imperious abroad as they were at home, and the Chinese generals dependent upon them.[53] In particular, led by their military attaché Yegorov, the advisers resisted what seemed a hare-brained scheme, given limited resources, of marching north to conquer central China.[54]

Soviet intelligence tended to exaggerate any bad news from the East or the West. And in China Soviet military intelligence (the Fourth Directorate) tended to duplicate the efforts of InOGPU (civilian foreign intelligence). It was therefore decided simultaneously to save money and divide activity in China into two: northern China (Manchuria and Mongolia) would be the focus primarily from the military point of view for the defence of the USSR; whereas China proper would be the focus of "the demands of our active policy in China and the study of the forces embattled there".[55]

People's Commissar for Foreign Affairs Chicherin, for one, had read too many hair-raising intelligence reports to believe tales of "temporary setbacks . . . compared to the successes achieved by the whole liberation movement, by the parties as by the trades unions".[56] Morale was un-doubtedly high. On 10 February 1926 Comintern representative in China Grigorii Voitinskii gave a full progress report to the presidium. He claimed that in Shanghai "the Communist Party organised the trades unions, created a press and led the union movements in this mas-sive port". It had 4,500 members, of whom 60% were industrial workers. And its influence extended far beyond its membership; the press counted 50,000 sales a week. To achieve all this they had burrowed in-side the Guomindang, extending their reach as they did so. With some exaggeration, Voitinskii boasted that "the Communist Party effectively leads the Guomindang".[57] What he failed to see, however, was that Sun Yat-sen's cunning and steely successor, Chiang Kai-shek, hitherto iden-tified as a leftist, was also very much aware of what had been going on and determined to reverse the process.

No one could question who bore the brunt of the onslaught. The estimated value of British capital in China stood at £350 million: over £20 billion at today's valuation. The total of British and British India's exports to China in 1926 amounted to £33.2 million: nearly £2 billion today.[58] And that was after the boycott had made serious inroads into the numbers. Further potential losses were incalculable. Here the die-hards in the Conservative Party agreed entirely with the Bolsheviks. "British imperialism has recently suffered a massive defeat as a result of this," Voitinskii boasted; "a defeat such as it has not had since the time of the opium war. That Hong Kong has ceased to be the basic transit port, that it has been smashed economically, has delivered an enormous moral defeat to British imperialism not only in Southern China but also throughout China. It has inflicted a massive defeat on the English im-perialists in the colonies as well, such as India."[59]

On 18 March a committee was set up by the Politburo under the chairmanship of Trotsky to look into the position of Japan. Chicherin was a member and summed up the significance of recent events in China for international relations as a whole:

> During the previous period the world Powers were so focused on the Ruhr, reparations, resolving the results of the war by the various par-ties, and, finally, Locarno, that it was not possible to turn attention more intensively to the Far East. In this connexion comrade [Mikhail] Trilisser [for InOGPU] cited the words of English ministers—I don't remember now who these were—that Locarno had to a greater de-gree distracted attention from the Far East. The sudden change, no-ticeable in the Far East and starkly visible in the English press, is that instead of intermittent attention and relegating the handling of Far Eastern affairs to embassies and consulates, now Far Eastern affairs have been placed at the centre of attention of the world Powers, and on their part an offensive has opened right down the line.[60]

In two days Chiang Kai-shek took action. He launched a mini coup d'état, liquidating the Communist-dominated strike committee that had effectively run the campaign of protest since the Shanghai massacre. By late July no issue took up more Politburo time than that of China, not least because the management of Chinese affairs had been reallo-cated from the People's Commissariat for Foreign Affairs (Narkomin-del) to the China Committee of the Politburo.[61]

The General Strike in Britain

Events then further complicated the emerging conflict between the Soviet Union and Britain over China. It might have seemed that no more damage could be inflicted on Soviet relations with Britain—until, that is, the advent of the general strike, a desperate measure launched by the Trades Union Congress in support of the coal miners who had been striking in vain for over a year to hold on to the existing value of their wage packets. The government had been subsidising wages out of taxation, but finally ditched that policy at the end of April 1926 as too costly an open-ended commitment.

The background to this was that as an industrial country Britain was heavily dependent on foreign markets. Only one-seventh of the population was engaged in agriculture. International trade was thus essential. Britain had two million unemployed and had had to spend £100 million to keep them afloat. The economy was rapidly deflating under the impact of returning the pound sterling to parity with the price of gold, a policy pushed by the Treasury and the Bank of England, which were indifferent to increased unemployment consequent upon an uncompetitive rate of exchange.[62] This compounded a long-standing problem. A high pound benefited only the trade in financial services profiting circles in the City. Demand for raw materials now plummeted as exports dried up. Chancellor of the Exchequer Winston Churchill, who unwisely consented to the primacy of the pound sterling, later described the attitude of Sir Otto Niemeyer at the Treasury as that of "letting everything smash into bankruptcy and unemployment in order that reconstruction can be built upon the ruins".[63] He blithely gave way none the less.

Anger peaked when the owners locked out the miners at the beginning of May 1926. Called at one minute to midnight on 3 May, the strike brought the country to a halt. Four days later Prime Minister Stanley Baldwin bewailed the fact that "Constitutional Government is being attacked" as England embarked upon "the road to anarchy and ruin".[64] This had its effect on the reformist leaders of the Trades Union Council (TUC), who took fright. In the privacy of Comintern headquarters, however, hopes rose to new heights. Zinoviev claimed the temporary stabilisation of capitalism had come to an end: "events taking place now in England are the most important events since the Russian Revolution," he gushed.[65] Zinoviev was not alone in becoming over-excited. The prospect of Britain on its knees made all the sacrifices Russia had made since 1917 seem worthwhile. It was hard to suppress the sense of exhilaration. Stalin was no doubt surprised, however, to receive from the Anglophobe Chicherin, who had in 1918 been imprisoned by the British, the draft of an article, "The directions of the English revolution".[66] Despite the heightened tension in relations over China, the Russians, swept up by the dramatic new turn of events, acted recklessly out of ideological fervour. On 4 May the Politburo instructed the Soviet trades union council to write out a cheque for £26,000 (250,000 roubles, or over £1.5 million at current value) in aid of the general strike. Received on 5 May, it was rejected out of hand by Walter Citrine, the acting general secretary of the TUC.[67]

The reformist trades unions did not have the stomach for a prolonged strike that threatened the constitutional order. Their interests were exactly the reverse of the Bolsheviks'. But the miners were a major and radical presence within the unions represented. The TUC thus hastily called a halt to the strikes on 12 May, though the Russians continued to subsidise the miners to the tune of something approaching £200,000 all told through to March 1927—nearly £12 million at today's valuation—and the collapse of their industrial dispute.[68]

Containment of the Soviet Union in Europe

Meanwhile in China Soviet military advisers directed by Borodin were arming and training the movement's forces to drive north from the southern stronghold, Canton. No direct means existed for the British to retaliate in China, which was too vast and where British military power was too limited. One favoured option, that of bombing Canton from Hong Kong, would have little lasting effect, for example. London had no idea how to proceed. Responding to Russian policy in late July, in London the Committee of Imperial Defence deliberated at length on the Russian danger and the difficult question of how to deal with what it called "an ever-threatening menace to civilisation", but to no satisfactory conclusion.[69]

On 28 July 1926 the comments of Sir William Tyrrell, the permanent under-secretary, underscored a crucial theme: "I assume as common ground that ever since the Bolshevist régime was established in Russia its activities have been mainly directed against this country, and that in every part of the world we have been met by its persistent and consistent hostility." It was his view, and not his alone, that "our overthrow is the chief aim and object of Moscow". The clash of policy between Britain and the Soviet Union was "unbridgeable". War, however, was not an option, because of public opinion and the lack of military capability—the massive army that had been rapidly mobilised in 1914 was no more. The only means of containing Bolshevism was through diplomacy. By undermining the Soviet–German entente, the British were securing Europe: "we look upon the policy embodied in the Locarno treaties as laying the foundations for a settlement of continental conditions which offers the best prospect for our most effective protection against the common danger from the East".[70]

This policy was elegantly outlined by the young high-flying diplomat Harold Nicolson in a cabinet paper:

Europe to-day is divided into three main elements, namely, the victors, the vanquished and Russia. The Russian problem, that incessant, though shapeless menace, can be stated only as a problem; it is impossible as yet to forecast what effect the development of Russia will have on the future stability of Europe. It is true, on the one hand, that the feeling of uncertainty which is sapping the health of Western Europe is caused to no small extent by the disappearance of Russia as a Power accountable in the European concert. On the other hand, the Russian problem is for the moment Asiatic rather than European; to-morrow Russia may again figure decisively in the balance of continental power; but to-day she hangs as a storm-cloud upon the Eastern horizon of Europe—impending, imponderable, but, for the present, detached. Russia is not, therefore in any sense a factor of stability; she is indeed the most menacing of all our uncertainties; and it must thus be in spite of Russia, perhaps even because of Russia, that a policy of security must be framed.[71]

The Locarno Pact was signed on 1 December 1925. It treated Germany and France as equals. Britain guaranteed both (along with Belgium) against aggression by the other party. In so doing, as Nicolson suggested, the British sought to undercut the Rapallo relationship between the Germans and the Russians, since Germany was also now to be admitted to the League of Nations. Marchese Pietro della Torretta, the Italian ambassador, understood from the Foreign Office that the pact guaranteeing the French, Belgian and German frontiers to the West had as its target the neutralisation of Moscow's "disturbing activity deployed everywhere and particularly in Germany, in Central Europe and in the Near and Far East" that "constitutes a really serious danger for the domestic peace of various countries and for world peace".[72] But the unanswered question remained: was Britain prepared to go further? What about the option of war in order to stem Bolshevik agitation in the Far East?

Summing up the situation throughout China in January 1927 the chiefs of staff—First Sea Lord Admiral Beatty, Field Marshal George Milne and General Sir Hugh Trenchard (Royal Air Force)—agreed that "in the last few months the situation has very much deteriorated. The further and serious disturbances which we apprehended in June 1925 have arisen. The Nationalist Government, working to a considerable extent under Bolshevist influence, has obtained control of the greater part of China south of the Yangtse. Two of the British Concessions on the Yangtse (Hankow and Kiukiang) have been evacuated. Shanghai is menaced in the near future."[73] "At present victory lay with the Bolsheviks," the hapless foreign secretary confessed to cabinet.[74]

Once the paramount sceptic, Stalin had somehow convinced himself that Hankow would "soon become the Chinese Moscow".[75] So no argument in favour of appeasing diehards in London was likely to win out. Austen Chamberlain summed up the British dilemma: "The Soviet Government . . . has some right to claim the Canton boycott as its most outstanding success outside its own borders since it came into existence. The loss to British trade and to the Colony of Hong Kong, in particular, has been very great."[76]

Britain Turns the Tables on Russia in China

Ultimately there was only one way out of the trap into which the British had inadvertently stumbled in 1925 by indiscriminately shooting unarmed Chinese—and that was to reverse course and turn the tables on the Bolsheviks by winning over local nationalism, thereby transforming it into a formidable barrier to Soviet penetration. Proposals ingeniously engineered by diplomat Owen O'Malley who, as an Irishman, had no sympathy for the plight of the China lobby, but who had served in Soviet Russia, overrode stubborn resistance when the British minister to China, Sir Miles Lampson, and the foreign secretary sought an easy way out of the problem. Well briefed, Chamberlain told cabinet, "The Chinese Nationalists are using the Russians for their own ends, and it may be expected that if the Kuomintang establishes itself as the Government of China and enters into relations with the Powers its need of Russian support will decrease and the influence of the Russians will wane."[77]

O'Malley and Chamberlain were right in the short term, though they had significantly overestimated the staying power of democracy in Japan, as events were to show (see chapter 4, below). None the less, Soviet policy in China finally met its match early in 1927. Events suddenly slipped out of control at the weakest link—the CCP. Its most radical members saw no reason to wait upon events. On 3 January the Chinese attacked the British concession in Hankow. In anticipation of the Guomindang army's arrival in Shanghai, the Russians were taken completely by surprise when the local CCP and trades unions launched a general strike, which they learned about only through the newspapers. This fateful decision had been taken on 18 March. Even the leaders of the CCP knew nothing about it. "A general strike against the background of the arrival of Nationalist Government forces has created a massive crisis of power," they reported.[78] This was bad news for Moscow; the British cabinet would not tolerate the surrender of Shanghai to violence, as it would have a "disastrous effect" on the British position in "China, Japan, India and throughout the East".[79] For London, this was the last straw.

Guomindang forces entered the city on 21 March, when it was economically paralysed. Chiang turned up five days later and met with leaders of the financial sector, who were willing to back him provided the

Communists were suppressed. The British, desperate to pre-empt the ultimate loss of Shanghai, now began to take more resolute measures and bombarded Nanjing, Chiang's stronghold, on 24 March. Four days later the Soviet Politburo instructed the Chinese leadership to call off the strike and any uprising they had in mind. But it was too late. Chiang decided to wipe out the Communist presence, and for this purpose he enlisted a ruthless criminal fraternity: the notorious Green Gang.[80]

It was the British who lurked behind the delivery of a series of blows that struck the Russians and their junior allies in China. On 31 March Churchill proposed that "it would not be at all out of keeping with the Chinese character, and might also be in harmony with the interests of Chiang Kai-shek and the Moderates, to consent to the expulsion of these Red Russians who are seeking to reduce China through Communism to Muscovite vassalage. At any rate, my feeling is that that is the point at which we should aim. With the malignant influence of the Red Russians out of the way we might soon be able to make a good arrangement with the native Chinese."[81]

On 6 April, and with the connivance of the diplomatic corps, northern warlord Chang Tso-lin's troops raided the massive Soviet embassy compound in Beijing. There they came upon a veritable treasure trove of incriminating evidence. Even they, however, were surprised to find not only one of the co-founders of the CCP, Li Dazhao, plus armaments, but an entire archive of top-secret material, including the addresses of Communist safe houses, incriminating correspondence with Moscow, and details of Fourth Directorate secret agents and payments.[82] Following up on the British cabinet's express determination not to let Shanghai fall to the Communists came the blockade of the Soviet general consulate in Shanghai on 7 April. Two days later Chiang declared martial law in the city. Beginning in the middle of the night on 12 April the Green Gang, dressed in army uniforms, took just seven hours to liquidate the Communists.[83]

The documents discovered in the Beijing raid on the Soviet embassy confirmed London's worst fears and suspicions. The material uncovered demonstrated conclusively to the Foreign Office that "Russian influence and infiltration in the Nationalist army was much more complete and

detailed than we had been inclined to believe". To its great embarrass-
ment, there were also copies of head of legation Lampson's correspondence with the Foreign Office itself.[84] The breach of diplomatic relations with the Soviet Union that followed, much to the regret of the
foreign secretary, came about on 26 May as the dam of back-bench
opinion within the Conservative Party finally burst; the result was a
surge of supressed anger, rather than a product of considered policy.
Quite apart from the impact of the Chinese revolutionary disturbances,
the party conference at Scarborough on 8 October 1926 had passed a
resolution calling for abrogation of the Anglo–Soviet trade agreement
of March 1921. Two hundred members of parliament had signed a peti-
tion to the same effect.

No immediate consequences were to be expected, though King
George V, who had lost his cousin, Tsar Nikolai, and Nikolai's family in
1918, and who had a tendency to meddle in government policy, twice
assured the German ambassador that were France and Germany to follow
Britain's example, the Soviet Union would collapse.[85] The threat of war
involving Poland in the autumn of 1926 had stirred fears within the Soviet
Union. The peasants began hoarding salt; food shortages were aggra-
vated. In September Commissar for Military and Naval Affairs Kliment
Voroshilov warned new officers of the Red Army, "We are in possession
of information which testifies that we are now in a situation where an
attack on us depends upon the smallest accidents."[86]

Yet the Soviet leadership had no reason to fear war. At the end of
January 1927 the Fourth Directorate produced a consolidated assessment of the international situation. Allowing for the deterioration in
relations with the West, the briefing concluded that "unresolved disputes
between our neighbours (the failure to form a Polish–Baltic alliance),
between Poland and Germany, and also the difficulty of joint action by
the Western Great Powers in support of our neighbours in a war against
us, make military action in the coming year 1927 unlikely".[87] Trotsky, losing his personal battle against Stalin, instead highlighted the dangers of
war even waged by neighbours Poland and Romania egged on from London. He wanted Comintern to mobilise the working class across Europe
on the basis of fears of a repeat of the outbreak of war as in 1914.[88] And by

raising a parallel between himself and "Tiger" Georges Clemenceau, who had taken power in France at the height of the world war in the name of prosecuting the fight more effectively, Trotsky played right into Stalin's hands. His days were numbered, much to the relief of the British.

The Bolshevik threat to their empire had traumatised those who owned and ruled Britain. The long-term consequences became evident only a decade hence. One immediate and symptomatic side effect was a noticeable indulgence towards fascism, because of its decisive suppression of Communists. Their most dangerous leader in Italy, Antonio Gramsci, was safely behind bars. The rest of the PCI leadership headed by Palmiro Togliatti found exile in Moscow. Alberto de Stefani, Italy's finance minister, reported to the prime minister (and foreign minister) Benito Mussolini from Paris on 7 January 1925 that "[i]n a discussion that I had today with [Winston] Churchill [then chancellor of the exchequer] . . . the latter expressed his sympathy for Your Excellency and his esteem for the energetic work carried out by Your Excellency in suppressing Bolshevism".[89]

Early in 1927, by which time Mussolini's régime had become a machine of merciless repression of the left, the anti-Semitic *Morning Post* published a leading article entitled "The Fascist Ideal": "When MUSSOLINI took hold of Italy, democracy, delirious with Communism, was swiftly and bloodily ruining the country. And because every other nation is menaced by the same disaster, the example of Italy is peculiarly illuminating, as 'a contribution to civilisation.' Signor Mussolini believes—and he is not alone in that conviction—that sooner or later other nations must resort to some expedient equivalent to the Fascist purge."[90] Such attitudes resonated into the 1930s. They carried with them a deep-seated reluctance to oppose the fascist powers that paraded along the front line against Bolshevism.

4

The Manchurian Fiasco, 1931

We have argued that it would ill suit Japanese interests to have Manchuria in a state of chaos which would probably end in some form of Soviet domination over the whole of the North down to Changchung.

—LINDLEY (TOKYO) TO MARQUESS OF READING (LONDON), 30 OCTOBER 1931[1]

After the trauma the British suffered in China during the 1920s, subsequent complications arising from Japan, though naturally unwelcome, were treated on another scale of concern. The illusion took hold that, compared with the impossibly complicated business of dealing with the Communist threat, other rivals were fundamentally reasonable, played by the old rules and were therefore manageable in their conduct and limited in their ambitions. But nothing could have been further from the truth, as the British were soon to discover.

The Wall Street Crash

The postwar system of collective security centred on the League of Nations could work only if the great powers on its council behaved responsibly in pursuit of their own national interests and in indifferently sanctioning those states that misbehaved. Thus the entire structure in Geneva hinged upon the decisions of a few who would act without bias and in everyone's long-term interest, regardless of conditions prevailing at home and abroad. In the conduct of international relations, this was too much to ask. And what the impact of the Great Depression clearly demonstrated from 1929 was that if the world economy and the international trading system broke down, so did the open-ended commitment to maintaining the international political order.

The international political order was new, so few could be blamed for assuming too much for lack of realism, and these were confined almost entirely to the English-speaking world. But the international economic order was the same as it had always been throughout the nineteenth century. Trading cycles brought major economic depressions in the wake of unbridled commercial booms, most recently in 1873. In the United States, since the creation of the Federal Reserve Bank in 1913, successive Republican administrations had sensed no need for constraint in operating a policy of easy money. As a result the economic boom of the late 1920s pivoted precariously on massive private indebtedness that grew and sustained a stock-market bubble. Between 1925 and 1929 an unprecedented sum of $50 billion in new public offerings was issued on Wall Street. Borrowing to buy them on the margin was no problem even for those of modest means. Investment houses readily facilitated easy credit to members of the public who had no way of covering their debts should the market drop. Bust inevitably followed boom. Having reached unprecedented heights for over four years, as brokers lent $6 billion on the margin, the US market abruptly crashed over two sessions once some of the 450 investment trusts began cashing in to show profits for the year that September, inadvertently shattering blind confidence that the market would forever rise to new heights. The reckoning came on 24 October 1929 when more than 1,600,000 shares were traded within thirty minutes of the market opening; 441 shares hit new lows and only two reached new highs. It represented the most severe decline of prices in the history of Wall Street—only for this record to be topped by a factor of fifteen five days later when, in a deluge of 16,410,000 shares changing hands, there were 551 new lows and no new highs.[2]

Financial collapse yanked the US economy down with it. By the summer of 1931, and with a run on gold, the Great Crash also wrenched the rug from under the German economy, bringing the tottering British economy along with it. Americans, desperate to meet calls on their own loans, sought redemption of the extensive short-term loans that had been propping up German industry since the Dawes Plan of 1924. The German government, habituated to the reckless printing of money to meet its financial obligations since July 1914, had incautiously returned to old habits, as a result of which middle-class savings were wiped out by hyperinflation in 1923. The state thereafter made no attempt to limit the ceaseless expansion of credit. Moreover, even before the crash on Wall Street, as early as 1928 growing unemployment had been pointing to more troubled times. And given Germany's pivotal role in European trade no one was going to escape unscathed from the chaos that resulted.

Britain, by now clinging on as the leading power in Europe, was one of the most heavily dependent upon foreign trade; of the major economies, only the Netherlands was more exposed. The British economy had been in secular decline since its currency was fixed uncompetitively to the gold standard in 1925 in order to sustain the dominance of London in world financial markets. This had made British manufactures too expensive for export. The severely deflated economy now found itself especially vulnerable to the drastic protectionist measures taken by the US government. And, as in Germany, a bad situation was made far worse by drastic cuts in government expenditure, especially wages, to balance the budget.

The underlying fear was, understandably, that a continuation of the Great Depression, if unchecked, would sweep capitalism aside. Reassurance was not enough. US Secretary of State Henry Stimson heard from his Italian counterpart Dino Grandi comforting news that the Communist Party had no hope of gaining any foothold in Italy. "Nor in America is there any danger of Bolshevism," Stimson retorted, not to be outdone, "because in the United States the working classes are the most hostile towards Communism." Displaying his innate caution, however, he added that "it is in the interests of every one of us to defend the capitalist régime and demonstrate that this crisis is temporary and not innate to the capitalist system. Therefore we must also speedily overcome it."[3]

These were the conditions in which the entire postwar edifice optimistically constructed to guarantee against aggression by the Central Powers at Paris in 1919 was effectively hollowed out from within on the eve of Hitler's ascent to power. The League of Nations, from which the United States had excluded itself—having deserted the nest at birth—was now exposed for what it was: an empty shell. Once exposed as such, the revelation dealt a tremendous psychological blow to those statesmen seeking to defend the postwar territorial status quo.

Japanese Aggression

The test came when the Japanese recklessly embarked upon the military occupation of north-eastern China (Manchuria). The excuse was a terrorist incident contrived at Mukden along the South Manchuria Railway on 18 September 1931. The pretence was a backhanded compliment to the new world order. Although nominally a democracy, Japan was on the cusp of becoming a militarised state, which meant that at the League of Nations plausible, polite civilians fronted for the warrior caste—a turn of affairs for which the rest of the world was utterly unprepared, and which for a long time it found impossible to recognise and then used every excuse for doing nothing to counter.

Japanese aggression in Manchuria struck as a bolt from the blue. Very few followed and fully understood Japan's political trajectory to the extremity of nationalism with the onset of the Showa Depression in 1930 and the severe deflation and growing unemployment that had rapidly taken hold in the country. But whereas in Europe such conditions made for caution, in Japan Foreign Minister Baron Shidehara's attempted appeasement of China aroused within the military the spirit of aggression. Indeed, Shidehara's policy of appeasement itself ultimately prompted the conspiracy in Mukden. A leading authority on Japanese foreign policy has pointed out that the Manchurian crisis "was manufactured because the diplomats were in measurable distance of resolving the China problem—or were thought to be so".[4]

What was that "problem"? Since the mid-1920s China had succeeded in rectifying the more extreme elements of extra-territoriality that the

British had forced on the country as a result of the opium wars of the 1840s. Britain had sensibly accepted that of the two main dangers, Chinese nationalism and Chinese Bolshevism, the former, if satiated, could block the latter, though at the price of concessions from British interests. But Communist penetration in particular was viewed by the Kwantung Army command as a mortal threat to "sacred" interests in Shantung and Manchuria.

During the heady revolutionary years of the mid-1920s the Soviet Politburo had worked to hold back the Chinese Communist Party (CCP) from asserting itself in Manchuria in an "attempt to obtain a breathing-space here, and that in fact means 'put to one side' the issue of the status of Manchuria; i.e., in effect accommodate to the fact that Southern Manchuria will remain for the time being in the hands of Japan". This display of unprincipled opportunism was potentially very embarrassing, the Soviet Politburo acknowledged. It could lead to "a mendacious construction on the part of inadequately informed elements to the effect that the interests of China are being sacrificed for the purposes of settling inter-state relations between the USSR and Japan".[5]

Chinese Communists Alarm Moscow

Yet the Kremlin could never be entirely certain of its control over the CCP. After Communist bases in the cities had been wiped out in 1927 the party that re-emerged was disaggregated and fell prey to a kind of lunatic extremism that threatened Soviet interests in the region, which inevitably also worried the Japanese. In 1930 the leadership of the CCP was taken over from the illiterate general secretary Xiang Zhongfa by a young and ruthless fanatic, Li Li-san. Li took at face value the extreme revolutionary rhetoric spewing out of Moscow from 1928. Not a modest man, he styled himself as the new Lenin destined to bring about world revolution from its base in China. He launched proposals for all-out assaults on a series of cities; in so doing he refused to take criticism from Comintern advisers such as Gerhart Eisler (code name Roberts) in Shanghai, and he ruled out Mao Tse-tung's preference for capturing the countryside through guerrilla warfare before laying siege to urban areas.

Eisler was scathing in his criticism: "On every question his method was to give an abstract philosophical response and his total underestimation of the leading organisational role of the party and his inability to understand how to work with the masses given the stance he has taken at the present time is a brake in the future development of the party."[6]

At a CCP Politburo meeting on 2 August 1930 Li had obtained agreement to the organisation of uprisings in Wuchang (where one had already taken place but was about to be overthrown), Beijing, Tientsin, Harbin (in Manchuria) and elsewhere "with the support of the Russian Red Army and war against the imperialists". From Shanghai, Comintern's executive was warned that "the situation is serious, critical".[7] To buttress their case against Li, the Profintern (Red Trades Union International) representative in Shanghai sent his chief Solomon Lozovsky incriminating quotations from Li. The most damaging, because it touched directly on Soviet state interests, read as follows: "An uprising in Manchuria forms the prologue to international war. This would mean a war by Japan against the USSR . . . Our strategy must be to provoke an international war . . . Comintern may consider this incorrect but I am convinced it is correct."[8]

On 12 August 1930 the Far Eastern Bureau telegraphed Comintern's executive with a warning that "the [CCP] Politburo insists on uprisings and asks for your speedy decision".[9] From Sochi on the following day Stalin wrote, "The lurch by the Chinese is unrealistic and dangerous. A general uprising in China is in the current situation nonsense . . . The Chinese have already made fools of themselves rushing to seize Changsha. Now they want to make fools of themselves all over China. This cannot be permitted."[10] In Moscow on 25 August the Politburo discussed the problem after a comprehensive presentation of the issues by Comintern. It approved a long, accusatory telegram to the Chinese Communist leadership. Given that the preconditions for success were absent, the telegram rejected and condemned Li Li-san's plans to seize the big cities, including Hankow, Shanghai, Beijing and Mukden (the main city within the Japanese sphere of influence in southern Manchuria), as "the most harmful adventurism".[11] Stalin was not against revolutionary activism in principle, but only as long as it was profitably directed and did not touch directly on Soviet state interests.

The Japanese had reason to be concerned at the radicalisation of CCP activity not only within China proper but also within their own sphere of influence in Manchuria, and here the Russians were directly culpable. In 1929 they had faced a threat to their hold over the Chinese Eastern Railway (CER), which ran through northern Manchuria. At that time Stalin suggested "organizing an uprising by a revolutionary movement in Manchuria".[12] And in a letter from Comintern's political secretariat to the CCP, highlighting the importance of mobilising the peasantry in general, Manchuria was pointed to as a region that should receive attention.[13] Nothing immediate resulted, but Communist cells began springing up like mushrooms in the political shadows, despite repeated and intensive measures to suppress them. The Communist Party, though small, was significantly expanded by the incorporation of Korean Communists who had hitherto been separately organised under their own banner. They threatened to turn the region into a "fireball".[14] To the Japanese this was inevitably an alarming development.

Special operations were also launched from Moscow to neutralise the Kwantung Army's intelligence activity against Soviet targets and to ascertain Japanese intentions in the region. On 17–18 November 1930 the Russians kidnapped the Japanese officer running the military intelligence office at Pogranichnaya, at the south-eastern tip of the CER. He was brought into the Soviet Union to Khabarovsk, where he was interrogated.[15] To say the least, the disappearance of their head of station would have heightened Japanese concerns. Resurgent Chinese nationalism itself could no longer be ignored in Japanese eyes. The local Chinese warlord Chang Hsueh-liang, whose father had recently been assassinated by the Japanese, had in 1929 retaliated by aligning himself with Chiang Kai-shek's nationalist movement.

American Isolationism and European Indifference

The omens were not good. Disinclined to wait upon events, the Kwantung Army command had therefore lashed out unilaterally. But only with Japan at peace was there a chance that nationalism and Communism in China could remain separable. This was a point emphasised to Japanese officials by the British ambassador to Japan, diehard anti-Bolshevik Sir Francis Lindley. Lindley, who had served as consul-general in Russia with the counter-revolutionary forces in 1919 before they were defeated, "argued that it would ill suit Japanese interests to have Manchuria in a state of chaos which would probably end in some form of Soviet domination over the whole of the North down to Changchung".[16]

Although he was still clinging to office by his fingertips, gone was the dominance of peacemaker Shidehara. Before long anyone in Tokyo who attempted to keep the armed forces (and in particular fanatical junior army officers) in check was promptly despatched with an assassin's bullet. Even so, the Western powers bent over backwards to give Tokyo the benefit of the doubt as though the civilians still held real power.

At the League of Nations in Geneva the Chinese government, the object of Japanese aggression, was effectively dismissed out of hand and disingenuously treated as though it bore some responsibility for the Manchurian crisis. Nothing was done to put an end to Japanese aggression. And, far from satisfying Japan, Western and Russian attempts to alleviate the tension merely whetted its appetite. Particularly in the West, the costly, naïve delusion sustained by those who knew nothing about Japanese politics was that somehow "world opinion" would oblige Japan to behave in a civilised way. When news of the Japanese attack came into Washington DC on 19 September 1931, Secretary of State Henry Stimson was deeply immersed in sorting out debt repayments with America's economic partners. "I went over and had a talk with the President about it and found that he thoroughly agreed with me in my caution," Stimson recorded in his diary.[17] The Americans understood that it was the Japanese army that had precipitated the crisis, but they deluded themselves into thinking that by ingratiating themselves with the Foreign Ministry under Shidehara they could ensure that the military were brought back under civilian control. They simultaneously discouraged any decisive action from the League of Nations, which was scorned for "bungling ahead" and "trying to butt in and do something".[18] Not surprisingly the British embassy in Tokyo dismissed the Americans as "completely passive".[19] And not for the last time.

As it slowly dawned on Stimson that the crisis was more serious than he had believed and that Japanese diplomats were leading him down the garden path, he realised he had missed his chance. Hoover had no interest in foreign policy. Stimson now faced the problem that the president was "so busy over his domestic and financial problems that he is not thinking out ahead the problems of international relations to the extent that he has been hitherto".[20] Stimson's hands were tied. Hoover, he believed, had no understanding of "what it means to him in his administration to have Japan run amok and play havoc with its peace treaties, so his main proposition . . . was not to allow under any circumstances anybody to deposit that baby on our lap; and second, not to get ourselves into a humiliating position, in case Japan refused to do anything to what he called our scraps of paper or paper treaties".[21]

But how much was Stimson himself prepared to risk? In the Far East as in Europe, the Western powers feared that undoing the status quo would unleash the forces of disorder. Bolshevism still loomed in the background as the likely beneficiary. And the Americans, out of deeply rooted hostility and suspicion, had yet even to recognise the Soviet régime. Siren voices from Western Europe tended to reinforce their fears.

The US government was alerted by Prime Minister Pierre Laval to the ever present dangers of Communism in Europe. Laval, who was not unaware that frightening the Americans might make them more conciliatory in debt negotiations, "dilated on the real pacific feeling of France, of horrors at any war at all, and the fact that the French Army under the present situation in Europe, the unsettlement in Middle Europe and Sovietism in Russia, was after all the defense against Bolshevism".[22] The French army was, like all armed forces in the capitalist world, a prime target for subversion from Moscow. Only three years earlier Comintern had amplified "Instructions on working within the forces" to sections worldwide. "Work amidst the ranks of the armed forces of the bourgeoisie is necessary not only from the viewpoint of the struggle against war", it advised, "but also in general from the viewpoint of every genuine revolutionary struggle. The fundamental degradation of the armed forces of the bourgeoisie is an absolutely necessary precondition for seizing power by the proletariat." Action was essential in order to turn an imperialist war into a civil war. It was defined as "one of the most important tasks of Communist Parties". For this purpose a special apparatus was required within each Party to inject cells into the armed forces.[23] Stimson was not unaffected by French alarmism. Not surprisingly therefore he formulated his proposals to Hoover for action in the Far East according to his "own view that the relations we had with Japan were most important, because Japan really stood as our own buffer against the unknown powers behind her on the mainland of China and Russia".[24] Those "powers" were obviously Communist, as Stalin's Russia could be defined in no other terms. But Hoover did not take the bait.

Japanese aggression in Manchuria had not been entirely unforeseen, though the brutality of the offensive came as an unpleasant surprise. In retrospect Hoover acknowledged that the threat of "Bolshevist Russia to the north" and "a possible Bolshevist China" on Japan's flank put Japan's independence "in jeopardy".[25] Yet he saw no remedy to the situation other than that which the Japanese chose unilaterally.

Soviet Isolationism

US isolationism was matched by Soviet isolationism. The Soviet Union was no different from any of the great powers in taking the line of least resistance to Japan, and for good reason. The aggression against the Chinese on Russia's eastern flank could not have come at a more unfortunate time. The forced collectivisation of agriculture was still in progress and industrialisation had been hastened at such a pace that it led to acute bottlenecks in the economy. Any immediate new military requirements would place unexpected and heavy burdens on a system already strained to the limits. Stalin did not have much understanding of economics, but this was obvious even to him.

He was down south, as was usual every autumn, at a datcha in Sochi when news reached Moscow of Japanese forces occupying Manchuria. On 20 September Stalin ordered that initial decisions on what moves to take be reversed until more information came in.[26] His grasp of the international situation was woefully weak, however, based as it was upon assumptions of an active capitalist conspiracy against the Soviet Union.

This can be seen in his bizarre explanations for the Japanese occupation that sped by telegram on 23 September from Sochi to Kaganovich and Molotov, who were running the Politburo between them:

1. The most likely of all is that Japan's intervention is being carried out by agreement with all or some of the great powers on the basis of expanding and strengthening spheres of influence in China.

2. It is not to be excluded, though unlikely, that America kicked up a row defending Chang Hsueh-liang against Japan, as, given the current situation, it could also guarantee for itself "its share" of China without coming to blows with Japan, even with the agreement of the Chinese themselves.

3. It is not to be excluded and likely even, that the Japanese have an agreement to intervene, with some influential militarist groups in China such as Fyn or Yan Sishan or old Mukdenites similar to Chan Tsunchan, or all of them together.

Caution was to be the watchword. It could be a trap. Stalin went on to say that Soviet military intervention was "of course, to be excluded". Diplomatic intervention was currently "pointless" as it could "just unite the imperialists, whereas it is to our advantage that they fall out with one another". The furthest he would go was to target a barrage of propaganda at the Japanese, the League of Nations and the United States, among others, though taking care that in the official government newspaper *Izvestiya* the tone should be "ultra-careful". Indeed, the Japanese were to be asked to keep Moscow informed.[27]

On 25 September the Politburo called on its embassies in the region for an accurate update. They were firmly told, "[D]o not undertake any steps and do not give any explanations without instruction from Moscow."[28] Two months later Stalin wrote to Commissar for Military and Naval Affairs Voroshilov reminding him that the Japanese issue was both "complicated" and "serious". The outlook was bleak. Tokyo was evidently in pursuit of not only Manchuria "but also Beijing", intent on forming a government to counterpose to Nanjing. "Moreover", Stalin continued, "it is not to be excluded and is even likely that it will reach out to our Far East and possibly also to Mongolia." Japan might not move against the Soviet Union that winter, but in the future "it could make such an attempt. The wish to reinforce its position in Manchuria would push it in that direction. But it will only be able to reinforce its position in Manchuria if it succeeds in fostering hatred between China and the USSR." That would require it to help Chinese warlords seize the CER, Outer Mongolia and Russia's maritime province, putting in place puppets totally dependent upon Japan. Stalin defined Japanese aims as fourfold: (a) to safeguard Japan against "the Bolshevik infection"; (b) to render a rapprochement between the USSR and China impossible; (c) to create for itself an extensive economic and military base on the mainland; and (d) to make this base self-sufficient for war with America.

Without such a plan Japan would find itself "face to face with American militarisation, China in revolution, and a rapidly growing USSR pushing towards the open sea". The Japanese believed that waiting a couple of years inevitably meant that they would leave it too late to pre-empt disaster. Only the failure of the United States to act (which Stalin thought unlikely), the failure of the Chinese to mobilise against Japan (which he also thought unlikely), the failure of a powerful revolutionary movement to emerge in Japan (no sign of this so far) and the failure of the Soviet Union itself to take pre-emptive military and other measures would make it possible to carry out their plans.[29]

At the end of March 1932 the Soviet ambassador in Tokyo, Alexander Troyanovsky, advised Moscow that Japan's general staff were convinced that neither the United States nor the USSR was willing or able to fight, but that in due course they might become so. Hence Japan had to move quickly. He warned Moscow that the "slightest change in the international situation" might easily result in "dragging us into a war". Apparently it was only the intervention of Japan's navy—which had the Americans always in its gunsights—in the form of Admiral Kato that forestalled precipitate military action against the Soviet Union.[30] Looking back years later Molotov recalled how at that time in the Far East security was "neglected and the Soviet Union could undoubtedly expect many surprises".[31]

In response to the threat, and with the first fruits of industrialisation to hand, the build-up of Soviet forces in the region was intensive. Within four months, as of January 1932, the number of men stationed in the Soviet Far East had risen from 42,000 to 108,610; of planes, from 88 to 276; and of tanks, from 16 to 376.[32] But much more would be needed in the event of war. Late in April 1932 Radek let it be known "that the Soviet Government were getting extremely anxious about the position in Manchuria and feared war with Japan in the near future . . . He was convinced that if hostilities did break out Poland and Roumania would come in on the side of Japan. This would lead to complications in Europe to which it was impossible to forsee any limit." This was clearly an oblique reference to the Rapallo relationship and what Germany might do if the Russians were at war with Poland. Radek added that Moscow "had spent milliards of roubles in the last seven months to prepare against a danger it foresaw from the outset of the conflict. These preparations had strained the country's resources, and compelled the government to alter its five-year plan. The whole programme for the metallurgical industry had been changed owing to production for war purposes. They had stored enough stocks of corn to feed the army for a year, and this and the necessity for transporting supplies to the Far Eastern army accounted for the present food shortage [famine] and general tightening of conditions." Radek insisted that they would "remain strongly on the defensive" as the five-year plan's completion was the highest priority "and would not shed the blood of the workers for any material interests in Manchuria. If there were a genuine revolutionary movement there, that of course would be a different matter."[33] Japan's refusal on 13 December 1931 to accept the Soviet offer of a non-aggression pact confirmed existing fears.[34]

Worried as they all undoubtedly were, Stalin none the less had a problem restraining subordinates in the Far East, whose escapades held dangerous implications for Soviet security. In the summer of 1932 a sabotage unit of the OGPU made up of ethnic Koreans was sent into Korea to blow up railway bridges. Hearing of the operation, Stalin called on Kaganovich for the punishment of those concerned: "Speak to Molotov and take draconian measures against offenders from OGPU and the Fourth Directorate (it is entirely possible that these people are agents of our enemies in our midst.) Demonstrate that there [in the Far East] Moscow still has the power to punish offenders."[35] Other such provocations also prompted outbursts from Stalin: "It is clear that such issues and 'incidents', which carry the risk of 'suddenly' unleashing a war, must be handled, down to the tiniest details, by Moscow alone."[36]

Japanese expansion into Inner Mongolia in January–February 1933 certainly kept the Russians on their toes. In April 1933 Lieutenant Colonel Suzuki of the Japanese Bureau of Military Affairs told the Marquis Kido Kōichi, the emperor's closest advisor, that "there are two kinds of enemies, an absolute enemy and a relative enemy. Since Russia aimed to destroy the national structure of Japan, he cited Russia as the absolute enemy."[37] The Russians were both an old geopolitical rival and a new revolutionary interloper. Comintern was, of course, trying its best to destroy the monarchy and empire, though in Japan itself it never had any chance of success. In 1931 more than 280 members of the party (including the leadership and the Tokyo district chiefs) had been arrested in two waves, on 15 March and 16 April.[38]

The League of Nations Farce

The Western response to Japanese aggression was debilitated by the Depression. In Britain the resistance to increasing public expenditure—indeed sustained pressure to cut it—and the consequent obsession with reducing military expenditure were inseparably linked to the delusion that disarmament was the best palliative for the deterioration in international relations. The British government, without whom any containment of Japan was impossible, was cutting the pay of the armed forces at every rank. The brief mutiny of the British fleet at Invergordon that resulted on 15–16 September 1931—hailed enthusiastically by Comintern as "a genuine about-turn in the sentiments of the masses in the direction of revolutionary class struggle"[39]—and the much-delayed decision of 21 September to decouple the pound sterling from the price of gold thus meant Japan faced no deterrent to continuing its seizure of Manchuria.

The British were not of one mind about the problem, either. They had traditionally barred the way to Japanese colonisation of Manchuria not out of any moral consideration but because of the danger that it might well precipitate war with Russia, at a time when Russia was an ally. The difference was that now Russia was under the Bolsheviks. Britain was also primarily an imperial power, so eagerness to support the League of Nations and its treasured principle of non-aggression came a long second to the protection of core interests overseas. Britain's minister at the embassy in Beijing had, indeed, back at the height of the Chinese revolution in the mid-twenties, written of Manchuria: "There is ... no reason why we should boggle any longer at its absorption by Japan as and when favourable opportunities occur, and every reason why we should give Japan plainly to understand that we are prepared to support her absorption of Manchuria, or at least of the Chinese Eastern Railway, by any means which do not expose us to military dangers or legitimate reproach. My impression of the Japanese is that they would place a high value on assurances of this kind."[40]

The British knew well how to kick an inconvenient ball into the long grass: set up a committee. The Lytton Commission, established to investigate the obvious, took a year. It reported to the autumn 1932 session of the League Assembly. Foreign Secretary Sir John Simon had the reputation of being a brilliant advocate, which, in political life, was, however, seriously handicapped by a reputation for saying whatever was convenient at any given time and a "lifelong inclination to sit on the fence".[41] There was also something oddly whimsical about him even as a member of the House of Commons Chess Circle, where one performance elicited the comment that if Simon "had not by inadvertence thrown away a position where the win was within his grasp" the victory would have been all the greater.[42] As in chess, it seems, so in foreign affairs, first in play against imperial Japan, and later Nazi Germany. On 7 December Foreign Minister Matsuoka Yōsuke described Simon's speech at Geneva as "magnificent", because "he explained in perfect English what I have been trying to say in my halting way from the beginning".[43]

The US secretary of state, though not without his own failings, was justifiably contemptuous of Britain's attitude. When the Italian ambassador to Britain Dino Grandi met Stimson in Geneva he found him "furious" at the British for refusing to support a united front that the Americans belatedly called for against Japan. "The United States", Stimson declared, "will never allow the Open Door régime in China, in which every state in Europe has an interest together with America, to be compromised. Suffice to say that the past year, that has been the worst for American trade, American exports to China have doubled. All the Western states in America are in ferment. Europe takes no account of the situation in the Pacific, and in particular pays no regard to Japan's domestic condition. After eighty years of a policy of modernisation, Japan has fallen back under the domination of a dangerous military caste. The best quality politicians have been assassinated or find themselves under continuous threat for their lives."[44] And even though the Americans did nothing about the Japanese, they had no illusions about them. Indeed, when Japan's ambassador Debuchi Katsuji glibly began excusing renewed aggression in Jehol by saying "that in any event Japan had no territorial ambition south of the Great Wall", Stimson caustically "reminded the Ambassador that a year ago he had told me Japan had no territorial ambitions in Manchuria". Debuchi had, after all, confessed only weeks before that Tokyo was "in the control of a group of younger officers, none of them of a higher rank than a Lieutenant-Colonel".[45]

The Russians had hoped that the Americans would step in, as they had done after a Japanese army of 70,000 men entered the Soviet Far East in 1918 and then refused to leave when the other intervening powers did so. Comintern's secretary for the region was the Finn Otto Kuusinen, whose wife worked as an officer for the Fourth Directorate in the Far East. Kuusinen later recalled, "We were rendered a small amount of help from another state, a very doubtful friend, namely the United States. They, that is one of the participants in the intervention, at that time demanded the removal of Japanese forces from Siberia. Just as at the time of the conclusion of the peace at Portsmouth [New Hampshire, in 1905]!" The Russians certainly did not count on the United States once again intervening to their advantage. "None the less", Kuusinen continued, "in so far as it is a question not of a direct fight with the Soviet Union, but primarily a fight for Manchuria and China, it is impossible to dispute the existence of a certain exacerbation of deep contradictions, antagonism between Japanese and American imperialism." Would this lead to war between them? "I do not think that such a turn of events will occur directly in the immediate future," he argued. "We do not see sufficient grounds for such a supposition. On the contrary, there are some grounds for saying that for the immediate future there will not be open war between Japan and America. But this does not exclude the fact that on both sides there are very active preparations for a coming war, and at present, a conflict is developing partly by other means, that is of a financial and economic nature, and partly by other forces, those of the Chinese."[46]

Moscow Launches the Anti-War Movement

Faced with continued Western inertia and the need on the diplomatic level to appease the Japanese, Comintern launched a mass-based anti-war campaign matching the Soviet state's array of non-aggression pacts stitched together by the new people's commissar Maxim Litvinov at Narkomindel. Comintern resolved at its political committee meeting on 27 April 1932 that "the further growth of the danger of war and intervention against the Soviet Union" had "not met with the necessary determination . . . The successes thus far of anti-war work are still completely inadequate." There was as yet no "real mass movement". It was therefore agreed to hold an international anti-war congress on 28 July during an anti-imperialist armaments week "on the widest basis". A small subcommittee set up to supervise the project, including Willi Münzenberg and a representative from the West European Bureau in Berlin, was to be chaired by KPD leader Ernst Thälmann or his representative. The agenda would focus on the war in China, intervention against the USSR and world war.[47] As the deadline approached, the congress was moved to a three-day event in Berlin in August. Münzenberg was to act as secretary to the committee and the Hungarian Lajos Magyar was added to its tightly restricted list of members. The stipulation made was that the resolutions of the congress must not be "purely

Communist but appear independent"; on the other hand, they should focus on the Japanese problem.[48]

Nothing confused the Communist rank and file more than the fact that direct collaboration against fascism with the Socialist International and its branches was forbidden as heresy, yet they were supposed to open their arms to these same enemies alongside sundry liberal pacifists at an "independent" congress, in the name of defending the Soviet Union and fighting for peace. But, as one Comintern official pointed out, "Of course, there is nothing bad in succeeding, through some means or other, in deceiving the class enemy. But the trouble is that by such manoeuvres the enemy is not outwitted and one may cause considerable bewilderment within one's own ranks."[49] The congress eventually convened in Amsterdam on 27–29 August, with 2,200 delegates from twenty-seven countries.

The need for peace was genuine. The coincidence of Japanese military intervention in the Far East with a crisis in Soviet agriculture and transport, as political unrest within the party loomed on the horizon, made Moscow unusually anxious. One crucial success obtained the following year that relieved some of the anxiety was diplomatic recognition of the Soviet régime by the United States once Democrat Franklin Roosevelt took office. The move broadened Roosevelt's range of options in foreign policy, even though he was unable to exercise any of them for the time being. By the same token, at one stroke recognition complicated Japanese plans. The potential for a closer relationship between Moscow and Washington emerged as a new possibility that Tokyo had to take into account, even though the new US administration was as averse to foreign entanglements as the old. For despite their continuing ideological differences, which would plague relations for years to come, both the Russians and the Americans saw the evident need to stiffen China's resolve against the predatory Japanese. Diplomatic notes were exchanged between Moscow and Washington on 16 November 1933, though when Litvinov asked Roosevelt "what he thinks of an agreement with us on joint action in the event of a danger to peace", he was told that this was out of the question.[50]

In the meantime, Soviet interests dictated that Europe had to remain a house divided. The one eventuality that Stalin desperately needed to forestall was the healing of postwar wounds that could make possible an entente between governments hostile to world revolution: the long-standing bogey of a common front against the Soviet Union. Averting such an outcome put a premium on Stalin's ability to foster division and exacerbate Germany's uneasy relations with its neighbours. This was ultimately the job of Comintern, which could penetrate the parts that others could not reach. However, combined with the apparently irresistible appeal of the far right, the policy pursued of focusing more on the "social fascists" than the real fascists effectively made the rise of Hitler a foregone conclusion. Allowed to follow their own instincts, the KPD, certainly General Secretary Ernst Thälmann, would most likely have buried the hatchet with the social democrats. But that was something Moscow would not tolerate.[51]

5

Stalin's Gamble on German Nationalism

Germany is not Bulgaria.

—STALIN, 7 AUGUST 1923[1]

Having demonstrably failed to revolutionise Europe and China, the Soviet Union had turned inwards. Committed to ruthless *Realpolitik*, Stalin had lost hope that Soviet isolation could simply be relieved by an indigenous German revolution—a revolution that Trotsky in exile still believed feasible. Stalin's order of priorities broke with those of Lenin and Trotsky, neither of whom believed that building socialism in one country was possible, whereas Stalin saw it as the overriding priority for Russia. Having outflanked both the left and the right, and having isolated all forms of opposition within the party, in 1929 Stalin proceeded to impose the collectivisation of agriculture and five-year plans of industrialisation, including the building of vast new cities beyond the Urals in the rural backwaters of Siberia. The entire venture was brilliantly advertised to gullible intellectuals in the West—the example of a planned economy—before it had even left the drawing board. It was prematurely hailed by utopian British socialists Beatrice and Sidney Webb as the dawn of a "new civilisation". In Britain the Labour Party in coalition with the Liberal Party and aided by a secret Soviet subsidy won the general election on 30 May—13.4 million votes against 8.5 million for the Conservatives. Ramsay MacDonald returned as prime minister.[2] On 1 October diplomatic relations with the Soviet Union were resumed without preconditions.

The Top Priority of Dividing the Germans

Stalin was by then propelling his revolution from above at full speed. The primitive socialist accumulation of capital squeezed out of working-class living standards and from the impoverished peasant yielded the foreign exchange to buy Western machinery to modernise industry and rearm Russia as the agricultural surplus went for export.

In order to stave off any foreign threat to the revolution at home, the Soviet Union's potential adversaries had to be neutralised. This presented a difficult challenge when Moscow's foreign enemies, anxious about the advance of Bolshevism through Comintern, now sounded the alarm at the frightening prospect of Russia being fortified into an industrialised state. Moreover, not all parts of every major capitalist economy benefited from rising Soviet demand in the Great Depression. Some suffered grievously from the dumping of Soviet commodities, particularly grain, onto a falling market. And as conditions worsened, people turned to the extreme right rather than to the left for their salvation (farming communities in Germany became strong supporters of the Nazis). And Stalin was not averse to dealing with the extreme right.

It was at this point that several interests pointed in the same direction: Stalin's reluctance to allow the German Communists their own head of steam in case matters got out of hand and precipitated a Western intervention to sustain the status quo; the need to have a peaceful international context while the domestic situation was restabilised; and the rise of the far right within Germany. Two further complications then came into play that reinforced Stalin's new German policy. France replaced Britain as the main enemy because its empire in the Far East exploded in a revolution backed by Comintern. And the Japanese, as we have seen, invaded north-eastern China.

In Germany, thanks to the Communists splitting the vote from the left, the social democrats had lost the presidency to the nationalist reactionary Field Marshal von Hindenburg in May 1925. Hindenburg clung staunchly to fixed ideas of his own. Thereafter the social democrats increasingly lost control over the fate of the Weimar Republic. Coalition with the nationalists was workable under a moderate conservative nationalist like Stresemann. But Stresemann died at the worst possible moment: just before the crash on Wall Street, at the very time he was most needed. And when in March 1930 the social democrats and the nationalists fell out over payments to the growing numbers of unemployed, the fragile coalition that Stresemann had single-handedly managed to stitch together fell apart. Hindenburg promptly snatched this rare opportunity and inserted a puppet minority régime under the Centre Party leader Heinrich Brüning, which ruled by emergency decree when both the nationalists and the social democrats failed to support it in the Reichstag. Weimar's flawed constitution paved the way for authoritarian government and ultimately for Hitler.

Meanwhile in the Soviet Union the focal point of Stalin's attention was the forced collectivisation of agriculture. Only massive exports of grain could release the hard currency necessary to pay for capital goods that would give the Soviet Union the level of industrialisation appropriate to a major power. And the collapse of commodity markets in the spring of 1929 meant that ever greater quantities had to be exported in a falling market to bring in the foreign exchange Stalin sought. He had originally thought to collectivise just 20% of farms over five years. Now he persuaded the party's Central Committee plenum in November 1929 of the need to take over all the most important regions: the Lower Volga, the Middle Volga and the North Caucasus. Resolutions were brought forward by the Politburo on 5 and 30 January 1930 for "liquidating kulaks [rich peasants] as a class". Implementation was put in the hands of OGPU under Yagoda, which soon meant the physical liquidation of those peasants resisting the process.[3]

Belting hell-for-leather for collectivisation threatened Soviet defences because the army, manned by the strapping sons of wealthier peasants, ultimately had to back up OGPU in brutal enforcement measures.[4] The Soviet state had not been so vulnerable from within since the Kronstadt revolt in March 1921. And it was at this point that a crisis developed in relations with France, whose allies along the Soviet border were closely monitoring the disastrous side effects of collectivisation.

France Makes a Bid for Hegemony

A sense of urgency took hold in Moscow when France, largely untouched by the Great Crash, came into direct collision with the Soviet Union. France, unlike Britain, was not yet weakened by the Great Depression. The head of the Bank of England, Montagu Norman, exerting pressure at home to cut wages and the state budget, correctly judged "Belgium and France as not being economically affected by the situation and standing in a class by themselves".[5] After Britain's abject retreat from its position as the foremost antagonist of Soviet power, France stepped in with hegemonic plans for European federation.

In late March 1930 Britain's prime minister Ramsay MacDonald dined with the French foreign minister Aristide Briand, whose intentions were scarcely peaceful. Briand "said France wants to be the biggest military power in Europe and wishes to be able to fight any two nations in Europe successfully and rather expects to fight Italy and Germany. Furthermore, France has now planned to be the economic center of Europe, shaping her development for that purpose."[6]

The Soviet reaction was predictable. "For us any, even partial, stabilisation of capitalist states is dangerous", wrote the Soviet ambassador in Vienna, "especially if it is accomplished under France's leadership."[7] The French had been subsidising their satellites in Eastern Europe—Poland, Czechoslovakia, Romania and Yugoslavia—to tighten the ring around Germany. Collectively the French system far exceeded residual German military capability even if, in the event of war, certain allies opted out in rivalry with others (the Czechs and the Poles had been at odds since 1920). However, although the Depression had thus far left France substantially untouched, Norman noted that Russia remained "the greatest of all the dangers" and "all of the other little countries around Russia ... were in the terrible position that they were not getting help from the capitalist system to stand the expenses of remaining capitalistic; that they were being kept out by tariffs and other things from the natural development which they should have, and all the time they wobbled and wavered Russia was beckoning to them to come over to her system."[8] Not surprisingly Norman later became a staunch supporter of appeasing Nazi Germany.

French Indochina Revolts

What tipped France into confronting the Soviet Union was Comintern meddling. The French empire had begun to show signs of vulnerability comparable to those once faced only by the British. Hitherto Soviet aid to rebels in French North Africa had been merely a manageable irritant. Similarly, the involvement of the PCF (Parti communiste français) general secretary Jean Cremet in spying for the Soviet intelligence services on French armaments industries through the latter half of the 1920s had prompted internal police action and the suppression of the PCF, but was seen as containable. Now, however, the stakes were raised considerably and in an unexpected form. The ground was laid for more serious reprisals against Moscow and the promise of much worse. The trouble emerged in the Far East.

On 9–10 February 1930 Vietnamese nationalists who were regulars in the French colonial army attacked a garrison at Yen-Bay. The economic condition of the subjugated population, who worked predominantly in plantations, mines or textile factories, had seriously deteriorated. Prices for rice and clothing on the domestic market were rising, while employers were cutting wages and dismissing staff. Unfortunately for the rebels the nationalist party had not co-ordinated the action with any other party or section of society. The mutiny was therefore easy for the authorities to suppress. But this was by reputation *la plus belle colonie*, and now it suffered the first armed uprising in Indochina under French rule. Although this had nothing to do with Comintern—the newly unified Vietnamese Communist Party had not been warned in advance of the timing of the revolt—the Communists of course did everything to fan the flames once it had occurred.

Comintern was quick to take advantage. In August Governor-General Pasquier notified Paris that "new agitators coming from Canton are arriving clandestinely in Indochina. The department knows from the latest monthly reports of the Sûreté's political branch that the Far Eastern section of the Third International has been in effective charge of the Indochinese Communist movement for four months."[9] By the end of the month the party was instructed to drop "traces of individual terrorism; by this terrorism the Communist Party looks like the nationalist parties . . . in order for the Party to differ entirely from other parties, it must give up the habit of individual terrorism".[10] This was the aspect highlighted by the French governor-general in his lurid publicity.[11]

Though the Vietnamese Communist Party was young—before the revolt it had only five hundred members and forty cells, containing around three thousand workers in a country of five million[12]—it was estimated in Moscow that under its general secretary Nguyen Ai Quoc (later known as Ho Chi Minh) there had occurred 218 peasant uprisings and 74 strikes and workers' demonstrations through to the end of 1930.[13] The crackdown was not long in coming, however, with a wave of arrests inside and outside Indochina, culminating at the end of the year and into the New Year in Bangkok (Siam) and Hong Kong (China). It was thus only a matter of time before Ho was caught up in the tentacles spread by French secret intelligence in liaison with their British counterparts, the Guomindang and others.

When the leader of the Russian counter-revolutionary movement, General Kutepov, was kidnapped on the streets of Paris in January by InOGPU operatives, it left the French government embarrassed but unmoved. Yet it did not take long for the French foreign minister Briand to complain to the Soviet ambassador, Valerian Dovgalevsky, about the uprising in Indochina.[14] French indignation exploded. By mid-May Paris learned that the entire movement appeared to be in the hands of the Communists. And on 13 June, rather as happened with Britain in its response to the May Thirtieth Movement in China in 1925, the colonial minister, François Piétri, addressed the Chamber of Deputies in righteous anger at "the action of Bolshevik Communism, led and paid for by the permanent agency which the propagators of the Third International maintain in Canton".[15]

It took only one more issue to end French tolerance, and that was the Soviet dumping of goods below cost price on the falling domestic market—a much greater problem for French satellites in Eastern Europe, as major commodity exporters. Trade between France and the Soviet Union was small because the French government refused to back any credit until the Russians repaid their pre-revolutionary debts. In 1930 the existing trade balance turned sharply to French disadvantage and on 3 October the government restricted imports from the Soviet Union. The minister for commerce and industry, Auguste Flandin, a Germanophile whom the Russians nicknamed the "minister for dumping", toured Europe to gather support.[16]

Stalin Becomes Aware of Nazi Potential

As a result of the threat whipped up by the French, Soviet military planning highlighted France and its main allies Poland and Romania along with Britain as the most likely enemies.[17] Buttressing the Rapallo relationship with Germany thus became a high priority, and that meant at all costs keeping the French away from a German embrace. And under the Brüning government, elected in March 1930, the Germans were tempted. This made the Nazis, by virtue of being Brüning's main adversaries, an object of special interest to Stalin. Information picked up by secret intelligence pointed in that very direction. In London on 19 October 1930 Churchill, now on the back benches, told Prince Otto von Bismarck, the counsellor at the German embassy in London, that "the burgeoning industrialisation of the Soviet state presents a great danger to the whole of Europe that can be dealt with only through the establishment of an alliance with the whole of the rest of Europe and America against Russia". The fact that Churchill also "made sharp remarks about national-socialism" that would, in his opinion, "significantly worsen Germany's position abroad, especially in relation to France" must, however, have been music to Stalin's ears when he received a copy of the conversation from foreign intelligence on 30 November.[18]

Indeed, Brüning was seeking better relations with France through American mediation. In so doing he had no hesitation in identifying Germany to the US government, which still at that point had no diplomatic relations with the Soviet Union, as a bulwark against Communism. "[President] Hindenburg backs Bruening on the question that Germany is facing a Russian menace," reported the US ambassador to Germany Frederic Sackett, a solid Republican businessman. "They believe that eventually Russia will be compelled by public opinion to take back Bessarabia and that this will reopen the whole question of the spread of Bolshevism throughout Europe. In this maelstrom Germany will be the buffer state and must be ready to defend itself and the rest of Europe against Bolshevism."[19]

Inevitably these events had a dramatic effect on Soviet policy towards Germany and, more specifically, on the directives given to the KPD. Berlin was protesting loudly at the upsurge in Communist activism. "From the Soviet point of view", diplomat Hans Heinrich Herwarth von Bittenfeld at the German embassy in Moscow noted, "Brüning's foreign policy was firmly centred on the West. His overriding concern was to undo those clauses of the Versailles Treaty that were damaging to Germany."[20] And the social democrats, though out of office, fully supported this goal. Stalin therefore had more than one reason to sustain a Comintern policy formalised at its sixth congress in 1928: that "social fascist" (social democratic) leaders were thus indistinguishable from fascists. They were therefore inappropriate as allies against the fascists, though the SPD rank and file should be seduced away from their own leadership into a united front with the Communists. Within the KPD the far left made social fascism priority number one over fascism proper.

Imposed on the KPD as its general secretary by Stalin to avoid the emergence of more assertive alternative leaders from the right, Ernst Thälmann, hero of the Hamburg uprising in 1923, faced direct insubordination from the left. It had been agreed that the Germans should decide their own best course of action except where Moscow deemed intervention absolutely necessary.[21] Thälmann's problem was that Comintern's executive committee was the final arbiter in any dispute; if Stalin and Molotov felt strongly about any issue of policy, their view could easily be enforced. Article 13 of Comintern's statutes, voted in at the sixth congress in 1928, made the executive's decisions "obligatory for all sections" and stipulated that they "must immediately be put into effect." Parties were explicitly downgraded to the status of mere "sections".[22]

The German Communist Party in Disarray

In March 1930 Thälmann tried to discipline the disobedient ultra-leftist Paul Merker after Merker had appealed to the Comintern executive to make the doctrine of social fascism the centrepiece of Communist policy. Merker's main opponent in the leadership, Hermann Remmele, asserted, to the contrary, that the label applied only to some social democratic leaders. The dispute prompted the leading Comintern secretary Pyatnitsky—"the boss"—to seek the support of Stalin—"the big boss"—for a decision that only nominally reprimanded Merker and in effect constrained Thälmann, who was told to consult Moscow before disciplining recalcitrant factionalists on the left.[23] This emasculated Thälmann and inevitably encouraged others such as the ever ambitious Heinz Neumann in a barefaced attempt to unseat the general secretary.

Not only was Thälmann instinctively averse to Merker's extremism; he was equally opposed to the kind of opportunism favoured by Radek. Radek had introduced the so-called Schlageter line in 1923: backing German nationalism when France and Belgium occupied the Ruhr to secure reparations and humiliate Germany.[24] Having supported Trotsky, and now offering advice to Stalin on foreign policy, he dusted off the Schlageter line. Comintern should back German nationalism.

In response to the Young Plan for reparations payments, in 1929 Alfred Hugenberg, leading the National Popular Party (DNVP), mobilised the far right, including the Nazis, into pressing for a "freedom law" that would end all reparations. Although there was sufficient support to bring about a vote in the Reichstag, as a proposal it failed miserably. Yet it helped legitimise the Nazis as a party and this had important consequences less than a year later. Neumann was impressed. He triumphantly returned from a trip to Moscow in early July 1930 with a brilliant solution to the KPD's dilemma when faced with Nazi rivalry: Stalin's instruction that the KPD raise "the national question" and, in so doing, Thälmann said, "whack the national socialists".[25]

Comintern followed up with written instructions after a meeting on 18 July that without precedent included both Stalin and Molotov. The KPD now had to raise its struggle against the Nazis to the same level as its campaign against the socialists.[26] But Thälmann, in whom Stalin never confided, could not at this stage understand why it was necessary to beat the nationalist drum. Surely the promise of the proletarian revolution was enough? He did his best to talk Stalin out of the nationalist line later at a meeting in December, but to no avail.[27]

The unforeseen success of the Nazis in the Reichstag elections on 14 September 1930 inevitably confirmed Stalin in his judgement and strengthened Neumann's position immeasurably. Their number of seats increased out of all proportion and against every expectation from 12 to 107. An inquest was held at a session of Comintern's executive committee presidium on 28 October. Pyatnitsky led the charge. "Why have the national-socialists received so many votes?" he asked—"so many votes that it was unexpected not only to us, who are not taken up solely with the German question all the time, but also to the German comrades themselves". At this point a voice was raised from the floor: "And to the national-socialists themselves." "Perhaps," echoed Pyatnitsky, "even for the national-socialists. They thought that they would receive 3,500,000 but that they received 6,400,000 was a complete surprise." Why was this? Here Pyatnitsky raised the issue of the nationalist party leader Hugenberg's campaign against the Young Plan. Instead of "beating the fascists where they find them", the KPD should be reasoning with them. The party came late to the program of "national and international liberation".[28]

This extraordinary piece of opportunism, which made no sense at all in terms of revolutionary objectives, inevitably aroused resistance within the ranks. At Comintern opposition to the new tactics was vociferous. Ruggero Grieco from the Italian Communist Party said "people's revolution" was not a Communist term. The KPD should return to the term "proletarian revolution". Comintern secretary Manuilsky, a trimmer by nature, announced that the KPD was an exception by virtue of the exceptional conditions in which it had to operate. Similarly, he argued, the Italians had been right to raise the slogan of a constituent national assembly on the basis of soviets as a point of transition and Comintern had been wrong to insist it be dropped.[29] Of course, Germany ceased to be the exception. That was the way Comintern worked. By the end of the year other parties had senselessly adopted the slogan without discrimination since otherwise its purely opportunistic tactical purpose would become apparent to all.[30]

Thälmann did his level best to restrict the new policy's application to propaganda and effectively to forestall its impact overall. But he was trying to swim against the tide. The Soviet ambassador's annual report noted that "the growth of anti-Soviet opinion and the fascisisation of Germany, particularly among political parties, obliged even left-of-centre Wirth, formerly Minister of the Interior, to deliver a speech in parliament against 'cultural Bolshevism' with a threat to make the prolongation of the Berlin Treaty dependent upon the behaviour of the German Communist Party and Comintern".[31] Stalin might not be able to revive pro-Soviet sentiment in Berlin, but he could at least bolster hostility towards France, Britain and the United States.

Laval and Briand Visit Berlin

The Brüning government had succumbed to a mortal crisis with a run on the Reichsmark as American creditors called in their loans to Germany. Throughout June 1931 vast sums in gold were withdrawn from accounts earmarked in London, Paris and New York, to meet German obligations. As much as $107 million—nearly $2 billion at today's value—was withdrawn in three days (9–12 June). The run began again a week later.[32] Britain could not meet its own obligations to the United States without German reparations. The only way it could do so would be to remove the parity of the pound sterling with gold, doing which proved only a matter of time. The financial crisis had finally reached global proportions. The German government resorted to ruling by emergency decree to staunch the flow and simultaneously sought to patch up relations with France (hitherto relatively immune to the crisis, though no longer) as a matter of urgency. In late September, for the first time since 1878, the prime minister and foreign minister of France, Laval and Briand, paid an official visit to Germany. The Russians were inevitably nervous lest the Rapallo relationship be sacrificed on the altar of a Franco–German entente for the settlement of outstanding reparations payments.

In such circumstances the tension between Thälmann's foot-dragging on the issue of nationalism and Moscow's priorities came to a head over the tactics to adopt when the Nazis forced a plebiscite to oust the social democratic government of Prussia. The vote was due on 9 August 1931. Under Thälmann's direction, on 15 July the KPD leadership decided as a matter of principle to abstain.[33] Any association with the Nazis was ruled out. Even the more radical Neumann appeared to go along with the decision.[34] "Some" of the comrades in Moscow at Comintern's secretariat also thought this the correct line to take: probably the moderate Kuusinen and doubtless the sinuous but not unintelligent Manuilsky.[35] But as soon as word spread, others—probably the leftists Pyatnitsky and Vil'gel'm Knorin, egged on by Neumann[36]—appealed over the heads of the German leadership to Stalin.

Wilhelm Pieck was both a member of Comintern's ruling presidium and its political secretariat. His attempts to win support in Moscow for Berlin's viewpoint, notably his argument that bridging the gap with the SPD's supporters would be impossible if the Communists went ahead in support of the plebiscite, fell on deaf ears. It would mean at the very least acting in parallel with the Nationalists and Nazis.[37] Indeed, it promised to obliterate once and for all the possibility of seeking a united front "from below" with the socialist rank and file.

The Prussian plebiscite proved a dangerous fiasco that destroyed any chance of a united front against fascism in Germany and yet failed to make the KPD a credible voice for nationalism. A great victory was declared by Comintern and the KPD—Neumann, indeed, claimed that the central government and the Prussian administration were now "peeing in their pants"[38]—even though insufficient numbers voted to oust the SPD from power in Prussia.[39] All this did was to alienate social democrats even further, and not just them. The shortfall was attributable not least to the fact that core Communist districts failed to participate. This was, indeed, a serious matter. Most supporters of the KPD were simply unwilling to throw out the socialists. The doctrine of social fascism was thus effectively being ignored among the rank and file of the party. Stalin's opportunism had tipped the largest Communist party in Europe, and therefore Moscow's best asset, into prolonged crisis.

The Manchurian Crisis and Events in Germany

Events in the Far East exacerbated the Kremlin's sense of being boxed in on all sides. As we have seen, on 18 September the Japanese overran north-eastern China. If anything this threat accentuated Stalin's determination to keep France at odds with Germany, even though plagiarising Hitler's nationalist platform proved disastrously ill-conceived while the Nazis continued from strength to strength.

The danger now became one of a simultaneous attack on the Soviet Union from the Far East by Japan and a Franco–German rapprochement in the West directed at Moscow. As PCF general secretary Maurice Thorez remarked, "The French bourgeoisie has taken advantage of the fact that the other capitalist countries were hit more speedily and more deeply by the crisis to firm up its positions relatively for the time being."[40] Evidence was not hard to obtain. France seemed a likely ally for Japan. In June 1932, for instance, the Japanese offered the French "a valuable guarantee against Russia; it would ensure the security of Indochina against Communism".[41] And as Comintern secretary Manuilsky pointed out, "If Germany is the weakest link in the capitalist chain, France is the strongest link in the capitalist chain and, from this follows a whole series of social and political consequences."[42]

Before long Manuilsky could be heard acknowledging that fascism had not been blocked in Germany as "some comrades" had asserted, and that "in fact in no country had the growth of fascism been brought to a halt". Worse still, the party in Germany appeared to be all over the place. On 17 November 1931 the KPD daily *Die Rote Fahne* spoke of

Social Democracy as the main menace. Five days later it named the Centre Party.[43] Comintern's German policy was in tatters. But the underlying reason for the chaos was unmentionable, even within the walls of Comintern: Soviet state interests, as conceived by Stalin, had to be served. At all costs the Centre Party and the Social Democratic Party of Germany had to be removed from the levers of power or the convergence between debt-ridden Germany and the Entente would continue, leaving Moscow isolated and therefore vulnerable to the emergence of a hostile coalition.

The KPD was lambasted for not doing enough to combat the Nazis, who were seen by the party as fundamentally "anti-capitalist" and passively making gains on the back of dissatisfaction with government.[44] They were seen as doing a better job of exploiting discontent, the implication being that the Communists should learn from them. Indeed, Thälmann made a Freudian slip in rating Hugenberg's nationalist party against "the not so right-wing [sic] party of the Nazis".[45] Inevitably the KPD was bewildered and demoralised by signals from Moscow. As late in the day as 10 April 1932 Stalin was still insisting that "the main blow" should be aimed at Social Democracy.[46] And this was after the presidential elections of 12 March, when Hitler obtained 30.1% of the vote against Thälmann's tiny 13.2% and Hindenburg's 49.6%.

The disconcerting spectacle all too visible to Comintern was that the Nazis were making alarming headway in recruiting from workers in enterprises where the Communists had been predominant. It soon became obvious where former KPD activists were going. KPD party membership rose as never before, but these were new members. Moreover, the numbers voting Communist in key working-class districts of Berlin such as Wedding and Friedrichshain were lower than in the May 1928 elections. All of this was cause for "serious alarm".[47] In this respect Thälmann's speech to Comintern's executive committee on 19 May was scarcely reassuring.[48]

Thälmann was inevitably depressed by the outcome of the elections. It was a defeat generally recognised as such within Comintern, despite Pyatnitsky's attempts to lighten the blow with reassuring denials. Yet Thälmann clearly understood that his hands were largely tied by

Comintern's commitment to the doctrine of social fascism. The KPD could not block the election of a Nazi to the Prussian Landtag "because it is not permissible to enter into horse-trading with Social Democracy and even less with the Centre as the governing party". Moreover, his analysis of the Nazi Party and its growing popularity was bleak but spot-on:

> The question is: why has the National Socialist Party such a colossal following? It is not only a question of the party being so active. It is not only a question of it conducting massive agitation and propaganda; it is not only a question of the millions provided by the bourgeoisie for these elections and other elections; but it also has to do with the existence of chauvinist and nationalist sentiment in Germany. . . . The Hitler movement positions itself as the movement that fights against the system and enables it to mobilise expressions of discontent and anti-capitalist opinion in Germany (general opposition to the Versailles system is also very strong) into their ranks.[49]

Stalin Distracted

Even diehards at Comintern headquarters momentarily began to suspect that they might be on the road to catastrophe when a new coalition government emerged on 1 June 1932 under the leadership of Franz von Papen for the Centre Party. With defeat staring him in the face, Knorin, the ultra-leftist heading Comintern's Central European secretariat, panicked and raised the alarm: "Our party must now make every effort to reorganise itself in expectation of being outlawed. History has never known an instance of an 800,000-member party being forced underground. But we are now faced with . . . such a possibility." Knorin now openly admitted that "Germany has a decisive significance for Comintern. Should fascism succeed in wiping out the resistance of the working class, should fascism succeed in forcing our party underground for a long time . . . then this would mean a colossal growth of the reactionary camp, it would mean fascism across the face of Europe."[50] Indeed.

Yet nothing was done. Under Stalin a highly centralised dictatorship was unsteady on its feet. The crisis exacerbated Stalin's brutal temper. It invaded the home, culminating in his wife's suicide on 9 November. The massive gambles made in 1929 in high-speed industrialisation and the forced collectivisation of agriculture looked in danger of failing. By the end of 1932 and for the first time since the ousting of Trotsky, Stalin faced internal opposition that, because of the crisis, doubtless appeared much more of a threat than it actually was. One early symptom of this was that from late November 1931 half of all Politburo meetings were closed; until then specialists and members of the Central Committee had invariably been seated in the antechamber, the walnut room, and summoned as required.[51] The summer of 1932 was entirely taken up by coping with the famine. The priority was that of "feeding the workers and the Red Army with grain".[52] Deprived of seed corn, and with most livestock consumed in desperation, the peasants starved. Moreover, to compound the Politburo's difficulties, rearmament, previously delayed and denied, was now pushed ahead at breakneck speed.[53]

On 4 April 1932 Stalin had told Thälmann's nemesis, Neumann, that he was preoccupied with military matters and that left no time for Comintern.[54] At this stage of the Depression other governments were increasingly sensitive to Comintern activity because of its international reach, even though the organisation was at its most sectarian and was therefore losing rather than gaining members. In May the Swiss minister in Rome had an audience with Mussolini, who in a bid to dominate the table played the anti-Communist card: "He told me that the four European great powers, France, Germany, England, and Italy, have to restore order in Europe; otherwise we are heading for one of the most serious social crises, the bolshevisation of Europe. Bolshevik propaganda is pervasive everywhere in all guises. Our bourgeois class is itself completely penetrated. Throughout Europe, not excluding Italy, the working class is convinced that the Bolshevik régime has succeeded."[55]

It is by no means certain that knowing this would have reassured the Soviet leadership; rather the reverse is possible. The common fear of Bolshevism without doubt cemented relations between the antagonistic capitalist powers. Secret intelligence indicated that the German government was seeking common ground with the French at Soviet expense.[56] Indeed, at the Lausanne conference of the major European powers on 29 June Papen, who counted on the Americans to ease reparations payments, proposed military conversations with the French for common action against the Soviet Union—a proposal that was, no doubt to Stalin's relief, dismissed out of hand.[57] Anxious not to make matters worse, given Papen's fierce anti-Communism, Stalin vented his fury at "disastrous" attacks launched on the Papen government by the Soviet press.[58] The consequences of his immediate priorities soon became apparent.

Comintern's secretariat was largely on its own. It was frozen in place by Stalin's previous decisions without any flexibility permitted to improvise policy for the KPD. In addition, Stalin's habit of confiding in Neumann, who had nominally been in the dock since the spring of 1930 over his ultra-leftism, seriously undermined the authority both of Comintern's secretariat and of Thälmann. Only shortly after he had made the case for anticipating a fascist coup Knorin, along with Pyatnitsky, refused to go along with a proposal made by Thälmann, who wanted to stop the election of a Nazi as chairman of the Prussian parliament even by means of voting for a socialist or Centre Party candidate and had the agreement of the majority within Comintern's secretariat.[59]

In Moscow the heightened vigilance during that summer proved all too brief. It dropped precipitously when the Reichstag elections on 6 November 1932 fortuitously delivered a rise in votes for the KPD and a fall in support for the Nazi Party. This inevitably sent a welcome wave of euphoria through Comintern and the German Communist leadership, who were now tempted to believe that the crisis was finally past. It proved a fatally beguiling mirage. One clue to the staying power of unrealism was the obviously demoralising consequence of acknowledging how far policy hitherto had been misdirected.

Of course, Stalin did not really want the Nazis in power, but he had need of them to neutralise the socialists and the Centre Party, which the Communists were insufficiently powerful to do. He was now reassured by the emergence of General Kurt von Schleicher, the "political brains" of the Reichswehr, the "social general". Schleicher early on had been involved in establishing the Rapallo relationship on the military front under Seeckt, and he now became chancellor on 3 December. It seemed highly probable that a populist like Schleicher, with the power of the Reichswehr behind him, would be right-wing enough to alienate the French and to steal the thunder from the Nazis, but not fiercely anti-Communist. The Rapallo relationship with the Russians would be safe in his hands. The fact that the Reichstag elections on 6 November had seen a rise in votes for the KPD and a fall for the Nazi Party also induced a euphoria within the German Communist leadership that proved a fatally misleading distraction.

Litvinov had an amicable talk with Schleicher on 19–20 December and was assured of Berlin's continuing commitment to the German–Russian friendship "in political and, as he pointedly said, in military contacts, to which Litvinov enthusiastically agreed". But Schleicher also took the opportunity to point out that the KPD was at cross purposes: on the one hand, it opposed the Versailles Treaty; on the other, it objected to the rearmament of Germany.[60] This was not a discussion Litvinov wanted to have. None the less, he took away with him Schleicher's beguiling reassurance that "he in his capacity as Chancellor is the guarantee that pre-existing Soviet–German relations will be sustained in so far as they depend upon Germany. He, and the entire Reichswehr, cannot imagine any other kind of relations with us."[61] And that was all Stalin wanted to hear.

6

The Impact of Hitler

Germany has a decisive significance within Comintern.

—HEAD OF COMINTERN'S CENTRAL EUROPEAN
LÄNDERSEKRETARIAT[1]

The Schleicher guarantee proved worthless. Everyone had miscalculated except Adolf Hitler, whose advent to power on 30 January 1933 proved entirely unexpected. It sent shock waves through Europe. It created a crisis within Comintern, as it divided its leadership. It also handed anti-Communism a charismatic leader who could exploit to the very limit the underlying fears that Moscow had mercilessly generated across the continent and beyond since 1917. On appointment as chancellor of Germany, Hitler had within reach what he had set out to do a decade earlier when he first outlined his global ambitions on paper. Initially Social Democracy thought it would be spared. However, the speed, the brutality and the deftness with which Hitler moved during the subsequent years took everyone by surprise.

Dismissed by most foreign politicians and diplomats as a ranting fool and an unstable demagogue, inside eighteen months Hitler crushed the organised labour movement, extinguished the opposition of every other political party, wiped out his immediate rivals and embarked upon wholesale rearmament accompanied by the abrupt removal of Germany from the League of Nations.

Since the unification of Germany in 1871 no one could disagree as to the country's significance. It was central to the continent's future by virtue of economic weight, geographical position and the overwhelming size (and growth) of its population, at 67 million. France was only two-thirds that size, at 41 million. And the KPD was still the largest Communist Party in Europe, though not for much longer. An immediate program for rearmament was the first item destined for Hitler's agenda on 8 February.[2] Barely three weeks later he announced that "the KPD is taking to extremes. The fight against it must not be limited by legal considerations."[3]

Yet the reports emanating from Soviet military intelligence, the Fourth Directorate, as late as 4 March were scrupulously nuanced. It seems to have been the intention of "the old man", director Jan Berzin, to offset the panic and disarray evident in Comintern, where Pyatnitsky, with whom he was close, was the only official trusted to receive such information. The report began with a memorable maxim. "On 30 January", Berzin reassured his immediate boss, Voroshilov, "Hitler did not win power, he was only allowed it." According to Soviet secret agents this happened only through the intervention of Papen. Moreover, Hitler could keep Hindenburg onside only by forming a coalition with Hugenberg. In addressing the heads of the Reichswehr on 3 February—reported by Soviet military intelligence that very day— Hitler emphasised that he had to hand a shadow government formed in opposition, and that the tasks for the Reichswehr were purely external. As to the fight against the enemy at home, he could count on his loyal storm troopers. Hitler was thus trying to edge the Reichswehr out of the political arena. By secret instruction on 11 February he arranged for the storm troopers to march on Berlin. At the same time Hugenberg's nationalist paramilitaries—the *Stalheim*—were locked out of any Nazi activities. The latest information, however— that Blomberg, in charge of the Reichswehr, would answer only to Hindenburg—indicated the limits of Hitler's power.[4] By implication Berzin, like Pyatnitsky, wanted Moscow to wait and see whether the German military would neutralise Hitler or even remove him from the Chancellery.

Events were already rapidly overtaking Soviet intelligence assessments. In cabinet on 2 March Hitler's right-hand man "Captain" Hermann Göring had already outlined the mass measures to be taken against the KPD on the basis of records of plans seized the night before.[5] And three days later the elections—with the Communists suppressed—handed the Nazis a majority in the Reichstag; though it required the votes of the National Party and the Catholic Centre Party for the two-thirds necessary on 23 March to pass the Enabling Act that effectively turned Germany into a dictatorship.

A Tentative Change of Line Is Reversed

As already indicated, the immediate reaction to Hitler's arrival in power was thus not uniform, even within Comintern. Before Berzin's report had come in, a "closed" meeting of the political secretariat, with no official minutes taken, had been summoned on 21 February to consider the *Einheitsfrontmanöver der Sozialdemokratie*: the proposal issued on 6 February by seven independent European labour parties for joint action against the threat from Hitler. This was followed by an appeal from the hated Second International. The result of what must have been a bitter debate was a controversial proposal by Comintern secretary Manuilsky for a complete about-turn in policy in order to meet the threat within Germany. Manuilsky then took the proposal to Comintern's presidium on 28 February. He argued that they should respond positively to soundings for joint action and forge a united front against fascism. Manuilsky's main argument repesented a complete volte-face in terms of policy since 1928: that no longer was Social Democracy a threat. On the contrary, it was "in panic and complete prostration". Its "inheritance" was at stake.

Not only did Manuilsky refer to these as proposals from the political secretariat; he also made barbed remarks—including an intriguing reference to leftist Profintern chief Lozovsky ("For the first time I agree with you")—as well as veiled references to those seeking to restrict a united front to Germany alone. Communist parties should not huddle in corners. "Germany is not Yugoslavia; it's not Bulgaria; it's not Spain;

it is a decisive country for capitalism, positioned in the heart of capitalist Europe. . . . We are people of high principle when we sit in the Turkish baths [*v vannoi*] at Comintern scrutinising every form, every word, peer at every mistake through a magnifying glass." This may have been a necessity, but now they were in "another era". Manuilsky thought everyone would be critical of this major new advance. "Why, comrades? Because people are inclined to think in categories which we have had to endure . . . for a number of years. And I have to say, comrades, that without doubt this conservatism in thinking puts pressure not only on every individual person but even and particularly on entire parties." The rise of fascism in Germany was "a fact of major international significance". And, Manuilsky added, most unusually in a Comintern forum but evidently to indicate support from higher up, that "the Soviet Government has already through Litvinov's statements signalled that for German fascism there would be international political consequences of one kind or another."[6]

The proposal was delayed by over a week, however, and when it did appear its impact had been effectively neutralised, larded with hostility towards Social Democracy that vitiated any genuine attempt to settle differences with the Second International—though it did "recommend that Communist Parties issue to the appropriate central committees of Social Democratic parties a proposal for joint action against fascism and the offensive by capital".[7] This was, Manuilsky claimed, "without question one of the most important steps that we have taken in the last number of years".[8] But it had been sabotaged. His hopes crashed unceremoniously. Manuilsky "lacked the necessary authority", he confessed to Georgi Dimitrov a year later.[9]

The projected turn-around at Comintern therefore failed, and it took more than a year for it to be attempted again. Stalin was now extremely risk-averse. He sat on the fence, saying nothing in public. Pyatnitsky— uniquely privy within Comintern to Soviet military intelligence from Berzin—although mystified by the absence of any resistance to Hitler was inclined to underestimate the chances of his régime succeeding, even after the KPD was harried into submission. He had obtained a rare meeting with Stalin along with the diehard Knorin on the evening of 28 February, after Manuilsky had presented his radical proposals, and doubtless put the case against making the offer.[10]

Pyatnitsky's attitude was no secret. He dismissed Hitler's rise to power as "a passing phenomenon".[11] After pursuing a policy that had inevitably led up to this disaster, he and his supporters could scarcely argue anything else. And when German representative Fritz Heckert also took to the podium to argue that Hitler would not last long, he did so blurting out an unsettling truth that others were anxious not to confront: "Were we to admit that this government had a long future, then we would have to acknowledge that our whole outlook on the disintegration of capitalism in the current situation is incorrect."[12] Precisely.

Britain Refuses to Guarantee France

Just as the Manchurian crisis had paralysed Britain's Far Eastern policy, so too did Hitler's first year in power leave Britain's entire European policy at a dead point. The Nazi menace tore away the mask of aloofness symbolised by Curzon's effortless superiority in the 1920s. But unfortunately it failed to make the British any more trusting of the French, whom Curzon had reined in from dismembering Weimar Germany. Britain now drifted into the doldrums of self-doubt. "I'm convinced that our so-called 'policy' has been a complete disaster since 1919", reflected Alexander Cadogan, early in 1938 to be permanent under-secretary.[13] Worse still, the moral and intellectual vacuum that had emerged with the Great Depression had made possible the advent to power of politicians accompanied by personal advisers who understood nothing of international relations but who sought to impose simplistic solutions upon a disoriented and demoralised bureaucracy.

From this sense of unease there followed hasty proposals to unravel the Versailles settlement that were bizarrely unrealistic. Prime Minister MacDonald, the ineffectual Labour Party leader of the coalition governing Britain, met Mussolini in Rome in late March 1933. Together they attempted to steal a march on events by belatedly pressing the issue of a revision of the Versailles Treaty that, after making one concession after another, would inevitably entail territorial redistribution through peaceful means. Of course, this would be excusively at the expense of others. Yet how were its obvious victims—Poland and the Little Entente— likely to react? The Poles and the Balts could, of course, veto any such project when presented with proposals at the League of Nations in Geneva. Having ostentatiously tried to render these countries powerless, the British and Italians managed to hand back to them the decision as to whether to proceed. The Swiss minister stationed in Paris, represent-ing a country entirely inactive except on international financial matters but always interested in the state of play, made a tart observation: "It is becoming more and more evident that the Anglo–Italian projectile that left Rome has traced the same trajectory as the Australian weapon called 'a boomerang' which, thrown into the air, comes back to land at the point of departure."[14]

The Weimar Republic that Hitler so brusquely supplanted had few well-wishers. Dismissed as "a travesty" even by foreign onlookers one would have expected to have been sympathetic, it was blotted out in an instant. No one bothered to attend the funeral or even to send flowers. When the new cabinet appeared, Soviet eyes were glued on the pres-ence of known enemies Papen and Hugenberg and the absence of their most prominent sympathiser, Schleicher. From Moscow, the German ambassador Herbert von Dirksen explained that "the resignation of Schleicher, in whose Russian outlook so much faith had been vested here, and the appointment of the Hitler/Papen Cabinet has triggered off agitated alarm. The anxieties about Mr. von Papen have not dimin-ished at all and the National Socialist Party is taken to be fiercely anti-Soviet—perhaps not entirely wrongly." Those who had talked to Lit-vinov, Krestinsky and Radek were aware of worries about the presence of the extreme nationalist Hugenberg in the cabinet. Dirksen thus an-ticipated the anti-Communist foreign policy Hitler was to adopt.[15]

When on 1 March the cardinal archbishop of Munich Michael von Faulhaber spoke to Papen, whom he mistook to be "a sincere Catholic", Papen was unhesitating about dealing harshly with Moscow. "It is not possible", Papen insisted, "to stamp out Bolshevism in Germany with-out simultaneously dismantling the financial underpinning of German Bolshevism from Russia; without breaking off diplomatic relations with

Moscow; without terminating industrial contracts with Russia; without deporting Russian agents of Bolshevism, especially students; without forbidding in Germany Russian pamphleteering and radio broadcasts from Moscow."[16] This was precisely what Stalin feared.

But Papen, like Schleicher, was far too devious for his own good. The Russians were right to worry more about Hitler who, now in office, no longer had any reason to contain his vitriolic sentiments towards the Soviet Union. On the contrary, when Britain's ambassador, Permanent Under-Secretary Sir Robert Vansittart's brother-in-law Sir Eric Phipps, met him, Phipps was struck that "even when pretending to fear a Russian attack [Hitler] spoke of Russia with supreme contempt, and declared his conviction that Germany was vastly superior to her both militarily and technically. At times he ground the floor with his heel, as though crushing a worm."[17]

Hastily adjusting to the new realities, Foreign Minister Konstantin von Neurath confirmed that Hitler was intransigent on only three issues: 1) the Jewish problem; 2) Communism; and 3) the Austrian problem.[18] The public expression of the second of these sentiments, hitherto withheld for fear of alienating the supporters of the Rapallo relationship, was now on full display. Yet not everyone, even outside the walls of Comintern, was convinced that Hitler's régime would last. Reporting to Mussolini, the press officer at the Italian embassy in Vienna suggested early in August that "within many political circles and within those of the Austrian Government the belief is common that the Hitler Government will have a very short life in Germany". Behind this lay "mistakes, abuses of power, the presence of a great number of Communists in Hitlerite organisations etc.".[19]

An infinite variety of rationalisations now emerged to back up a policy of "watchful waiting". Britain, too, had no conception of the scale of the problem it was about to face. Its ministers of state still dreamed wistfully of disarmament, rather more to save taxes and sustain deflation than from deep moral conviction. The intense preoccupation with the state of the economy, war debts and imperial affairs distracted government departments along Whitehall from developments in continental Europe, even though early, violent anti-Semitic outbursts in Germany throughout 1933 did occasion momentary alarm upon the reading of newspapers at the breakfast table. The tendency took hold to rationalise it all away, not least because Britain's leaders were without exception inward-looking. Even the former prime minister Lloyd George, whose thirst for power had by no means diminished as much as his capacity to understand the world, repented the Versailles Treaty which he had fought so hard to secure.

Reacting to renewed pressure on Britain from France for a mutual assistance pact, in 1930 Lloyd George had complained to the Americans that "France had always been militaristic and grasping" and stated that Britain "would never assent to adding anything to her Continental commitments [sic]".[20] Guaranteed to capture and mirror fleeting opinion, in September 1933 he coldly and fatalistically laid out an argument that was to become all too familiar throughout Europe, particularly from the mouths of British politicians and officials—that Hitler was the only alternative to a Communist revolution:

> If the Powers succeed in overthrowing Nazism in Germany, what would follow? Not a Conservative, Socialist or Liberal regime, but extreme Communism. Surely that could not be their objective.
>
> A Communist Germany would be infinitely more formidable than a Communist Russia.[21]

This dramatic assessment of Hitler's value to Britain—even though published only in a local newspaper—was not just that of Lloyd George. He was quicker and less inhibited than most to say what others were merely thinking. It was an unwritten assumption that had lodged itself firmly in the minds of fellow politicians. It found an echo in the relatively lenient treatment of Italy when Mussolini challenged the League of Nations Covenant in October 1935 by invading Abyssinia (Ethiopia). At a stroke it inhibited any forceful measures to sustain the territorial status quo. It was not just the sulphuric whiff of rhetoric issuing from the mouths of extinct political volcanoes; it had also penetrated the Foreign Office at every level. The red-headed young Robert Hadow, then first secretary at the embassy in Vienna, argued that weakening Hitler would lead towards a Communist Germany "led by utterly unreasonable men—which I do not consider Hitler to be". He insisted, "I prefer to help Hitler rather than risk having a worse alternative in his place!"[22]

The right was obsessed with Communism. The centre and centre-left were racked with guilt, because of not only the Versailles Treaty but also the failure to compensate the Germans for it while there was still time. The younger members of the Foreign Office were perhaps the most affected. Cadogan believed that "we should have made concessions ... to Stresemann, Brüning, etc.—especially at the time of the Disarmament Conference ... we destroyed Stresemann and Brüning and made Hitler".[23] And one rising talent, "Ted" Carr, reared in the pro-German sentiment of the Edwardian era, finally resigned in March 1936 in the face of what was deemed anti-German opinion at the top, epitomised in the person of the permanent under-secretary Vansittart, whose French prose was infinitely more fluent than his English, and whose anti-German bark was invariably worse than his bite.[24]

Hitler had been ushered into office by President Hindenburg, who was emblematic of the Prussian military establishment—men like Schleicher, who arrogantly deluded themselves that they could simultaneously use, contain and control a populist agitator like Hitler to their own ends. Hitler then surprised them all, however, when he crushed the KPD overnight, rapidly cemented his position through a hurried election and then outlawed all political parties other than his own.

On 1 May 1933 Hitler addressed a gigantic rally of a million and a half enthusiastic supporters in a speech not untypically laced with hysterical rhetoric but entirely devoid of substantive content. The papal nuncio in Berlin, Cesare Orsenigo, was frankly astonished: "What for us foreigners comes as so surprising is the rapidity with which the people, who otherwise have a reputation for being above all cold and hard to arouse emotionally, have, however, reacted to the new régime to a mystical degree. In effect Hitler's government has the masses now completely in his hands and can take them where he wants." Comintern thus faced a challenge of unprecedented dimensions. But Moscow clung on to what was for it a hope and for Catholics, as stated by the nuncio, a veritable nightmare: "If these people, now so excited by the idea of an imminent restoration of the economy, are deceived, and already many fear so, we should not be surprised if by way of reaction national socialism turns into ferocious Bolshevism."[25] All too often anxious observers looking at Nazism consoled themselves that at least it was not Bolshevism.

Hitler did not exactly impose himself on the people of Germany so much as pander to deep-seated needs and awaken the nation's darkest desires. His was a deeply disturbed mind, misshapen and disfigured by unsettled times. He soon set about meeting widespread demands for full employment, a living wage and national dignity, initially with funds raised by Schleicher. Ultimately the humiliation of a vengeful peace in 1919 and the widespread material deprivation of the Great Depression a decade later had delivered the country into Hitler's outstretched hands. As one of his fiercest critics, Britain's ambassador Phipps, regretfully acknowledged only two years after the Nazis seized full power, "Were a general election to take place to-day in conditions of complete freedom, it is not unlikely that Herr Hitler would receive a considerable majority of the votes."[26] Indeed, Comintern secretary Pieck, never one afraid to express an opinion, acknowledged on 1 April 1936 that, although the official results of the German elections were doubtless false, almost 100% of voters had gone to the polls and "roughly ⅚ of the population voted for the fascist list. It is not that the German population have fallen in love with the fascist system," he said, "not that the German people have, for instance, been supportive of Hitler's provocative politics. But Hitler has succeeded, with the aid of his hypocritical stance for peace, in duping the people concerning his actual war aims."[27]

There was no revolutionary situation. And it was obvious that Comintern had failed disastrously even while it heaped blame on the social democrats. Manuilsky alluded to the problem early in November 1932: "We have to address one question extremely important for us as members of the RCP(b) [Russian Communist Party (Bolshevik)]. At every enterprise of ours workers commonly pose the question: why has the revolution been delayed in a whole range of capitalist countries; and in Germany especially did not the German Communist Party fail to take advantage of the revolutionary situation; are these not due to the failings of Comintern's leadership?"[28] Within party ranks some spoke out

more critically. Martemyan Ryutin, a Siberian—notoriously individual-
istic even under Soviet rule—and the son of poor peasants, who was
expelled from the party in 1930, was foolhardy enough to express in print
what others would say only in private. Comintern was in crisis, he asserted, even while the objective conditions for revolution were at a peak.
Why? "Comintern, from being the headquarters of the world proletarian
revolution, which in fact it was under the leadership of Lenin, Zinoviev
and to a certain extent even under the leadership of Bukharin, after the
defeat of all opposition and Lenin's associates, after the consolidation of
Stalin's personal dictatorship in the Soviet Communist Party and Comintern, was turned into Stalin's chancellery for the affairs of Communist Parties."[29] Similarly, Vissario "Besso" Lominadze, a Georgian member of the Central Committee, was attacked for asserting that Stalin
viewed Comintern as "a talking shop (*lavochka*) that continues to exist
only while we provide for it". He also derided the staff of Comintern as
"weak" and dismissed it as "an empty space, a nonsense".[30]

Tacitly accepting that Comintern was in crisis, its mouthpiece *International Press Correspondence* (*Inprecorr*) somewhat pathetically argued
that "the more successes—even including successes bought with
sacrifices—Soviet diplomacy achieves, the more quickly will it be possible to hand over Hitler and Mussolini's frock coats and silk hats to the
revolutionary museum, and hand over Hitler and Mussolini to the Revolutionary tribunal".[31] In the absence of an effective Comintern strategy,
Moscow's flirtation with bourgeois France was therefore inevitable and
soon became hard to miss. At the League of Nations in Geneva Litvinov
left onlookers with the distinct "impression of having it off with the
French", the Italians quipped, not without a trace of envy.[32]

Knowledge of Hitler was sparse outside Germany—even in the Soviet Union, which had been so closely tied to it within the Rapallo relationship. *Mein Kampf*, which had hitherto sold badly, was still available
only in German. Those who could read the book, particularly those
Communists who were of Jewish parentage, reacted with horror: they
were the dual target of Hitler's hysterical rage. It was therefore no accident that the task of Russian translation was undertaken by no less a
figure than Zinoviev, formerly president of Comintern, from his place
of internal exile in the town of Kustana in distant Kazakhstan. It was

published in a restricted edition available only to those in power, and it was quoted by Bukharin at the Seventeenth Party Congress in January 1934. Stalin was given a copy for his personal library.[33]

A staunch realist and also Jewish, Litvinov had no wish to conceal his concerns about the Nazi takeover. Having for some time feared what was now taking place, he stopped off en route from Geneva to Moscow to see his German counterpart Neurath on 1 March. No one else within the Soviet hierarchy had remained so self-consciously disinterested in the activities abroad of allied Communist parties, whatever the degree of provocation. Few others were capable of exerting such enormous self-control. This occasion, however, was to be a unique exception. Litvinov's inhibitions appear to have vanished. Neurath, taken aback by his indignation at the repression of the KPD, because he was usually so calm and collected, could not resist needling him:

> He [Litvinov] came immediately after the events of the preceding days in Berlin and to speak about the measures against the Communists. Mr. Litvinov commented that the actions taken against the German Communists have excited great alarm in the Russian press and in Moscow.
>
> I expressed to Mr. Litvinov my surprise that he should get so upset that the German Government brings to account the German Communists for their action in in setting fire to the Reichstag in plain sight. Up to now he has always assured me that German–Russian relations would in no way be influenced by the German Government restraining German Communism.... Mr. Litvinov thereupon answered that, following the alarm in Moscow in the summer of the previous year over proposals from the then Reich Chancellor von Papen to Mr. Herriot to join in an alliance, one might suppose that the conflict with Communism and with the East are one and the same.[34]

Catholic Anti-Communism

Litvinov could take heart from the fact that the Soviet Union was not alone in its concern, though he could not seriously expect that other states which had long feared the spread of Communism in Central Europe would greet the suppression of the KPD with anything other than profound relief. And not just secular states. Pope Pius XI had insisted to the archbishop of Avignon on 15 October 1932 that there was no danger of war, but only that posed by Bolshevism, a subject he spent some time dilating upon. The French ambassador Charles-Roux pointed out that he and several others had been subjected to a similar diatribe from the pontiff.[35] On 7 March 1933, after the arrest and imprisonment of KPD officials and the suppression of the party, Pius told the French ambassador to the Vatican that "I have changed my mind about Hitler as a result of the tone that he has adopted recently in talking about communism. This is the first time, one can say, that a government spokesman has made himself heard denouncing Bolshevism in such categorical terms and that unites with the stance of the Pope."[36] And when Engelbert Dollfuss, effectively dictator of Austria, came to see him that Easter, the pope surprised him by asking outright, "Are the Reds still in the town hall?" (The socialists had previously attained about 60% of the vote in Vienna.)[37]

Catholic solidarity with the new régime in Germany soon spread northwards. On returning to Bavaria in April, Cardinal Faulhaber, formerly opposed to the Nazis because of their racism, assured bishops that "the Holy Father has praised the imperial chancellor Adolf Hitler for having taken a stance against communism".[38] On 20 July, and in spite of the arrest of some forty-five priests by the German authorities, a *Reichskonkordat* was concluded between the Nazi régime and the Vatican, signed by Vice Chancellor Papen and Secretary of State Cardinal Pacelli. Pius told Papen that "although he did not approve of many measures taken by the Hitler Government which were against the principles of Christian charity, he was induced to give his approval to the Concordat in expectation of the advantages the Bishops, the priests and German Catholics could reap and from the undoubted service rendered to humanity and to religion by the current government of the Reich in fighting with such energy against Communism and blocking its expansion in Europe".[39] And, as we have already seen, it was not just the holy church that was relieved.

It was assumed that Hitler was also to some extent the prisoner of his allies, the Reichswehr. For some time the illusion prevailed that the military were merely tolerating Hitler; that they, indeed, would have the final word. For this reason the extensive visit to the Soviet Union of a German military delegation under Lieutenant General Alfred von Vollard-Bockelberg from 8 to 25 May 1933 was seen as a litmus test of German good intentions. With Stalin's assent the delegation was shown the full range of facilities for the production of Soviet armaments—but, as it turned out, solely for the purpose of deterrence. On 13 May Ambassador Dirksen gave dinner for the visitors. The entire revolutionary military council of the Soviet Union led by Voroshilov and Tukhachevsky turned up. Bockelberg did what was expected of him by his hosts and declared without reservation that "the Reichswehr wishes to preserve pre-existing German–Soviet relations and that he has succeeded in exerting the appropriate influence on Hitler in that direction".[40]

Russia Turns to France and Its Allies

Stalin's consent to such lavish hospitality indicated nothing, however. Hitler had purposely taken a fiercely hostile line against Moscow. He appeared to be acting irresponsibly. Indeed, from the Italian point of view, the Germans were foolishly driving the Russians into the hands of the French. In contrast the Italians, anxious lest the fascist experiment in Germany run adrift through lack of savoir faire on the part of its inexperienced chancellor, did their best to advise the Germans to follow the line taken by Italy, smugly boasting that it "has always maintained a clear distinction between the Soviet Government and the Third International, that is to say, fighting against Communism at home while maintaining abroad normal and satisfactory relations with the Soviet Government".[41]

With no idea how speedily Hitler would free Germany from the constraints of the Versailles Treaty, the Russians assumed they could press the Reichswehr to subdue Hitler by denying it access to its customary military facilities in the Soviet Union. Just in case this tactic failed, however, they also ostentatiously opened the door to the French. In April the first French military attaché, Colonel Edmond Mendras, arrived in Moscow, while the Russians appeared to be trying in vain to save their relationship with the Germans. That summer, however, the Rapallo relationship was abruptly sundered on Stalin's orders. In its place Voroshilov and Tukhachevsky both separately proposed "technical collaboration" between France and the Soviet Union. In September the French aviation minister Pierre Cot came to see the Russian production facilities at plants 22 and 24. The French came away impressed—all the more so because their own defence industries were lagging in production—though they were not at this stage ready to commit to anything.[42]

It made sense for Moscow to respond to entreaties from Paris for an anti-German combination. Frustrated by the failure of the Germans to mend fences they had wilfully broken, Stalin and the Politburo went ahead with a complete realignment in favour of the territorial status quo they had so long condemned. On 19 December it was agreed that the Soviet Union should join the League of Nations and conclude "a regional agreement on mutual defence against aggression on the part of Germany". Participants might include Belgium, France, Czechoslovakia, Poland, Lithuania, Latvia, Estonia and Finland, "or some of these countries but the participation of France and Poland is obligatory". It was simultaneously made clear that France had initiated the entire project, which was nicknamed the "Eastern Locarno" after the Locarno Pact of 1925 that had, against its wishes, guaranteed only West European frontiers. It was additionally provided that the participants of the intended treaty would be "obliged to render each other diplomatic, moral, and, where possible, material support also in the event of military attack not envisaged by the agreement itself".[43]

For France the Soviet Union was never the preferred partner. Britain was infinitely the better choice, if choice were to be had. On 8 June Lord Londonderry, secretary of state for air, and Norman Davis, US delegate to the League Disarmament Conference, met the French to persuade them of the virtues of disarmament in order to appease the Germans. But neither was able "to satisfy M. Daladier of the will or the power to give France the equivalent in security of what both are asking of her in disarmament".[44] Heading the Central Department in the Foreign Office, Orme Sargent pointed out that "from the point of view of 'security' France would, I have no doubt, attach a whisper by Great Britain vastly more value than to the most substantial promises and pledges from Lit-vinoff". This was no idle boast. But the British were utterly unavailable and had no intention of taking any initiative—even "a whisper"—tending towards the containment of Nazi Germany. France was thus on its own. Worse than that, the British, with no illusions about French motives, exerted their utmost influence "to prevent the Franco–Russian alliance". "The French", they noted, "invented the present scheme of a multilateral mutual guarantee pact because, having failed to obtain any further guarantee as regards 'security' from us, and having lost faith in the Polish alliance, they felt compelled to accept Russia's offer of co-operation when proffered."[45] No one could deny that the British knew exactly what they were doing, though they had as yet no clear idea as to the longer-term consequences of their actions.

Poland Rejects Soviet Overtures

The problem for France was Poland. Although their participation was an important precondition for the plan's success, the Poles had long ago adopted a policy of attempting to balance between the Russians and the Germans. The point of balance was never attained, however. From May 1926, when Marshal Piłsudski seized power, Poland tilted against the Russians rather more than against the Germans. But Poland also had a sizeable German minority and a bad reputation for mistreating minorities—including Byelorussians and Ukrainians, whom the Russians had been surreptitiously arming in an extended and undeclared guerrilla war. The bulk of Polish defences were thus constructed to deal with the threat from the east. Crucially the Poles now saw no substantial difference between Hitler's Germany and Weimar Germany, and certainly no difference at all between Stalin's Russia and Lenin's Russia.

It was entirely consistent, therefore, for Poland to recoil from French entreaties that it come to terms with the Soviet Union for an alliance against Germany. The truth was, as the French ambassador to Warsaw reported, Piłsudski "does not believe in an immediate danger from Hitler".[46] The famed precautionary measures taken to reinforce the Polish garrison at Westerplatte in Danzig on 6 March had merely been a warlike display intended to meet fears expressed by the domestic opposition. Polish alarm at Hugenberg, the extreme nationalist and Germany's economy minister, exceeded fears of Hitler who, as Austrian-born, was mistakenly taken to be less concerned about Danzig than were the Prussians around him. The Poles turned for reassurance to the Russians in a blaze of publicity merely to enhance their bargaining position, but simultaneously they turned to the Germans in the greatest secrecy for a deal.

Chief editor of the semi-official newspaper *Gazeta Polska* Colonel Miedziński, the subordinate most trusted by Piłsudski, visited Moscow from 30 April to 3 May 1933. His task was "to assure the Bolsheviks that there was no way Poland would ally with the Germans in any kind of aggressive action against the Soviet Union". He was received by Radek, who now ran the Central Committee's Bureau for International Information. What he told Radek—and "conviction" was the word of the day—turned out to be entirely untrue and in retrospect deliberately designed to mislead.

Miedziński said the Polish leaders believed "that Germany will go to war with them, but they themselves did not want to force events". They were "convinced that we [the Russians] were not interested in their being weakened vis-à-vis Germany, as they are also determined not to be a tool of alien interests against us. He is convinced that the Germans will try to foment complications between ourselves and Poland."[47] The Russians fell for it and did perhaps more than the Poles ever really intended them to do, without an iota of reciprocity. To Stalin their position seemed entirely logical, but only if one assumed they were acting purely out of *ragion di stato*; that they had overcome their fear of Communism.

After his guest departed Radek published a sensational article in *Pravda* on 10 May entitled "The Revision of the Versailles Treaty". With one blow Soviet policy since 1919 was struck down for all to see. "The road towards the revision of the predatory and agonising Versailles peace goes along the route to *a new world war*," Radek intoned. The "*international proletariat—the enemy of the Versailles peace—cannot be on the side of those imperialist forces which seek to bring about a new division of the world in the conflagration of a new imperialist war*".

Radek then reciprocated Miedziński's visit by touring Poland from 6 to 21 July, ostensibly en route to see his neglected mother. The Germans, the French, the British and the Italians signed the Four-Power Pact while he was there—on 15 July. Yet it had no real significance. It was an empty frame put up by hollow men. Italy's foreign minister Baron Pompeo Aloisi captured the spirit of this phony gesture when he wrote that "the content of the new instrument of European political life has less importance than the simple fact of its existence".[48] Germany was being treated as an equal. But the pact also underlined that countries to the east were on their own, as had Locarno nearly a decade earlier. So the Poles had even more incentive to reach an understanding with Germany before Hitler rearmed his country.

Judging by the decisions he took and the assumptions he made about Polish willingness to align with the Russians against the Germans, Stalin grossly overestimated the strength of Polish nationalism—the purely national interest—and seriously underestimated the overriding power of anti-Bolshevism.[49] Radek emphasised to the Poles Stalin's keen interest in continuing conversations. He suggested that the Germans could take one of two courses of action: either invade and occupy Poland en route to the USSR or, and this continued to be the Soviet preoccupation in the years to come, negotiate German control over the Polish corridor to East Prussia and thus give Berlin a springboard for attacking the Soviet Union. But the Poles did not see things this way. Radek tried bribery. It was a sign of Soviet eagerness that he even offered Poland a free hand against their mutual neighbour Lithuania. Since 1920 when the Poles summarily annexed its capital Vilnius—where Piłsudski was born—the Lithuanians had stubbornly refused to sign a peace treaty recognising its loss. The Russians had hitherto stood by them, but now Radek remarked in Polish, "Róbcie sobie z nimi co chcecie" (Do what you want with them), adding in Russian, "Puskai penyayut sami na sebya" (They have only themselves to blame).[50]

Radek had barely left Polish soil, however, when Berlin began negotiating a special relationship with Warsaw. On 20–21 July Papen presented to Mussolini "his idea of an agreement with Poland at the expense of Russia, which he judges possible. At every era in history there is one country that pays for the others. Latterly it was the Germans; in the near future it will be the Russians. That will permit Germany and Poland to resolve the question of the corridor [from Germany through Poland to East Prussia] and all the other burning questions on the Eastern front."[51] Negotiations were conducted in the strictest secrecy. Hitler's propaganda chief Joseph Goebbels found that the Polish ambassador Józef Lipski was "opposed to Bolshevism. Tactfully opposed to France. For a modus vivendi with Germany. [Believes] Hitler is sincere."[52]

The process did not take long. On 26 January 1934 the Polish and German governments startled Europe with a joint declaration of non-aggression that followed some months of secret talks. The agreement served "as a cushion against Russia", Hitler told the Italians.[53] It represented a surprising rapprochement between hitherto sworn enemies and from both sides purposefully cut directly across all French and Russian hopes of building an Eastern Locarno or, failing that, a multilateral mutual assistance pact that encompassed France's allies in Eastern Europe. The Baltic states, now perilously isolated, were left with little room for manoeuvre. Having made this move, the Polish foreign minister Józef Beck warned Vilhelm Munters, secretary general of neighbouring Latvia's Foreign Ministry, that Poland considered "any attempt" to include the Soviet Union in a general pact "on equal footing with the other Great Powers" as "directed against its most vital interests" and would be resolutely opposed.[54] Beck apparently believed that because Hitler was Austrian, he had none of the anti-Polish sentiments of his Prussian contemporaries.[55] The Politburo proposals of December 1933 showed every sign of being dead in the water. Moscow had to find another way to block the German road eastwards.

The failure of France's potential ally, the Soviet Union, to find common ground with Poland against Germany left a hole gaping in the Franco–Soviet project for a multilateral pact of mutual assistance that had been accepted by the Politburo on 19 December 1933.[56] This did not mean that France intended to give up, however. On the contrary, military co-operation with the Soviet Union remained top priority. According to Alexis Léger, secretary general at the Quai d'Orsay, for "nearly two years . . . the general staff, supported by a considerable section of political opinion, had been urging that it was folly for France not to conclude a bilateral agreement with Russia which was there for the asking". The point was "to have Russia's vast industrial resources at her disposal".[57] Moreover, and this was also no small matter, although the Red Army was widely regarded as useless for offensive operations even before Stalin executed his leading officers, the "principal value" of a Franco–Soviet pact "in the eyes of informed opinion" was "that it would deny to Germany the possibility of exploiting the massive resources of Russia. If, therefore, it did not bring Russia into the war on the side of France and her allies, it would at least keep her out of it altogether."[58]

Finally, on 24 April 1934 the French went ahead and formalised their offer of a bilateral pact to the Russians. Although the Soviet Union declared itself willing, it sought an extension to cover its near neighbours the Baltic states, Estonia, Latvia and Lithuania, which were now intimidated by Poland. They formed an important front line against potential German aggression against the USSR and the Russians were not going to let them fall into hostile hands, as events were to demonstrate in 1939–40. France initially agreed to this condition. But on 18 May the Russians learned that it would no longer be achievable, despite pressing the issue to the very last.

The impact of Poland's shift towards Germany can be seen in the order of priorities given to Soviet secret intelligence. On 25 May 1934 the Politburo agreed that "the centre of gravity in the work of military intelligence shift towards Poland, Germany, Finland, Romania, England, Japan, Manchuria, China". With respect to other states—including France, Czechoslovakia and Italy—the study of their armed forces would be *pro forma*, relegated to "legal means" carried out by military attachés.[59] The worm had turned.

As plans progressed, recognition of the Soviet Union by Romania and Czechoslovakia became a reality on 9 June. The Russians promptly moved ahead with joining the League of Nations on the condition that compulsory arbitration was permissible only with regard to territorial issues arising after entry (this was in order to leave open the reannexation of Bessarabia from Romania). On 14 July 1934 the Politburo formally agreed on a tripartite pact between France, the Soviet Union and Germany (nominally included so as not to alienate Britain), "guaranteeing an Eastern regional pact".[60]

Emboldened by its entente with Poland, however, on 8 September Germany turned down the suggestion of such a pact. Instead Berlin pressed for a bilateral trade agreement with Moscow. Its motive was blatantly suspect. By telegraph from Sochi on 15 September Stalin noted that the Germans appeared to be desperate for a bilateral deal: "It is not we who need this done quickly, but the Germans who, by means of a treaty with us, want to spoil the game in Europe, smooth over the bad impression given by their rejection of the Eastern Pact, sow mistrust towards us among the French and improve their domestic situation." Stalin advised slowing down, as the Germans "need a treaty with us more than we do".[61] At the same time Narkomindel was instructed, "Do not hurry with the initiative for a pact without Germany and Poland"— until, that is, Litvinov had finished soundings in Geneva.[62]

There Beck promptly followed the German example.[63] Polish thinking was now clear to Moscow. At the very time the Eastern Pact was being hawked about Europe, the Russians had good reason to fear an attack from Japan. On 18 October, when they learned more of Polish calculations, the interconnection between the European and Far Eastern theatres became painfully apparent. The foreign department of the NKVD (InO GUGB) learned that "Poland in its foreign policy at the current time is acting from the deep conviction that war between the USSR and Japan will break out in the not so distant future and that this situation will in turn signal fundamental changes in Europe". Looking ahead, Poland sought to avoid any "shocks" and would therefore base its policy on purely bilateral security arrangements, as it had with Germany in "taking advantage of the latter's serious condition. . . . Were Poland to join with the French policy of rapprochement with the USSR, it would turn into a second rate factor in international politics. . . . Poland considers that the Eastern Pact is aimed at the encirclement of Germany by France and the USSR; in a plan such as this Poland, in agreeing with France's policy, would turn into a weapon of Franco-Soviet policy." Thus Poland would "delay replying to the question of the Eastern Pact, wanting to conceal its real intentions as long as possible".[64]

Poland was, however, playing with fire. Beneath the unruffled surface of self-confidence fundamental weaknesses were multiplying. The country faced a crisis in public finances. It had fallen behind militarily as a result of Piłsudski's resistance to modernising the armed forces. The glorious campaign of 1920 lived on in legend, but the armies of 1923 that had surpassed both German and Russian capabilities had lost their edge. The world had decisively entered the age of automation with the appearance of armoured divisions, artillery and aviation. Neighbouring rival Czechoslovakia had pressed well ahead. Between 1926 and 1935 the Polish air force actually declined by 50%; anti-aircraft guns and anti-tank weaponry failed to keep up with requirements. Motorisation, already backward, seriously stagnated.[65]

Moscow decided it would wait no longer. Suspicions of Polish intentions now peaked. After a briefing from Narkomindel and with evident reluctance, on 2 November the Politburo resolved to "recognise as possible the conclusion of the Eastern Pact even without the participation of Germany and Poland in the event of France and Czechoslovakia or France alone agreeing to it". Moreover, the Russians were determined not to legitimise any German rearmament which would breach the Versailles Treaty unless Berlin joined the Eastern Pact.[66] And when the French prime minister, Louis Barthou, the inspiration behind the Franco–Soviet rapprochement, and the visiting king of allied Yugoslavia, Alexander, were assassinated in Marseilles on 9 December, Stalin had no doubt: "In my opinion the murder of Barthou and Alexander was at the hands of German–Polish intelligence." The aim was to shift policy, as with the assassination of Austria's Chancellor Dollfus on 25 July. "To me that's clear", Stalin wrote. "I consider this version the closest to the truth."[67]

The entire thrust of Soviet policy, however, necessarily brought Russia directly into collision with the British, who sought to appease Hitler and to buy time by agreeing to German rearmament.

British Appeasement of Germany

Although sceptical, Sargent, now assistant under-secretary overseeing the Central European department in the Foreign Office, did believe in "a common policy of co-ordinated defence" against Germany. Otherwise

Hitler would "accumulate a sufficient amount of force behind him to enable him to achieve his objectives one by one by the silent threat of force, but without even the use, or even the display, of force". But where Sargent proved completely mistaken, and in this he was certainly not alone, was with respect to how much time Britain had at its disposal. Seriously underestimating the sheer raw energy of German nationalism roused by the Nazis, Sargent argued that Hitler would require "decades" to be able to fight a war of aggression. He therefore posited that Germany intended "an aggressive *policy* and not an aggressive *war*".[68] This was a comforting distinction without a difference. Ample time seemed available before British rearmament would be urgently required. This was the rationale for the snail's pace taken by the Foreign Office in reaction to events. And bear in mind that Sargent was one of the more perceptive realists within its upper reaches. Britain thus appeared essentially passive while others, such as France and the Soviet Union, seized the initiative. That Britain actually had some kind of policy alternative crystallised only when France and Russia ran too far ahead and hastened to substitute a lesser alliance system for the containment of Germany and in so doing ran headlong into British objections and determined obstruction.

The predominant British view was epitomised by Carr, then first secretary in the Foreign Office and very much by temperament and experience an appeaser of Germany. He recalls how "a growing body of opinion came round to the view that the only effect of the French understandings with Italy and the Soviet Union was to isolate and encircle Germany and to perpetuate the inequalities of the Versailles Treaty—in short, to maintain those very conditions which had been largely responsible for the Nazi revolution".[69] Behind this, of course, lay the untested assumption that Hitler was a leader of only limited aims and therefore entirely amenable to reason—a blinkered, perhaps typically British fallacy. Thereafter everything Britain did worked to that assumption. In place of encirclement as a policy, the Foreign Office instead decided "to break the ring round Germany, to engage in friendly discussions of her grievances, and to bring her back to the League of Nations".[70] This worked to the advantage of Germany since, as the French foreign minister Pierre Laval pointed out to the minister for League of Nations affairs at the Foreign Office, Anthony Eden, "Hitler's tactics were to try to make arrangements with one Power at a time".[71] And, unfortunately for the French, the British thought themselves strong enough and sufficiently knowledgeable to risk going it alone if necessary; in the end, if uncooperative, France could be left to fend for itself.

At a meeting with Prime Minister Étienne Flandin and Laval in Paris on 22 December, Foreign Secretary Simon finally insisted that "things could not be allowed to drift", though in fact that was precisely what British policy had been doing since January 1933. And, of course, it was better to drift than to follow dutifully in the wake of the nearest German man-of-war. Simon's suggestion that Hitler would "come forward himself with proposals to settle the armaments question and invite us to negotiate with him on the subject" seems in retrospect ludicrously naïve and hopelessly wide of the mark.[72] Knowing British attitudes all too well, the Politburo sensibly resolved that it would "exert pressure on France to take into its own hands negotiations with Germany without relying on England to mediate".[73] This choice had its risks, however. Moscow and London were heading for a collision over the handling of Germany. A tug-of-war between the two over France soon took centre stage.

Soviet Mistrust of Poland

Thereafter, although direct evidence was lacking, the Russians became increasingly certain that they faced a hostile combination. Litvinov told the Italian ambassador that the Polish–German non-aggression protocol "must at least have been supplemented by oral understandings and perhaps secret clauses. It is impossible for it to be otherwise": understandings including, perhaps, a sphere of influence in the Baltic or Ukraine. Litvinov, who had grown up on the eastern edge of what was now Poland, found it very hard to keep his voice steady on this subject.[74] Rumours were rife. The US military attaché in Berlin wrote to his ambassador that "past reports have indicated the probability of the existence of a military agreement in regard to the acquisition by Poland of the Ukraine in exchange for the Corridor".[75] French intelligence reported on a conversation with Poland's foreign minister Colonel Beck after a session of the Council of the League of Nations at the end of January 1935. There Beck "gave to understand that he did not himself understand what Marshal Piłsudski had in hand and that he did not agree with certain undertakings contracted by Poland towards Germany alongside the non-aggression protocol". Among these undertakings, the report continued, "there existed in particular a secret clause in the Polish–German agreement by which Poland would not contract to sign any agreement without prior authorisation from the Ministry of Foreign Affairs in Berlin".[76]

According to Soviet human intelligence reports from a "reliable" Polish source, "the English are sure that there exists between Poland and Germany some kind of secret agreement linking their European policies and obligations for mutual assistance".[77] This was also the belief at the Quai d'Orsay.[78] The Polish military attaché in Paris, Colonel Bleszinski, himself credited far-reaching goals in Eastern Europe for the agreement with Germany. The fact that Polish Generals Galler and Sikorski also believed it to be an alliance had an unfortunate impact on Moscow.[79] It therefore came as a comfort that Soviet military intelligence, the Fourth Directorate, reliably reported directly from sources in the German embassy that Göring, on his visit to Poland (27–31 January 1935), was rebuffed by Piłsudski when he proposed an alliance.[80]

But how much had Beck really understood of the marshal's reasoning? Barely more than forty years old at the time and poorly educated, Beck was a man of enormous vanity and was widely dismissed in both London and Paris as a fool. German propaganda chief Joseph Goebbels more charitably thought him "young and impressionable".[81] Less forgiving was the Countess Łubieńska, who was married to Beck's cabinet secretary: "Even in Polish, he never knows what he wants to say," she quipped.[82] Certainly conversing with him was exhausting. Beck spoke Polish to a fault, but France's Ambassador Noël recalls a problem working out exactly what he was saying: "It was like trying but failing to hold onto an eel slipping through one's hands."[83]

The fact was that Beck shared what ideas he had with very few in his own foreign ministry. And for good reason. With the exception of the ambassadors to France and Germany, most Polish officials were totally opposed to the rapprochement with Hitler.[84] Inevitably speculation was rife and an odour of suspicion lingered. Whatever Beck thought he was up to, and to this day no one really knows for certain, the assumption that something more sinister lurked behind the joint declaration with Germany formed the basis of Soviet military planning in Europe through to the end of 1938. It makes a striking appearance in a memorandum on war plans sent to Stalin by commanders Tukhachevsky— soon to become Marshal—and Uborevich on 5 February 1935, even after Göring failed to obtain what Hitler wanted from the Poles.[85] The Soviet war games in the autumn of 1936 were conducted on the same basis.[86] In thus antagonising the Russians, Piłsudski and Beck were playing for high stakes based on very uncertain knowledge.

Poland's junior ally Romania was as much in the dark as everyone else. Ambassador Constantin Vișoianu, newly arrived in Warsaw at the beginning of 1936, sounded out all his foreign counterparts for some convincing explanation of Beck's policy. He himself was close to Foreign Minister Nicolae Titulescu. "I have got the impression", he told Valters, Latvia's ambassador, "that they all are of completely the same opinion about Poland's policy. . . . Poland's current foreign policy does not seem transparent and understandable to anyone, it is mysterious. . . . If today you asked a French person if he can rely on Poland, he would say no. You can ask the same question to us, the Romanians, or the English— you will always get the same reply that it cannot be relied on. Recently I talked to England's ambassador to this country. His reply did not differ from that of the others at all, he just made a helpless gesture and added [that] nobody understood Poland's policy. For us, Poland's military allies, such [a] question is particularly important and we need to know exactly what . . . Polish–German relations are like. We do not know. . . . Neither does France. . . . The only thing Poland achieves by such [a] policy is distrust."[87]

Piłsudski died on 12 May 1935 and took with him the intuition and the reasoning behind his foreign policy. Thereafter, as Galeazzo Ciano noted four years later, "The only voice that counts in Poland is that of a dead man, Marshal Pilsudski [*sic*] and there are too many who are fighting for the right to be the true custodians of his word."[88] He had, apparently with no great enthusiasm, designated as his successor General Edward Rydz-Śmigły. But no one was really big enough to fill the old man's shoes. The struggle for power among the ruling colonels continued through the succession until it petered out a year later. Pilsudski saw his chosen successor as one of the most able in the field of battle, but he was far from convinced that Rydz-Śmigły had the political insight to ascertain "the adverse motives of a potential enemy".[89] Rydz-Śmigły fully understood that the next war required total mobilisation—indeed, his assessments were as innovative as those of the Germans—but as time rapidly slipped by in the 1920s, when change was still affordable, he failed to convince his superiors of the sacrifices necessary to turn such ideas for reform into reality. Whereas Beck had an instinct for what the Italians call *piccola politica*, Rydz-Śmigły's lack of tactical agility became ever more apparent once he became the first among equals.[90]

Thus, even though Rydz-Śmigły took the rise of German power more seriously than Beck did, and tried earnestly to win back the French after they signed their alliance with the Russians, nothing concrete resulted. He therefore fell in behind Beck, however reluctantly; his anti-Bolshevik instincts ultimately left him with little choice. Pius XI had a long conversation with the Polish-Prussian aristocrat Bogdan Hutten-Czapski, whom he had known while serving as nuncio in Poland immediately after the war. Pius greatly lamented the death of Pilsudski. On many occasions Pius had "noted that the Marshal, despite having been imprisoned by the Germans for a long time, did not create an anti-German policy and he believed that the true enemy were the soviets. . . . Naturally, were the Marshal still living, he would have been displeased at the blow from France with whom you have a kind of military alliance, which has however now drawn up a treaty of sorts with the soviets."[91] And when the new commander-in-chief visited Berlin on 16 February 1936, he told Göring he did not doubt that "in the event of any kind of complications arising in Europe the USSR would make use of them to precipitate social unrest and revolution. In the event of a conflict Poland is determined not to side with the USSR."[92] He repeated this to Jan Szembek, Beck's assistant, at the end of September: "If we are forced to favor one side over the other, Rydz stated that it certainly would not be with the Bolsheviks."[93]

Jan Łukasiewicz had been Polish ambassador to the Soviet Union before moving to France in 1936. He had no doubts as to how matters stood: "For Poland, the Bolsheviks are much more dangerous than the Germans, and Moscow than Berlin." When the French prime minister Barthou originally proposed the so-called Eastern Locarno that would guarantee borders in the east as the Locarno Pact of 1925 had guaranteed those in the west, the Polish government had been utterly contemptuous. "If Mr Barthou had known the history of Polish–Russian relations over the centuries better and, in particular, after the division of Poland, he would never have proposed conclusion of a mutual assistance pact with the Soviets," the ambassador pointed out.[94]

This deep-seated hostility to Bolshevism was common to the entire Piłsudski camarilla, even the most moderate among them. The views of the commander-in-chief were so widely shared among the colonels who ruled the country that a vigorous open debate about the country's orientation never took place, even within the inner core. Soon those outside Poland came to understand this. When the newly appointed head of Polish intelligence (the II Department), Colonel Tadeusz Pełczyński, visited France to see Maurice Gauche, chief of intelligence assessment at the Deuxième Bureau, hopes were momentarily raised in Paris that business could at last be done, until he showed no interest at all in what really interested the French. Pełczyński's purpose was entirely political. He was there to sound the alarm. He warned Gauche: "The Russian danger is the most threatening and steadfast. Russia will make use of the first opportunity that presents itself to invade Poland and remain there; the Red Army has become an instrument of menace, continuously increasing its military might. The Red [High] Command maintains a concentration of 10 to 15 divisions on our border. What Russia wants is the extinction of the Polish state; the Reds would perhaps allow us the name of Poland and our language; but from a spiritual point of view we would be utterly wiped out." Pełczyński did not credit the possibility of a Soviet–German entente for the time being, "given that Hitler is stubbornly opposed to it".[95]

The consequences of this mindset were alarming. The gloomy prognosis in effect deprived Poland of any freedom to manoeuvre, thereby unthinkingly handing Hitler carte blanche. The Poles had inadvertently relinquished all alternatives. They could be counted out as a potential block to German ambitions. When a few years later, during 1937 in the first wave of Stalin's terror campaign against suspect foreign elements, the NKVD began rounding up suspects to be imprisoned or shot, a unique instruction went out from chief Nikolai Yezhov personally— and it must have emanated from Stalin—to arrest "absolutely all Poles" regardless of status.[96] In Soviet minds there *were* no friendly Poles, even Communist Poles. Consider that the Polish Communist Party was one of only two sections of Comintern that were completely liquidated (the other being Korean). They paid the ultimate price for having been too close to the Russians as former comrades in the Russian Social Democratic Labour Party.

Sir John Simon in Berlin

The Polish leaders were, of course, not alone in having their heads in the sand. The integrity of the British government's position was not helped when on 11 March 1935 a leading article appeared in *The Times* that backed the position of Lord Lothian in favour of German rearmament. He had been to see Hitler on 29 January. The editorial argued, "Since the Government are facing facts, let the fact also be faced that the restriction of German arms to the Versailles level has gone past retrieval. . . . If it is the intention of the British Government to get Part V of the Versailles Treaty superseded by a system in which all are equal, then no purpose is served by harping upon a breach of the Treaty—a breach moreover for which it is unfair to blame Germany alone."[97] Within three days, on 14 March, as part of his divide-and-rule tactics Hitler invited Foreign Secretary Sir John Simon to Berlin. The invitation had barely been accepted when, two days later, Hitler announced full-scale rearmament in open defiance of part five of the Versailles Treaty.

And how could London have been surprised? Had this not already been sanctioned by *The Times*, long viewed as the mouthpiece of the Foreign Office? His hopes dashed, Simon duly arrived in Berlin accompanied by Eden and serviced by William Strang and Ralph Wigram from the Central Department of the Foreign Office, for two days of meetings (25–26 March). Watching in bewilderment, the Russians had to make do subsequently hosting a visit to Moscow by the more junior Eden— clearly nothing more than a sop to keep them within the frame.[98]

In Berlin the British grandly opened with a principled statement of protest against Hitler's defiant prelude. They outlined their principles— either co-operation on peace and security had to be "general" or Europe would be divided "into two camps". Very impressive, no doubt. But then, true to form and to Simon's mixed record of incompetence and opportunism, within a matter of hours they caved in completely and took whatever Hitler was willing to offer.

Most of the discussion was taken up by Hitler's intermittent mono-logue directed against the Soviet Union and Comintern. Whereas Eden, who had a soft spot for the left, insisted that Bolshevism was a purely domestic matter, Hitler correctly pointed to Comintern's worldwide operations and insisted on his first-hand experience of them as "one who had seen Bolshevism in Germany". Moscow, not Berlin, was the most likely source of war. Hitler expressed his firm conviction that in the future "co-operation and solidarity would be urgently necessary to defend Europe against the Asiatic and Bolshevik menace" because "in ten years time . . . Russia would be a very formidable Power".[99]

Simon's visit, outlined to cabinet, was a failure. Indeed, in the eyes of some foreign observers, it was "more a fiasco".[100] Yet Eden's trip to Moscow—the first time a British minister of any description had made such a journey or met Stalin—was not deemed significant enough even for a briefing to cabinet. After all, what Stalin had to say to Eden did not exactly harmonise with mainstream Foreign Office opinion. Eden found Stalin—with Ambassador Ivan Maisky interpreting—insistent that the situation was more perilous than in 1913 because two sources of danger now existed: not only Germany but also Japan. Japan was just taking a pause before renewing its aggression. Stalin had no confidence

in non-aggression pacts signed by Germany, since it treated international obligations so lightly. How could one trust the Germans? In contrast, a collective mutual assistance pact could bind them in. "Here we
are six people in the room. Imagine, for instance, if comrade Maisky
wanted to attack one of us. What would happen? With our joint strength
we would beat up comrade Maisky." "That's why Maisky is being so un-
assuming," quipped Molotov, unkindly. It was a form of insurance, Stalin continued, given that Germany would break out from the chains of
the Versailles Treaty sooner or later. He then gave Eden another lesson
in Hitler's practice of playing off one state against another. The Germans
were entirely disingenuous. A year earlier they had offered a 200 million
mark credit. The Russians had agreed to negotiate. Yet almost at once
rumours began circulating that Tukhachevsky and Göring had met in
secret to prepare a plan to attack France. "What sort of politics is that?"
Stalin remarked. "It is petty politics." And had not Eden been subjected
in Berlin to talk about the danger of war from the Soviet Union? "And
do you not know", Stalin said, "that at the same time the German government agreed to supply us with credits such products—about which
it is awkward even to mention—armaments, chemicals etc.?" Eden was
suitably appalled. Stalin concluded by emphasising the importance of
Britain's role and responsibility. "A small island indeed upon which
much depends. If this tiny island told Germany: we are giving you no
money, no raw materials, no metals; then peace in Europe could be
guaranteed." To which Eden had no answer to offer.[101]

The contents of the discussion made no impact at all in London
among the few who read them. The British appeared to be utterly disoriented. There was still no fully thought-out policy. Once it began to
dawn that Germany was not conforming to "reasonable" expectations,
the British government showed every sign of grasping at straws. In
Western Europe a wide divergence emerged between public displays of
solidarity against Germany and the unabashed pursuit of individual
advantage. On 11–14 April 1935 Prime Minister MacDonald, Mussolini
and Flandin met at the Palazzo Borromeo on Isola Bella in Stresa with
their respective foreign ministers to reaffirm the validity of the Locarno
Pact and the independence of clerical-fascist Austria, the gateway to

the Balkans. Sargent hoped that "we will at Stresa do all we can to prevent the conclusion of a direct Franco–Russian military alliance directed against Germany".[102] That was doubtful without offering the French some measure of security. And it was not to be. On the contrary, Simon and Eden, wafting into the political stratosphere, had opened negotiations with Hitler in the utterly utopian hope "that Germany might be brought into a peaceful organisation of Europe, and that she might be induced to give full and active and loyal support to the league as a member thereof".[103] Nothing that followed dissipated the air of unreality integral to British policy or French determination to follow their own interests regardless. Thereafter, having made the requisite gesture, the participants discreetly went their separate ways. Hitler could have hoped for nothing better.

A Franco–Soviet Alliance

Britain was adamantly against an alliance in defence of France. Indeed, the only branch of its armed forces that failed to receive priority for rearmament was the army, which indicated that a military commitment to war on the continent was not exactly a desirable option (if an option at all). On the other hand the only alliance on offer to the French—from the Russians—was viewed as entirely obstructive of peace in Europe. At the Foreign Office Sargent fretted that the British "should warn the French Government that they cannot approve of a Franco–Russian alliance, and that the existence of such an alliance might render the operation of the Treaty of Locarno very difficult".[104] Sargent could not see what the French imagined that they could gain from an alliance with the Russians, yet he never really asked them. Worse still, given the nature of the Nazi régime, Sargent saw a war by Germany against the Soviet Union as inevitable: "The need of expansion will force Germany towards the East as being the only field open to her, and as long as the Bolshevist régime exists in Russia it is impossible for this expansion to take merely the form of peaceful penetration." Sargent was definitely the most intelligent among his peers. He therefore carried some authority beyond his rank. And on his view—and this did not change until late

August 1939—an entente between Berlin and Moscow was impossible, as for Hitler the fight against Communism was a fundamental principle on which he could not compromise "without destroying the *raison d'être* of his system".[105] Furthermore Sargent strongly held that a Franco-Soviet entente "can . . . only lead to one ultimate result namely a European war". In such a war "the Soviet Government in their capacity of agents of the Third International [Comintern], would probably be the only beneficiaries".[106] Once again, the issue of Bolshevism reared its ugly head.

Thus it was to the barely concealed fury of leading British officials, utterly frustrated at their inability to stop the inevitable, that a Franco–Soviet pact of mutual assistance was signed on 2 May. This was followed by the interlocking Czechoslovakian–Soviet pact two weeks later. Were Germany to attack Czechoslovakia, the ultimate effect of the two pacts would be that France would have to attack Germany and thereby breach the Locarno Pact of 1925 which guaranteed the border between France and Germany. In which case, what would Britain do? Faced with a conflict between its commitments under Locarno and under the prior commitment to the League of Nations Covenant (article 16), presumably it would be obliged to come to France's assistance. Were this to be the case, Britain's entire German policy would be mortgaged to French priorities constructed without even tacit consent.

From the British embassy in Berlin, where the initial shock of Hitler's revolution had worn off, Ambassador Phipps, now adjusting to new realities, was reduced to damage limitation. London had no appetite for confronting the Germans. He proffered the tactical objection that by "erect[ing] too much barbed wire, whether along Hitler's southern or eastern frontier, we will head the beast back to the west". Sargent commented with respect to this that a "great deal" could be said for Britain making no commitments to defend Eastern Europe. Once again he added that he could not bring himself "to believe in either the willingness or the ability of the Bolshevik Government to maintain peace if it ever came to be threatened in the west".[107]

A further complication arose that served merely to confirm existing suspicions, not only in Paris but also in London, that the Russians were pursuing the same dual policy they had conducted since Lenin's day—but with an added twist. On this occasion the general secretary of the Soviet Communist Party made a commitment with regard to the activities of a Comintern section that would not be honoured. In conversation with Stalin, Laval is reported to have "spoken out quite strongly . . . about the Comintern encouragement of Communist subversive propaganda, especially in the French army".[108] For his part Stalin knew Laval saw the pact as a bargaining chip rather than a full alliance. At a meeting with French trades union leader Léon Jouhaux in November 1937 Stalin recalled that "when Laval came here, in this very room we put the question to him: does he envisage that the pact is a defensive political alliance? Laval looked at Léger, Léger at Laval; then Laval replied: 'No, it is a peace pact.' . . . At times I ask myself the question," Stalin reflected pessimistically, "what this pact can do for us."[109]

The Russians were thus sceptical that the pact had much value; it could be just small change for the French, so they were disinclined to sacrifice much in return for it. On signature and at the express request of Laval, Stalin stated publicly and unequivocally "his complete understanding and approval of the defence of the state carried out by France and the maintenance of its armed forces at a level commensurate with the needs of its security".[110] Apparently the French magician had finally pulled the rabbit out of the hat. But Laval had not allowed for the strength of Bolshevik opinion. Stalin's statement was not going to bind the French Communist Party and to reverse long-standing policy without causing disarray within its ranks, and the French had the largest Comintern section in Europe. The French government were completely naïve in its thinking. This became strikingly and embarrassingly apparent within hours of Stalin's momentous statement being reported in the press.

Leading the French Communist delegation at Comintern, André Marty reported to its presidium that Stalin's statement "provoked lively emotion in the country [France] . . . some anxiety and a great deal of trouble".[111] Indeed, the very day Stalin's words appeared in print the PCF leadership called a meeting of Communists from the Paris region at the famous dance hall on the Avenue de l'Observatoire, the Salle Bullier. It was attended by some five thousand people. As reported in *l'Humanité*, Thorez reassured comrades that, despite what Stalin said, nothing had changed. Times had been bad: "Today as well, it's hard, I know. Stalin's words are reverberating like a clap of thunder. The class enemy is using them in unspeakably bad faith. It claims they conflict with what we are doing, what we are saying, what we are writing." Yet what Thorez went on to say did exactly that: "Communists do not have confidence in the government of the bourgeoisie to conduct a policy of peace and given that the army may be used against the working class within the country, to oppress the population in the colonies, and, at the moment, against the Soviet Union, our party maintains its opposition to the return of two years' [military service] and its refusal of war credits."[112]

Further, open discussion appeared in Comintern's *Inprecorr* on 18 May. And what this made clear to the world was that the Soviet Union predicated its "peace" policy upon transforming the domestic politics of its partners. In other words, Litvinov's collective security strategy was to be mortgaged on overturning capitalism in the countries with which Moscow sought an alliance. With respect to support for the defence budget of France the editorial on "The Franco–Soviet Pact" declared, in what appears to have been a clumsy translation from Russian,

> Our struggle must be conducted not *against* the weapons, but rather for control of the weapons. . . . The struggle for peace thus simultaneously passes into the struggle for power, for only a people which has shaken off the rule of the bourgeoisie and of the big landlords will represent the invincible power which is necessary in the present stage of tremendously developed war technique in order successfully to secure its national independence.

Stalin's words of reassurance to Laval were thus in effect a dead letter as soon as they were uttered. And Litvinov's strategy, subjected to a wrecking ball tossed in from the fundamentalists at Comintern, now teetered in the balance. The French prime minister could not have been entirely surprised. He would have been woefully uninformed to have believed that Stalin would endorse French rearmament given that he, Laval, "regarded the French Army as a great safeguard against Communism".[113] As Marty asked the seventh congress of Comintern on 14 August, "What guarantees have we that the French army will not be used to-morrow against the workers and peasants as was done in Belgium, in Geneva and in Asturias? [see below, pp. 207–208]."[114] Until France was ruled by a régime acceptable to Comintern—at the least an alliance of the left—the PCF would not vote for the defence budget in the Chamber of Deputies. As late as mid-May 1936, even after the Germans reoccupied the Rhineland, Jacques Duclos spoke for the PCF in denying the government a vote for military expenditure because "up to now a vote for these sums would unquestioningly have meant support for imperialist goals".[115]

Laval in turn had retaliated by delaying ratification of the mutual assistance pact. And Stalin had no intention of calling the PCF to order. (After all, the reoccupation of the Rhineland indicated that Hitler could just as easily strike west as he could strike east.) This sleight of hand illustrated the basic ambiguity of the Soviet Union as a power. Contrary to the supposition of many then and later, the régime under Stalin, like it or not, still incubated the bacillus of revolution, as Trotsky in exile always acknowledged. Trotsky was always careful to craft his criticism of the USSR in terms of Stalin's bureaucratic deformation of the Soviet system, not in terms of a change in its identity and ultimate purpose as heir to the October Revolution. Stalin chafed at these limitations and before long sought to throw them off through a policy of terror, but he never entirely succeeded in spite of the death toll he attained.

The visit to Paris of Colonel Rogers of British intelligence at the end of May, coming as it did straight after signature of the Franco–Soviet pact, was no accident.[116] It gave him a platform to air the organisation's assessment of the Soviet Union to his opposite numbers, to clarify exactly where London stood and how it viewed the future. His words are worth recalling, not least because the Russians purloined a copy and thus had a good sense of what they were dealing with.

On the view of his government, French and British talks with the Russians were merely a means of exerting pressure on Germany:

In the mean time the fundamental trend of British policy in relation to Russia remains as it was. The existence of the USSR in its present form is incompatible with Britain's interests. London, of course, did not believe in Hitler's assertions that the USSR will soon try to move westwards. All British information contradicts this and the situation of the USSR at the present time is not such as to enable it to contemplate offensive operations to the west. However, the British are assessing the growth of Soviet military capability and think that the USSR with its dangerous doctrines and its powerful army may sooner or later become a serious factor in respect of all conflicts in Europe and Asia. The liquidation of this growing danger is entirely in the interests of Britain. The British will in no way attempt to do this with their own hands and will not take part openly in any anti-Soviet combinations. In this respect Hitler's hopes merely indicate how badly informed German diplomacy is. But should there emerge the possibility of defeating the Bolsheviks by any combination of forces, then the British will look upon it with sympathy and will at the decisive moment themselves take part in it. If another government forms in Russia, then the possibility is not to be excluded that Britain will support it, thereby finally re-establishing the balance of power in Europe.

In this context, Rogers is reported to have said, "Hitler's declarations of his irreconcilable attitude to the Bolsheviks have therefore made a forceful impression on British Ministers. In London they believe that the centre of European politics will gradually shift to Berlin and that, given that Germany is becoming the strongest power, its sentiments have to be taken into account."[117]

This was a firm but polite shot across the bows. France and Britain were evidently drifting even further apart. More was to come. After the Franco–Soviet pact was signed, on 18 June 1935 the British served notice of their own priorities by brazenly breaching part five of the Versailles Treaty in legitimising German rearmament at sea through the Anglo–German Naval Agreement, which allowed Berlin to build up naval forces to 35% of the British level. The US ambassador to London, Robert Bingham, reported "bitter resentment in France".[118] The French had good reason to be horrified. The common front of sustaining the Versailles settlement had been sundered. In acting this way Britain was signalling that it would not allow France to veto the latent option of a rapproche-ment with Germany. Unilateralism in Paris could just as easily be matched by unilateralism in London.

Not only Poland but also Romania and Yugoslavia, the Baltic states and Finland still stood aloof from the proposed alliance system that the French were attempting to construct. Czechoslovakia alone had come in with France, which left a major flaw in the system: Soviet troops could come to the aid of the Czechs through Romania only. Moreover, the Czechs most certainly did not want or envisage the Red Army ar-riving on their doorstep without a French military presence. Romania's possession of Bessarabia was still disputed by the Soviet Union, and no one could conceive of the Red Army passing through both for fear of Bolshevism and Soviet territorial claims. Moreover, Poland had a sepa-rate alliance with Romania and subjected its neighbour to close scrutiny born of intense mistrust. Even Czechoslovakia had agreed a mutual as-sistance pact with the Soviet Union only on the precondition that, in the event of war, France would come to its aid first. Such was the inten-sity of anxieties about the threat of revolutionary war, unchanged since the previous decade. These countries well understood that Lenin's shelving of that option in the autumn of 1920 came about after the re-treat from Warsaw demonstrated that the Russians did not have forces on the ground sufficient to carry revolutionary war to victory. The con-comitant of this was that once they had acquired such a capability, they would put it to good use and force Communism into Central Europe and, if possible, beyond. This was the Napoleonic option of revolution-ary war put into effect by the only Communists who could succeed: Russian forces armed to the teeth.

7

Italy Breaks Out

One must bear in mind that early on the French government had not
fully realised what the "free hand" that it gave could and must mean
before long.

—"FRANCIA: SITUAZIONE POLITICA NEL 1935":
ITALIAN FOREIGN MINISTRY.[1]

Italy demonstrated that, with fascism in power, its international relations could not be reduced to the predictable regularity of state interests
(*ragion di stato*). Other states became aware of this only when Hitler's
rise to power gave Mussolini a choice. Any coalition against Germany
in Western Europe required the active involvement of Italy. But in Britain and France settled expectations of Italian fascism were destined for
deep disappointment. Through most of the 1920s Mussolini, aided by
Foreign Minister Dino Grandi, worked at making fascist Italy a reliable
standing member of the European club of great powers. Its relations
with Britain were bolstered by philo-fascist sentiments among diehards
in the ruling Conservative Party under Baldwin, whom Churchill once
hailed, without irony, as Britain's Mussolini. Indeed, "[i]f I had been
Italian", Churchill waxed, "I am sure I should have been whole-heartedly
with you from the start to finish in your triumphant struggle against the
bestial appetites and passions of Leninism." England, of course, had its
own way of doing things. "But that we shall succeed in grappling with

Communism and choking the life out of it—of that I am completely sure." In this respect Mussolini's fascism "has rendered service to the whole world".[2] But this was an Italy that kept its fascism at home, not on delivery for export. Abroad it generally behaved like the capitalist democracies, though it took a little settling in after the bombardment and brief occupation of Corfu in 1923.

The Essence of Fascism

A decade later, even more than with respect to Nazi Germany, anti-Bolshevik antipathies among the democracies sustained the grand and comforting illusion that Italy was "reasonable". After all, its behaviour generally suited the interests of the Entente. Were Italy won over and turned against Germany, then a grand alliance of Western powers would be feasible. This was the illusion of the Stresa summit, dispelled abruptly by Britain's decision to go it alone with the Anglo–German Naval Agreement very shortly thereafter.

But the assumption that Austria's continuation as an independent state was more important to Mussolini than building an empire neglects the trajectory of Italian history and the complex reasons why Italian fascism took hold. It was not just the unhappy product of a bad war epitomised by a catastrophic defeat at Caporetto (October–November 1917), with ten thousand dead and nearly a quarter of a million so demoralised that they willingly surrendered. This was, indeed, so bad for the country's reputation that to his intense shame the Italian military attaché in London found it the only subject of conversation with his hosts. "It ['Caporetto'] seems to be almost the only Italian word that they [the English] can pronounce", General Mario Caracciolo dolefully reported.[3]

There was more to all this than Caporetto. The entire canvas of disappointed hopes stretched further back to the prewar dominance of a corrupt liberalism unable to compete internationally for colonies, incapable of coping with the pace of economic growth; the backwardness of the Mezzogiorno; and then the unexpected advent of universal suffrage on the back of a state that had been patched together hastily from above in the north under Count Cavour and a constitutional monarchy.[4] Unification had failed to glue the people together through the kind of blood sacrifice anticipated earlier. On a relatively small land mass deprived of natural mineral resources, a massive haemorrhaging of people to both North Africa and the Americas in search of employment meant that Italy was in no position to compete with its more powerful neighbours. The decision to enter the First World War had brought nothing but grief, aggravating the country's existing dilemmas. In drawing up the Paris peace settlement the Entente and the United States, in particular, had deliberately ignored Italy's demands for contiguous territory. The Italians were self-evidently not a high priority for their allies. Their government had also unforgivably given every appearance of being excessively pro-German when the French sought revenge.

Mussolini's impulse to smash the prevailing system, his militant anti-reformism and his fierce anti-parliamentarianism had been just as evident when he had been a socialist. The biographer Gaudens Megaro noted, "His anti-democratic fascism is the child of his anti-democratic socialism."[5] Most have subsequently assumed that it was only because Mussolini had been alienated by Britain that the common front against Hitler's Germany did not eventually fall neatly into place. To say the least, this is questionable. When Neville Chamberlain became prime minister in 1937 and bent over backwards to appease the Italians, ceding everything he could (including his own dignity) in the process, the net result was zero. The presupposition that Italian concerns about German expansion were more important than Mussolini's imperial ambitions and the deeply rooted sense of international injustice that gave rise to fascism in the first place may well have been an egregious error.

What drew Rome and Berlin closer grew with the years, to the point in 1938 that they became barely distinguishable once Mussolini officially adopted Hitler's racist ideology, was that fascism meant something. Even before the Nazis took power in Germany, Göring, Hitler's chief adviser on foreign and domestic politics, spoke at length to the Italian ambassador to Berlin about the latest developments "and of the affinity of this movement with Fascism, of the common goal of fighting Communism and Social Democracy".[6] In early March 1933 Hitler, who had a bust of Mussolini in his office in the Brown House (Munich), told the Italian ambassador that now liberalism had had its day it would have to give way to "ideas proclaimed by your Leader. We are thus marching towards the realisation of fascism—complete fascism—bearing in mind that our own situation is naturally different from that in Italy and requires measures suiting our circumstances."[7] This affinity tightened down the years, despite evident clashes of personality, particularly once Mussolini realised that he would eventually have to concede to the German annexation of Austria. And by that time, with Germany seriously rearmed, Hitler had emerged self-confidently as the more powerful icon of fascism.

Although there was never much to show for fascist doctrine in the domestic realm that was distinctive other than the idea of the corporate state, in international relations this was not the case. A doctrine had emerged that was startlingly original. It turned the ideas of Karl Marx on their head. It was the brilliant writer and agitator Enrico Corradini—even now hardly known in Britain or France—who first articulated Italy's international dilemma. Corradini's thinking before the First World War left an indelible imprint on the fascist régime that emerged after it. His core thesis was expounded at the first Nationalist congress in Florence on 3 December 1910. "We have to start by recognising this principle: there are proletarian nations just as there are proletarian classes. Italy is materially and morally a proletarian nation." Within Italy it was socialism that aroused the working class, and "just as socialism taught the proletariat the value of the class struggle, we have to teach Italy the value of the international struggle".[8]

Ideology and Geopolitics

Where ideology took hold, geopolitics lay not far behind. The Italians attending the Paris Peace Conference identified France as the main enemy, the Mediterranean as the battlefield. And this made it all the more likely that the Italians would receive no territorial rewards originally envisaged for fighting alongside the Entente instead of the Central Powers. Later, when the Spanish monarchy was overthrown and a republic installed on 14 April 1931, Foreign Minister Grandi was alarmed. He prematurely anticipated a French ascendancy meaning that "war in the Mediterranean" would be "lost before the fighting. . . . The new Spanish situation could alter the balance in the Mediterranean to our disadvantage and that of England." His only consolation was that Spain was immune to Communism.[9] He was wrong on both counts. And the Italians were never really committed to the postwar status quo. Mussolini had contemplated leaving the League of Nations as early as November 1933.[10] Why should he have been thinking of doing so if his intentions were entirely beneficent and he had no *arrière pensée*?

Retracing the image drawn by Corradini of a proletarian state holding its own among the plutocrats, the Italian Foreign Ministry published an unusual article in the official *Corriere Diplomatico e Consolare* on the eve of Mussolini's return to the Palazzo Chigi as foreign minister in the summer of 1932. Its message should have been taken more seriously. Italy was presented as the poverty-stricken Mezzogiorno writ large. Entitled "The Italian Problem", the article argued that hitherto "on every occasion that men of good will have called on our good will, Italy has always been the first to respond":

> Yet Italy, too, has a problem of its own to put to the world. It is not less exalted nor less serious than that of security [France], than that of liberty [Germany], than that of updating economic relations with neighbouring states. This is the problem of living that fully encompasses our existence and our future.
>
> The problem of peace, of peace of mind and of work, for a population of 42 million inhabitants that will be 50 million in a dozen or so years. Can they exist, live, prosper together in a land that is half of that of the French, that of the Spanish, that of the Germans; that does not have the riches of primary produce; that does not have the resources to supply its own essentials[?][11]

It is perhaps also easily forgotten that Italy was an irredentist power, bullying the papacy and recklessly ruffling the feathers of its neighbours, particularly Austria and Switzerland, by supporting extravagant claims

for territorial annexation and unification with the fatherland. Italy's anxieties about German ambitions for an *Anschluss* with Austria by no
means overshadowed its own imperial dreams. Choosing between the
two was not difficult for Mussolini. Amid the conundrum about containing Nazi Germany came his dash for Abyssinia (Ethiopia), to en-
large his empire in East Africa from one half of neighbouring Somalia
to a much greater whole.

In directly breaching the League of Nations Covenant, Mussolini's
actions followed the gratifying precedent of Japan's blatant, unopposed
annexation of Manchuria in 1931–32: another piece of the semi-colonial
world snatched in front of an international audience that offered not the
slightest resistance. Britain's reluctance to ensure observance of the
Covenant's provisions against aggression was evident when Baldwin
cynically imposed mild sanctions—avoiding an oil embargo—sufficient
to neutralise leftist support for the League on the eve of an election
while not forcefully bringing Italy to heel. In the event, of course, this
unhappy compromise succeeded in alienating Italy without achieving
anything to rescue Ethiopia.

Much is made of a by-election held in the constituency of Fulham
(London) in October 1933 that destroyed a substantial Conservative
majority and turned it into a substantial majority for the Labour Party.
The Germans had just walked out of the Disarmament Conference
and the League of Nations at Geneva. The *West London and Fulham
Gazette* noted that "the masses were scared at the prospect of another
war".[12] The loss to the national government was widely taken as a key
indicator that the population was as a whole peace-minded and would
not tolerate rearmament. Yet the Foreign Office noted, "If Russia and
France were anxious as to our attitude in the future, they ought to
mark with great satisfaction the recent outburst of British public opinion in support of the League . . . where the British public were convinced that a flagrant act of unprovoked aggression was being threatened or committed, it would express itself with overwhelming force
in support of the obligations of the Covenant."[13] But not all ministers
thought this to be progress, as became evident once Italy broke out of
the constraints set in 1919.

The African Obsession

On 22 March 1932 General Emilio De Bono, minister for the colonies, on his return from a visit to Italian Eritrea, had warned Mussolini that Ethiopia was strengthening its military capabilities. He recommended the launching of an offensive before Ethiopia had enhanced its power.[14] On 20 January 1934 the chief of the general staff, Marshal Pietro Badoglio, intolerant of the delay, instructed Mussolini in similar terms, referring also to the *vendetta di sangue* (blood feud) that had to be settled as a result of Ethiopia's defeat of Italian forces back in 1896.[15] Before the year 1934 was out and under intense pressure from the military, Mussolini had resolved upon "the total conquest of Ethiopia [Abyssinia]". Italian forces duly moved on 2 October 1935. As long as he produced a fait accompli, Mussolini did not expect Britain or France to intervene. All they needed, he believed, was a little reassurance.[16]

Unexpectedly, however, British public sentiment rose to fever pitch. The US ambassador to Poland found to his surprise on visiting Britain in the autumn of 1935 that "the Government is attempting to restrain the demand for more aggressive action".[17] But once again fear of Bolshevism reared its head as a restraining factor. When a fellow of All Souls, Oxford, challenged the foreign secretary with the idea that a vessel of sufficient tonnage could be scuppered along the Suez Canal to cut off Italian support for its troops, Sir John Simon retorted, "We couldn't do that: it would mean that Mussolini would fall!" "That was what was at the back of their minds," recalled A. L. Rowse: "the anti-Red theme that confused their minds where they should have been thinking in terms of their country's interests and safety".[18] The fear of chaos consequent upon the downfall of a fascist régime was sustained in relation to Germany as well as Italy.

The Times was widely regarded across Europe as "the organ of His Majesty's Government".[19] And this created considerable difficulties for the Foreign Office, not infrequently thrown onto its back foot and forced to fend off allegations about shifts in British foreign policy. Rowse tackled Geoffrey Dawson, a life fellow of his college and editor of *The Times*, on the subject of appeasement. Why, he asked, was Dawson so set against Mussolini's Italy, when Germany represented the crucial threat to the peace of Europe, more powerful than every other power put together? Rowse could scarcely believe Dawson's answer, which shocked him deeply: "To take your argument on its own valuation—mind you I'm not saying that I agree with it—but if the Germans are so powerful as you say, *oughtn't we to go in with them?*"[20] And *The Times* was leading, not following establishment opinion.

The Abyssinian war that broke out on 3 October 1935 and its aftermath demonstrated to Britain that Italy was, to say the least, on a path entirely different from that of world peace. The British had finally woken up to the fact that the days were over when Italy could be counted on automatically as a friendly and submissive power. Eden had his eyes elsewhere. Only too attentive to public opinion, he seized the moment to assert the role of the League of Nations in defence against aggression, only to find, and complain about, other states holding back from imposing sanctions under Article 16 of the Covenant. Those such as the former colonial secretary Leo Amery, a hardline realist and another fellow of All Souls, held firmly to the view that the problem lay not with members of the League who did not act as the Covenant required of them, but with the Covenant itself. South African prime minister Jan Smuts was one of those who believed strongly that, on the contrary, the member states were failing the League. Amery remonstrated with his friend: "If you try to place a hundred weight load on a cardhouse and it collapses it is no use saying that the cardhouse is all right and that it could substitute entirely different nations as for the nations that exist to-day you might perhaps have a Covenant in which Article 16 would be workable. But you have not."[21]

Amery was also anti-Communist. The Franco–Soviet pact was for this very reason anathema. The pope, too, was "obsessed by a fear of bolshevism" that "colours his whole policy and outlook".[22] Even his attitude to the Italian attack on Abyssinia was affected by this. Hugh Montgomery, the British chargé d'affaires at the Holy See, noted with interest that the French ambassador, Charles-Roux, was forever "informing whoever cared to listen that the views of M. Laval and His Holiness as to the conflict and the best means of settling it were practically identical". Thus the wrecking of the Paris peace proposals in December 1935 "was undoubtedly a great blow to the Vatican".[23] Pius XI was a patriot, and his Italian church—notably the cardinal archbishop of Milan and Archbishop Monreale in Sicily—were openly supportive of the Italian war effort. Besides, the pope "consistently desired peace above all things, being afraid that the fall of fascism might result from an unsuccessful war, and that a Communist or anti-clerical régime might seize power, with disastrous results for the Papacy."[24] This was neither the first nor the last time that the inner fragility of fascism was taken as a reason not to offer direct armed resistance against it.

The Impact on Moscow

Italy's isolation provided Germany with the ideal opportunity to begin forging a common axis in international relations on a shared ideological platform. It would be a mistake to assume that, just because the Italian Communist Party had been crushed within Italy, Mussolini could feel entirely secure about the threat that Comintern posed. Why else did he keep the Party's sickly leader Gramsci behind bars and dying from lack of timely medical intervention? The fact that Soviet ambassador Vladimir Potemkin pleaded repeatedly for his release merely confirmed his importance to Mussolini. The birds had already flown, he insisted. The Italian secret police were very efficient. Potemkin's cleaner supplied Mussolini with the contents of the ambassador's wastepaper basket including the neatly scissored contents of the letters from his wife in Moscow. And access to the mail of Soviet intelligence officers to and from Rome was comforting in that he could tell what was going on. But it also reminded him that forces were continually at work to undermine the régime he had established. Moreover, the rise of Hitler had accentuated widespread hostility in the Soviet press towards fascism in general. This prompted complaints from the Italian ambassador in Moscow, Bernardo Attolico, who lamented this turn for the worse. In response Deputy Commissar Nikolai Krestinsky frankly acknowledged that the Bolsheviks were conducting a decisive ideological struggle against all bourgeois ideas from Social Democracy to fascism.[25]

The Russians and the Italians had tried to patch up relations with a Pact of Friendship, Non-Aggression and Neutrality, after much haggling, on 2 August 1933.[26] They had hitherto both done their best to keep ideological conflict out of inter-state relations. The issue under debate had been whether a clause should be included that would provide against "indirect" aggression as well as direct aggression by either party; the former term aimed at encompassing Comintern as well as the Soviet government. Following established practice, Krestinsky had persisted in his opposition to the clause and the Italians ended up conceding to Soviet wishes.[27] Yet Moscow, faced with German enmity, was actually working hard to make friends across Europe. It wanted to avoid unexpected crises arising from Comintern operations and was willing to make concessions to appease potential partners.

The Soviet military attaché, an officer in the Fourth Directorate, was not a happy man. He was "very critical" of the pact with Italy because Moscow wanted him to curtail his activities. On the basis of intercepting his communications with the NKVD in Moscow, in September 1933 the Italian government uncovered instructions telling him to hold back on Bolshevik propaganda in the Italian colonies. Instead his work was to be shared with the Soviet trade delegation in Milan and he had accordingly been in touch with a woman attached to the Soviet consulate there: the mistress or lover of a Communist militant in exile, Guido Picelli. The attaché commented bitterly that Mussolini had "played" the Soviet authorities.[28]

The problem for Soviet diplomacy was that the core objective of Comintern's Popular Front strategy launched at its seventh congress in August 1935 was aimed, of course, not merely at isolating German fascism but at combating fascism in general. This inevitably swept Italy and Germany into the same camp, even while Soviet diplomats were doing their best to separate them. In practice Comintern proved itself ineffective, though effective enough to alienate the Italian régime. "We have to admit", Dimitrov told Comintern insiders in March 1936, "that we were unable to build a more or less serious campaign against the imperialist war in Abyssinia."[29] Both Comintern and Soviet diplomacy, just like that of the British, fell between two stools: annoying the

Italians sufficiently to alienate them without decisively prompting them to back away.

The Germans were naturally not slow to alight upon this obvious area of common interest between themselves and the Italians. Hitherto co-operation between the police forces of Europe against the threat represented by Comintern had been conducted entirely informally. On 1 January 1932 a report by the Fourth Directorate in Moscow referred to the fact that "for the past two years we have had and now face a continuous onslaught; such organisations as the 'Intelligence Service', 'Scotland Yard', the [French] 'Sûreté Genéral', the [Romanian] 'Siguranţa' etc. have acted as a united front. This police international makes itself felt more and more both in the sense of heightened measures of surveillance and provocations as well as through mutual exchange of information by the organs of the security police of various countries."[30]

Italo–German Police Collaboration

The Germans tried to take matters one step further. States secretary at the Ausamt Bernhard von Bülow wrote to Ambassador Ulrich von Hassell in Rome on 15 November 1935, "I would like to sound out the Italian Government as to whether it favours the idea of the German and Italian political police working together for the purpose of a joint struggle against Bolshevism. Should it prove possible, the German Government would like to invite the departments involved to a conference in Berlin to initiate a secret agreement on international political criminality as a whole." Hassell was to add that such an agreement already existed with Hungary and the idea was to bring on board other states with such an agreement.[31] The subject was raised with Count Rogeri, the head of the Italian Foreign Ministry's political department. On 12 December the Germans were informed that Mussolini was in principle willing, on condition that no other parties were included before a decision was taken as to how the proposal was to be effected. Senior official at the Italian Foreign Ministry Baron Aloisi was keen to participate in person; moreover, he expressed the wish that the co-operation not be confined to police activity but have a view to major political questions.[32]

Mussolini's agreement was relayed to Heinrich Himmler, the minister for state security, by Bülow, who took the opportunity to emphasise that in addition to police co-operation he had in mind "general foreign policy grounds for making haste with the opening of German-Italian discussions for a joint struggle against Bolshevism". Mid-April 1936 was the date he suggested. The meeting in Berlin would have to be held in the strictest secrecy.[33] Both sides were eager to get started. In late February Mussolini's representative, an Italian general—it is uncertain exactly who this was—held meetings in Berlin with Admiral Canaris (Abwehr), General von Blomberg (Wehrmacht) and Joachim von Ribbentrop (the Nazi Party Außenpolitisches Amt) to survey the international situation and military affairs. And in Himmler's absence Gruppenführer Reinhard Heydrich stood in to discuss close collaboration against the common enemy, Comintern, by means of closely co-ordinating separate police activity—German, Italian, Hungarian, Polish and Finnish—run through the SS.[34]

On 1 April Himmler signed a secret agreement with his Italian counterpart Arturo Bocchini. It provided for both the exchange of intelligence information and the extradition of political undesirables from other countries.[35] Germany already had understandings of some kind with Greece, the Netherlands, Japan, Poland, Hungary, Denmark, Romania, Brazil, Argentina and Uruguay. The rapprochement with Germany went beyond purely police matters, as the Germans had intended. It also facilitated a series of talks at the Villa d'Este on Lake Como concerning the Alto Adige, the thorniest issue dividing the two countries.[36] The agreement cut directly across the "horizontal" line of Italian foreign policy in Europe, which was marked by protocols extending economic co-operation with Austria and Hungary on 17 March 1934 and amplified as soon as 23 May 1936.[37]

Italy Dumps Austria

The Italians went on to concede to Germany predominance over Austria with the conclusion of a friendship agreement on 11 July. They rationalised it as "delaying, even for a brief period of time, a blow of some kind from Germany, as it would now be inconvenient for Italy to get involved in a fight".[38] Others saw it the same way. "My impression is that the rapprochement between Italy and Germany is deeper and more serious than you and we together suspected", noted Deputy Commissar for Foreign Affairs Nikolai Krestinsky to the Soviet ambassador in Rome. "Italy", Krestinsky went on, "puts a good face on playing a bad hand and does not give the impression that it has suffered a defeat. But in fact that is the case. Italy, tied up in Abyssinia and not having liquidated its conflict with England, could not allow itself the luxury of putting up armed resistance to Germany and was under pressure not to protest against the German–Austrian agreement." He believed the agreement also served an anti-Soviet purpose. "The anti-Soviet focus lies in the fact that Italy will not block Germany from strengthening its anti-Czech policy, and in the fact that Germany even without a formal Anschluss can, in the absence of Italian resistance, spread its influence into the Balkans, in order at a time of its own making to carry out an offensive against us through the Balkans."[39] The shift towards fascist solidarity was marked more than symbolically on 10 June by the banishment from the Palazzo Chigi to the embassy in Washington DC of Mussolini's under-secretary, the pragmatist Fulvio Suvich—"a sceptic as to the value of ideology in international relations".[40] He was replaced by Galeazzo Ciano, who was openly anti-Semitic like Mussolini and vociferously supported an axis with Berlin. Ciano dismissed Suvich as "an unscrupulous businessman from Trieste who conducts the anti-German and Central European policy of his clientele of Jewish bosses".[41]

Germany Marches into the Rhineland

Meanwhile, Hitler had made a daring move to demonstrate that the Locarno Pact of 1925 that bound together France, Belgium and Britain in a multilateral security guarantee was effectively redundant. In London as far back as mid-January 1935 the cabinet had already dropped the Rhineland as a British concern in spite of the warning that this would "almost mean that we are encouraging Germany to regard part of the Locarno Treaty as a dead letter". But advice like this met with a shrug of the shoulders. Not surprisingly the head of the Central Department concluded, "Nothing is less certain than that we would be ready to resist . . . an open violation of the Zone."[42]

On Saturday 7 March 1936, when German troops marched in, it came as no surprise in London. MI6 had obtained the details of the operation and of the diplomatic moves Germany would take afterwards.[43] But the government, now under Baldwin, chose to do nothing to forestall it. At the Foreign Office some could barely stifle a yawn. Carr's diary told it all: "Germans occupy Rhineland. Home to lunch."[44] "I remember clearly", he wrote years later, "that I refused to be indignant. . . . This was a rectification of an old injustice, and the Western Powers asked for what they got."[45] Yet, morality aside, the reoccupation of the Rhineland and its subsequent fortification meant that France could no longer contemplate striking at Germany's most vulnerable point in order to stand by its allies in Eastern Europe. It meant that Hitler had effectively weakened the chance of having to fight on two fronts simultaneously. This was, indeed, what the armed forces in Britain had predicted.[46] What this meant strategically was clearly explained by the British chiefs of staff: "The reoccupation by Germany of the Demilitarized Zone has increased the practicability of a sudden attack on France and Belgium if Germany were to decide to make such an attack, and, at the same time, has rendered it more difficult for France to launch an offensive to assist her allies if they are attacked by Germany. These developments have created a feeling of uncertainty and alarm throughout Europe."[47]

Those like former colonial secretary Leo Amery, born in India, held to the view that the British were "not a European power".[48] But faced with little alternative, he had regarded the Stresa Front as the only path to take in order to restrain Hitler and had therefore opposed resistance to Italy over Ethiopia. "All the most pessimistic prognostications which we both entertained about the Abyssinian business in its effect on the general situation have come true," Amery wrote to his friend Jacques Bardoux. "Hitler has seized upon the unfortunate Franco–Soviet Pact in order to startle Europe by yet another act of audacious violence. Inevitably", he added, "France and Russia are drawn more closely together while we, no less inevitably, adopt a feeble and hesitating attitude which

France must think an ill return for the pledges given as against Mussolini's."[49]

Apart from the moral sentiment that the Germans were justified in reoccupying their back garden, in London well-heeled young officials such as Gladwyn Jebb also shared fears of Bolshevism. And with respect to the fascist régimes, the assumption—though rarely stated—was that "all dictatorships are by nature temporary".[50] Indeed, Jebb recalled that he and others like him were "unduly impressed by the danger of chaos in Germany if the Nazis were overthrown, or, in a general way, if both dictators [Hitler and Mussolini] were successfully opposed by the democracies. But as it seemed to me then, the economic situation in Germany would be so unfavourable in such an event that the U.S.S.R. would be able to fish in troubled waters, and the end result might very well therefore be a semi-Communist Germany in alliance with a Communist Russia, which would represent, ultimately, a force capable of extending its influence over the whole of Western Europe, and might even do so before America, abandoning isolation, was prepared to re-enter the European ring. In other words, I shared apprehensions which have often been ascribed to the more palsied of the French and British *bourgeoisie*."[51]

Comintern Reacts

In Moscow the seventh congress of Comintern—for this see the next chapter—had in August 1935 inaugurated an anti-fascist front and yet it had barely addressed the emerging danger of war. Although commentators focused on the fact that Hitler had moved westward with the reoccupation of the Rhineland and that therefore Britain and France should not safely assume he would necessarily direct his ambitions towards the East, the alarm bells nevertheless rang out in private. "Frankly," Dimitrov confessed, "in the course of a number of years we talked about the danger of war." But now they all faced "an obviously concrete danger of war that, tomorrow or the day after, could break out"; yet Comintern had made not even "elementary preparations for that possibility". His de facto deputy Palmiro Togliatti had touched on the problem at the seventh congress but no advance had been made. So Dimitrov opened a debate within the presidium of Comintern's executive committee with a view to "discussion within a small circle in the secretariat or in a special committee of the presidium" before reaching a decision.

Most speakers, such as Thorez, did not even broach the subject. What Togliatti had to say to the assembled was that "war could break out in the [Far] East and in Europe at any moment. That is what is new ["Das ist das neue Moment"]." Sanctions, even military sanctions, had to be supported ["Das braucht unbedingt der Fall zu sein."]. Yet no one directly addressed the embarrassing paradox that faced sections of Comintern given the prevailing party line. The British Labour Party and Liberals were freely pilloried and mocked for demanding sanctions but simultaneously refusing to contemplate military sanctions against Italy. But the fact was that all Communist parties also openly opposed military spending and in fact proudly undermined national defence—as the PCF's response to Stalin's assurances to Laval had so publicly demonstrated—even when their rulers allied with the Soviet Union.

The general secretary of the British Communist Party, the popular Harry Pollitt, was the only one with the common sense and the courage to grasp the nettle and plead for something to be done. Pollitt boasted of his party's successes in penetrating the defence industries and effectively undercutting their profitability through industrial action: "In the work the Party is doing in the aircraft industry [that took the major share of defence expenditure], now the key industry in the country so far as war preparations are concerned, there we have a leading position. Every strike has been led by the Party, and every strike we have won . . . in 13 of the main aircraft factories in the country, we now have 17 Party cells." But Pollitt was too intelligent not to see that the long-standing line of subverting defence was ultimately in conflict with the formation of a Europe-wide alliance system to deter and if necessary defeat Nazi Germany, though he delicately refrained from saying so. Instead he called for more clarity. The policy on war had led to confusion. The latest events had "complicated" matters "which are not even clear to the

Party". "Whilst the 7th Congress gave a much clearer lead in its war resolution", Pollitt said, "in the light of the subsequent developments, we have not yet got clear enough, nor does it now answer, some of the questions now coming up." In Britain 11.5 million had signed up to the Peace Ballot but 80% voted for sanctions against aggression. When he was speaking at a rally, Pollitt was asked point blank whether the party supported military sanctions against Italy. "Don't dodge, Harry," a member of the audience insisted.[52] And the problem for them all was that some of those strongest against Mussolini were also the strongest opponents of sanctions against Germany for occupying the Rhineland. In this sense, the Popular Front against fascism faced a profoundly difficult paradox.

From this discussion there arose a set of recommendations formulated on 1 April 1936. It began with a firm reassertion of doctrine, the defence of the working class: "Only proletarian power is in a condition to guarantee reliable defence against damage to its independence." It also repeated the warning that Communists would take "no political responsibility whatever for defence measures" by bourgeois governments and "will oppose the military budget as a whole". So, for example, Pollitt would have to continue to oppose the British military budget. However, some movement was apparent. The difference from before was twofold. First, Comintern would now "not rule out justified motivation for abstaining from voting for those measures of a defensive nature that make it difficult for the aggressor to attack (for example the reinforcement of frontiers)." Second, faced with "a direct threat" from a fascist aggressor, Communists would seek "the immediate establishment of a Popular Front government" that would "guarantee control by the masses over the defence of the country and would facilitate an increase in the defence capability of the people against a fascist aggressor".[53] In other words, some element of flexibility was now permissible, according to circumstances. But it did not take someone of military training to point out that leaving it until an attack was imminent before increasing defence capability was scarcely of much help to a beleaguered state, particularly in an age of highly mechanised warfare. The problems France would have building a credible defence in the second half of the

1930s were to demonstrate the impracticability of Comintern policy even when stretched to the limits of permissible flexibility. The bottom line was that unless a Popular Front government was actually under attack, Moscow was unwilling to subscribe to anyone's defence beyond Soviet borders, even if the country concerned were allied to the USSR. This stance underscored the unalterable fact that the Soviet régime operated in an international states system that it saw as illegitimate and inherently hostile to Bolshevism. And nothing that occurred during the rest of the decade did anything to undermine this assumption.

8

The Paradox of the
Popular Front

The aim of our fight against fascism is not the re-establishment
of bourgeois democracy but winning Soviet power.

—GEORGI DIMITROV[1]

Those opposed to fascism but also opposed to Communism faced a
cruel dilemma. What emerged as the Popular Front did not solve the
problem. Inaugurated at Comintern's long-awaited seventh congress in
August 1935, the Popular Front policy was not an entirely new strategy
but, as Dimitrov privately referred to it, "a tactic of the united front" in
pursuit of "Soviet power". None the less, whatever the original intention, appearances mattered; they were sufficiently beguiling to encourage a degree of self-deception in those most fearful of fascism. The
Popular Front was thus sufficient to transform Comintern sections in
the Western world from small and increasingly isolated sectarian out-
posts of revolutionary rhetoric into mainstream political parties that
seriously threatened to challenge and overturn the capitalist order.[2]

By December 1936 the French Communist Party counted its membership at 282,000—an increase of over 400% since the beginning of
the year—95% of whom were working-class. And sales of the daily
l'Humanité stood at 419,000.[3] Even in Britain, where the Labour Party

dominated the left through the trades union movement that created it, this wind of change could be felt. The nationwide shop stewards movement within the trades unions affiliated to the Labour Party grew directly out of the Communist Party which gave it something of a whip hand in industrial disputes. The proposal that individual Communists could apply for Labour Party membership was raised each year at the party conference but, though supported by the block vote of the miners, predictably failed, as did the proposal to join the Popular Front. None the less, "M.I.5. believed that the threat from the C.P.G.B. was becoming greater than before because it was acquiring a cloak of respectability from its Popular Front policies and its prominence in the anti-Fascist crusade. In 1935 M.I.5. argued that the new tactics 'show a distinct tendency by the Comintern to face realities and to adopt methods which, had they been exploited consistently since its inception, would certainly have produced far greater results."[4]

That said, the Popular Front embraced a fundamental contradiction. Was it intended to contain Hitler in particular or to block the advance of fascism in general? The distinction mattered because standing up to Mussolini was not at all the same as containing Hitler; nor, indeed, was resistance to the rebellion of the far right in Spain which emerged in 1936. Sooner or later a choice had to be made as to the greater danger, and Comintern strategy made that difficult, if not impossible, as the ideological fall-out from the Franco–Soviet pact made apparent.

France Divides

Complications originally arose from the fact that the Popular Front policy originated not in Russia but in France. As Thorez reminded his colleagues in March 1936, "our party was and still is the one that initiated it and breathes life into it".[5] But how did this happen? In France the Great Depression did not hit until 1931, hard, but late compared with the rest of Europe. What impressed onlookers was that France, of all states, seemed immune, being the closest to economic self-sufficiency.[6] But, as elsewhere, widespread immiseration inevitably followed the crash. By 1936 the total national income taken by wages had fallen to 30%.[7]

From a peak of 580,000 workers on strike in 1930, the figure plunged to 48,000 a year later. And the nature of industrial unrest had also changed.[8] Mass unemployment and stifling deflation imposed by business awakened traditional anarcho-syndicalist sentiment expressed in incremental political strikes.[9] The timing could not have been less fortunate. The domestic political system, once so firm, was fragmenting at the very moment Hitler came to power.

The left had itself split well before then. Communists and socialists had long been at loggerheads—the former in secular decline, the latter remorselessly on the rise. The rift between the two parties, PCF and SFIO, was impossible to bridge until the threat that emerged in the form of Nazi Germany was taken more seriously. Up to the moment that Hitler crushed the KPD at the end of February 1933 an element of ambiguity remained. France was identified by Hitler as the main enemy. But the German social democrats, still hoping to hang on while the KPD was broken by the Nazis, refused to allow the Second International to respond to overtures from Comintern, which of course more comfortably reverted to its former hostility. Meanwhile in France continued division on the left opened an avenue of opportunity to the far right.

Fascism was infectious. The emergence of extreme nationalism in Germany had inspired the assertiveness of various fascist parties in France—the Camelots du Roi, the Jeunesses Patriotes, the Croix du Feu, Solidarité Française and the Francistes—into attempting to destabilise the Third Republic. The moment chosen was "l'affaire Stavisky", a scandal of corruption in government, which broke in January 1934 and brought down the ruling coalition. Not to be outdone by a wave of strikes protesting wage reductions, the extreme right deluged Paris on 6 February. Some twenty thousand poured in and set fire to the Ministry for the Navy. Two days later the French Communist Party reacted by calling on supporters to take back the streets the following day and congregate at the Place de la République. The Socialist Party refused to co-operate but the demonstration took place none the less.

Nothing illustrated better the transcendent importance of ideology in international relations than the fact that Mussolini, who should by all rights have been most concerned to keep France solid to counterbalance Germany, was, on the contrary, enthralled at the prospect that "the French crisis . . . is ultimately weakening the positions of Social Democracy throughout Europe and also in Austria". Indeed he fully expected that the crisis "will have a long and troubled growth".[10] This was plainly international fascist solidarity. It completely undercut the traditional norm of *ragion di stato*. This was a fundamental change to the nature of international relations from that prevailing up to the October Revolution. What mattered was the make-up of society and the form of society and economy; not the balance of power as such, but what lay on the scales, and that was defined ideologically. The problem was that statesmen and diplomats had serious difficulty adjusting to these new realities. This was why Mussolini had ousted Grandi from the Italian Foreign Ministry and taken it over himself. Whereas those in the Foreign Office, badly burned by Comintern in the 1920s, realised that Soviet foreign policy was at root dictated by revolutionary priorities, they had yet to understand that fascism was not merely a decorative cover for customary geopolitics. They were soon to discover so, however, and the game was played out in France, Austria and then Spain.

A turning-point in the French disturbances came when the socialist trades union organisation, the CGT, to the left of the SFIO, called for a twenty-four-hour general strike. It took place on 12 February with Communist backing and brought four million French workers (60% of the national total) out for the "day of the barricades".[11] At this point the far right made a tactical retreat from the stage: *reculer pour mieux sauter*.

The PCF was, of course, not independent: it was a section of Comintern. From 1928 the degree of latitude it possessed was largely at Stalin's discretion. The only way in which the threat from the far right could be deterred was if the Communists were permitted to form a united front with the socialists. At this stage only a united front from below, exclusively with the rank and file, was permissible. Pollitt, the talented leader of the minuscule British Communist Party and therefore very anxious to break out of the sectarian shell, wrote to Moscow on the eve of the fascist seizure of the streets, expressing "some doubts" about PCF tactics. He was, however, admonished by "Bob" (Stewart) at Comintern headquarters: "You consider that our French comrades should have agreed to negotiate with the socialist leaders regarding joint actions in the struggle against fascist reaction which is maturing in France", but the PCF were correct. A united front from below presented the socialists with a fait accompli, exposing their leaders for making approaches to the Communists while simultaneously talking to the government.[12]

Austria Taken by Clerical Fascism

Two other events converged with the crisis in Paris to create a climate uniquely conducive to co-operation between socialists and Communists against the common enemy, fascism. At Riccione, Austria received a guarantee of its independence, underwritten by Italy. But in return the Austrians had to embrace fascist rule. The president, Wilhelm Miklas, and chancellor, Engelbert Dollfuss, accordingly dismissed parliament on 5 March 1933, taking the path to dictatorship at the urging of Mussolini. This brought to a head long-standing tension with the Socialist Party, headed by the pacifist Otto Bauer, who was once disparaged by the papal nuncio Enrico Sibilia as "more than a Jew, . . . a pagan and ultra-Marxist".[13] After destroying constitutional democracy by dismissing parliament, in October 1933 Miklas received from Pius XI the rare honour of being awarded the Order of Christ.[14] And, as the British noted, "behind the velvet glove of Dr. Dollfuss was now the mailed fist of Major Fey", his vice-chancellor.[15] On 11 February 1934 Mussolini urged Dollfuss to move against the socialists. The events in France provided "the most favourable moment to act on all fronts and to rally the Austrian people around the new State". Mussolini hoped that the chancellor "has this feeling and that he will act accordingly".[16]

The following day right-wing paramilitaries allied to the régime— collectively known as the Heimwehr—along with the police, raided a hotel in the town of Linz where the socialists stored arms. The socialists fought back. Disorder spread rapidly to Vienna and elsewhere. A general strike was called and martial law was declared. In the capital the police and the Heimwehr again attacked the socialists and their paramilitaries, who defended themselves successfully until bursts of artillery fire destroyed their makeshift fortifications, including vast blocks of social housing for the working class that had not been cleared of women and children. The French approached the Vatican to intercede for clemency. On 16 February, however, Pius XI told Cardinal Secretary of State Eugenio Pacelli that "the Holy Father wishes the Chancellor [of Austria] to do everything that must be done to re-establish order once and for all. It was a mistake made by [former chancellor Ignaz] Seipel who at a given moment [a socialist uprising in 1927] could have removed the Socialists from Vienna; but he did not have the courage to accomplish it. Harshness can be merciful."[17] "I rejoice . . . to see the town hall or the local government of Vienna free from the real tyranny of the reds," Sibilia assured Pacelli.[18]

The measures dictated by the vice-chancellor were manifestly vindictive. The social democrats had suffered a heroic defeat. Yet Comintern was elated. Hitherto the social democrats had refused any co-operation with the Communists because they were not democratic. Now everything had changed. Oskar Grossmann, the Austrian Communist Party's representative, highlighted the undoubted fact that "the unfortunate wall that so long stood between ourselves and Social Democratic workers was broken down. The atmosphere has changed to one of friendship and comradeship."[19]

These two sets of events were what was needed to convince Stalin to alter Comintern's course and to accept that he had to reverse out of the cul-de-sac of "social fascism" because collaboration with Social Democracy was essential. The question was how far he was willing to go in seeing the policy renounced. The trouble was that the old guard led by Comintern secretary Knorin read events differently. Knorin saw no need at all for a change in strategy. The violent turn of events in Austria was taken as evidence of "the masses turning from reformism to Communism". France was even more important, as the most stable capitalist state on the continent. It was one of the main victors of the world war. The dramatic outbreak of violence in Paris demonstrated that it was "a country in which the whole evolution of international contradictions has led to a great exacerbation of domestic contradictions". In other words, the disruption of the European states system resulting from Hitler's rise to power was increasing strains within those states and those strains would lead inexorably to revolution: "The more rapid the preparations for war will be, and fascism and war are tightly intertwined, the more rapid will be the growth of the revolutionary crisis."[20] German fascism was seen as the ice-breaker, fragmenting what had held bourgeois society in one piece and charting the course to revolution.

Georgi Dimitrov Convinces Stalin

Manuilsky never had the strength of character, the stature or the prestige to lead Comintern out of its morass. Someone else would have to do so, and that person was Bulgarian Communist leader Georgi Dimitrov. On 27 February 1934 Dimitrov, who had been in charge of Comintern's West European Bureau in Berlin when arrested for the Reichstag fire, was released from prison after the Nazis failed to find him guilty at a show trial. Dimitrov had already become an invaluable international emblem for the anti-fascist cause worldwide thanks to Willi Münzenberg's press machine that went rapidly into action after Dimitrov's incarceration. Stalin needed a heroic figure to turn the international Communist movement around after the speedy and humiliating destruction of the German Communist Party at the hands of the Nazi régime in March 1933.

On 7 April 1934 Dimitrov finally had a meeting with Stalin in the Kremlin, and in a matter of weeks he was put in charge of the crucial Central European secretariat, ousting the diehard Knorin.[21] With the May Day parade in progress Stalin summoned Dimitrov onto the podium as a grand public gesture of approval. This one symbolic act demonstrated to all that he was in favour. Thereafter his main rival Pyatnitsky lost access to the Kremlin and a year later lost all control over his financial and organisational empire in Comintern. As to future strategy and tactics—"on this question, there is still nothing in my head", Stalin confessed to Dimitrov on 21 June. "Something must be prepared!"[22]

For Dimitrov the events in France and Austria pointed in one and the same direction: ending "social fascism" and building a broad united front against fascism. He told Austrian Ernst Fischer, a militant social democrat who had now joined the Communist Party as a result of the repression, that he had made a good decision: "The February battles in Vienna and Paris marked the beginning of a new era."[23] But Stalin dragged his feet, thus giving hope to the fundamentalists, when he was asked to accept that France, in particular, forge "a united front also 'from above'".[24]

On the other hand the deep scepticism Stalin showed about the prospects for revolution in Western Europe revealed to Dimitrov an open-mindedness that he had never anticipated. This brusque realism cut through the revolutionary dogmatism that had overhung Comintern since 1928, when Molotov took it on. It gave Dimitrov a unique opportunity. Stalin's well-concealed stance was not a long way from that of Pollitt and, indeed, Litvinov. Stalin realised that the working class of Europe were far too attached to bourgeois democracy to accept Communism through violence, and with that admission the assumption made dogma since 1928 that the only reason for the lack of revolution in Western Europe was betrayal by Social Democracy tacitly fell away by default.[25] Yet this startling revelation was far too controversial to be shared with anyone but Dimitrov. Thereafter no one else from Comintern was admitted to see Stalin in order to make an alternative case to that now presented by Dimitrov. Effectively, therefore, Dimitrov had become the gate-keeper and played a free hand—until, that is, betrayed by events, like Litvinov, he ultimately lost Stalin's confidence.

In Austria, as we have seen, the willingness of socialists to use force against a repressive clerical-fascist government was a clear indication of change which Dimitrov seized upon in trying to turn the direction of Comintern policy around. On 23 June the political secretariat issued a resolution recognising the Austrian party's "successes in the task of winning over Social Democratic workers to the side of Communism" and pressed it to go further "in drawing into its ranks former functionaries of Social Democracy", with a view to a congress of unification even before the seventh congress of Comintern was due to meet.[26] Dimitrov used the unique influence he now wielded to insist on an about-turn elsewhere: a united front at all levels across Europe between Communists and socialists. In so doing he immediately roused stiff resistance from the old guard—Knorin, Kun and the man he most feared, Pyatnitsky—but he found equally firm support from the ever agile and unscrupulous Manuilsky, the Finn Otto Kuusinen and, conditionally, the new Machiavelli at Comintern Togliatti, who had good reason to rue the day the Italian party failed to find common cause against Mussolini.[27] Stalin, keeping his own hands as free as possible, tasked Dimitrov with reframing Comintern tactics, but having done so, typically, left him to fight it out for himself.

A French Innovation

The PCF was initially slow to realise that Comintern's direction was changing so dramatically and at such speed. A party conference was due to take place on 24–26 June 1934 at Ivry. In anticipation, Comintern sent its advice on 11 June. It called for specific recommendations to enhance the united front against fascism and for an end to vacuous generalities. It also pressed for action to win over the petty bourgeoisie, incorporating all those not actually fascist but previously identified as such. In particular, the army should be drawn in through the establishment of anti-fascist cells among the younger officers, as "in the last analysis its actions will determine whether fascism does or does not triumph in France".[28] And within three days no less a figure than Manuilsky, finally witnessing the changes take effect that he had deemed necessary in February 1933, formally acknowledged that "up to now . . . all of our instructions were such that Social Democracy was our main enemy. The point is that, ignoring the struggle against fascism, we have concentrated all our fire on Social Democracy and that, by fighting Social Democracy, we are thereby smashing fascism."[29] These words would have been condemned as heresy only a few months before they were uttered. A complete reversal of the party's policy was well under way. This meant that an instruction issued only a matter of a few days earlier could effectively be out of date by the time it was to be implemented.

In what started to become a habit, Moscow learned what took place in France only from the pages of the Communist daily, *l'Humanité*. Thorez's speech was later printed in the PCF's journal *Cahiers du Bol-*

chévisme, on 1 July. He had clearly argued that "we want to forestall employees in the big cities, the civil servants, the middle classes—small shopkeepers, artisans—and the mass of working peasants from being won over to fascism". He underlined the importance of winning against fascism. So far so good. But he had undermined his primary message by merely adjusting the tone while sustaining the existing line. He made matters worse by referring to "our goal, soviets in France", which flatly contradicted his simultaneous assurance that *"the united front is not a manoeuvre"*.[30] Logically, if joining the united front meant furthering the victory of Communism, then the socialists, let alone the middle classes, would have nothing to do with it. So announcing this publicly was to say the least unhelpful, if not obtuse. In haste, nothing had been properly thought through.

Comintern's reformers were naturally not at all pleased. Advice had been ignored. Had it even been read? A blistering reprimand was telegraphed to Paris after Comintern's political committee met on 4 July: "On the basis of reporting in *l'Humanité* we consider that the national conference and in particular Thorez's speech insufficiently reflected our instructions."[31] The humiliation of this rebuke seems then to have galvanised in Thorez and other Politburo members a stubborn determination to make a distinctively radical mark on policy. Most striking of all was Thorez's subsequent expression of a sentiment wholly suppressed for the previous decade and a half: "we love our country".[32]

The continuing disagreements in Moscow and the pace of events in Western Europe led by default to improvisation. The delays in summoning the seventh Comintern congress—the previous one had been held in 1928—and Dimitrov's intermittent hospitalisation after his incarceration in Germany made flexibility and some degree of delegation unavoidable. On 4 September Stalin and the Politburo decided to postpone the congress again, until March 1935: "The special complexity of the current international situation requires a fundamental discussion beforehand of the political and tactical problems in all sections of Comintern."[33]

Dimitrov's vision had collided head-on with the pre-existing orthodoxy. Three days later he called on Stalin to buttress his own stance.

"Having familiarised myself more closely with the situation in Comintern", Dimitrov wrote, "I have come to the conclusion that improvements occurring in the world labour movement and the tasks facing the Comintern, especially on the issue of fighting for the unity of the working class against fascism and the threat of war, demand a speedy adjustment to change the working methods of the leading organs of Comintern." This Delphic suggestion actually amounted to a plea for help, asking Stalin to weigh in on his side. Dimitrov continued,

> After exchanging opinions with leading comrades within Comintern I have become convinced that this adjustment is impossible to bring about without the intervention and assistance of yourself and the Politburo of the Central Committee of the Russian Communist Party. This is all the more necessary because resolution of these questions is complicated by the evident conservatism and bureaucratic routine that has accumulated within the leadership of Comintern as well as the unhealthy relationships between comrades directly participating in the leadership of Comintern.[34]

Stalin was not eager to get overtly involved, however. His disengagement had consequences as events took on a life of their own. And they ran much further ahead than anyone, including Stalin, had anticipated.

To win over the middle classes, which the PCF was supposed to do, would require splitting the more moderate wing of the Radical Socialist Party from hardliners like Prime Minister Gaston Doumergue and overt reactionaries like General Pétain and Pierre Laval. Accordingly, in September secret talks opened between Politburo member Julien Racamond and a leading Radical, Édouard Daladier. This immediately prompted strictures from Comintern against taking the initiative.[35] On 16 September the instructions read, "In accordance with promise to DIMITROW [sic] do not put forward proposals. Instructions will follow in a few days."[36]

Nothing came in, however, and for good reason. Battle lines had firmed up within Comintern's inner leadership between the steadfast proponents of radical change headed by the ailing Dimitrov, backed by Manuilsky, Kuusinen and Togliatti, and the doctrinaire diehards Pyatnitsky, Kun and Knorin, the last of whom Dimitrov had supplanted as head of the crucial Central European secretariat. Stalin had yet to pronounce. And Dimitrov, in poor health, still had no formal status other than as head of the Central European secretariat and member of Comintern's ruling executive committee.

At Comintern on 27 September Manuilsky, who headed the Latin secretariat, finally lost his patience and exploded in an onslaught against those opposing the new, united front line: "Take the French Communist Party. It has now decided to vote for the Radicals if necessary at the elections." This was a deliberate provocation. The Hungarian hardliner Kun was so appalled, the minutes read, that his eyes nearly popped out of his head. Was this not the same, Kun asked, as the socialists supporting the Brüning government that ruled by emergency decree in Germany (1930–32)? Manuilsky brusquely retorted that he could not see what all the fuss was about. "What's the difference", he asked rhetorically, "between our tactic towards Social Democracy [in 1930–32] and the tactic of voting for the Radicals and the Socialists?" The point, however, was that "we do not treat bourgeois democracy and fascism ... as equal", though this did not mean an end to the class struggle.[37] What was at issue was a fundamental shift in tactics—not a renunciation of purpose.

On 3 October Comintern elaborated upon the strategy of splitting the Radical Socialists. The political secretariat reasoned that Prime Minister Doumergue was aligning "the petty bourgeois masses against the working classes and the united front". It strongly advised the PCF to "unmask very energetically DOUMERGUE's manoeuvres deploying all our anti-fascist efforts among the working class and with the campaign already under way against the threat to trades union rights and the fascist reform of the state".[38] Conversations with Daladier resumed. And, in opposition to Doumergue, Daladier suggested that the only way to defeat fascism was to create a united front between the working class and the middle class. This would be a "popular front". The term made its first appearance in l'Humanité five days later. Comintern was not pleased. The French comrades claimed—all too conveniently at the very moment the issue of strategy had come to a head—that problems had arisen over decrypting communications from Moscow. The matter was so urgent that Togliatti was sent to Paris with a letter dated 20 October from the executive committee insisting that on no account was there to be a united front with the middle classes. The united front could be expanded only to "the labouring masses of the population . . . the majority of the population".[39] But, ignoring pleas for restraint, and aware no doubt of the split in Moscow as yet unresolved by Stalin, Thorez threw caution to the winds and unilaterally launched the *Front populaire* in a speech at Nantes on the eve of the Radical Party congress in the town, on 24 October 1934.

Togliatti had tried—perhaps not as hard as he might—but failed to restrain him. Clément (Evžen Fried), Comintern adviser and friend to Thorez had formerly been a leftist rebel in his own party until sent to manage the French comrades. He ostentatiously washed his hands of the entire affair.[40] From Moscow Comintern once more urged restraint and then on 31 October a telegram—a week too late—rapped them all on the knuckles: "Any participation by bourgeois parties in the anti-fascist front must be excluded in advance," it insisted, clearly cutting across Manuilsky's own preferences and reasserting the old line still sustained by Pyatnitsky and others.[41]

The problem was that the fundamentalists who had had Comintern in their grasp since 1928 still believed that revolution was not just possible but probable in Western Europe, even in the face of fascism. By backing Dimitrov, Stalin had inadvertently opened Pandora's box. Echoes of opposition to Dimitrov's innovations could be heard within the Soviet Communist Party itself. On trial, Yefim Yevdokimov, a former Chekist posted to the North Caucasus, arraigned alongside Zinoviev and Kamenev for criticising the régime's policies, told the court in January 1935,

> We accused the Party leadership of not taking measures to activate the international Communist movement, falsely claiming that the Central Committee [Politburo] was putting the brakes on the development of this movement. As an example I will cite my conversation with Zinoviev at the end of 1934. Zinoviev accused the CC of hand-

ing over the initiative in the leadership of the labour movement in France to the Second International.[42]

With accusations in Moscow of a sell-out, the PCF still did not budge, however. Stalin sat back and watched from a great distance. Thorez justified his speech with the argument that he was calling for "something much bigger" than "parliamentary struggle"; it was, he said, "a matter of expanding our anti-fascist base".[43] The impact of the Thorez rejection of sectarianism made itself felt within France in a matter of months.

Only the dogmatists of the left had failed to foresee the obvious. Communism was being given a facelift; it was actually being rehabilitated for its own good. The diehards at Comintern resisted all change to the bitter end—no doubt counting on support from hardliners Molotov and Kaganovich, perhaps even Stalin, whose fence-sitting must have become increasingly uncomfortable. From Paris Togliatti tried to split the difference between the two factions. "We propose", he wrote on 3 December 1934, "also to allow into the anti-fascist front groups of Radicals from below who are overtly in political disagreement with the party leadership."[44]

Although Stalin still reserved his own position, it gradually became known in Moscow and was then assumed that Thorez met with his approval. A fierce debate then took place at the plenum of Comintern's executive committee, where the majority voted in favour of the Thorez policy.[45] Finally, on 16 January 1935 approval came through from the Comintern secretariat.[46] The Nantes speech was now to be formalised as policy at the seventh congress of Comintern, scheduled for July 1935.

The Party in France had much ground to make up as a result of the sectarianism dictated by Comintern, which had been showcased at the sixth congress, in 1928. This had reached its nadir in 1932, at a time when socialists were still targeted as "social fascists", with membership at a mere 32,000. Prospects were now much brighter. Sales of the daily l'Humanité rose from 189,832 in January 1935 to 249,516 by November—good, though not good enough. But some measure of success can be found in the fears expressed on the right. The municipal elections in France closed on 12 May 1935. From across the English Channel Lord Rothermere, who owned the Daily Mail, was anxious that France had become "disorganised". The "elections yesterday show that extreme Socialism and Communism are making great strides," he warned the like-minded Winston Churchill.[47]

The PCF was certain that, in order to succeed, the *Front populaire* had to become a movement at the level of the factory and not just parliament, through the formation of Popular Front committees at every place of work. It also had to raise bread-and-butter issues, including personal freedom, to acquire "a more human face", as Politburo member Jacques Duclos declared. And Duclos was second only to Thorez in the party hierarchy. At the same time, rivalry with the socialists kept bubbling to the surface. Duclos, for instance, took the view that the SFIO had been "dragged" into the *Front populaire* and that at every opportunity the socialists avoided unity of action. They seemed more preoccupied with having Communist agitators disarmed, rather than their fascist counterparts.

On this issue socialist leader Léon Blum was accused of conniving with the reactionary prime minister Pierre Laval and talking "crap" (*cochonnerie*). The Radicals had no liking for the Communists either, but their ideological preferences were offset by "a strong pro-Soviet current in the Radical Party as also among the mass of the French population". It was they who had originally pressed for an alliance with Moscow that Laval had reluctantly found himself concluding on 2 May 1935. That show of public opinion was avowedly of "considerable help" to the PCF.[48] Indeed, Mussolini privately described the leader of the Radical Party Édouard Herriot as "the most ill-starred man for France. . . . He is preparing his country for the road to Bolshevism."[49] Opponents of the Popular Front policy on the left in Moscow were unconvinced, however. Solomon Lozovsky, head of Profintern, for one, did not believe that Radicals could be counted on.[50]

The *Front populaire* Wins Power

But what if the coalition of the left actually won at the ballot? Would Communist parties enter a coalition government as a minority? This was the question that was to bedevil Comintern thereafter. It did not take long before the first test took place. In France the *Front populaire* won a general election in two rounds, on 26 April and 3 May 1936. The SFIO secured the largest vote at 1,922,123. The PCF obtained an unprecedented 1,503,125. The Radicals dropped 24% from their portion of the vote in 1932 to 1,401,974.

Working-class almost to a man, the Communists elected were, however, still only the junior partners. But their membership was rising rapidly, from just 80,000 in January 1936 to 185,000 in July.[51] By January 1937 it had hit 280,000.[52] Just over a week after victory at the polls, at Comintern's secretariat the delicate issue was raised as to whether the PCF should enter the governing coalition. Dimitrov was evidently pleased: it was a "more significant" victory than expected. But he was also adamant that the PCF leadership were correct in deciding against such a risky move: "It is a question of expediency and not a question of principle. That must be made clear." He clarified this point: "Had the victory of the popular front in France been more striking, had more of the masses been united, had the socialists and Communists a greater majority in parliament, had a Communist–socialist government been created, on which we could depend to begin the fight in parliament against fascism, then we could have taken this initiative." Yet, as matters stood, Communist participation would have alienated the Radicals and provoked attacks from the far right.[53] This stance was later ratified by the presidium of Comintern's executive committee.[54] The party could plausibly be accused of seeking power but evading direct responsibility, a position it became sensitive to in the weeks that followed. But this was not least due to fears of a fascist backlash.

Clément (Fried), adviser to the PCF, and Dimitrov both saw the far right as the imminent threat. On 22 May 1936 Comintern's secretariat demanded that the party take seriously "the preparation of a fascist coup d'état", on the grounds that "this danger will worsen in the future".[55] The exaggerated fears of the far right entirely obscured the extent to which France had altered course and was fast driving left. Dimitrov could not get himself to see the fundamental shift in opinion that the electoral victory indicated. To him and his subordinates in the secretariat, "this government is not yet a Popular Front government in the full sense of the decisions of the 7th World Congress".[56] None the less the PCF came out in "complete and unfailing support" of the new government.[57] Thus Moscow was completely unprepared and was taken aback by what followed.

Class consciousness was not something manufactured and exported from Moscow. Given the unexpected victory of the *Front populaire*, French workers were now no longer willing to tolerate lock-outs—a notable feature, for instance, at the manufacturers of Citroën through 1935.[58] Metalworkers (*métallos*), for example, were notoriously dismissed at seven francs an hour to be rehired at five. Beginning on 11 May 1936 and picking up pace three days later, a movement to occupy the factories gradually spread to a series of automobile and aviation plants. By 26 May it encompassed massive enterprises such as Nieuport, Sauté Harnet, Renault (which supplied tanks, armoured cars and aircraft engines to the French armed forces), Hotchkiss (which produced almost all the machine guns for the army), Hispano-Suiza and Lavalette. This amounted to almost all the metalworkers of the Paris region. That day a heated session of the PCF Central Committee took place. André Marty hailed the movement as the biggest since Russia's in 1917. The occupations relentlessly gathered momentum and spread to Lille, Dunkirk, Marseilles and beyond. The action peaked on 5 June, with a quarter of a million downing tools. Families included, the strikers in Paris accounted for one-fifth of the city's population.[59]

"What is it?" asked Simone Weil, the uncompromising young Marxist intellectual. "A revolutionary movement? But everything is calm. A movement for better conditions? But why so deep, so general, so strong, and so sudden?"[60] No one had the answer. Head of civilian counter-intelligence (Deuxième Bureau) Lieutenant Colonel Mermet was not one to miss the opportunity to pin unrest on the PCF. But it was obvious that the PCF had lost control. It had previously found during a big strike at Citroën that "the party sometimes disappears as a party in these [strike] movements".[61] The same appeared now to be the case. The socialist trades union body, the CGT, was now united with the Communist CGTU (Confédération générale du travail unitaire). Mermet confessed that it was "trying to put the brakes on the movement but it appears to be outflanked by its rank and file".[62]

Socialist daily *Le Populaire* emphasised that "it is a question, we repeat, of spontaneous action supported, once known, by the leaders of the metallurgical trades union".[63] This opinion was echoed by the secretary general of the CGT, Léon Jouhaux, addressing its Comité Confédéral on 16 June: "As you know, and as you could have yourselves said, the movement was unleashed without anyone knowing exactly how or where."[64] None the less, preceded by an organised mass demonstration at the well where the communards were massacred in 1871, it was bound to stir deep unease among men of property. The Communist daily *l'Humanité* asked rhetorically: "Should one not be surprised that after the electoral victory of the Popular Front 250,000 Parisian metal workers rise up against pressure from their bosses?"[65]

When the newly elected Chamber of Deputies sat for the first time on 2 June, the threat to established order was already hard to miss. *Le Temps*—the French establishment's most authoritative mouthpiece—expressed great alarm. The majority of those elected were, it asserted, "inspired by the theory of revolutionary illegality", and as such they were responsive to "those they call the 'popular masses', whose power is exerted outside Parliament and even, on occasion, against Parliament". Deputies were thus answering not to the assembly "but to the demands of categories of people who are in fact factions organised for the purposes of conspiracy and violence".[66]

While Blum tried to delay the enforcement of an agreement on the owners, in late May he received a visit from Benoît Frachon, himself formerly a *métallo*, now secretary of the CGT but no longer a member of the PCF Politburo (he and Racamond had to step down in order to be able to sit on government committees). Marty pointed out that "Blum understood that a mass movement stood behind Frachon and that behind that stands the Communist Party".[67] Yet it took further strike action to convince the employers that all was lost.

Although prepared reluctantly to concede that spontaneity lay behind the occupations, *Le Temps* held trades unions to account for adopting syndicalist tactics that accentuated the "revolutionary character of the movement". The occupation had, it argued, "unleashed disruptive forces that move beyond the reach of the trades unions".[68] At the

Italian embassy a sense of déjà vu prevailed. Ambassador Vittorio Cerruti reflected that Blum's government was "looking to take conciliatory measures that we are familiar with from the period of liberalism in Italy. In fact they are giving in to the will of the Communists."[69]

"The anarchy has lasted long enough," *Le Temps* intoned on 5 June. The trades unions were "visibly engulfed by the flood. The same is true of the socialist and communist members of parliament." The crisis increasingly resembled "a revolution". Whether or not the resemblance was also reality, it certainly appeared to be heading in that direction. The deputy chief of the army general staff, General Victor-Henri Schweisguth, took the same alarmist view.[70] Yet Mermet did not see any of this as orchestrated: "It seems at the moment the executive and legislature have been overtaken by the power of the people." He added that the CGT was trying "to put the brakes on the movement. But it appears not to be much listened to." [71] None was more disturbed than the timorous PCF leadership. What was perhaps so unnerving was the "absolute discipline" displayed by those occupying the factories, assiduously safeguarding property and avoiding manifestations of violence. "Never has one seen anything like it," Marty gushed. On the other hand, he had to admit that "this strike movement has seemed to many comrades unexpected, inopportune".[72] Indeed, on 11 June Thorez spoke out for caution: "Though it is important to lead well the struggle for better conditions, it is also important to end it at the right moment. We must even accept a compromise in order to preserve all our forces, and especially in order to counteract the panic campaign carried on by the reactionaries."[73]

Even when the first great wave of strikes ceased that day, domestic counter-intelligence at the Deuxième Bureau was alarmed at the workers' extraordinary self-discipline.[74] The ultimate impact of the *événements* was to remind everyone that the social peace in France hung by a thread. From exile Leon Trotsky brashly declared that "the French revolution has begun".[75] The Swiss ambassador, for one, was by no means alone in believing that France had undergone not just a strike "but a revolution; not just a change of government but a complete transformation of the political order [*einen Regimewechsel*]". And he wondered what the outcome would be if the Popular Front experiment met with failure. Would a coalition between socialists and Communists be willing to hand back power or would they end up installing a leftist dictatorship, giving a boost to the trend towards authoritarian solutions?[76] Former prime minister Laval perversely but triumphantly took consolation from the fact that "the Communists have shown themselves unsure of being able to count on a consensus in the country. He considers the excesses committed useful because they have opened the eyes of many people."[77]

British Fears of the *Front populaire*

In Britain attitudes within the Conservative Party towards the Soviet Union had softened somewhat since the frosty atmosphere of the late 1920s. But scratch the surface and the old fears readily resurfaced, even among senior figures in the Foreign Office who had tended to be more relaxed about such matters. And the advent of the *Front populaire* on the back of the Franco–Soviet pact did a great deal more than irritate a wound that had never healed. Sargent, now under-secretary of state, who had resolutely opposed the pact on the grounds that it made a settlement with Germany more difficult, had already expressed serious qualms about what was occurring in France even before the election of the Popular Front.[78] He was one of the most class-conscious of the officials—indeed, known to be something of a snob—and was certainly not averse to expressing his sentiments. The "extreme Left" in France were, he noted, "of course in the pockets of the Bolsheviks and are play-ing the Russian game, no doubt with the help of Russian money".[79]

Prime Minister Baldwin was not one to take an active interest in for-eign policy, but he had been burned by the searing experience of the Chinese revolution and the general strike during his first period of office from 1924 to 1929. Tom Jones, the Welsh deputy secretary to the cabinet, spent a weekend with the Baldwins at Chequers on 23 May 1936, before France experienced its bewildering workers' revolt under the *Front populaire*. Jones detected in Britain "signs of a more vigorous attempt to come to some sort of an alliance with Germany which would not alienate

France". Of course, the Franco–Soviet pact complicated matters but Jones felt sure Britain would "have to choose between Russia and Germany and choose soon". Hitler, on Jones's view, was worried by Russia: "He is therefore asking for an alliance with us to form a bulwark against the spread of Communism." Baldwin, recorded Jones, "is not indisposed to attempt this as a final effort before he resigns after the Coronation [of Edward VIII] next year [1937], to make way for Neville Chamberlain".[80] And very soon after he stepped down from office as the newly ennobled Earl Baldwin, the former prime minister did not hide "his preoccupation with France" and "added that for him there had never been a greater enemy of the world than Bolshevism".[81]

Thus the calamitous divide that the Bolshevik revolution had created was not so easily or so speedily bridged, even in the face of German assertiveness. The impact of Commissar Litvinov's importuning, assiduously reinforced by Ambassador Maisky's inexhaustible socialising across the entire political spectrum, needed reinforcing by a broad public relations campaign in which the Bolsheviks could sustain a soothing image and refrain from revolutionary action where opportunity presented itself.

A junior minister at the Foreign Office, Anthony Eden, had begun to shift from the the consensus that Germany was much misunderstood and deserved the benefit of the doubt to a more realistic assessment of where the Nazis were heading. His superior Sir John Simon, however, was of a different mould. He held out to Hitler the prospect of a deal on air force limitation in return for a more general European settlement. When Hitler showed himself willing to take the deal without the quid pro quo, Eden of course protested. But Simon characteristically gave way. "Simon toys with [the] idea of letting G. [Germany] expand eastwards," Eden surmised. Eden himself was naturally "strongly" opposed. "Apart from its dishonesty," Eden noted, and this was where an acute realism aligned with his political instincts, "it would be our turn next."[82] Simon none the less drew consolation from Hitler's obsession with marching through to Eastern Europe.

Eden's reading of the situation was not far from that of Litvinov: to both, peace was indivisible. But it found no echo in cabinet. Whereas

Hitler could count on an official visit from the foreign secretary, Stalin merited only the arrival, unheralded, of the more junior Eden. Moreover, Permanent Under-Secretary Vansittart remarked upon "a lot of domestic opposition", even to the low-key Moscow visit. In an awkward echo of the 1920s, and giving a clear sign that the ambitious young minister felt the need to guard his back, Eden asked the Russians to commit to ending Communist propaganda in the empire.[83]

Not untypical of Conservative opinions was that of Lord Londonderry, one of Churchill's innumerable cousins. He was an extraordinarily wealthy man, with more than most to lose were genuine socialism to take power. Londonderry was of the view that Germany was the lesser evil: "that if the Nazi regime in Germany is destroyed, Germany will go Communist and we shall find a lining up of Communism between France, Germany and Russia".[84] Détente with Moscow was a reality, but an entente still hung uneasily in the balance. The slightest reinforcement of old fears could tip the scales, and the Germans knew and understood the British well.

Even though he should have been alert to the dangers Hitler represented, Sargent painted the decision of the French to align with Moscow in May 1935 as an unmitigated disaster. As late as November 1934 he was convinced that Hitler did not want war and that Germany would in any case not be ready for one "for some years yet".[85] So from that stance a Franco–Soviet alliance looked not only unnecessary but provocative. But there was more to his thinking. Something else had come to mind; a kind of substitute alibi. As he explained only a few months later, "[t]he need for expansion will force Germany towards the east as being the only field open to her, and as long as the Bolshevist régime exists in Russia it is impossible for this expansion to take merely the form of peaceful penetration".[86]

From London's vantage point Germany was invariably seen as the more likely partner and as willing to talk if the price were right. The overwhelming consensus tended in that direction. Even Wigram at the head of the Central European Department, usually portrayed as a diehard anti-German, worried lest even the appearance of a political rapprochement with Moscow would arouse suspicion in Berlin, and that the cabinet would not contemplate the prospect of rapprochement while hope remained of assuring peace by any other means.[87]

The *événements* in France further tipped the scales. From London Vansittart wrote in search of reassurance, "We want to know how far the swing to the left has really gone and if you think that it has at all endangered law and order, or the regime." Ambassador Sir George Clerk, however, was in no mood to put his mind at rest; quite the opposite: "It is extraordinarily reminiscent of the early days of the Russian Revolution, with Blum as an unconscious Kerensky and an unknown Lenin or Trotsky in the background."[88] Clerk really should not have worried so much. Although Marty freely acknowledged that the strikers were "the body and soul of the proletariat of Paris", he also admitted—though only within the walls of Comintern headquarters—that "this strike movement has seemed unexpected, inopportune to many comrades".[89]

Back in Paris nerves were unquestionably on edge within government. At a meeting of the left in the Chamber of Deputies the socialist interior minister stared at Ramette, the PCF Politburo member leading the Communist faction, and declared that the government would "maintain order without regard to and against everyone". Responding, and not the kind of man to be pushed around, certainly not in the current atmosphere, Ramette stood up and said that this would be possible only when the bosses gave the workers what they demanded. The law should also be imposed on the fascist leagues. Backing off, the interior minister then softened his tone.[90] Bourgeois deputies had every reason to feel the balance had swung far to the left. And even the PCF Politburo sounded defensive about the strikes.[91] The pressure was on to reach a settlement.

In an atmosphere of heightened tension a settlement between workers and bosses was finally signed at the prime minister's residence, the Hotel Matignon, on 7 June, forced through by Blum under direct pressure from the PCF. However, although sustained for decades to come, before long the deal proved illusory in respect of real wages. The cost of food had, even by early July, risen in the shops by 15%–20%. Smaller businesses went bankrupt. The addition of multiple days free from work could not be clawed back by industry, but the cost of living caught up with (in 1937) and then overtook (in 1938) the wage increases. The devaluation of the franc on 1 October 1936 by more than 20% saw to that. So pressure from the shop floor for higher wages mounted, particularly in industries associated with the war effort. And the CGT, backed by the PCF, stood four-square behind these demands. Inflation grew alarmingly from 7.7% in 1936 to 25.7% in 1937, 13.6% in 1938 and 17.8% in 1940, and as ever it fell hardest on the poor.

Something decisive had none the less happened that would take decades to reverse. Before 1936 capitalism indisputably dominated France. But no longer. And it was not the parlous state of the economy which, though serious, rendered the Blum experience "so dangerous, so threatening and even tragic", as the Swiss embassy reported, "but *more the emotional and clearly revolutionary atmosphere* in which he operates". The most flagrant violations of Republican law and order, the attacks on property and the right to work were cited as worsening a situation that was already alarming as the factory occupations continued unimpeded.[92] Marcel Cachin claimed that the PCF had told the workers that "this is not the only means of fighting; there are other methods. One needs to be prudent. In winning obvious advantages one must understand that this is only one stage and that later we will continue the class struggle."[93] But that continuation was precisely what the existing social order fretted about. The delay scarcely made business owners more confident about investing for the future.

Moreover, anxieties lest the trauma of June 1936 recur never entirely vanished despite reassurances from leaders of the PCF. A revolutionary culture had manifestly taken hold from below. The workers had come to accept Communism, "its flag, symbols and salute in a way which astonishes the impartial onlooker", the Irish ambassador noted, to his acute discomfort. "The Red Flag, the singing of the Internationale, the Communist salute of the closed fist are now as common in France and in certain quarters much more common than the tricolour and the singing of the Marseillaise."[94] A third force that was not completely under anyone's control emerged on the back of the PCF's policy of adapting to the middle-class mindset. This assimilation was evident at the 14 July celebrations in Paris with the eastern section of the city including the

Place de la Nation, the Place de la République and the Place de la Bastille "invaded by a frenzied crowd, decked in red and three-coloured flags, filing past members of the government and partying until late into the night to the endless repetition of the Carmagnole, the Internationale and the Marseillaise".[95] By the end of the year no fundamental change was evident. The "burning issue" remained "that of occupations of factories by striking workmen".[96]

The corrosive impact on foreign policy was noticeable in every direction. The combination of France's pact with the Soviet Union and incipient revolution at home was too much for Britain to swallow. France was effectively to be counted out. The guardians of Britain's security now warned that "what British opinion is not prepared to accept is the leadership of France over the whole field of foreign politics, or to admit responsibility for all the liabilities which she has been accumulating since the war in the shape of alliances on the farther side of Germany".[97]

Although he was apparently the beneficiary, for Stalin this was rather too much too quickly. He had an instinctive aversion to events taking place under foreign Communist auspices that he could not control were they to reach the point of revolution. Indeed, the Kremlin was no more optimistic than Whitehall. It was reported that Blum was not considered a weighty enough figure to lead French interests abroad. Moscow would have much preferred the pro-Soviet Radical Édouard Herriot or the stronger socialist Vincent Auriol (later president of France). The Italian embassy—as ever, unusually well informed—reported that "the wave of strikes, breaking out it seems spontaneously as a result of the unbridled demagogic rivalry during the election campaign, has prompted anxiety among leading circles and whether for reasons of foreign policy or considerations of domestic policy of the Communist Party". The Franco–Soviet pact was Moscow's "fundamental interest". Therefore it was crucial that "the French Government showed itself as 'strong' as possible in the international arena; above all free of domestic preoccupations". The conclusion was "that the Blum Government risks being of no use either for the purpose of Soviet foreign policy or for the French Communist Party, or, basically, for the reinforcement of the Popular

Front". The pessimistic prognostications that permeated Soviet official-
dom were of eventual collapse and a fierce reaction.[98]

Domestically, the prospect of spontaneous disorder from the left inevitably also raised intense anxiety about the possibility of a backlash from
the far right. Towards the end of June a letter to Blum and to Daladier had
called on the three parties—Radical, Socialist and Communist—to make
an appeal to the country in response to the atmosphere of civil war that
the fascists were trying to create.[99] Resistance to the Popular Front saw
the bourgeoisie stoop to new depths. The fact that Blum was Jewish, as
were a number of his ministers, led to a venomous resurgence of anti-
Semitism to an extent not known since the prosecution of the Jewish
Captain Dreyfus at the turn of the century.

Since the war the French left had identified closely with pacifism and
anti-military sentiment. The officer corps, in contrast, remained self-
consciously bourgeois. Minister of War Édouard Daladier was thus
under sustained pressure from the right and from the general staff to
ban the the socialist paper *Le Populaire* and the Communist paper
l'Humanité from the barracks.[100] The seventh congress of Comintern
had after all passed secret resolutions on the need to democratise the
armed forces and purge them of "fascist elements", particularly among
the officer corps and non-commissioned officers.[101] This policy continued even after the Germans entered the Rhineland and France ratified
the Franco–Soviet pact. In May Jacques Duclos, effectively number two
in the PCF leadership, told the press that "up to now" voting for military
expenditiure "would have indisputably meant sustaining imperialist
objectives". Only if certain reforms were introduced, Thorez added,
could the Communists be induced to vote for the budget.[102]

Fears of a coup by the armed forces were thus not entirely ground-
less. On the outbreak of the factory occupations the government discussed with the general staff whether force should be applied to end the
disorder. In the event Blum's advocacy of forced compromise between
employers and employees prevailed.[103] Much later, on 3 December,
Daladier sent a telegraphic despatch to officers commanding the various
military districts of Paris instructing them what to do in the event of
"disturbances of an insurrectional nature".[104] Usually very well informed,

and since his brief, bitter experience as ambassador to the Soviet Union was trenchantly anti-Communist, US Ambassador William Bullitt was acutely sensitive to the slightest signs of growth in Bolshevik influence, of which there were many. He welcomed the fact that Daladier "has taken pains to send all members of Communist cells in the Army first to jail for sixty days and then to the eastern garrisons". Daladier also confided to Bullitt that "he had urged Blum twenty times to cut loose from his Communist supporters and base himself on the Socialists, Radical Socialists and some of the Center Parties".[105] Blum, however, feared being pushed further to the right. This was the same month the PCF firmed up its support for him and finally voted for the defence budget.

These dramatic events made themselves felt far to the south. Beyond the Pyrenees, a spontaneous revolution was under way that the weak leadership of the Popular Front (*Frente Popular*) government in Spain was incapable of restraining. The reporting from the British embassy in Madrid was as alarmist as it had been from Paris only a month or two earlier. A disturbing indicator for the *Front populaire* government in France, and a straw in the wind, was the fact that in Spain its embassy, without exception—until the arrival of the new military attaché, Henri Morel—instinctively took the side of the rebels.[106]

9

Spain and the Schism of Europe

Can the League, or can Great Britain, do anything to prevent the
schism of Europe into two rival camps of Fascism and Communism?

—*THE ECONOMIST*[1]

On 18 July 1936 the outbreak of civil war in Spain and the splitting of
Europe into ideological blocs set back any hope of creating an effective
alliance that could contain Nazi Germany. After hearing that Berlin and
Rome had agreed on an anti-Bolshevik platform for co-operation in
secret intelligence that June, the French ambassador to Italy Charles de
Chambrun pleaded with Foreign Minister Ciano for closer relations
with France. He repeated more than once "his personal conception,
according to which 'horizontal' agreements [between states] lead to
peace, whereas 'vertical' ones [between states of only one type—fascist
on fascist, for example] would inevitably lead to a war".[2] This was surely
a fundamental truth of the interwar era. But the plea nevertheless fell
on deaf ears.

The steadfast attempts by those such as Chambrun to detoxify the
conduct of international relations had no effect. It was not just a ques-
tion of fascism. For nearly two decades relations between the Soviet
Union and the other states of Europe had been fundamentally unstable.
On the advent of the *Front populaire* the overthrow of capitalism by
Bolshevism remained the order of the day. The British propertied

classes, and not only they, had always dreaded the prospect of the Russians advancing into Central Europe—indeed, anywhere in their direction (or towards India). Those in the West who abjured class warfare and favoured classical balance-of-power politics divorced from ideology—the so-called "classicists"—now faced further difficulties. Not only was the Soviet Union unacceptable because of its mission as the harbinger of revolution but so too, increasingly, was its ally, France. Gladwyn Jebb, then a rising star at the Foreign Office, has since explained that "differing views between ourselves and the French as regards the correct treatment of Italy, to say nothing of the right policy to pursue in Spain, had put some of the 'classicists' in a rather difficult position".[3]

France itself faced an unenviable dilemma. Were the Spanish rebels to win, the fascist powers would threaten the *Front populaire* government on three sides, its prestige drastically reduced and the number of divisions it could mobilise lowered by at least six.[4] The civil war in Spain thus further complicated Britain's relations with the France of the *Front populaire*. Already allied to Moscow, Paris was ideologically at one with Madrid. Moreover, Mussolini had decided that now was the moment to raise aloft the banner of international fascist solidarity, as he had in February 1934, and to submerge lingering geopolitical differences with Germany over Austria in an ambitious quest to dominate the Mediterranean and create a *mare clausum*.

Spain resembled France in its anarcho-syndicalist heritage. But it differed in that islands of industrialisation to the north (Catalonia, Asturias and the Basque Country) were flanked by a massive and impoverished peasant hinterland to the south. It was also dissimilar in the degree of violent instability experienced in recent years. An aspirant fascist dictatorship in the 1920s under Primo de Rivera failed to root itself in the political culture. It was followed by the overthrow of the hapless monarch, Alfonso XIII, and the installation of a republic in 1931. And it was not just the vertical division by class that threatened the new order; no less fractious was the horizontal division by nation. Both Catalonia and the Basque Country sought home rule at almost any price. Spain was thus an intricate mosaic that was brittle to the touch.

Abortive Revolution, 1934

The birth of the republic proved an unexpected disappointment to its more radical proponents in that the electorate turned out to be far more conservative than anticipated. To the astonishment and fury of the left, against expectations the elections handed government over to the right. There the pro-fascist CEDA (Confederación Española de Derechas Autónomas) was led by José María Gil Robles. Though a constitutional-ist, he was also a self-proclaimed admirer of Hitler. He won a majority at election in 1933 but, because the leftist president Alcalá-Zamora re-fused to make Gil Robles prime minister, the more moderate conserva-tive Alejandro Lerroux was instead asked to form an administration. The coalition in due course collapsed and a new one was formed under peacemaker Ricardo Samper in April 1934. But this too foundered for want of support.

In hasty pursuit of an anti-fascist united front, Comintern fixed upon the flamboyant socialist leader Francisco Largo Caballero and offered him a meeting with the PCE and Comintern representatives "in another country" to discuss Spain.[5] On 3 October 1934 Gil Robles finally over-turned a second coalition that was too vacillating. This time he de-manded seats in the cabinet. After Hitler's tidal wave of repression, the violent clashes with the fascist leagues in Paris that February and the bloodshed in Vienna, the left was not about to give him the benefit of the doubt. An attempt was immediately made to overturn the new gov-ernment by means of a general strike. Plans were laid for 4 October. However, it rapidly collapsed through most of the country, including nationalist Barcelona, the capital of Catalonia, when the far right mo-bilised its own supporters. Asturias proved the exception. Here, on the north coast of Spain, events went further than even the left ever expected.

It was later claimed by Comintern secretary Manuilsky that "the gov-ernment provoked the Spanish workers into fighting prematurely".[6] Nonetheless, on 7 October Comintern had issued instructions that Communists should broaden the "mass strike and the armed struggle of the workers". The PCE was told to "approach the Left republican

party of AZANA [*sic*] and the Catalonian Left . . . with the proposal to
create a whole anti-fascist concentration composed of the alliance of
the workers with these parties in order to [secure?] the overthrow of
the LERROUX Government".[7] Asturias, in contrast to the rest of Spain,
housed a well-entrenched Communist Party. Unlike Catalonia, the anarchists were relatively weak. Of twenty-nine factory committees, the
PCE held twenty-two. The socialists called their supporters out onto
the streets, but the Communists increasingly made themselves felt.
Strikes had already begun over living standards: attempts to cut wages
and introduce labour-saving measures leading to more of the same.
Every day new disputes broke out over a variety of demands and before
long the entire mining zone had downed tools. Insurrection then
brought together socialists and Communists, who fought alongside one
another in spite of their sharp differences, under the recently formed
Alianzas Obreras (workers' alliances).

The only misgivings expressed at Comintern headquarters took the
form of regret that "we had hostages and nowhere it appears other than
Turon did we inflict red terror against the bourgeoisie". In the mining
town of Turon, unperturbed by any moral qualms, a Cheka sprung up
"which worked decisively and liquidated counter-revolutionary elements".[8] In the Asturian revolt priests were killed—some in a most hor-
rific manner—churches burned down, a cathedral vandalised. The
papal nuncio recorded that this was "the most extensive and most serious revolutionary movement that Spain had seen in many years".[9]
Around fifteen thousand troops despatched by General Francisco
Franco in Madrid went in to quell the revolt with savagery, deploying
notoriously brutal Moroccan troops and thereby reviving dread memories of the medieval Arab invasion and occupation of Spain. Most leading Communists managed through foresight to escape the bloody retribution that followed; the socialists, not so well organised, were less
fortunate. The losses amounted to 1,375 dead and 2,945 wounded.[10]

At Comintern Manuilsky declared that the rising could be compared
to the abortive Russian revolution of 1905 in its national significance. "It
demonstrated to the Spanish proletariat the need to take up arms for
the overthrow of bourgeois authorities," he asserted. "This is no small

lesson."[11] The impact of the revolt on the left was to demonstrate that Communists and socialists had objectives similar enough to warrant close political collaboration on the political stage. To the right it had a galvanising effect on the awareness of a standing threat of repeated insurrection from both socialists and Communists. The lessons were not lost abroad, either. Colonel Sir John Shute, MP, a British businessman, in conversation with the Duke of Alba recalled that the rising had been a "rehearsal" for what was to come, "the infinitely more awful Red Revolution, when the civilisation of Spain and the world was shaken to its roots".[12]

The Election of the *Frente Popular*

On 9 January 1936 the PCE reported to Moscow that parliament was being dissolved, elections were imminent and the prospects were of "a stiff fight". A Popular Front campaign on the French model was rushed into being on 15–16 January 1936, though there were scarcely any funds. The Spanish Party had no more than 48,000 francs. Comintern responded by despatching 200,000 francs via Paris, but they did not arrive on time.[13] It was thus to everyone's complete surprise that the *Frente Popular* won the majority at the elections on 16 February 1936. An electoral system that had previously worked to such advantage for the right now worked to the advantage of the left. With a difference of only four hundred thousand votes the left gained more than 250 seats in the Cortes and the right only 150. A military coup attempted on the following day failed. On 18 February Comintern adviser Codovilla reported that "the victory of the Popular bloc is overwhelming".[14]

The new government formed on 19 February was led by a moderate Republican, the writer Manuel Azaña. The circumstances were inauspicious, however. Mass demonstrations with calls to release the thirty thousand arrested in the revolt of October 1934 and clashes with the police had already begun in Madrid and regional capitals. Foreign observers were alert to the likelihood of serious further disturbances.[15] The departing prime minister, Gil Robles, asked the president not to hand over power and, facing obdurate refusal, headed across the frontier for the safety of fascist Portugal.

At the Holy See, on his arrival as minister at the British mission, D'Arcy Osborne had been "at once struck by the Vatican's obsession with communism".[16] Events in Spain did everything to magnify preexisting fears. The nuncio in Madrid, for one, did have genuine reasons for alarm. The shock of the bloody revolt in Asturias (1934) was never far from anyone's mind as a taste of things to come. Cardinal Tedeschini told Pius XI, "In my opinion Communism has in recent days officially and forcefully emerged on the Spanish horizon." Azaña had already embarked on a series of concessions to the extreme left, including amnesties, even for those once condemned to death. Should he continue in that direction, Tedeschini feared, then the worst could be expected.[17] Indeed, by the end of the month he had told the counsellor of the British embassy in Madrid "that he thought the situation far more serious than that of 1931 and, fearing that his life might be in danger from Communist elements as a result of a military *coup d'état* which might occur at any moment, asked whether he could, if necessary, seek asylum in His Majesty's Embassy".[18]

Everywhere the streets were teeming with youths dressed in red, clenched fists in the air. "The demonstration this Saturday", Tedeschini wrote, "although smaller, made the greatest and most awful impression. It was the glorification of prisoners and the glorification of crime. Here the one receiving the greatest applause was a woman known by the pseudonym 'La Pasionaria' and she made a point of striking the most extreme pitch, calling for the head of this or that politician. Whoever saw this demonstration was certain that she was to be feared!" In Madrid the Communists, although a small party with only fifteen deputies in the Cortes, had received more than half the votes from the local population.

Worse still, the nuncio was firmly convinced that there was "no difference between Communism and Socialism".[19] "Demonstrations," Tedeschini added, "permitted and carried out with great show mainly in the capital, not only under the eyes of the authorities but in their presence and therefore with their consent, have effectively emboldened the extreme parties, and have given the impression that the Government either has not the power or has not the will to maintain order because it is indebted to them."[20]

Land seizures were retrospectively legitimised by the Instituto de Reforma Agraria, which the government had brought into being. A Spanish politician told the Swedish ambassador that he was "very pessimistic about the situation. A large part of the nation has slid over to the left and the situation in Spain at present is very reminiscent of that prevailing in Russia under Kerensky."[21] "The authorities", relates the former Communist Tagüeña, "were overwhelmed and were unable to oppose illegal acts, terrorism, the burning of churches. . . . Public order had fundamentally broken down".[22] A rising tide of reports came in from parishes across the country of the burning of churches and monasteries and the widespread intimidation of the clergy, to the point that they were given leave to dress as laymen to disguise their calling.[23] The pope strongly complained of the prevalent violence to the new Spanish ambassador at the Vatican on 4 May.[24] Not surprisingly, along with the great landowners, the clergy almost to the man—and also the nuns—consolidated to form one of the strongest pillars of the new order Franco brought into being. Panic had set in among those with most to lose. The number of those fleeing into fascist Portugal was so great as to give rise to the epithet "chicken run". Tagüeña recalls, "The impatience of the victors and the fear of the defeated inevitably led to a climate of violence across the entire country."[25] "Spain is heading for civil war", the Irish ambassador noted as early as 17 April, "unless the Government takes very prompt measures to render excesses impossible."[26]

In Moscow there also emerged an underlying tone of rising concern. The Bolsheviks were not about to be taken in by appearances, as too much was at stake. Red Madrid, where terrified foreign diplomats lived and reported from, was not typical of Spain. No one at Comintern exaggerated the government's legitimacy: plainly it was "not a government of the popular front but a bourgeois government of the left". Indeed, Comintern welcomed it only as the lesser evil in the face of a greater danger. The gap in consciousness between its leadership and the wild expectations of the rank and file of the tiny PCE was thus colossal. This sense of caution was increasingly reflected in the defensiveness of the instructions sent to the PCE: "in spite of the fact that it is not a popular front government we consider that you should support the AZANA [*sic*] Government against attacks and possible coups d'état from reactionaries, so that it may carry out the electoral programme of the popular front".[27] For his part, Azaña had for some time viewed the PCE as a "relatively weak force", so it had never entered much into his calculations.[28]

He was right to do so. Buoyed up by this heady atmosphere, the Spanish Communist Party was out of its depth and poorly advised. General Secretary José Díaz commanded respect in Moscow, but his health was chronically bad and he was unable to manage everything his role required. His éminence grise, the Italo-Argentinian Vittorio Codovilla (nicknamed comrade "Codo") was condemned in no uncertain terms by Comintern secretary Marty for behaving like a *cacique*—a local party boss—instead of merely an adviser from Comintern. Despite Dimitrov's insistence that such advisers not act like petty dictators, as they had done up to 1934—"Turkestanis", as they were known—"Codo" arrived at work at nine, wrote the editorials for the party paper, *Mundo Obrero*, delegated tasks to Politburo members as subordinates and gave audience to regional party secretaries, sending them on their way with his instructions.[29] Even before events broke, in other words, the PCE was fundamentally dysfunctional. The crisis just made this fact all the more apparent to Moscow. Inevitably it was only a matter of weeks before the Russians took it in hand.

The British Overreact

But would knowing that the Communists proper were weak and badly led have changed anything for the rebels or the Western powers? As events soon demonstrated, the cleavage of Spain ran too deep and the high spirits extended well beyond Moscow's ability to contain them. It was not Russia's role through Comintern that was of concern, so much as the revolution itself, which began to carry all before it, including the PCE, just as the lesser unrest was to do in Paris. In response to the groundswell of unrest bubbling up from below, encouraged by the more radical anarcho-syndicalists, the PCE reported that the Azaña government "under pressure from the masses" was going "even further" than the Popular Front program. "The revolutionary position is developing rapidly. The solution of the land-problem by revolutionary methods will not be long in establishing itself with the development of the struggle, and the problem of power."[30]

Contrary to expectation, the response was quick and blunt. Extravagant hopes had to be stilled. Comintern was "much alarmed because deeds are being perpetrated which are helping the cause of the anti-revolutionists, such as frequent clashes between the masses and the armed forces of the Government", adding the advice: "Do not on any account let yourselves be provoked, do not precipitate events, as it would be harmful to the revolution at this moment and would only lead to the triumph of the anti-revolutionaries." The PCE was left in doubt: "The creation of soviet power is not the order of the day."[31]

This was certainly not what was generally believed. In London the fleeting access to Comintern cyphers from 1934–36 had been discovered by the Russians in late August and curtailed with the despatch of fake messages that would mislead the British. So all the Foreign Office had to rely upon when they realised this was the none-too-accurate guesswork of its diplomats. In Spain during the disorders of late March, the British ambassador Sir Henry Chilton was as nervous as the nuncio. Like Clerk in Paris, Chilton and his good colleague the Swedish ambassador in Madrid likened the prevailing unrest to the situation in Russia "prior to the Bolshevik Revolution". His prognostications became ever more gloomy. A coup was to be expected from the far left in order to "set up a Soviet Republic, in which case the lives and property of no one will be safe". Similarly, the consul-general in Barcelona, the heartland of anarcho-syndicalism, reflected on the "considerable risk of revolutionary chaos in Spain, when efforts might even be made to set up Soviet governments in part of the country". The British, heavily invested in the regional status quo, also credited the possibility of a spill-over into Portugal under its fascist dictator António de Oliveira Salazar. From Lisbon Ambassador Charles Wingfield reported that "Spain was in for a prolonged period of red rule", with the likelihood that "communism in Portugal would become a danger".[32] And MI6 took the firm view that "the establishment of a Soviet regime in the Iberian Peninsula is hardly a happening which anyone can view with equanimity for military, political or economic reasons".[33]

The British had reason to worry. In Moscow Dimitrov struck an optimistic note, sensibly hedged with caution. In Spain, he told a meeting of the Comintern secretariat on 5 June, "good weather has broken out. The sun is shining. How long this will last, no one knows. We would like this to continue until the final victory of the proletarian revolution. Whether this comes about, we have no idea."[34] Possessed of a mere twenty thousand members in a country of some twenty-four million, the PCE was in no condition to head a revolution, however, even though by late May its membership had quadrupled.[35] The bulk of the organised working class belonged to either the socialist (UGT) or the anarchist (CNT) trades union. On his own initiative Politburo member Jesús Hernández came to Moscow with "Codo", ostensibly to "correct" policy. But in practice the pair boasted of their (very limited) successes, including raising local militias, mobilising local authorities on behalf of the unemployed and recruiting army officers as party members. Their only misgivings appeared to be with respect to lack of progress in relations with the anarchists and the notorious problem of Catalan separatism.[36] More significant, however, were rumours reported by the Italian consul in San Sebastián on 23 June of an insurgent movement emerging on the far right under German auspices.[37]

Dimitrov fully understood the urgent need to deflate the prevailing euphoria. Having encouraged the government to undertake necessary reforms, including land redistribution, the Spanish comrades were told to pay more attention now to the dangers from the far right. For their part the Spanish agreed "that there is such a danger and that this danger is growing". If they ignored it, Dimitrov insisted, "this entire program of yours won't be worth a brass farthing".[38] The stern rebuke was reinforced a week later with the added stricture that the party should "not be posing yet as an immediate task a transition from completing the bourgeois democratic revolution to a socialist revolution".[39] The Spanish comrades were also strongly advised, following the French example set by Thorez, to convince women that the party was not anti-Catholic.[40] But that was easier said than done.

Civil War

By mid-July the political temperature had shot up to the scorching level of a Madrid summer. The new leader of the monarchists, José Calvo Sotelo, was assassinated by Captain Moreno, a leftist police officer, on 13 July. Moreno had also planned to assassinate Gil Robles but could not find him at home. Comintern judged the situation "very critical". It cautioned that "the danger comes from the anarchist leaders who persist in prolonging the strikes with the idea of bringing the workers face to face with the Government".[41] On 17 July the party was advised "to do what you have omitted to do before, due to the lack of firmness on the part of your allies in the Popular Front, that is to say, taking full and immediate advantage of the present alarming situation, create, in conjunction with the other parties of the Popular Front, alliances of workers and peasants, elected as mass organisations, to fight against the conspirators in defence of the workers' and peasants' militia".[42]

But events were fast moving out of control. Only the previous day the Italian consul-general in Tangier reported that "following the murder of Deputy Calvo Sotelo a new insurrection is being prepared in Spain that will be carried out by General Franco, now governor of the Canaries".[43] It was around this time that Italy's foreign minister Ciano told the Soviet ambassador that an uprising from the right was to be expected in the very near future.[44] Indeed, on 17 July Franco flew into Spanish Morocco from the Canaries to begin the revolt with the same brutal troops he had deployed to crush the uprising in Asturias. This was the first step in a larger plan. Within two days Morocco had fallen to the rebels. On 20 July in Tangier Franco pressed the Italian military attaché with some urgency to provide aircraft for the transportation of his foreign legion to the mainland.[45]

There the revolt centred to the south-west on Seville. Orazio Pedrazzi, the Italian ambassador in Madrid, predicted that "Spanish democracy is being drowned in a civil war that will make way for either reaction of a military type or a socialist radicalisation of an increasingly Bolshevik kind".[46] It was not, Pedrazzi emphasised, "a simple military coup as before. . . . The picture facing us is as follows: on one side the

Popular Front, on the other hand the other forces of the nation that can go on no longer. Farmers tired of the invasions and disorder from Bolsheviks in the countryside; builders tired of the endless strikes; the lower middle class saturated by agitation; Catholics and priests threatened every day of their lives as are their possessions; this is the bloc that is coalescing around the rebel army that has at its head the most notable and popular generals in Spain."[47]

The rebels needed help and sought it primarily from Italy. The day of Pedrazzi's despatch, 20 July, the ex-king of Spain Alfonso XIII described to Mussolini "the enormous importance of the Spanish movement. Modern pieces of aviation are needed", he wrote, "and with the purpose of obtaining them Juan La Cierva (the inventor of the compass [helicopter]) and Luis Bolin, people who have my complete confidence, are en route to Rome". The bearer of the letter, the Marqués de Viana, would explain everything in detail.[48] Once again the Italian attaché in Tangier pressed his superiors in Rome for aid. Fascist forces were being repulsed. Regulars had disembarked at Cádiz and were on their way to Córdoba. Further south, Málaga was a centre of resistance.[49] But officials in Rome were disinclined to give the rebels what they needed and told Luccardi in Tangier to turn them down or tell them to wait.[50] Mussolini was clearly weighing the odds and was not to be bounced into a premature decision with momentous consequences, given that he had, in effect, finally persuaded the British to accept defeat over the Italian conquest of Abyssinia. Franco unsurprisingly saw Mussolini as myopic, given the influence Italy and Germany could have over Spain were the rebels to win.[51]

Franco and Anti-Communism

Backed into a corner, Franco then played his trump card—anti-Communism. He told the Italian consul-general in Tangier that the aim of the rebels was not party political, but "to save Spain from Bolshevism and form a government in the fascist mode. He is convinced", Pier De Rossi argued, "that he is fighting not only for the future of his country but for the peace of Latin people and this section of the Mediterranean, because the arrival of Bolshevism in Spain would inevitably translate to serious disorder in Portugal, as yet unfit to defend itself, and to an unstable structure in France."[52]

What made Italian assistance more probable was news from the naval attaché in Paris that came through on 22 July. The Spanish government had sent emissaries to Paris in search of twenty-five bombers plus ammunition, artillery pieces, machine guns and rounds. Blum and leftist diehard aviation minister Pierre Cot were in favour but the more moderate foreign minister Yvon Delbos—with an ear to London—was resistant for fear of international complications. The French ambassador in Madrid, who favoured the rebels, was also seeking ways of sabotaging the request.[53] A day later Cerruti reported that Blum and Cot had decided to supply weapons without consulting the cabinet.[54] But Mussolini was not likely to ignore any form of French aid to the republic. The French, driven by a sense of ideological solidarity and a determination to bolster their like-minded neighbour, had unthinkingly lit a fuse that would ultimately detonate an uncontrolled explosion. French involvement tipped the balance towards Italian intervention. Earlier that year Mussolini declared that, on the one hand, Britain was "our enemy"; on the other, "France has betrayed us".[55] Ideological and geopolitical considerations pointed in the same direction. Cardinal secretary of state at the Vatican Pacelli noted that "certainly Mussolini and Hitler are at odds but it is inevitable that if Spain goes Bolshevik, if France is turbulent, then Italy will feel all the more thrust towards Germany as the only door open".[56]

Throughout the following week confusion reigned, however. Communications were down across most of the country; to telegraph Rome the Italian ambassador to Spain was driven to San Sebastián, where all the ambassadors were now quartered. The Russians had no idea what was going on. They had no ambassador in Spain, nor even a newspaper correspondent. Although there had been no shortage of warnings that a rebellion was on the cards, Comintern was itself entirely "unprepared, taken by surprise".[57] Without aid from Mussolini, however, the rebels were in trouble. On 20 July, much too complacent for his own good, General Secretary of the PCE José Díaz reported that the "military insurrection was crushed. In a few parts of the country the struggle is still developing, but there is nothing definite. The fight was fierce and to the death. It was the workers' militia that decided the victory."[58] Only hours later the more prudent "Codo", alert to Moscow's concerns, sounded a more cautious note. "The development of the fight", he reported, "shows that the insurgents have a complete military plan and a majority in the army. The situation continues to be difficult." The rebels held Morocco, the Canaries, Seville, Córdoba, Valladolid, Navarre and more. They were targeting Madrid.[59] Fearing that the government might prove ineffective, Comintern ordered the formation of a committee in defence of the republic.[60] "You must listen to us every three hours," Moscow insisted.[61] "We are listening all the time", came the tetchy response.[62]

Comintern was right to worry that the Spanish comrades had taken off into a fantasy world. Perhaps this was not surprising. The party had in recent years been growing, Dimitrov noted, but "its cadres are not particularly qualified politically; they do not have a great deal of political experience".[63] At a meeting of Comintern's secretariat in September Dimitrov angrily read out telegraphic exchanges immediately after the coup—including an absurdly self-congratulatory message from Madrid celebrating the fact that they had got hold of a printing press, and an excitable reference to a message from Codovilla about wiping out "kulaks" (rich peasants) in Valencia, as though this were the Soviet Union undergoing collectivisation.[64]

Three days after the coup Díaz persisted in his misplaced optimism. He assured Moscow he was "convinced that we shall crush the enemy decisively, and that this will be the first step in the realisation of the revolutionary democratic programme".[65] In a bizarre gesture, and with a lot still to learn about self-control, he declared that he would ask to join the government. This suggestion evidently met with no response. And on 23 July he solemnly announced that "the fascist insurrection is definitely crumbling!"[66] This elicited an abrupt reprimand. Comintern swiftly retorted, "You must not allow yourselves to be carried away by the initial successes."[67] Within Madrid the mob likewise got carried away. "In fact, the government scarcely exists," wrote Fontanel, the Swiss chargé d'affaires, sheltering some fifty-five terrified nationals within the walls of the embassy from the madness in the streets.[68] Factories were being raided by armed mobs, who swarmed into hotels demanding meals. Almost all the churches were burned to the ground. "The red terror is spreading everywhere to some degree," noted Fontanel. "I really fear that Bolshevism is taking over for a period it is impossible to foresee those parts where the rebellion has not made itself felt." He added, "It takes, as you know, little time to destroy what the years have put in place. The red militia are taking over the restaurants and hotels, threatening the owners in a tone of people certain of what they are about."[69] And he was not just worrying about his lunch.

As we have seen, this lofty air of triumphalism worried Moscow, too, as it spelt complacency in the face of a growing menace. Díaz and Codovilla were once again reprimanded on 24 July, and in no uncertain terms:

> Your information is insufficient; it is not concrete but sentimental. Once again we ask you to send us serious and effective information.
>   We insist that you:
>
> 1. Concentrate everything on the most important needs of the moment, i.e., the speedy suppression and the final liquidation of the fascist uprising.
> 2. Avoid any measures that could undermine the unity of the Popular Front in the fight against the rebels.
> 3. Forestall any tendency towards overestimating our own strength and the strength of the Popular Front and towards underestimating the difficulties and new dangers.
> 4. Don't rush ahead and clash with the stance of the democratic régime and don't desert the ranks of the struggle for a genuinely democratic republic.
> 5. For the time being it is possible to get by without the direct participation of Communists in the government; it is advantageous not to enter the government thereby making it easier to sustain the unity of the Popular Front. Join the government only in the extreme event that it is absolutely necessary for the purposes of suppressing the uprising.

6. We consider it now valuable that when suppressing the uprising one has to unite all forces both of the popular militia and the regular forces of the republic, to raise the question of replacing the regular army with a people's militia; all the more so because in the current fighting a new republican army is being forged; together with the popular militia it will form the fulcrum of the republican régime against foreign and domestic enemies. Use every means to attract loyal officers from among the republicans to the side of the people and induce units of rebels to cross to the side of the Popular Front. The government has to issue an amnesty for those that immediately desert the ranks of the rebels and come over to the side of the people.

Dimitrov copied the telegram to Stalin, who approved it for despatch.[70]

In Spain desertion from the armed forces was led by the most senior officers. The republic no longer had a general staff.[71] Moreover, the Italians calculated that the rebels could count on 7,000 officers but the republic only 260.[72] The balance of power did not look good. Defence of the existing order had to take priority. Moscow did all it could to put its foot on the revolutionary brake. Contradicting advice given only a day before, no doubt after Stalin had been consulted, the PCE was instructed not to raise a popular militia but to stick with the official defence of the republic. Land could be confiscated without compensation, but this was to apply only to rebels, as punishment.[73] At the end of the month Dimitrov held meetings with Pollitt, Thorez and others to counteract the "inertia" with which the coup had been received. Although the PCE had warned well in advance that a coup was likely and Comintern's press had repeatedly publicised the threat, "Communist Parties were unprepared, the Spanish events took them by surprise."[74]

France Flip-Flops on Aid to Spain

On 25 July France had hastily decided to aid the republic, only to countermand instructions two days later (evidently under direct pressure from London).[75] Italy then committed itself to help the rebels.[76] The most immediate task was to ship in troops from Morocco to the mainland.[77] The French foreign minister had told missions abroad that they would not intervene in the internal affairs of other countries, but private industry none the less supplied planes to the Spanish Republic.[78] On 28 July the rebels were told that munitions were on their way from Italy.[79] And, after much pleading with Berlin, on 29 July German aircraft began arriving in Cádiz, along with eighty-five officers and specialists.[80] In the German capital the French ambassador was struck by the manner in which "leading circles of the Reich follow with passion the events that are unfolding in Spain". What was most apparent was the "greater degree of harshness than ever with which they attack the USSR". This bore all the marks of an emerging crusade.[81]

It was not just Franco who framed the rebellion in terms of the fight against Bolshevism. So too did Mussolini. "No one should be surprised if today we raise the flag of anti-Bolshevism. For that is our old flag! For we were born under that sign!" More significantly to those on the right of the British political spectrum, Mussolini speciously insisted that "it is time to put an end to holding Fascism and democracy in opposition to one another".[82] Elsewhere events seemed to moving in the same direction. On 4 August, confronted by the prospect of an indefinite general strike threatened by Communist deputies, the prime minister of Greece General Ioannis Metaxás, with the connivance of King George II, whom he had restored to the throne only the year before, declared a state of emergency that was to all intents and purposes a coup d'état. Metaxás told the Italian minister in Athens, Raffaele Boscarelli, to tell Rome that "it was a dictatorship that I have myself instituted in agreement with the sovereign. . . . I was inspired by Italy's example and I hope that your government will look on with sympathy at the road I propose taking in the interests of my country."[83] But however corporatist Greece became, it was unlikely to be able to wean itself from British influence and wholly adopt the Italian model. Greece was well within the gunsights of the Royal Navy. But it was a sign of the times, none the less.

Cardinal Secretary of State Pacelli, as well-informed as ever, told the French ambassador that before the outbreak of the civil war in Spain anti-Communist solidarity had played its part in consolidating relations between Germany and Italy, but that "it has since become the dominant factor". Moreover, Pacelli remarked, the civil war itself was exerting "a profound impact . . . in the eyes of countries whose domestic make-up is reckoned to be the most targeted by Communism and even in the eyes of various other countries that are less officially anti-Communist". Here Pacelli referred to Portugal, Belgium and France.[84] As if to illustrate the cardinal's comments, André François-Poncet, the staunchly conservative French ambassador in Berlin, told his opposite number from Italy that "the establishment of a Communist government in Spain would of itself be a legitimate cause for concern and thus European intervention".[85]

British Conservative Sympathy with the Rebels

As we have noted, a crucial obstacle to the French supply of arms to the Spanish government was Britain, already deeply suspicious of its neighbour because of the latter's mutual assistance pact with Moscow, the election of the *Front populaire* government and its benign attitude to the occupation of the factories in Paris and beyond. Most Conservatives—even those such as Churchill who were fully committed against the appeasement of Hitler—instinctively took the side of Franco in the struggle. On 26 July, the day after the French government resolved to aid the Spanish Republic, Baldwin forthrightly "told Eden . . . that on no account, French or other, must he bring us in to fight on the side of the Russians".[86] This, passed across the Channel, explains why the French rapidly reversed their course as abruptly as they had taken the initial decision. Three days later the Italian chargé d'affaires Count Leonardo Vitetti spent several hours with Leo Amery. A highly intelligent man, a prize fellow of All Souls, Oxford, Amery had no illusions about Hitler's Germany. As colonial secretary (1924–29) he had, however, always been more pragmatic than fellow ministers such as Churchill about the dangers of Bolshevism. No longer.

Vitetti met Amery at the House of Commons. "The Spanish revolution", Amery insisted, "has brought to the forefront of our policy the problem of the defence of Europe from the menace of Bolshevism.

There is no one in England that is not convinced that Spanish Communism has been organised from Moscow and there isn't anyone deluded about the danger of growing Soviet influence in France hastening the dissolution of the structure of politics in France. We are alarmed by the policy of the Popular Front and by the consequences Franco–Soviet collaboration could have for Europe. The Franco–Soviet pact constitutes at this moment the greatest obstacle to any attempt at collaboration in Europe, and England must make every effort to induce France to abandon it." Amery did not want to find Britain "exposed to having to defend Russia" and certainly not to "allow itself to be dragged into a war with Germany because of a Russo–German conflict". The pact constituted "a danger not only to peace but also to the social stability of Europe". For this reason, he concluded, "France had to choose between Russia and the West European Great Powers".[87] Such views were shared by the palace. King Edward VIII was described by a friend as "pro-German, against Russia, and against too much slipshod democracy".[88] Later, his hand-picked equerry, Dudley Forwood, recalled, "We were not averse to Hitler politically. We felt that the Nazi regime was a more appropriate government than the Weimar Republic, which had been extremely socialist [sic]."[89]

Vitetti talked to Churchill just over a week later. The ambassador found Churchill troubled by conflicting loyalties—not wanting to see a parliamentary system in Spain succumb to a dictatorship but wholly averse to Communism. Churchill was also preoccupied with the danger that Italy would demand bases in the Balearic Islands or Morocco in return for aiding the rebels. But, once reassured on this point, he reverted to old fears. "In arming the Communists", Churchill said, "the Spanish Government has assumed a tremendous responsibility. . . . Comintern's tactics are exposed clearly in Spain, consisting of favouring the advent of a weak government that can be overturned easily by force and establish a soviet régime. The bolshevisation of Spain would be a veritable disaster for Europe and would give the Soviet Government a new impulse dangerous to every country." And for France to intervene would be "truly suicidal". France was, he said, "copying the Soviet Russians. Blum, as the government of France, conducts a policy of neutrality, and as the Popular Front the policy of intervention. Moscow as a government conducts a policy of neutrality and as Comintern incites, finances and arms Spanish Communism against Europe and against the British Empire."[90]

Vitetti also reported Eden's implausible denial that he had "exerted pressure on Blum to persuade him not to furnish arms to the Spanish Government. None the less the opinion is widespread that he had made Blum understand what a sinister effect French intervention in the Spanish revolution would have on Franco–British relations."[91] The Italians were delighted at this turn of events. After talking to Ciano, the Polish ambassador to Italy reported home that "in Paris just as in London there is by all accounts anxiety prevailing at the fascist, Germanophile attitudes resulting from the Spanish uprising."[92]

That very day a telegram from Moscow to Paris calling for substantial support for the government in Madrid emphasised that "defeat of the Spanish Republic would be defeat for France's Popular Front".[93] Two days later Thorez reported that the Germans were "feverishly" arming the rebels.[94] Comintern was slow to respond, though its weekly, *Inprecorr*, finally appeared on 1 August with an entire issue impressively devoted to Spain. And a last-minute decision was made in Moscow on 3 August for a mass demonstration in Red Square in support of the Republic.[95] Only four days later the Russians informed French comrades that troops were disembarking from Morocco, with direct German and Italian aid also arriving, at a time when the *Front populaire* had acted forcefully in favour of neutrality. This "creates a great danger for the outcome of the Spanish people's struggle", Comintern hastened to warn the PCF.[96]

The greater need for urgency is apparent from Vitetti's telegram to Ciano on 5 August, not long after the French government raised the idea of an agreement on non-intervention. "The main preoccupation of the English at this time is to obtain from France an undertaking not to assist the Spanish government and renounce once and for all any idea of intervening in the revolution," he wrote.[97] In London suspicion of the French had not abated. Secretary of the Committee of Imperial Defence Sir Maurice Hankey rejected the idea of any alliance with France which, he insisted, was "half-riddled with discontent and communism" and tied to the Russians who aimed to "force Bolshevism on a shattered Europe".[98]

Vansittart stayed with his brother-in-law, Phipps, at the British embassy in Berlin for a fortnight from the end of July and passed through Paris on his return in mid-August. Deeply Francophile, Vansittart confided to the secretary general at the Quai d'Orsay, "M. Blum must remember, as I had told him in Paris, that the British Government was upheld by a very large Conservative majority, who were never prepared, and now probably less than ever, to make much sacrifice for red eyes. The Russian aspect of Spain could not fail to make a difference in these sections of English feeling." Vansittart warned that should France move "further to the Left" he "was by no means sure of the effect of such a development on my own countrymen".[99]

What will have made matters worse for the British was that the Russian military began angling once more for consultations with the French general staff. Invitations to do so had been made on 29 May 1935 and were repeated more than once before Deputy Commissar for Defence Tukhachevsky made the proposal to a senior French officer observing the autumn manoeuvres in Byelorussia that September. But the French were too nervous to accept, as were the Czechs, for fear of upsetting the Germans.[100]

Meanwhile the Italian consul-general in Barcelona reported on the ever more blatant arrival of planes, bombs, and armoured cars along with hundreds of volunteers by the day from France, including Italians in exile.[101] Inevitably this prompted a response. Not everyone waited on Moscow's word. The cause of the Spanish Republic excited a latent internationalism among those who themselves had been subjected to fascist repression and had been driven abroad. Disgusted by the inaction around him, Carlo Rosselli of Giustizia e Libertà, a tiny but vociferous group of Italian exiles, announced that "the Spanish revolution is our Revolution". He did not restrict himself to words. He immediately set about organising a group of Italian volunteers in Barcelona: the Ascaso column that fought for the first time on 28 August. The slogan Rosselli made famous before he was assassinated in 1937 was "Today

Spain, Tomorrow Italy".[102] Others, Italian Communists, also joined military formations in the Catalan capital.[103]

Comintern Aid?

Such spontaneous displays of internationalism were the exception rather than the rule, however. Leading Italian Communist Luigi Longo recalls that "at the outbreak of the Franco revolt there was some hesitation on the part of Communist parties from various countries to undertake fundamental assistance to the armed struggle of the Spanish republicans".[104] The PCF, the party most affected, was one of the most insular. It had instinctively reacted to the coup in terms of what it meant for France, where fascists might be tempted to copy the Spanish example.[105] And even then it proved difficult to impress upon party leaders and their officials a sense of urgency comparing to enjoyment of the newly established salaried summer break.

Not just the leaders of the CGT but also others were out of town, leaving Duclos to hold the fort (Thorez was in Russia), putting pressure on Blum and others to aid the Republic. Not surprisingly Comintern official Ernő Gerő sent a telegram to Moscow on 3 August, the first line of which read, "Up to now the French have carried out next to nothing of the directives concerning Spain."[106] On 8 August Comintern's *Inprecorr* appeared with the desperate plea: "Not Passive Sympathy but Active Help for the People of Spain". On 10 August the insurrection briefly reached the top of the PCF's Politburo agenda.[107] But, as Spanish delegates turned up at the Gare d'Orsay on 31 August to meet with their French counterparts, only Marty was there to greet them; the other Communist leaders were still on holiday. Moreover, no interviews with *l'Humanité* had been arranged. Marty was understandably incensed. Unquestionably the PCF had, in Marty's carefully chosen words, "no sense of the gravity of the situation".[108]

By 21 September matters not only failed to improve, but had if anything worsened. Spain had slipped to as low as sixth on the agenda of the French Politburo, and as late as 8 October the attention of the leadership still focused on "economic demands, in the first instance of the unemployed and the middle classes"—though this may have had less to do with ignoring Spain and more to do with preventing the far right from making trouble at home.[109] The significance of this would appear to be borne out by Thorez's remark at the Central Committee meeting on 16 October to the effect that in France "a violent counter-offensive from reaction" was blocking the progress of the *Front populaire*.[110] Comintern's secretariat was pressing ahead, however. On 7 August a more sober report from Díaz had finally acknowledged that it would be "a long and hard struggle".[111] And the shortages of men and matériel were dire. Sending technical personnel from France was said to be impossible because "it would create a great scandal".[112] From Spain came news that the situation was "very critical because of the non-delivery of arms".[113]

The government in Catalonia was devoid of officers for its fifteen-thousand-strong militia (mainly anarchists). Indeed, the situation was desperate when Vladimir Antonov-Ovseenko arrived in October to take up his post as the Soviet consul-general in Barcelona. He had no hesitation in confessing to his British opposite number that he thought Franco's military "were bound to win".[114] In the Basque Country they were also severely short of ammunition. The Republic as a whole was desperately short of pilots. On 11 August Comintern contacted Earl Browder, who worked as a Soviet military intelligence officer as well as secretary of the Communist Party USA. Could he find pilots? Some were found but at first they never made it out of Paris to Spain; chaos reigned.[115] The Italian consul-general in Barcelona did, however, soon report the arrival of thirty French bombers at the Llobregat airport, the French pilots staying on in Spain after delivery.[116]

Stalin Procrastinates

The Soviet government proper still hung back from action, though straws were appearing in the wind. On 9 August Voroshilov appointed Brigade Commander (tank corps) Vladimir Gorev, a former anarchist but an experienced officer in the Fourth Directorate, as adviser to the Republic, and Bruno Windt, a member of the KPD, also from the Fourth, as his radio operator.[117] On 10–11 August Mikhail Kol'tsov for

Pravda and Ilya Ehrenburg for *Izvestiya* were also despatched to Madrid.[118]

On 13 August Gerő reached the capital but was told to return to Paris with all the detail he could muster on the coup and on German and Italian aid for the rebels.[119] Despite Marty's activism Comintern had thus far done little more than issue declarations. Nevertheless Moscow was being irrevocably, albeit reluctantly, sucked into the maelstrom. In the Politburo, with Stalin out at his datcha on the coast of the Black Sea, his hatchet man Lazar Kaganovich was charged with responsibility for Spanish affairs.

On leave in London the first secretary at the British embassy in Berlin, Ivone Kirkpatrick, shocked by what he had seen in Germany, openly expressed his disgust at the Foreign Office, "which he says is spineless and at sixes and sevens".[120] Even the more intelligent and more experienced, however, had signally failed to adjust their antennae to the new realities—not least because they could not stomach the prospect of any close association with Moscow. From 21 September 1936 Sargent, the under-secretary of state, was one such.

Sargent had in late 1936 belatedly sought to revive a Concert of Europe, having done his best to block the multilateral Eastern Locarno project pushed by the Russians in 1934. What he foresaw, as did *The Economist*, was the division of the continent into ideologically opposing camps. Spain was the catalyst, but France, as he saw it, was the real problem. Yet Sargent, the son of a gentleman of independent means, was, unsurprisingly, resolutely anti-Communist. So what he proposed inevitably had an anti-Soviet edge to it. Indeed, its gist anticipated a line of appeasement that came to be identified with Neville Chamberlain, based as it was on assumptions about the motives for German and Italian policies that bore little relation to the facts on the ground and which necessitated, on the part of the British, pressure to force the French into line.

Sargent suggested strongly that "we ought to be able to strengthen the French Government in its efforts—or indeed bring pressure to bear to force it—to free itself from Communist domination, both domestic and Muscovite. Even though this might involve at a certain stage something very like interference in the internal affairs of France, surely it would be worth while running this risk?" As to the two fascist powers, however, the task lay in removing their "feeling" of being isolated. "Moreover," Sargent continued, "in so far as the fear of the spread of Communism is bringing Germany and Italy to co-operate, this fear is centred not so much on what is going to happen in Spain as on what is going to happen in France. Both Governments, for different reasons, dread the prospect of a France weakened or paralysed by Communist infection." To Sargent this pointed in the direction of "(1) our preventing France by hook or by crook from 'going Bolshevik' under the influence of the Spanish civil war; and (2) our freeing Italy from the feeling of isolation and vulnerability which the Abyssinian Affair has left her with".[121] The focus on France was reported by the US ambassador in London, where he found everyone "more anxious and apprehensive than I have ever seen them before". He also found "grave reason to apprehend a blow-up in France".[122]

The Poles, too, looked on anxiously at the drift of events in France that autumn, even though they as yet had little to worry about for themselves. The Russians had no means of exerting pressure on them, at least not through Comintern. The entire Polish political system was closed to Communists; the party had split in 1926, when its leaders mistakenly supported Piłsudski's coup d'état, and since then it had been penetrated by agents of the state. The situation had reached a point of no return, in Comintern's opinion, and the secretariat resolved "to abolish the Polish section of Comintern" on 31 January 1936.[123] Thereafter the ruling clique of colonels faced no orchestrated Communist opposition. Stalin had done their work for them.

Sargent's assessment of the European situation was matched by that of Hankey, secretary to the cabinet, who feared a war fought in the company of a France "half-riddled with discontent and Communism" and thereby indirectly allied with the Bolsheviks, who aimed "to . . . force Bolshevism on a shattered Europe".[124] The Italians naturally played up the threat from Moscow. In Rome Ciano told susceptible Polish diplomats that he was "alarmed by Spain and the size of the outflow of soviets into Europe".[125] While in London the newly appointed German ambassador Joachim von Ribbentrop played the same ominous refrain to Jan Szembek, Poland's deputy secretary of state for foreign affairs.[126]

According to US military intelligence in Berlin the German government "witnessed with dismay the lack of decisive success which the Generals have secured up to August 21st and believes that the weight of military ponderables is slowly shifting to the side of the government. It further recognizes that if aid is given the rival parties by the other European states, France, which adjoins Catalonia, can through its geographical position bring far more aid to the government than could Germany and Italy by sea and air to the Generals."[127]

Meanwhile the Republican government in Spain was rocked by crisis as a result of unpreparedness and ineptitude. The charismatic leader of the socialists, Largo Caballero, emerged from the shadows to challenge the Giral administration. He wanted the Communists in with him. This was reported to Moscow on 1 September. But Comintern still desperately wanted to avoid an administration entirely focused on the left. It preferred a government based around the Republicans, though allowing for the participation of Largo Caballero, fellow socialist Indalecio Prieto and two (unnamed) Communists. Duclos, who was in Madrid, was asked to persuade Largo Caballero of this more moderate solution to the crisis. The arguments of Duclos focused on the need to keep Britain from rallying to the side of the rebels and to forestall "the threat of German and Italian intervention".[128] Largo Caballero went ahead and formed a new administration on 4 September, handing two ministries to the PCE.[129]

Events were moving fast and not to Comintern's advantage. Moscow's priority and that of the PCF was to avoid destabilising the Franco–Soviet pact and therefore it was vital to avoid at all costs unseating the *Front populaire* in Paris. Prime Minister Blum had succumbed to a deep pessimism. His gloomy reasoning was outlined in an apologia written much later, after the fall of France: "Civil war in France", he recalled, "could have preceded a foreign war . . . with little chance of victory for the Republic. That is to say, Spain would not have been saved but France would have turned fascist. . . . That would have meant the conquest of the European continent by Hitler without striking a blow."[130] Sensitive to Blum's dilemma, on 23 August 1936 the Russians acceded to the non-intervention agreement signed by Britain and

France on 15 August in the vain hope that Italy and Germany could be persuaded to desist from aiding Franco.

The issue of foreign military aid, in both men and matériel, was critical. Without aid from Italy and Germany, particularly air power, the rebels would have floundered. Of three hundred planes, two hundred lay with the Republic, as did the fleet, though not its officer corps, who deserted to the rebels.[131] The French government under Blum had with British encouragement initiated a non-intervention agreement which they applied to themselves. Similarly the Second International was under pressure from the British Labour Party to hold back from granting aid.[132] When Ehrenburg reported to Stalin after arrival in early September, he instanced the fact that outside Madrid "there is no front, there is no line, only outcrops. One can drive directly down a fine highway directly to the enemy without encountering any outpost along the road."[133] But the flow of Italian and German armaments to the rebels left the Republic in a potentially disastrous plight.

Germany and Italy Commit

On 26 August the chiefs of military intelligence from Italy and Germany, General Mario Roatta and Admiral Wilhelm Canaris, convened in Rome to negotiate the co-ordination of aid to Franco. It was envisaged that this would as far as possible reach the rebels via neighbouring Portugal. They signed an agreement two days later.[134] As noted above, Portugal was a fascist state under Salazar. The Italians reported that "the Communist danger that threatened to come from Spain was for Portugal . . . a very loud wake-up call". The reaction to it was apparently so sudden and decisive as to cause acute tensions with Britain, its age-old ally.[135] The Italians feared that in the event of Franco's defeat any unrest in Portugal would receive every means of support from Madrid.[136] Elsewhere in Europe, Austria, Switzerland and Sweden all handed the protection of their Spanish interests to the Germans.[137]

The Portuguese ambassador in London, Armindo Monteiro, assured the British of "the horror with which Soviet Russia is regarded in Portugal. Owing to her own past experiences [unspecified], Portugal regarded

Russian influence as a kind of disease which must at all costs be kept from her coasts."[138] "It is not only the fate of Spain that is at stake", the Portuguese government advised the British. "It is clear that Communist and Anarchist militias are perpetrating methods of a reign of terror, destroying the rich patrimony of Spain, public and private, the accumulated riches of many generations, in obedience to a preconceived plan. They have carried out mass assassinations of persons belonging to classes considered undesirable."[139]

On 26 July 1936 Salazar told General Mola, Franco's ally on the mainland, that he could count on Portuguese solidarity. On 1 August Salazar followed this up with his expressed wish to support the uprising "with all means at his disposal" (as a result of which Lisbon became a commercial base for Franco's acquisition of arms).[140] The first load of munitions flew out of Lisbon on 27 July. "Portugal has aided the rebels as far as it has been able to," reported the Republic's ambassador to Lisbon as early as 6 August. "They have been given every kind of facilities for transit through Portugal." Claudio Sánchez added that "the Portuguese government's panic at our possible triumph that would result in a Portuguese revolution as an immediate corollary could take them even further".[141]

As the Germans and Italians negotiated their respective contributions to the rebel aid effort, Stalin was finally persuaded that it was time to act. On 28 August the Politburo discussed the idea of sending Communist volunteers to fight. The decision was delayed, however.[142] The following week Churchill wrote to his wife Clementine, relieved that "the Spanish Nationalists are making progress. They are the only ones who have the power of attack. The others can only die sitting. Horrible! But better for the safety of all if the Communists are crushed."[143] Churchill's problem was how to square a potential alliance with the Soviet Union against Nazi Germany with his hostility to Communism. He tried hard to believe that the trial and execution of Old Bolsheviks in Moscow spelt an end to revolutionary internationalism. On 16 October Churchill published a piece in the *Evening Standard*. "The Communist Schism" suggested that the Germans had been subsidising Stalin's enemies.

Churchill was heavily dependent upon Desmond Morton of MI6, now in charge of its offshoot, the Industrial Intelligence Centre, for data on German rearmament and advice. Morton did not pull his punches: "I personally cannot agree that the Government of Moscow has changed its original intentions and objective one iota. Time after time in the past the Jekyll and Hyde theory has been put into practice in a manner impossible to a nation with the least moral consistency. The old game was the denial of responsibility for the activities of the IIIrd International [Comintern]. Now my information states that in destroying the well known leaders of the latter, the Soviet Government has retained in its own hands, secretly, the machinery. Through that machinery the Soviet Government is distributing funds to the Spanish Communists and other disruptive forces."[144] If he accepted this discomforting assessment, Churchill was left with a cruel dilemma.

In Moscow, as Morton predicted, far from the public eye contingency plans were now set into motion to send armaments, as Giral had requested. On 14 September the Fourth Directorate (military intelligence) and the InO (foreign intelligence) produced a plan entitled Operation X (pronounced 'kha' in Russian) for the supply of weapons.[145] Yet for two weeks the plan remained on the drawing board. On 16 September Comintern's ruling body held a meeting. Major decisions had to be reached. British Communist Party leader Pollitt was consistently pushing for action on Spain. He attacked "all" sections of Comintern for being too slow in reacting to events. He placed most of the responsibility on the French and doubtless added the British just to show even-handedness. "For two entire weeks", Pollitt said, "practically nothing was done. In the meantime these two weeks had decisive significance." And it was not just in Paris and London that complacency reigned. "In Moscow I talked to many comrades who considered the victory of the Spanish Government inevitable." But time was on the side of the fascists.[146]

Stalin Sends Arms

The following day Comintern's secretariat decided to create what became known as the International Brigades, an international army of volunteers to defend the Republic.[147] Far behind the scenes at one of his datchas in Georgia, Stalin finally made a commitment. The Soviet government proper now moved into action. On 19 September Soviet military intelligence was instructed to buy twenty thousand rifles, ten million rounds and ten aeroplanes in the United States, using Mexicans as cover (Mexico was pro-Republic).[148] For this purpose, $1,175,000 was released—$21,277,812 at today's value.[149] On 28 September Thorez reported that the first thousand volunteers had been recruited.[150] Time was pressing. Stalin had delayed to the last possible minute. That day Toledo fell. The eighty-mile road north-east to Madrid was now completely open.

On 29 September the Politburo at last agreed—with Stalin speaking by telephone from Sochi—that arms shipments should be delivered from the Soviet Union. The head of foreign intelligence, the InO GUGB, Artur Artuzov, set in motion a top-secret operation created by Boris El'man. For these purposes a special unit, Section X ('kha') was set up with the Fourth Directorate, which was also then under Artuzov's control.[151] As the Spanish ambassador reached Moscow on 7 October, heavy armaments—under the guise of "special machines"—were being loaded on board the *Komsomol* in Odessa for shipment to Cartagena. They arrived in Spain on 15 October, scarcely in secret. When the vessels tied up they were greeted by crowds in an atmosphere of "mass hysteria" at the first sight of a tank on board.[152] That very day the Soviet chargé d'affaires in London presented an ultimatum to the committee overseeing the non-intervention agreement: "The Soviet Government has no alternative . . . but to declare that should breaches of the non-intervention agreement not cease immediately, it will consider itself free from the obligation arising out of the agreement."[153] By then the calls had gone out to all sections of Comintern for volunteers.[154] They were codenamed "postcards".

The cost of the armaments was to be met from the Republic's gold supply. On 9 October the Russians were asked if they could take, store and release in order to meet various obligations overseas 500 tons of gold and some 100 million–250 million gold pesetas.[155] Three days later the Politburo agreed.[156] It was decided to offset the risk in transhipment by spreading the load among several vessels returning after offloading aid to Spain. In the utmost secrecy 510,080 kilograms were shipped from

Cartagena to Odessa and arrived in Moscow on 5 November.[157] With that the die was cast. While formally observing the non-intervention agreement, the Soviet government as well as Comintern was now deeply committed to saving the Republic from the rebels. By mid-December the Russians had spent $32,921,382 under Operation X. Losses in men amounted to 19% of pilots and 17% of tank crew—thirty-six dead in total.[158]

Comintern's surging commitment was now bolstered by substantial aid shipments from the Soviet government proper, though no real distinction could be drawn between the two. Franco noticed the openness with which Soviet armaments were arriving in Spain by mid-October. The challenge to him had expanded. He faced not just Red Spain but Russia itself.[159] Meanwhile in Albacete, in Spain's south-east, the first three thousand men destined for the International Brigades had been assembled; two thousand of them had already made up four battalions. They consisted of Italians, Germans, Frenchmen, Poles and various Balkan nationals. Around 80% were Communist or socialist. "Every evening", Longo recalls, "groups of 30–40 volunteers left from Paris and arrived at the Pyrenees." They came from all over with what little they could find to sustain them. One metallurgical worker from Paris even brought his motorcycle, as he had heard of the transportation shortage at the front. Those who had come in from Poland, Germany and the Balkans underwent an even more dramatic passage.[160]

There were crucial problems, however. Volunteers lacked automatic weapons and artillery, one-third had insufficient military training and officers of sufficient experience were few in number. By mid-November it was expected that another two thousand would have joined up.[161] And without those in place to train them, volunteers were easy targets. To remedy the deficiency, in Moscow the International Leninist school at Comintern gave those from fascist countries special military training to serve as officers in Spain. In addition several hundred political émigrés were trained by the NKVD, and a smaller number went to the Red Army for rapid training to serve in tanks and communications.[162] The despatch of trained personnel from the Soviet Union on diplomatic passports was no easy business, however. It became more and more difficult for Narkomindel to obtain transit visas. Where possible Czech passports were obtained even for those unable to speak the language. Crossing Poland or Germany was almost impossible, and although the Austrians and the Swedes were initially generous, by January 1937 it had to be accepted that the flow would cease, at least by land.[163]

By sea, of course, the Russians increasingly faced attack from Italian submarines. On 24 October the secretary general at the Quai d'Orsay Alexis Léger called in the Soviet chargé d'affaires, Hirshfeld, to tick him off for his government's blatant supply of aid to the Republic. Léger professed concern lest Russian shipping be intercepted at sea and conflict occur with the Germans or the Italians. And how could the supply of aid be squared with sitting on the non-intervention committee in London? Hirshfeld was nonplussed and acknowledged the truth of what was said. "Whatever happened, however," he said, "the Russian Government were now prepared to go to any lengths to help the Government of Madrid. They had come to the conclusion that they could not afford to see the proletarian régime in Spain suppressed, and though they might already be too late they were going to do everything in their power to enable them to resist General Franco and to prevent the establishment of another Fascist régime." During the course of his oration, Léger speculated as to Stalin's motives for taking such risks and suggested his behaviour was understandable "if he was to hold his own against the growing opposition of the ideologists of the Russian Revolution."[164] No answer was of course forthcoming.

Germany and Italy Raise the Stakes

At a meeting on 6 December staged in the Palazzo Venezia and chaired by Mussolini, Canaris gave a short briefing. The German espionage chief did not think it would be easy for Franco to meet his objectives even if the rebels seized Madrid. "It is obvious that the resistance of the Spanish reds has been galvanised by the USSR and the Third International and that without Bolshevik *matériel* the reds could achieve nothing." But he did not think they could form an organic army that could command a serious offensive "in the grand style" or take the operational initiative. What Germany and Italy could do, which the Russians would not, was to despatch large military units. Mussolini believed that the way forward lay seaward, in the interception of Soviet shipping. In the air the Germans would supply the bombers, the Italians the fighter planes.[165]

As German and Italian intervention became more blatant, the French and British governments became ever more committed to enforcing non-intervention, primarily against those aiding the Republic. The Spanish events played into the hands of the Germans and Italians at the expense of the Russians.[166] Boris Shtein, the Soviet ambassador in Rome, drew the obvious conclusion that Spain was "cementing" the Italo–German relationship. "With respect to this problem in particular one may speak of a parallelism and a coincidence of interests between Italy and Germany. With respect to this problem neither side has made any concessions to the other side; nothing of its own has been given up; no sacrifice made. In Berlin it has been said that both governments wish one and the same, think one and the same and will continue to do one and the same."[167] Ideological solidarity was the order of the day. Mussolini personally underscored this conclusion, telling the nuncio in late November "that the international situation had reached a peak of tension and that in his opinion it was more acute than in 1914. Hitler has had enough of Bolshevism."[168]

Whereas the civil war drew Germany and Italy together, it had the opposite effect on the British, the French and the Russians. The supporters of the Republic were united only precariously. Nothing illustrated better the gulf that separated Moscow from mainstream opinion in the European democracies. Too conscious of the need to keep the French onside, the PCF advised Dimitrov to back away from attacking Blum. In early December Thorez was reminded that "it is not convenient in current circumstances to force a government crisis and even less so to bring down the Blum government".[169] But that day, 5 December, PCF deputies none the less abstained on a government vote. The PCF's Georges Cogniot was despatched to Moscow to explain why they acted in this way. Comintern's executive repeated its message to the French on 14 December. But two days later Stalin, who had the final word on this as all else, told Dimitrov that criticism was fine: Blum was a "charlatan. . . . This is not Caballero."[170]

The incentives for German and Italian involvement grew rather than diminished as the war continued. Mussolini told Göring in January 1937 that "in the Spanish question Italy intends to venture to the extreme limit without, however, reaching the stage of a general war". Blum and his colleagues "wish to avoid it and demand and cry out for 'aeroplanes and arms for Spain', which they do purely and only for domestic political reasons. England also fears a wider conflict, and Russia will certainly not let things go beyond the limit."[171]

Those domestic reasons included the overwhelming presence of the French Communist Party, which was riding high. Contrasting the pre-election period with the establishment of the Popular Front government in May 1936, Marcel Cachin described his briefing to the ruling presidium of Comintern on 3 February as "a victory balance sheet". The PCF had 60,000 members in January 1936 and 282,000 by December. Its membership was the largest of all French political parties, with 50,000 more than its rival, the socialist SFIO. It dominated various trades unions in industries such as metallurgy, construction and rail. It brokered secret talks between the two Internationals on behalf of Dimitrov. For Paul Vaillant-Couturier, editor in chief of *l'Humanité*, "Cachin very justifiably said that fascism had seen its surge that had swollen formidably in the period that preceded the elections drop following the June strikes". For the PCF the anxieties of the previous autumn had evidently subsided, though not completely. The fascists "have serious enough roots in the army and air force". The army general staff was "not essentially fascist. The vast majority of troops . . . are anti-fascist. But there are middle-ranking officers, captains, majors and a certain number of colonels who are plainly registered with fascist organisations." And within the air force an eye had to be kept on Minister Pierre Cot's own entourage, according to Roger Salengro, Blum's minister for the interior. But the party was set upon becoming an integral part of the governing system, even in matters of defence: "On the committees where we work, whether on the army committee, whether on that for the air force, we play an important role." Furthermore, Vaillant-Couturier added, "I will be teaching you nothing in reminding you that the French national flag [*le Tricolore*] flies alongside the red flag in our demonstrations and that the *Marseillaise* is sung after the *Internationale*."[172] And Vaillant-Couturier was a founding member of the PCF.

What made for Soviet caution was news of systematic pressure from the British embassy in Paris on the Quai d'Orsay to co-operate more closely with Britain and to revise the Franco–Soviet pact by gutting it of any real commitment to defend the Soviet Union. In fact Eden was reported to have asked that the French issue a declaration to that effect. The US ambassador Bullitt was told of this by Foreign Minister Delbos.[173]

The fact that Stalin sent in not his own troops but only international volunteers, albeit reinforced by officers from the armed forces "advising" the Republicans, was indicative of his restraint. The main effort was thus borne by Comintern. And there the results initially seemed encouraging. Reviewing events over the past fifteen months in September 1937, "Codo", advising the PCE, took evident pride in stating that "our little party has grown into a large mass party, playing a decisive role in the country".[174] Those were his last words before Togliatti finally succeeded in getting him withdrawn to Moscow, seeing him as "in love with himself, ambitious . . . he demoralised the Spanish comrades as he did everything for them, even to the point of getting them cars". Worse than that, "he personally formed ties with the leaders of other parties [including Largo Caballero]; this discredited the Party; it brought the leadership of the Party into contempt". Togliatti continued, "He lacks political tact; he turned the leadership of the Communist Party of Spain against all the leaders of the other parties instead of co-operating with them."[175] Marty was of the same mind. He sardonically remarked that "Comrade Codo considers the party as his property".[176] None the less the PCE had ballooned on the back of the civil war, from 46,000 members in March 1936 to 118,763 in July, 142,800 in December and 328,978 by August 1937.[177]

The extraordinary growth of the PCE was attributable to its leading role in the defence of Madrid and in the widening of the *Frente Popular* to take in the anarcho-syndicalists despite the differences between them in matters of revolutionary priorities. Those differences proved hard to contain as Comintern insisted on greater commitment to defending the status quo and the complete abandonment of the revolution while the civil war proceeded. Reporting on events, Ernő Gerő told the presidium of Comintern's executive in late December 1936 that "at the beginning of the civil war, relations between Communists and anarcho-syndicalists were extremely tense. In the minds of many of our comrades it appeared that the anarchists had to be dealt with summarily [*raspravit'sya*] at an early stage and later it would be possible to seriously get to work in the fight against fascism."[178]

Whereas the anarcho-syndicalists were seen as errant brothers rather than renegades—Russian anarchists had ended up in Soviet military intelligence, where their daredevil activism was valued—those identified as Trotskyists (POUM) were never given an inch. There could be no doubt where the POUM stood. Bourgeois democracy and fascism marked different ends of the same capitalist spectrum. Revolution—a workers' government, the dictatorship of the proletariat—was the priority in Spain, "not the maintenance of the democratic republic". The Popular Front was just a front for reformism.[179]

Seen as exploiting fissures within the *Frente Popular*, the POUM were dealt with accordingly. Gerő's comment resonated with Stalin's current obsession: "The Communist Party of Spain has conducted a big struggle against Trotskyism; it has succeeded in almost liquidating the Trotskyists in Madrid." In Catalonia, however, the young Socialist United Party (Communist) mistakenly entered government along with the Trotskyists—an error later corrected.[180] Overall, however, as the Italians noted with a certain satisfaction, "The reds are more divided than the whites; opposing factions collide with one another menacingly and established authority runs the risk of being swept away at any moment."[181]

The Russian Elephant in the Room

Comintern was above all concerned to ensure that the left in Spain was seen to be defending bourgeois democracy rather than conducting a revolution. Only this would outflank Franco's propaganda. Back in late

November 1936 Togliatti's secretariat warned, "The Communist Party hitherto has been unable to allay among the wide democratic nationalist masses the general lack of clarity about the fact that in Spain the fight is not for sovietisation but for a constitutional republican order, for national independence and for peace."[182]

This was more easily said than done, however. Comintern did not control the revolution under way. The PCE leadership and "Codo" explained to Moscow, "Our party has correctly fought against various attempts at premature revolution in the towns and the countryside (against socialisation, forced collectivisation, against egalitarian communism). But you have to take into account the fact that the majority of these incidents have occurred because the civil war in Spain has taken on a profoundly class character and the masses in general want to produce and head production themselves." Account had also to be taken of the fact that "the vast majority of landowners—large and medium, large entrepreneurs, representatives of finance capital etc.—took an active part in the struggle on the side of fascism".[183]

A crucial element was the manner in which Moscow's emissaries increasingly took charge when they found their hosts disorganised or at odds with one another.[184] The Politburo had reason to reprimand Ambassador Rozenberg in late December 1936. He was supposed to be there to help the Spanish government "and not to try to tie it to this or that decision . . . *the ambassador is not a commissar, but, at most, an adviser*". But it is important to note, despite the categorical tone of the despatch, that the emphasis was more upon making the Spanish "feel" they were in charge rather than making sure they really were directing the course of events.[185] The Russians were now, after all, effectively running Republican Spain.

As the war proceeded the Russian role became ever more blatant, as did the role of Comintern. Acting under camouflage was something that needlessly burdened Togliatti, who judged openness an asset rather than an inconvenience in terms of cementing his authority. The Russians, on the other hand, given their addiction to secrecy, rarely found transparency congenial. A further and not unimportant reason for keeping matters secret was that in the world of diplomacy the British were most anxious to close down the civil war at almost any price. And Blum, in particular, found that the civil war complicated the almost impossible job of easing class tensions within France.

In Moscow Litvinov, who had had no confidence in world revolution since 1918, found himself in the cross-hairs of the ideological battle. To the US ambassador he "vigorously" expressed his "failure to understand why England and France were 'continually bothering' with Hitler in Germany; that he could not understand why they should project notes and questionnaires and constantly stir up the German situation and thereby accentuate Hitler's importance and 'feed his vanity' into his self-conception that he (Hitler) is the dominating figure in Europe; that he thought they ought to let him 'stew in his own juice' . . . . He seemed to be very much stirred about this and apprehensive lest there should be some composition of differences between France, England, and Germany."[186] And this was before Neville Chamberlain had even entered 10 Downing Street as prime minister. "As regards Spain", the British ambassador reported, "M. Litvinov declared in reply to a question that the Soviet Government had no interest in Spain whatever. They did not care what form of government was set up in Spain even if it were a Fascist Government such as had been established by General Primo de Rivera, as long as it was not a Government under the direct orders and control of Berlin or Rome." He added, no doubt in the face of strong headwinds at home, "that the Soviet Government's foreign policy had perhaps been rather too forward in furthering collective security. They would now play their part with others, but would not take the lead."[187]

But matters had gone too far already. There existed no "neutral" source for mediation. Asked about rumours that the British and French were calling on the Vatican for that purpose, Cardinal Pacelli echoed the most recent encyclical—*Divini Redemptoris*—of 19 March 1937 in a vehemently negative response to enquiries from the Italian ambassador: "I replied that the Holy See would willingly see anything that could lead to an end of such an atrocious war but has not undertaken any role; in addition I noted that the Communists in the regions occupied by them have completely destroyed everything to do with religion."[188] Not that the Holy See was prepared to accept anything to help Germany by of-

ficially recognising the Franco régime at a time when Hitler was perse-
cuting the Jesuits.

The lame but well-intentioned attempt by Eden to end Italian attacks
on Republican shipping at a multilateral conference convened at the
little village of Nyon in mid-September 1937 was effectively a failure
because the Italians simply refused to attend. The agreement reached
was therefore meaningless and the Italians intensified rather than reduced their efforts, suffering no adverse consequences for doing so. By
that time Franco's forces controlled the "magnificent heavy industry" of
northern Spain. "The fall of Bilbao and of Santander is thus the greatest
setback that we have undergone since the beginning of the war," André
Marty told Comintern's presidium; "it is this that may have the most
serious consequences". Troops were deserting and morale in the International Brigades was weakening—"extremely serious symptoms
in such a sensitive organism", Marty remarked. And it was not just
the battlefield that worried Marty: "The most difficult is not always the
front. The most difficult job is in the rear: in the workplace, in the
villages."[189]

Britain Aims at Appeasing Italy

Now back in Moscow, Codovilla correctly saw that the alienation of
Britain and France from the Republic was due to two factors: "the pro-
tracted nature of the war and the evident reinforcement of the achievements of the people's revolution that excites fear in the governments of
these countries faced with the revolution developing in Spain".[190] The
British navy tasked at Nyon with interdicting Italian vessels was none
too happy for these very reasons. First Sea Lord Admiral Lord Chatfield
objected more fundamentally to his government's policy of denying
belligerent rights to Franco even though he had complete command of
local waters by the end of 1936. As far as the admiral was concerned, the
policy was adopted "mainly" to satisfy the French. Indeed, on Chatfield's view his fleet's sympathies lay entirely with the rebels.[191] The Republic was thereafter ever more in the hands of the Russians. This might
have made for a more effective war effort. But this was obtained at the

high price of Soviet dominance at a time when the worst excesses of Stalinism were on open display.

For the Republic a false dawn broke with the failure of Franco in the new year to launch a great offensive on the central front. The Republicans had seized Teruel on 8 January 1938. The Italian War Ministry lamented that "the hope of victory" had returned to the Republic; that the balance between the two sides, once favourable to Franco, was more equal in terms of technology owing to invaluable foreign aid; and that "time is working in favour of the Reds".[192] Teruel was in itself not much. But in the larger scale of things it indicated that a rebel victory required substantially more support from Germany and Italy until success could be assured.[193] This was, as ever, soon forthcoming.

Oliver Harvey, a rather more liberal private secretary to the new foreign secretary, Lord Halifax, than others would have preferred, noted early in June that the British were "praying for Franco's victory and bringing all the influence they can bear on France to stop the inflow of munitions to Barcelona".[194] Halifax was no exception. He believed the civil war made it easier to find common ground with Germany, because the Communist role would cause the British to see Germany "as an ally of ours and of all order-loving folk [sic]".[195] The pressure from London under Chamberlain was unremitting. On 13 June French Prime Minister Édouard Daladier finally closed the frontier to arms traffic heading into Spain. Thereafter the Republic was doomed.

10

A United Front against Japan

In military circles in Russia—Soviet military officers have told me this
themselves—the defeat of 1905 still rankles, and one thing that the Soviet
army desires is good relations with Europe, in order that they may have
their hands free to get their own back on Japan as soon as possible.

—MINUTE ON LT. COL. HAYES (MI2)
TO COLLIER (FOREIGN OFFICE)[1]

A keen distinction can be drawn between the ideological schism that
had opened up in Europe over Spain and the state of affairs in the Far
Eastern theatre, where the Japanese alone felt that they faced the urgent
need to repel the advance of Bolshevism.

Here, in stark contrast to the 1920s when a bleak lesson had been
learned from the failure of the Chinese revolution, Stalin resolutely sub-
ordinated the needs of the local Communist Party to the needs of Soviet
state security. This was the sort of behaviour the Western powers instinctively understood. Whereas Soviet military intervention in Spain
was seen by Britain as entirely disruptive and primarily ideologically
motivated, Soviet military intervention in China to sustain armed opposition to the Japanese was seen as sound reasons of state. The immediate threat of Bolshevism to British and French interests had long since
disappeared when the CCP was forced to trek to the distant north-west
to escape Chiang Kai-shek's guns. The Soviet military as such were thus

not entirely unwelcome in the region as far as the Western powers were concerned. The Japanese believed that they alone were neutralising the threat of Bolshevism in the region, as Stalin had explicitly recognised at the height of the Manchurian crisis back in the fateful autumn of 1931, and that was in fact true by 1936. The crucial fact for the Western powers, including the United States, was that Bolshevism to the north distracted Japan from moving south against French Indochina and the British colony of Malaya en route to the ultimate goal of seizing the oil of the Dutch East Indies to make Japan self-sufficient for war.

China's Communists on the Run

From 1927, when Chiang Kai-shek turned on the Communists and wiped them out in the major cities, the remnants re-formed in the countryside—notably in Kiangsi province, where from November 1930 Chiang once again began a campaign of suppression. American military intelligence reported, "By this time the scattered Reds had been busy in those areas neglected by the Government, where the peasant population suffering from local misrule welcomed any form of government which promised some amelioration of their lot." Eradication was a complete failure, not least because the Japanese occupation of Manchuria proved a major distraction. "The more the suppression the more the banditry," many areas reported. But after the conclusion of a truce with Japan in May 1933, Chiang was able to concentrate on his task. And he succeeded—to a point. As the Americans reported, "A small but apparently well organized force of Reds under Chu [Teh] and Mao [Tse-tung] made a remarkable march across Hunan, Kweichow and northern Yunnan, made a feint toward Yunnanfu, turned suddenly north and by June 1935, turned suddenly and by June 1935 had united in western Szechwan with other Reds under Hsu Hsiang-ch'ien which had also been moving west across northern Szechwan."[2]

The drive to the north-west was in search of safety closer to the Soviet Union. By the winter of 1935 they had reached Shensi, re-emerging embattled and bedraggled, a shadow of their former selves. Secret contacts were launched and sustained with the Guomindang in Shanghai to discuss the formation of an anti-Japanese front, but they never went anywhere. Once they had beaten back a combined offensive by Chang Hsueh-liang, who headed the sixty-seventh army for the north-east and the seventeenth, north-western army headquartered in Sian, under Yang Hu-cheng, they set about building a new revolutionary base area.

The remnants of the Red Army were not exactly the Jeffersonian farmers that naïve young New Deal American emissaries sent out by President Roosevelt, like Marine Captain Evans Carlson and, later, foreign service officer John Service, believed them to be. But in Russian terms these were predominantly peasants and therefore not really Bolsheviks at all. They were, as Stalin later quipped, not real Communists but "margarine Communists".[3] The leftist American journalist Edgar Snow had spent four months in Paoan with Mao. His reports were "colored by a decided-Communist bias". He implausibly claimed that the Reds were "no longer opposed to capitalism, but to imperialism".[4] Colonel Joseph Stilwell, the US military attaché, also took the view that Mao's party "can hardly be said to represent pure communism". None the less he correctly saw that "these leaders have proved themselves to be expert organizers and dangerously capable of leading a major revolution if a propitious occasion should present itself".[5] And even with the remnants of the party holding out in the distant north-west, Japan continued to fret. In November 1935 the Russians had decrypted a Polish despatch from Shanghai citing the Japanese ambassador's pessimism about the possibility of defeating Communism in China without striking at its Soviet roots: "In Japanese circles the opinion is increasingly hardening that only an attack on the USSR could radically call a halt to the development of the Communist movement in China. This opinion is inflaming the Kwantung Army Command."[6]

The Chinese Communists Consolidate

In a desperate situation, faced with renewed and more heavily armed offensives, the CCP inevitably saw the Japanese as a secondary enemy until Chiang Kai-shek could be turned around. And that was not a stance that Stalin could accept. Secure radio contact with Moscow was not safely restored until June 1936 and only then was Comintern able to begin exerting pressure for unity against Japan on the lines dictated by its seventh congress.[7] Up to that point the slogan remained, "Resist Japan and Oppose Chiang Kai-shek". The party needed all the political guile it—meaning Chou En-lai—could muster and a great deal of luck in order to hold off extinction at the hands of the Guomindang and its allies. In the circumstances, the advice from Moscow was, not to put too fine a point on it, utterly redundant; more than that, it was largely detrimental to finding a workable solution.

A unique opportunity arose. A colonel from Chang Hsueh-liang's army who was taken captive by the Communists revealed to Chou En-lai that Chang was interested in collaboration against the Japanese. Soundings began on 21 January 1936.[8] They continued through to March when, finally, with Mao Tse-tung's blessing, Chou En-lai took charge of negotiations personally. On 18 March the CCP issued a ceasefire.[9] In the meantime his subordinates had also been in touch with Yang Hu-cheng, via contacts forged in the 1920s.[10] On 5 April 1936 Chou told the Chinese Politburo that now was the moment to move in alliance with both armies against Chiang Kai-shek. But it soon became apparent that Chang was not yet ready for such a drastic about-turn, as Chiang Kai-shek had not explicitly rejected resistance to Japan.

The Chinese Communists pressed further east towards Ningsia on the Great Wall in order to establish a road corridor through to Inner Mongolia and the empty landscape of the Gobi desert so that aid could reach them directly from the Soviet Union via Outer Mongolia. But not only were the forces sympathetic to the Communists in neighbouring Gansu defeated in battle by Chiang's armies; the entire strategy envisaged came under fire from Comintern. The Russians had no intention of supplying aid separately to the Communists. At a meeting of the secretariat on 23 June Dimitrov insisted that the CCP instead focus on coming to terms directly with the Guomindang against the Japanese; that it "create a situation in China so that Chiang Kai-shek would be driven into this kind of anti-Japanese front".[11] The ambiguity in this particular instruction then opened the path to machinations that before long horrified Stalin—the kind of loss of control that his terror campaign within the Soviet Union was designed to stamp out once and for all. But of course his arms were never long enough, they could not reach abroad, to enforce his priorities.

It became increasingly obvious to Mao Tse-tung that the Chinese Communists were there to serve Soviet interests; not the other way around. On 10 August 1936, a year after Comintern's seventh congress had called for an anti-imperialist front against Japan, he finally discarded its slogan "Resist Japan and Oppose Chiang Kai-shek". But Moscow was still displeased. Two days later the Chinese Politburo resolved to push on with its earlier, provocative plans to open up a route to the Soviet Union. Not for nearly a fortnight was word of this plan then despatched to Comintern. The CCP must have known the Russians would not approve of it. Although formally pressing for co-operation with Chiang, the CCP was simultaneously counting on a purely bilateral relationship with the Soviet Union. This was apparent when, on 5 October, Chou and Mao wrote to Chang Hsueh-liang that a year had passed since contacts were opened with Chiang Kai-shek, to no result.

Chiang Kai-shek was now ordering Guomindang forces to attack the Communists in Shensi and Gansu. "We are left with nothing other than for the purpose of self-defence to respond with a counter-offensive," the letter continued. Chang was asked to call a halt to attacks on the Red Army and inform Chiang Kai-shek that conditions had to be established for talks about joint action against Japan. But the Guomindang was mobilising squadrons of bombers for a massive assault on the Communist base area and when confronted by Chang Hsueh-liang, Chiang Kai-shek refused to give way. Chou outlined all this to the Politburo on 13 November. They prepared for the worst.[12]

On the diplomatic front the Japanese shored up their common interests with Germany. An anti-Comintern pact was signed by Japan and Germany on 25 November 1936. The initiative had originated with the Germans. More than a year earlier, in October 1935, Ribbentrop, heading the Nazi Party foreign office, had approached the military attaché at the Japanese embassy, Oshima Kenkichi, with the suggestion of some kind of alliance against the Russians. Ribbentrop said that he hoped to draw in the British as well. Informal negotiations continued into

December, but the Japanese military were doubtful of its value. Once the Japanese felt ready, however, it was the Germans who played coy. Finally, the Japanese general staff recognised that the ratification of the Franco–Soviet pact had made the Soviet Union a "more decisive" factor in its calculations.[13] In turn the Spanish Civil War seemed to make the agreement more a matter of urgency for Germany.

Both antagonists were closing in on the Russians. Official, implausible denials issued from Tokyo that a secret protocol named the Soviet Union as the target of the pact immediately prompted threats from Moscow to publish the text. Ambassador Yurenev, in Japan since March 1933, immediately called a halt to the negotiations with Foreign Minister Satō Naotake. But, with Stalin's terror unleashed in Moscow and complications arising from intervention in the Spanish Civil War, the Russians were not actively seeking further foreign complications. A frontier clash on the Amur River led Moscow to back down in subsequent negotiations on mutual withdrawal—only for the Russians to face humiliation at the hands of the Japanese who, within days of the agreement, seized territory that both sides had evacuated.[14]

When Chiang Kai-shek flew north to pressure generals Chang and Yang into military action against the Communists, they arrested him and called on the CCP to come and discuss further action. There were demands to put him on trial and execute him, a sentiment that was strong within the Communist camp. And whereas Moscow panicked at the news—more CCP adventurism—Mao and his men were inclined to drive home their unexpected advantage at Chiang's expense. Doubtless what alarmed Stalin most was that these events followed so soon after signature of the Anti-Comintern Pact and that with no notion of the consequences for Moscow the victorious rebels raised "the slogan of alliance with the USSR". Comintern immediately demanded that the CCP stand down, a recommendation that came as "a bolt from the blue".

Chiang's release was secured after he agreed to reorganise the national government, cease the anti-Communist offensive and ally with the Red Army against the Japanese. Closer contact between Communists and Guomindang then became a mainstay from February 1937, a fact even acknowledged by the CCP on 22 June. "Nanjing has ended military attacks on the Red Army", Chou En-lai conceded. "It has lifted the economic blockade on our region and is now supplying three-fifths, or $300,000 of the $500,000 of the monthly food allowance due to our troops as units of the national army. If the talks succeed, we expect our forces will receive the full amount."[15] The Communists formally joined Guomindang forces against the Japanese as the Eighth Route Army. Meanwhile, it appears, the Soviet ambassador in Nanjing, Bogomolov, was acting out of line and encouraging Chiang to believe Moscow would stand firm behind him against the Japanese at a time when the Japanese took the bit between their teeth in suppressing Chinese resistance once and for all.

The Marco Polo Bridge Incident: War

Unlike in the Manchurian crisis of 1931, the shooting incident that occurred on 8 July 1937 on Marco Polo Bridge (Lukouchiao) ten miles west of Beijing and gave rise to fighting between Chinese and Japanese troops is believed to have been spontaneous. The American naval attaché in Tokyo, however, reported, "Many circumstances point to the fact that the present trouble in North China was either instigated by the Japanese or that they are using the incidents to further their aims and ambitions in that area."[16] Certainly the Japanese reacted aggressively after the incident by launching a major campaign from their base in occupied Manchuria to conquer the whole of northern China—under General Doihara, the provinces of Jehol, Hopei and Chahar had already been incorporated into a buffer zone through a blend of terror and cajolery. Even before the "incident", General Isogai, chief of the military affairs bureau of the Japanese War Ministry, had warned the British that "Japan was not antagonistic towards the Nanking [Nanjing] government but was sceptical over its real attitude towards the suppression of communism". More specifically, "[w]hile the Nanking government's attitude with regard to the special relations between Japan, Manchukuo and north China, to the control of anti-Japanese activities and the suppression of communism remained unsatisfactory, the Japanese government could not remain indifferent."[17]

The inflation of nomenclature tells all. "Incident" in Japanese is *jihen*, which means a conflict short of war. At the outset the Japanese called the shooting at Marco Polo Bridge the "Lukouchiao Incident". This was subsequently and tellingly renamed the "North China Incident"; then the "Sino–Japanese Incident"; and, finally, the "China Incident", as the Japanese relentlessly expanded their military offensive and took advantage of events.[18] Indeed, on 17 August the Japanese cabinet accepted that this was a war in all but name and reversed the policy of not extending the conflict.[19] Hitherto Japanese aggression could be seen as "local". But this now turned out to be something entirely different in scale. The first question was how the Chinese would react. The second question was how the British and the Americans would respond.

British Attempts to Appease Japan

By September 1937 the large-scale campaign that was unfolding took in about five hundred thousand Japanese troops and extended one thousand miles from north to south. It also included a naval blockade of the entire coastline. The Americans had no intention of sticking out their necks and did not expect the British to do so either.[20] From the perspective of London it was seen as good reason to accelerate rather than abrogate the policy of appeasing Japan that Chamberlain, when chancellor of the exchequer and now as prime minister, had tirelessly pursued. Overriding the objections of the Foreign Office in 1934–35, Chamberlain was aided and abetted by permanent under-secretary at the Treasury Sir Warren Fisher in launching the Leith-Ross mission to China (1935–36). The flimsy hope was of raising a major loan to reform the Chinese currency in return for Chiang Kai-shek's recognition of Manchukuo (Japanese-occupied Manchuria). This was, of course, categorically denied in parliament. Sir Frederick Leith-Ross arrived in Shanghai in September 1935. "He does not know the first things about the political situation here," complained British Ambassador Alexander Cadogan. "God save us from our amateur diplomats."[21] The same could equally be said of the latest foreign secretary, Sir Samuel Hoare, who had enthusiastically gone along with Chamberlain's pet scheme, hoping for a division of China into spheres of influence—Japan in the north and Britain in the south—"whilst we still have some bargaining counters".[22] The mission was a complete failure, not least because the Japanese were bent on controlling north China unilaterally through a series of puppet warlords and sought to weaken Chiang's government in Nanjing, to the south, in order to neutralise it as a military factor. This would mean, Sir Frederick Leith-Ross finally realised, the "eventual disruption of Chinese credit and trade and ultimately possibly some fresh wave of communism". Only "big guns" could knock sense into the ruling Japanese military.[23] That meant the United States. But Chamberlain was not listening. It was an ominous sign of things to come as events in Europe began to unfold in Chamberlain's hands.

The British thus diplomatically accepted Japan's description of the fighting in China as the "Sino–Japanese dispute". Not without dissent, this was very much the determined approach of Britain's controversial new ambassador, Sir Robert Craigie, who arrived in Tokyo on 3 September 1937. Like his counterpart in Berlin, Sir Nevile Henderson, with respect to Germany, Craigie took the view, despite overwhelming evidence to the contrary, that Japan had no real desire for territorial expansion. The British, after all, still had an estimated investment in China of £13.75 billion (at today's value) and no effective way of protecting it. They could not even protect their own ambassador, Sir Hugh Knatchbull-Hugessen, whose car, a few miles south of Shanghai en route from Nanjing, was on 26 August strafed by machine-gun fire from a Japanese aircraft—apparently in the belief that it was a military bus despite the fact that the Japanese authorities had been notified in advance and that the Union Jack was painted on the roof of his own vehicle and the two accompanying him. Knatchbull-Hugessen ended up in the Shanghai Country Hospital until 25 September 1937. It was a revealing symptom of the abrupt collapse of Britain's standing in China publicised for all the world to see, inconceivable only a decade earlier.[24] Such was the speed with which international relations were transformed between the world wars.

Chamberlain warned the cabinet that he "could not imagine anything more suicidal than to pick a quarrel with Japan at the present moment when the European situation had become so serious. If this country were to become involved in the Far East the temptation to the Dictator States to take action, whether in Eastern Europe or in Spain, might be irresistible."[25] This position was reiterated just over a year later when the foreign secretary dared to propose a £3 million loan to China (£194 million at today's value) but without any quid pro quo for Japan. Chancellor of the Exchequer and former foreign secretary Simon, who had argued the Japanese case so well in 1931, thus protested against the proposal on the grounds that the Japanese would see it as support for the Chinese war effort. Chamberlain hastily agreed and, as reported, insisted that "we should then have to face the question whether we were prepared to go to war with Japan. At the present moment he felt that the position in Europe was not sufficiently stable to justify us incurring this risk."[26]

The United States had taken Britain's measure accurately—the US Treasury had by far the best intelligence in the area. It had correctly judged Soviet interests and the policy that flowed from them. "Soviet Russia is much more involved in the Far East than it is in Spain," Treasury Secretary Morgenthau's secretary wrote. Soviet assistance to China was therefore likely to be much greater, he predicted. "China is in effect fighting Russia's war", he continued, "and Russia fully realizes that every additional blow administered to Japan will make her own position that much stronger." It was thus to be expected that the Russians would offer all aid short of war.[27] This assessment was accurate in spite of the Soviet Union's self-inflicted wounds.

Stalin Terrorises His Own Armed Forces

From the Soviet position the timing of the Japanese offensive could not have been worse. The only advantage was that it infuriated the Germans because it threatened to bog down their only ally in the Soviet Union's rear and thereby gave the Russians a military advantage vis-à-vis any offensive intended by Germany in Central Europe. What relieved both the Germans and the Japanese was that Stalin now found it hard to accommodate the weight that his armed forces had now acquired within the Soviet Union. They demanded a greater voice in policy at a time when Stalin sought the greatest freedom of manoeuvre. Marshal Tukhachevsky, in particular, appeared to think that his opinions mattered.

In August 1936 Stalin had arraigned his old rivals Zinoviev and Kamenev on trumped-up charges of treason and terrorism. On 29 June Yagoda had presented Stalin, Molotov and Yezhov with testimony—we do not know how exactly it was extracted—by one Dreitser, formerly a Trotsky bodyguard, and one Pikel', formerly a manager in Zinoviev's secretariat and at Comintern. The NKVD claimed that "in October 1934 Dreitser received an instruction in Moscow written personally by Trotsky: 'Remove [*ubrat'*] Stalin and Voroshilov, develop work organising cells in the army etc.'" Whether this was a confession extracted by torture is a matter of surmise. It was also claimed that Dreitser was told to organise terrorist groups to target party leaders.[28] Trotsky had certainly argued in print a year before that the "bureaucracy can be compelled to yield power into the hands of the proletariat vanguard only by *force*".[29] And Stalin was not about to wait.

On 11 June 1937 Stalin moved swiftly against the Red Army officer corps, purging it from top to bottom, beginning with Tukhachevsky—presumably in the spirit of Voltaire's admonition after the British executed Admiral Byng in 1757 that from time to time one has to kill an admiral in order to encourage the others. Once the terror spread directly through the Red Army high command, Western estimates of Soviet military power (vis-à-vis Germany's) that already assumed the Russians were incapable of an offensive now seriously began to doubt the Soviet capacity even for effective defence, particularly when faced with the threat of a two-front war. And that soon emerged as a real possibility.

After the Lukouchiao Incident the Soviet Union's ambassador to Japan, Yurenev, moved to Berlin, where his expertise could be put to good use monitoring the German relationship with Japan, for it was here that the influential military attaché Oshima had negotiated the Anti-Comintern Pact. The execution of the Red Army leadership was clearly not the moment for unilateral initiatives from the Soviet embassy in China directed against Japan. Yet Ambassador Dmitrii Bogomolov, along with the military attaché, Major Lepin, had been engaging in talks about a possible bilateral mutual assistance pact even before Lukouchiao. US Naval Intelligence caught wind of the fact that, on the subject of aid to China, "there has been a wide divergence of opinion among Soviet Russian officials in China and in the Soviet Government".[30] When Stalin became aware of what was going on behind his back, Bogomolov's actions prompted a severe reprimand from Litvinov on 19 July. Bogomolov was instructed that "in forcing this question at the present moment the Chinese are trying to get us involved in a war with Japan".[31] Stalin's suspicions were reflected in London. The British assessment was that in Soviet military circles "the defeat of 1905 still rankles, and one thing that the Soviet army desires is good relations with Europe, in order that they may have their hands free to get their own back on Japan as soon as possible".[32]

The Politburo discussed the matter on 29 July and two days later Bogomolov was told that the most Moscow would countenance was a non-aggression pact as anything more direct could risk war with Japan. Finally, within days of Yurenev's successor Slavutsky, formerly consul-general in Manchuria, arriving in Tokyo, on 21 August the Russians signed the pact. Yurenev had warned Moscow a year earlier that "in current international circumstances England is counting on a Japanese–Chinese war assured that we will inevitably be drawn into it".[33] The unfortunate Bogomolov was recalled and left China on 27 September, followed by Lepin on 7 October. Both were arrested on arrival and executed, following the path of many others.

It was clear that Stalin was intent on avoiding any direct military engagement with the Japanese. While the Far Eastern command under Marshal Vasilii Blyukher was spared the firing squad for the time being, resistance from the Chinese tied down Japanese forces. The French ambassador reported a senior Soviet diplomat saying that it had "the effect of reducing the pressure which it exercises on our Manchurian frontier".[34] As in Spain against the Germans, so in China against the Japanese: the Russians needed a firebreak to stave off the inevitable conflagration. In 1938 therefore the Soviet Union supplied China with 597 planes, 827 tanks, 3,825 machine guns and 700 trucks. The following year it gave China credit for more than 300 planes, 500 artillery pieces, 5,700 machine guns, 50,000 rifles, 850 trucks and other military supplies.[35] The French ambassador reported from Moscow Deputy Commissar for Foreign Affairs Potemkin's remark that the situation in China was "splendid" and that he was "counting on resistance by this country for several years, after which Japan will be too enfeebled to be capable of attacking the USSR".[36]

II

The Appeasement of Germany, 1937–1939

> Conservative circles are, it is true, worried about the strength of Germany; but their greater fear is of Bolshevism.
>
> —GÖRING'S WORDS TO MUSSOLINI,
> 23 JANUARY 1937[1]

How was it that so many distinguished and apparently intelligent people managed to get matters so badly wrong? A large part of the story was an overriding and debilitating preoccupation with Bolshevism. But there were others who were quite simply naïve, and had a deep-seated reluctance to see evil for what it was. In late February 1936, just before Hitler invaded the Rhineland, the celebrated liberal guru Arnold Toynbee was granted an audience with Hitler. On Toynbee's return to the Royal Institute of International Affairs a German Jewish colleague from Balliol College, Oxford, Albrecht Mendelssohn Bartholdy, heard at first hand how impressed the distinguished professor was with the German dictator. And he was appalled. Summing up Toynbee and people like him, Bartholdy despaired: "It is quite hopeless; they simply don't understand."[2] Toynbee was not untypical of trusting intellectuals of his class.

Neville Chamberlain Takes Charge

After outstaying his welcome, Baldwin finally stepped down as prime minister in May 1937. His successor was the ambitious and authoritarian former chancellor of the exchequer Neville Chamberlain, long impatient for the highest office and imbued with implacable self-belief that he could do the job better than anyone else. After listening to him over lunch a friend, Leo Amery, portrayed his manner of working: "I gather he runs the Cabinet much more on the lines of a big factory, calling up the heads of departments to see him individually and getting them well primed to do what he wants them to do (and probably also what he wants them to say) before the Cabinet Meetings."[3]

The inner group of the Conservative Party under Baldwin, which included Geoffrey Dawson at *The Times*, did not have much interest in Europe. They were predominantly isolationist in spirit. They may have been reared as imperialists; indeed, some had been influenced by Viscount Milner's glowing vision of the imperial future. But the First World War had also left its mark. Outside parliament Dawson, a politician by nature if a journalist by trade, led the pack. Certainly in a position to know, he listed the "inner ring of the Cabinet" under Baldwin as Conservatives Neville Chamberlain and Lord Halifax, Liberals Sir John Simon and Walter Runciman and, trailing, for Labour, Ramsay MacDonald.[4] All of them except MacDonald, who died in 1937, came to be closely identified with the policy of appeasing Germany. Only Simon, a Liberal in name only, had any experience as foreign secretary, and his tenure was widely recognised by others as having been nothing short of calamitous, beginning with the Manchurian crisis.

Chamberlain was always something of an odd one out. He had not fought in the war that brought the empire to its zenith, though he had organised conscription for military service; scarcely a prestigious role when others put their life on the line. Indeed, the impact the conflict made upon him was entirely negative. He was effectively an isolationist rather than an imperialist, as his China policy demonstrated, especially in respect of continental Europe. "The political temper of people in this country", he intoned, "is strongly opposed to Continental adventures." From this followed a very definite consequence: "Owing to our geographical position it is unnecessary for us to maintain a large army ready for war at a moment's notice."[5] It was thus not so much money—though he obsessed about sustaining a balanced budget, still the received wisdom of the day—as the priorities for expenditure that determined Chamberlain's attitude to war as chancellor of the exchequer.

After dropping the gold standard, the British economy grew at a healthy 3.6% from 1932 to 1938. None the less the chancellor was always looking to cut government expenditure to reduce government debt and personal taxation. Deeply sceptical of rearmament and a great advocate of a long-term understanding with Berlin, Chamberlain's closest adviser was Sir Horace Wilson. Wilson was an able and "highly ambitious" but provincial labour economist, who as principal private secretary had made his mark helping Prime Minister Baldwin settle the general strike in 1926. He and Chamberlain shared a vision and he rapidly became the new prime minister's *éminence grise*.[6] He had no experience whatever in foreign affairs but, as with the permanent secretary at the Treasury Sir Warren Fisher, whom Wilson later succeeded, that never held him back. Businessman Lord Woolton recalled Wilson gaining power and influence "unequalled by any member of the Cabinet except the Prime Minister".[7] In many respects, he played the role of obsequious courtier. Harold Nicolson, a penetrating observer of human nature at its less than finest, hit the nail on the head with his jibe that Wilson's advice was "never inconvenient".[8]

After the war Sir Alexander Cadogan came to regret that Chamberlain, a man he had once so much admired, shared Wilson's simplistic belief that the conduct of foreign policy resembled business negotiations.[9] And looking back in 1940 Anthony Eden told Ambassador Maisky, "You know, the greatest difficulty for me at this time was to convince my friends that Hitler and Mussolini were not quite similar in psychology, in motive and methods, in their entire cast of mind anything like English 'business men or country gentlemen'. This they could never get themselves to believe. They thought that I was 'biased' against the 'dictators' and that I didn't wish to understand them . . . Some of our statesmen even after me attempted to communicate with 'dictators' as with 'business men'. The results are obvious."[10]

The dominant assumption was that "reasonable men"—a term much favoured by leader writers at *The Times*—would in the end reach agreement with other "reasonable men" because all men were at bottom "reasonable" in the balancing of mutual interests. How else could one expect business to be done? Interviewed in 1962, Wilson clarified the far-reaching aims that he and Chamberlain had had with respect no less to Nazi Germany than to fascist Italy: "Our policy was never designed just to postpone war, or enable us to enter war more united. The aim of our appeasement was to avoid war altogether, for all time. Our method was to seek reasonable agreements with all European powers. There was no reason why we should exclude Germany from such an agreement."[11] Having Wilson at his ear meant that Chamberlain rarely had to listen to truly expert advice at close quarters unless explicitly requested; in his mind specialists were an unwelcome hindrance to clear thought.

The journalist Philip Kerr, former personal secretary to Lloyd George in 1919 and later elevated as the Marquess of Lothian, expressed much the same view of Wilson as had Cadogan. In conversation with Maisky in 1936 Lothian also alluded to the fact that Chamberlain was "very naïve in questions of foreign policy".[12] But this, of course, was only part of a much larger problem. There were strict limits to the extent to which the rational meeting of interests was applicable to the conduct of international relations. And here the Bolshevik menace reared its head. Chamberlain never believed that Wilson's approach to foreign affairs could ever work with the Soviet Union. This was the single exception. It was, at root, a question of "us" (Western/Central Europe) versus "them" (the Bolsheviks). And in this attitude Chamberlain was by no means alone. Indeed, Wilson went so far as to reflect that Hitler "had an extraordinary amount of political wisdom. He saw more clearly than most people the danger of the Russian advance."[13]

Still writing leaders for James Garvin at the Astors' other newspaper, *The Observer*, Lothian favoured the same course of action as did Chamberlain with respect to Hitler's Germany, but he was also demonstrably Machiavellian. So was Garvin. In 1933 Garvin had no illusions: German rearmament was "inevitable". The Germans wanted to "get back every-thing. . . . This people is blinder than it was before 1914." On his view, "We must be stronger or perish."[14] But Britain had done much less re-arming than it should have by 1937, so Garvin saw appeasement as in-evitable, as did Lothian. Bullitt, the American ambassador to Paris, hav-ing had Lothian to stay the night on 8 January 1937, reported to Roosevelt, "He is convinced that Hitler will not accept peace except at the price of domination of Eastern and Central Europe and the Balkans . . . Kerr personally would like to see Germany get that domina-tion and is absolutely opposed to any armed interference by England to prevent it."[15] Rarely, outside Russia, had Bullitt heard anything so bluntly stated. But what some were prepared to be candid about, others held close to their chest from a sense of shame and fear of exposure to those who saw it as unjustifiable prejudice.

The Roots of Appeasement

Not unlike Baldwin, Chamberlain confessed privately to "the most pro-found distrust of Russia".[16] In late 1938 he wrote of "the Russians stealth-ily and cunningly pulling all the strings to get us involved in war with Germany (our Secret Service doesn't spend all its time looking out of the window)".[17] The secret service was, of course, also deeply anti-Communist, ill-informed on matters Soviet and, except for a handful of years, able only to intercept but not read Comintern communications. The blame for that, as we have seen, lay with the Conservative govern-ment in 1927, which had revealed to the world that it could decrypt Soviet cyphers. From 1934 to 1936 an agent within Comintern gave the British access but that ended when the Russians were tipped off by their spy in the Foreign Office, Donald Maclean. Thereafter it was largely a question of guesswork fitting long-held preconceptions, flavoured by tidbits from British Communist Party headquarters on King Street. Chamberlain's comment that the Russians were trying to lure the Brit-ish into war with Germany is a striking example of mirror-imaging, as this was precisely what Stalin believed Chamberlain was doing to the Soviet Union. And as we have seen, Chamberlain's distrust was certainly not exceptional within the Conservative Party; it was the norm. Nicolson, as usual, saw what was happening with open eyes. He quipped that "people of the governing classes think only of their own fortunes, which means hatred of the Reds. This creates a perfectly artificial but at present most effective secret bond between ourselves and Hitler. Our class interests, on both sides, cut across our national interests."[18]

This was, indeed, an acute diagnosis of an underlying motive force behind appeasement. No one faced with Germany really wanted war. The question was how long it could be postponed, and at what price. Even after the forced Anschluss between Germany and Austria in March 1938 the young Tory MP Ronald Cartland "was amazed how many of colleagues were still terrified of the Communist bogy, and how few realised the imminent danger to this country of the continual strengthening and diplomatic successes of Germany".[19] This was, surely, a key factor in the strength and persistence of appeasement. And it should occasion no surprise. These attitudes were deeply embedded in the bitter domestic and imperial turmoil of the 1920s, when Chamberlain served as health minister, and in which the Russians were caught red-handed on more than one notorious occasion. As chancellor under Baldwin, Chamberlain was summed up by Amery as being "keen on good relations with Japan, on reducing European commitments to a minimum, to getting Russia out of Europe and dropping coercion out of the League".[20] It is unlikely that a better description of his attitudes will ever be found.

Here Amery, originally a friend to Neville's distinguished father Joseph, was able to exert his influence, though only to a limited degree. First of all, he favoured ditching any reliance on the League, "the chapter of humbug and make-believe which has bedevilled our foreign policy in recent years". "I think it was old Lord Salisbury", he wrote, "who said that there is nothing so fatal as sticking to the carcases of dead policies and it seems to me that that is what we are still doing to a considerable extent, trying to move in a new direction and yet dragging the old carcase of Collective Security after us." Instead he strongly favoured, as did Chamberlain, that they "get down to business" with Mussolini. All collective security would result in, he suggested, would be an "Anglo-Franco-Russian combination crystallizing against us the German-Italian-Japanese combination which for us at any rate is far the most dangerous conceivable".[21] Chamberlain was, indeed, working behind his foreign secretary's back in trying to appease Mussolini, but where he differed from Amery was in wanting to do the same with Hitler. And whereas Amery strongly wished to see the British army beefed up, Chamberlain had a firm aversion to any continental capability at all being developed. "Progress with Italy is blocked at the moment by the Spanish situation," Chamberlain explained to Amery in mid-November. "On the other hand," he wrote, "progress with Germany ought not to be delayed because we are, there, in the face of a rising market and the longer we delay, the higher will be the terms asked."[22]

The commercial metaphor is enlightening. And in this respect Chamberlain and Amery were entirely at odds: "The real difference here", Amery advised, "is that we can hardly meet Germany without alienating France and that in the present position we cannot afford to do." He added, "Remember that France will be much more easy to detach from Russia and to persuade her to take a moderate line over Central Europe if she is once more in reasonable relations with Italy. Stresa was the high water mark of success of our diplomacy in Europe." He also pointed out that "In the main I am certain that Germany can only be satisfied in Europe. That means as a minimum our disinterestedness in any quarrel she may have with Russia over the Baltic States."[23] A key concern that he shared with Chamberlain was the need to remove the Russians from the picture and leave them to face the Germans alone. In a subsequent letter to the Australian politician Richard Casey he went on to say that "[i]f we could win around Italy, a must [sic: much] easier task I believe [than winning around Germany], we should then so strengthen the French position that France might drop the Soviet pact leaving Germany free to see what she could do in that quarter."[24] In other words, turn the Germans eastwards.

The only notable exception to the anti-Communism so prevalent on the Tory side of the House of Commons was Churchill, who, though leading the anti-Bolshevik lobby at the outset, had with Hitler's accession purposefully cast aside his long-standing detestation of Moscow to focus on the immediate threat to the empire from Berlin. As we have seen, this abrupt turn-around in Churchill's attitude came under a severe test with the rebellion in Spain. The Duke of Alba, a distant cousin of Churchill's, was a descendant of James II, and thus had among his thirteen titles that of the Duke of Berwick. His magnificent home in the very centre of Madrid, the Palacio de Liria, had been ransacked and burned down by fanatical supporters of the Popular Front in the heady summer of 1936. Alba found himself in England at the time of Franco's revolt. Indeed, on 10 July he was a guest of Edward VIII at St. James's Palace.[25] Unable to return home, he became Franco's unofficial emissary— recognised as such by the British government in November 1937—having been led to believe by Franco, falsely as it turned out, that a nationalist victory would immediately restore the Spanish monarchy.

Alba was the greatest landowner in Spain, with more to lose from revolution than any of his fellow countrymen; a staunch monarchist, "Jimmy" was also intimate with the royal family in Britain; all of which gave him enviable access that no mere ambassador could ever obtain. Glancing back wistfully from his lofty perch to the last days of Queen Victoria, the golden era when he was educated at the Jesuit Beaumont College in Windsor, and gifted with "perfect English", Alba had good reason to regret the irreversible deterioration of political life in Britain since the halcyon days of Lord Salisbury.[26] He lamented that Britain, once a great country run by a "group of families", had since gone rapidly downhill to become a country run by a "group of men" powerful in politics, the City and the press.[27] A very able but diffident man (who had briefly been Spain's foreign minister in the twilight of monarchy, from February 1930 to February 1931), Alba did not tolerate fools gladly and was definitely no socialite. But in the cause of an anti-Communist Spain he resolutely set himself the objective of winning over those in British society to whom he had easy access by privilege of birth.

In London Alba was both a symbol and a magnet. The effect of the Spanish revolt within Britain was to reinforce the anxieties stimulated by the *événements* in France, bringing everyone back to the fundamentals of the 1920s. Regardless of the rise of Nazi Germany, was one anti-Bolshevik or not? Churchill, of course, had instinctively sided with

Franco and had to be talked out of voicing overt support for the Spanish insurrectionists in the House of Commons, by the Soviet ambassador Maisky. "I think I ought to let you know", Churchill warned André Corbin, the French ambassador, "that in my judgement the great bulk of the Conservative Party are very much inclined to cheer the so-called Spanish rebels."[28] Indeed, when in January 1937 Eden, who had something of a deaf ear, innocently commented in cabinet that, were Franco to succeed in taking Madrid, there would be a considerable backlash in Britain, Sir Kingsley Wood indignantly "pointed out that many people in this country would be equally troubled if the Bolshevists achieved a victory".[29]

At the Conservative Party Foreign Affairs Committee on 15 July Nicolson noticed that "the enormous majority are passionately anti-Government and pro-Franco".[30] Newly elected MP Henry ("Chips") Channon told his local newspaper that he himself was "very pro-Franco". Channon also confided to his diary that it would be "a disaster for Conservatism if he [Franco] is defeated by the forces of Communism and anarchy, which dominate the Madrid government".[31] Baldwin, though deemed weak "in the face of the Communist menace", nevertheless was himself strongly anti-Communist and "expressed himself in terms of great sympathy for [Franco's rebels fighting for] Spain".[32] Hoare similarly told Alba that "from the very beginning I have been on your side".[33] Alba also found Viscount Cranborne, the future Lord Salisbury and at that time parliamentary under-secretary at the Foreign Office, "very friendly".[34] Garvin at *The Observer* was just as sympathetic, and so was Lord Salisbury's personal secretary Philip Farrar, a notorious reactionary, who opined after Eden was unceremoniously ejected from the cabinet in February 1938 that "all the individuals in the government wish for the victory of our [Alba's] cause because of the danger of a Red Spain that could infect Portugal". Lord Chancellor the Viscount Hailsham, the agriculture minister W. S. ("Shakes") Morrison and the hopelessly ineffectual minister for co-ordination of defence Sir Thomas Inskip (once unkindly compared to the horse Caligula appointed as consul) also counted themselves on side.[35] One of the few exceptions was Francophile First Lord of the Admiralty, formerly the minister for war, Duff

Cooper.[36] Cooper, unlike his colleagues, was given to frequent outbursts of vituperative hostility towards Nazi Germany.

Most importantly perhaps for Alba, King George VI also discreetly drew alongside. From the winter of 1936, Alba had on two occasions encountered him as Duke of York on country-house weekends, no doubt not entirely by accident. Now king, his initial diffidence had by the summer of 1937 given way to a more confident manner. Out dining in town at one of the homes of former aviation minister the Marquess of Londonderry, Alba was abruptly invited into a neighbouring room to discuss Spain. During the subsequent three quarters of an hour, the king was particularly interested to know what nature the régime would take after the struggle was won by the rebels and, in particular, the fate of the monarchy. Alba said there was not yet any question of a restoration which he himself always favoured. On Germany, he added his "belief that Hitler is sincere when he says that he does not wish a conflict with the Western Powers".[37]

The connections between France and the Soviet Union by alliance and the ties both had to the fate of the Spanish Republic further exacerbated British ideological ambivalence towards the French. The Popular Front itself was anathema, even as it demonstrably weakened. In June 1937 Blum fell from office. Radical Camille Chautemps took over, but Blum and the socialists supported him for want of anything better. The change put the PCF on notice that the government was drifting away from "its base in the Popular Front". Dunant, the Swiss ambassador to France, quipped that this was "not a simple question of politics but rather more, as they say, a question of mathematics". The country was, quite simply, going broke; its credit was ruined.[38]

The PCF was of course instructed to put pressure on Chautemps to sustain *Front populaire* priorities. At the same time, however, Comintern was adamant that the "Communists do not approve at present the growing wave of strikes", which it attributed to provocation from the far right and the Trotskyists.[39] But as far as Britain was concerned, the damage had already been done. Even those still convinced of the ultimate need of an Anglo–French alliance despaired of what the Popular Front had done to the French defence effort. Comparing French and British rearmament in November 1937, the Committee of Imperial Defence reckoned that "recent nationalisation measures introduced in France and internal labour disputes have temporarily reduced French capacity for industrial expansion in emergency, particularly in the case of aircraft . . . the present condition of the French aircraft industry is deplorable".[40]

It did not help the credibility of the left in Britain that, while pressing forcefully for armaments to be exported in aid of the Spanish Republic, they were exerting themselves to the utmost to oppose rearmament at home. In mid-August 1937, for instance, oblivious to such contradictions, Comintern's executive approved the British Communist Party's call for unity "against the National Government, fascism and war" bent on "rearmament" and co-operation with the fascist powers. It condemned the Labour Party for only abstaining on the vote for the defence budget.[41] It was therefore difficult for anyone in London to see the Russians as doing anything other than undermining British security.

Meanwhile Chamberlain's secret back channel to Mussolini, operating between Sir Joseph Ball and Ambassador Grandi from October 1937, began to trouble the Foreign Office.[42] As the situation deteriorated, the left-leaning head of the News Department, the Australian Reginald ("Rex") Leeper, had grown very pessimistic at what he saw as Britain's "policy of continual surrender" towards Mussolini: although fellow reformist Eden stood firm, the others "especially Chamberlain are surrenderers, and in any case are terrified of Bolshevism . . . Sam Hoare is among these".[43]

It was not merely that Chamberlain held to the line of appeasing Germany and Italy while at all costs avoiding any contact with the Soviet Union. He also sought to bully his colleagues and force other states into adopting the same policy. In so doing the prejudices he freely expressed were such as to shock those correspondents who participated in his off-the-record briefings. Former lobby correspondent James Margach recalls, "Any questions put across the table about, say, reports of persecutions of Jews, Hitler's broken pledges or Mussolini's ambitions, would receive a response on the well-established lines; he was surprised that such an experienced journalist was susceptible to Jewish-Communist propaganda."[44] Chamberlain's instincts were consistently authoritarian. Indeed Eden, though not exactly an objective witness, always suspected that the dictators appealed to him in some unconscious and deep-seated way. Chamberlain's support for Ball's anti-Semitic, anti-Bolshevik and pro-appeasement magazine *Truth*, which he strongly recommended as reading matter to his sisters, indicates that his largely undisclosed inclinations lay, indeed, uncomfortably close to the far right.[45]

British Unilateralism

The Times had indicated in July 1936 that the British government, certainly under Chamberlain, was not going to allow its foreign policy to be led from Paris. On the contrary, when Lord Privy Seal Viscount Halifax, former viceroy of India and staunchly "anti-Russian", took himself off "informally" to Germany on Chamberlain's behalf as a guest of the German Hunting Association on 8 November,[46] the French were not even forewarned of his going. Foreign Minister Delbos correctly saw this trip as an informal probe for a bilateral understanding.[47] Halifax was hosted by Göring and visited Hitler at Berchtesgaden, where he thought it appropriate to congratulate the dictator on performing what he described as "great services in Germany". Halifax added that Hitler "also, as he would no doubt feel, had been able, by preventing the entry of communism into his own country, to bar its passage further west".[48]

Halifax confided to Channon that he "liked all the Nazi leaders, even Goebbels! whom no one likes. He was much impressed, interested and amused by visit. He thinks the regime fantastic, perhaps too fantastic to take seriously."[49] And Halifax did not doubt they were "genuine haters of Communism". He believed it vital that Britain "get on with them".[50] Ever confident in his judgement but devoid of experience, Halifax took a relatively benign view of German "beaver-like activities" which he considered "less harmful than (say) a military invasion of Austria".[51] Despite claims to the contrary, Sargent noted, the visit did have "a definite political significance".[52] The French, deeply offended, were astounded at such insouciance. This was for them the first of several unpleasant surprises sprung by Chamberlain.

The arrival in London on 29 November of Chautemps, the French president of the council, and Foreign Minister Delbos, for consultations, threatened to ruffle British complacency, however. Delbos was en route to Eastern Europe. The British would have preferred that he had stayed at home. The French were alarmed "that Germany was aiming at the absorption of Austria and part of Czecho-Slovakia", Chamberlain reported. "At one time", he added, "it looked as though they were going to press the British Ministers to adopt some more forthcoming attitude in Central Europe." But, thanks to British discouragement, they backed off, to Chamberlain's great relief.[53]

France was thus increasingly isolated: cut out by British unilateralism and simultaneously cold-shouldered by the Russians. In Moscow Litvinov was himself subject to investigation by the NKVD and expecting to be arrested along with many of his subordinates at any moment; he was living on borrowed time. The forward policy of collective security he had talked Stalin into four years before looked dangerously overexposed. It was, after all, dead in London. And when he tried to invite Delbos to Moscow as a continuation of his East European tour, the Politburo bluntly instructed Narkomindel that if the issue were to be raised, "reply that we don't understand why now in particular Delbos needs to visit Moscow. We ourselves should not take any initiative."[54]

The Kremlin's attitude was increasingly becoming one of "fortress Russia". As such it was not so much pro-German as completely xenophobic, as the show trials indicated: after all the bulk of those arraigned for treachery were artificially linked to the Germans as conspirators. Indeed, on 21 December Stalin and the Politburo took a tough line with Germany because it had held back from exporting manufactures of military significance under the credits arranged in 1935.[55] Woefully short of raw materials for their accelerated weapons programs, the Germans offered the Russians a credit of 200 million marks, superseding the credits of 1935 that had not been entirely exhausted. Berlin was thus on notice from Moscow. But what struck foreign observers more was the fact that both Leningrad Party Secretary Andrei Zhdanov and Chairman of the Council of People's Commissars Molotov launched attacks on France at the Supreme Soviet while avoiding direct criticism of Germany. And when *Le Temps* correspondent Luciani—who was in the pay of the Quai d'Orsay—visited Litvinov, now under immense pressure from his superiors, he was treated to a "violent diatribe" directed at the French foreign minister and was warned "that if the French did not mend their ways the Soviet Government might well be driven into the arms of Germany".[56]

The reorientation of Britain's policy explicitly towards a bilateral understanding with Germany relegated the Soviet Union to the sidelines. Those in Britain that the Russians felt they could depend upon, at least as attentive listeners, were also being systematically cold-shouldered by the supporters of Chamberlain, and this inevitably reinforced the sense of isolation in Moscow. One such was Vansittart. At the Foreign Office Halifax had been obliged to work uncomfortably close to him. A larger-than-life figure, he was an implacable opponent of appeasing Germany and a regular at Ambassador Maisky's informal lunches. It took Wilson nearly a year to have the permanent under-secretary pushed upstairs.[57] Wilson then usurped Vansittart's functions when the latter was appointed "chief diplomatic advisor": a title without precedent, without office and without function, as demonstrated by the fact that Chamberlain did not speak to him once in the two subsequent years.[58] Vansittart was supplanted at the Foreign Office by his deputy Cadogan, "a tame and colourless civil servant" in the words of Eden.[59] Cadogan loathed "Van", and took his place in spite of resolutely negative lobbying by Fisher from the Treasury, an opponent of appeasement.[60] Arguably the rightful heir by virtue of expertise was Sargent, a man steeped in knowledge of Central Europe and more in line with Fisher's robust views on Germany. Sargent was definitely not Wilson's cup of tea. Moreover, he had managed throughout his career to avoid all foreign postings. He was also tainted by dangerous proximity to Vansittart.

Cadogan was a much more malleable man: collegial, from the top drawer, the son of an earl no less, conventional, solidly anti-Bolshevik and a firm believer in revising the Versailles Treaty. At an audience with Edward VIII in mid-May 1936 the king said, "Anyhow, we must have peace." "Oddly enough," Cadogan noted, "he hit, spontaneously, on my remedy: 'We must get away from Versailles.'"[61] Cadogan's was a world of benign, liberal rationalism. The assumption was that foreign states-men worked along the same lines as the sensible British. "Let us break down this awful wall of reserve between us and Germany," Cadogan confided to his diary in January 1937.[62] This suited Chamberlain admi-rably. No better match could have been found.

New Year 1938 thus saw Cadogan firmly in the saddle, with the odd one out, the younger, ambitious but irresolute Eden, now fully exposed to Chamberlain's line of fire. Vansittart, whom Eden himself found ir-ritating, had warned Eden that he might be next. Eden was boxed in by Chamberlain's unilateralist instincts and his easily expressed irritation at France's commitment to the Soviet Union. More open minded than most leading Conservatives, Eden rightly noted in November 1937 that relations with the Russians were held back "if only on account of the feelings about Communism held by many people in Great Britain".[63]

As we have seen, Stalin had told Dimitrov in 1934 that he did not be-lieve Communism would advance in either Britain or France of its own volition, given the democratic traditions of both countries. Moreover, as time went on Stalin had become ever more conscious of the continuity between himself and the Romanov dynasty, though with a Bolshevik twist. To a larger audience that was understandably terrified of putting a foot wrong, on the anniversary of the October Revolution in Novem-ber 1937, Stalin felt uninhibited about delivering a heretical confession on this count: lauding the tsars for building such "a massive state", he also pointed out that in Britain "nothing can be done because the middling rank and file side with Labour. The French Party is conducting the right policy but the socialist party is none the less very strong."[64]

Then there was the crucial issue of rearmament, to which the British cabinet was not wholeheartedly committed, particularly with respect to land forces. Eden was bluntly advised that a "great many of your col-leagues, and the public servants who work for them, have no idea of the real urgency & danger of our position. Nothing but a really great shake-up in the Cabinet seems to me capable of getting the necessity of rear-mament seen in the right light & pace. It is surely of no use for the Chancellor to say that he cannot afford more than £200,000,000 for upkeep. A larger sum—for a while at least—will be cheaper than destruction." Chamberlain was shown this but, in keeping with his nature, decided not to circulate it to cabinet.[65]

What happened was all too easily predictable. On Sunday 20 February the cabinet was "in almost continuous session in the afternoon and evening over the growing sense of divergence between Anthony [Eden] and Neville [Chamberlain], brought to a head by an approach on Friday from [Italian ambassador Dino] Grandi".[66] Eden's resignation was in on Monday. Halifax was a welcome replacement; as Wilson recalled, the new foreign secretary "wasn't a man of courage; he didn't readily take responsibility".[67]

The political differences between Halifax and Eden were marked; their preferences were entirely incompatible. Whereas Eden, a believer in collective security, sought to work in tandem with France in alignment against Italy and Germany, Halifax—in line with Chamberlain's preferences—rejected the French connection and preferred unilateral action.[68] Halifax was wholly averse to any attempt at multilateral coordination to contain Italy or Germany. He did not believe in containment at all. Indeed, he went further than that: he believed in diplomacy divorced from military capability—a position his illustrious predecessors would have regarded as pure folly. He advised Loraine, then ambassador to Italy, that "the lesson that we all have to learn is . . . about influence being better than power".[69] This was, to say the least, a catastrophic assumption to make in, of all times, the Nazi era. Halifax also believed that Europe's problems should be solved "piecemeal". And his underlying premise, like that of Chamberlain and Wilson, was one of rational liberal economics. At the very time the prime minister was dismissing the notion that rearmament on any major scale could be afforded, his closest colleague Halifax envisaged large-scale financial aid to the fascist powers. The contradiction in saying that one could not afford rearmament but one could afford massive foreign aid never seemed to occur to him. He talked airily about "assisting Italy and Germany through the transition period back to normal relationships with the other powers of the world". And he grasped, mistakenly, at what he misunderstood to be Roosevelt's agreement that the new approach of appeasement adopted by London was "right". On this, at least, he was abruptly and firmly put in his place. The Americans may have been impotent, thanks to isolationism in Congress, but they had few illusions about stark reality. This was most certainly so in the case of Under-Secretary of State Sumner Welles, who brusquely took to task the British ambassador, Sir Ronald Lindsay: "I have never indicated in our previous conversation that the president or any responsible officials of this Government had undertaken to determine or much less say to the British Government that they considered its procedure 'to be right'."[70]

Britain's relationship with France was, of course, crucial to safeguarding the security of the home islands. But Chamberlain's own prejudice against France was that it scarcely amounted to anything of importance and would therefore not constitute a reliable ally. Once again the judgement turned not only on finances but also on the problem of subversion: France was, Chamberlain believed, "in a terribly weak condition being continually subject to attacks on the franc and flights of capital together with industrial troubles and discontent which seriously affects her production of all kinds and particularly of arms and equipment".[71] He was not wrong, of course; but deserting France in the face of a resurgent Germany would not make matters any better. In fact it made them a good deal worse.

Permanent Under-Secretary at the Foreign Office Cadogan also thought the *Front populaire* and the "Red" Government in Spain "awful".[72] He was by no means the exception in the Foreign Office. Sir Francis Lindley, who had served as consul-general in Russia in 1919 and later as ambassador to Japan, which had long ago locked up all its Bolsheviks, wrote a prominently displayed letter to *The Times* on 7 August 1936. There he referred to the Soviet régime's "settled policy . . . to organise, finance, and arm those who agree with its social aims in every country of the world. The full implications of this policy of Moscow", he continued, "have never been grasped in this country. Its unavoidable result is to bring the opposed foreign extremists into the field and to endanger the peace of the world. Spain may well not be the last of the fruits of the action of the peace-loving Soviets." In a rebuttal to criticism of his letter, on 22 August Lindley made two points: the first, that Soviet agents had long been "preparing 'heavy civil war' (the technical Bolshevist expression) in Spain. The second is that the Government, though democratic and properly elected, has never governed. From the outset it tolerated, if it did not encourage, the grossest outrages by its most ardent supporters." Lindley was, indeed, in the best of company. From Ankara Ambassador Sir Percy Loraine confided to a friend, "Obviously my private sympathies, which must be carefully kept under an official bushel are entirely Franquista." Indeed, he wanted to entertain King Alfonso of Spain as his house guest. Loraine's cousin Sir Lancelot Oliphant was head of the Eastern Department and did not relish the idea, however, countering that the Foreign Office as a whole was under attack because of "our alleged leanings to the Right in matters Spanish".[73] Halifax himself had no doubts about the "beastly Bolshevik point of view".[74]

When Joseph Kennedy, Roosevelt's choice, arrived as ambassador to London, he was entertained by both Chamberlain and Halifax. Subsequently Kennedy told the Soviet ambassador that Chamberlain's policy was one of coming to terms with Germany and Italy through concessions and that he had no intention of retreating from it. At this point Kennedy shrugged his shoulders and exclaimed, "I don't know if there exists in the world anything that the Premier is prepared to fight for."[75] The German seizure of Austria naturally made no difference.

On 10 March a group of Austrian schoolchildren out on the slopes of the Alps noticed by chance German troops moving across the mountains. The following day the clatter of the German Eighth Army entering Vienna took the British by surprise. France, the guardian of the postwar status quo and guarantor of Austrian independence, was stupefied. And when its chargé d'affaires in Rome phoned the Palazzo Chigi to seek co-operation against Germany, he was humiliated by Ciano's refusal to see him.[76] The Germans knew that, however much the French wanted to exact retribution, the British would have no hand in it. In Berlin Göring's "research" office (under cover as the *Reichsluftfahrtministeriums-Forschungsamt*), the most effective cryptanalytical department in Germany, had as a matter of fact obtained the British diplomatic cipher and were aware of Britain's decision. Göring told Hitler that the "French indeed wanted to go into action without any reservation and so pressed most hard on the British. I can send you the decoded cables . . . Today

France tells its ministers in the various countries it can do nothing because England refused".[77] The *Forschungsamt* was, indeed, entirely accurate.[78]

In an extraordinary display of contempt for the chief architects of the Versailles Treaty that Hitler was ripping apart, the unpopular German ambassador to London Ribbentrop and his wife were being entertained as guests of the king and queen and then having lunch with Chamberlain while all this was going on. Apparently, according to Leeper at the Foreign Office, Ribbentrop "had been told in very clear terms what this country thought of it." "Before or after lunch[?]", quipped the director of the BBC, Sir John Reith.[79] But the Germans had calculated correctly. The Vatican's secretary of state had noted, back in 1936, that "After the blow in the Rhineland, the Nazis have gained much in Austria ... England has no sense of the Austrian problem."[80] The Germans understood their British counterparts well enough, even those hostile to Berlin. After all, was it not the noted Germanophobe Vansittart who had told Count Grandi several years earlier that "the problem of Austria is of 90% interest for Italy and only indirectly for Great Britain".[81] In the intimate world of diplomacy such juicy tidbits from on high were bound to circulate.

To the surprise of its readers, on the first occasion since 1933 *The Times* actually expressed shock at Hitler's behaviour. Printing House Square had not thus far become completely insensible to the use of force by the Hitler régime. The pious deputy editor Robin Barrington-Ward, who regarded the British as, in the words of the Book of Common Prayer, "tied and bound by the chains of our sins" and had hitherto seemed willing to accept whatever Hitler did as justifiable, finally woke up, at least for a brief moment.[82] In "A March and The Moral", the leader that appeared on 14 March, Barrington-Ward acknowledged "the view, which has been common to most thoughtful Englishmen, that she [Austria] was destined sooner or later to find herself in close association with the German Reich". But he added, "What is so deeply resented here and throughout the civilized world ... is that it was thought necessary, for the sake of a Dictator's prestige, to reverse the whole process by applying to it the physical strength of the bully, and in so doing to arrest other hopeful movements towards a stable peace."

Yet the Germans, though aggressive, were none the less seen as vulnerable. Halifax's dream of extensive economic assistance to help them out indicated as much. It was not at this stage so much from fear of Germany that the British refused to act. No assessment existed to the effect that the Germans were anything like ready for a major war. On the contrary, the strains and stresses of an economy stretched to the utmost by hasty rearmament were only too apparent. The fears derived instead from a very different quarter: fascism was fragile, Communism strong. Gladwyn Jebb, now private secretary to the permanent undersecretary at the Foreign Office, and therefore liaison with MI6, argued that were Britain, France and Russia to oppose the Anschluss with force, "it still seemed that a total collapse of the Germans, which might then be achieved, could only result in a Russian absorption of Poland and the probable extension of Russian power westwards in an alliance with some Russophile government in Germany".[83] It is thus a mistake to assume that because Chamberlain and Halifax behaved as supplicants they necessarily saw themselves as weak in respect of Germany.

With Austria under the boots of the Wehrmacht, Czechoslovakia, which was signatory to a mutual assistance pact with both France and the Soviet Union, now stood perilously exposed on the front line. One-third of its population lay in the western part of the country, the Sudetenland, with German troops now to the south. No doubt fortuitously, Barrington-Ward's 'in-sorrow-not-in-anger' editorial had appeared beside a leader on "The Moscow Trial" of Stalin's latest victims from among the Old Bolsheviks. Hitler's timing was, as ever, perfect, in that the Communists of the Soviet Union under Stalin's despotic hand were absorbed in cannibalising themselves; not least did the show trials revolt those in the West looking to Moscow as a potential ally. No appetite existed in Moscow for further foreign complications when it was believed that both Britain and France were willing if not eager to see Nazi German armies advance eastwards. Any unilateral measures on the part of the Soviet Union would, it was believed, play into the hands of those seeking to encourage Hitler to move even further in that direction.

The crisis that emerged over the fate of Czechoslovakia now brought to a head Britain's resolute determination to bind Germany along with

Italy into an inescapable embrace. It also highlighted the issue of the "beastly" Bolsheviks, because in Moscow "the hitlerisation of Austria" was seen as having "predetermined the fate of Czechoslovakia". In the memorable words of Litvinov, "The Anschluss has already guaranteed Hitler hegemony in Europe independently of the future fate of Czechoslovakia."[84] The crucial question that gripped everyone's attention was whether the Russians would defend the Czechs if the Germans attacked. The target of Hitler's ambition, Czechoslovakia, was itself no less concerned at the prospect of the Red Army speeding to its aid than were the British. Fears that a new war in Europe would result in the rapid expansion of Bolshevism across the continent were as keenly felt in Prague, the next victim of German predation, as in London and Paris—and the Czechs were allies of the Russians. On 9 April Alexandrovsky, the Soviet ambassador to Czechoslovakia, recorded the surprise of President Edvard Beneš "when people say that they don't understand the vacillation and blackmail of England and France, for instance, on the question of Spain, the issue of aid to Czechoslovakia etc. The secret is simple. Europe, for instance, knows what were the consequences of world war 1914–1918 even for the victors. Another such war would mean arming many millions. The experience of the Russian revolution, the collapse of Austria-Hungary, the German revolution; the social turmoil in the victor countries were already a sufficient lesson. And at that time there did not yet exist such a 'noxious' institution as Comintern. Now it not only exists, but it has issued the slogan that imperialist war should be turned into civil war, turning the weapons received against one's own bourgeoisie. Who now would willingly get embroiled in a world war?!"[85] Indeed. Chamberlain himself could not have expressed it better.

At Comintern Dimitrov had reacted swiftly to meet the incoming threat. Austria was first on the agenda. Hitler's *coup de main* had been all the easier, he wrote, because the working class had been disarmed and suppressed successively by Chancellors Engelbert Dollfuss and Kurt Schuschnigg. Leaving no doubt in anyone's mind, Dimitrov also held "[j]ointly responsible for the removal of Austria's independence . . . the reactionary circles of France and above all the Conservative English

Government, that have indirectly backed Hitler's invasion". Comintern's secretariat now resolved that Austrian Party members should "remain within every legal organisation and organ of the workforce, to hold on and immediately join all those newly created". It also insisted on "the closest contact with Catholics" in order to win over the peasantry; advising that comrades join existing Catholic organisations and establish contact with leaders of Catholic institutions. Part of the Party leadership should leave the country for a certain period and be relocated and appointed to the leading organs of the Spanish, Czechoslovakian and French parties. It was important also that they acquire legal status in their countries of adoption.[86] The shutters were hastily closing, however. Having issued a declaration that, in his despair, he believed to be "the last call to Europe for co-operation", Litvinov wrote that "we will adopt and pursue a position of little interest in the future development of the affairs of Europe". Four countries lay in Hitler's path: not just Czechoslovakia, but also Romania, Poland and Hungary. If the four did not get together, they would be taken one by one, in Litvinov's expert opinion.[87]

Stalin was averse to taking any bold initiatives abroad. As a result of his own paranoia, the Red Army was in no condition to contemplate significant offensive operations beyond Soviet borders. Contingency plans were nevertheless pursued. Soviet military intelligence followed up enquiries as to whether Romania, the only feasible avenue for the Red Army to pass through into Czechoslovakia, would be willing to allow passage. Buda, the Czech military attaché, had spoken to King Carol. The Fourth Directorate's *resident* in Bucharest, under deep cover as the TASS correspondent, reported Carol's reply: "In the event that the Red Army crosses through Romania, he (Carol) will restrict himself to a declaration of protest to the League of Nations, but Romania will remain on the side of the Czechs."[88] As a next step, on 14 May Stalin agreed to a proposal from Voroshilov to send an inspection team into Czechoslovakia to check on its fortifications.[89] And on 29 May the Artillery Directorate's military team reported in from Prague.[90] But, as Litvinov had already indicated, everything hinged on the French mustering their allies in Eastern Europe to facilitate the defence of Czechoslovakia. And the Romanians, flapping like loose sails in the wind, were under sustained pressure from the Poles to resist the French. Worse still, Litvinov reported to Stalin that Poland did not conceal its determination to use a German assault on Czechoslovakia to seize Czech territory (Teschen) inhabited by ethnic Poles. Russia could take action to hinder Polish intervention, but for that it needed to know whether France would consider that an attack on Poland required it to act under the terms of the Franco–Polish alliance.[91] Meanwhile, in Moscow on 28 May the Fourth Directorate reported in "On the unity of action of Romania and Poland on the Czechoslovakian question".[92] And the French themselves, under sustained pressure from the British to do nothing to aid the Czechs, showed themselves unwilling to step forward to meet the Russians half way.

France Hesitates

The initiative lay beyond Russian confines, in France; provided the Kremlin's long, clammy hand did not rein it in and provided the French held firm against British pressure. In Paris the Anschluss had caught everyone by surprise amidst a governmental crisis. Thorez had accepted the collapse of the *Front populaire* and wanted to join the Radicals in a national unity coalition. On 18 March he sent Comintern the following message:

> Political circles in France are hurriedly preparing to form a government of national unity made up from representatives of every party with the exception of small pro-Hitler groups. The Communist Party obviously proposes to take part in the government. This proposal will be made in the course of the next few days, and if the international situation worsens still more, then the question of reorganising the government will come to the fore even earlier. We consider inevitable co-operation with parties that were not part of the Popular Front. . . . Shouldn't we send a delegation over to you in this instance to join in discussing this question?[93]

Stalin also saw the telegram, and after discussion two days later involving Georges Cogniot from the PCF, Dimitrov and Manuilsky gave

Thorez the bad news that the secretariat was "against the participation of Communists in a government of national unity". Only war would make this possible.[94] Thorez, however, was not about to throw hope to the winds, even as the outlook became ever bleaker. In Spain Teruel had fallen, this time to Franco, leaving Republican forces exhausted. The Republicans had lost any chance for command of the air. Soviet planes were no longer a match for the Germans' in speed and manoeuvreability both vertically and horizontally.[95]

Sentiment among those close to the levers of power in Britain was irredeemably hostile to Moscow and what it stood for. In late April the celebrated thriller writer John Buchan, governor-general of Canada, indicated to Amery that "[o]ur chief anxiety in European affairs is France's alliance with Russia. I do not like any commitments with that collection of blood-stained mountebanks."[96] When Sir Horace Wilson was, after the war, justifying appeasement to Samuel Hoare, he argued that what was not being appreciated was "the extent to which Neville Chamberlain and your Cabinet colleagues were bound to realise the weakness of France and the state of mind of Daladier & co—a weakness which we knew had been increasing steadily since the Blum 'socialisation.'"[97]

On 9 May Communist Deputy Florimond Bont had a meeting with Daladier and was confronted with the realities of British policy. Yet, as Daladier explained to Bont, the shoe was on the other foot. The plain fact was that France's will to resist Germany was serially undermined by Britain. The French were being disciplined by the British, who gave little or no consideration to their wishes. In stark contrast to Foreign Minister Bonnet, Prime Minister Daladier, though suspicious of the Communists with whom he had initiated the *Front populaire*, did try to stand firm against Hitler. But in Paris the uneasy sense that the British were rapidly drifting away had now taken hold. In explaining why France held back from helping Republican Spain Daladier said, "I have to take into consideration relations with England and Chamberlain." Daladier had found Chamberlain in a peculiar state of mind, but one entirely consistent with that which the US ambassador Kennedy had encountered. Chamberlain puzzlingly asserted that others were planning to encircle

Germany (a reference to the Franco–Soviet pact). In response Daladier insisted that it was precisely the other way around. Chamberlain, however, was convinced that the way forward was to talk to Germany and regulate issues in dispute. The discussion left Daladier decidedly unhappy, as did Chamberlain's "notion that it was impossible to co-operate with the Soviet Union"; a thought which he elaborated upon further. For although Daladier did not value the Red Army highly, he did respect its air force in action, such as had been demonstrated in Spain.[98] Nonetheless, resentment at the Communist Party's continued disruption of the French defence effort burned deep. The tension was palpable. When the Soviet ambassador Yakov Surits, due to travel to Moscow shortly, raised with Daladier the interminable delays in fulfilling Soviet orders for defence equipment, the prime minister snapped back, "Tell Stalin how the business of military defence is being disrupted."[99]

Within the Foreign Office there was considerable disagreement about what to do. But Chamberlain, along with Wilson and Ball, head of the Conservative Research Association which doubled as an informal offshoot of MI5, was, as Jebb describes, "more than ever convinced that some general and lasting arrangement with both dictators—as opposed to a sort of 'holding operation' as regards the Nazis which was certainly the most I was prepared to contemplate—was not only desirable but possible without any very exceptional rearmament effort on our part. Though we had our differences inside the Office," Jebb continues, "there was hardly a Foreign Office official who could swallow this preposterous theory, and we watched, therefore, with some dismay the goings on in No. 10 [Downing Street] and heard with trepidation the rumours regarding the missions of the mysterious emissaries (and notably the self-appointed one of Ivy Chamberlain to Mussolini) who might, for all we knew, be about to conclude some bargain which could weaken the whole diplomatic position of the country."[100]

Not everyone in the British Communist Party believed the situation so urgent as to trim its ideological sails. In mid-April at the request of British comrades in Moscow and very much in the spirit of Harry Pollitt, Comintern had issued a decision as to the importance of clarifying to everyone the "treacherous character of the policy of the Chamberlain

Government, particularly its pro-fascist foreign policy. The Party, therefore, must conduct a systematic mass campaign to expose Chamberlain's policy which is cunningly covered by a mask of peace." To this end
the Party was instructed to broaden its reach to encompass even dissatisfied Conservatives. Members were also instructed to join the "anti-
aircraft defense [sic] movement".[101]

Chamberlain resisted to the last any expenditure on rearmament
above and beyond what had already been hammered out. He did not
win every battle: he lost the fight against the establishment on 25 May
of a Ministry of Supply that was intended to rationalise and expedite
rearmament. Yet elsewhere his grip on policy held firm, notably over
exerting maximum pressure on the Czechs to secure a compromise with
the Germans. Although it was not made explicit to the French, the
prime minister's office was entirely hostile to Prague. "From the start
we were up against the fundamental difficulty that Czechoslovakia had
no business to exist as it was," Wilson shamelessly recalled many years
later.[102] Had the French any idea of the extent of this hostility, they
would have fully understood that the British, far from assisting the
Czechs in any way, were actually doing quite the opposite.

The Russians, meanwhile, were formally standing four-square with
the Czechs, though Stalin no less than Beneš was most reluctant to face
the prospect of a unilateral collision with Germany. He had not given
up on Britain entirely only because he took a more Churchillian view
of British power and influence than Chamberlain and Halifax ever did.
Just as he had done with respect to Poland, he underestimated the
strength and depth of anti-Communism within the British élite. On 5
June he told the US ambassador "that the reactionary elements in
England, represented by the Chamberlain government, were determined upon a policy of making Germany strong, and thus place France
in a position of continual, increasing dependence upon England; also
with the purpose of ultimately making Germany strong against Russia.
He stated that in his opinion Chamberlain did not represent the British
people and that he would probably fail because the Fascist dictators
would drive too hard a bargain."[103] It was evidently in this expectation
that Stalin retained Litvinov on borrowed time at Narkomindel.

With a German attack on Czechoslovakia in prospect and the British refusing to engage, Poland had to consider the possibility of Soviet military intervention not by land, which neighbouring Romania was less likely to permit unconditionally, but by air. The Russians could only accomplish this were Romania to grant them permission to fly over the country to reach Czech airfields. The Poles did their level best to prevent this happening. All of a sudden the Russians found that an agreement on even a regular air route for civilian transport through to Romania had been delayed *sine die*. The initial tendency in Moscow to withdraw from its forward policy was now considerably reinforced. The Russians possessed a massive air force, though no longer at its most competitive technologically, as it had been in 1936. Provided Stalin was prepared to take heavy losses—and he usually was—from faster and more agile German fighter planes, it could certainly still wreak a great deal of damage—a fact even Chamberlain grudgingly acknowledged. On 17 September he told Hugh Dalton that the Red Army could not do much. "In the air, no doubt, the Russians *could* do a great deal, but *would* they?"[104]

Soviet Air Power Forward Based

A clear sign that the Russians were drawing in their horns politically came on 11 May 1938, when Comintern's secretariat issued strict instructions to the Czechoslovakian Communist Party that the German minority must be made to feel at one with the Czech state and that the government's attempts to place national unity in opposition to a separate German identity was misplaced.[105] And on 11 August Litvinov warned the Soviet ambassador in Prague:

> Of course, we are extremely interested in the preservation of Czechoslovakia's independence, in hindering the Hitlerite drive to the South-East, but without the Western Powers it is doubtful whether we would be able to do anything serious, and those Powers do not consider it necessary to seek our assistance, ignore us and decide everything concerning the German-Czechoslovakian conflict among themselves.[106]

He had good reason for his reserve. Even moderate appeasers in Britain like Jebb felt that "we could hardly invoke Russia at this point for the purpose of restraining Hitler without a danger of bringing Russia right into Europe and prejudicing the possibility of eventually, after we had ourselves rearmed, restraining him without such an unfortunate result".[107] The crucial issue for London, as ever, was at all costs to keep the Bolsheviks out of Central Europe.

Although resolute against anyone's assumption that the Soviet Union would have to support Czechoslovakia regardless, ignoring potential objections by overflying Romania, Stalin began the discreet deployment of pilots and planes onto Czech soil. In early July a report about this came into Warsaw from an agent of Polish military intelligence, though this was initially unverified.[108] It was followed up by what seems to have been an intensive operation to clarify the true state of affairs.

On 1 August a memorandum from the head of military intelligence Major General Tadeusz Pełczyński to the chief of the general staff Major General Wacław Stachiewicz detailed numbers of planes and personnel, enclosing a map of their deployment across the country. Intelligence estimated the number of aircraft at 160, 120 of which were centred on Prague. Service personnel and instructors were listed at 180.[109] A later report, on 10 August, listed bombers, including eleven at Brno.[110]

Given that the Czechs had been and were still buying SB bombers from the Soviet Union—though only the frames into which they inserted their own engines—it is not entirely clear that all of the aircraft were to be manned by Russians, but certainly many would have been. Contingency planning, including a complete survey of conditions on the ground in Czechoslovakia, made good sense for the Soviet Union. But it is unlikely that Stalin seriously contemplated anything so radical as unilateral intervention; not least because it was a well-worn assumption since Lenin's day that the other great powers would look upon any such move as the ideal moment to unite against the Bolsheviks in order to wipe out this common scourge once and for all. Many Conservatives in Britain were indeed, as we have seen, not entirely averse to the prospect of Germany under Hitler acting as the bulwark against the spread of Bolshevik influence westwards. Moreover, the recent Soviet military success in battle at Lake Khasan against the Japanese, a much less formidable foe than the Germans, had been a far from stellar performance, even in the air.[111]

The full-scale demoralisation of the Red Army through decapitation and relentless terror was at its height. Commissar for Defence Voroshilov celebrated the fact that "[t]hroughout 1937 and 1938 we had to ruthlessly purge our ranks, mercilessly cutting out the infected parts of the organism through to living, healthy tissue, cleaning it of loathsome, treacherous mildew".[112] And the lesson of the civil war in Spain was that much more needed to be done in order to keep pace with German technology. This was most obvious with respect to air power, the Messerschmitt 109-E outpacing its rival Ilyushin-15 and Ilyushin-16s in Spain, with further improvements to come. On 21 January 1938 Commander of the Air Force Colonel-General Aleksandr Loktionov and his deputy Yakov Smushkevich together with member of the Military Council Kol'tsov called for immediate remedial action. They pleaded with Voroshilov on the basis that "if at the start of the war in Spain we had an obvious advantage in the quality of matériel (fighter planes), the Germans and Italians have currently caught up with us, and even gained a slight superiority for themselves".[113]

Moreover, although it is now accepted that in the face of Hitler's determination to go to war over Czechoslovakia his own military command were completely at sixes and sevens over whether to oppose him and even launch a coup d'état, no one outside Germany, let alone inside, had any confidence that such a revolt could succeed.[114] The most that can be said is that, were Germany to go to war and face not only Czechoslovakia but also the British, the French and possibly also the Russians, its economy and its military readiness in the west as well as the east were not such as to inspire much confidence in a speedy victory, if victory at all.[115]

This, Litvinov as a former soldier, fully understood.[116] And as someone who never doubted his own courage, even to the point of sleeping fully dressed with a gun under his pillow in case the secret police came for him late at night (he had a horror of being led away in his pyjamas), lack of moral fortitude was not something he readily sympathised with in others.[117] Thus when the US ambassador in Moscow "suggested that perhaps the democratic countries, including England and France, did not wish to hazard a firm position until they were prepared adequately, he [Litvinov] stated that neither Germany nor Italy was prepared adequately. To my expression of surprise, that Germany was not prepared from a military point of view, he stated again that their information was positive that Germany was not ready, even in a military sense, leaving out of consideration the economic background."[118] Indeed, the *Westwall* had not yet been completed as a barrier against the French army, and not for want of accelerated effort. Hitler's armoured divisions were not yet what they were to become by 1940 (thanks in part to Czech tank production that the Germans by that time controlled). The Luftwaffe's bombers were deployed for action in Central/Eastern Europe. And the economy was spluttering from shortages in key raw materials for war, uncertain supplies of food and bottlenecks in transportation.[119]

Odd as it may seem in retrospect, the British would have done almost anything so that Germany could avert the prospect of war on two fronts. At the most important meeting held to discuss Britain's options during the Czechoslovakian crisis, on 30 August, Chamberlain and Halifax ruled out delivering any warnings or threats to Germany that carried with them the possibility that aggression would mean war. Halifax insisted that Czechoslovakia could not be saved. More than that, he coolly argued that even trying to rescue the Czechs would achieve nothing. Entirely rhetorically, Halifax "asked himself whether it was justifiable to fight a certain war now in order to forestall a possible war later". But here he clashed directly with the Earl Winterton, who "thought we underrated the capacity of Czechoslovakia to defend herself". Indeed, even Sir Nevile Henderson, the hitherto resolute appeaser as ambassador to Berlin, pointed out that the Germans were anxious about the Soviet air force. Moreover, Minister of Health Walter Elliot "found it difficult to accept the view that, if Germany attacked Czechoslovakia, we should put pressure on France to localise the conflict. He was very doubtful whether this was the right course, since this might be the last opportunity of standing up against German aggression." And whereas Halifax believed that the incorporation of Czechoslovakia with its non-German nationals would actually weaken Germany, First Lord of the Admiralty Duff Cooper thought that it would, on the contrary, "enormously strengthen it". Like Halifax, Chamberlain obsessively insisted that it was "very important not to exacerbate feeling in Berlin against us", even though Henderson's advice—and he was in a position to know—was that Britain "was the one country of which Germany was afraid".[120]

Because of its alliance with Czechoslovakia, the issue of how to tackle France was an extremely delicate one. Under the Locarno Pact Britain was committed to aid France in the event of attack, but it was equally committed to assist Germany in the event of an attack by France even in defence of another state. Chamberlain and Halifax were determined that France should not attack Germany were the latter to attack Czechoslovakia. Indeed Simon, now chancellor of the exchequer, seemed averse to defending France at all. Reining in the French became as important a priority as forcing the Czechs to concede to Hitler's demands. But this was made absolutely clear only to Kennedy, the US ambassador. At the end of August Assistant Secretary of State Adolf Berle updated Roosevelt on Chamberlain's determination to go it alone even were the French to fight for Czechoslovakia: "Kennedy cables from London that he talked to Neville Chamberlain just after the Cabinet Meeting; that Chamberlain opposed the group in the British Cabinet which advocated [a] declaration of war should Hitler march; and that he would definitely not go to war until he was absolutely forced to even though France went."[121] French Foreign Minister Georges Bonnet—not the most reliable of men and in 1938 pursuing a tactic of duck and cover—told Ambassador Bullitt the exact opposite;[122] but Chamberlain was certainly the one to be believed, given Bonnet's notoriously loose relationship with the truth.[123]

The Czechs Are Disowned by the British

On 7 September an editorial appeared in *The Times* that rapidly became notorious. Entitled undramatically, if not arcanely, "Nuremberg and Aussig", and drafted by leader writer and arch-appeaser Leo Kennedy as a secondary contribution to the leader columns, it could easily have slipped by unnoticed but for its explosive content. It had been abruptly seized upon and "heavily revised" by Dawson later that night.[124] And Dawson most certainly knew what he was doing. As the official history of *The Times* notes, what now took pride of place "was universally regarded . . . as inspired by a high official source".[125] The most controversial paragraph ran:

> [I]t might be worth while for the Czechoslovak Government to consider whether they should exclude altogether the project, which has found favour in some quarters, of making Czechoslovakia a more homogeneous State by the secession of that fringe of alien populations who are contiguous to the nation with which they are united by race. In any case the wishes of the population concerned would seem to be a decisively important element in any solution that can hope to be regarded as permanent, and the advantages to Czechoslovakia of becoming a homogeneous State might conceivably outweigh the obvious disadvantages of losing the Sudeten German districts of the borderland.[126]

"There was a hubbub, as I fully expected over the morning's leader," wrote Dawson, apparently unperturbed; "reactions in Prague and Berlin and the F[oreign] O[ffice] went up through the roof. Not so however the Foreign Secretary, who came and lunched with me at the Travellers [Club] and had a long talk."[127] This open display of solidarity was scarcely accidental in a club heavily frequented by diplomats, domestic and foreign. The official history of *The Times* notes that Halifax was "a tried and intimate friend of Dawson's, an old member of the circle of Imperialist Conservatives in which Dawson had moved for a generation, and a Yorkshire neighbour".[128]

Evidently to lend at least the appearance of consulting the Russians, Halifax called in the Soviet ambassador the following day, hardly expecting the lashing he then received from Maisky's sharp tongue. When Halifax alluded to the danger that the Sudeten Germans could reject the latest Czech compromise (put together with Chamberlain's close colleague and emissary, shipping magnate Lord Runciman), Maisky sarcastically suggested that this might have something to do with *The*

Times's editorial. With as much "fervour" as he could muster—"and even that did not amount to much", Maisky noted sourly—Halifax disingenuously conceded that the editorial was a great pity but had nothing to do with the views of the British government. "The trouble was", he said, "that no one believes our denials." Exactly, and not without good reason. Maisky correctly concluded that the leader amounted to a sounding for a forthcoming deal at the expense of Czechoslovakia's territorial integrity.[129]

British and French evasiveness on the subject of Czechoslovakia barely concealed blatant attempts to sell the Czechs down the river. Spreading the word that the Russians would never abide by their treaty with Czechoslovakia was seen as the most effective means of doing so. Meanwhile, as the Soviet ambassador in Paris learned on 3 September, the British were actively discouraging any French contact with the Russians, particularly of a military nature: "One of the Ministers (I don't know who, but I think it's Chautemps) said at the council that from discussions with Englishmen in authority, he gained the distinct impression that above all they fear the intervention of the USSR in European affairs, apprehensive lest the success of Soviet arms may pave the way towards Communism in Central Europe."[130] This certainly fits with what we already know about the attitude of the diehard appeasers. The crucial factor was thus not a dismissal of the Soviet Union as a military threat because of Stalin's terror, but rather the lingering fear and suspicion that his armed forces had sufficient firepower to intervene and snatch whatever was going.

The thinking and assumptions behind British policy on Czechoslovakia occasion no surprise. At Printing House Square Dawson "was certainly influenced too by the thought that Nazi Germany served as a barrier to the spread of Communism in the West".[131] This was the settled view common to all of the main appeasers. The Palace was no exception. The Duke of Windsor was notoriously "very pro-German".[132] The Duke and Duchess of Kent stood not far off.[133] And on 13 September, with his trip to Germany in sight, Chamberlain wrote to a sympathetic King George VI of his aims. Chamberlain clearly understood that the king, whom he briefed every week, was, like his mother Queen

Mary, herself a German, at root sympathetic to Berlin and anti-Bolshevik to the core. In meeting Hitler, Chamberlain, confident of royal support, said he would outline "the prospect of Germany and England as the two pillars of European peace and buttresses against Communism".[134]

Chamberlain's motivations could scarcely have been made more explicit. His loyal parliamentary private secretary Lord Dunglass (later Prime Minister Sir Alec Douglas Home) recalled, "One of Neville Chamberlain's motives in trying to dissuade Hitler from war and in doing so risk slipping over the edge of reconciliation into the pit of appeasement, was that he felt certain in his mind that if Europe weakened itself in another war, Russia would try to dominate the continent of Europe."[135] And this was scarcely a secret within the Foreign Office. Diplomat Geoffrey Thompson noted in a letter to Claude Bowers, the US ambassador to Spain, that Chamberlain was inspired by "the mawkish dread of communism".[136] Secretary of State for India the Marquess Zetland, a member of the Anglo-German Fellowship that lobbied vigorously for appeasement, also "wondered what sort of regime would exist in Germany after a world war. Might it not be even more dangerous to us than the Nazi Regime?"[137]

At Chamberlain's request, MI6 under the highly politicised Admiral "Quex" Sinclair—supposedly a purely intelligence gathering institution—readily produced policy proposals that supported the dismemberment of Czechoslovakia to "forestall the inevitable".[138] In direct contrast Vansittart, now effectively only a reluctant witness forced onto the sidelines, argued strongly but in vain that "[i]f we lend ourselves to the beginning of this process, the future is fairly obvious—in two stages. In the first Russia will be evicted and retire into sulky isolation. In the second she will be penetrated by Germany, and Bismarck's traditional policy of close Russo–German relations will follow. The consequences to Europe are too obvious to need enlargement here."[139]

Hitler persistently upped his demands so that the other powers effectively handed him the Sudetenland on a plate. In an act of desperation at the prospect of peace unravelling and in the knowledge that the German armed forces were preparing an invasion, on 15 September Chamberlain flew in to see Hitler at Berchtesgaden to avert war. But

Hitler, fixed on settling the problem through war, was unappreciative and if anything irritated rather than flattered by the gesture. None the less Chamberlain wrote to his younger sister Ida that he "got the impression that here was a man who could be relied upon when he had given his word".[140] Meanwhile, at Geneva for a session of the League of Nations Richard ("Rab") Butler, Halifax's parliamentary under-secretary, assured Chips Channon that "there would be no war, no matter what people said: he had implicit faith in Halifax and Chamberlain, both were linked together by an understanding; either would do a dishonest deed to reach a high goal. The ultimate object is all that counted."[141]

In anticipation of a further summit between Chamberlain and Hitler, and under intense pressure to save his country, on 19 September President Beneš put two questions to the Soviet ambassador, Alexandrovsky. In Moscow the Politburo was updated and on 20 September resolved the following answer to Beneš's questions:

1. To Beneš' question whether the USSR, according to the treaty, will render immediate and genuine aid to Czechoslovakia should France remain true to it and also render aid, you can in the name of the Government of the Soviet Union give an answer in the affirmative.

2. You can give an affirmative answer also to Beneš' other question—whether the USSR, as a member of the League of Nations, come to the aid of Czechoslovakia on the basis of articles 16 and 17 should, in the event of an attack by Germany, Beneš turn to the Council of the League of Nations with a request for the implementation of the above articles.

3. Inform Beneš that we are simultaneously making known to the French Government the contents of our response.[142]

This reply was immediately telegraphed to Alexandrovsky by Deputy Commissar Potemkin. It was conveyed to Beneš by telephone at 7 that evening, during a session of the government at which the Anglo-French ultimatum was being discussed. After repeating the answer twice more, Beneš seemed satisfied with the reply and two hours later the foreign minister's chief secretary, Ina, told Alexandrovsky that the Czechs were turning down the Anglo-French proposals.[143]

During the meeting Prime Minister Milan Hodža outlined the Soviet answer, pointing out that for the League to act, defining Germany as the aggressor would require unanimity from the League Council. The Russians had said they would be satisfied if only a majority of members agreed to the motion. "However," the minutes record Hodža as saying, "in present circumstances, in particular, if one bore in mind the statement from France and Britain, it was clear that this path was uncertain and did not promise positive results. When, in these conditions representatives of our army were asked, they stated that a conflict in isolation would mean collapse for Czechoslovakia; especially because it would entail the danger of a possible attack by other, neighbouring states. Thus a possible change of opinion of the other states in the Little Entente was borne in mind." The Czechs decided to rescind the note sent to the British and French the day before that rejected the solution to the crisis proposed by London and Paris. The prime minister therefore proposed, after discussion, that they now accept the terms offered.[144]

The Czechs Capitulate

Czechoslovakia went ahead but only on certain preconditions. Beneš explained to Alexandrovsky that his government had agreed to concede to Germany a section of territory with a German population above 50%; this would, however, have to be determined by an international committee and no German forces could enter the country until it was done. But, clearly not confident that the British and French would obtain Hitler's agreement, Beneš then enlarged upon his original request for Soviet intervention. First, in the event of a German invasion, would the Russians be willing to send in the air force and land troops without waiting for a decision from the League of Nations? What would be the size of the intervention and what would be the timing? Second, if Czechoslovakia turned to Romania requesting that the Red Army be allowed through, would the Soviet Union send in land forces and what would it do if Romania objected? Third, Beneš had received a demand from Poland to make a decision about the Polish minority. How would the Soviet Union react to a Polish attack on Czechoslovakia? An agreement would have to be drawn up. Beneš asked for an immediate reply because he doubted that Chamberlain would succeed in persuading Hitler to accept Czech conditions.[145] There was no way Stalin was going to commit the Soviet Union to a war against Germany with no likely allies while Britain and France sat back to take advantage of the outcome. Beneš could not have been entirely surprised never to have received an answer.

Prague had effectively surrendered before a shot was fired. Unfortunately for the Czechs, having handed the country's fate over to London and Paris, there were no limits to Chamberlain's appetite for concessions when he flew in on 22 September and Hitler once more raised his demands. To Field-Marshal Jan Smuts, Amery poured out contempt for his old friend the prime minister: "It was really a great mistake for anyone, only accustomed to the ordinary decencies of Cabinet and Parliamentary discussion, and with such little knowledge of the detailed and background history of Central Europe, to think that he could stand up to a single-handed discussion with Hitler. The trouble is that his relative success over the Italian agreement had made Neville think that he was up to the job of a Foreign Minister, which, with all his good qualities, I fear he is not."[146]

Indeed, the harder Hitler pressed, the more inclined was Chamberlain to give way. "Hitler's memo. now in," wrote Cadogan in his diary on 24 September. "It's awful. A week ago when we moved (or were pushed) from 'autonomy' to cession, many of us found great difficulty in the idea of ceding people to Nazi Germany. We salved our consciences (at least I did) by stipulating it must be an 'orderly' cession—i.e. under international supervision, with safeguards for exchange of populations, compensation, &c. Now Hitler says he must march into the whole area *at once* (to keep order!) and the safeguards—and plebiscites! can be held *after*!" The "inner cabinet" met. "P.M. made his report to us. I was completely horrified—he was quite calmly for total surrender." And Halifax was at one with Chamberlain, just as Butler had foreseen.[147]

Far too late Amery, who had had no idea of what the prime minister was capable of, wrote to Chamberlain astonished at "the demands that the Czechs should, in advance of any orderly and international impersonal settlement, immediately hand over the predominantly German speaking areas to the German Army: in other words that they should abandon their only defensive line before they have time to construct even the rudiments of a new one, as well as abandon all their own friends in the ceded districts to the tender mercies of their political opponents without giving them even a few weeks to make arrangements for clearing out." This would, he emphasised, be "an act of folly and cowardice". Were Chamberlain to go ahead on this basis, he warned, "there would be a tremendous revulsion of feeling against you".[148] If there is one explanation as to why Amery was never offered a post by Chamberlain when war finally came, this letter is it.

On 26 September Wilson left for Berchtesgaden for further clarification. On the following day Chamberlain broadcast his horror, not that Britain was without flinching mutilating another country and handing over millions into the hands of the Gestapo, but, true to form, that "we should be digging trenches and trying on gas-masks here because of a quarrel in a far-away country between people of whom we know nothing". While insisting that a deal on Czechoslovakia could still be done, Wilson also told Hitler that he "had often been struck, as had many others in England, by a speech in which Herr Hitler had said that he regarded England and Germany as bulwarks against disruption, particularly from the East".[149] Conscious that he was in a commanding position, Hitler then invited Chamberlain to Munich, along with Mussolini and Daladier. In the early hours of 30 September they had between them agreed to partition Czechoslovakia, ceding the Sudetenland in its entirety to Germany. This was the achievement that Chamberlain heralded as "peace with honour".

Britain's international standing was in shreds. Roosevelt, safely at a remote distance from events, summed up a not uncommon view when he said that "the Anglo-French note to [the] Czechoslovakian Government was the most terrible remorseless sacrifice that had ever been demanded of a State".[150] Beneš was understandably very bitter. He told his personal secretary Prokop Drtina that "[t]hey [Britain and France] think that they will save themselves from war and revolution at our expense. They are wrong."[151] Utterly deluded, however, Chamberlain seriously believed "he had now established an influence over Herr Hitler and that the latter trusted him and was willing to work with him".[152] And the doubts of those friends of Chamberlain who questioned whether this was true were undercut by their antipathy to the French, enhanced by their close association with the Russians: so deep did this antipathy go. Amery, a strong anti-Communist for whom this was a policy that he had "always favoured" wrote, "The real justification for Neville's policy is no doubt a profound conviction that the French entanglement with Czechoslovakia and Russia had to be liquidated at all costs whatever the injustice to the Czechs or the humiliation to ourselves."[153]

It is often claimed that Chamberlain was seeking to buy time to rearm. The evidence, however, is all to the contrary. Wilson doggedly insisted that "[t]he aim of our appeasement was to avoid war altogether, for all time."[154] Moreover, the prime minister had always felt that too much was being spent on armaments, and when the War Office and the Air Ministry immediately now pressed for more expenditure, Wilson advised Chamberlain that "we must hesitate before departing too far from the aggregate sum approved, reluctantly, by the Cabinet earlier in the year".[155] Clearly Wilson resented even the existing level of expenditure, let alone an increase. And he was listened to despite Britain's immense wealth, the greater part of which was to be liquidated in the coming world war. Again true to form, on 31 October Chamberlain told cabinet of his determination to establish the kind of relations with Germany and Italy "which will lead to a settlement in Europe and a sense of stability. A good deal of false emphasis has been placed . . . in the country and in the Press . . . on rearmament, as though one result of the Munich Agreement has been that it will be necessary to add to our rearmament programmes . . . it may be possible to take active steps and to follow up the Munich Agreement by other measures." He also hoped that "one day we shall be able to secure limitation of armaments, though it is too soon to say when this will prove possible."[156]

No. 10 had not in fact been seeking to buy more time for further re-armament by appeasing Hitler at Munich. Indeed, "[Chamberlain] thought armaments were a wasteful form of expenditure," Wilson re-called.[157] And as before, the prime minister was still in search of the means of settling relations permanently with Germany on a more ami-cable basis. Thus on 1 November Amery found fellow members of the House of Commons "rather depressed by the lack of any indication of a really bold policy of rearmament. It looks very much as if he [Cham-berlain] is still pinning his faith to appeasement and only prepared to do as much rearmament as public opinion insists upon."[158] Indeed, do-mestic public opinion was equally dismayed. As the Americans noted later in 1940, "Public opinion in England has been in advance of Cham-berlain in all of the crises that preceded the war."[159] The *News Chronicle* published a poll at the beginning of November 1938 showing that 72% of the population called for more expenditure on armaments. More-over, though it remained unpublished under pressure from the usual quarters not so far from Downing Street and for fear of upsetting the government line, 86% expressed disbelief at Hitler's assertion that he had no more territorial claims to make.[160]

Moscow Draws the Lessons

An early sign of the shift in the Kremlin's thinking to more deep-seated suspicions was the fact that Soviet naval intelligence now allowed for a further contingency in its planning for war: the prospect of Britain as a covert ally of Germany. "From an analysis of the current military-political situation in Europe it follows that the main organiser and inspiration for war against the Soviet Union in the West is Fascist Germany evidently under the patronage of England and France."[161] British policy on Spain certainly fitted the pattern. There the Republic was on its knees. Looking ahead, the prime minister finally found time to meet Franco's informal envoy, the Duke of Alba, at a dinner on 25 October 1938 dutifully ar-ranged by Chamberlain's sister-in-law. During the extended conversa-tion Chamberlain expressed what Alba described as "sympathy for our ideology".[162] After 9–10 November—*Kristallnacht*—any expressions of sympathy for fascism became more difficult, however: torches were put to Jewish businesses throughout Germany. The lives and property of all Jews were now in the hands of marauding Nazis. Amery immediately wrote in horror to Halifax calling on the government to take in fifty thousand refugees and then redistribute them to other recipient countries.[163] The famous *Kindertransport* resulted, a singular achievement that saved the lives of so many, but unfortunately left most of the rescued children's parents behind in Germany to face mass deportation to concentration and then extermination camps. Amery also called on Home Secretary Hoare to mobilise.[164] But at the year's end he expressed to Smuts "great anxiety about the slowness of rearmament and the inadequacy of our policy against air attack".[165]

On 28 January 1939 Butler, who somehow even after *Kristallnacht* found the "anti-German bias in London"—but evidently not the anti-Semitic persecution that prompted it—"depressing", wrote to his sons that he was "more confident ... about the desire for peace in Germany, and that we ought still to endeavour and will be able to secure reasonably satisfactory results without war by a conciliatory method of approach though certain dangers must be acknowledged. ... An early success for Mr. Chamberlain on a peaceful basis seems most important if we are not to see Winston Churchill and others in the Cabinet, and a complete anti-German bloc leading to a world war to decide, at the expense of many millions, whether Winston or Hitler should take first place." He wrote that he was "certain that war is not inevitable and that Hitler himself does not wish to start any large-scale bloodshed". He was certain too that "[n]either Hitler nor Ribbentrop are likely to be quite as inhuman as featured", and believed that "even the effect of Miss [Unity] Mitford's frequent meetings with the Fuhrer should not be underestimated". Flying to Berlin, he noted, "is so easy now, that anyone can go there for a few days, and I would not at all mind going back shortly".[166]

Hitler's invasion of Czechoslovakia on Wednesday 15 March 1939 should not have come as a bolt from the blue, except to the truly deluded. And deluded is precisely what Chamberlain was, along with Halifax. At MI6 'C' had concluded in February that Europe would remain peaceful; that rumours of a threat from Germany were false information spread by the Bolsheviks and Jews in their own interests.[167] Exactly a week before invasion the prime minister had appeared at a dinner hosted by the 1936 Club made up of senior Conservatives. Channon, an enthusiastic supporter, noted that Chamberlain "sees no crisis on the horizon, all seems well: he thinks the Russian danger receding and the dangers of a German war less every day".[168] And on 9 March, Amery noted, Chamberlain had given lobby correspondents an "astonishing optimistic interview . . . without even consulting the Foreign Office".[169] Hoare, with the prime minister's explicit encouragement, then delivered a surreal speech to his constituents in Chelsea the following day, welcoming the dawn of "a golden age . . . five men in Europe, the three dictators and the Prime Ministers of England and France . . . might in an incredibly short time transform the whole history of the world".[170] The Foreign Office was speechless. So too, doubtless, were many of the voters who heard him.

Instead of forestalling the inevitable, however, the Munich settlement had actually hastened its arrival. Hitler no longer had to contend with the only natural defences in the form of heavily forested mountains that afforded the Czechs natural protection from Germany and Austria. Furthermore, the Russians lost their only incentive to come to Czechoslovkia's defence in some form, even by air: the phantom Soviet aircraft that had apparently been there in August had mysteriously returned home. The massive Škoda armaments company in Plzeň, one of the world's largest exporters of weapons, including tanks, was now in the hands of the Germans, who ramped up production to contribute one third of the German panzer forces that were used against the French in the spring of 1940. Back in September Czechoslovakia also had at its disposal 418 tanks of its own manufacture,[171] though the general impression was that alone they could have held out for only a few weeks at most.

The assessment by Iverach McDonald, the very well-informed diplomatic correspondent of *The Times*, is worth quoting:

To say, as was so often said in excuse of Chamberlain at the time, that he had no option but to agree to Hitler's terms for the dismemberment of Czechoslovakia is in fact to make the most powerful condemnation of the government's policy over the years, including the slowness in rearmament and the reluctance to consider alliances until too late. Moreover, before the disparity in arms between Germany on the one side and Britain and France on the other is accepted as overwhelming proof that the Munich settlement was inevitable, the wider European picture should be considered. At least the significance of what was lost should be recalled. Munich not only removed Germany's immediate and ever-recurring fear of a war on two fronts but it neutralised a well-equipped Czechoslovak army of thirty-eight divisions— this at a time when Britain had only two divisions ready, or nearly ready, to be sent to the Continent. We sacrificed in Czechoslovakia a greater weight in armoured strength than Britain and France together had a year later, and Germany's lead in arms was growing. Britain and France had to pay dearly in 1939 and 1940 for the time they claimed to have bought in 1938.[172]

Butler balefully lamented that "after the invasion of Bohemia . . . he [Chamberlain] decided in his own mind that no agreement could be come to with the Nazis except on some new and certain basis".[173] What that basis should have been is hard to tell. Poland was clearly the next target, however, and the British government, utterly unprepared for such an eventuality, rapidly began improvising in a desperate search for any solution that would hold off negotiations with the Russians that were demanded by the opposition. The presupposition of those demanding talks with Moscow was not that the Red Army was in any condition to launch an offensive, but the likelihood that the Russians might find common cause with the Germans; something that even "realists" like Sargent in the Foreign Office never believed could happen. At the very least, the threat of Soviet air power would make Berlin think twice about invasion. In Warsaw speculation that Moscow and Berlin could act jointly against Poland was, prematurely dismissed out of hand. Apprehensions about such a possibility were current among the French military and conveyed to Under-Secretary of State for Foreign Affairs Mirosław Arciszewski. Undaunted, however, he confidently insisted that no such possibility actually existed because of "Hitler's irreconcilable stance towards Bolshevism and the USSR".[174] In the meantime "day after day" Halifax kept postponing a meeting with Maisky "about the threat to Poland".[175] Moreover, across the English Channel the highly opinionated US ambassador Bullitt, still embittered as a result of his brief tenure in Moscow, reinforced Polish obduracy when he showed his "repugnance and contempt" with respect to the Soviet Union in conversation with the Polish ambassador in Washington DC.[176]

Britain Unilaterally Guarantees Poland

Without warning, to the alarm of Wilson and against the advice of the chiefs of staff, who said that without the Soviet Union it would be meaningless, on 31 March Chamberlain made an abrupt about-turn and issued a unilateral guarantee to Poland.[177] The Soviet government naturally objected that a unilateral guarantee made it easier for Poland to resist creation of a multilateral security pact to defend one and all against Germany. Yet nothing was quite as it appeared. The commitment to the Poles was less a matter of any sympathies towards Poland than a means of blocking out the Russians. As Wilson confessed, "We disliked the Poles. They were an awful nuisance . . . The Government had to deal with some very difficult people."[178] It was certainly not the sign that many had hoped for, that Chamberlain had finally abandoned appeasement. Indeed, the leader that appeared in *The Times* on 1 April completely undermined the credibility of the guarantee. It argued that the "new obligation which this country yesterday assumed does not bind Britain to defend every inch of the present frontiers of Poland. The key word in the statement is not integrity but 'independence' . . . Mr Chamberlain's statement involves no blind acceptance of the *status quo*." In other words a new Munich agreement dismembering Poland could not be ruled out. The leader was written by Leo Kennedy and amended by Dawson on the basis of a full briefing by Cadogan. Kennedy "wrote the leader entirely on the lines of our talk and of what he [Cadogan] told me".[179]

In Moscow every suspicion was confirmed. Litvinov for one believed that the guarantee, made without reference to the Soviet Union, would provide Colonel Beck with an opportunity to strike a deal with Hitler "at the expense of Lithuania and the Baltic area".[180] Litvinov, who was unquestionably the most Anglophile member of the Soviet government, thought it possible that "Chamberlain is prompting Hitler to direct his aggression to the north-east. Chamberlain is counting on us to resist the occupation of the Baltic area and expecting that this will lead to the Soviet–German clash he has been hoping for."[181] The French had already refused to guarantee the Baltic states in July 1935.[182] The Poles saw these countries as destined to play the role of Belgium in 1914.[183]

Poland was now in an invidious position, the target of German hostility but still too distrustful and fearful to turn for help to the Soviet Union. Beck was otherwise isolated in that Poland's closest ally, Romania, felt excluded from his deliberations. In early March the Latvian ambassador in Warsaw summed it up:

> After Beck's unsuccessful trip to Galaţi last autumn [18–19 October 1938, to meet King Carol of Romania] all the mutual contacts that Romania and Poland as allies must maintain as well as opportunities of bilateral co-operation had slackened off and the atmosphere between Warsaw and Bucharest was rather cold and reserved. The extra-tours made by Poland's Minister of Foreign Affairs to Berchtesgaden, visits and hunting trips by Ribbentrop, the Union of Front Combatants, Germany's Chief of Police and Chief of SS Himmler, the urging of Hungarians towards the Carpathian Ukraine, the concentration of Polish agents and secret dislocation [deployment] of storm-troopers in the Carpathians were not agreeable to Romania.[184]

The Romanian foreign minister Grigore Gafencu's visit to Warsaw in early March made no substantial difference. Romania and Poland no longer had much to say to one another. They had drifted off in different directions.

To follow up on Chamberlain's initiative and irrevocably determined to avoid any arrangement involving the Russians, Beck arrived in London for talks that took place between 4 and 6 April 1939. He bluntly told the British that "in view of the grave tension between Moscow and Berlin, it would be dangerous to bring Russia into any discussions. He recalled what Marshal Piłsudski had said, namely, that when thinking of Germany and Russia it was necessary to take into account not only their interests, but their ideologies".[185] Indeed.

On 14 April French Foreign Minister Georges Bonnet, hitherto a sinuous appeaser, handed the Soviet ambassador in Paris, Yakov Surits, proposals for a tripartite agreement for mutual assistance in the event of France coming to the aid of Poland or Romania against Germany. In response Litvinov framed a more complete tripartite pact that would guarantee all states from the Baltic to the Black Sea and presented the draft for discussion with Stalin on 16 April. The revised offer went to the British ambassador Sir William Seeds the following day.[186] At the Foreign Office Butler was horrified. "The Russian proposal is extremely inconvenient," he minuted. "We have to balance the advantage of a paper commitment by Russia to join in a war on one side against the disadvantage of associating ourselves openly with Russia." The whole point of negotiating with the Russians was, Butler noted, "to placate our left wing in England, rather than to obtain any solid military advantage". He added, "We have . . . asked the Soviet [Union] whether they would declare that in the event of any act of aggression against any European neighbour of the Soviet Union, which was resisted by the country concerned, the assistance of the Soviet Government would be available, if desired, in such manner as would be found most convenient. The Soviet Government now confront us with this proposal."[187] In response, the British lapsed into stony, embarrassed silence. Laurence Collier, heading the Northern Department at the Foreign Office responsible for the Soviet Union, minuted on 28 April, "I cannot help feeling that the real motive for the Cabinet's attitude is the desire to secure Russian help and at the same time to leave our hands free to enable Germany to expand eastwards at Russian expense if we think it is convenient."[188]

Litvinov Is Sacked

The tripartite pact proposals were Litvinov's last throw. An alternative had unexpectedly arisen; something Stalin and Molotov had long been waiting for. The road towards an understanding with the Germans was now within sight. The very day that Litvinov handed Seeds the Soviet offer—which received no response for weeks—the Soviet ambassador in Berlin, Aleksei Merekalov, had a chance meeting with the states secretary at the Ausamt Ernst von Weizsäcker, who, after discussing purely economic matters, suddenly interjected that he was "willingly ready to exchange opinions on the overall political situation and to answer all questions of interest to the ambassador". He went on to ask whether the USSR felt its interests were being damaged in any respect, which Merekalov denied. Merekalov proceeded to ask how Weizsäcker saw the future of relations between Germany and the Soviet Union. At this point, pressed for a quotable commitment, the states secretary was jocularly evasive.[189] No more was heard, for the moment.

At the end of April and behind the back of Halifax, Chamberlain met lobby correspondents "for another of his sunshine tours", one of them recalls. "Reassure public opinion, he urged us; the worst was over and there would be no more shocks or surprise coups by the dictators—he was convinced of their good intentions. Have a good holiday, he advised us, free from worry and concern."[190] Of course, none of this made matters easier for those in Moscow trying to hold the line against the less remote possibility of a deal with Berlin. The boil was now lanced. At the beginning of May and in Stalin's presence, Litvinov came to blows with Chairman Molotov, whom he had always regarded as a fool, but who increasingly had Stalin's ear. It was his last act in office.

On 3 May an announcement went out to the Soviet Union's leading ambassadors stating that Litvinov had had to resign as a result of his disloyalty to Molotov, stemming from "a serious conflict" between them.[191] That could scarcely have come as a surprise. The surprise was that Molotov was installed in his place. The sinister Georgii Malenkov, who compiled the lists for Stalin of those to be shot, moved into Narkomindel, interviewed one by one those unfortunates listed by Litvinov as his most trusted subordinates and then sacked them, which meant interrogation and a labour camp or execution. Few survived this process. Stalin's removal of Litvinov had less to do with his being Jewish—after all Molotov's wife was unashamedly Jewish and they shared the home with his mother-in-law, who was expansively Zionist—than with the fact that Litvinov was obviously being led down the garden path by the British. Rather late in the day, Chamberlain hypocritically complained that "the Russians changed their Foreign Secretary just at a critical time. They got rid of Litvinov who, after all, was a man of the world. Negotiations with Molotov are not at all easy. He has never been out of Russia in his life. He sits up on a higher chair than the rest when negotiations take place, and this does not create a very friendly atmosphere. He only makes curt statements, rejecting or objecting to this or that proposal of ours. There is no real discussion."[192]

Yet Chamberlain, signally tone deaf, failed to draw the correct conclusions from Litvinov's dismissal. By now Stalin had no trust whatsoever in the prime minister's judgement or intentions. As Maisky suspected, Chamberlain was forever "looking for a hole in the hedge".[193] And as if to underline Stalin's deep suspicion, that same day Vansittart warned that "Horace Wilson and Chamberlain are still where they were . . . active and ready at any time to start up appeasement again and to sell the Poles as they sold the Czechs".[194]

Belatedly, on 4 May a leader appeared in *The Times* entitled "Poland and Russia", which grudgingly accepted that some kind of common front with Moscow might after all be necessary, but then undercut this unusually expansive gesture with the bald assertion that "Danzig is really not worth a war". In other words, a settlement with Germany that would result in the dismemberment of Poland was most certainly not to be ruled out. No longer did Moscow mince words. On the same day Comintern instructed French comrades to focus on support for collective security. "Taking this path the Party will determine its stance in relation to the Daladier-Bonnet government depending on what policy the government carries out: political capitulation or a policy of resisting the aggressors."[195]

The Germans now took a more decisive step. The Russians had a hearty dislike of Papen. His momentary chancellorship of Germany in the heady summer of 1932 had been associated with the fearful prospect of a Franco–German entente. As Germany's newly appointed ambassador in Ankara, he had come down in the world and had to follow orders instead of dishing them out. On 5 May, one day after Litvinov's dismissal was announced, Papen paid a visit to the Soviet ambassador Aleksei Terent'ev, and dropped the unexpected suggestion that Stalin and Hitler were very similar. Papen added that he saw no issues that could hinder "a rapprochement" in relations between the two. All that stood in the way was Poland, as Danzig had to be returned to Germany.[196]

Meanwhile from Berlin Soviet chargé d'affaires Astakhov reported that Hitler was determined to take Danzig. It could be done "without war", he wrote, through psychological pressure and "blackmail Munich style" as the Germans believed that the British and French had no intention of defending Poland.[197] It certainly encouraged the Germans to know that the Duke of Buccleugh, a convinced appeaser and friend of Butler's, who met Ribbentrop on a visit to Berlin from 15 to 18 April, was easily comforted by reassurances that the Germans wanted only Danzig and the Corridor. Butler assured Buccleugh that he was "much relieved to know of and realise your work and attitude".[198]

In London Chamberlain certainly did not want the chiefs of staff to say whether or not an alliance with Moscow was a good idea. Instead they were carefully asked only for an appreciation of Soviet military capabilities, which was hardly likely to be very positive. After Stalin had murdered so many senior and middle-ranking Soviet officers, heads of military-industrial enterprises and teams of inventive engineers, leaving the remainder paralysed by fear, the cabinet could scarcely have expected a clean bill of health from such an assessment. Nor did they receive one. The chiefs concluded that there was no question of "any substantial Russian military support to Poland". On the other hand, the Soviet Union did possess thirty cavalry divisions, mainly horse but with nine thousand tanks, along with a hundred infantry divisions. And, despite the terror, the Soviet air force and its fighter planes had excelled in the initial phase of the Spanish Civil War. Indeed, the chiefs of staff reckoned that in attacking Poland German air defence would face a problem from that quarter. But the crucial point they had to make, and which Chamberlain, Halifax and most of the other ministers certainly did not want said and refused to believe, was that there were "very grave military dangers inherent in the possibility of any agreement between Germany and Russia".[199]

Under Molotov's management Soviet policy had not yet changed in substance, but only in form and tone. Absolutely no discretion was permitted even to the most senior of subordinates. The pressure was on the Western democracies to close the front against Germany or take the consequences. On 4 May, the day of Litvinov's abrupt dismissal, Comintern's secretariat issued instructions that were a symptom of a coming shift of line. The PCF was told to speak out "resolutely" for a government of "national defence" and "for the reinforcement of France's defence capability and armaments". At the same time, however, the Party had to insist upon sustaining the benefits to the workers of the Popular Front, obtain further concessions on living standards and revive the stance sustained before the Popular Front had come to power on the issue of rearmament: "the Party will demand necessary guarantees that arms will not be used against the workers or to conduct a counter-revolutionary war".[200] The British and French governments were not privy to these instructions as Comintern cyphers were unreadable, but they scarcely needed to be, as their results were all over the front pages of the Communist press.

The Russians still seemed dogged in pursuit of the right agreement with the French and the British. Despite hints, the Germans had yet to offer anything concrete. Halifax, still treading water far out of his depth in European affairs, had received reports of secret negotiations between Moscow and Berlin. Yet he and Chamberlain were still in no hurry. Halifax, firmly convinced he was right, "found it difficult to attach much credence to these reports, which might be spread by persons who desired to drive us into making a pact with Russia". And even though he acknowledged "the bare possibility that a refusal of Russia's offer [of an alliance] might even throw her into Germany's arms", his greater fear was that a tripartite pact—Britain, France and the USSR—would "make war inevitable".[201] The underlying assumption remained that the Russians had nowhere else to go because Hitler would be incapable of overcoming his firmly rooted prejudices even were Stalin able to do so. Indeed, back in November 1938 Halifax had insisted that "Soviet Russia can scarcely become the ally of Germany as long as Hitler lives".[202] If Stalin believed that the substitution of the notoriously stubborn Molotov for the more accommodating Litvinov would suffice to convince the British to take him more seriously, he was sorely mistaken.

After further delay a counter-offer belatedly came in to Moscow from the British on 8 May. But once again there was no sign of full reciprocity. The proposals did not meet Soviet concerns about the security of the Baltic states against German penetration, signs of which had already been apparent for some time. Sir Ivone Kirkpatrick, formerly counsellor at the embassy in Germany, now heading the Central Department at the Foreign Office, bitterly joked about his superiors' high-handed attitude and their blatant ignorance of how to manage foreign affairs: "At the beginning our Government thought they were inviting the Russians to join the Turf Club and that they would fall over themselves with delight. The Russians, on the other hand, felt that they had a valuable oriental carpet to sell and were dissatisfied with the price offered."[203] The Germans, of course, were much more interested in the carpet than were the British. Molotov was brutally frank with Germany's ambassador, Friedrich-Werner Erdmann Matthias Johann Bernhard Erich Graf von der Schulenburg. When Schulenburg spoke of trade, Molotov retorted that "to achieve success in economic negotiations the appropriate political basis had to be established". Molotov's remark took Schulenburg completely by surprise.[204]

The Russians had yet to decide which way to jump. One figure who hoped the British and French would join them was Commissar of Defence Voroshilov. On 12 May 1939 Colonel Firebrace, the British military attaché in Moscow, had occasion to visit him. They had not seen one another since April 1938. Firebrace handed over an invitation to attend British army manoeuvres in September. Voroshilov was "friendly and direct" and, not unlike Litvinov, with whom he had been on good terms, "the Marshal said that he was a realist and that he thought it necessary to close the front against Germany . . . it only depended on us [the British] whether or not it would be closed". He emphasised that Germany was "in a very difficult economic and financial position".[205] This was the moment for the British to step forward with concrete proposals that met the needs of both parties. Chamberlain's abiding purpose was, however, as he confided to his sister Hilda, to "keep Russia in the background without antagonizing her".[206]

But would the Russians not realise that their role was merely back-stage? To Chamberlain that scarcely mattered. When pressed by the Labour opposition as to the danger that negotiations with Moscow could break down, the prime minister's complacent response was, "Well, I don't think that would be the end of the world."[207] So alienating Moscow did not really matter after all. This much was obvious to Admiral of the Fleet Lord Chatfield, Inskip's capable successor as minister for the co-ordination of defence. As we have seen with respect to Spain, Chatfield was one of nature's conservatives. He none the less dismissed Halifax's complacency and the tendency to find every excuse to avoid an alliance with Russia because of objections from various countries. At the cabinet's foreign policy committee on 16 May Chatfield argued that "failure to reach an agreement with Russia might result in Russia standing aside in a future European war and hoping thereby to secure advantage from the exhaustion of the western nations". And, having given Poland a unilateral guarantee against Germany without having consulted Russia, for fear of upsetting the Poles, "we had pressed Russia to give a guarantee to Poland without offering her any quid pro quo". This left Chamberlain unconvinced, as did the joint chiefs' anxiety "that Russia should not, in any circumstances, become allied with Germany. From the military point of view such an eventuality would create a most dangerous situation for us."[208] The issue of ideological preference was scarcely concealed. Halifax's private secretary Oliver Harvey under-stated the obvious when he noted that it was "difficult for a British Conservative Government to negotiate an agreement with a Russian Communist one".[209]

Moscow Told of German Intentions

It was on 17 May that Stalin received news from the head of what was now called the Fifth Directorate (Intelligence) of the Red Army. Courtesy of Rudolf von Scheliha, working at the German embassy in Warsaw, the Russians had the transcript of a briefing given by Ribbentrop's leading specialist on Eastern Europe, Peter Kleist. The briefing proved a brilliant prediction of what actually was to happen. It disclosed Hitler's words to Ribbentrop that, "turning aside from ideological considerations", if Poland did not capitulate in the next few weeks Germany would attack and Poland would be smashed "in 8–14 days". Preparations, however, would be delayed to the last minute, July–August. The conflict could be "localised ... England and France, as before, are not ready to come out on the side of Poland". If Germany acted speedily, then the British would merely parade the fleet and the French would just rattle their sabres.[210] If Intelligence were to be believed, the Russians now had a deadline to sort out their relations with the Germans; a deadline of which the British and French were oblivious.

That very day Chatfield told cabinet that he "thought that the danger which would result from a possible Russo–German combination outweighed the disadvantages which might be expected to result from the hostile reactions of Spain, Portugal, Italy, Japan and possibly other countries, to an agreement between this country and Russia".[211] Chatfield was not far from the truth. At around this time Schulenburg was told by Ribbentrop that Berlin now believed Comintern was no longer of importance and that therefore ideological barriers between Germany and the Soviet Union had fallen.[212] In London, however, Cadogan noted a few days later that the prime minister "hates it" (the idea of an alliance with the Russians) and that he was by no means alone: Simon and Halifax felt the same way.[213] Amery noted that "[t]he trouble with Neville is that he is being pushed all the time into a policy which he does not like, and hates abandoning the last bridges which might still enable him to renew his former policy".[214]

The further Chamberlain was moved away from appeasement and the greater the pressure to move towards the Russians, the more he dragged his feet, and the more he dragged his feet, the more elaborate became his effort to sabotage any understanding with them. The good news that, in answer to further enquiries from the Foreign Office, "both Poland and Rumania have now intimated that they do not wish to stand in our way as regards negotiation of a tri-partite pact with Soviet Russia" was thus not exactly the kind of thing that he wanted to hear.[215] He therefore sought ever more justifications for avoiding an alliance with Moscow. He told the Polish ambassador of his scepticism that the Russians had either the ability or the will to launch a large-scale military offensive.[216] The least one can say about this is that statements such as these were unlikely to encourage the Poles into entering into any defence arrangements with Moscow; rather the reverse. The young diplomat Geoffrey Thompson fortuitously found himself in the same hospital as Chamberlain's wife Annie. Her brother-in-law, Lieutenant Colonel Cole, came to visit and, on learning that Thompson worked at the Foreign Office, strongly expressed his outlook on the situation in Europe: "that the last thing we desired was internal trouble in Germany, as the alternative to Hitler was 'communism, with which France is already rotten'".[217] Thompson did not have any difficulty guessing where such sentiments may have originated.

The last recorded justification that Chamberlain offered for not lining up with the Russians, given on 24 May, was surely the most desperate, if not the most ridiculous: that Roman Catholics all over the world were "strongly opposed" to the idea. For a Protestant prime minister of an overwhelmingly Protestant country, formerly lord mayor of a city notable for its Quaker roots and notorious for its Masonic practices, this was certainly a first. And were any engagement with the Russians impossible to avoid, Chamberlain added, then it should be made conditional on article XVI of the League of Nations Covenant because article XVI would have to be revived in the near future and this conveniently "introduced an element of a temporary character into the arrangement without special mentioning of a time limit".[218] This particular ruse was the poisonous concoction of arch-appeasers Butler and Wilson.

Meanwhile Chamberlain's host at Whitsun (Pentecost), Sir Francis Lindley, diehard anti-Bolshevik and former ambassador to Japan, launched into a diatribe at the very idea of alliance with Moscow at the foreign affairs committee of the Conservative Party. Of course, it leaked out, as was no doubt intended, and confirmed the opinion that this must, indeed, be Chamberlain's view as well.[219] No wonder Moscow saw his foreign policy as "pro-fascist". Although Comintern welcomed the fact that the British Communist Party rejected the planning of compulsory military training—approved in parliament on 26 May—it suspected dubious pacifist motives: "the Party created the impression that the British people, irrespective of what government is in power in Britain, does not want to take big military obligations upon itself in defence of peace and the independence of countries threatened by fascism".[220] Just as in France, so in Britain, heightened mistrust of the democracies' intentions made the extent of Communist support for rearmament conditional upon the orientation of each government's foreign policy. But this threat was hollow if the government were run by a man who had no interest in further rearmament and indeed, regarded it as provocative to the Germans.

Early in June Maisky arrived back from Moscow, doubtless surprised and deeply relieved at having averted the grisly fate of his erstwhile colleagues. Almost all of the Litvinov crowd who had survived the terror, except for Surits in Paris and Kollontai in Stockholm, had now disappeared into the night. Beatrice Webb solicitously asked the ambassador about his meeting with Stalin. "From his sullen expression and monosyllabic reply I gather that he has no particular liking for the idolised leader of the masses."[221] Meanwhile from within MI6 Soviet spy Guy Burgess reported on a damning conversation with Wilson to the effect that "[i]n government circles the opinion expressed is that England never thought about concluding a serious pact with the U.S.S.R. The prime minister's advisers openly say that Great Britain can do without a Russian pact."[222] Indeed, Butler noted that Wilson, whom he absurdly considered "the Burleigh of the present age"—his "power is very great"—still hoped "in his heart . . . to come to an understanding with Nazi Germany".[223]

It is not hard to imagine what Stalin and Molotov made of all this. The Germans were apparently confident that the British would do nothing to bale out Eastern Europe. Rudolf Hess, who ran the Nazi Party apparatus, assured his trusted adjutant that "with a sword in our hands we will take from the East everything that we need". And when Karl Heinz Pintsch suggested that John Bull would not just stand by and let it happen, Hess insisted that "we have firm assurances that in the face of our campaign in the East the English, although they will remain in the West weapons in hand, will undertake no action against Germany".[224]

Within a decade of the events described, the historian Lewis Namier, himself once a Jewish refugee from inhospitable Eastern Europe, put it in a nutshell:

> It had been a mistake on the part of the British Govermnent, so quick, unstinting, and easy about terms when handing out guarantees to second and third-rate Powers, to have treated Soviet Russia like a suppliant, and to have started off with suggestions which were both ludicrous and humiliating; it was a further mistake to have gone on haggling about every concession, which rendered it ungracious and unconvincing; it was a third mistake to have sent a junior official to negotiate with Russia, and, later on, Service men of less standing than were sent, for instance, to Poland or Turkey. Behind it all was a deep, insuperable aversion to Bolshevist Russia, such as was not shown in dealings with Hitler or Mussolini; and whether it was justified or not, it was certainly not conducive to success in very difficult negotiations.[225]

On 12 June another safe pair of hands from Chamberlain and Halifax's point of view, William Strang—who had briefly served in Moscow but had no Russian to speak of—was sent out from London to assist Ambassador Sir William Seeds. Both the prime minister and his foreign secretary approached the Russians, Butler noted, "with a sense of distaste, Halifax because of his religious and gentlemanly views, the P.M. because he dislikes Russian politics, fears contamination, and despises Soviet inefficiency".[226] Stalin later that year recalled how unserious the British were: "they sent some sort of clerk, Strang, who every day presented a new variant, printed in advance".[227] Not surprisingly Strang found the Russians to be "most disagreeable and tiresome to negoitiate with" and Molotov, in particular, completely unapproachable.[228] On 16 June the Politburo formally decided to reject the one-sided British proposals that Moscow guarantee the security of other states but that the security of the Baltic states be left unresolved. It also insisted that in any agreement provision be made that would prevent any signatory from making a separate peace.[229] The Germans at last decided to wait no longer. On 17 June Schulenburg called on Astakhov in Berlin. He said the time had come to improve relations and took out of his pocket the Ausamt record of the Weizsäcker conversation, the text of which appeared much more categorical than Astakhov recalled it to have been. Schulenburg said that he understood that the Russians would be wary, but that German intentions were "sufficiently serious". He could not speak for Hitler, whom he had not seen, though he could speak for Ribbentrop.[230] But from the German embassy in Warsaw, news reached Moscow that although Hitler had told Ribbentrop of a new Rapallo, he also viewed this as "temporary . . . a pause . . . for the next couple of years . . . the precondition to resolving problems in Western Europe".[231] Stalin would have done well to bear in mind the fact that Hitler saw this about-turn to be of very limited duration.

If this were true, then Moscow was on shaky ground giving Hitler his own way in Western Europe. Stalin did not like taking open-ended risks in foreign policy. On the other hand the British were not serious about an alliance. When Maisky saw Halifax on 23 June, the Soviet ambassador faced a baffling accusation that the Russians were raising "superfluous difficulties" over the security of the Baltic states. He retorted by asserting Moscow's right to the equivalent of a Monroe Doctrine over its near neighbours, which did nothing to lessen the foreign secretary's general irritability.[232]

Indeed, there was nothing "superfluous" about the Baltic states, except perhaps to a provincial Englishman. On 10 July, when drawing up a threat assessment for future negotiations with the British and French, Chief of the General Staff Boris Shaposhnikov noted that of all the dangers the Russians faced "the most pressing . . . is if German aggression is directed against the USSR making use of the territory of Finland, Estonia and Latvia".[233] By then the Soviet negotiating position vis-à-vis the British was notably hardening. Maisky had forever been encouraging Stalin to await Churchill's arrival in office as prime minister after a palace coup. Even rumours that Chamberlain would have allowed Churchill and Eden into cabinet had proven misleading, however. This was music of the future. Russia had run out of options. Maisky reported that "Chamberlain at heart remains an 'appeaser' as before. The concessions towards a 'new direction' are being made and will be made only against his wishes because he has to under very heavy pressure from public opinion."[234] That very day, 10 July, the prime minister told General Edmund Ironside "that it seemed impossible to come to an understanding with Russia".[235] And on 15 July Chamberlain confessed he was "glad to say that Halifax is at last getting 'fed up' with Molotov . . . If we do get an agreement as I rather think we shall, I am afraid I shall not regard it as a triumph."[236]

Finally, the walls began to close in. On 19 July Halifax at last recognised that "discussions of some kind were proceeding between the German Government and the Soviet Government". But this did not mean that the foreign secretary wanted talks to make progress in Moscow, as we shall see. Chamberlain, true to form, responded that "he could not bring himself to believe that a real alliance between Russia and Germany was possible".[237] The prime minister no doubt found support in his stubbornness from MI6, which reported that it had "nothing to show that any political conversations are taking place between Berlin and Moscow". It added that the idea of a Soviet–German agreement was after all "very hypothetical".[238] Nothing could have been more misleading. Reports had been dismissed incautiously within MI6 on the supposition that the person leaking information on Soviet–German contacts could not possibly have access to such high-level sources: a classic example of secret intelligence being shunted aside because it did not fit with preconceptions and prejudices. Chamberlain was still deluding himself that "Hitler has concluded that we mean business and that the time is not ripe for the major war".[239]

Unable to halt the drive towards an understanding with Moscow for fear of losing office under a barrage of growing discontent, the prime minister instead resorted to subterfuge behind the backs of the Foreign Office, just as he had done in private pursuit of a rapprochement with Italy in 1937–38. On this occasion he used the good offices of Helmut Wohltat, German minister for export, attending a whaling conference in London. The secret soundings were made by Wilson along with Robert Hudson, a junior minister for overseas trade. The grandiose proposal was for a division of economic spheres of influence, which involved directing the Germans towards eastern and south-eastern Europe, accompanied by non-aggression pacts that would "enable England to free itself from obligations in relation to Poland". Wilson was looking to the long term: five years.[240] The German ambassador Dirksen was persuaded to follow up when on 3 August Wilson invited him home. During a two-hour conversation Wilson "went into some detail about the fact that entering into confidential negotiations with the German Government carried with it a major risk for Chamberlain. If anything of it became known, this would result in a gigantic scandal and Chamberlain would doubtless be forced to resign." Chamberlain, Wilson underlined, could not speak out for appeasement without being forced from office; only Hitler was in a position to do this. It was made explicit to Dirksen that the previous talks should be viewed as "an official démarche" to which a German reply was expected. Contacts made with other governments—obviously a reference to the Russians—were only a means of helping matters along. They would "fall away as soon as the one important goal worthy of sacrifice is obtained: agreement with Germany".[241]

The British press was, however, aggrieved at being so tightly controlled by Downing Street. It broke the news.[242] A scandal duly ensued. Chamberlain, of course, had a sustained record of such underhand subterfuges—the very reason for Eden's resignation the year before. Jebb recalls, "What cannot be justified is the installation in No. 10 of a small machine which acts completely independently of, and quite often at variance with, the official machine, including its representative in the cabinet. Halifax should never have consented to such a system. A Prime Minister running foreign policy through the medium of an éminence grise is a recipe for disaster."[243] Even those who had supported appeasement so loyally and so diligently were upset. Cadogan was absent when the news of Hudson's activities broke. And Jebb quietly vented his fury: "The immediate effect of this piece of super-appeasement", he wrote, "has been to arouse all the suspicions of the Bolsheviks, dishearten the Poles . . . and encourage the Germans into thinking that we are prepared to buy peace . . . I must say I doubt whether folly could be pushed to a further extreme."[244] But more was to follow.

On 25 July Ribbentrop, with a deadline approaching for war with Poland, was uninterested in anything the British had to offer, and was instead preoccupied with the Soviet failure to respond to German approaches. Karl Schnurre, the head of the German economic delegation to the Soviet Union, invited Astakhov along with Babarin, the deputy head of the Soviet trade delegation, to talk informally over dinner on 26 July.[245] At this "intimate dinner" Schnurre candidly underlined Germany's willingness to come to terms on everything, including the Baltic and Poland. Astakhov reported, "To my question whether Schnurre was certain that his words reflect the sentiments and aims of those at the top, he stated that he was speaking on direct instruction from Ribbentrop."[246]

Anglo–Soviet Military Conversations

Still concerned to disarm his opponents, Chamberlain reluctantly agreed that military conversations could be opened with the Russians even though political negotiations had gone nowhere. Seeds offered this to the Soviet government on 25 July as an appetiser, which, for want of anything better, they duly accepted; though not with any great enthusiasm. Chamberlain was still not serious, and neither was Halifax. They did not send any of the chiefs of staff. Instead, three days later Admiral Sir Reginald Plunkett-Ernle-Erle-Drax emerged from obscurity to be told he would head the military mission to Moscow. It took another three days to draft his instructions, which did not include plenipotentiary powers to conclude any agreement, nor details as to how Britain could aid the Russians in the event of war.[247] How would the delegation actually get to Moscow? The notion of flying via Stockholm or Helsinki was for no good reason ruled out, although it soon became evident why: "A warship was suggested, but the Foreign Secretary thought this would have the effect of attaching too much importance to the Mission." By now those destined to head it had become decidedly cynical about the entire escapade. General Ismay suggested, tongue-in-cheek, that "they might bicycle", and Drax, with a less incisive sense of humour, volunteered that "there is also a route via Vladivostok".[248] If those conducting the talks were so cynical about them, the Russians were unlikely to be less so.

Finally HMS *Exeter* was selected as an appropriate vessel. The team, including Major General Haywood for the army and Marshal Charles Barnett for the RAF, were briefed by "C" from MI6, who, to say the least, was not optimistic. On 2 August they were seen by Chatfield, the three armed services ministers and Halifax. Echoing Sinclair's sentiments, "the Foreign Secretary then remarked that on the whole it would be preferable to draw out the negotiations as long as possible". The team followed this up by meeting and greeting their French counterparts under General Doumenec before a further briefing from Sinclair, who unexpectedly announced that Chamberlain would like to see them. "The Prime Minister", Drax recalled, "seemed to be somewhat worried and uneasy about the Russian situation and said that the House of Commons had pushed him further than he had wished to go." And with that heartening thought, the mission embarked on 5 August only to find that the maximum speed of the *Exeter* was a meagre 13 knots (just under 15 miles per hour).[249] But the main trouble was that Drax "gathered that General Doumenec's instructions were to the effect that at all costs an agreement must be reached with Russia".[250] Once again, the British were about to let down the French.

Maisky attended the send-off for the Anglo–French military missions at St. Pancras Station, from which the railway connected to the docks at Tilbury. The ambassador was enthusiastic, because at last something for which he had worked so many years was in motion; but he had good reason to reflect that the inclinations of the appeasers had nothing to do with the progress being made. Quite the opposite: in an outburst of candour discreetly confided to the pages of his daily record, Maisky wrote,

> The bourgeoisie and the Palace have no love for but hate 'Soviet Communism'. Chamberlain was always ready to drown the USSR in a teaspoon of water. We on the Soviet side also have no sympathy for 'the top ten thousand' of Britain. On the contrary, the century-long traditions of the past, the recent experience of the Soviet period, ideological habits, all combine to imbue our attitudes towards the

rulers of England; in particular towards the Prime Minister, the focal point of entirely justifiable suspicions and mistrust.[251]

In the meantime, one of Chamberlain's great admirers, Lord Kemsley, owner of *The Sunday Times*, had taken himself off to Berlin with the encouragement of Wilson, Halifax and Henderson.[252] Here the press baron expressed views identical to those of Chamberlain. On 25 July, in conversation with Nazi ideologue Alfred Rosenberg, he insisted that "England and Germany must never go to war again. Were that to happen, Soviet Russia would be the only winner remaining and Europe's culture would certainly be destroyed." He added, with a suitably naval metaphor, that Chamberlain's government was negotiating with Moscow only "to take the winds out of the sails of the Opposition". At dinner Lady Kemsley let her hair down and in a disgraceful aside suggested that "only the Jews would benefit from war between Germany and England".[253] Two days later, with the military mission still a mere proposal, Kemsley, now fully primed, followed this up with a prized meeting with Hitler. Here, he confidently emphasised that Chamberlain "looked upon the Munich Agreement not merely as a settlement of the Sudeten matter, but as the forerunner of a different relationship with Germany in the future".[254] Hope sprang eternal. Butler insisted to Buccleugh that "[w]e on our side have got to be ready for anything, as we know that Germany will expand if she gets a chance, but we also believe that Hitler is going to have one more look around to see how much he can get without war before he takes an irrevocable decision".[255]

News of the coming talks between the Russians, British and French had the effect of prompting the Germans to come clean about their intentions. Following the Schnurre dinner, on 2 August at a meeting with Weizsäcker at the Ausamt, Astakhov was invited in to see Ribbentrop. After a lengthy monologue, Ribbentrop finally came to the point: "We can come to terms without difficulty on every problem relating to territory *from the Black Sea to the Baltic*. Of this I am convinced. (This, R[ibbentrop] repeated in various forms several times.)" He could scarcely have been more direct. As to Poland, he continued, "rest assured about one thing—Danzig will be ours . . . We do not regard the armed forces of Poland as serious . . . For us a military campaign against Poland is a matter of a week or ten days." The Germans wanted to negotiate in Berlin.[256]

With the British and French delegations expected, the Russians were more optimistic than before about building "a dam against Germany" but, when asked what might come of the talks, Deputy Commissar for Foreign Affairs Lozovsky—previously head of Profintern—said only that this was "difficult to foresee".[257] The young and inexperienced Pavel Fitin had been appointed head of Soviet foreign intelligence—the Fifth Department of the GUGB NKVD (formerly the InO GUGB)—on 13 May, and was immediately thrown into events. On 7 August, four days after Astakhov despatched Ribbentrop's words and two days after the British delegation left on their slow boat to Leningrad, Fitin reported to Stalin that in the very near future—any day after 25 August—Germany would attack Poland.[258] No wonder Ribbentrop was so insistent on the need to negotiate. But the Soviet leadership was waiting to see whether the British and French could be persuaded to be forthcoming. The instruction issued to the Soviet negotiators that same day was simple: agreement was "impossible" if "free passage of our forces through the territory of Poland and Romania is excluded". Moreover, since American aviator Charles Lindbergh's visit in 1938, no foreigners had been or would be allowed to see military enterprises or military units unless and until they were "our allies".[259]

The Russians remained studiously cautious with respect to all parties. A key indicator of this came when, in communicating to Molotov on 11 August, Astakhov used the word "negotiations", and Molotov abruptly deleted it and substituted "conversations".[260] Still prepared to wait and see how the first day of negotiations with the British and French went, on 12 August Molotov sent a blunt, temporising telegram to Astakhov: "A list of subjects does not interest us. Negotiating them requires preparation and step by step transition from the trade credit agreement to other issues. We prefer to conduct talks on these questions in Moscow."[261] He had good reason to be careful. The Germans could after all be playing them along, as were the British, whose military mission was finally arriving, along with the French, in Moscow that very afternoon.

The following day, the British and French met the Soviet delegates: Commissar for Defence Voroshilov, Chief of the General Staff Commander Shaposhnikov, Commissar for the Navy Admiral Kuznetsov, air force chief Commander Loktionov and Deputy Chief of the General Staff Smorodinov.

It took just two days for the Russians to reach stalemate with the British and French, who had nothing to offer. Not only had Drax no power to sign an alliance, but he had not even been provided with any credentials. In the words of Admiral Kuznetsov, "the opening of the negotiations prompted serious mistrust and this mistrust grew as the negotiations progressed".[262] No doubt to Drax's chagrin, Voroshilov immediately announced that he would like to see rapid progress and that his team were available any number of hours. He produced his own credentials, indicating that his delegation could sign a military convention on behalf of his government—whereas Drax and Doumenec would have to refer to their home governments for any agreement. The Russians also outlined their order of battle: 120 infantry divisions, 16 cavalry divisions, 5,000 heavy guns, 9,000–10,000 tanks and 5,000–5,500 aircraft. Mobilisation could be completed in eight to twenty days. On 14 August Voroshilov tabled the key question: could the Red Army pass through Poland and Romania? To which no answer emerged.[263] And when the British and French could offer nothing in return, Voroshilov, having raised the need to have passage through Poland via the Wilno gap and Galicia and through Romania, bluntly stated on 16 August, "We are not gathered here to make abstract declarations."[264]

The Russians reluctantly bided their time until the Germans were ready. They took the Soviet armed forces more seriously than did Chamberlain, being genuinely worried lest the Soviet air force deny Göring's Luftwaffe command of the air. Indeed, the Russians could deploy 460–550 bombers and 465–575 fighters on their western front;[265] and in his diary for the day upon which the pact between Germany and Russia was signed Rosenberg recognised that it removed "the threat from the Russian air fleet in the German-Polish conflict."[266] On 17 August and under intense pressure from Berlin, Ambassador Schulenburg indicated that the Soviet terms for an agreement were acceptable, including the proposed term of twenty-five years. Molotov then said a protocol should be added. On 19 August the Russians gave the Germans a full draft, though it was not until the following day that Hitler finally committed and sent Schulenburg a message for Stalin agreeing to a non-aggression pact with a supplementary secret protocol. The draft became the Nazi–Soviet pact.[267] News of this, set alongside the inadequate British stance on negotiations, finally sealed the fate of a strategy that had waited in the wings since Eden's visit to Moscow in 1935. Stalin summed it up in conversation with Dimitrov, Zhdanov and Molotov in the privacy of his office, after signing up with Hitler: "We preferred agreements with the so-called democratic countries and therefore conducted negotiations." But the British and the French had wanted the Russians to do their work for them "at no cost!"[268]

A warning had come into the Foreign Office from Washington DC several days before, but the telegram was lost among others of lesser importance occupying the in-tray for far too long.[269] The third secretary at the American embassy in Moscow, Charles Bohlen, had anticipated the news after briefings from junior diplomat Herwarth at the German embassy.[270] Herwarth had also warned the third secretary at the British embassy, yet we have no record of this in any despatch from the ambassador, and the secretary was later killed in the war leaving no trace of what he did, if anything. The Poles had also picked up from the Latvians talk "among certain English circles" that Russia was going to come to terms with the Germans. But in Riga Foreign Minister Vilhelms Munters had dismissed this as wild fantasy. In his words, "Only a fool would imagine such a thing."[271] Such fools were evidently in short supply: MI6, for example, remained convinced that Stalin and Hitler could never come to terms and opposed Britain's negotiating with the Russians.[272]

London was equally complacent, and with far greater consequences for all. When Jebb at the Foreign Office weighed up possibilities he noted that it made sense for Moscow to sign a pact with Berlin only assuming "that a German attack in the West would result in an inconclusive war in the West". He goes on to reflect that states "are not always guided by what appears to a rational observer to be their interests".[273] That was certainly true of British policy. And what Jebb did not fully understand was that the Russians had no expectation of a definitive outcome to war between Germany and the West (see below, pp. 334–335). Their calculations were rather different. Moscow had invariably held to a vastly inflated view of British power, adding up every imperial asset, economic and military. That was why Stalin persisted with the idea of an alliance.

Meanwhile, on Monday 21 August Halifax arrived at the Foreign Office early and by 11.30 that morning he was at No. 10 with Cadogan. His diary tells us what followed: "'C' [the head of MI6] tells us that he has received an approach suggesting that Göring should come over to London if he can be assured that he will be able to see the Prime Minister. It was decided to send an affirmative answer to this curious suggestion, and arrangements were accordingly set in hand for Göring to come over secretly on Wednesday, the 23rd. The idea is that he should land at some deserted aerodrome, be picked up in a car and taken direct to Chequers. There the regular household is to be given *congé* and the telephone to be disconnected." The following day, with Halifax, Cadogan, Wilson and Chamberlain at Downing Street, a "final draft of the letter to Hitler is approved". But then everything went awry: news of the Nazi–Soviet pact came in. It took a while for the shocking consequences of the utterly unexpected entirely to sink in. The following day Halifax noted, "The German idea has, temporarily at least, faded out." Hitler sent word that the scheduled meeting with Göring would not be "immediately useful".[274]

The Nazi–Soviet Pact

On 23 August Ribbentrop arrived in Moscow to sign a non-aggression pact with Molotov. There could have been no great satisfaction for Vansittart in saying he had warned of this, but he had written the following minute soon after signature of the Franco–Soviet pact in 1935: "Unless M. Laval completely destroys the confidence of Russia . . . a Russo–German agreement is possible, but not probable. It would become far more probable if we too took the road to Berlin prematurely. And if we did, and brought about an anxious Russian bid to Berlin, and then failed ourselves? Much care is indeed required in all these great businesses."[275] But, of course, no leading member of cabinet, all rank amateurs in the business of foreign policy, had taken Vansittart sufficiently seriously. He was dismissed, literally, as hopelessly Francophile and Germanophobe. The responsibility for what happened lay entirely with Chamberlain's men.

The blunt message from Moscow was put plainly by Deputy Commissar Lozovsky in conversation with the Swedish ambassador: "that no one can any longer pronounce on important questions concerning international relations—and above all questions concerning Eastern Europe—without the active participation of the Soviet Union".[276]

As late as 27 August the appeasers were still barrelling down the road to Berlin. Halifax's secretary, Harvey, expressed himself "terrified of another attempt at a Munich and selling out on the Poles. [Sir] Horace Wilson and R. A. Butler are working like beavers for this."[277] As a diehard proponent of appeasing Germany, Butler was the one who, despite long illness, took a first-class degree, actually spoke German, and did so with loving precision. Informal soundings were conducted by Halifax with the Swedish businessman Dahlerus, Göring's intermediary, on 25 and 27 August, with a visit to No. 10 on 30 August, the idea floated being that a plebiscite could be offered on Danzig. Halifax expressed concern only "that any proposal Hitler may make should not be couched in the form of a Diktat to the Poles".[278]

The Russians knew what was happening. On 29 August Astakhov reported from Berlin Ribbentrop's message that "before Henderson's departure for England he expressed to Hitler the wish of the English [sic] government to resolve the Polish question by peaceful means and improve relations between Germany and England. Hitler replied that he would like to improve relations with England, but the Polish question must sooner or later under any conditions be resolved." He also promised that he would not abandon his friendly relations with the Soviet Union and would not take part in any international conference without Soviet participation. "On the issue of the east all of his decisions would be taken together with the USSR."[279]

The pact naturally exacerbated the anti-Bolshevism of the appeasement camp and totally undermined pro-Soviet sentiment on the left.

Having endured the news of the terror, this came as a final blow for some. Those who had swallowed their doubts in the name of the Popular Front against fascism now had to confront the reality of Soviet state interests. In her endearingly egocentric manner, the devoted fellow-traveller Beatrice Webb reflected the sentiment of those who had clung on in hope through Stalin's bloody purge when she wrote on 25 August, "The German-Soviet Pact seems a great disaster to all that the Webbs have stood for. Even Sidney is dazed, and I am, for a time at least, knocked almost senseless!"[280] In London, war now seemed inevitable. At *The Times* all hope was lost, even though the lessons were still unlearned. "What folly, folly, folly, this is . . . An unforced evolution in Germany is what Europe needs," wrote the wretched deputy editor Barrington-Ward, devoid of any understanding as to how this could take place under a totalitarian régime.[281]

The right, of course, believed themselves completely vindicated, particularly after the Russians seized eastern Poland. Arthur Rucker, Chamberlain's devoted principal private secretary and a man devoid of international experience, that autumn confided to his colleague John Colville that "Communism is now the great danger, greater even than Nazi Germany".[282] If anything, news of the pact, bad though it undoubtedly was, had acted as an accelerator to diehard appeasers. Hitler was, however, too impatient to wait for what the British had to offer. On 1 September Germany attacked Poland. And because it failed to respond positively to an ultimatum from Britain, a state of war was declared between the two on Sunday 3 September 1939.

12

War, 1939–1940

> What would be so bad about extending the socialist system to new
> territories and populations as a result of the defeat of Poland?
>
> —STALIN[1]

Hitler's rapid annihilation of Poland was possible only because he had
finally come to terms with Stalin. Had the Poles found a way of putting
to one side their differences with the Russians, it would not have been
so easy for the Germans, given their need for command of the air. But
as far as Beck was concerned it was by no means as simple as it was for
Hitler to act purely in terms of *ragion di stato*, because the Poles also
faced Bolshevism in its ugliest form: the return of the Red Army to Polish soil with a revolution from above and the persecutions that this
would certainly entail. Memories of the scare in 1920 were still all too
fresh, and those who had escaped across the Russian border served to
amplify them with their own horror stories.

The full extent of Soviet–German collaboration and Stalin's hopes
for it were by no means evident for some time. Not just one pact, but
two were agreed by the Soviet Union and Nazi Germany. Furthermore,
as became clear in 1940, the Kremlin fully expected a third pact to follow
in due course. The abrupt change in tone towards the Nazi régime
within Moscow was startling. From August 1939 fascists were no longer
called fascists. The word disappeared from Soviet propaganda. To their

obvious distress, emigré German Communists found themselves con-
gratulated at the workplace on "their" successful invasion of Poland.[2]

The first treaty—the non-aggression pact with a secret protocol
signed on 23 August 1939—marked the complete bankruptcy of Chamberlain's appeasement policy, the ultimate aim of which had been to
keep the Russians out of Europe to avert the threat of Bolshevism. Instead, as Beneš had warned would happen, it brought the Russians back
in, and on terms the British were powerless to limit. The policy, itself at
root ideological, gambled on the unfounded supposition that Stalin and
Hitler were inherently incompatible for ideological reasons; that *Realpolitik* had no place at all in the vocabulary of either party. It also failed
to take account of the shared provenance of both Bolshevism and fascism that had once so excited the father of anarcho-syndicalism, Sorel.
Thus Western statesmen and officials could not see that the common,
underlying hostility of Moscow and Berlin to liberal values and bourgeois democracy could bind them; let alone the overriding logic of geopolitics. Faced with the dire prospect of war with Germany, on Chamberlain's behalf Wilson turned to US Ambassador Kennedy, asking that
he intercede with Roosevelt, whom Chamberlain had hitherto consistently and openly cold-shouldered. Britain was not in a position to press
Poland to back down, he suggested; but the United States could.[3] London was desperate. Another Munich was in the offing.

The second treaty between Germany and the Soviet Union—the
Friendship Pact of 28 September—followed the German invasion of
Poland from the west on 1 September and the Soviet invasion from the
east on 17 September. It demonstrated that the Soviet Union's entente
with Germany was here to stay, intended for the long term. The indications are that the Russians counted on several years at least. The Friendship Pact, which inter alia handed Lithuania over to the Soviet sphere
of influence, underlined that there was to be no turning back. Hitler was
not only free to conquer most of Poland. He also had *carte blanche* to
seize whatever he liked in Western Europe, were he able to do so;
though Stalin thought this unlikely, given his reading of the balance of
power. The Soviet régime believed that it may have saved itself from the
prospect of major war, for the foreseeable future at least.[4] Not only that;

it had also given itself an unexpected opportunity for the territorial expansion of Soviet power.

Kremlin Calculations

In the interval between the two pacts, Stalin could never be certain that Berlin would actually follow through with the commitments it had undertaken. These were anxious moments. Co-ordination between the new turn in Soviet state policy and Comintern strategy thus remained incomplete until this uncertainty had been fully resolved. The test would come when the Red Army entered Poland and made direct contact with the Wehrmacht. The pact almost ready, Comintern's executive committee secretariat issued a resolution on 22 August in anticipation of the dismay and confusion within Communist ranks that news of it would inevitably prompt. It falsely, and no doubt deliberately, indicated that the pact did not rule out "the possibility and the necessity of an agreement between England, France and the USSR for jointly repulsing aggression". In other words, no change to Comintern's line should be anticipated.[5] This may have lightened the blow. None the less, the entire international Communist movement was thrown into unprecedented disarray. Thorez recalled later that the reaction was one of "surprise and complete confusion". Gone was the notion impressed during the years of the Popular Front that throughout Europe the Communist Party line could be identified with the national interest. Instead all that remained was "loyalty to the Soviet Union, to the Communist International; to Stalin".[6] Togliatti, charged with Western Europe, hastened to Paris, sending word that the line to follow in the meantime would be that of Clémenceau in 1914: full support for the war but severe criticism of the inadequate conduct of hostilities.[7] More would be required, however, in the face of general disorientation and demoralisation that was likely to worsen once Stalin had made a final decision on Comintern's directives. Togliatti thus anticipated reconstituting the defunct West European Bureau in the French capital to rein in the bewildered rank and file and ensure that Communist parties closed ranks once the new, definitive policy line arrived from Moscow.[8]

The Kremlin was taking a leap into the unknown that would inevitably sell short the interests of the world Communist movement in return for concrete territorial gains. The Soviet leadership straddled a belief both in the fundamental crisis of capitalism and the need, short-term, for expediency at almost any price. Hence the *Realpolitik* towards Berlin. Britain, the cornerstone of capitalism in Europe, was manifestly not serious about allying with Russia against Germany. On the other hand, Stalin was by no means sure that Hitler would triumph. He "said that Germany could be beaten and then England's position will be unclear".[9] His hope was that "it would be fine if at the hands of Germany the position of the richest capitalist countries (especially England) were shaken", for "Hitler, without understanding it or desiring it, is shaking and undermining the capitalist system. . . . We can manoeuvre, pit one side against the other to set them fighting with each other as fiercely as possible."[10] The capitalist world's disaster would be a Bolshevik opportunity. In this context it is worth recalling what Stalin had said, unreported to the public, on 5 April 1927: "At the time of [the] October [Revolution] imperialism was split in two coalitions, into two camps . . . This struggle within imperialism harmed imperialism and weakened it. It was precisely because this struggle was taking place, because the imperialist front was broken, that we, the Russian Communists, succeeded so easily in then slipping through to socialism. That was precisely why. Without that we could have been beaten."[11] A fascinating echo of such sentiments emerged in distant Beijing, from the mouth of Soviet chargé d'affaires Nikitin in June 1940 as the Russians expanded into the Baltic and the Balkans. Nikitin candidly revealed to the US ambassador that the Nazi–Soviet pact of August 1939 was based on the hope that war between Germany and the West would lead to the mutual exhaustion of both sides, "leaving Russia safe from external menace in Europe".[12]

War

On 1 September, at the time Hitler struck Poland, Italy was not ready for war; neither were the French (psychologically) nor the British (materially). Twenty years too late France now pressed for a conference to examine how differences over the Versailles Treaty might be settled peacefully. But Hitler was having none of it. The Italian foreign minister Ciano, with the co-operation of the French and British ambassadors in Rome, attempted to find a way out of the crisis through further negotiations with Germany. But Hitler would not retreat from Poland and, although Halifax seemed willing to compromise, Chamberlain, burned more than once by Hitler, now stood firm, absolutely averse to further concessions.[13] Moreover, the House of Commons was in no mood to let him take any other course.

The spirit of defeatism persisted, however. For instance, both King George VI and Hoare (now Lord Privy Seal), to whom US Ambassador Kennedy spoke, expected German, not necessarily Hitler's, peace proposals within months. In addition both expressed the opinion that continuation of the war "means complete economic, financial, and social collapse and nothing will be saved after the war is over".[14] On the part of London and Paris no one wanted to begin fighting. The Poles were on their own. The French were not willing to risk an offensive against Germany's *Westwall* and all the British could offer was air cover over Western Europe. It was Chamberlain's fault. He had always vigorously resisted creating a land army for action on the continent, opposed conscription until it was forced upon him and, thanks to his sustained unilateralism, the level of trust between the allies—never great—had in the meantime if anything worsened rather than improved.[15] Inevitably the French felt let down. Minister of Finance Paul Reynaud told the US ambassador that "it was his belief that the clear object of Sir John Simon [his British counterpart] was to see French resources exhausted before there was serious weakening on the part of Great Britain, so that at the end of this war, Great Britain could control the situation absolutely".[16] Not the best start to a wartime alliance.

Moreover the spirit of appeasement had by no means vanished. It had become too engrained as a habit of mind. At the end of September Kennedy reported from London a German opinion that "if Hitler goes, Germany might very well go communistic and be a menace to Europe". Halifax, he said, shared the view that "if this war continued it will mean

Bolshevism all over Europe".[17] "Ronnie", Lord Brocket, a friend of Chamberlain's, who was viewed as so dangerous that his butler was discreetly put in place by MI5, wrote to Butler urging acceptance of mediation from "the two sovereigns" (of Belgium and the Netherlands).[18] And the Duke of Buccleugh continued to badger Butler to re-engage with the Germans. It was "wrong", he wrote, "to turn everything down flat". In response Butler would not rule out talks, but "[a]s you know we feel there is real difficulty in coming to any understanding with those who are at present in charge of Germany, and from whom we can get no chance of security".[19]

The fate of Poland was predictable after Molotov had dismissed it as a bastardised state when addressing the Supreme Soviet on 31 August, foreshadowing its fourth partition. The war against it took only a matter of weeks. The campaign culminated in the terrorisation of Warsaw by the Luftwaffe on 25 September with the dropping of 560 tons of high explosive and 72 tons of incendiary ordinance, the like of which had never been seen before. Britain and France looked on from afar, aghast at the speed with which Polish resistance collapsed, as their own men were called to the ranks. "No one", Molotov said later, candidly acknowledging that this included the Russians, "could believe that the Polish state would display such feebleness and . . . rapid disintegration . . . The ruling circles of Poland made a lot of noise about the 'solidity' of their state and the 'might' of their army. However, a brief blow against Poland, initially by the German army and then the Red Army, proved enough for nothing to remain of this misshapen offspring of the Versailles Treaty, living at the expense of suppressed non-Polish nationalities. The 'traditional policy' of unprincipled manoeuvring between and playing off of Germany and the USSR turned out to be a failure and was completely bankrupt."[20] "Poland was a great country," Stalin muttered contemptuously. "Where is Poland now?" Where *were* their leaders to be found?[21] Stalin, no doubt recalling at first hand the rout of the Red Army in 1920, personally respected Polish soldiers and equipment but was "amazed at the utter bankruptcy and confusion of their officer corps".[22] These were the men who had ruled the country since 1926.

Comintern Finally Changes Line

The British cabinet now had its back against the wall, its defiance of Hitler stiffened only by Chamberlain's determination not to be fooled again and bolstered by the much delayed return of Churchill to its ranks. Would Britain cave in and compromise? Stalin had been anxiously waiting to see whether it would. At first no substantial change was made in Comintern policy. Dimitrov had no doubt about how difficult it would be to sell the new line to the international movement: "I must point out", he wrote to Zhdanov on 5 September, "that with this line we are facing and especially the tactical positions and political tasks of Communist Parties under new conditions, we will encounter exceptional difficulties".[23] Dimitrov no longer had much say in anything. On 8 September a telegram went out to the Czechoslovak Communist Party from Gottwald in the name of Comintern's secretariat. It was also directed to the PCF; these were, however, only initial theses that anticipated what would reach all parties by the end of the month. It read:

> The present war is an imperialist war, an unjust war, with respect to which the bourgeoisie of all the belligerent states are equally culpable. In no country must the working class nor, even less the Communist Party, support the war. The bourgeoisie is not waging the war against Fascism, as Chamberlain and the party leaders of Social Democracy maintain. The war is turning out to be between two groups of capitalist countries for the domination of the world. The international working class can in no way defend Fascist Poland, which has refused help from the Soviet Union and oppresses the other nationalities.
>
> The Communist Parties have fought against the supporters of Munich, because they preferred a genuine anti-Fascist front with the participation of the Soviet Union, but the bourgeoisie of England and France have repulsed the Soviet Union in order to conduct a predatory war.
>
> The war has changed the situation fundamentally. The division of states into Fascist and democratic has now lost its former signifi-

cance. Accordingly, tactics must change. The tactic of Communist Parties in all belligerent countries at this stage of the war is to come out against the war, to expose its imperialist character; where there are Communist Deputies present, they must vote against war credits, explaining to the masses that the war will bring them only trouble and ruin. The governments which declare their countries neutral, but seek to profit, support war by other countries—like the government of the United States in Japan and China—must be exposed. Communist Parties must above all launch a decisive offensive against the treacherous policy of Social Democracy.

Communist Parties, in particular, the French, the English, the Belgian and the US parties, that have hitherto acted contrary to these views, must immediately correct their political line.[24]

But Comintern communications were down and remained so with respect to the British Communist Party until the invasion of the Soviet Union. Douglas Springhall, a member of the British Communist Party's executive, happened to be in Moscow and was hurriedly briefed by Dimitrov and Marty, taking the new line back home with oral instructions that the Party must desert the ranks and oppose the war.[25] Nothing damaged the reputation of Comintern's sections more than the ultimate betrayal of their country for another whose motives were quite plainly entirely self-serving.

The decisions taken, the rationalisations followed. Dimitrov himself, no doubt following Stalin, privately expressed the view that a German victory was "improbable". Stalin made a curious remark to the Germans at the conclusion of the Friendship Pact on 28 September, and given that he never made off-the-cuff remarks devoid of significance, it should be taken seriously: he told Schulenburg that "if, in spite of expectations, Germany relapses into a serious condition, then it can be assured that the Soviet people will come to Germany's aid and will not allow Germany to be crushed. The Soviet Union is interested", Stalin emphasised, "in a strong Germany and will not allow Germany to be wiped off the face of the earth."[26] He was not being disingenuous or ironical; certainly not on so important a matter.

Odd as it may seem, this statement reflected a recurrent Marxist-inspired underestimation of the Nazi Party as a classless, amorphous institution that would one day break down into its constituent elements (including a mass of former members of the KPD) and a grossly mistaken estimation of the international balance of power. Behind it all lurked a firm conviction based on the not too distant past and reflecting the very fears that Chamberlain felt so intensely: that war would generate revolution, as it had in 1917. Hoare said as much to Ambassador Maisky on 31 October.[27] Even moderately minded Liberals in Britain such as Lieutenant Colonel Murray, who had been Sir Edward Grey's parliamentary private secretary in 1914, noted "the gathering forces of a communistic invasion of thought and ideals".[28]

At Comintern the Hungarian economist Jenő Varga gave an opinion on the likely outcome of an Anglo–German war that almost certainly expressed a consensus shared with the Kremlin, as he rarely overstepped that mark:

> There is a lack of objective data. It is difficult to say. My view is: the peculiarity of this war, where there has in fact not been any fighting with the exception of naval engagements, is . . . caused by the fact that on the one hand Hitler cannot risk any defeat while he fears the domestic political consequences of the first major defeat and, on the other hand, that both Chamberlain and Daladier have similar fears of the possible domestic political consequences of defeating Hitler and as a result wriggle back and forth, without making up their mind, without conducting a genuine war. That is in one respect a weakness of the Hitler regime and of the regime of finance capital, whereby I believe that of the three countries, Germany, France and England, the power of the bourgeoisie is intrinsically stronger in England . . . England is of the three countries the strongest point today.[29]

This analysis of the balance between Germany and the Anglo–French coalition was not only completely wrong, but it had major implications for the amount of time in hand that the Kremlin believed would be needed should the Nazi régime fail to collapse and for Soviet forces to be brought up to a level that could sustain the country's defence against an adversary perhaps considerably strengthened economically and militarily by war. Planning in Moscow began on the basis of an assumption of no war with Germany for several years. Far from identifying with Poland and its speedy collapse, the Russians, despite the Finnish debacle (see below), still saw themselves as in the premier league. All of this began to become clear even before the end of 1939, and was to be revealed as a glaring deficiency by the time of Hitler's spring offensive in Western Europe.

The occupation and sovietisation of eastern Poland raised the spirits of those who saw the expansion of Communism as an end in itself. From his place of exile in distant Mexico Trotsky, the unrelenting optimist, began to think his lingering hopes for the Soviet Union were not unjustified after all. Paradoxically, perhaps, the reactionary despot Stalin was after all set to play the role of Napoleon:

> [I]n the regions that must become a component of the USSR, the Moscow government will take measures to expropriate the big property-owners and to nationalise the means of production. Such acts are more likely not because the bureaucracy is true to the socialist program, but because it does not wish to and is unable to share power and the privileges connected with the old ruling classes of the occupied regions. Here an analogy presents itself. The first Bonaparte brought the revolution to a halt with the aid of military dictatorship. However, when French forces invaded Poland, Napoleon signed a decree: 'Serfdom is abolished.' This action was not dictated by Napoleon's sympathies for the peasants, but by the fact that the Bonapartist dictatorship rested not on feudal but bourgeois property. Since Stalin's Bonapartist dictatorship rests not on private but on state property, the Red Army's invasion of Poland must virtually bring with it the liquidation of private capitalist property in order thereby to bring the régime of the occupied territories into line with the régime in the USSR.[30]

Trotsky was right. Stalin, like Napoleon, found himself leading a revolutionary war, even though his primary motivations were geopolitical. Since 1936 he had sedulously reduced Comintern to a residue of its former self. But without purposefully seeking to do so, he had expanded Communist domains by the bayonet, as in 1919–20. This formed the prelude to what was to happen on a grand scale as the Red Army drove out the Wehrmacht from Eastern Europe in 1944–45. Kazys Škirpa, the Lithuanian ambassador to Germany, noted that "Soviet Russia's intervention in the Polish–German war not only facilitated the collapse of Poland, but also, one may say that as a consequence of this everything in the eastern part of Europe has been turned on its head. In addition the possible future intervention of Soviet Russia in the military conflict between bourgeois European states threatens them all with totalitarian communism."[31] Ambassador Maisky also noted that on both sides in the war the fear of a Communist revolution was apparent.[32]

Finland at War

This was precisely what Chamberlain and the other appeasers had anticipated, dreaded and so desperately wanted to avert, at almost any price. Stalin was set on recalibrating the balance of power in Europe to Soviet advantage, and with it the correlation of forces between Communism and capitalism; a nightmare that horrified Chamberlain's private secretary Arthur Rucker, who went so far as to declare that "Communism is now the great danger, greater even than Nazi Germany. All the independent states of Europe are anti-Russian, but Communism is a plague that does not stop at national boundaries, and with the advance of the Soviet [Union] into Poland the states of Eastern Europe will find their powers of resistance to Communism very much weakened. It is thus vital we should play our hand very carefully with Russia, and not destroy the possibility of uniting, if necessary, with a new German Government against the common danger."[33] Indeed, feeling was rising so high that on 23 October the war cabinet was asked to consider "the relative advantages and disadvantages which would accrue to us if either formally or informally, we were to declare war on the USSR as the result of Soviet aggression against Finland or against any of the other Scandinavian countries".[34]

The war with Finland was not a primary objective for the Soviet Union, but the tragic result of failed diplomacy in desperate times. In September 1936 Voroshilov had warned visiting French generals Schweisguth and Vuillemin that the Finnish and Estonian borders were perilously close to Leningrad.[35] The attack on Finland in 1939 was preceded by intensive attempts to negotiate Soviet hegemony over all Baltic states. But resistance to any kind of sovietisation was intensely felt there: compared to the Russians, the Germans at first sight appeared the lesser of two evils. Estonia was ethnically and politically close to Finland; the foreign minister of Estonia told the Polish ambassador, "A month of Soviet occupation is worse than four years of German occupation."[36] None the less, out of fear Estonia gave way and reluctantly signed up with the Russians. Finland was the only one to hold out. Referring to the Gulf of Finland, Molotov told Estonian Foreign Minister Karl Selter on 24 September,

> Twenty years ago you made us sit in this Finnish 'puddle'. You don't think that this can last . . . forever. . . . The Soviet Union is now a great power whose interests need to be taken into consideration. I tell you—the Soviet Union needs enlargement of her security guarantee system; for this purpose she needs an exit from the Baltic Sea. If you do not want to conclude with us a mutual assistance pact, then we will have to use . . . other ways, perhaps drastic; perhaps more complicated. I ask you, do not compel us to use force against Estonia.[37]

Latvia was the next in line, on 5 October. In the meantime, immediately after the Friendship Pact with Germany was signed, the Lithuanians had been summoned to Moscow. Resistance again did not last long. "You argue too much," Stalin warned.[38] They conceded on 10 October. The following day *Pravda* boasted of "an iron belt of Soviet defence throughout the Baltic region". But the Russians were still nervous: the British Communist Andrew Rothstein, a TASS correspondent linked to Soviet military intelligence and a true believer in the need for Stalin's terror, had invited the head of news at the Foreign Office to lunch. There he appealed for direct ministerial contact—on the part of

Churchill or Eden—with Moscow. Rothstein said it would be warmly received. This followed Churchill's speech of 1 October, when he described Russian policy as a product purely of cold self-interest.[39] But nothing came of it. The government was if anything more hostile now to the Soviet Union than it had been through most of the 1930s.

More than a year after the Russians had opened secret talks with Finland on the subject of Soviet defence needs, Helsinki could scarcely have been surprised by the Kremlin's pressure for negotiations; nor by its demands. Stalin's determination that Leningrad be secured had been reinforced by a report from the Fifth Directorate of the NKVD on 1 June. Its *rezident* in Helsinki, Boris Rybkin, reported that the head of the department for mobilisation of the Finnish general staff "in conversation with our source" said the following:

> Should England really conclude a pact with the USSR then we will have war. Germany will wait only until the harvest is brought in . . . In this war Germany will not move against Finland, and we can maintain our independence and neutrality for the purpose of becoming an outpost in the fight against Bolshevism and the Soviet Union . . . If with the aid of our coastal artillery and fleet we can prevent the Soviet fleet and air force from getting into the Baltic Sea, we can be absolutely sure that after the war's end our independence will be reinforced in relation to Germany.

Moreover, it was assumed that even were Soviet planes to penetrate and bomb some targets, "the Red Army will be unable to enter Finland. In a German war with the USSR, even if England is against Germany, the Red Army could not sustain a long war given the absence of qualified leaders."[40]

It must have been clear to Stalin that the Finns did not take Soviet military power sufficiently seriously. The terror had wrought so much damage. The issue for the Finns was how much of a risk they were prepared to take now that the Germans had apparently abandoned them to the Russians. Some measure of concession would at least abate any threat from the Soviet side. The fundamental issue in dispute between Finance Minister Väinö Tanner and diplomat Juho Paasikivi was whether Soviet territorial demands, comparatively limited in scope, were just the thin end of the wedge or, as the Russians claimed, the entire extent of their ambitions.

Molotov expected to negotiate directly with Foreign Minister Eljas Erkko coming as a plenipotentiary. He was immediately disappointed. Erkko was a diehard anti-Communist and had no wish to go. In his place the Finns chose their minister in Stockholm, the 69-year-old former politician Juho Paasikivi. A strong conservative and a formidable negotiator, Paasikivi had headed the first cabinet after the civil war between reds and whites and he had led the delegation to the peace talks with Soviet Russia in 1920. He was a staunch realist, steeped in knowledge of Russia, including the language.[41] Paasikivi sought out Baron Carl Mannerheim's assessment. Mannerheim, Finland's most senior military officer and a veteran of the tsarist army, was anxious to avert war with Russia because of the weakness of Finnish defences.[42] But President Kyösti Kallio and social democrat Väinö Tanner, who had run the previous, secret talks into the ground, severely limited Paasikivi's room for manoeuvre. On 11 October, as a precaution, all men of serving age were called up for duty, just as Paasikivi arrived in Moscow to negotiate.

On 12 October the talks opened at the Kremlin in Molotov's room, at the other end of the corridor from Stalin's, at five o'clock in the afternoon. A stand-off swiftly ensued. Stalin pointed out that in 1919 Yudenich was able to attack Petrograd from the south coast of Finland and that same year the Royal Navy had bombarded Kronstadt from its base at Koivisto (Björkö) and sunk two battleships. He asked whether the entire Gulf of Finland should not be closed to traffic. Molotov suggested a lease on a site in the Gulf for thirty years.

The Finns had granted a nickel concession in Petsamo to Britain for ninety-nine years. The Russians insisted that the border with Petsamo be altered to Soviet advantage. They also wanted Hogland and Hangö. In return they were offering to trade territory—forest—in Eastern Karelia. As instructed, Paasikivi resisted. "You are extraordinary people, you Finns!" Stalin protested. "Bitterness towards tsarist Russia was completely justified, but you have no reason to transpose that to Soviet Russia. Do you really think that the country of the tsars would have negotiated with you in this manner? Far from it." Paasikivi insisted he had to consult with his government. It was six o'clock in the afternoon, and Molotov suggested they reconvene in five hours. Paasikivi refused.[43]

The Finns delayed until 14 October before issuing a reply. Discussion retraced the previous course. Finally, exasperated, as a man who never tolerated fools gladly, Paasikivi asked the Russians to come clean about what they really feared. Molotov said that "for the present we have good relations with Germany, but everything could change". Unwilling to take that heretical thought any further, he added, "England could also send a powerful fleet into the Gulf of Finland." Moreover, doubling the distance of Leningrad from the Finnish frontier in Karelia to seventy kilometres, in return for which the Russians would trade twice as much territory as that lost by Finland, seemed to them reasonable. "We do not fear you", Stalin persisted, revealing his underlying concerns, "but Germany and England could anyway bring pressure to bear forcing you into attacking Leningrad."[44]

Within the Finnish war cabinet on 15 October, divisions hardened as the issues were thrashed out. Tanner feared the risk of war much less than did Paasikivi, though he was willing to concede something. However, Foreign Minister Erkko and Defence Minister Juho Niukkanen were adamant that compromise was completely out of the question regarding ceding military bases to the Russians. Erkko, convinced Finland would find support elsewhere (he had British relatives), insisted that they refuse any bases, that the Russians were bluffing. He refused moreover to acknowledge that the Soviet Union was "a great power". Mannerheim rebutted these assumptions, but was in turn undermined by the defence minister. Niukkanen believed that granting bases would be the prelude to a complete takeover.[45]

On 22 October conscription in Finland was completed. The following day negotiations resumed in Molotov's study. On this occasion Tanner accompanied Paasikivi. From six to eight o'clock in the evening no progress was made. Stalin insisted that there was no alternative to Hangö as a base to block the entrance to the Gulf of Finland. The Finns also refused to retreat from the existing border north-east of Leningrad.

Talks broke up and resumed at eleven o'clock that night, but they remained at stalemate.

On 25 October the Finnish government issued an order to mine the coastline. Back in Helsinki the following day Paasikivi suggested a counter-proposal of a base at Jussarö, but Erkko refused to accept it, threatening to resign if the others agreed with Paasikivi. Mannerheim's fears were still disregarded. Meeting on 28 October, the defence minister insisted that Finland's army was "first class". And even though Erkko reported for the first time that other countries suggested that Finland compromise, the suggestion went nowhere.[46] Further meetings at the beginning of November in Moscow failed to accomplish anything. The Finns were on their own.

By the end of October Stalin was already telling his subordinates that "we will have to fight Finland".[47] The Soviet threat assessment for the Baltic now realistically included "the possibility that given the influence of England on the Scandinavian countries, Sweden will not remain neutral and will be drawn into war on Finland's side".[48] On 10 November, just after the Finnish delegation returned home, the chief of staff of the Leningrad military district warned Voroshilov that "by dragging out talks with the Soviet Union the Finnish government hopes to play for time in order to mobilise its armed forces and material resources and to enlist assistance from England and the Scandinavian countries in the event of war with the Soviet Union".[49] Less than a week later an ominous caricature appeared in *Komsomol'skaya pravda* entitled "In Paris". It showed Polish leaders Colonel Beck and General Sikorski at a hotel door in tatters. Beck is gesturing down the street. Beneath was the caption: "Let's wait for Mr Erkko, you'll see he's following in my footsteps." That day, 15 November, Voroshilov ordered the deployment of Soviet forces along the Finnish frontier, though almost a week later Erkko still appeared to be convinced that the force of world opinion "seems to be restraining the Russians".[50]

That was always rather unlikely. The decision to open hostilities was made in the Kremlin. If all went well, in a speedy war, there was not much to worry about. Stalin saw no alternative, but Rothstein was hastily despatched to see William Ridsdale at the press department of the

Foreign Office, presumably to take the political temperature in case Moscow was about to walk into a trap. Ridsdale reported, "Soviet circles for some reason or other are in a markedly nervous condition; among their other fears seems to be one that Germany and the Western powers may yet get together and treat Bolshevism as their common enemy."[51]

Later Stalin asked,

> Was it possible to get by without a war? War was necessary as peace negotiations with Finland produced no results and Leningrad's security had to be guaranteed; no question, for it was a matter of the security of the homeland. Not only because Leningrad represents 30–35% of the defence industry of our country, and the fate of our country depends upon the integrity and defensibility of Leningrad, but because Leningrad is the second capital of our country. To break with Leningrad, for it to be seized and to have, let's say, a bourgeois, a white government appear there, that would mean handing a relatively serious base over for a civil war within the country against the Soviet authorities.

In answer to implicit criticism that he had acted too quickly, that the campaign could have been postponed and undertaken with greater preparation, Stalin insisted that his decision was justified by the international situation. The three major powers of Europe "had each other by the throat"; that was the moment to strike. It would have been "very stupid" and "politically shortsighted" to let that opportunity pass without acting.[52]

The ageing "Bolshevik Venus" Alexandra Kollontai, whom the US ambassador whimsically belittled as "a kindly old lady addicted to tea and [the Victorian novelist] Anthony Trollope" was the Soviet ambassador to Sweden.[53] On 22 November she flew in to Moscow to see Molotov. Flanked in Stockholm by a minister-counsellor and a first secretary working for the Fifth Directorate of the NKVD, Kollontai knew what courage was all about. Molotov did not much like her, but it was after all she who had introduced him to Polina Zhemchuzhina, his beloved wife.[54] However, as the Swedish ambassador Vilhelm Assarasson discovered, Kollontai's influence in Moscow was not quite as strong as the Swedes liked to flatter themselves it was.[55] "Have you come to plead for your Finns?" Molotov sneered. Indeed Kollontai had, arguing, among other things, what damage war would do for the Soviet Union's reputation amid "progressive forces" throughout the world. This elicited more scorn from the naturally abrasive Molotov: "You honour England and France as 'progressive forces', do you?" Kollontai got nowhere; she was an unwelcome messenger from another world of which few traces remained in Moscow.[56]

The Red Army struck Finland after faking a border incident, German-style, at two o'clock in the morning on 30 November. The fighting was intense. Helsinki was stupefied by an attack it had casually dismissed as highly unlikely. The government fell. On 1 December Tanner, now foreign minister, "immediately made plain his intention to seek negotiations with Moscow", though simultaneously asking Stockholm to join them in fortifying the Åland islands before the Russians took them.[57] The Swedes saw through this ploy, naturally preferring that the Russians and the Finns negotiate rather than being tricked into colliding with Moscow. Unsurprisingly Tanner found the Russians coolly indifferent to entreaty. Indeed, in an outburst of unjustified optimism, on 2 December the Soviet government recognised a bogus "People's Democratic Republic" under the leading Finnish Communist at Comintern, Kuusinen, whose second wife Aino, a military intelligence officer, had been arrested and imprisoned by the NKVD only the year before.[58] A foretaste of things to come.

Simultaneously the Russians published an account of Molotov's meeting with Laurence Steinhardt, the US ambassador, which included a firm rebuke to the Finns. "As to the resignation of the Cajander government and its replacement by Tanner's," Molotov said, "this event unfortunately improves nothing. . . . Mr Tanner was and remains the evil genius who disrupted the Soviet–Finnish negotiations. Had the negotiations on the Finnish side been led by Mr. Paasikivi, without the participation of Mr Tanner, as it was in the first phase . . . then the talks would clearly have culminated in an appropriate agreement. The participation of Mr Tanner in the negotiations spoiled everything and evidently tied Mr. Paasikivi's hands."[59]

The Swedish ambassador in Moscow, Wilhelm Winther, was told that Stockholm had taken on the role of protective power at Tanner's request. But when Winther finally returned to his post on 4 December, he received a brush-off: Sweden, Molotov insisted, had no business in that role. Moscow no longer recognised the government in Helsinki. The news was published in *Pravda* on the following day.[60]

In Stockholm Kollontai knew it would be bad but was nevertheless horrified at the disastrous turn of events, fearing lest Sweden join Finland against the Soviet Union. She called on the cabinet secretary at the Foreign Ministry, Erik Boheman, and found him "in an extremely nervous state" but able unofficially to talk "between old friends". The strength of feeling over Finland could, given the prevailing state of mind in Moscow, arouse suspicions not that Sweden wanted to intervene, but that Britain was involved. It had to be borne in mind, she noted, that Moscow was not terribly well informed about how the world felt. The Russians could not, for example, understand that "a little country like Finland would think to defend itself against a Great Power like Russia if Finland hadn't counted on direct assistance from another Great Power, i.e. England". Thus the mood in Sweden could be seen as "an attempt from the side of the English to force us [Sweden] into a war with the Soviet Union". Kollontai wondered if anything could be done to calm Swedish opinion. Boheman reassured her that Sweden had no intention of intervening, but that for historical reasons the two countries were close, and that the Russians should look to the long term and negotiate, as the Finns were willing to do.[61]

The British, and certainly Chamberlain, were at first loath to enter into another conflict, but not for want of sympathy towards Finland. Few could doubt prevailing attitudes to "the Soviet menace".[62] Indeed, when the Russians attacked Finland Chamberlain's personal secretary Rucker lamented the fact that "after the last war the statesmen of Europe did not see Russia was the great menace and did not make friends with Germany on that basis".[63] Thomas Snow, the minister at the British legation in Helsinki, had recommended that Britain defend Finland against the Soviet Union. He also openly declared that, as a partner of Hitler, Stalin was "a more likely winner than Herr Hitler and, if left to his own devices, is accordingly possibly the greater menace of the two".[64] Indeed, on 22 December Halifax asked that the Foreign Office consider the option of war with the Soviet Union.[65]

Behind the scenes Halifax's creature, Parliamentary Under-Secretary Butler, was still playing with the idea of concluding peace with Germany. His friends were determinedly anti-Bolshevik. The author Arthur Bryant had been asked by Butler what the government ought to do. Bryant was

> of the opinion that if Hitler is in a devil of a hole, out of which our firm attitude offers him and Germany no escape save a Phyrric [*sic*] victory over us or ultimate Bolshevism, we are in as awkward a one . . . As its old possessing and middle class was destroyed in the Inflation, there is now little or no possibility of an industrialised nation like Germany meeting a second defeat without going Bolshevist. We shall thus have a solid Bolshevist bloc from the Pacific to the Rhine. . . . Russia's leaders have never abandoned their possibility of spreading Bolshevism by the Marxist expedient of a prolonged world war culminating in revolution. By their patient and subtle manoeuvres last summer they precipitated that war. They are now endeavouring to prolong it.[66]

Such speculation could also be heard in Moscow, though only behind closed doors. On 29 November, Dimitrov, ever the optimist, argued that "[t]he pact is exerting a revolutionary influence on Germany. The National Socialist Party", he insisted, "is not a homogeneous but a heterogeneous party." Within Germany, the Soviet Union and the issue of socialism were back on the table for discussion, he asserted. Moreover, he ruled out a speedy peace between Germany, Britain and France: "This is most unlikely." The second possibility, that "Germany will achieve victory through a long war" was "even less likely", because "Germany will be too exhausted by it". The third possibility was the one the British appeasers had always feared, that in the course of the war with the British and French underpinned by the Americans, the growth of anti-fascist sentiment and nationalist resistance in Germany would bring down the Hitler régime, leading to general exhaustion. This would "not be so bad for the working class in Germany".[67] The assumption, however, was that the Soviet Union should and could, in the meantime, remain aloof.

Meanwhile, on 10 December Finland took Soviet aggression to the League of Nations, now a moribund organisation that had not condemned Nazi Germany's invasion and conquest of Austria, Czechoslovakia and Poland. Typically Butler, who had attended the League since working for Halifax, was designated by London to lead the charge. British hypocrisy was much in evidence. Halifax himself had no time for an institution that he had derided as "largely a sham" back in 1937.[68] The British and French, morally compromised by the appeasement of Germany, evidently hoped to shore up what remained of their dignity by the expulsion of the Soviet Union, which took place a mere four days later. Chamberlain above all sought "reprobation".[69] Behind the scenes the American ambassador to France, Bullitt, not one to avoid the limelight and now an extreme anti-Communist who saw himself as an avenging angel, was encouraging the League, an organisation the Americans had long ago spurned at birth, to condemn the Russians. Bullitt worked through Daladier, who was himself desperately clutching at straws in Paris.[70] To say the least, this was not a dignified spectacle.

There were also practical objections. Sweden opposed League action on the grounds that it would drive the Russians further into the arms of the Germans. But the Swedes set a pattern by falling in with the French and the British when pressed.[71] Committed to sustaining a posture of neutrality, unlike neighbouring Norway, which argued for direct intervention in Finland, Sweden would not intervene in the war directly on the side of the Finns for fear of the Soviet navy, given "the exposed situation of the country", with its industries and population centres perilously close to the coastline. However, it was "disposed to help Finland and ready to afford all necessary facilities for help from other countries". But, and this was a bizarrely unrealistic caveat, everything had to be done "privately".[72] The recruitment and despatch of thousands of volunteers inevitably undercut that pious aspiration.[73] The Swedes were none the less careful to secure German assent to the passage of volunteers from "the Western Powers" through Sweden before implementing the understandings reached with Finland's supporters.[74]

For her part, Kollontai had already protested that such actions were "not only incompatible with Sweden's policy of neutrality, but may also lead to undesirable complications between Sweden and the Union of Soviet Socialist Republics".[75] The consequences for Sweden could be serious, given its vulnerability at sea and the fact that the Germans needed to be assured that its iron ore was readily available to their own war effort. Indeed, on 22 February People's Commissar for the Navy Admiral Kuznetsov anticipated the worst, and requested "preparation of an operational plan of action against Sweden".[76]

The Soviet Union would have to pay a high price if the Finnish war continued. The longer it lasted, the more damage was done to the Soviet Union's diplomatic position, now over-exposed worldwide. The Soviet–Finnish war did not merely distract the world from the German danger; it also threatened to wreck the carefully balanced attempts to incorporate the Baltic states as protectorates.

Still smarting from his personal failure to convince Finland that the way forward was through timely territorial concessions, Stalin met Estonia's chief of staff, Laidoner, along with its ambassador, in the early hours of 12 December. According to the account given to the Swedes, Stalin, at his most diplomatic, showed himself to be very anxious to explain that the war came about only because the Finns were unyielding, and that he quite understood why "populations related to the Finns [Estonia]" inevitably sympathised with them.[77]

The Soviet performance in war was nothing less than disastrous, however. Stalin was unprepared for both the determination of the Finns and the obstructive terrain under heavy snow that lent itself to a kind of partisan warfare on skis which the Russians had never before encountered. In a rash display of exuberance, Stalin had thrown aside Chief of Staff Boris Shaposhnikov's original plans for invasion, which had required a heavy deployment, and chose instead to encourage the officer commanding the Leningrad military district, the over-eager Kirill Meretskov, to improvise his own strategy.[78] Unfortunately for the Russians, as Marshal Georgii Zhukov noted in his memoirs, "in practice

I. V. Stalin poorly understood issues of military strategy; even worse was his understanding of managing the battlefield".[79] This remained so at least until the battle of Stalingrad in 1942–43.

In the Far East, at war with the Japanese, Commander Zhukov had miraculously succeeded in overcoming the severe damage wrought by Stalin's purge of the military. He had done so through massive deployments of combined arms. Nothing had been left to chance. The stakes were too high. In Finland, however, bad planning showed through when Stalin insisted on minimal force allocations. Incompetence was manifest from top to bottom, as evident in military intelligence as in battle planning. At a plenum of the Central Committee on 27 March 1940, reviewing the record of failure Voroshilov had no choice but to acknowledge "Ignorance of the actual situation in Finland . . . Unpreparedness for such a war . . . Our casualties: 230,000, including 52,000 killed . . . The Finns: 70,000 killed and 200,000 wounded". An extraordinary number of Soviet aircraft—1,200—that the Russians could ill afford to dispense with were also lost.[80]

Britain Heads for War with the Soviet Union

The reputation of the Soviet armed forces had hit its lowest point since 1920. Moreover, Stalin's eventual victory ensured that the Finns would be on the side of the Germans for a return round when Hitler finally attacked the Soviet Union. The entire cost of this damaging episode had yet to be counted. The Russians had meanwhile inadvertently stumbled ill-equipped into more than one minefield. First Lord of the Admiralty Winston Churchill, hitherto someone Stalin believed he could perhaps work with, "thought it would be to our [British] advantage if the trend of events in Scandinavia brought it about that Norway and Sweden were forced into war with Russia. We would then be able to gain a foothold in Scandinavia with the object of helping them, but without having to go to the extent of ourselves declaring war on Russia."[81] Prime Minister Chamberlain also wanted the focus of the Germans to shift to Scandinavia.[82]

The Russians certainly believed the British were working in that direction. Sweden found itself sandwiched between Britain and France on the one hand and Russia and Germany on the other. With the British supplying indirect military aid to Finland at the end of the year, the French baying for blood and the Swedish general staff demanding direct intervention, the cabinet in Stockholm sought to bring the conflict to an end with an approach to Berlin asking for German influence to be brought to bear on Moscow.[83]

The fallout from the Finnish war was catastrophic. The atmosphere around the Soviet embassy in London had not been worse since the days of the Munich settlement. The political barometer had plummeted to new lows. Early extravagant hopes of separating Moscow from Berlin had given way to long-standing fears of Bolshevism moving in on the ruins of a civilisation destroyed by war. The barriers to Anglo–French intervention were rapidly falling. The Jewish secretary of state for war Leslie Hore-Belisha was a staunch reformer who had fallen out with the more conservative generals who had the ear of the king (some, like Lieutenant General Pownall, fiercely anti-Semitic and very anti-Bolshevik). He was brusquely sacked by Chamberlain on 4 January 1940. The following day, emboldened by Red Army setbacks, London decided to help the Finns on the model of the Italian and German intervention in Spain.[84] Hore-Belisha's removal also made possible Anglo–French plans laid by Generals Weygand, Gamelin, Gort and Ironside for attacking the Soviet Union, a scheme that notoriously included bombing the oilfields of Baku in Azerbaijan.[85]

As anti-Soviet sentiment rose, Maisky reported on the underlying preoccupations of the British establishment, which had begun to realise that the war against Germany might be "very long and exhausting"; that "the military outcome remains to the highest degree unclear and that the likelihood of revolutionary disturbances in Europe as a result of the war are becoming almost certain". Some of those who favoured widening the war, he suggested, believed it to be "especially dangerous should, at the end of the war, the USSR remain 'out of the ring'; as a result turning into a European hegemon with all the international political and domestic social consequences at the very moment that all the remaining bourgeois governments are weakened and exhausted". For them it would be better to draw the weakened Russians directly into the conflict to weigh down the Germans; particularly if the Americans came in.[86]

With military action against Soviet forces now "seriously contemplated",[87] Chamberlain deluded himself with the thought that "once our Hurricane aircraft, and other foreign aircraft, are in action on the Finnish side 'there won't be a Russian left in Finland.'"[88] But, even before this extravagant expedition could get under way, Sweden began pressing for a negotiated solution. And here Stalin held the distinct advantage. Moscow was up to speed on Anglo–French preparations thanks to Soviet spy John Cairncross, at that time private secretary to Maurice Hankey, minister without portfolio and member of the war cabinet, and could thereby time its moves on the diplomatic front.[89]

On 26 January Swedish Foreign Minister Christian Günther called in on Kollontai. He emphasised that Sweden and the Soviet Union had an identical interest in keeping Sweden completely neutral. "However," he emphasised, "the longer the war lasts, the more difficult it becomes to restrain the activists and to resist pressure from outside." The Finns were, he said, "effectively defeated" and would go for any terms. "Sweden is prepared to offer full co-operation to the [Soviet] Union in the search for a path to peace." In response Kollontai gave the official line that no peace could be obtained with the White Finns. Günther expressed regret: "Should the activists gain the upper hand over our policy, and with the war dragging on that is inevitable, then the Great Powers will not stand on ceremony. Now there is still time to avoid a general war; soon it will be too late." But within two days Molotov replied to Kollontai's telegram, making a crucial concession:

> In principle we do not exclude the possibility of a compromise with the Ryti-Tanner government. As to the tactical side of the question, we need to take the measure of the Ryti government's concessions, without which there is no point in talking about a compromise. In this respect one must take into account that our demands will go beyond the terms we offered at the time of the negotiations with Tanner and Paasikivi, as since the negotiations with the latter blood has been shed; shed not through our fault, but the shedding of blood

requires additional guarantees for the security of the USSR's borders. One also must take into account that what we have refused the Kuusinen government can in no way be agreed upon for the Ryti government.[90]

On 5 February Tanner arrived in Stockholm and met Kollontai secretly in a room at the Grand Hotel to make an offer to Stalin. But it by no means met Moscow's demands; whereupon Tanner proved even more unforthcoming. The explanation given by Günther was news that the French were determined to intervene but that the Swedes were resisting their entreaties.[91] Further attempts by Tanner, meeting Kollontai incognito on 27 February, to press the Russians into reducing their demands merely delayed progress. London and Paris were working in the other direction. The Swedes became ever more convinced that the Finns were quite prepared to saddle their neighbours with war in order to obtain their terms.[92]

Finally, on 7 March a full Finnish delegation including Prime Minister Risto Ryti arrived in Moscow under Swedish cover and with no photographs on their identity papers. Talks took place in Moscow on 8 and 10 March. The terms were, as expected, far worse than those of October 1939. The Swedes, evidently in order not to discourage the Finns, had not shown them the full extent of Soviet demands which had been conveyed by both Molotov and Kollontai to Foreign Minister Günther and Ambassador Assarsson respectively on 6 March.[93] But the Finns had little choice in the matter. On 12 March 1940 the war was settled on Soviet terms; though ultimately to no lasting advantage, since this left Finland with a score to settle. *Pravda* the following day featured an editorial on the peace agreement: "Those tasks that the Soviet Government set itself have been resolved. The security of our north-western frontiers, especially the security of the largest centre of workers in the world, Leningrad, has been totally guaranteed."[94]

The day that peace was signed Sir Victor Mallet, recently appointed British minister to Sweden, came up the staircase at the Swedish Foreign Ministry as Kollontai came down. They stood together face to face for a moment in embarrassed silence until he commented on the fine weather they had been having, before they continued on their way. Mallett came formally to request the passage of British troops through to Finland, a request simultaneously made in Oslo.[95] It was too late, however. The Russians had narrowly averted the landing in Finland of an Anglo–French expeditionary force, with untold consequences for all those concerned.

Hitler Invades Western Europe

Assured of no further distractions to the north-east, and in the full knowledge that the Soviet armed forces had been dealt a humiliation even in victory, on 9 April the Wehrmacht attacked Denmark, and then Norway. Given Swedish warnings, this should not have taken London by surprise.[96] In the Balkans nerves were rattled. Stalin was determined that the Soviet Union should become a Danubian power in order to block Germany's advance in south-eastern Europe. The Soviet chargé d'affaires told the Latvian ambassador to Bucharest that on the issue of Bessarabia the Romanians had to come to terms. "The Russians are still waiting in vain for the Romanians to make proposals in this regard. But if something happens in this region, Soviet Russia will not idly remain a peaceful observer 'twiddling its thumbs'. A rather unambiguous view. About the Romanian military . . . my Soviet colleague spoke in a rather scornful manner: 'What are they (Romanians) going to defend themselves with? Are they going to put living meat against steel and iron, like the Poles did?'"[97]

Meanwhile in Britain the House of Commons had finally had enough of Chamberlain. The Labour opposition would not serve in government with him as prime minister; indeed, they did not want him in government at all. On 7 May Amery had carried with him to the debate the famous words of Oliver Cromwell with which he dismissed the Rump Parliament. When, after much hesitation, he finally delivered them, he brought the house down.[98] Chamberlain was finished. The king, on Chamberlain's advice, given in final recognition that his erstwhile adversary had been right where he himself had been consistently wrong about Hitler, called upon Churchill to head a new government. And not a moment too soon.

On 10 May 1940 the Germans sliced through Belgium and Holland. The king of the Belgians unilaterally surrendered without elected authority or consultation with Britain and France, undermining the prestige of the monarchy after the war. As Belgian and French forces succumbed to the German advance, the Kremlin's anxiety was hard to conceal. On 22 May the French chargé d'affaires in Moscow reported a conversation with a Baltic diplomat in which Molotov was heard to express his concern about the situation and to go so far as to hope for an allied recovery.[99] Too much should not be read into this indiscretion, however. The Russians were not much impressed when, at the inept insistence of Labour Party leader Clement Attlee, who had been invited into government on 10 May, the British hastily decided to send Independent Labour Party veteran Sir Stafford Cripps to Moscow as ambassador; a baffling blunder on London's part, given that the Bolsheviks naturally regarded him as "a Menshevik".[100] They would, on past form, have preferred a full-blown Conservative; preferably a hereditary peer, someone of standing with the establishment.

Between 28 May and 2 June one quarter of a million British troops were heroically evacuated by scores of privately owned vessels from the shores of Dunkirk, followed by over one hundred thousand Frenchmen. The battle for France had been lost by the Entente. Paris fell on 14 June. Molotov acknowledged that it was "not without the assistance of the pact with the USSR, that Germany was able to carry out so speedily and with such military glory its operations in Norway, Denmark, Belgium, Holland and France".[101] The sudden and complete collapse of France could be explained by inadequate rearmament, the lack of mechanised forces, an air force out of date compared with that of the Germans and poor generalship. But this was not all. As Defence Minister Marshal Pétain had not been far from the truth when he blurted out that the country "was putrefied by politics".[102] Precisely: the fierce anti-Communism generated by the Nazi–Soviet non-aggression pact reflected an inner malaise that had rotted the entire body politic. Churchill picked up this aspect in conversation with Maisky, organised through the intervention of TASS correspondent Rothstein.

Churchill saw Maisky on 3 July. They surveyed the progress of the war, and Britain's chances, which Churchill "thought good".[103] More importantly for Maisky (and Stalin), Churchill "categorically and force-fully refuted rumours about the possibility of peace talks". He insisted Britain would fight to the end, "a matter of life or death for England and the British empire". In passing, Churchill related the following: on the evening of 16 June just after the resignation of Reynaud, Laval was sitting in a restaurant in Bordeaux. Next to his table sat the celebrated American journalist Hubert Knickerbocker, who had once been kicked out of Nazi Germany. Laval invited Knickerbocker to join him and asked him what he thought of Pétain's government opening peace talks with the Germans. Knickerbocker believed France should fight on or lose her status as a great power. To this Laval responded that Knickerbocker did not understand that Hitler had nothing against France; he just hated the Bolsheviks and was merely waiting for the right moment to wipe them out, "and we will help him do it".[104]

More Attempts to Appease

Churchill's reassurance that Britain would not follow in French foot-steps to secure a peace was critical, for those most avid for appeasement had by no means given up. In January the Marquess of Tavistock made a fool of himself trying to elicit peace proposals from the German embassy in Dublin—a fact that was leaked to the press—and he continued to do so into February, despite the hopelessness of the effort.[105] In March Butler, whose Germanophile sentiments seemed to grow rather than diminish as the war proceeded, gave dinner at Claridges to Jay Moffat, chief of the West European Division at the US Department of State. Butler is reported to have "said the Christian revival was giving Halifax his chance, and that he alone could prevail against useless and unwarranted punishment of the German people".[106] Just how far out of touch with reality Butler was came as no secret to the Americans. Secretary to the Treasury Morgenthau's intelligence appreciation for Europe in late March included the observation from Captain William Puleston that "[p]ublic opinion in England has been in advance of Chamberlain in all of the crises that preceded the war".[107] And Butler's errant behaviour did not go unnoticed. Cadogan confided to his diary that "RAB is the most baleful man. A craven pacifist, a muddle-headed appeaser and a nit-wit, he talks defeatism to Pressmen. I'm on his tracks—we have put C[harles] Peake [handling the press at the Foreign Office] on to them. I shan't be able to stand too much more. Can the Party [a revealing and interesting slip of the tongue] find none better than this?"[108] Halifax, however, typically, clung on to Butler until removed as foreign secretary and despatched to serve as ambassador to the United States in July 1941. There was good reason for this: Butler's instincts were those of his master.

The urge to make a compromise peace with the Germans among those who were opposed to Churchill was if anything strengthened by the fall of Paris on 14 June. In Moscow Stalin had prevented the PCF from fighting the German invader and directed it instead to focus its fire entirely on the two hundred families dominating the country. Comintern proposals to go further were delayed and continuously watered down. Worse still, when the Germans took control, Jacques Duclos, without reference to Moscow, arrived from Brussels with Maurice Tréand, "the fat man" responsible for security within the PCF, trusted by the NKVD. Tréand tried to open negotiations with the Germans (18–20 June) but his emissaries were promptly arrested. Otto Abetz of the Ausamt then stepped in and overruled the Wehrmacht. He took up the talks with the long-standing legal adviser to Soviet institutions in France, Robert Foisson, on behalf of the PCF. The proposal was that the Communist daily *l'Humanité* be published, on the grounds that the Belgian Party was releasing its own newspaper, *Eulenspiegel*, under German occupation. This "basic line" was ex post facto approved in Moscow on 17 July,[109] though Comintern was careful to warn the French just two days later that they must be alert to the "danger of being compromised". "Passive resistance" was the only form of resistance to the Germans that Moscow authorised.[110] On 5 August Comintern further warned that the PCF was open to manipulation by the German authorities, by leaving them in peace, exaggerating the strength of the Party in negotiations with Pétain and Laval to obtain better terms and discrediting the Party, thus isolating it from the masses.[111] Duclos was dismayed, indeed "astonished that they could think that we could become playthings in the hands of the occupier".[112] Collaboration had already collapsed, but damage had been done.

Just three days after the fall of Paris, while the outcome of Franco–German peace talks was still uncertain, Butler talked to the Swedish minister, Börn Prytz, at the Foreign Office.[113] Prytz recorded,

> During the conversation today with Butler at Foreign Office he confirmed that France had capitulated . . . Britain's official attitude will for the present continue to be that the war must go on, but he assured me that no opportunity for reaching a compromise peace would be neglected if the possibility were offered on reasonable conditions and that no 'diehards' would be allowed to stand in the way in this connection. He thought that Britain had greater possibilities of negotiation than she might have later on . . . During the conversation, Butler was called in to see Halifax, who sent me the message that 'common sense and not bravado would dictate the British Government's policy' [quoted in English] . . . It would appear from conversations I have had with other members of parliament that there is an expectation that, if and when the prospect of negotiations arises, possibly after 28 June, Halifax may succeed Churchill.[114]

Halifax's surreptitious fight with Churchill was over the prospects for a compromise peace. It had after all been Chamberlain who had recommended that the king call for Churchill rather than Halifax when he himself finally threw in the towel as prime minister. After Germany's assault on Poland, to the consternation of his diehard supporters, Chamberlain shifted abruptly from favouring appeasement to an obstinate refusal even to consider any offer from Germany while Hitler remained in power. Communicating to Lord Arnold in January Chamberlain had insisted there was no weakening in the government's resolution; only when Hitler was convinced would he negotiate a lasting peace. Lord Brocket, for example, complained to fellow appeaser Bryant that he found Chamberlain "most obstinate".[115] And the reaction of many, including Butler, bordered on hysteria when the news came in that the king had called for Churchill. Whereas the enigmatic Halifax epitomised cool rationality and the spirit of pragmatic compromise, Churchill incarnated the fiery eighteenth-century aristocratic temperament, where the passions held sway. What Halifax's tribe did not understand was that, in competing with Hitler, "rationality" did nothing but sustain delusions of reciprocity and undermine morale.

Before long the substance of the Butler–Prytz conversation had been disseminated among Swedish envoys, including the ambassador to Berlin, and thereby reached the Germans. Prytz reported that "Butler has experienced unpleasantness, since suspicion of defeatism is a serious matter in these days". Indeed, not unexpectedly, when Churchill eventually learned of it he sent a polite shot across Halifax's bow, writing on 26 June that "Butler held odd language to the Swedish Minister and certainly the Swede derived a strong impression of defeatism".[116] Since Butler had actually consulted Halifax during his meeting with Prytz, the foreign secretary's polite enquiry to Butler about the conversation was nothing more than cynical pretence.

The only rationale for an Anglo–German entente was anti-Bolshevism, following the model epitomised by Vichy. Not long after the fall of Paris the young Roger Makins recorded, "What happened at Bordeaux was a coup d'état engineered by the most corrupt elements in France [Pierre Laval and Pierre Badouin] making use of famous names [Philippe Pétain and Maxime Weygand]." As Colville, Churchill's private secretary, noted, "It is accepted here that the anti-Bolshevik feelings of Pétain, Weygand etc., were exploited by Laval and Badouin".[117]

Meanwhile the Duke of Windsor was positioning himself as "the king over the water".[118] Indeed, lunching with Cadogan and others on 10 July, George VI expressed himself somewhat defensively as "amused at 'C''s report of the Quisling activities of 'my brother'!"[119] On the previous day the foreign department of Soviet state security, perhaps on the basis of the same intelligence, sent its counterpart in the Red Army a report that "[t]he former English king, Edward, together with his wife Simpson, are currently in Madrid where they are in contact with Hitler. Edward is conducting negotiations with Hitler on the question of forming a new English government, the conclusion of peace with Germany conditional upon establishing a military alliance against the USSR".[120] The king's private secretary briefed Guy Liddell of MI5: the Duke of Windsor had "expressed the view, which I understand he has expressed elsewhere, that the whole war was a mistake and that if he had been King it would never have happened. He clearly rather felt himself in the role of mediator, if his country had finally collapsed, but he did not think the moment opportune for any sort of intervention. He seemed to believe that he understood the German people far better than anyone else."[121] Obliged by Churchill to become governor of the Bahamas, the duke arranged a codeword with his former host in Portugal, Espirito Santo Silva, himself a German agent, in the event that he were needed, should Britain succumb to the Luftwaffe in the Battle of Britain that summer.[122]

On the other side of the continent the lightning speed with which Hitler overran Western Europe had come as a nasty surprise to the Kremlin, which had counted on serious resistance by the French. Molotov, not the brightest of men, gave away his own side's anxiety in awkwardly congratulating ambassador Schulenburg on the fact "that Hitler and the German Government could scarcely have expected such speedy successes".[123] The Soviet consul at Kalgan, northern China, likely as not an intelligence operative confident that he could speak out of the official line, told the Americans that Germany's victory against France had upset Russian calculations made in August 1939 that Germany and the West would exhaust one another in war.[124]

Faced with this calamity, Stalin rationalised the situation and took the long view. He reflected that "Germany cannot dominate Europe without command of the seas and in any case she has not the strength to dominate all Europe". Stalin consoled himself that he did "not believe, either, that such is her intention from what the Germans have told him", though he added that he was "not so simple as to rely on their statements, but rather on the facts". He none the less held it as a rule, of great relevance when peace was achieved in 1945, that "[w]hoever dominates Europe will dominate the world".[125]

The Soviet Union Expands

Others in Moscow were more candid. Early in June 1940 the Red Army swooped in to seize the territorial gains allocated to the Russians in the two pacts with Germany, having previously satisfied themselves with only eastern Poland. In the Kremlin late at night on 30–31 June the deputy prime minister of Lithuania Vincas Krėvė-Mickevičius was told bluntly, "You should begin now to initiate your people into the Soviet system which in the future shall reign everywhere, throughout all Europe, put into practice earlier in some places, as in the Baltic nations, later in others." And from the indelicate intelligence officer Vladimir Dekanozov, deputy commissar for foreign affairs, the prime minister also heard that the war would put "all Europe into our hands, like so much ripe fruit".[126]

From Berlin it looked as though "Russia's action was predicated on the belief that the end of the war is near at hand" and that before the conclusion of a new territorial settlement Moscow needed to have its troops in place on the ground.[127] On 26 June Russian troops descended upon Northern Bukovina, hitherto not included within the scope of the non-aggression pact's secret protocol. The Germans strongly objected. The territory contained ethnic Germans and the invasion demonstrated conclusively that the Russians were determined to hold a bridgehead on the Danube.

Stalin had too much respect for the British Empire to anticipate that it could be beaten, though others did. On 4 July Deputy Commissar Solomon Lozovskii talked to Sweden's senior foreign ministry official Boheman, who foolishly suggested that after Germany had defeated Britain in the next few weeks, the Germans would take her fleet and the government would move to Canada. To this Lozovskii more cautiously retorted that the outcome of the war was for the time being hard to predict, as Britain still commanded massive resources.[128]

Hitler had yet to invade Britain. But he took the view that henceforth the Russians would only get stronger, so on 31 July he made a provisional decision to attack the Soviet Union at some indefinite point in the future. His opinion, according to Rudolf Hess's personal adjutant, was that after the fall of France, Britain was more likely to come to terms if Germany attacked the Soviet Union. Indeed, in August, with the Battle of Britain at its height in the skies above the home islands, contacts were renewed in Geneva between appeasement diehards led by the Marquess of Tavistock, now Duke of Bedford, and the Germans led by Albrecht Haushofer, son of Karl, Hess's foreign policy adviser. According to Hess's assistant, Bedford made it a precondition that peace negotiations be contingent on German renunciation of the Nazi–Soviet pact, and that both Hitler and Hess agree to this; but only after Germany had taken the Balkans.[129] That moment was not to not arrive until April 1941.

On 27 September, to deter American intervention, Italy and Japan joined Germany in a formal alliance, the Tripartite Pact. Hitler had his eyes fixed on the Balkans, a major source of oil and grain for the German economy, as a matter of urgency. Careful not to provoke the Germans beyond the limit, Comintern exercised restraint. Its instructions to the Romanian section, for instance, cautioned against anything that would draw the country into the war, but at the same time insisted that they oppose "the transformation of the country into a dependency of German imperialism".[130] Little more than a fortnight after these instructions were issued, on 7 October, unwilling to risk waiting further, Hitler sent his forces in to seize control of the Romanian oilfields.

In Moscow opinion now began to shift against Berlin. This rapidly became apparent within Comintern. The Spanish Communist Tagüeña recalls Manuilsky lecturing Spanish students that autumn: he "told us that the war was inevitable because Russia considered the Balkans its chief sphere of influence". And Marty spoke enthusiastically about Britain's resistance to German bombing from the air.[131] Although the official press was tongue-tied, Comintern's *World News and Views* argued on 19 October that "Germany's plans for domination in the Near East and over the Balkans menace a vital interest of the USSR in the Black Sea, quite apart from the well-known aspirations of German imperialism for Ukrainian wheat and Caucasian oil".

Molotov Visits Berlin

The Germans invited Molotov to Berlin for talks with Hitler, reciprocating Ribbentrop's two visits to Stalin in 1939. The date set was for 11 November. Stalin was seriously worried. He unexpectedly revealed his underlying concerns to the rest of the leadership a few days earlier. The leadership had lingered over dinner for three and a half hours. But just as everyone was getting up to go, Stalin took the floor. He spoke in a way

that Dimitrov, for one, had never experienced. Now alert to dangers on
the horizon, Stalin warned of a prevalent complacency. They had to
catch up with their rivals. They had beaten Japanese forces at Khalkhin
Gol, but "our aircraft proved inferior to the Japanese aircraft for speed
and altitude". He went on, "We are not prepared for the sort of war being
waged between Germany and England . . . It turns out that our aircraft
can stay aloft for only thirty-five minutes, while German and English
aircraft can stay up for several hours! . . . If in the future", he warned,
"our armed forces, transport and so forth, are not equal to the forces of
our enemies (and those enemies are all the capitalist states, and those
which deck themselves out to look like our friends!), then they will
devour us." Stalin now busied himself every day meeting the designers
of aircraft.[132]

Molotov, less intelligent than "the big boss", appears to have been
more complacent, believing that Germany could not afford to confront
the Soviet Union. Even before leaving for Berlin to draw a line at the
German encroachment into Finland and the Balkans, he forcefully expressed the view that Germany's fight with Britain would be long and
hard, as the British—for whom he had no liking—had at their disposal
"infinite riches and means of resistance".[133] Zhdanov, too, categorically
insisted that because both sides in the war were bogged down, the Soviet Union need not worry about invasion.[134] This *idée fixe* was not
erased, moreover, but reinforced when Molotov arrived in Berlin. Entirely unfamiliar with Germany at first hand, he could not speak or read
German although he was by no means alone in having once made the
effort to learn. Molotov also had a level of confidence in his own abilities
that was not entirely justified, on the view of those who worked closely
with him. Marshal Ivan Konev, indeed, described him as "extremely unintelligent".[135] Litvinov thought him a fool and told him so on more
than one occasion.[136]

Molotov's directives, thrashed out with Stalin, were to clarify Germany's plans, particularly in relation to its allies, Italy and Japan; to de-
lineate "the USSR's spheres of interest" in Europe, the Near East and
Central Asia; to ensure that Germany kept out of Finland; to assure the
Soviet Union's status as a Danubian power; to protest at the unilateral

introduction of German troops into Romania; to assert the inclusion of Bulgaria within the Soviet sphere of interest and the introduction of Soviet troops into the country (to enhance Moscow's position on the Black Sea); and to make clear that both Turkey and Iran should not be touched without reference to the Soviet Union. The entire formulation was apparently predicated on a grand settlement of issues, including secret protocols on the model of 1939.[137]

Molotov left Moscow at a quarter to seven in the evening on 10 November, accompanied by a full delegation that, apart from senior Soviet diplomats, included the deputy commissar of aviation, Alexander Yakovlev, and Vsevolod Merkulov, Beria's deputy commissar at the NKVD. They arrived at Małkinia on the new German frontier at eight o'clock in the evening the following day. They reached Berlin and were met by Ribbentrop at eleven o'clock in the morning of 12 November at the Anhalter Bahnhof, finding the station decked in German and Soviet flags, with an orchestra playing a march. The meeting with Hitler took place at three o'clock that afternoon in an annexe of the magnificent Bellevue Palace, in the Tiergarten, where Bismarck had lived.[138] The summit was preceded by tedious preliminaries, courtesy of Ribbentrop. The Germans insisted that Britain could not hold out, and that even if the Americans came into the war they would be unable to find a foothold on the European continent.[139]

With Hitler present, Molotov laid down a marker intended to impress the Germans with the bold assertion that "the Soviet Union as a great and powerful country cannot stand aside from the resolution of the most important questions in Europe as in Asia". But the talks rambled along without any real focus as it became increasingly obvious that Hitler was not ready for a grand bargain.[140] On 14 November they were even further prolonged, to no real consequence. Hitler, implausibly, pretended not to be fully informed about German penetration of either Finland or Bulgaria. Moreover, Hitler seemed intent on muscling in on any revision of the Montreux Convention dealing with entry and egress with respect to the Black Sea, even though Germany was not a riparian power. The Germans also appeared to be ostentatiously redirecting the Russians away from Europe and towards the Indian Ocean.[141]

The final day of talks was hosted by Ribbentrop at the Wilhelm-strasse, where he boasted once again about Britain being finished. But an air raid warning interrupted proceedings, an explosion occurred, the glass rattled. Ribbentrop promptly escorted them all down to the bun-ker, and when he resumed his monologue on the theme of Britain's defeat, Molotov, never the diplomat, could not resist the riposte: "If England is beaten, why are we sitting in this shelter? And whose bombs are dropping so close that we can hear their explosions even here?"[142] As soon as Molotov had left, Hitler, exasperated by the irritating waste of his time, began immediate preparations for the invasion of the So-viet Union.

Molotov, entirely insensitive to the impact he had on others, was also rather too impressed with his own performance in Berlin. He came away assured that Hitler was more concerned to destroy Britain than to in-vade the Soviet Union. The official Soviet historian Dmitrii Volkogonov later came to the conclusion that after the trip Molotov "continued to insist that Hitler would not attack the USSR" and that Stalin had come to rely upon his judgement about foreign policy.[143] This accords with what the US ambassador Steinhardt reported to Secretary of State Cordell Hull on 7 December: "It has been ascertained from heretofore reliable sources that the anti-German propaganda which was being spread in party circles prior to Molotov's visit to Berlin . . . has been abandoned since the visit." The ambassador also learned that Comin-tern instructions to foreign Communist parties to revert to anti-fascism had been cancelled.[144]

Hitler Resolves to Invade the Soviet Union

Thus it must have come as something of a shock to discover that no sooner had Molotov departed than Hitler became ever more intent on entrenching Germany in the Balkans and in Finland. Worse still, his invitation to the Russians appeared to have been a ruse to give the pub-lic appearance of Soviet complicity in German expansionism. The So-viet embassy in Germany had no doubts: "The coincidence of Germany's activity in the Balkans with the timing of comrade Molotov's departure is an attempt to show evidence of complete agreement by the USSR with the principles of the tripartite pact, with the 'new order' in Europe, etc.; and, doubtless, as the most effective means of pressure on Balkan states with the aim of fully subordinating them to its will and its wishes."[145] The visit evidently also rattled others in Moscow. Molotov felt obliged to reassure Dimitrov that "we concluded no agreement and assumed no obligations whatever with the Germans" who "wanted to portray us as having approved their plans in the Balkans".[146]

To the north, Germany also appeared to be working towards uniting Sweden, Norway and Finland against the Soviet Union.[147] But the first direct clash between Moscow and Berlin came over Bulgaria, which was the obvious route for German armies aiding the failing Italian invasion of Greece. On 25 November the general secretary of Narkomindel went on a special mission to King Boris of Bulgaria with the offer of a pact of mutual assistance to counter the Germans. Dimitrov was summoned the same day to Stalin in the Kremlin where, in the presence of Molotov, he was told that "[i]f the Bulgarians do not accept our offer, they will fall entirely in the lap of the Germans and Italians and will then perish. . . . This offer must be made widely known in Bulgaria."[148]

It was an inept move. At this point, with Stalin distracted by anxiety at the lack of military preparedness, the Kremlin appears to have been in disarray. Dimitrov immediately circulated the news to the secretary of the Bulgarian Communist Party, Vasil Kolarov, including the fact that the offer had been made to the tsar and former prime minister Bogdan Filov. He also suggested that the Russians would back territorial claims against Greece.[149] But when Bulgarian Communists began disseminating leaflets about the offer of the pact, the campaign ordered by Stalin backfired completely. On 28 November Molotov belatedly phoned Comintern from Stalin's office to call a halt. Dimitrov instructed the Bulgarian comrades "to stop the harmful stupidity".[150] A mere five days after the proposal was made, Popov, the Bulgarian foreign minister, politely but coldly informed Soviet ambassador Lavrishchev that the offer had been rejected.[151]

Molotov understood that the Bulgarians feared being drawn into the war.[152] But it would be wholly misleading to believe that the Russians were similarly fearful. Their aim was still unilateral expansion. At the close of the year Molotov had a long meeting with Italian ambassador Rosso, in which he strongly asserted the Soviet Union's rights as a Danubian power, given that the Soviet Union had annexed Bessarabia from Romania. He also asserted "the pre-eminence of Soviet interests in the Black Sea". Recalling the Crimean War (1853–56) and the landing of British (1918) and French (1919) troops, Molotov pointed to the recent reinforcement of Britain's positions in the eastern Mediterreanean, notably its occupation of Crete. If this were important to Italy, Molotov continued, "Russia can no less ignore it and had to be concerned. . . . The country that is threatening is always England," he added. "Not just Italy but also the USSR cannot ignore the problem represented by naval power in the eastern Mediterranean."[153] Clearly Soviet thinking was still locked into the axis with Germany and Italy rather than open to any alternative, despite rivalry with Berlin in the Balkans.

Early in the new year, 1941, Dimitrov urgently turned again to Stalin for advice, asking to see him to review proposals to place the Bulgarian Communist Party on the alert. Stalin phoned him at two o'clock in the morning the following day, 14 January, approving the new line. Comintern then immediately telegraphed the Bulgarian comrades:

> The intervention of German forces into Bulgaria under preparation confronts the Bulgarian Communist Party with an extraordinarily difficult and complicated task. Having a massive influence in the country, it cannot pass over in silence such an act on the part of Germany carried out with the agreement or connivance of the Bulgarian Government.

The Party had to "expose the responsibility of Tsar Boris and the government who, by rejecting the Soviet proposal of a mutual assistance pact, are directly liable for the resulting situation, and in this respect ever more forcefully underscore the need for a mutual assistance pact between Bulgaria and the USSR." A widely disseminated TASS statement denying that the transfer of German troops had been agreed with the USSR was to be used "to paralyse the deceiving of the masses by government circles".[154] None of this proved effective. And on 1 March the Bulgarian government agreed that German forces could enter the country. Bulgaria joined the Tripartite Pact between Italy, Germany and Japan.

Stalin's Balkan policy had come apart at the seams. In a sense this was unavoidable, since Italy's invasion of Greece in June 1940 was predictably a failure, and Germany was increasingly drawn in to resolve the problem. After Bulgaria fell to the Germans, Yugoslavia was obviously next, and here the Russians trod carefully, not wishing to fall into a trap that would bring them into direct confrontation with Berlin. But, as Kollontai told Cabinet Secretary Boheman in Stockholm, the Soviet government was concerned none the less lest Yugoslavia suffer the same fate as Bulgaria. Should Germany proceed with further operations in the region, the Soviet Union would have to retaliate by some means short of war; for example, economic sanctions.[155] When on 18 February the Turkish ambassador saw Deputy Commissar Andrei Vyshinsky, the ex-Menshevik, formerly the notorious prosecutor at the show trials, he seemed "very nervous and uneasy at the prospect of the forthcoming negotiations on the Balkans".[156]

After German troops entered Bulgaria and Yugoslavia was offered membership of the Tripartite Pact, the Yugoslav ambassador to Moscow, Milan Gavrilović, warned Vyshinsky of his country's impression "that the USSR is consigning the Balkans and Yugoslavia to the German sphere of influence. This impression of the USSR's stance must, in the opinion of Gavrilović, be allayed."[157] At this point, on 27 March, in a futile gesture that hastened the inevitable, the British used both MI6 and the Special Operations Executive to launch a coup that succeeded in unseating Paul the Regent and bringing young King Peter to the throne, ejecting the cabinet that had led Yugoslavia into the Tripartite Pact.[158] But it came too late. The new foreign minister Momčilo Ninčić stayed loyal to the pact for fear of alienating the Germans. The Russians were understanding; less so the British.[159] Belgrade now expressed an interest in signing a treaty of friendship and non-aggression with Moscow. But the Yugoslavs were intent on much more. The timing could not have been worse, because Stalin was bending over backwards to avoid provoking Germany.

On 3 April, as instructed from Belgrade and accompanied by Gavrilović, Božin Simić and Colonel Dragutin Savić arrived in Moscow and told a startled and risk-averse Vyshinsky that "our government wants and expects an alliance with the USSR". The Yugoslav delegation had even brought along with them a draft treaty, including a secret clause (3) concerning military assistance. When asked what kind of aid the Russians would be expected to render, Simić answered, in Russian, "Everything that can be delivered by air."[160] Vyshinsky promised a reply the following day. But when that day dawned he had to tell his guests that there was no question of an alliance; certainly at such short notice.[161] After some textual changes on 4 April a friendship pact was agreed and signed the following day, leaving Simić, for one, very unhappy.[162] The ink applied to this innocuous piece of paper was barely dry when on 6 April Germany impatiently invaded Yugoslavia. To say the least, this gave every impression of Soviet impotence. It certainly made no difference to Hitler's Operation Barbarossa, timed to follow completion of the Balkan campaign.

13

The Invasion of the Soviet Union

What guarantee is there that the German Government, which
so lightly breaks its international obligations, is going to observe a
non-aggression pact?

—STALIN[1]

Hitler's luck seemed almost limitless. The only enterprise to fail thus far
in his triumphal march towards European domination was Operation
Seelöwe (Sealion) for the invasion of Britain in the summer of 1940. It
certainly helped that the quality of statesmanship with which Hitler had
to compete throughout Europe was well below his own. Chamberlain
was by no means alone in being blind to reality. And there was nothing
like the reception of unwelcome secret intelligence to illustrate the rule
that the mind screens out information failing to fit well-entrenched
preconceptions.

The Politburo and not just Stalin firmly believed that Germany would
not attack before Britain was defeated: "that sentiment was not only
Stalin's, but also mine and that of others", Molotov said, excusing his
own colossal misjudgement many years later.[2] Indeed, although Litvinov
had been warning of invasion up to the very last minute, in his official
position as Soviet ambassador months afterwards in December 1941 he
pointed out to his American hosts that "[m]y government did receive
warnings as to the treacherous intentions of Hitler with regard to the

Soviet Union, but it did not take them seriously and this not because it believed in the sacredness of Hitler's signature, or did not believe him capable of violating the treaties he signed, and the oft-repeated solemn promises he made, but because it considered that it would have been madness on his part to undertake war in the East against such a powerful land such as ours, before finishing off his war in the West."[3]

No end of Soviet intelligence reports pointed directly to a surprise attack from Germany. But what Stalin feared above all was that his own forces in their zeal for action would inadvertently provoke a German attack. This nervousness also afflicted Comintern and its sections. With respect to occupied France, for example, the Party had backed away from its initial stance of de facto collaboration with the invader, yet instructions from Moscow as late as 8 January 1941 were that "conditions for liberating the French people from under the yoke of the occupiers have, however, not yet matured". Comintern was still looking to "the mutual weakening of the warring groups" (Britain and Germany). Instead, the PCF was supposed to concentrate its fire on the collaborators. It could only stand back and appreciate the work of De Gaulle's resistance which, although "anti-democratic", was "weakening the occupiers, frustrating the fulfilment of their plans", and was thus "objectively playing a positive role".[4]

What Litvinov did not, of course, disclose publicly was that to warn Stalin was risky and continuing to press such warnings upon him could prove fatal. Certainly Molotov did not at the time wish to hear any such news. He was much too publicly associated with the entente with Germany. Both he and Stalin were irrevocably committed to it for the foreseeable future. And for others trapped in positions of responsibility it was like watching an ancient Greek tragedy unfold while they could do nothing to forestall the inevitable. In March 1941 the Swedish diplomat turned politician Gunnar Hägglöf sat next to Ambassador Kollontai at lunch. She was a friend. Kollontai politely asked about Hägglöf's recent trip to Berlin. He told her that the Germans were preparing to invade the Soviet Union. Tears welled up in her eyes and after a moment's silence she said, "Be quiet, my dear Mr Hagglof [sic]. You have no right to tell me this and I have no right to listen to you."[5]

Churchill Warns Stalin

Too much is usually made of the warning that came in to Stalin from Churchill. On the slender basis of what was to hand—mainly Luftwaffe redeployments to Poland—on 30 March the Government Code and Cypher School suggested the possibility of a German move against the Soviet Union "either for intimidation or for actual attack".[6] Yet the British had yet to accomplish the massively complex task of breaking most of Germany's Enigma machine ciphers, through which its armed forces communicated. Moreover, there was, of course, a very big difference between intimidation and attack. So what Churchill had was the result of conjecture. Churchill's own apparent certainty was also typically based on inspired intuition, reinforced by a heavy dose of self-interest. None the less, he wrote to Stalin, "I have sure information from a trusted agent that when the Germans thought they had got Yugoslavia in the net, that is to say after March 20, they began to move three out of the five Panzer divisions from Roumania to southern Poland. The moment they heard of the Serbian revolution this movement was countermanded. Your Excellency will readily appreciate the significance of these facts."[7]

This somewhat cryptic warning to Stalin was then rendered even more dubious at the hands of its inept messenger, Cripps. Ambassadors sometimes think they know better; even or especially those with no training at all in diplomacy. Churchill's message was deliberately delayed for sixteen days, arguably for the best of motives. As a result Stalin received it only after a puzzling delay, on 19 April.[8] Given the intensity of Stalin's suspicions at the best of times, however, it made no difference to his judgement because it flatly contradicted what British military intelligence was saying as well as what the Foreign Office believed; information Stalin received as a matter of course through his efficient intelligence network in London.

Another crucial event contributed to catastrophic miscalculation, and that was the Soviet Union's détente with Japan. After Japanese forces attacked on 28–29 May 1939 at Khalkhin-Gol on the Chinese border with Outer Mongolia, Commander Georgii Zhukov, maximising the element of surprise, finally succeeded in surrounding them and wiped them out in a series of battles using combined arms between 20 and 31 August. Although the Japanese then unleashed an air bombardment, the engagement so shattered their confidence in the power of the Kwantung Army that the entire command were forced into retirement.[9]

As a result of this unexpected humiliation, the Japanese had to reassess the Soviet order of battle. Japan had only forty-one army divisions and now calculated that as many as forty-six would be needed to fight the Russians again with any prospect of success. Moreover, the Nazi–Soviet non-aggression pact concluded that fateful month had relieved Stalin of an immediate danger of war in Europe. In Tokyo a war on two fronts had therefore to be ruled out. The Germans as ever had shown themselves entirely inconsiderate of Japanese needs. Clearly they had no intention of incorporating vital Japanese interests in their decision-making. For reasons of race, if for no other, Hitler viewed the Japanese merely as a useful distraction for the European powers, rather than as equals with whom he should co-ordinate policy. For the Japanese, however, war in the north was incompatible with war to the south. They had no realistic alternative but to come to terms with the Russians. Foreign Minister Arita Hachirō was therefore instructed to negotiate with Moscow. The concessions he demanded were utterly unrealistic, as were those of Prime Minister Togo. Stalin had no intention of ending aid to the Chinese. And the Russians were not at all interested in a non-aggression pact, which did not go far enough as insurance against the prospect of war on two fronts in the more distant future.

A neutrality pact was at last agreed with Japan on 13 April 1941. As suitors, the Japanese were anxious to resolve all outstanding disputes with the Russians before contemplating an inevitable war with the Americans. Signature indicated that in the event of further complications in Europe, Moscow could at least avert the threat of a two-front war. Even though the new, impulsive and bullishly self-confident foreign minister Matsuoka Yōsuke had been to and from Berlin as he attempted to patch up a deal with the Russians, he failed to pick up hints that Germany was about to attack the Soviet Union. So Japanese miscalculation inadvertently intensified Stalin's scepticism about warnings of an invasion. As Matsuoka subsequently confessed to his colleagues, "I concluded the Neutrality Pact because I thought that Germany and Soviet Russia would not go to war. If I had known that they would go to war, I would have preferred to take a more friendly position towards Germany, and I would not have concluded the Neutrality Pact."[10] Matsuoka subsequently spoke belatedly in favour of attacking the Soviet Union. But by now his judgement was seriously in doubt; nor would such a course have solved Japan's problem of a possible war on two fronts while still bogged down in China.

The other side to Stalin's reasoning was, as already indicated, what he read from secret intelligence sources in London. The official historian of British intelligence notes that "the Whitehall authorities had been slow to reach agreement on the conclusion that Germany would make an attack on Russia, an undertaking which she had been preparing throughout the previous winter. Even when they had settled their differences, a bare three weeks before the attack, they were still failing to understand that what Germany had been preparing was not war in the event of the breakdown of negotiations, and after the despatch of an ultimatum, but an unconditional invasion, a surprise assault."[11] This was an assessment that the Russians had access to through their spy rings in Whitehall, and it turned out to be wholly misleading.

The 'experts' in the Foreign Office were actually completely in the dark, though incapable of admitting that they were merely engaged in idle speculation underpinned by Anglo-Saxon logic. The young Fitzroy Maclean in the Northern Department, a larger than life personality and a fervent anti-Communist, having experienced both the chaos of the *Front populaire* in Paris and the mind-numbing show trials in Moscow, typically dismissed out of hand "these rather misleading rumours of Soviet–German tension".[12] In a memorandum on "Military Indications of German Intentions towards Russia" dated 17 January, Maclean insisted that "[t]he military evidence available does not at the present support the view that Germany intends to attack Russia. The most significant factor against this view is the low proportion of divisions of the field army in Poland. German troop dispositions and other military preparations in the neighbourhood of the Russian frontiers cannot at the moment be described as anything but normal."[13] The Germans began shifting forces eastwards from the end of that month.[14]

Utterly frustrated at the failure of his "special mission", Cripps had been trying to browbeat the Russians with the threat of a German invasion since June 1940. But he had cried wolf so often that no one in Moscow could afford to take him seriously. In desperation Cripps had come around to seeing that Stalin could be roused only by generating "the fear that we may conclude a separate peace on the basis of German withdrawal from occupied territories of Western Europe and a free hand for Hitler in the East". Not a complete fool, he realised "of course that this is a most delicate matter to be handled through round about channels. Nevertheless I consider it our most valuable card in a very difficult hand and I trust some means may be found of playing it. Soviet talent for acquiring information through illicit channels might surely for once be turned to our account."[15] The success of this tactic, however, presupposed that the Russians were not reading his mail.

Hess Flies into Britain

Assessments such as these, that may well have reached Moscow courtesy of spy Donald Maclean in the Foreign Office, were further reinforced by the unexpected flight of Rudolf Hess to Britain on the night of 10 May. No worse combination of circumstances could have been contrived. In fact, as Hess explained to his adjutant Karlheinz Pintsch in the strictest secrecy, he was as early as January "determined to fly to England to bring to a conclusion the talks begun in August 1940". This was described to Pintsch as "Hitler's decision", though it appears from the incomplete evidence to hand that Hitler, otherwise distracted, may have given only vague, general assent in the months preceding the flight, rather than explicit approval on the very eve of the mission. Hess was extremely self-important and not a good listener, let alone one who could take a hint. He was utterly convinced that his own appearance in Britain would "reinforce the position of those English politicians who were aiming at the immediate conclusion of peace with Germany and that his mission would be successful". Thereafter he diligently set to work "intensively" preparing the "political and economic proposals" he would bring with him. Preparation involved Ernst Bohle, head of the Nazi Party's Auslands-Organisation (AO)—"foreign organisation"—and Hess's brother Alfred, deputy head of the AO, the ministerial director of foreign trade at the Economics Ministry Eberhard von Jagwitz and Karl Haushofer. Hitler's secretary Martin Bormann was reportedly also kept up to date on Hess's preparations. Detailed measures undertaken for the flight involved other significant people, including Professor Messerschmitt, who provided a Bf Me-110 heavy fighter aircraft, plus provisions for training and special equipment, daily weather reports and so on. Reichsleiter Alfred Rosenberg was summoned by Hess to Munich from Berlin hours before his planned departure from the aerodrome at Augsburg that evening, as was Alfred Meyer, the gauleiter of Northern Westphalia, from Munster. This was not exactly an impromptu personal escapade improvised at the last moment.

The impending invasion of the Soviet Union hung over everything. In March 1941 Hess described his main aim as "to free up forces engaged in the West that could be used against Russia". On the back of advice he had received, Hess dictated eight proposals he would deliver to the British via the Duke of Hamilton, who was a friend of Churchill:

A. Germany will drop all claim to its former colonies in Africa;

B. Germany is willing and ready to limit its fleet, recognising England's command of the sea;

C. Germany is not interested in the defeat of the British Empire worldwide;

D. Germany is prepared to render England full support in preserving its position as a world Power;

E. Germany is prepared to render England full support in forestalling a world economic crisis after the war;

F. Germany demands England return private German assets abroad frozen since 1918 not itemised in the bill for reparations;

G. In return for these assets, after the conclusion of peace England must supply Germany with raw materials;

H. Germany undertakes the obligation to put an end to the
danger of the Bolshevisation of Europe threatening from
Russia and will be granted freedom of action in the East which
accords with the conditions set by the English at the talks in
August 1940 in Geneva.[16]

Guy Liddell, director of counter-espionage at MI5, was thus right when
he wrote that the "statement in the press about Hess being mad would
merely have been put over to cover up the fact that the Germans are
putting out peace-feelers".[17]

Cripps, however, though ignorant of Hess's real mission as he was of
much else, now had the bright idea of suggesting that the purpose of the
secret visit was indeed to negotiate a peace with Britain predicated on the
invasion of the Soviet Union by Germany.[18] Initially this option was sensibly rejected by Assistant Under-Secretary Sargent. But on further reflection and discussion with MI6, Sargent foolishly relented, against his better
judgement. A "whisper" went out along the lines that Cripps had suggested.[19] On 10 June, just before Hitler struck, Sir Christopher Warner,
now heading the Northern Department, reassured Cripps: "We are putting it about through covert channels that the Hess flight indicates growing split over Hitler's policy of collaboration with the Soviet Union."[20]

This subterfuge boomeranged not just at the time, but throughout the
war. At the very least it completely undermined Churchill's attempt to get
Stalin to sit up and take notice, because Stalin had access to the correspondence between Cripps and London. In the longer term, after the
Germans invaded, it led to even greater damage as it continuously fed
Stalin's obsession with Hess as a latent peace contact with Hitler. This
became most evident when Stalin was at the end of his tether during the
fateful battle of Stalingrad, where the ultimate fate of the Soviet Union
would be decided.[21] On 13 June 1941 TASS publicly denied the rumours
that Germany would attack the Soviet Union and sourced them to Cripps,
which demonstrated just how utterly counter-productive his endless
warnings were and what a liability he had by then become.[22]

What came in from Berlin to the Kremlin was much closer to the
truth. But Stalin and Molotov had made up their minds that Hitler

would never go back on his judgement expressed in *Mein Kampf*, that a war on two fronts would be fatal. Moreover, extensive German disinformation proved effective. The Soviet ambassador Dekanozov reported on rumours of war impending between Germany and the Soviet Union. They appeared simultaneously with rumours of far-reaching concessions by the Russians to hold it off.[23] And when yet one more warning from a source considered reliable by Fitin came in from Berlin, Stalin scrawled on the covering letter: "To [People's Commissar for State Security] Comrade Merkulov. You can send your 'source' from the German Luftwaffe Staff to fuck [his/your] mother. This is not a 'source' but a purveyor of disinformation. I. St."[24] Fitin was risking his life to save his country and paid for his courage when he was summarily dismissed without a pension at the end of the war.

The Invasion Materialises

In a surprise attack German forces struck by air and by land through the morning mist minutes after sunrise on 22 June. They were greeted by the enforced inertia of the Soviet forces in place and later widely welcomed as liberators by the peasantry that had suffered so badly from collectivisation at the hands of Stalin; though this honeymoon lasted only until the German mistreatment of the inhabitants as *Untermenschen*—subhumans—became the norm for the occupying forces.

Three hours into the attack Dimitrov arrived at the Kremlin to find Molotov, Voroshilov, Kaganovich and Malenkov in Stalin's office. Stalin was outraged that "[t]hey attacked us without declaring any grievances, without demanding any negotiations; they attacked us viciously, like gangsters".[25] And Molotov called on Ambassador Schulenburg and demanded to know, "Why did Germany conclude a non-aggression pact yet breach it so easily?"[26] It was a lament all too reminiscent of Neville Chamberlain, but with far less excuse. Rearmament at a higher technological level had yet to be put into mass production. The "Stalin line" of fortifications ripped out with the occupation of the Baltic states had not yet been completed along the new western perimeter of the Soviet Union.

At noon in Litvinov's study where he and his wife were playing a round of bridge with a friend and dummy, their little puppy crawled over to the radio and accidentally turned the knob. The unmistakeable sound of Molotov's high-pitched voice could be heard addressing the country in the face of disaster and concluding solemnly, "Victory will be ours."[27] Stalin evidently delayed his own appearance in the vain hope that matters might soon improve and he could deliver better news. But the situation did not get better; it got a good deal worse. Finally he could procrastinate no longer and delivered a broadcast to the nation on 3 July. Both he and Molotov revealed their own hubris and appalling neglect in naïvely accusing Germany of treachery. It took five more days for the man who had been right all along in his fears about Germany, Litvinov, to be allowed to broadcast, and then in English and to foreign audiences only. In stark contrast to Stalin and Molotov's jejune lamentations, Litvinov bluntly reiterated what he had long been telling everyone: "No agreement or treaties, no undertaking signed by Hitler and his henchmen, no promises or assurances on their part, no declarations of neutrality, no relations with them whatsoever can provide a guarantee against a sudden unprovoked attack. . . . His strategy is to mark down his victims and strike them one by one in the order prompted by circumstances." Hitler "intended first to deal with the western states so as to be free to fall upon the Soviet Union".[28]

There was more. On this occasion Litvinov was also provided with a unique opportunity in private to remind the once deluded British of exactly what he had predicted. It was 26 July. German bombs were raining down on Moscow. The sirens sounded. Ambassador Cripps was visiting the Kremlin and on entering one of the air raid shelters he bumped into Litvinov. The former commissar wished to be remembered to Eden, now foreign secretary in place of the noble Lord Halifax. Litvinov, who was reported to be "enjoying a position of some importance in the Kremlin", though that piece of information was certainly exaggerated, asked whether Eden could recall a conversation they had had in Brussels "when he [Litvinov] predicted that this situation would arise".[29] Indeed, on 9 November 1937 Litvinov had told Eden that "there were two alternatives before the world; either the Powers who had

territorial possessions and no territorial designs must draw closer together than they had done hitherto and combine their action, or Germany, Italy and Japan would one day virtually dominate the world and
Britain and France would be reduced to playing the rôle of second-class
Powers in Europe."[30] Though suffering the consequences along with the
rest of the country, at least Litvinov had the satisfaction of being right.
But that came as little compensation for the Soviet people, now subjected to further horrors, even worse than those already experienced
under Stalin, this time at the hands of the savage Germans.

Guidelines issued to Hitler's troops directly reflected the spirit, indeed
the very letter, of *Mein Kampf*. They underlined Hitler's long-held purpose. Why else would he take such an enormous gamble, having won so
much so easily in the West? Had he really feared the United States, he
would most certainly have never ventured East. Colonel-General Erich
Hoepner issued the following order for Armoured Group 4:

> The war against Russia is an essential phase in the German nation's
> struggle for existence. It is the ancient struggle of the Germanic
> peoples against Slavdom, the defence of European culture against the
> Muscovite-Asiatic tide, the repulse of Jewish Bolshevism. That strug-
> gle must have as its aim the shattering of present-day Russia and must
> therefore be waged with unprecedented hardness. Every combat ac-
> tion must be inspired, in concept and execution, by an iron determina-
> tion to ensure the merciless, total annihilation of the enemy. In par-
> ticular, there must be no sparing the exponents of the present Russian
> Bolshevik system.[31]

Another order to troops intoned:

>   1. Bolshevism is the mortal enemy of the *National Socialist
>   German people. Germany's struggle is aimed against that
>   disruptive ideology and its exponents.*
>   2. *That* struggle demands ruthless and energetic action against
>   *Bolshevik agitators, guerrillas, saboteurs, Jews* and the complete
>   liquidation of any active or passive resistance.[32]

Both Reichsmarshal Göring and the Führer himself strongly believed
that a German invasion "would cause the entire Bolshevik state to

collapse".[33] They were by no means exceptional in this mistaken assumption. Indeed, the "prevailing view in diplomatic circles in Moscow" was that "Russia could not hold out against Germany for more than three or four weeks".[34] After the Germans invaded, this bleak and melodramatic assessment underwent no substantial revision for several months, through to the "grand skedaddle" from Moscow in October. Many British MPs vented the opinion that "[t]he Red Army at most will last three months".[35] And journalist Alexander Werth recalled, "British military experts at War Office or Ministry of Information briefings very clearly suggested they did not think the war in Russia would last more than a few weeks or, at most, months."[36]

One of the few to take a contrary view was diplomat Rex Leeper, who had studied Russian under Litvinov while teaching him English when the latter was exiled in Britain during the First World War. And Leeper was perhaps the first to see that the victory of Soviet forces would present the world with a dilemma that it had not confronted since the Spanish Civil War. Speaking largely if not wholly of British opinion, Leeper ventured that "[t]he hopes of many millions of people rest on the success of the Russian armies. Since a fortnight ago [22 June] there has been something of a revolution in men's minds. . . . It is not too much to suggest that the relief and consequent enthusiasm felt for a Russian victory will make many people forget the excesses and brutalities of Communism." And he cautioned that "[s]uch a wave of relief and enthusiasm might carry people far beyond the bounds of clear reasoning both here and elsewhere."[37]

Conclusions

A crucial lesson in the history of international relations has hitherto too frequently been overlooked. And that relates directly to the experience of the Bolshevik revolution and the reaction to it. This is not something that can be understood by looking only at English-language sources in Europe, let alone ignoring the Russian sources beyond them.

Moreover the analysis of international relations in the twentieth century cannot successfully be reduced to the simplicity of traditional balance-of-power politics without doing serious damage to the truth. The unimaginative application of our understanding of inter-state relations in one epoch to an entirely different era may to some traditionalists seem sound, but it can only deceive.

As we have seen, the Bolshevik revolution, like the French Revolution over a century earlier, shook the very foundations of international relations. The allied war of intervention of 1918–19 failed to crush it for lack of resolve and the absence of public support in Britain and the United States. Once the drive for revolution in Europe petered out in the early 1920s, and once the same occurred in Asia well before the end of the decade, it was widely assumed by *bien pensant* British liberals that Bolshevik Russia would, under sustained pressure to conform from its more powerful neighbours, sooner or later miraculously revert to being a "normal" country.

This uncontested assumption grew out of the comforting determinism of classical economics at the roots of nineteenth-century liberalism. It gave the predominantly Whiggish officials in the Foreign Office a comforting rationale for the much favoured policy of doing nothing: "watchful waiting", as they preferred to call it. Thus the exile of Trotsky after the triumph of Stalin was completely misread. Stalin was the man the Foreign Office much preferred. The only real difference between the two in terms of international relations, however, was that whereas Trotsky believed foreigners had the capacity to make their own revolutions, because the capitalist world was on its last legs, Stalin equally firmly believed that foreigners were too incompetent to manage it without direct military assistance from the Soviet Union, because the underlying conditions were by no means as propitious as Trotsky supposed.

However, once it was realised in 1936 that Bolshevism was back, spearheaded by Comintern's Popular Front in France and Spain, the reaction, certainly in Britain, was so resolutely hostile that no question could arise of an alliance with the Soviet Union to contain any aggression from Nazi Germany on the continent of Europe. At this crucial point Britain's imperial trauma of the 1920s reinforced fears for the fate of Europe that fascism never rivalled. Mussolini was assumed to be fundamentally sound at home where he kept Bolshevism in its place and Gramsci in prison, though provocative in his foreign ambitions. Hitler's breaches of the Versailles Treaty, even the reoccupation of the Rhineland, were seen as the necessary rectification of recent injustices; fascism in Germany, as in Italy and then in Spain, was viewed as a necessary antidote to revolutionary excesses.

In some senses the official British interpretation was justifiable. Comintern did indeed see the Popular Front not just as a necessary obstacle to the expansion of fascism, but also as the most effective path to revolution. Having realised that the Russians had not put to one side their revolutionary ambitions, but if anything given them new impetus, the British abandoned any notion of a value-free geopolitics. Having done so, they then blandly assumed that the same ideological fixation which now possessed them would also render impossible a rapprochement between Hitler and Stalin.

Having themselves awoken to the transcendence of ideas, the British would allow for nothing more important than ideology in the minds of others. They thereby left the door ajar for the Nazi–Soviet pact in 1939.

This was a grievous miscalculation with untold consequences. But did those ruling Britain ever learn the lessons? Whereas disasters such as the Japanese attack on Pearl Harbor in 1941 led to committees of enquiry, diplomatic disasters are quietly buried in the archives, with the intention that the details not be revealed before the death of all concerned.

The historian should of course always exercise caution before concluding that history teaches us anything in general that could have practical application to the particular. The British and the Americans have tended to assume that decision making is rational; that any departure from rationality must be a temporary aberration, remediable merely by effort, time and patience. This attachment to a belief in the dominance of reason accords with a shared culture, steeped in the world of commerce, where pragmatism rules the roost and differences of interest are overcome through compromise—a feature reinforced during the postwar period by the behaviourist psychology ("Skinnerism") that has been dominant in the major American universities. Yet this rationalist approach is deeply flawed, in that it assumes our own sense of reality has itself not been undermined by distortions of vision. Even when insurrectionist régimes display a steadfast determination to undermine the workings of the entire international system, the tendency has invariably been to assume that "common sense" will sooner or later return and reaffirm its natural dominance. The British thus relapse into "watchful waiting", while the Americans succumb to "strategic patience".

The lessons drawn by Americans from nuclear deterrence—that under the terrifying threat of mutual annihilation governments will behave "sensibly"—make for reassuring reading, and inevitably tend to reinforce faith in the idea of rationality conditioned by force of circumstance. When faced directly and immediately with extinction, it has seemed even the most irrational actor will draw back from the brink: Soviet ruler Nikita Khrushchev, for instance, did eventually back down during the Cuban missile crisis in October 1962, abandoning his high-risk bid to outflank US defences and force the allies out of Berlin. And let us hope good sense and the instinct for survival continue to hold true among new nuclear powers; though such instances may very well turn out to be the exception rather than the rule.

When the ayatollah Khomeini's fundamentalist revolution broke out in Iran in 1979, the inclination in London and Washington was to hang on until the fire burned itself out. They had failed to see what was coming, despite the evidence staring them in the face. Thereafter, having made the initial error as to what might happen, diplomats and spies both promptly followed through with the second misjudgement, about what would ensue: the Islamist revolution, as with the Bolshevik revolution in 1917, did not just peter out. It had been a long time coming and it did not lack ready tinder. The "moderates" did not take the place of the "extremists"; rather the reverse. Extremism instead became thoroughly institutionalised without being moderated. Moreover, as in 1919, the fanatics proceeded to spread the revolution abroad with a speed, a vigour, a discipline and a determination that took everyone aback. The Islamic fundamentalists had won, after all.

On the part of the industrialised capitalist democracies, this was effectively a re-run of the errors of judgement made decades before. The dynamism of fundamentalist Islam is with us still. What was missing in the analysis of the international system was that its constituent elements, states, were assumed in practice to be precisely what they were not: clever, articulated machines, like businesses operating in the market, the behaviour of which are open to prediction; not organisms, life forms that evolve according to inner dynamics affected by ethnicity and traditional culture.

The tendency to assume like-mindedness has invariably proved overwhelming, and wrong. Society is, and always was, a complex organism. Ideology and cultural tradition always belonged more to the realm of organisms than that of machines. This matters, because ideologies in the international system, once activated, can completely undercut predictability, as they do not operate within the parameters of more settled states. The assumption that the system is run by rational actors thus falls apart because the calculation of what is rational is contingent on culture and historical evolution. The difference is fundamental between, at its most extreme, a country taken over by fanatics bent on revolutionary change and a country governed by complacent, well-entrenched élites with much to lose. The former still believe they can deliver a shot that the opponent cannot return; the latter just hope that their own delivery lands the ball in the opponent's service box.

This leaves us with an uncomfortable thought. Could Bolshevism or fascism ever re-emerge? Ideas at the extreme ends of the spectrum do not just disappear. They can vanish momentarily from our field of vision through evaporation from the surface. But suddenly without warning they may condense and descend upon us as an unexpectedly destructive storm. Such ideologies do not find a mass following while economies are in equilibrium. But history tells us that this state of balance cannot be expected to continue indefinitely.

The Great Crash of 1929, just like those of 1873 and 2008, was not an exception to the economic system. Major recessions are as recurrent in capitalism as are wildfires in a forest, burning away unproductive brush to clear the ground for reseeding. The response by government to the crisis of 2008, under pressure from the élite, was to prop up the banks but not the consumer with vast loans for which the state (ultimately future generations of taxpayers) assumed the burden of the debt. The result was a feeble, anaemic Japanese-style economic recovery, as a re-distribution of national wealth was effected to the disadvantage of the citizen. The Trump revolution in the American economy recharged the machine from below by cutting taxes and regulation, but the world economy up to 2020 was still floating on an unprecedented sea of public and private debt, which complicated and magnified the impact of the collapse when the world was hit by the coronavirus. Since the reflation of the world economy from the crash of 2008, no serious attempt had been made to shrink the global burden of debt, which is more than 50% greater than a decade before, topping $255 trillion. Rather the reverse.

An economic depression is not the only danger. To combat the economic effects of the previous recession and to fight off the economic damage wrought by locking down the economy to fight the coronavirus, the major economies issued credit on an ever increasing scale, flooding the markets with ready money, so that this time corporate and public debt will increase to reach levels previously unknown and ultimately high inflation will result. The final consequences are unknown at the time of writing. The problem with massive public debt is that when it reaches over 90% of gross national product it cuts a country's rate of growth in half; and this threshold will be far exceeded by all the major economies before the crisis is over. Easy money also results in the irresponsible accumulation of debt that cannot ultimately be offset by the proceeds of profitable investment, not least because it rewards the inefficient along with the efficient producer. The problem is global. The interconnectedness of the global financial system was revealed in 2007–8, as a world crisis spun out of financial collapse in the economy of Iceland, a tiny country with a population not much larger than that of Des Moines, Iowa.

Once the market becomes aware that debts may not be met on any scale, confidence in repayment collapses, bringing down entire financial houses and threatening the global banking system. Once the dominoes begin to topple, there is nothing to stop them completing their collapse. Should global indebtedness continue to accelerate, then the next crash will far exceed the last one. It could once again be driven by an economy hitherto ignored by most as unimportant, apparently standing on the margins of the world financial system. States become brittle when the economy and the financial system begin to fail.

The lesson of the interwar years is that in political life the extreme can all too easily become mainstream. And that feeds back into the economy, in that the confidence to invest will be undermined by political instability, and all the more so by revolutionary extremism. Fringe political groups that appear under the leadership of the mentally unstable during a boom can all too easily become popular when the economy faces bust—either through mass unemployment or runaway inflation—and not just the working class but also the middle classes fall prey to their worst fears of dispossession. Eventually the inflationary impact of vastly expanding the money supply worldwide will undermine confidence in fiat currencies and reduce the value of savings in those currencies to an appreciable degree, if not to zero.

Within the EU the rise of right-wing populism in France and Germany has yet to threaten the existing political order. Britain's next destination is unknown. In China, the highest debtor in the world, the lid on political dissent and economic freedom has been rammed tight; only explosions in Hong Kong showed the potential for mass disorder in a major city. Even within the United States, the world's second largest debtor but still the world's most successful economy, the broad social consensus that emerged unsteadily from the Vietnam War has once again broken down. Riots stoked by extremist organisations have been tolerated by local authorities in New York and Washington state; the reaction among the middle classes is seen in the widespread increase in gun ownership, where escaping the city is not a practical option.

Quite apart from other alarming symptoms of international political instability, notably Iran's bid for hegemony over the Middle East, the threat of an all-out tariff war, with untold consequences for the buoyancy of trade across the globe, weighs on the market. We have good cause to worry. All the more reason, then, not to ignore contemporary history. The bare bones of the archival record—the skeletal past—alone, vital as they are, give us the framework, but little of the essence. The meat of history comes to us only through the restoration of the prevailing ideas and dominant assumptions of an era, and the way in which these interacted with material life to push us to the edge of disaster. Writing the origins of the Second World War in ignorance of them cheats subsequent generations. History does offer warnings, if we care to recognise them for what they are.

NOTES

Preface

1. A. Taylor, *The Struggle for the Mastery of Europe, 1848–1918* (Oxford: Oxford University Press, 1954) and *The Origins of the Second World War* (London: Hamish Hamilton, 1961).

2. L. Hunt, *The New Cultural History* (Berkeley: University of California Press, 1989), p. 1; and K. Thomas, "The Tools and the Job", *Times Literary Supplement*, 7 April 1966.

3. Thomas later backed off from his youthful zealotry: K. Thomas, "History Revisited", *The Times*, 11 October 2006.

4. C. Thorne, *The Limits of Foreign Policy: The West, the League and the Far Eastern Crisis of 1931–1933* (London: Hamish Hamilton, 1972). J. Gittings, "Rules of the Game", *New York Review of Books*, 17 May 1973. Thorne's *The Approach of War 1938–39* (London: Macmillan, 1967) was written before most of the documents were available. Yet he successfully built upon an inestimable advantage obtained from direct access to witnesses such as Lord Stockton (Harold Macmillan) on the periphery of the tragedy.

5. V. Bogdanor, review of *The Triumph of the Dark*, *New Statesman*, 18 November 2010.

6. Z. Steiner, *The Triumph of the Dark: European International History 1933–1939* (Oxford: Oxford University Press, 2011), p. 1,048.

7. Quoted in Thorne, *Approach of War*, p. 17.

8. See J. Haslam, *No Virtue Like Necessity: Realist Thought in International Relations Since Machiavelli* (New Haven: Yale University Press, 2002).

9. K. Arrow, "Risk Perception in Psychology and Economics", Technical Report No. 351, October 1981. A Report of the Center for Research on Organizational Efficiency, Stanford University.

10. The five most notorious Soviet spies emanating from Cambridge University were Kim Philby, Donald Maclean, Guy Burgess, John Cairncross and Anthony Blunt. See J. Haslam, *Near and Distant Neighbours: A New History of Soviet Intelligence* (Oxford: Oxford University Press, 2015). The Russian foreign intelligence service, for whom they worked, is now releasing onto the world wide web classified documents relating to their operations, at www.cambridge5.ru.

Introduction

1. From Keynes's notes for "8 Lectures on Company Finance and Stock Exchange", Lent Term 1910: UK. Cambridge. King's College, Modern Archives, John Maynard Keynes Papers, UA/6/3/4.

2. *The Times*, 4 January 1919. Arno Mayer predicated his magnum opus on this postulate: A. Mayer, *The Politics and Diplomacy of Peacemaking: Containment and Counterrevolution at Versailles, 1918–1919* (New York: Knopf, 1967). The war in Vietnam for a while made it inconceivable for those on the left, certainly in the United States, to write the history of international relations with society left out; though that consciousness soon passed.

3. Dunant (Paris) to Mota (Bern), 10 March 1921: *Documents diplomatiques suisses, 1848–1945*, Vol. 8, ed. A. Fleury et al. (Bern: Benteli, 1988), doc. 50.

4. Letter to Molotov, 14 August 1921: *Komintern i ideya mirovoi revolyutsii. Dokumenty*, ed. K. Anderson et al. (Moscow: Nauka, 1998), doc. 86.

5. A term used within Comintern. For example, in a memorandum by the Czechoslovakian Communist Fried, 6 August 1927: *Komintern protiv fashizma: dokumenty*, ed. V. Dam'e et al. (Moscow: Nauka, 1999), doc. 50.

6. Secret telegraphic instruction from the Russian Communist Party, 22 October 1923: *Deutschland, Russland, Komintern. Dokumente 1918–1945*, Vol. 1, ed. H. Weber et al. (Berlin: De Gruyter, 2014), doc. 95.

7. V. Lenin, *Pol'noe sobranie sochinenii* (Moscow: Gosizdat, 1963), Vol. 42.

8. W. Yen, *An Autobiography* (Shanghai, 1946), p. 363. Republished by St John's University Press of New York in 1974.

9. Speech to the Ninth Conference of the Russian Communist Party, 22 September 1920: Russia. Moscow. RGASPI, Arkhiv Kominterna, f. 44, op. 1, d. 5. For some reason omitted from the published Russian version—*Politburo TsK RKP(b)–VKP(b) i Komintern, 1919–1943. Dokumenty*, ed. G. Adibekov et al. (Moscow: Rosspen, 2004), doc. 30—but included in the more extensive German translation: *Deutschland, Russland, Komintern*, Vol. 1, doc. 32.

10. Trotsky (Moscow) to Ioffe (Shanghai), 20 January 1923: *VKP(b), Komintern i natsional'no-revolyutsionnoe dvizhenie v Kitae. Dokumenty*, Vol. 1, ed. M. Titarenko et al. (Moscow: AO "Buklet", 1994), doc. 58.

11. Austen Chamberlain, 3 March 1927: *Hansard. Parliamentary Debates. Commons*. 5th Series, Vol. 203, col. 633.

12. *Documents on British Foreign Policy 1919–1939*, 2nd Series, Vol. 6, ed. L. Woodward and R. Butler (London: HMSO, 1957), doc. 247, footnote 1.

13. For the military implications: M. Howard, *The Continental Commitment: The Dilemma of British Defence Policy in the Era of the Two World Wars* (London: Martin Temple Smith, 1972).

14. *Financial Times*, 19 April 1927.

15. *Morning Post*, 9 April 1927.

16. Ibid., 29 April 1927.

17. K. Jeffery, *MI6. The History of the Secret Intelligence Service, 1909–1949* (London: Bloomsbury, 2010), p. 740.

18. In conversation with the Swiss minister in Rome, 3 January 1933: Wagnière (Rome) to Motta (Bern), 3 January 1933: Switzerland. *Documents diplomatiques suisses, 1848–1945*, Vol. 10, ed. J.-C. Favez et al. (Bern: Benteli, 1982), doc. 225.

19. H. Weber, "Die deutsche kommunistische Emigration in Moskau", *Die Politische Meinung*, No. 443, October 2006, p. 56. Weber worked in Comintern headquarters at the time.

20. E. Nolte, *Der europäische Bürgerkrieg 1917–1945: Nationalsozialismus und Bolschewismus* (Berlin: Propyläen, 1987).

21. G. Ciano, *Diario 1937–1943*, ed. R. De Felice (Rome: Rizzoli, 1980 edition), pp. 52, 53, 54. Donald Watt always took this line in undergraduate lectures (1970–71). The tradition at the London School of Economics continued. See M. Knox, *Common Destiny: Dictatorship, Foreign Policy, and War in Fascist Italy and Nazi Germany* (Cambridge: Cambridge University Press, 2000), p. 144 and footnote. In his published work, Watt omitted anti-Bolshevism entirely as a factor even with respect to dismissing the Russians as a potential ally in 1939: D. Watt, *How War Came: The Immediate Origins of the Second World War, 1938–1939* (London: Heinemann, 1989). In contrast, ex-diplomat and historian of Soviet Russia E. H. Carr, who was well acquainted with the appeasers at the time (being one of them) and a friend to William Strang who was despatched to Moscow for negotiations early in 1939, refers to "fear of Bolshevism" as "one, at any rate, of the factors" in the fateful decision of that year not to invoke Russia "as the counterweight to Germany": *From Napoleon to Stalin and Other Essays*, 2nd edition (London: Macmillan, 2003), p. 34. Although he left the Office in 1936, Carr maintained contact with senior officials over lunch at the Oxford and Cambridge Club, notably Strang and Laurence Collier. Watt's American counterpart Gerhard Weinberg blithely dismissed Bolshevism as merely "a tool, first of domestic and later of foreign propaganda by the National Socialists. Hitler explained to his associates that this was a device for the consumption of others": G. Weinberg, *The Foreign Policy of Hitler's Germany: Diplomatic Revolution in Europe, 1933–36* (Chicago: University of Chicago Press, 1970), ch. 1, footnote 40.

22. E. Hobsbawm, *The Age of Extremes: A History of the World, 1914–1991* (New York: Vintage, 1996), p. 125.

23. Mayer, *Politics and Diplomacy of Peacemaking*, p. 31.

Chapter 1. Crossroads to World Revolution, 1917–1920

1. Interviewed by Lt. Col. W. Stewart Roddie, 3 March 1920: UK. London. National Archives, CP 831.

2. "Letters from France. 1 The Spiritual Crisis", by Paul Valéry, *The Athenaeum*, 11 April 1919. The letters were commissioned by editor Middleton Murray and first written in English, though they have usually been quoted in French.

3. J. Talmon, "The Legacy of Georges Sorel", *Encounter*, Vol. 34, No. 2, February 1970, pp. 47–60; F. Stern, *The Politics of Cultural Despair: A Study in the Rise of the Germanic Ideology* (Berkeley: University of California Press, 1974); and R. Wohl, *The Generation of 1914* (Cambridge, Mass.: Harvard University Press, 1979).

4. Letter, 5 March 1917: G. Sorel, *"Da Proudhon à Lenin" e "L'Europa sotto la tormenta"*, ed. G. De Rosa (Rome: Edizioni di Storia e Letteratura, 1973), p. 613.

5. Ibid., "Chiarimenti su Lenin", p. 417.

6. See V. Bovykin, *Frantsuzskie banki v Rossii: konets XIX–nachalo XX v.* (Moscow: Rosspen, 1999).

7. "Istoricheskie Sud'by Ucheniya Karla Marksa", 1 March 1913: V. Lenin, *Pol'noe sobranie sochinenii*, Vol. 23.

8. Quoted in J. Haslam, *Russia's Cold War: From the October Revolution to the Fall of the Wall* (New Haven: Yale University Press, 2011), p. 3.

9. "Western and General", No. 110, 12 March 1919: UK. London. National Archives, CAB 24/150.

10. Stated to the British representative of the Red Cross, Abrahamson, and reported to London by Sir Charles Marling, 30 March 1919: "Western and General", No. 113, 2 April 1919: ibid.

11. Quoted in E. Carr, *German–Soviet Relations between the Two World Wars, 1919–1939* (Baltimore: Johns Hopkins University Press, 1951), p. 9.

12. For the most vivid, detailed account: Mayer, *Politics and Diplomacy of Peacemaking*, pp. 133–166.

13. "Western and General" No. 103, 22 January 1919: UK. London. National Archives, CAB 24/150.

14. "Western and General", No. 102, 15 January 1919: ibid.

15. "Western and General", No. 103: ibid.

16. Quoted from Communist Party archives in D. Volkogonov, *Lenin: Life and Legacy* (London: HarperCollins, 1994), p. 394.

17. Telegram from the Central Committee of the Russian Communist Party, 24 December 1919: *Die Weltpartei aus Moskau. Der Gründungskongress der Kommunistischen Internationale 1919. Protokoll und neue Dokumente*, ed. W. Hedeler and A. Vatlin (Berlin: Akademie Verlag, 2008), doc. 1.

18. Session of Comintern's executive committee, 18 June 1920: Russia. Moscow. RGASPI, Arkhiv Kominterna, f. 495, op. 1, d. 6.

19. Karl Radek (Berlin) to Lenin, Chicherin and Sverdlov (Moscow), 24 January 1919: *Deutschland, Russland, Komintern*, Vol. 1, doc. 11.

20. Quoted in E. Carr, *The October Revolution: Before and After* (New York: Vintage, 1971), p. 57.

21. A. Ransome, *Russia in 1919* (New York: Huebsch, 1919), p. 218.

22. Ibid., p. 228.

23. These are in Krasin's papers, which I inspected with a view to purchase on behalf of the Centre for Russian and East European Studies at Birmingham University in the late 1970s. Unfortunately the deal did not succeed.

24. Zinoviev to the Orgburo of the RKP(b), 26 March 1919: Russia. Moscow. RGASPI, Arkhiv Kominterna, f. 495, op. 18, d. 5. For internal reference by the Fourth Directorate (military intelligence) to the Big House, see Berzin (Moscow) to Bronin (Shanghai), 15 January 1935: "The fact is that formally the Big House itself has no means of communication": *"Delo Zorge"*. *Telegrammy i pis'ma (1930–1945)*, ed. A. Fesyun (Moscow: Serebrannye niti, 2018), p. 75.

25. "Protokol No. 1. Zasedanie Ispolnitel'nogo Komiteta Kommunisticheskogo Internatsionala ot 26-go marta 1919 g.": Russia. Moscow. RGASPI, Arkhiv Kominterna, f. 495, op. 1, d. 1., J. Carswell, *The Exile. A Life of Ivy Litvinov* (London: Faber and Faber, 1983), p. 91.

26. Session of Comintern's executive committee, 18 June 1920: Russia. Moscow. RGASPI, Arkhiv Kominterna, f. 495, op. 1, d. 6.

27. 1st session, 7 August 1920: "Vtoroi Kongress Kommunisticheskogo Internatsionala. Stenograficheskii otchet". Russia. Moscow. RGASPI, Arkhiv Kominterna, f. 495, op. 1, d. 7.

28. Lenin's speech to the 9th conference of the Russian Communist Party, 22 September 1920: Politburo TsK RKPb)–VKP(b) i Komintern, 1919–1943, doc. 30.

29. The Poles, likely as not assisted by the British and French, who now employed the leading tsarist cryptographers, successfully broke all Soviet secret communications, thus making the Red Army vulnerable at every turn: Haslam, *Near and Distant Neighbours*, p. 24.

30. This is not typically included in Lenin's collected works—"Zapiska V. Lenina po povodu rukopisi stat'i K. Radeka", 6 October 1920: *Komintern i ideya mirovoi revolyutsii*, doc. 52.

31. Quoted by People's Commissar for Enlightenment Anatoly Lunacharsky, 26 February 1922: M. Cachin, *Carnets 1906–1947*, ed. D. Peschanski, Vol. 3 (Paris: CNRS, 1998), p. 161.

32. Report on concessions to the Russian Communist Party (Bolshevik) Group at the 8th Congress of Soviets, 21 December 1920: V. Lenin, *Collected Works* (Moscow: Progress, 1966), Vol. 31, pp. 461–534. (Note that the report on concessions is dated eight days before the main report to the congress and is contained in Part 1 of the proceedings.)

33. Jeffery, *MI6*, p. 194.

Chapter 2. Europe at the Brink

1. Told to L. Fischer, *Men and Politics: An Autobiography* (London: Jonathan Cape, 1941), p. 71. Fischer, a "progressive" and a sympathiser with the Bolshevik régime until 1939, obtained unprecedented access to senior officials. He was given archival documents in the late 1920s that we have only very recently been able to glimpse ourselves.

2. 8 August 1918: *Die II. Internationale 1918/1919. Protokolle, Memoranden, Berichte und Korrespondenzen*, ed. G. Ritter (Berlin: Dietz, 1980), Vol. 1, pp. 636–637.

3. "Western and General", No. 111, 19 March 1919: UK. London. National Archives, CAB 24/150.

4. E. Carr, *The Bolshevik Revolution 1917–1923*, Vol. 3, (London: Macmillan, 1953), pp. 309–311.

5. Ibid., p. 139.

6. "Aufzeichnung des Chefs der Heeresleitung im Reichswehrministerium Generalleutnant von Seeckt", 26 July 1920: *Akten zur deutschen auswärtigen Politik, 1918–1945*, Series A, Vol. 3, ed. W. Bussmann et al. (Göttingen: Vandenhoeck & Ruprecht, 1985), doc. 218.

7. Quoted from the German Foreign Ministry archive: S. Gorlov, *Sovershenno Sekretno. Moskva–Berlin 1920–1933. Voenno-politicheskie otnosheniya mezhdu SSSR i Germaniei* (Moscow: IVI RAN, 1999), p. 39.

8. Ibid., p. 44.

9. From Stresemann's unpublished papers, quoted in H. Gatzke, "Von Rapallo nach Berlin. Stresemann und Die Deutsche Russlandpolitik", *Vierteljahrshefte für Zeitgeschichte*, No. 4, 1956, p. 2.

10. "Giants and Pigmies (From the Papers of Comrade X)" in Ypsilon, *Pattern for World Revolution* (Chicago and New York: Ziff-Davis, 1947), p. 38. Ypsilon was the *nom de plume* of Karl Volk (Johann Max Rindl) and Julian Gumperz.

11. *Komintern protiv fashizma*, p. 66, footnote 2.

12. In the mid-twenties Trotsky was subjected to a vicious diatribe by the opportunist Kun. His devastating retort made sense only in Italian: "La maniera di Béla non è una bella maniera".

13. Kun to Lenin, 6 May 1921: *Komintern i ideya mirovoi revolyutsii*, doc. 71.

14. D. Volkogonov, *Lenin: Life and Legacy*, pp. 401–402. Someone working for Thomas later testified, "The money was usually kept at Comrade Thomas's apartment. It was in trunks and suitcases, cupboards and occasionally thick files, left lying on his bookshelves or behind books. The money was doled out in our apartments late at night in cardboard boxes weighing as much

as ten to fifteen kilogrammes each."—ibid. Thomas was naturally indignant at the "dissatisfaction" and the patent lack of trust shown in him—complaint sent to Zinoviev, 26 September 1920: *Deutschland, Russland, Komintern*, Vol. 1, doc. 33.

15. Lenin (Moscow) to Zekin and Levi (Berlin), 16 April 1921: ibid., doc. 38.

16. F. Borkenau, *World Communism: A History of the Communist International* (Ann Arbor: University of Michigan Press, 1962), p. 220.

17. The Genoa conference itself failed in part because the French refused to concede anything to Germany and in part because Britain would not forgive Russian pre-revolutionary debts.

18. Radek (Berlin) to Narkomindel and the Politburo (Moscow), 11 February 1922: *Komintern i ideya mirovoi revolyutsii*, doc. 93.

19. Gorlov, *Sovershenno Sekretno*, p. 73.

20. Houghton (Berlin) to Hughes (Washington DC), 23 October 1922: *Papers Relating to the Foreign Relations of the United States, 1922*, Vol. 2, ed. J. Fuller, (Washington DC: US GPO, 1938), doc. 138.

21. 23 November 1922: USA. *Congressional Record*, 66th Congress, 3rd Session, Vol. 63, p. 49.

22. Quoted in D. Gescher, *Die Vereinigten Staaten von Nordamerika und die Reparationen 1920–1924. Eine Untersuchung der Reparationsfrage auf der Grundlage amerikanischer Akten* (Bonn: Röhrscheid, 1966), p. 125.

23. 23 May 1922: UK. London. National Archives, CAB 29 (22).

24. Ibid.

25. There exist half a dozen accounts of the great inflation in English alone. But the classic and very detailed contemporary explanation is C. Bresciani-Turroni, *Le vicende del marco tedesco*, *Annali di Economia*, Vol. 7, 1931, pp. v–xxiv, 1–596. Bresciani-Turroni had served on the Berlin staff of the Reparations Commission in 1920, as head of exports control in 1921 and then as economic adviser to the agent-general of reparations until 1929. An English translation of a revised version appeared in 1937 under the title *The Economics of Inflation. A Study of Currency Depreciation in Post-War Germany* (London: John Dickens, 1937).

26. H. Nicolson, *Curzon: The Last Phase 1919–1925. A Study in Post-War Diplomacy* (London: Constable, 1934), pp. 374–376.

27. G. Sandys, "Notes on the Fascisti Movement", enclosed in Joynson Hicks to Cecil Harmsworth, 19 April 1921: UK. London. National Archives, FO 371/6174.

28. Lenin to Stalin about the situation in Comintern, 23 July 1920: *Politburo TsK RKP(b)–VKP(b) i Komintern, 1919–1943*, doc. 25.

29. Lenin's speech to the 9th conference of the Russian Communist Party, 22 September 1920: ibid., doc. 30.

30. Despatch from the commercial secretary, 9 September 1920, contained in Kennard (Rome) to Curzon (London), 10 September 1920: UK. London. National Archives, FO 371/6174.

31. Report by Greenway enclosed in Kennard (Rome) to Curzon (London), 24 September 1920: ibid.

32. The legendary ostrich runs purposefully in the wrong direction, into danger rather than out of danger: D. Livingstone, *Missionary Travels and Researches in South Africa, including a sketch of sixteen years residence in the interior of Africa* (London: John Murray, 1857), p. 145. Those reared in late Victorian Britain imbibed this story in the nursery.

33. British consul-general (Milan), W. Churchill, 15 September 1920: UK. London. National Archives, FO 371/6174.

34. Greenway report, 24 September 1921: ibid.

35. "Annual report on Italy for year 1920", enclosed in Buchanan (Rome) to Curzon (London), 20 January 1921: UK. London. National Archives, FO 371/6184.

36. "Il movimento dei metallurgici", *L'Ordine Nuovo*, 2 October 1920.

37. P. Alatri, "La Fiat dal 1921 al 1926", *Belfagor*, Vol. 29, No. 3, 31 May 1974.

38. "Annual report on Italy for year 1920", enclosed in Buchanan (Rome) to Curzon (London), 20 January 1921: UK. London. National Archives, FO 371/6184.

39. G. Spadolini, *Il mondo di Giolitti* (Firenze: Le Monnier, 1970), p. 220.

40. M. Montagnana, *Ricordi di un operaio torinese* (Rome: Rinascita, 1949), p. 91.

41. *Il Popolo d'Italia*, 25 October 1922.

42. R. De Felice, *Mussolini il fascista. 1. La conquista del potere 1921–1925* (Turin: Einaudi, 1966), pp. 359–386.

43. Statement, 28 October 1930: Russia. Moscow. RGASPI, Arkhiv Kominterna, f. 495, op. 2, d. 168.

44. "Italienische Frage", 20 February 1923: Russia. Moscow. RGASPI, Arkhiv Kominterna, f. 495, op. 2, d. 16.

45. Quoted in P. Spriano, *Storia del partito comunista italiano*, Vol. 1 (Turin: Einaudi, 1967), p. 260.

46. Speech, 15 November 1922, quoted in ibid., p. 240.

47. N. Zhukovskii, *Posol novogo mira* (Moscow: Politicheskaya Literatura, 1978).

48. "Protokol PB No. 36", 10 November, followed by "Protokol PB No. 37", 23 November 1922: Russia. Moscow. RGASPI, f. 17, op. 3, d. 323.

49. "Protokol PB No. 48", 8 February 1923: ibid. RGASPI, f. 17, op. 3, d. 334.

50. "Protokol PB No. 50", 19 February 1923: ibid. RGASPI, f. 17, op. 3, d. 336.

51. Note from the Russian representative in Italy to the general secretary of the Italian Foreign Ministry, 27 February 1923: *Dokumenty vneshnei politiki SSSR*, Vol. 6, ed. A Gromyko et al. (Moscow: Politizdat, 1962), doc. 117.

52. Cited from the archives of the Italian Ministry of the Interior: G. Petracchi, *La Russia rivoluzionaria nella politica italiana: le relazioni italo–sovietiche 1917–25* (Rome and Bari: Laterza, 1982), p. 237.

53. "Protokol PB No. 10", 14 July 1924: Russia. Moscow. RGASPI, f. 17, op. 3, d. 450.

54. "Protokol PB No. 30", 23 October 1924: ibid., f. 17, op. 3, d. 470.

55. "Protokol PB No. 32", 5 November 1924: ibid., f. 558, op. 2, d. 55.

56. *Akten zur deutschen auswärtigen Politik*, Series A, Vol. 7, ed. W. Bussmann et al. (Göttingen: Vandenhoeck & Ruprecht, 1989), doc. 226.

57. Zinoviev and Bukharin's private letter to Brandler and Thalheimer, 27 July 1923: *Deutscher Oktober 1923. Ein Revolutsionsplan und sein Scheitern*, ed. B. Bayerlein et al. (Berlin: Aufbau, 2003), doc. 3.

58. Entry, 15 February 1922: Cachin, *Carnets 1906–1947*, Vol. 3, p. 107.

59. First draft of notes on "The Situation in Germany and our Tasks", 15 August 1923: *Deutscher Oktober*, doc. 7.

60. Quoted in P. Makarenko, "Nemetskii Oktyabr' 1923 g. i sovetskaya vneshnyaya politika", *Voprosy istorii*, No. 3, March 2012, pp. 36–55.

61. Stalin's remarks, 20 August 1923: *Deutscher Oktober*, doc. 9.

62. Politburo debate on the German revolution, 21 August 1923: ibid., doc. 10.

63. Published on 10 October 1923 in *Die Rote Fahne*. "I hope one day we will be able to transfer the entire dictatorship to you foreigners, and shift the Executive Committee from Moscow to Berlin or Paris", Zinoviev told Jules Humbert-Droz in 1921: Ypsilon, *Pattern for World Revolution*, p. 38.

64. Secret Central Committee plenum, 22 September 1923: *Deutscher Oktober*, doc. 21.

65. Letter from Berlin, 29 October 1923, to the Politburo and Comintern's executive committee in Moscow: *Komintern i ideya mirovoi revolyutsii*, doc. 115.

66. Shklovskii (Hamburg) to Zinoviev, Stalin and Litvinov (Moscow), 30 October 1923: *Politburo TsK RKP(b)–VKP(b) i Komintern, 1919–1943*, doc. 124.

67. Ibid., p. 243, footnote 1.

68. Ibid., p. 249, footnote 1.

69. "Protokol PB No. 57", 27 December 1923: Russia. Moscow. RGASPI, f. 17, op. 3, d. 405.

70. Statement in reaction to the decisions of the Politburo of 27 December 1923 and of the Central Committee plenum of 15 January 1924: *Komintern protiv fashizma*, doc. 26.

71. Report to Comintern's executive, 11 February 1924: *Komintern i ideya mirovoi revolyutsii*, doc. 120.

72. Quoted at length by Krestinsky: *Politburo TsK RKP(b)–VKP(b) i Komintern, 1919–1943*, pp. 250–251.

73. Yu. Denike, "The Situation in Germany", 22 February 1924: Russia. Moscow. RGASPI, f. 504, op. 1, d. 187.

74. 15 September 1923: Gorlov, *Sovershenno Sekretno*, pp. 81–82.

75. Quoted in A. Thimme, *Gustav Stresemann* (Frankfurt am Main: Goedel, 1957), p. 108.

76. Quoted in Gatzke, "Von Rapallo nach Berlin", p. 8.

77. Entry, 23 October 1931: USA. New Haven. Yale University Library, Henry Lewis Stimson diaries, Vol. 18, p. 167.

78. W. Link, *Die amerikanische Stabilisierungspolitik in Deutschland 1921–32* (Düsseldorf: Droste, 1970), p. 138.

79. "Conditions in Bavaria—The National Socialist Labor Party—Service Report", 25 November 1922: USA. College Park. National Archives, US Military Intelligence, Germany, 002928-001-0329.

80. Reprinted in Spanish: E. Xammar, *El huevo de la serpiente. Crónicas desde Alemania (1922–1924)* (Barcelona: Acantilado, 2005), pp. 204–208. It has been argued that, because Xammar made no mention of the interview in his reminiscences, it must have been fabricated. This is just speculation. Xammar may have had good reason for not wishing to recall the event. He had dismissed Hitler as a monumental fool; not exactly indicative of a journalist with much foresight, as he wished, no doubt, to be remembered.

81. We now have an invaluable, comprehensively edited version in two volumes: Hitler, *Mein Kampf. Eine kritische Edition*, ed. C. Hartmann, T. Vordermayer, O. Plöckinger and R. Toppel (Munich and Berlin: Instituts für Zeitgeschichte, 2016). We still lack anything like this in English translation.

82. E. Bloch, "My Patient, Hitler", *Collier's Weekly*, 15 and 22 March 1941.

83. Quoted in V. Ullrich, *Hitler*, Vol. 1: *Ascent 1889–1939* (New York: Knopf, 2016), p. 109.

84. T. Ryback, *Hitler's Private Library. The Books that Shaped his Life* (London: Random House, 2010), p. 69.

85. O. Plöckinger, ed. *Quellen und Dokumente zur Geschichte von "Mein Kampf" 1924–1945* (Stuttgart: Franz Steiner, 2016), doc. 6.

86. H. Rollin, "Sous le signe de la croix gammée", *Le Temps*, 6 June 1933.

87. These encyclicals formed a sequence as Stalin's revolution from above took hold: *Miserentissimus Redemptor* (8 May 1928), *Quadragesimo anno* (15 May 1931), *Caritate Christi compulsi* (3 May 1932), *Acerba animi* (29 September 1932) and *Dilectissima Nobis* (3 June 1933).

88. Cardinal Secretary of State Pacelli's record of the conversation, 2 February 1930: *L'archivio della nunziatura apostolica in Italia 1 (1929–1939). Cenni storici e inventario*, ed. G. Castaldo and G. Lo Bianco (Vatican City: Archivio Segreto Vaticano, 2010), p. 732.

89. Haslam, *No Virtue Like Necessity*, p. 169.

90. Ibid., pp. 167–168, and 176–178.

91. Ibid.

92. Ullrich, *Hitler*, p. 477.

93. Hitler, *Mein Kampf*, p. 326.

94. Ibid., p. 330.

95. Chicherin (Wiesbaden) to Stalin (Moscow), 22 March 1929: *Sovetskoe rukovodstvo. Perepiska 1928–1941*, ed. A. Kvashonkin et al. (Moscow: Rosspen, 1999), p. 69.

96. Memorandum, 28 July 1926: UK. London. National Archives, CP 303 (26).

Chapter 3. Subverting Great Britain and Its Empire

1. *The Diaries of Sir Alexander Cadogan, O.M., 1938–1945*, ed. D. Dilks (London: Cassell, 1971), p. 132. "Great Britain and the British Empire (and India in particular) were the prime target of the campaign of subversion which the Comintern carried out until the Fascist threat compelled it to adopt a radical change of policy in the middle of the 1930s.": F. Hinsley and C. Simkins, *British Intelligence in the Second World War*, Vol. 4 (London: HMSO, 1990), p. 18.

2. Record of a conversation between Stalin, Molotov and Ribbentrop, 27–28 September 1939: *SSSR i Litva v gody vtoroi mirovoi voiny*, Vol. 1, ed. A. Kasparavičius et al. (Vilnius: Leidykla, 2006), doc. 42.

3. Trotsky to the Politburo, 5 August 1919: *Politburo TsK RKP(b)–VKP(b) i Komintern, 1919–1943*, p. 30, footnote 3.

4. For the story: Haslam, *Near and Distant Neighbours*, ch. 3.

5. Communiqué No. 01574 to the Comrades of the Communist Party of Great Britain, contained in Directorate of Intelligence (Home Office), "A Monthly Review of Revolutionary Movements in British Dominions Overseas and Foreign Countries", No. 34, August 1921: UK. London. National Archives, CAB 24/125.

6. *Command 2895* (London: HMSO, 1927).

7. Report on concessions at the 8th Congress of Soviets, 21 December 1920: Lenin, *Collected Works*, Vol. 31, p. 72.

8. Enclosure in Curzon (London) to Hodgson (Moscow), 2 May 1923: *Documents on British Foreign Policy 1919–1939*, 1st Series, Vol. 25, ed. W. Medlicott and D. Dakin, (London: HMSO, 1984), doc. 53.

9. Hodgson (Moscow) to Curzon (London), 13 May 1923: ibid., doc. 68.

10. Chicherin to Stalin, 10 May 1923: *Dokumenty vneshnei politiki SSSR*, Vol. 6, doc. 170.

11. G. Bennett, *The Zinoviev Letter: The Conspiracy That Never Dies* (Oxford: Oxford University Press, 2018). The legacy of suspicion meant that the Foreign Office thereafter refused to take MI6 revelations entirely on trust. I gathered as much from conversation with E. H. Carr.

12. M. Alekseev, *Sovetskaya voennaya razvedka v Kitae i khronika "kitaiskoi smuty" (1922–1929)* (Moscow: Kuchkovo pole, 2010), p. 51. The archives on these activities are still not open to outsiders.

13. G. Vidal, "L'affaire Fantômas (1932). Le contre-espionnage français et les prémices de la préparation à la guerre", *Vingtième Siècle. Revue d'Histoire*, No. 119, 2013/3, https://www.cairn.info/revue-vingtieme-siecle-revue-d-histoire-2013-3-page-3.htm.

14. *Dokumenty vneshnei politiki SSSR*, Vol. 7, ed. A. Gromyko et al. (Moscow: Politizdat, 1962), doc. 275.

15. Reported in the *Morning Post*, 28 November 1924.

16. *New York Times*, 30 November 1924.

17. Graham (Rome) to Chamberlain (London), 11 December 1924: UK. London. National Archives, FO 371/10502.

18. Chamberlain (London) to Rumbold (Madrid), 16 December 1924: ibid.

19. Record of a conversation with Winston Churchill copied to Austen Chamberlain, 10 January 1925, quoted in M. Gilbert, *Winston S. Churchill*, Vol. 5: *The Prophet of Truth, 1922–1939* (London: Heinemann, 1976), p. 122.

20. Quoted in ibid., p. 227, footnote.

21. Debate on the Address, 9 February 1927: *Hansard. Commons*. 5th Series, Vol. 202, col. 159.

22. A. H. Hamilton-Gordon, 26 November 1926: UK. London. National Archives, FO 371/11777.

23. C. Orde, 29 November 1926: ibid.

24. UK. London. National Archives, FO 371/11006. For Smith and Ricardo: Haslam, *No Virtue Like Necessity*, pp. 144–147.

25. Krasin (Paris) to Chicherin (Moscow), 7 December 1924: *Dokumenty vneshnei politiki SSSR*, Vol. 7, doc. 281. For the Polish armed forces: M. Hauner, "Military Budgets and the Armaments Industry", M. Kaser and E. Radice, eds, *The Economic History of Eastern Europe 1919–1975*, Vol. 2 (Oxford: Clarendon Press, 1986), p. 100.

26. Report from the Eastern Department of the executive to the presidium, 16 May 1925: *VKP(b), Komintern i natsional'no-revolyutsionnoe dvizhenie*, Vol. 1, doc. 151.

27. Vilenskii-Sibiryakov to Comintern's executive committee, 1 September 1920: ibid., doc. 4.

28. Statement by Lidin to the Far Eastern Department of Comintern's executive, 20 May 1922: ibid., doc. 21.

29. Letter from V. Vilenskii-Sibiryakov, Soviet Russia's plenipotentiary in the Far East, to Comintern's executive committee in Moscow, 1 September 1920: doc. 3.

30. L. Tikhvinskii, *Put' Kitaya k ob'edineniyu i nezavisimosti 1898–1949. Po materialami biografii Chzhou En'lai* (Moscow: 'Vostochnaya Literatura', RAN, 1996), p. 73.

31. Stalin's speech to activists of the Moscow organisation of the Soviet Communist Party, 5 April 1927: *Problemy dal'nego vostoka*, No. 1, 2001, p. 157.

32. Statement by Lidin: *VKP(b), Komintern i natsional'no-revolyutsionnoe dvizhenie*, doc. 21.

33. Potapov to Chicherin, 12 December 1920: ibid., doc. 7.

34. Quoted in A. Kartunova, 'Politicheskii obraz Sun Yatsena v perepiske I. V. Stalina i G. V. Chicherina s L. M. Karakhanom (1923-mart 1925 gg.)", *Problemy dal'nego vostoka*, No. 1, 2010, p. 127.

35. Ioffe to Karakhan, 30 August 1923: *VKP(b), Komintern i natsional'no-revolyutsionnoe dvizhenie*, Vol. 1, doc. 28.

36. Resolution of the IV Congress of Comintern, not later than 5 December 1922: ibid., doc. 49.

37. Maring, speaking at a session of Comintern's executive committee, 6 January 1923: ibid., doc. 56.

38. Stenographic report of a meeting of the presidium of Comintern's executive committee, 29 December 1922: ibid., doc. 53.

39. "Iz Protokola No. 53, Zasedaniya Politburo TsK RKP(b)", ibid., doc. 64.

40. Trotsky's comments transcribed by Baranovsky, 27 November 1923: ibid., doc. 97.

41. To the presidium of Comintern's executive committee, 4 April 1923: ibid., doc. 71.

42. Stalin (Moscow) letter to Karakhan (Beijing), 16 June 1924: *Perepiska I. V. Stalina i G. V. Chicherina s polpredom SSSR v Kitae L. M. Karakhanom. Dokumenty, avgust 1923 g.–1926 g.*, ed. M. Titarenko et al. (Moscow: Natalis, 2008), doc. 58.

43. Borodin's report to a Soviet Politbuto committee meeting in Beijing, 15 and 17 February 1926: *VKP(b), Komintern i natsional'no-revolyutsionnoe dvizhenie v Kitae*, Vol. 2, ed. M. Titarenko et al. (Moscow: AO "Buklet", 1996), Part 1, doc. 21.

44. Letter from Chicherin (Moscow) to Karakhan (Beijing), 2 June 1925: *Perepiska I. V. Stalina i G. V. Chicherina*, doc. 152.

45. Letter from Voitinsky (Moscow) to Karakhan (Beijing), 22 April 1925: *VKP(b), Komintern i natsional'no-revolyutsionnoe dvizhenie*, Vol. 1, doc. 147.

46. Speech at Sverdlovsk University, 9 June 1925: *Leningradskaya pravda*, 23 June 1925.

47. *Perepiska I. V. Stalina i G. V. Chicherina*, p. 540, footnote 1.

48. For the story updated: Haslam, *Near and Distant Neighbours*, ch. 3.

49. Stalin (Moscow) to Karakhan (Beijing), 12 June 1925: *Perepiska I. V. Stalina i G. V. Chicherina*, doc. 154.

50. "Protokol No. 68", 25 June 1925: Russia. Moscow. RGASPI, f. 17, op. 3, d. 508.

51. "Direktiva pechati i TASS", 3 December 1925: *VKP(b), Komintern i natsional'no-revolyutsionnoe dvizhenie*, Vol. 1, doc. 201.

52. "Protokol No. 93. Zasedaniya Politburo TsK RKP(b)", 3 December 1925: ibid., doc. 201.

53. Commander Egorov, in particular, became the object of Karakhan's fury for his inability to adapt to Chinese conditions—Letter from Karakhan (Beijing) to Stalin (Moscow), 18 January 1926: *Perepiska I. V. Stalina i G. V. Chicherina*, doc. 177.

54. The the best account by far is E. Carr, *A History of Soviet Russia*, Vol. 3: *Socialism in One Country 1924–1926*, (London: Macmillan, 1964), pp. 799–832.

55. Recommended by the China Committee under Bubnov, head of the political directorate of the Red Army and member of the Central Committee of the Party, 17 May 1926: *VKP(b), Komintern i natsional'no-revolyutsionnoe dvizhenie*, Vol. 2, Part 1, doc. 52.

398 NOTES TO CHAPTER 3

56. Letter from Chicherin (Moscow) to Karakhan (Beijing), 15 January 1926: *Perepiska I. V. Stalina i G. V. Chicherina*, doc. 176.

57. "Iz stenogrammy obsuzhdeniya Kitaiskogo voprosa na zasedanii prezidiuma IKKI", 10 February 1926. "Protokoly NoNo. 47 i 48 (zakrytogo) zasedanii Prezidiuma IKKI, ot 10 fevralya 1926g.". Russia. Moscow. RGASPI, Arkhiv Kominterna, f. 495, op. 2, d. 65.

58. Sir Montagu Turner, company meeting of the Chartered Bank of India, Australia and China, *Morning Post*, 31 March 1927.

59. "Iz stenogrammy obsuzhdeniya Kitaiskogo voprosa na zasedanii prezidiuma IKKI", 10 February 1926. "Protokoly NoNo. 47 i 48 (zakrytogo) zasedanii Prezidiuma IKKI, ot 10 fevralya 1926g." Russia. Moscow. RGASPI, Arkhiv Kominterna, f. 495, op. 2, d. 65.

60. Chicherin (Moscow) to Kopp (Beijing), 23 March 1925: *Perepiska I. V. Stalina i G. V. Chicherina*, doc. 189.

61. Chicherin (Moscow) to Karakhan (Beijing), 25 July 1926: ibid., doc. 206.

62. The Cambridge economist Maynard Keynes had argued against a return to the standard at the uncompetitive rate chosen: Gilbert, *Winston S. Churchill*, Vol. 5, p. 99. And Churchill, as chancellor of the exchequer, soon had good reason to regret not taking Keynes's advice: ibid., p. 238.

63. Quoted in ibid., p. 289.

64. *The Times*, 7 May 1926.

65. "Protokoll Nr. 58 der Sitzung des Präsidiums des IKKI vom 7 Mai 1926": Russia. Moscow. RGASPI, Arkhiv Kominterna, f. 495, op. 2, d. 71.

66. Chicherin to Stalin, 8 May 1926: ibid., f. 495, op. 18, d. 452.

67. W. Citrine, *Men and Work* (London: Hutchinson, 1964), p. 91. For the Politburo's decision: "Iz protokola No. 23", 4 May 1926: *Politburo TsK RKP(b)–VKP(b) i Evropa. Resheniya "Osoboi papki" 1923–1939*, ed. G. Adibekov et al. (Moscow: Rosspen, 2001), doc. 57.

68. The total in roubles was 16,015,009: *Profosyuzy SSSR: Dokumenty i materialy*, Vol. 2, ed. N. Antropov (Moscow: Profizdat, 1963), doc. 327.

69. Dated 22 July 1926: UK. London. National Archives, CP 303 (26).

70. Memorandum, "Foreign Policy in Relation to Russia and Japan": ibid.

71. "British Policy Considered in Relation to the European Situation". Memorandum by Harold Nicolson, prepared by order of Austen Chamberlain, 20 February 1925: UK. London. National Archives, CP 106 (25).

72. Della Torretta (London) to Mussolini (Rome), 26 August 1925: *I documenti diplomatici italiani*, 7th Series, Vol. 4, ed. R. Moscati (Rome: Istituto Poligrafico dello Stato, 1962), doc. 110.

73. UK. London. National Archives, CP 4 (27), containing COS 59, "China Situation 1927" (January).

74. 4 February 1927: ibid., CAB 7 (27).

75. Stalin (Sochi) to Molotov (Moscow), 23 September 1926: *Stalin's Letters to Molotov 1925–1936*, ed. L. Lih et al. (New Haven: Yale University Press, 1995), Letter 28.

76. Chamberlain for the cabinet, 23 November 1926: UK. London. National Archives, China, CP 399 (26).

77. Chamberlain for the cabinet, 23 November 1926: ibid.

78. "Dokladnaya Zapiska T. G. Mandalyana, A. E. Al'brekhta, N. M. Nasonova i N. A. Fokina o Vtorom Shankhaiskom Vosstanii", 4 March 1927: *VKP(b), Komintern i natsional'no-revolyutsionnoe dvizhenie*, Vol. 2, Part 2, doc. 175.

79. UK. London. National Archives, CAB 2 (27).

80. Alekseev, *Sovetskaya voennaya razvedka v Kitae*, p. 203.

81. UK. London. National Archives, CP 111 (27).

82. Haslam, *Near and Distant Neighbours*, p. 34.

83. P. Coble, *The Shanghai Capitalists and the Nationalist Government, 1927–1937* (Cambridge, Mass.: Harvard University Council on East Asian Studies, 1980), pp. 28–30.

84. UK. London. National Archives, FO 371/12500

85. H. Dyck, *Weimar Germany and Soviet Russia* (London: Chatto and Windus, 1966), p. 90.

86. *Pravda*, 21 September 1926.

87. Report sent to Voroshilov, 29 January 1927: *Glazami razvedki SSSR i Evropa 1919–1938 gody: sbornik dokumentov iz rossiiskikh arkhivov*, ed. M. Ul' et al. (Moscow: IstLit, 2015), doc. 75.

88. L. Trotsky, "Tezisy o Vneshnei Politike", 19 April 1927: *Arkhiv Trotskogo. Kommunisticheskaya Oppozitsiya v SSSR, 1923–1927*, Vol. 2 (Moscow: Terra, 1990), pp. 249–250.

89. De Stefani (Paris) to Mussolini (Rome), 7 January 1925: *I documenti diplomatici italiani*, 7th Series, Vol. 3, ed. R. Moscati (Rome: Istituto Poligrafico dello Stato, 1959), doc. 662.

90. *Morning Post*, 29 January 1927.

Chapter 4. The Manchurian Fiasco, 1931

1. UK. London. National Archives, FO 262/1774.

2. *Wall Street Journal*, 2 July, 3 July, 3 August, 25 and 30 October 1929

3. Note by Grandi of his conversation with Stimson, 14 July 1931: *I documenti diplomatici italiani*, 7th Series, Vol. 10, ed. G. Carocci (Rome: Istituto Poligrafico dello Stato, 1978), doc. 393, footnote 1.

4. I. Nish, *Japanese Foreign Policy 1869–1942: Kasumigaseki to Miyakezaka* (London: Routledge & Kegan Paul, 1977), p. 177; also pp. 165–166.

5. "Voprosy nashei politiki v otnoshenii Kitaya i Yaponii", *VKP(b), Komintern i Kitai. Dokumenty*, Vol. 3, ed. M. Titarenko et al. (Moscow: AO "Buklet", 1999), p. 166.

6. Letter from Eisler to the Eastern secretariat of Comintern's executive committee, 23–25 June 1930: ibid., doc. 243

7. Telegram from the Far Eastern Bureau to Comintern's executive committee, 4–7 August 1930: ibid., doc. 263.

8. Stolyar's letter to Lozovsky, 5 August 1930: ibid., doc. 264; capitals as in the original.

9. From Shanghai, 12 August 1930: ibid., doc. 277.

10. Telegram from Stalin (Sochi) to Molotov (Moscow), 13 August 1930: ibid., doc. 278.

11. "Iz protokola No. 5 (Osobyi No.) zasedaniya Politburo TsK VKP(b)", 25 August 1930: *Politburo TsK RKP(b)–VKP(b) i Komintern, 1919–1943*, doc. 391.

12. Stalin to Molotov, 7 October 1929: *Stalin's Letters to Molotov*, ed. Lih et al., doc. 51.

13. Russia. London. RGASPI, Arkhiv Kominterna, f. 495, op. 3, d. 129.

14. Ah Xiang, "Communists and the Japanese Invasion of Manchuria": http://republicanchina .org/COMMUNISTS-AND-JAPAN-INVASION-MANCHURIA.pdf, p. 9.

15. Information from FSB archives: O. Shinin, "Provedenie organami gosudarstvennoi bezopasnosti aktivnykh meropriyatii v 1922–1941 godakh", *Problemy dal'nego vostoka*, No. 4, 2006.

16. Lindley (Tokyo) to the Marquess of Reading (London), 30 October 1931: UK. London. National Archives, FO 262/1774.

17. Entry, 24 September 1931: USA. New Haven. Yale University Library, Stimson diaries, Vol. 18, p. 63.

18. Ibid.

19. Lindley (Tokyo) to the Marquess of Reading (London), 30 October 1931: UK. London. National Archives, FO 262/1774.

20. Entry, 30 September 1931: USA. New Haven. Yale University Library, Stimson diaries, p. 77.

21. Entry, 9 October 1931: ibid., p. 111.

22. Entry, 23 October 1931: ibid., p. 173.

23. "Instruktsiya po rabote sredi voisk", 7 July 1928: Russia. Moscow. RGASPI, Arkhiv Kominterna, f. 495, op. 20, d. 727.

24. Entry, 15 October 1931: USA. New Haven. Yale University Library, Stimson diaries, p. 136.

25. H. Hoover, *The Memoirs of Herbert Hoover*, Vol. 2: *The Cabinet and the Presidency 1920–1933* (New York: Macmillan, 1952), p. 369.

26. "Iz protokola No. 63", 20 September 1931: *VKP(b), Komintern i Yaponiya. 1917–1941*, ed. G. Adibekov and K. Vada (Wada) (Moscow: Rosspen, 2001).

27. Stalin to Kaganovich and Molotov, 23 September 1931: *Politburo TsK RKP(b)–VKP(b) i Komintern, 1919–1943*, doc. 404.

28. "Protokol PB No. 64", 25 September 1931: Russia. Moscow. RGASPI, f. 17, op. 3, d. 850.

29. Stalin to Voroshilov, 27 November 1931: *Sovetskoe rukovodstvo. Perepiska 1928–1941*, doc. 91.

30. Quoted in J. Haslam, *The Soviet Union and the Threat from the East, 1933–41* (London: Macmillan, 1992), p. 7.

31. In conversation with the Lithuanian foreign minister Urbšis and ambassador Natkevičius, 8 October 1939: *SSSR i Litva v gody mirovoi voiny*, doc. 51.

32. M. Alekseev, *"Vernyi Vam Ramzai". Rikhard Zorge i sovetskaya razvedka v Yaponii. 1933–1938 gody* (Moscow: Algoritm, 2017), p. 41.

33. "Note of a conversation with Karl Radek", 20 April 1932: enclosure in Sir John Pratt (Geneva) to Foreign Office (London), 26 April 1932: *Documents on British Foreign Policy, 1919–1939*, 2nd Series, Vol. 10, ed. W. Medlicott et al. (London: HMSO, 1969), doc. 270.

34. Haslam, *Soviet Union and the Threat from the East*, p. 8.

35. Quoted in Shinin, "Provedenie organami".

36. Kaganovich to Stalin, 2 June 1932 and Stalin to Kaganovich, 5 June 1932: *The Stalin–Kaganovich Correspondence 1931–36*, ed. R. Davies et al. (New Haven: Yale University Press, 2003), docs 24 and 26.

37. Haslam, *Soviet Union and the Threat from the East*, p. 9.

38. Central Committee, Japanese Communist Party, *Sixty-Year History of Japanese Communist Party, 1922–1982* (Tokyo: Japan Press Service, 1984), p. 61.

39. "Blizhaishie zadachi partii v kampanii protiv ekonomii", final text approved by the political committee of Comintern's executive, 28 September 1931: Russia. Moscow. RGASPI, Arkhiv Kominterna, f. 495, op. 20, d. 37.

40. Owen O'Malley, "CHINA", 10 June 1926: UK. Cambridge. Churchill College Archives, Strang Papers, STRN 4/4.

41. *The Memoirs of Lord Gladwyn* (London: Weidenfeld and Nicolson, 1972), p. 48.

42. *The Times*, 26 November 1925.

43. Said to the correspondent of the *New York Herald Tribune*: *The Commercial and Financial Chronicle*, 10 December 1932.

44. Grandi's record of the conversation, 19 April 1932: *I documenti diplomatici italiani*, 7th Series, Vol. 12, ed. G. Carocci (Rome: Istituto Poligrafico dello Stato, 1987), doc. 21.

45. Memorandum by Stimson, 5 January 1933: *Peace and War. United States Foreign Policy 1931–1941* (Washington DC: US GPO, 1943), doc. 11

46. Kuusinen's statement on the Japanese question at a meeting of the Comintern executive's presidium, 2 March 1932: *VKP(b), Komintern i Yaponiya*, doc. 358.

47. "Protokoll No. 238 Politkomissii Politsekretariata IKKI", 27 April 1932: Russia. Moscow. RGASPI, Arkhiv Kominterna, f. 495, op. 4, d. 186.

48. "Protokoll (B) Nr. 245 der aussordentlichen Sitzung der Politkommission des Politisches Sekretariat IKKI am 31. Mai 1932: Russia. Moscow. RGASPI, Arkhiv Kominterna, f. 495, op. 4, d. 188a.

49. Quoted in J. Haslam, *Soviet Foreign Policy 1930–33: The Impact of the Depression* (London: Macmillan, 1983), p. 91.

50. Quoted in Haslam, *Soviet Union and the Threat from the East*, p. 34.

51. The classic account, unaccountably ignored by most Germanists, is still T. Weingartner, *Stalin und der Aufstieg Hitlers* (Berlin: De Gruyter, 1970). In English, the most reliable remains E. Carr, *Twilight of Comintern, 1930–1935* (London: Macmillan, 1982).

Chapter 5. Stalin's Gamble on German Nationalism

1. To Zinoviev, 7 August 1923: *Deutscher Oktober*, doc. 5.

2. The subsidy appears to have been arranged by Arthur Henderson, who became foreign secretary. MacDonald knew nothing of this until March 1931. Stimson's diary records that the Canadian prime minister, Richard Bennett, had "just learned from MacDonald in London that MacDonald had only just discovered that half of the campaign funds for the Labor Party in the last campaign came from Russia through Snowden and Henderson; and that he, MacDonald, was scared and shocked at the discovery": entry, 30 March 1931: USA. New Haven. Yale University Library, Stimson diaries, Vol. 15, p. 4. If true, this might explain why senior Soviet diplomats were so utterly dismissive of Henderson when he tried feebly to bargain for the granting of full diplomatic recognition to the Soviet régime.

3. "Protokol PB No. 113", 15 January 1930: Russia. Moscow. RGASPI, f. 17, op. 3, d. 772; also, S. Kotkin, *Stalin. Waiting for Hitler 1929–1941* (New York: Penguin, 2017), p. 36.

4. N. Tarkhova, *Krasnaya armiya i stalinskaya kollektivizatsiya 1928–1933 gg.* (Moscow: Rosspen, 2010), pp. 138–141.

5. Entry, 8 April 1931: USA. New Haven. Yale University Library, Stimson diaries, Vol. 14, p. 221.

6. Entry, 23 March 1930: ibid., p. 17.

7. Quoted in Haslam, *Soviet Foreign Policy 1930–33*, p. 40.

8. Entry, 8 April 1931: USA. New Haven. Yale University Library, Stimson diaries, Vol. 15, p. 221.

9. Pasquier (Saigon) to Paris, 23 August 1930: France. Aix-en-Provence. Archives nationales d'outre-mer: Indochine, Nouveau Fonds, 326, 2636.

10. Công-Nhân, "Comment conquérir les masses?", *VO SAN* (The proletarian), No. 1, Paris, 31 August 1930.

11. Gouvernement général de l'Indochine, *Contribution à l'histoire des mouvements politiques de l'Indochine française. Documents*, Vol. 5: *La Terreur rouge en Annam, 1930–1931* (Hanoi: GGI, Direction des affaires politiques et de la Sûreté Génerale, 1933). The volume gives records of interrogations (without describing the torture employed). Tran Phu, general secretary of the Cong Sang Dang (Vietnamese Communist Party) was so badly tortured that he died the following year: Haslam, *Soviet Foreign Policy 1930–33*, p. 133, note 74.

12. "V frantsuzskoe byuro pri Kominterne", Ngien-Ai Kvak [Ho Chi-Minh], 27 February 1930: Russia. Moscow. RGASPI, Arkhiv Kominterna, f. 495, op. 154, d. 615.

13. Haslam, *Soviet Foreign Policy 1930–33*, p. 133, note 75.

14. Ibid., p. 35.

15. Ibid., p. 36.

16. Ibid., pp. 43–44. For Flandin's political orientation: Bullitt (Paris) to Roosevelt (Washington DC), 9 May 1939: USA. Hyde Park. Franklin D. Roosevelt Library and Archive, PSF, France, William C. Bullitt, 1939, Box 30.

17. O. Ken, A. Rupasov and L. Samuel'son, *Shvetsia v politike Moskvy 1930–1950-e gody* (Moscow: Rosspen, 2005), pp. 187–188.

18. Memorandum from foreign intelligence (InOGPU) to Stalin, 30 November 1930: *Glazami razvedki SSSR i Evropa 1919–1938 gody*, doc. 120. The German original can be found in *Akten zur deutschen auswärtigen Politik, 1918–1945*, Series B, Vol. 16, ed. H. Rothfels et al. (Göttingen: Vandenhoeck & Ruprecht, 1981), pp. 35–38. For the InOGPU's access to German traffic through the wife of a senior official, codename "Marta", see Haslam, *Near and Distant Neighbours*, pp. 45–47.

19. Entry, 27 August 1931: USA. New Haven. Yale University Library, Stimson diaries, Vol. 17, p. 181.

20. H. von Herwarth, *Against Two Evils* (New York: Rawson, Wade, 1981), p. 83. "Johnnie", as he was known, served at the German embassy in Moscow from 1931 to 1939.

21. Reference is made to this in a memorandum from Knorin, Manuilsky and Pyatnitsky to Stalin and Molotov, 28 October 1931: *Politburo TsK RKP(b)–VKP(b) i Komintern, 1919–1943*, doc. 406.

22. G. Berti, *I primi dieci anni di vita del PCI. Documenti inediti dell'archivio Angela Tasca* (Milan: Feltrinelli, 1967), p. 87.

23. Merker to Comintern's executive committee, 26 March 1930: Russia. Moscow. RGASPI, Arkhiv Kominterna, f. 495, op. 19, d. 522; reprinted in A. Gintsberg, "'Politsekretariat IKKI Trebuet":

Dokumenty Kominterna i Kompartii Germanii. 1930–1934 gg., *Istoricheskii arkhiv*, No. 1, 1994, pp. 150–152; note from Pyatnitsky to Thälmann, 4 April 1930: ibid., p. 152; telegram from the KPD secretariat to the Comintern executive's secretariat, 4 April 1930: ibid., pp. 152–153; private letter from the executive secretariat to the KPD. Central Committee, 26 April 1930: ibid., 153–157.

24. E. Carr, *A History of Soviet Russia*, Vol. 2: *The Interregnum 1923–1924* (London: Pelican, 1969), pp. 179–181.

25. Thälmann's report to a meeting of the Central Committee, 16/17 July 1930, quoted in B. Hoppe, *In Stalins Gefolgschaft: Moskau und die KPD 1928–1933* (Munich: Oldenbourg, 2007), p. 187. Neumann had attended the XVI Congress of the Soviet Communist Party as guest speaker at the end of June and it was here, behind the scenes, that Stalin discussed with him the way forward: ibid., p. 186.

26. Record of a meeting of the Soviet delegation to Comintern's executive committee, 18 July 1930: O. Khlevniuk, *Politburo. Mekhanizmy politicheskoi vlasti v 1930-e gody* (Moscow: Rosspen, 1996), doc. 388.

27. Hoppe, *In Stalins Gefolgschaft*, pp. 187–188.

28. "Protokoly NoNo. 27–28 Zasedanii Prezidiuma IKKI ot 28 oktyabrya i 19 noyabrya 1930 g.": Russia. Moscow. RGASPI, Arkhiv Kominterna, f. 495, op. 2, d. 168.

29. 6 April 1931: *Komintern i ideya mirovoi revolyutsii*, doc. 184.

30. Manuilsky, speaking to a session of the executive's political secretariat, 1 December 1931: ibid., doc. 186.

31. Reprinted in *Dokumenty vneshnei politiki SSSR*, Vol. 14, ed. P. Ershov et al. (Moscow: Politicheskaya Literatura, 1968), appendix, p. 48.

32. Entries, 6, 13 and 19 June 1931: USA. New Haven. Yale University Library, Stimson diaries, Vol. 16, pp. 133, 137, 163 and 194.

33. The claim made retrospectively by Pieck that Thälmann had actually left the issue open for discussion and that the vote for abstention took them all by surprise scarcely rings true: Pieck to an unknown member of Comintern's executive, 29 July 1931: *Istoricheskii arkhiv*, No. 1, 1994, pp. 158–159.

34. Thälmann's comment on 14 May 1932, quoted in Hoppe, *In Stalins Gefolgschaft*, p. 208.

35. Proof of Manuilsky's position can be found in the Comintern archive: ibid., p. 211, footnote 37.

36. Carr, *Twilight of Comintern*, p. 42.

37. Letter from Pieck to the KPD Central Committee, 20 July 1931: *Istoricheskii arkhiv*, No. 1, 1994, pp. 157–158.

38. Letter to Pieck, 15 August 1931, quoted in Hoppe, *In Stalins Gefolgschaft*, p. 218.

39. Resolution of the political secretariat of Comintern's executive committee, 18 September 1931: *Istoricheskii arkhiv*, No. 1, 1994, pp. 159–162.

40. Addressing Comintern's presidium, 17 January 1932: Russia. Moscow. RGASPI, Arkhiv Kominterna, f. 495, op. 2, d. 186.

41. The military counsellor of the Japanese delegation at the League of Nations, Colonel Kobayashi, made the offer to René Massigli, the French delegate, 9 June 1932: *Documents diplomatiques français, 1932–1939*, 1st series, Vol. 2, ed. P. Renouvin (Paris: Imprimerie National, 1964), doc. 3. The reponse was that France had to answer to the other great powers.

42. "Protokoll Nr. 52 der Sitzung des Präsidiums des EKKI am 26.September 1932". Russia. Moscow. RGASPI, Arkhiv Kominterna, f. 495, op. 2, d. 197.

43. Manuilsky's speech to the political secretariat of Comintern's executive committee, 1 December 1931: *Komintern i ideya mirovoi revolyutsii*, doc. 186.

44. Report from Knorin et al. to Stalin and Molotov, 28 October 1931: *Politburo TsK RKP(b)– VKP(b) i Komintern, 1919–1943*, doc. 406.

45. "Protokoll Nr. 47 der Sitzung des Präsidiums des EKKI am 19. Mai 1932": Russia. Moscow. RGASPI, Arkhiv Kominterna, f. 495, op. 2, d. 193.

46. Neumann's report to the KPD political secretariat on his recent conversation with Stalin, 10 April 1932: Hoppe, *In Stalins Gefolgschaft*, p. 294.

47. Letter from Pyatnitsky to Stalin, 10 May 1932: *Politburo TsK RKP(b)–VKP(b) i Komintern, 1919–1943*, doc. 410.

48. Ibid., p. 667, note 1.

49. "Protokoll Nr. 47 der Sitzung des Präsidiums des EKKI am 19. Mai 1932": Russia. Moscow. RGASPI, Arkhiv Kominterna, f. 495, op. 2, d. 193.

50. Addressing a meeting of Comintern's political secretariat, 11 June 1932: Russia. Moscow. RGASPI, Arkhiv Kominterna, f. 495, op. 3, d. 249.

51. *Stenogrammy zasedanii Politburo TsK RKP(b)–VKP(b), 1923–1938 gg.*, ed. K. Anderson et al. (Moscow: Rosspen, 2007), p. 676, footnote 29.

52. Speech to a joint session of the Politburo and the Central Control Committee, 27 November 1932: ibid., p. 661.

53. Haslam, *Soviet Union and the Threat from the East*, ch. 1.

54. Hoppe, *Stalins Gefolgschaft*, p. 311.

55. Wagnière (Rome) to Motta (Bern), 17 May 1932: *Documents diplomatiques suisses*, Vol. 10, doc. 167.

56. Report from InOGPU to the Council of People's Commissars, 24 June 1932: Russia. Moscow. Yeltsin Presidential Library. *Vtoraya mirovaya voina v arkhivnykh dokumentakh, 1933.* Arkhiv SVR Rossii, l. 154, photocopy: prlib.ru. Also Haslam, *Near and Distant Neighbours*, p. 43.

57. S. Schirmann, *Crise, coopération économique et financière entre États européens, 1929–1933* (Paris: Comité pour l'histoire économique et financière de la France, 2000), pp. 217–218.

58. Hoppe, *Stalins Gefolgschaft*, p. 312.

59. "Immediate. To comrade Molotov and comrade Kaganovich." 20 June 1932: Russia. Moscow. RGASPI, Arkhiv Kominterna, f. 495, op. 7, d. 126. Also, *Politburo TsK RKP(b)–VKP(b) i Komintern, 1919–1943*, doc. 414.

60. *Akten zur deutschen auswärtige Politik 1918–1945*, Series B, Vol. 21, ed. H. Rothfels et al. (Göttingen: Vandenhoeck & Ruprecht, 1983) pp. 481–482.

61. Quoted from Litvinov's record of the conversation: Gorlov, *Sovershenno Sekretno*, p. 293.

Chapter 6. The Impact of Hitler

1. Knorin, addressing the presidium of Comintern's executive committee, 1 April 1933: Russia. Moscow. RGASPI, Arkhiv Kominterna, f. 495, op. 2, d. 203.

2. *Akten der Reichskanzlei: Regierung Hitler 1933–1938.* Part 1, Vol. 1, ed. K.-H. Minuth (Boppard am Rhein: Boldt, 1983), doc. 19.

3. Ibid., doc. 32.

4. Report from Berzin and head of the Third Department, A. M. Nikonov, to Voroshilov, 5 March 1933: Russia. Moscow. Yeltsin Presidential Library. *Vtoraya mirovaya voina v arkhivnykh dokumentakh, 1933*. RGVA, f. 33987, op. za. d. 497, l. 59–63, photocopy: prlib.ru. For the report of 3 February: ibid., RGVA, f. 33987, op. za. d. 497, l. 18–23.

5. *Akten der Reichskanzlei*, doc. 41.

6. "Protokol No. 58 i stenogramma zasedaniya Prezidiuma IKKI", 28 February 1933: Russia. Moscow. RGASPI, Arkhiv Kominterna, f. 495, op.2, d. 202.

7. Issued in the name of Comintern's executive committee, 2 March 1933: published in *Pravda*, 6 March 1933; *Daily Worker*, 8 March 1933; *Rundschau über Politik, Wirtschaft und Arbeiterbewegung*, 11 March 1933.

8. Manuilsky: "Protokol No. 58 i stenogramma zasedaniya Prezidiuma IKKI", 28 February 1933: Russia. Moscow. RGASPI, Arkhiv Kominterna, f. 495, op. 2, d. 202.

9. Conversation, 25 April 1934: G. Dimitrov, *The Diary of Georgi Dimitrov, 1933–1949*, ed. I. Banac (New Haven: Yale University Press, 2003), p. 16.

10. *Na Prieme u Stalina. Tetradi (zhurnaly) zapisei lits, prinyatykh I. V. Stalinym (1924–1953 gg.)*, ed. A. Chernobaev et al. (Moscow: Novyi khronograf, 2008), p. 89.

11. "Stenogramma Sredneevropeiskogo L.S. IKKI: nemetskii fashizm", 26 March 1933: Russia. Moscow. RGASPI, Arkhiv Kominterna, f. 495, op. 28, d. 234. On Pyatnitsky: "Record of an interview with A. G. Krytov, 2 June 1988": USA. Stanford. Hoover Institution, Firsov Papers, Box 43. Krytov had worked as a Comintern executive committee assistant to the secretary of the Eastern Department.

12. Proceedings of the Central European regional secretariat, on German fascism, 26 March 1933: Russia. Moscow. RGASPI, Arkhiv Kominterna, f. 495, op. 28, d. 234.

13. Entry, 24 September 1936: UK. Cambridge. Churchill College Archives, Cadogan Diary, ACAD 1/5.

14. Dunant (Paris) to Motta (Rome), 28 March 1933: *Documents diplomatiques suisses*, Vol. 10, doc. 254.

15. Dirksen (Moscow) to Bülow (Berlin), 31 January 1933: *Akten zur deutschen auswärtgen Politik, 1918–1945*, Series C, Vol. 1, ed. H. Rothfels et al. (Göttingen: Vandenhoeck & Ruprecht, 1971), doc. 6.

16. *Akten Kardinal Michael von Faulhabers*, ed. L. Volk, Vol. 1, 1917–1934 (Mainz: Matthias-Grünewald Verlag, 1975), doc. 272

17. (Berlin) to Hoare, 16 December 1935: UK. London. National Archives, CP 13 (36).

18. Entry, 26 July 1933: Baron Aloisi, *Journal (25 juillet 1932–14 juin 1936)* (Paris: Plon, 1957), p. 141.

19. Morreale (Vienna) to Mussolini (Rome), 9 August 1933: *I documenti diplomatici italiani*, 7th Series, Vol. 14, ed. G Carocci et al. (Rome: Istituto Poligrafico dello Stato, 1989), doc. 77.

20. At lunch with Lord Reading and US Secretary of State: entry, 21 March 1930: USA. New Haven. Yale University Library, Stimson diaries, Vol. 14, p. 3.

21. *Western Daily Press*, 23 September 1933.

22. Letters to Sir Walford Selby and Captain Victor Cazalet, 9 January and 9 April 1934, quoted in L. Michie, *Portrait of an Appeaser: Robert Hadow, First Secretary in the British Foreign Office, 1931–1939* (Wesport, Conn.: Praeger, 1996), p. 23.

23. Sir Alexander Cadogan: entry, 21 October 1938: R. Bruce Lockhart, *The Diaries of Sir Robert Bruce Lockhart*, ed. K. Young (London: Macmillan, 1973), Vol. 1, p. 404.

24. J. Haslam, *The Vices of Integrity: E. H. Carr, 1892–1982* (London: Verso, 1999). Vansittart was, after all, the man who later proposed the notorious appeaser Nevile Henderson as ambassador to Berlin though his experience of important capitals amounted to less than one year in France.

25. Orseniga (Berlin) to Pacelli (Vatican), 2 May 1933: Vatican Secret Archive, AA.EE.SS. Germania, Pos. 643, fasc. 159, fols 122–123. Reprinted on the website of the German Historical Institute, Rome: www.dhi-roma.it.

26. Phipps (Berlin) to Simon (London), 1 April 1935: UK. London. National Archives, CP 13 (36).

27. Speech at a session of Comintern's executive committee, 1 April 1936: *Komintern protiv fashizma*, doc. 106.

28. Speech to Moscow Party activists: *Pravda*, 2 November 1932.

29. "Platforma 'Soyuza Marksistov-Lenintsev'" ('Gruppa Ryutina')", *Izvestiya TsK KPSS*, 11 (310), November 1990, p. 169.

30. "Stenogramma ob"edinennogo zasedaniya Politburo Ts.K. i Prezidiuma TsKK VKP(b) po voprosu 'O fraktsionnoi rabote tt. Syrtsova, Lominadze i dr.'", 4 November 1930: *Stenogrammy zasedanii Politburo TsK RKP(b)–VKP(b)*, p. 134.

31. *Inprecorr*, 15 December 1933.

32. Attolico (Moscow) to Rome, 22 February 1933, enclosed in 1° Affari Politici (Buti) to Paris, London, Berlin, Washington, Tokyo, 10 March 1933: Italy. Rome. Ministero degli Affari Esteri, Archivio Storico Diplomatico: Affari Politici 1931–1935, l'URSS: Busta N. 8, 1933. 1.1. Rapporti Politici: 1° trimestre, pos. 1.

33. Reissued for public distribution by S. Lobanov, who found a copy on a "special reserve" in a library of the CPSU Central Committee. A. Gitler, *Moya Bor'ba* (Moscow: T-Oko, 1992). For Zinoviev's role, see B. Khavkin, "Merzost', kotoruyu nevozmozhno zapretit' i nel'zya ne znat'", *Nezavisimoe voennoe obozrenie*, 15 January 2016.

34. "Aufzeichnung der Reichministers des Auswärtigen Freiherrn von Neurath", 1 March 1933: *Akten zur deutschen auswärtigen Politik*, Series C, Vol. 1, doc. 43.

35. Charles-Roux (Vatican) to Herriot (Paris), 16 October 1932: *Documents diplomatiques français, 1932–1939*, 1st Series, Vol. 1, ed. P. Renouvin et al. (Paris: Imprimerie Nationale, 1964), doc. 246.

36. Quoted in J. Hernández Figureiredo, "Avances y estado del comunismo en vísperas de la guerra civil española, según los informes inéditos del Archivo Secreto Vaticano", *Analecta sacra tarraconensia*, Vol. 83, 2010, p. 9.

37. Quoted in R. Klieber, "Die moralische und politische Schützenhilfe des Hl. Stuhles für den 'Staatsumbau' Österreichs 1933/34 im Lichte vatikanischer Quellenbestände", *Römische Historische Mitteilungen*, Vol. 54, 2012, p. 536.

38. Hernández Figureiredo, "Avances y estado del comunismo", p. 9.

39. Cerruti (Berlin) to Suvich (Rome), 15 July 1933: reprinted in L. Volk, *Das Reichskonkordat vom 20. Juli 1933. Von den Ansätzen in der Weimarer Republik bis zu Ratifizierung am 10. September 1933* (Mainz: Matthias-Grünewald Verlag, 1972), doc. 8.

40. Quoting from the Soviet record of proceedings: Gorlov, *Sovershenno Sekretno*, p. 299.

41. 1° Affari Politici (Rome) to Attolico (Moscow), 9 March 1933: Italy. Rome. Ministero degli Affari Esteri, Archivio Storico Diplomatico: Affari Politici 1931–35, l'URSS: Busta N. 8, 1933, 1.1. Rapporti Politici: 1° trimestre, pos. 1.

42. A. Lacroix-Riz, *Le Choix de la défaite. Les élites françaises dans les années 1930*, 2nd edition (Paris: Colin, 2010), pp. 203, 220–221.

43. "Iz protokola No. 151", 19 December 1933: *Politburo TsK RKP(b)–VKP(b) i Evropa. Resheniya "Osoboi papki" 1923–1939*, doc. 207.

44. *The Economist*, 17 June 1933.

45. Memorandum on the proposed Eastern Pact, 28 January 1935: *Documents on British Foreign Policy 1919–1939*, 2nd Series, Vol. 12, ed. W. Medlicott et al. (London: HMSO, 1972), doc. 380.

46. Quoted in J. Haslam, *The Soviet Union and the Struggle for Collective Security in Europe, 1933–39* (London: Macmillan, 1984), p. 13.

47. Radek's record of the conversation, 4 May 1933: Russia. Moscow. Yeltsin Presidential Library. *Vtoraya mirovaya voina v arkhivnykh documentakh*, 1933. RGASPI, photocopy: prlib.ru.

48. Entry, 18 April 1933: Aloisi, *Journal*, p. 111.

49. At around this time Stalin framed a brief dialogue of the subject of Poland's friendship that he never completed. What is most noticeable about it is his complete failure to consider the force of ideological motives behind Poland's foreign policy: "Stalin I. V. Beseda s pol'skim natsionalistom", *Istoricheskii arkhiv*, No. 3, 2015, pp. 97–98.

50. Quoted in Haslam, *Soviet Union and the Struggle*, p. 21.

51. Entry, 21 July 1933: Aloisi, *Journal*, p. 140.

52. Entry, 19 December 1933: *Die Tagebücher von Joseph Goebbels*, Part 1, ed. E. Fröhlich (Munich: Saur, 2006), p. 340.

53. Conversation reported by Major Renzetti, head of Alessandro Chiavolini's secretariat, Berlin, 3 February 1934: *Documenti diplomatici italiani*, 7th Series, Vol. 14, doc. 659. Chiavolini was Mussolini's secretary.

54. Sturdza (Riga) to Titulescu (Bucharest), 9 October 1934: *The Romanian–Latvian Relations [sic]. Diplomatic Documents (1918–1958)*, ed. S. Miloiu et al. (Târgoviște: Cetatea de Scaun, 2012), doc. 99.

55. J. Beck, *Dernier rapport* (Neuchâtel: La Baconnière, 1951), p. 29.

56. Litvinov's memorandum to Stalin and Politbuaro acceptance of Paul-Boncour's proposals: Russia. Moscow. Yeltsin Presidential Library. *Vtoraya mirovaya voina v arkhivnykh dokumentakh*. RGASPI, f. 17, op. 166, d. 510, l. 26–30, photocopy: prlib.ru.

57. Clerk (Paris) to Simon (London), 26 February 1935: *Documents on British Foreign Policy 1919–1939*, 2nd Series, Vol. 12, doc. 509.

58. Clerk (Paris) to Simon (London), 28 March 1935: ibid., doc. 663.

59. "Iz protokola No. 7", 25 May 1934: *VKP(b), Komintern i Yaponiya*, doc. 150.

60. "Iz protokola No. 10", 14 July 1934: *Politburo TsK RKP(b)–VKP(b) i Evropa. Resheniya "Osoboi papki" 1923–1939*, doc. 214.

61. Stalin to the Politburo, 15 September 1934: ibid., p. 316.

62. "Iz protokola No. 12", 23 September 1934: ibid., doc. 218.

63. Ibid., p. 318, footnote 1.

64. *Glazami razvedki SSSR i Evropa 1919–1938 gody*, doc. 150.

65. Polish statistics summarised in Kaser and Radice, eds, *Economic History of Eastern Europe*, Vol. 2, p. 100.

66. "Iz protokola, No. 16", 2 November 1934: *Politburo TsK RKP(b)-VKP(b) i Evropa. Resheniya "Osoboi papki" 1923–1939*, doc. 219.

67. Stalin (Sochi) to Molotov and Zhdanov (Moscow), 12 October 1934: Russia. Moscow. Yeltsin Presidential Library. *Vtoraya mirovaya voina v arkhivnykh dokumentakh, 1934*. RGASPI, photocopy: prlib.ru.

68. "Memorandum by Mr. Sargent on German Rearmament", 31 October 1934: *Documents on British Foreign Policy 1919–1939*, 2nd Series, Vol. 12, doc. 159.

69. E. Carr, *International Relations between the Two World Wars (1919–1939)* (London: Macmillan, 1947), p. 220. Carr resigned from the Office in March 1936.

70. Ibid., p. 221.

71. Patteson (Geneva) to Simon (London), 21 November 1934: *Documents on British Foreign Policy 1919–1939*, 2nd Series, Vol. 12, doc. 200.

72. Record of the meeting, 22 December 1934: ibid., doc. 311.

73. "Iz protokola No. 21", 11 February 1935: *Politburo TsK RKP(b)–VKP(b) i Evropa. Resheniya "Osoboi papki" 1923–1939*, doc. 220.

74. Attolico (Moscow) to Mussolini (Rome), 8 February 1934: *Documenti diplomatici italiani*, 7th Series, Vol. 14, doc. 675.

75. Lt. Col. Jacob Wuest to Ambassador William Dodd, 5 October 1934: USA. College Park. National Archives, US Military Intelligence, Germany, 0029828-020-0226.

76. The copy dated 30 January 1935 and obtained by Soviet military intelligence is in the French original: Russia. Moscow. Yeltsin Presidential Library. *Vtoraya mirovaya voina v arkhivnykh dokumentakh, 1934*. RGVA, f. 7k, op.1, d. 474, l. 53: prlib.ru.

77. Slutsky, deputy head, InO GUGB, report to Stalin, 1 April 1935: *Sekrety pol'skoi politiki 1935–1945 gg. Rassekrechennye dokumenty sluzhby vneshnei razvedki Rossiiskoi Federatsii*, ed. L. Sotskov (Moscow: Ripol, 2010), p. 12.

78. Memoirs of the French ambassador: L. Noël, *Polonia Restituta. La Pologne entre deux mondes* (Paris: La Sorbonne, 1984), p. 19. He took over the embassy six months after the German–Polish declaration.

79. From "reliable sources"—Slutsky, deputy head of InO GUGB NKVD (no date): *Sekrety pol'skoi politiki 1935–1945 gg.*, pp. 20–21.

80. Report enclosed in Artuzov to Voroshilov, 5 March 1935: Russia. Moscow. Yeltsin Presidential Library. *Vtoraya mirovaya voina v arkhivnykh dokumentakh, 1935*. RGVA, f. 33987, op. za. d. 745, l. 19–26: prlib.ru.

81. Entry, 27 September 1933: *Tagebücher von Joseph Goebbels*, p. 277.

82. Noël, *Polonia Restituta*, p. 76.

83. Ibid., p. 76.

84. From "reliable sources"—Slutsky, deputy head of InO GUGB NKVD (no date): *Sekrety pol'skoi politiki 1935–1945 gg.*, p. 20.

85. L. Samuelson, *Plans for Stalin's War Machine* (London: Macmillan, 2000), p. 159.

86. Ibid., p. 160.

87. Valters (Warsaw) to Munters (Reval), 21 February 1936: *Romanian–Latvian Relations*, doc. 114.

88. "Account of a trip to Poland and a conversation with Prime Minister Beck", 25 February–3 March 1939: G. Ciano, ed., *L'Europa verso la catastrofe. 184 colloqui con Mussolini, Hitler, Franco, Chamberlain, Sumner Welles, Rustu Aras, Stoiadinovic, Göring, Zog, François-Poncet, ecc. Verbalizzati da Galeazzo Ciano* (Milan: Mondadori, 1948), p. 416.

89. Quoted in R. Mirowicz, "Edward Rydz-Śmigły: A Political and Military Biography" (unpublished text translated and edited by G. Dziekoński, c. 1974), p. 109.

90. For Piłsudski's assessment: ibid., 154.

91. Reported to the Polish ambassador to the Vatican, Aleksander Skrzyński; quoted in M. Kornat, "Ricordi di Pio XI sul Maresciallo Piłsudski alla luce dei documenti diplomatici polacchi", in Q. Bortolato and M. Lenart, eds, *Nunzio in una terra di frontiera: Achille Ratti, poi Pio XI, in Polonia (1918–1921)*, (Vatican City: Pontificio Comitato di Scienze Storiche, 2017), p. 105.

92. Record of the conversation, 16 February 1937—obtained by a Soviet intelligence agent in the Polish Foreign Ministry and sent to Stalin and Molotov on 25 March 1937: *Sekrety pol'skoi politiki 1935–1945 gg.*, p. 182.

93. Mirowicz, "Edward Rydz-Śmigły," p. 198. Repeated to Germany's ambassador Moltke on 25 November: ibid., p. 201.

94. Quoted from the archives of the French Foreign Ministry: A. Lacroix-Riz, "Polen in der aussenpolitischen Strategie Frankreichs (Oktober 1938–August 1939)", *Polen und wir*, No. 3, 2014, pp. 11–17.

95. Quoted in A. Misyuk (Andrzej Misiuk), *Spetssluzhby Pol'shi, Sovetskoi Rossii i Germanii. Organizatsionnaya struktura pol'skikh spetssluzhb i ikh razvedyvatel'naya i kontrrazvedyvatel'naya deyatel'nost' v 1918–1939 godakh* (Moscow: Kraft, 2012), p. 142.

96. The precise words chosen by Yezhov: M. Jansen and N. Petrov, *Stalin's Loyal Executioner: People's Commissar Nikolai Ezhov, 1895–1940* (Stanford: Hoover Institution Press, 2002), p. 95.

97. *The History of "The Times"*, Vol. 4, (London: *The Times*, 1952), Part 2: 1921–1948, pp. 890–891.

98. "Iz protokola No. 23", 8 March 1935: *Politburo TsK RKP(b)-VKP(b) i Evropa. Resheniya "Osoboi papki" 1923–1939*, doc. 221.

99. "Notes of Anglo-German Conversations, held at the Chancellor's Palace, Berlin, on March 25 and 26, 1935": UK. London. National Archives, CP 69 (35).

100. Paravicini (London) to Motta (Bern), 28 March 1935: *Documents diplomatiques suisses, 1848–1945*, Vol. 11, ed. J.-C. Favez et al. (Bern: Benteli, 1989), doc. 107.

101. Record of a conversation between Stalin and Molotov with Lord Privy Seal Eden, 29 March 1935: *Dokumenty vneshnei politiki SSSR*, Vol. 18, ed. A. Gromyko et al. (Moscow: Politizdat, 1973), doc. 148.

102. Minute by Sargent, 1 April 1935: *Documents on British Foreign Policy 1919–1939*, 2nd Series, Vol. 12, doc. 678.

103. "Notes of Anglo–German Conversations": UK. London. National Archives, CP 69 (35).

104. Memorandum by Sargent on the proposed Eastern Pact, 28 January 1935: *Documents on British Foreign Policy*, 2nd Series, Vol. 12, doc. 380.

105. Memorandum on Russia's probable attitude towards a 'General Settlement' with Germany, and the Proposed Air Agreement, 7 February 1935: ibid., doc. 428

106. Minute dated 2 January 1936, quoted in P. Neville, "A Prophet Scorned? Ralph Wigram, the Foreign Office and the German Threat, 1933–36", *Journal of Contemporary History*, Vol. 40, No. 1, January 2005, p. 45.

107. Sargent, "Action on the Stresa Resolution, more particularly with regard to Germany", 24 April 1935: FO 371/18843, quoted in K. Neilson, "Orme Sargent, Appeasement and British Policy in Europe, 1933–39", *Twentieth Century British History*, Vol. 21, No. 1, January 2010, pp. 1–28, footnote 50 (section iv).

108. Chilston (Moscow) to Hoare (London), 22 June 1935: UK. London. National Archives, FO 371/19457.

109. End of November, 1937, Stalin, Molotov and Kaganovich: Russia. Moscow. Yeltsin Presidential Library, online, *Vtoraya mirovaya voina v arkhyvnikh dokumentakh*. RGASPI f. 558, op. 11, d. 390, photocopy: prlib.ru.

110. *Izvestiya* and *Le Temps*, 17 May 1935.

111. "Stenogramme. Zum Protokoll Nr. 86 des Präsidiums des EKKI vom. 27. mai 1935": Russia. Moscow. RGASPI, Arkhiv Kominterna, f. 495, op. 2, d. 228.

112. "Les Bolcheviks défendent la paix", *l'Humanité*, 18 May 1935.

113. This is what France's ambassador to the United States, Paul Claudel, told Secretary of State Stimson: entry, 9 October 1931: USA. New Haven. Yale University Library, Stimson diaries, Vol. 17, p. 114.

114. *Inprecorr*, 11 January 1936.

115. J. Duclos, "Réponses aux questions posées par les journalistes, à la Mutualité", *Cahiers du Bolchévisme*, Nos 8–9, 15 May 1936, p. 496.

116. Colonel G. H. Rogers was technically designated "War Office" when a member of the Interdepartmental Committee on Eastern Unrest, restricted to the most senior officials from relevant departments, in 1926. He was, however, listed next to the head of the Security Service (MI5), Colonel Sir Vernon Kell, also listed as "War Office". The Secret Intelligence Service (MI6) was listed separately: UK. London. National Archives, FO 371/11678.

117. Dated not later than 31 May 1935: Russia. Moscow. Yeltsin Presidential Library. *Vtoraya mirovaya voina v arkhyvnikh dokumentakh*. InO GUGB, ASVR l. 140–142, photocopy: prlib.ru.

118. Bingham (London) to Roosevelt (Washington DC), 28 June 1935: USA. Hyde Park. Franklin D. Roosevelt Library and Archive, PSF, Great Britain, Robert W. Bingham, Box 37.

Chapter 7. Italy Breaks Out

1. Quoted in R. De Felice, *Mussolini il duce. 1. Gli anni del consenso 1929–1936* (Turin: Einaudi, 1974), p. 165.

2. January 1927, quoted in Gilbert, *Winston S. Churchill*, Vol. 5, p. 226.

3. L. Longo, *L'attività degli addetti militari italiani all'estero fra le due guerre mondiali (1919–1939)* (Rome: Stato Maggiore dell'Esercito, Ufficio storico, 1999), p. 373.

4. The work of former fascist Roberto Vivarelli is enlightening in this respect: *Storia delle origini del fascismo*, Vol. 1 (Bologna: Il Mulino, 1991).

5. G. Megaro, *Mussolini in the Making* (London: Allen and Unwin, 1938), p. 293.

6. Baroni (Berlin) to Grandi (Rome), 21 January 1932: *I documenti diplomatici italiani*, 7th Series, Vol. 11, ed. G. Carocci (Rome: Istituto Poligrafico dello Stato, 1981), doc. 176.

7. Cerruti (Berlin) to Mussolini (Rome), 8 March 1933: *I documenti diplomatici italiani*, 7th Series, Vol. 13, ed. G. Carocci (Rome: Istituto Poligrafico dello Stato, 1989), doc. 182. The bust atop a column can be seen in the photograph opposite p. 374 of Ullrich, *Hitler*.

8. E. Corradini, *Il nazionalismo italiano* (Milan: Treves, 1914), pp. 67–68.

9. Quoted by R. De Felice in *Mussolini il duce. 2. Lo Stato totalitario 1936–1940* (Turin: Einaudi, 1981), pp. 360–361.

10. Motta (Bern) to Wagnière (Rome), 21 November 1933: *Documents diplomatiques suisses*, Vol. 10, doc. 358.

11. "Il problema italiano", *Corriere Diplomatico e Consolare*, 20 June 1932.

12. C. Stannage, "The East Fulham By-Election, 25 October 1933", *The Historical Journal*, Vol. 14, No. 1, March 1971, pp. 165–200.

13. 13 January 1935: UK. London. National Archives, FO 371/19452.

14. G. Rochat, *Militari e politici nella preparazione della campagna d'Etiopia. Studio e documenti 1932–1936* (Milan: Angeli, 1971), p. 26.

15. Ibid., appendix, doc. 7.

16. Haslam, *Soviet Union and the Struggle*, p. 60.

17. John Cudahy (London) to President Roosevelt (Washington DC), 11 October 1935: USA. Hyde Park. Franklin D. Roosevelt Library and Archive, PSF, Poland, Box 46.

18. A. Rowse, *Appeasement: A Study in Political Decline 1933–1939* (New York: Norton, 1963), p. 26.

19. Anthony Eden, Lord Privy Seal, notes, 7 April 1935: *Documents on British Foreign Policy 1919–1939*, 2nd Series, Vol. 12, doc. 701.

20. Rowse, *Appeasement*, p. 28 (original emphasis).

21. Amery to Smuts, 22 June 1936: UK. Cambridge. Churchill College Archives, Leo Amery Papers, AMEL 2/1/26.

22. "HOLY SEE. Annual Report, 1935", 9 January 1936: *Anglo–Vatican Relations, 1914–1939: Confidential Annual Reports of the British Ministers to the Holy See*, ed. T. Hachey (Boston, Mass.: G. K. Hall, 1972), p. 319.

23. Ibid., p. 311.

24. Ibid., p. 322.

25. A. Khormach, *SSSR–Italiya, 1924–1939 gg. (Diplomaticheskie i ekonomicheskie otnosheniya)* (Moscow: Institute of Russian History, RAN, 1995), p. 136; *Corriere della Sera*, 13 January 2016.

26. *Documenti diplomatici italiani*, 7th Series, Vol. 14, doc. 141.

27. Attolico (Moscow) to Rome. 15 August 1933: Italy. Rome. Ministero degli Affari Esteri, Archivio Storico Diplomatico: Affari Politici 1931–35: l'URSS, Busta N. 11, 1933. Rapporti Italia–URSS, 1.7.

28. Telegram from Rome to Attolico (Moscow), 12 September 1933: ibid.

29. Address to the presidium of Comintern's executive committee, 23 March 1936: Russia. Moscow. RGASPI, Arkhiv Kominterna, f. 495, op. 2, d. 238.

30. From the archives, quoted in Alekseev, *"Vernyi Vam Ramzai"*, pp. 104–105.

31. Bülow-Schwante (Berlin) to Hassell (Rome), 15 November 1935: UK. London. National Archives, GFM 33/3108/8039. In the German original.

32. Hassell (Rome) to Bülow (Berlin), 12 December 1935: ibid.

33. Bülow to Himmler, 11 January 1936: ibid.

34. S. Pelagalli, *Il generale Efisio Marras, addetto militare a Berlino (1936–1943)* (Rome: Stato Maggiore dell'Esercito, Ufficio storico, 1994), p. 14.

35. A copy was found in the Russian "trophy archive" of documents seized by the Red Army in 1945. P. Bernhard, "Der Beginn eine Fascistischen Interpol? Das deutsch-italienische Polizeiabkommen von 1936 und die Zusammenarbeit der faschistischen Diktaturen im Europa der Zwischenkriegzeit". *Themenportal Europäische Geschichte. Clio-online,* January 2010, https://www.europa.clio-online.de/essay/id/fdae-1535.

36. G. Leto, *OVRA: fascismo—antifascismo* (Rocca San Casciano: Cappelli, 1952), p. 162. Bocchini nicknamed Himmler "the laughing hyena".

37. V. Perna, *Galeazzo Ciano, operazione Polonia. Le relazione diplomatiche italo–polacche degli anni Trenta 1936–1939* (Milan: Lunk, 1999), pp. 39–40. However, Perna picks up the threads of Italo–Polish relations just after Italy has already effectively conceded to Germany on Austria, 11 July 1936.

38. The Italian ambassador to the Holy See, briefing Secretary of State Pacelli, 10 July 1936: M. Casella, ed., *Gli ambasciatori d'Italia presso la Santa Sede dal 1929 al 1943* (Galatina: Congedo, 2009), p. 198.

39. Krestinsky (Moscow) to Shtein (Rome), 17 July 1936: *Dokumenty vneshnei politiki SSSR,* Vol. 19, ed. A. Gromyko et al. (Moscow: Politizdat, 1974), doc. 223.

40. T. de Vergottini, "Fulvio Suvich e la difesa dell'independenza austriaca", *Rivista di Studi Politici Internazionali,* Vol. 60, No. 2 (238), April–June 1993, p. 260.

41. Quoted in ibid., p. 268, footnote 19.

42. Quoted in Neville, "A Prophet Scorned?", p. 43.

43. V. Kondrashov, *Voennye razvedki vo Vtoroi Mirovoi Voine* (Moscow: Kuchkovo pole, 2014), pp. 129–130. Some of the sources, not listed, come from intelligence agency archives in Russia.

44. Haslam, *Vices of Integrity,* p. 60.

45. Ibid.

46. At Wigram's suggestion, in January Vansittart obtained this analysis from the chiefs of staff just before events supervened: Neville, "A Prophet Scorned?", p. 45.

47. Committee of Imperial Defence. Imperial Conference, 1937. "Review of Imperial Defence by the Chiefs of Staff Sub-Committee, 289th meeting, 25 February 1937": UK. London. National Archives, CID 1305-B, also COS 560.

48. Amery to Beneš, 17 November 1933: UK. Cambridge. Churchill College Archives, Leo Amery Papers, AMEL 2/1/26.

49. Amery to Bardoux: ibid.

50. *La Victoire,* June 1931.

51. *Memoirs of Lord Gladwyn,* p. 55. Jebb wrote this from his notes composed at the time of these events. These notes are not to be found, however, in the Churchill College archive where his papers have been deposited.

52. Address to the Comintern's executive presidium, given on 25 March 1936: Russia. Moscow. RGASPI, Arkhiv Kominterna, f. 495, op. 2, d. 240.

53. "Materialy k Protokolu No. 10. Zasedaniya Prezidiuma IKKI", 1 April 1936: Russia. Moscow. RGASPI, Arkhiv Kominterna, f. 495, op. 2, d. 243.

Chapter 8. The Paradox of the Popular Front

1. Moscow, 21 July 1935: *Komintern i ideya mirovoi revolyutsii*, doc. 216.

2. The term "new orientation" was also used: Dimitrov, addressing a meeting of the Comintern executive's presidium, 23 March 1936: "Protokol No. 8 i stenogramma zasedaniya Prezidiuma IKKI ot 23 marta 1936 g.": Russia. Moscow. RGASPI, Arkhiv Kominterna, f. 495, op. 2, d. 238.

3. "Protokol No. 16 i stenogramma zasedaniya Prezidiuma IKKI ot 3 fevralya 1937": Russia. Moscow. RGASPI, Arkhiv Kominterna, f. 495, op. 2, d. 255.

4. Hinsley and Simkins, *British Intelligence*, Vol. 4, p. 18.

5. Address to the presidium of Comintern's executive committee, 23 March 1936: Russia. Moscow. RGASPI, Arkhiv Kominterna, f. 495, op. 2, d. 238.

6. *The Economist*, 15 July 1933.

7. Editorial, "M. Blum Faces a Storm", *The Times*, 5 June 1936.

8. A. Zhamaletdinova et al., *Zabastovochnaya bor'ba trudyashchikhsya konets XIXv.–70-e gody XXv. (Statistika)* (Moscow: Nauka, 1980), p. 173.

9. "Since 1931 the political character of strikes has not ceased to spread": comment by Gaston Monmousseau of the CGTU, 17 February 1934: "Procès-verbal de la réunion du Secrétariat du CEIC", No. 65: Russia. Moscow. RGASPI, Arkhiv Kominterna, f. 495, op. 2, d. 209.

10. Mussolini (Rome) to Preziosi (Vienna), 11 February 1934: *Documenti diplomatici italiani*, 7th Series, Vol. 14, doc. 683.

11. Report on the situation in France by former leader of the CGTU Gaston Monmousseau: "Stenogramme zum Protokoll Nr. 65 des Präsidiums des EKKI am 17. Febr. 1934": Russia. Moscow. RGASPI, Arkhiv Kominterna, f. 495, op. 2, d. 209.

12. Letter to Pollitt, 6 March 1934: "Procès-verbal 360. Commission politique du IKKI": ibid., f. 495, op. 4, d. 280.

13. Quoted from the Vatican Secret Archive in Klieber, "Die moralische und politische Schützenhilfe", p. 533.

14. Ibid., p. 552.

15. Selby (Vienna) to Simon (London), 17 February 1934: *Documents on British Foreign Policy 1919–1939*, 2nd Series, Vol. 6, doc. 293.

16. Mussolini (Rome) to Preziosi (Vienna), 11 February 1934: *Documenti diplomatici italiani*, 7th Series, Vol. 14, doc. 683.

17. Quoted in Klieber, 'Die moralische und politische Schützenhilfe", p. 562.

18. Ibid., p. 563.

19. Addressing the presidium of Comintern's executive committee, 17 February 1934: "Protokoll Nr. 65 der Sitzung des Präsidiums des EKKI am. 17 Februar 1934": Russia. Moscow. RGASPI, Arkhiv Kominterna, f. 495, op. 2, d. 209.

20. Ibid.

21. Dimitrov, *Diary*, p. 16.

22. Ibid., p. 24.

23. E. Fischer, *An Opposing Man* (London: Allen Lane, 1974), p. 263.

24. Entry, 20 May 1934: Dimitrov, *Diary*, p. 22.

25. Entry, 7 April 1934: ibid., p. 13.

26. Russia. Moscow. RGASPI, Arkhiv Kominterna, f. 495, op. 20, d. 17.

27. For Dimitrov's fear of Pyatnitsky: "Record of an interview with A. G. Krytov, 2 June 1988": USA. Stanford. Hoover Institution, Firsov Papers, Box 43.

28. "Tsentral'nomu komitetu KP Frantsii", drafted on 9 June and approved by summary vote after amendment a day later: Russia. Moscow. RGASPI, Arkhiv Kominterna, f. 495, op. 4, d. 294.

29. Manuilsky's speech at a meeting of a committee of Comintern's executive preparing for the seventh congress, 14 June 1934: *Komintern protiv fashizma*, doc. 88.

30. M. Thorez, "L'organisation du front unique de lutte", *Cahiers du Bolchévisme*, No. 18, 1 July 1934, pp. 773–774 (original emphasis).

31. "Protokoll (A) Nr. 386 der Sitzung der Politkommission des Politisches Sekretariat am 4.vii.1934": Russia. Moscow. RGASPI, Arkhiv Kominterna, f. 495, op. 4, d. 297.

32. Thorez, "L'organisation du front unique de lutte", pp. 773–774.

33. "Oprosom chlenov Politburo it 4.xi.34. Iz protokol No. 13 (Osobyi No) reshenii Politburo TsK VKP(b), 26 avgusta–14 sentyabrya 1934 g.": *Politburo TsK RKP(b)-VKP(b) i Komintern, 1919-1943*, doc. 443.

34. Dimitrov to Stalin, 6 October 1934: Russia. Moscow. RGASPI, Arkhiv Kominterna, f. 495, op. 73, d. 1. A copy can be found in the Firsov Papers at the Hoover Institution, Box 30, vol. 4.

35. Cited by F. Firsov, *Sekretnye kody istorii Kominterna 1919–1943* (Moscow: AIRO-XXI, 2007), p. 175.

36. Comintern (Moscow) to PCF (Paris), 16 September 1934: UK. London. National Archives, HW 17/13.

37. "Diskussiya po peredovoi v 'KI', posvyashennoi podgotovke v diskussii v svyazi s Up-m kongressom KI Zasedanie Politkomissii IKKI, 27/9/34": Russia. Moscow. RGASPI, Arkhiv Kominterna, f. 495, op. 4, d. 312.

38. Comintern (Moscow) to PCF (Paris), 3 October 1934: UK. London. National Archives, HW, 17/13.

39. Much of the detail is still missing. For the Daladier initiative: "24 octobre 1934: la naissance du Front populaire à Nantes", *l'Humanité*, 24 October 2014. For the decision of 19 October 1934: *Komintern i ideya mirovoi revolyutsii*, doc. 209. For the letter from the IKKI political secretariat to the CC of the PCF, 20 October 1934: *Komintern protiv fashizma*, doc. 96.

40. J. Duclos, "À la mémoire de mon ami Clément", *Cahiers de l'Institut Maurice Thorez*, No. 13, 1969, pp. 120–124; G. Cerreti, *Con Togliatti e Thorez. Quarant'anni di lotte politiche* (Milan: Feltrinelli, 1973), pp. 168–169; J. Haslam, "The Comintern and the Origins of the Popular Front, 1934–1935", *The Historical Journal*, Vol. 22, No. 3, September 1979, pp. 673–691.

41. Quoted in Firsov, *Sekretnye kody*, p. 176.

42. Quoted in Haslam, *Soviet Union and the Struggle*, p. 58.

43. Thorez (Paris) to Comintern secretariat (Moscow), 3 December 1934: *Communisme*, Nos 67–68, 2001, p. 93.

44. Clément (Paris) to Michel (Moscow), 3 December 1934: UK. London. National Archives, HW 17/13.

45. B. Leibzon and K. Shirinya, *Povorot v politike Kominterna* (Moscow: Mysl', 1975), p. 110.

46. Quoted by Central Committee member N. Pospielov, director of the Institute of Marxism-Leninism, in "Les Conclusions du VIIe Congrès de l'Internationale Communiste. A la lumière de l'experience du Front Populaire en France et le rôle de Georges Dimitrov", *Cahiers de l'Institut Maurice Thorez*, 1966–67, Nos 3–4, p. 136.

47. Rothermere to Churchill, 13 May 1935: *The Churchill Documents*, Vol. 12, ed. M. Gilbert (London: Heinemann, 1981), p. 1171.

48. "Sténographie des séances du sécretariat des pays romains du CEIC (sécretariat de Manouilski): rapport de Duclos sur la situation en France. Sécretariat Roman, Réunion du 5/1/36": Russia. Moscow. RGASPI, Arkhiv Kominterna, f. 495, op. 10, d. 1.

49. Nuncio in Rome, Francesco Borgongini Duca, to Secretary of State Pacelli (Vatican), 17 December 1935: *L'archivio della nunziatura apostolica*, p. 140.

50. 19 May 1936: "Sténogramme de la séance du Secrétariat du CEIC du 19 mai 1936. Procès-verbal": Russia. Moscow. RGASPI, Arkhiv Kominterna, f. 495, op. 11, d. 1089.

51. *Inprecorr*, 18 July 1936.

52. Ibid., 30 January 1937. Readership of the daily, *l'Humanité*, was much greater and stood at 420,000.

53. Dimitrov, 11 May 1936: "Procès-verbal no. 41 de la réunion du Secrétariat du CEIC": Russia. Moscow. RGASPI, Arkhiv Kominterna, f. 495, op. 18, d. 1086.

54. Agreed on 10 June 1936, though the directive was issued only on 20 July.

55. Quoted in G. Vidal, *La Grande Illusion? Le Parti communiste français et la Défense nationale à l'époque du Front populaire (1934–1939)* (Lyon: Presses Universitaires de Lyon, 2006), pp. 210–211.

56. Decision of the secretariat on the French question, 23 May 1936: Russia. Moscow. RGASPI, Arkhiv Kominterna, f. 495, op. 20, d. 573.

57. Resolution of 25 May 1936: *Inprecorr*, 6 June 1936.

58. A. Mahouy, "Le conflit Citroën", *La Révolution prolétarienne*, 10 June 1936.

59. "Obshchee polozhenie vo Frantsii. Otchet o plenarnom zasedanie TsK KPF, Protokol No. 12, Prezidium IKKI", 10 June 1936: Russia. Moscow. RGASPI, Arkhiv Kominterna, f. 495, op. 2, d. 246.

60. S. Galois [nom de plume], "La vie et la grève des ouvrières métallos?", *La Révolution prolétarienne*, 10 June 1936.

61. Briefing by Racamond and Mauvais, 15 May 1933: "Stenogramma zasedaniya frantsuzskoi komissii IKKI": Russia. Moscow. RGASPI, Arkhiv Kominterna, f. 495, op. 55, d. 27.

62. Quoted from the archives in G. Vidal, "L'institution militaire et la peur d'une insurrection communiste en 1936", *Communisme*, No. 69, 2002, p. 101.

63. *Le Populaire*, 27 May 1936.

64. *La Voix du Peuple*, 4th Series, No. 188, 1936, p. 302.

65. *l'Humanité*, 28 May 1936.

66. "Discipline Parlementaire et nationale", *Le Temps*, 1 June 1936.

67. "Obshchee polozhenie vo Frantsii. Otchet o plenarnom zasedanie TsK KPF, Protokol No. 12, Prezidium IKKI", 10 June 1936: Russia. Moscow. RGASPI. Arkhiv Kominterna, f. 495, op. 2, d. 246.

68. "Contrat Collectif", *Le Temps*, 2 June 1936.

69. Cerruti (Paris) to Mussolini (Rome), 29 May 1936: MAE, *I documenti diplomatici italiani*, 8th Series, Vol. 4, ed. R. De Felice and P. Pastorelli (Rome: Istituto Poligrafico dello Stato, 1993), doc. 131.

70. Quoted by G. Vidal, *L'Armée française et l'ennemi intérieur 1917–1939. Enjeux stratégique et culture politique* (Rennes: Universitaire de Rennes, 2015), p. 105.

71. Comment on 9 June: Vidal, "L'institution militaire", p. 103.

72. Marty, at the Comintern executive presidium, 10 June 1936: Russia. Moscow. RGASPI, Arkhiv Kominterna, f. 495, op. 2, d. 246.

73. *Inprecorr*, 20 June 1936.

74. Vidal, "L'institution militaire", p. 106.

75. "Frantsuzskaya revolyutsiya nachalas'", *Byulleten' oppozitsii*, No. 51, July–August 1936, p. 4.

76. Dunant (Paris) to Motta (Bern), 24 June 1936: *Documents diplomatiques suisses, 1848–1945*, Vol. 11, doc. 251.

77. Cerruti (London) to Ciano (Rome), 9 July 1936: *Documenti diplomatici italiani*, 8th Series, Vol. 4, doc. 490.

78. Neilson, "Orme Sargent", pp. 7–13.

79. Minute dated 19 March, on Clerk (Paris) to Foreign Office, 18 March 1936: UK. London. National Archives, FO 371/19894.

80. Letter to A. F., 23 May 1936: T. Jones, *A Diary with Letters 1931–1950* (London: Oxford University Press, 1954), p. 209.

81. Duke of Alba (London) to José Fernández Villaverde (Salamanca), 2 July 1937: Spain. Madrid. Archivo General de la Administración (Madrid), 54/6700, No. 12. Alba (for more, see below) met Earl Baldwin at a long "week-end" in a country house.

82. Entry, 26 March 1935: Eden's diary, quoted in D. Dutton, "Simon and Eden at the Foreign Office, 1931–1935", *Review of International Studies*, Vol. 20, No. 1, January 1994, p. 50.

83. G. Niedhart, *Grossbritannien und die Sowjetunion 1934–1939* (Munich: Fink, 1972), p. 332.

84. Letter to Churchill, 9 May 1936: I. Kershaw, *Making Friends with Hitler: Lord Londonderry and Britain's Road to War* (London: Allen Lane, 2004), p. 155.

85. Sargent to Churchill, 13 November 1934 and enclosure: M. Gilbert, ed., *Winston S. Churchill*, Vol. 5 *Companion*, Part 2, *Documents: The Wilderness Years, 1929–1935* (London: Heinemann, 1981) pp. 920–922.

86. Quoted in Haslam, *Soviet Union and the Struggle*, p. 47.

87. Ibid., pp. 335–336.

88. Quoted by D. Little, "Red Scare 1936: Anti-Bolshevism and the Origins of British Non-Intervention in the Spanish Civil War", *Journal of Contemporary History*, Vol. 23, No. 2, April 1988, p. 297.

89. Marty at the Comintern executive committee, 10 June 1936: Russia. Moscow. RGASPI, Arkhiv Kominterna, f. 495, op. 2, d. 246.

90. "Protokol zasedaniya Prezidiuma IKKI", 10 June 1936: ibid.

91. Procès-verbal, 4 June 1936: *Cahiers du Bolchévisme*, No. 10–11, 15 June 1936, pp. 753–756.

92. H. de Torrenté (Paris) to Motta (Bern), 10 September 1936: *Documents diplomatiques suisses*, Vol. 11, doc. 291 (original emphasis).

93. M. Cachin, "Nekotorye nashi dostizheniya", *Kommunisticheskii Internatsional*, No. 2, February 1937.

94. O'Brien (Paris) to Walshe (Dublin), 6 July 1936: *Documents on Irish Foreign Policy*, Vol. 4, ed. C. Crowe (Dublin: Royal Irish Academy, 2004), doc. 350.

95. Dunant (Paris) to Motta (Bern), 16 July 1936: *Documents diplomatiques suisses*, Vol. 11, doc. 267.

96. Bullitt (Paris) to Roosevelt (Washington DC), 8 December 1936: USA. Hyde Park. Franklin D. Roosevelt Library and Archive, PSF, France, William C. Bullitt, 1936, Box 20.

97. Leader, *The Times*, 6 July 1936.

98. Arone (Moscow) to Mussolini (Rome), 11 June 1936: *Documenti diplomatici italiani*, 8th Series, Vol. 4, doc. 237. The Italians, unusually, retained their diplomats in Moscow much longer than did others. Despite the differences between fascist Italy and Stalinist Russia, the Italians were able to cultivate their Soviet counterparts with relative ease; though the brutal mistreatment of Gramsci, imprisoned by the fascist authorities, did create recurrent tension.

99. "Décisions du Secrétariat", No. 146, 29 June 1936: France. Université de Bourgogne, *Fonds de la direction du Parti Communiste Français*: https://pandor.u-bourgogne.fr.

100. Dunant (Paris) to Motta (Bern), 20 July 1936: *Documents diplomatiques suisses*, Vol. 11, doc. 268.

101. Points 6 and 7 of the resolution on Dimitrov's speech, 20 August 1935: *Komintern i ideya mirovoi revolyutsii*, doc. 222.

102. J. Duclos, "Réponses aux questions posés par les journalistes, à la Mutualité", *Cahiers du Bolchévisme*, Nos 8–9, 15 May 1936, pp. 496 and 500.

103. This is what General Gamelin's secretary, Petiban, told the Italian military attaché, on 15 June: Barbasetti (Paris) to Cerruti (Paris), 16 June 1936: *Documenti diplomatici italiani*, 8th Series, Vol. 4, doc. 294.

104. Vidal, "L'institution militaire", p. 101.

105. Bullitt (Paris) to Roosevelt (Washington DC), 8 December 1936: USA. Hyde Park. Franklin D. Roosevelt Library and Archive, PSF, 1933–1945, Box 30. France: William C. Bullitt, 1936.

106. For Morel: A.-A. Inquimbert, *Un officier français dans la guerre d'Espagne. Carrière et écrits d'Henri Morel* (Rennes: Presses Universitaires de Rennes, 2009), ch. 6.

Chapter 9. Spain and the Schism of Europe

1. "Democracy and the Dictators", *The Economist*, 26 September 1936.

2. Exchange with France's ambassador, 29 June 1936: Ciano, ed., *L'Europa verso la catastrofe*, p. 28.

3. *Memoirs of Lord Gladwyn*, p. 59.

4. "Germany and the Spanish Civil War", 24 August 1936: USA. College Park. National Archives, US Military Intelligence, Germany, 002928-003-0001.

5. Comintern (Moscow) to PCE (Madrid), 22 September 1934: UK. London. National Archives, HW 17/26.

6. Addressing a session of the presidium of Comintern's executive committee, 25 January 1935: *Komintern i ideya mirovoi revolyutsii*, doc. 213.

7. Comintern (Moscow) to PCE (Madrid), 7 October 1934: UK. London. National Archives, HW 17/26.

8. Report on the uprising: "Stenogramma Zasedaniya Romanskii Lendersekretariat s ispanskimi tovarishchami", 1 December 1934: Russia. Moscow. RGASPI, Arkhiv Kominterna, f. 495, op. 32, d. 154.

9. Tedeschini (Madrid) to Pacelli (Vatican), 17 October 1934: *La II República y la Guerra Civil en el Archivo Secreto Vaticano*, ed. V. Cárcel Ortí, Vol. 3: *Documentos de los años 1933 y 1934* (Madrid: Biblioteca de Autores Cristianos, 2014), doc. 1,398.

10. J. Gil Robles, *No fue posible la paz* (Barcelona: Ediciones Ariel, 1968), p. 669.

11. Addressing the presidium of Comintern's executive committee, 25 January 1935: *Komintern i ideya mirovoi revolyutsii*, doc. 213.

12. Alba (London) to José Fernández de Villaverde (Burgos), 20 February 1939: Spain. Madrid. Archivo General de la Administración, 54/6700.

13. USA. Stanford. Hoover Institution, Firsov Papers, Box 32.

14. Codovilla (Madrid) to Manuilsky (Moscow), 18 February 1936: ibid., Box 37.

15. Danielsson (Madrid) to Stockholm, 17 February 1936: Sweden. Stockholm. Sveriges Riksarkivet, Utrikesdepartementet, 1920 års dossiersystem, HP 1, C, 90, Spansk Politik.

16. "HOLY SEE. Annual Report, 1936", 1 January 1937: *Anglo–Vatican Relations*, p. 361.

17. Despatch 7874, Tedeschini (Madrid) to Pacelli (Vatican), 1 March 1936: *La II República y la Guerra Civil en el Archivo Secreto Vaticano*, Vol. 4: *Documentos de los años 1935 y 1936* (Madrid: Biblioteca de Autores Cristianos, 2016), doc. 1,575.

18. "HOLY SEE. Annual Report, 1936", *Anglo–Vatican Relations*, p. 361. Further rumours of an impending coup reached the Swedish embassy: Danielsson (Madrid) to Sandler (Stockholm), 17 February 1936: Sweden. Stockholm. Sveriges Riksarkivet, Utrikesdepartementet, 1920 års dossiersystem, HP 1, C, 91.

19. Despatch 7875: Tedeschini (Madrid) to Pacelli (Vatican), 3 March 1936: *La II República y la Guerra Civil*, Vol. 4, doc. 1,576.

20. Despatch 7929: Tedeschini (Madrid) to Pacelli (Vatican), 27 March 1936: ibid., doc. 1,591.

21. Danielsson (Madrid) to Sandler (Stockholm), 4 March 1936: Sweden. Stockholm. Sveriges Riksarkivet, Utrikesdepartementet, 1920 års dossiersystem, HP 1, C, 129.

22. M. Tagüeña Lacorte, *Testimonio de dos guerras* (Barcelona: Planeta, 1978), p. 71. Tagüeña fled to the Soviet Union in 1939 along with many other leading Party members after fighting in the Civil War.

23. For the statistics from authoritative sources: M. Álvarez Tardío and R. Villa García, "El impacto de la violencia anticlerical en la primavera de 1936 y la respuesta des las autoridades", *Hispania Sacra*, Vol. 65, No. 132, July–December 2013, pp. 721–762.

24. Pacelli's notes of the meeting, 4 May 1936: *La II Republica y la Guerra Civil*, Vol. 4, doc. 1,614.

25. Tagüeña Lacorte, *Testimonio de dos guerras*, p. 68.

26. Kerney (Madrid) to Walshe (Dublin), 17 April 1936: *Documents on Irish Foreign Policy*, Vol. 4, doc. 332.

27. Comintern (Moscow) to the PCE (Madrid), 26 February 1936: UK. London. National Archives, HW 17/26. The Government Code and Cypher School (GCCS) had, in the person of Major John Tiltman, been intercepting and attempting to decrypt Comintern communications at least from 1930, with little success until it obtained cribs from a Comintern employee recruited in Berlin in February 1933 by Foley, MI6 head of station. Soviet intelligence became aware of this in late August 1936, apparently from Soviet spy Donald Maclean at the Western Department in the Foreign Office. The spy was Johann Heinrich de Graff, a German Communist and an officer in the Fourth Directorate of the Red Army (military intelligence): Jeffery, *MI6*, pp. 267–271. Dimitrov was informed on 26 August 1936: Dimitrov, *Diary*, p. 26. The NKVD decided to create a parallel cipher department with a new communications system, while sending disinformation through compromised channels: *Politburo TsK RKP(b)–VKP(b) i Komintern, 1919–1943*, p. 731. Thus one should not rely on British decrypts after August 1936, though a spy at Communist headquarters in King Street made reading possible again in 1939.

28. "Gilbert" from Comintern held talks with him on 26 September 1935 and sent his record of the discussion to Togliatti and Gottwald in October: "Sekretariat sekretarya IKKI Erkoli": Russia. Moscow. RGASPI, Arkhiv Kominterna, f. 495, op. 12, d. 92.

29. André Marty, "Notes sur le PCE", 11 October 1936: Russia. Moscow. RGASPI, Arkhiv Kominterna, f. 495, op. 12, d. 92.

30. PCE (Madrid) to Comintern (Moscow), 4 March 1936: UK. London. National Archives, HW 17/26.

31. Comintern (Moscow) to PCE. (Madrid), 9 April 1936: ibid.

32. Quoted in Little, "Red Scare 1936".

33. Quoted in Jeffery, *MI6*, p. 285.

34. At a meeting of the secretariat, 5 June 1936: Russia. Moscow. RGASPI, Arkhiv Kominterna, f. 495, op. 18, d. 1095.

35. Jesús Hernández: "Sténogramme de la réunion du Présidium du CEIC du 22 mai 1936": ibid., f. 495, op. 2, d. 245. These figures contradict those claimed in January—50,348: PCE (Madrid) to Comintern (Moscow), 31 January 1936: UK. London. National Archives, HW 17/26. The latest numbers were the correct ones, as evidenced by sums given in September 1937 (see below).

36. Manuilsky, normally in charge of the PCE, was off sick: "Sténogramme de la réunion du Présidium du CEIC du 22 mai 1936": Russia. Moscow. RGASPI, Arkhiv Kominterna, f. 495, op. 2, d. 245.

37. Pedrazzi (Madrid) to Ciano (Rome), 30 June 1936: *Documenti diplomatici italiani*, 8th Series, Vol. 4, doc. 414.

38. Dimitrov, referring to his notes: "Protokoll (A) Nr. 74 der Sitzung des Sekretariats des EKKI am 18. September 1936": Russia. Moscow. RGASPI, Arkhiv Kominterna, f. 495, op. 18, d. 113.

39. "Postanovlenie po ispanskomu voprosu", 29 May 1936: Russia. Moscow. RGASPI, Arkhiv Kominterna, f. 495, op. 18, d. 1092.

40. Comintern (Moscow) to the PCE (Madrid), 15 June 1936: UK. London. National Archives, HW 17/26.

41. Comintern (Moscow) to the PCE (Madrid), 13 July 1936: UK. London. National Archives, HW 17/27.

42. Comintern (Moscow) to the PCE (Madrid), 17 July 1936: ibid..

43. De Rossi (Tangier) to Ciano (Rome), 16 July 1936: *Documenti diplomatici italiani*, 8th Series, Vol. 4, doc. 541.

44. Shtein (Rome) to Krestinsky (Moscow), 13 August 1936: *Dokumenty vneshnei politiki SSSR*, Vol. 19, p. 758.

45. Luccardi (Tangier) to Ministry of War (Rome), 20 July 1936: *Documenti diplomatici italiani*, 8th Series, Vol. 4, doc. 570.

46. Pedrazzi (Madrid) to Ciano (Rome), 18 July 1936: ibid., doc. 565.

47. Pedrazzi (San Sebastian) to Ciano (Rome), 20 July 1936: ibid., doc. 575.

48. Alfonso XIII to Mussolini, 20 July 1936: ibid., doc. 577.

49. Luccardi (Tangier) to Ministry of War (Rome), 21 July 1936: ibid., doc. 578.

50. Roatta (Rome) to Luccardi (Tangier), 21 July 1936: ibid., doc. 582; and ibid., 21 July 1936: ibid., doc. 583.

51. Luccardi (Tangier) to Ministry of War (Rome), 23 July 1936: ibid., doc. 596.

52. De Rossi (Tangier) to Ciano (Rome), 23 July 1936: ibid., doc. 599.

53. Cerruti (Paris) to Ciano (Rome), 22 July 1936: ibid., doc. 589.

54. Cerruti (Paris) to Ciano (Rome), 23 July 1936: ibid., doc. 598.

55. In conversation with the nuncio, Francesco Borgongini Duca, 7 February 1936: *L'archivio della nunziatura apostolica*, p. 141.

56. Reflections after a conversation with the Italian ambassador, 8 August 1936: Casella, ed., *Gli ambasciatori d'Italia presso la Santa Sede*, p. 201.

57. Togliatti, "Bericht über die Durchführung der Spanien-kampagne der Kommunistischen Partein", 14 September 1936: Russia. Moscow. RGASPI, Arkhiv Kominterna, f. 495, op. 12, d. 92.

58. Comintern to the PCE, 20 July 1936: UK. London. National Archives, HW 17/27; now also reprinted in *SSSR i grazhdanskaya voina v Ispanii: 1926–1939 gody*, ed. S. Kudryashov et al. (Moscow: Vestnik Arkhiva Prezidenta Rossiiskoi Federatsii, 2013), doc. 1. Other telegrams have been omitted, however.

59. Comintern (Moscow) to the PCE (Madrid), 20 July 1936: UK. London. National Archives, HW 17/27.

60. Comintern (Moscow) to the PCE (Madrid), 20 July 1936: ibid.

61. Comintern (Moscow) to the PCE (Madrid), 20 July 1936: ibid.

62. PCE (Madrid) to Comintern (Moscow), 20 July 1936: ibid.

63. "Protokoll (A) Nr. 74 der Sitzung des Secretariats des EKKI am 18. September 1936": Russia. Moscow. RGASPI, Arkhiv Kominterna, f. 495, op. 18, d. 113.

64. Ibid.

65. PCE (Madrid) to Comintern (Moscow), 21 July 1936: UK. London. National Archives, HW 17/27.

66. PCE (Madrid) to Comintern (Moscow), 22 and 23 July 1936: ibid.

67. Comintern (Moscow) to PCE (Madrid), 23 July 1936: ibid.

68. Fontanel (Madrid) to Bonna (Bern), 23 July 1936: *Documents diplomatiques suisses*, Vol. 11, doc. 270.

69. Fontanel (Madrid) to Bonna (Bern), 29 July 1936: ibid., doc. 271.

70. Text of the telegram and Stalin's annotation: *Politburo TsK RKP(b)–VKP(b) i Komintern, 1919–1943*, p. 740.

71. Comintern (Moscow) to PCE (Madrid), 25 July 1936: UK. London. National Archives, HW 17/26.

72. A. Rovighi and F. Stefani, *La partecipazione italiana alla guerra civile spagnola (1936–1939)*, Vol. 1 (Rome: Stato Maggiore dell'Esercito, Ufficio storico, 1992), pp. 63–64.

73. Comintern (Moscow) to PCE (Madrid), 28 July 1936: UK. London. National Archives, HW 17/26.

74. Togliatti, "Bericht über die Durchführung der Spanien-kampagne der Kommunistischen Parteien", 14 September 1936, Sekretariat sekretarya IKKI Erkoli: Russia. Moscow. RGASPI, Arkhiv Kominterna, f. 495, op. 12, d. 92.

75. Delbos (Quai d'Orsay) to Auriol (Ministry of Finance), 26 July 1936 and Delbos to embassies in European capitals, 27 July 1936: *Documents diplomatiques français, 1932–1939*, 2nd Series, Vol. 3, ed. P. Mandoul et al. (Brussels: PIE–Peter Lang, 2005), docs 33 and 36.

76. Ciano (Rome) to De Rossi (Tangier), 27 July 1936: *Documenti diplomatici italiani*, 8th Series, Vol. 4, doc. 630.

77. De Rossi (Tangier) to Ciano (Rome), 27 July 1936: ibid., doc. 632.

78. Italian Military Intelligence to the Foreign Ministry, 27 July 1936: ibid., doc. 634.

79. Ciano (Rome) to De Rossi (Tangier), 28 July 1936: ibid., doc. 638.

80. Rovighi and Stefani, *La partecipazione italiana alla guerra civile spagnola*, Vol. 1, p. 81.

81. François-Poncet (Berlin) to Delbos (Paris), 22 July 1936: *Documents diplomatiques français*, 2nd Series, Vol. 3, doc. 10.

82. Milan, 1 November 1936: Rovighi and Stefani, *La partecipazione italiana alla guerra civile spagnola*, Vol. 1, p. 49.

83. 5 August 1936: R. Rainero, *L'Italie de Mussolini et le régime fasciste de Métaxas en Grèce (1936–1940)* (Paris: Publisud, 2014), p. 78.

84. The conversations took place on 6 and 8 August: Charles-Roux (Vatican) to Delbos (Paris), 9 August 1936: *Documents diplomatiques français*, 2nd Series, Vol. 3, doc. 113.

85. Attolico (Berlin) to Ciano (Rome), 20 August 1936: *Documenti diplomatici italiani*, 8th Series, Vol. 4, doc. 762.

86. Baldwin's words: entry 27 July 1936, Jones, *Diary with Letters*, p. 231.

87. Vitetti (London) to Ciano (Rome), 29 July 1936: *Documenti diplomatici italiani*, 8th Series, Vol. 4, doc. 641. Amery also expressed anxiety lest French commitments to the Soviet Union lead France into war with Japan. But the Franco–Soviet pact was deliberately contrived to avoid any such ancillary obligation, as was the Franco–Russian treaty of 1893.

88. 22 November 1936: H. Channon, *"Chips": The Diaries of Sir Henry Channon*, ed. R. Rhodes James (London: Weidenfeld and Nicolson, 1967), p. 85. Indeed, the king's official biographer, telling of the impact of the First World War upon the king, also says, "The only other principle which influenced him to a comparable extent was his belief that communism presented the greatest threat to the peace and stability of Europe.": P. Ziegler, *King Edward VIII. The Official Biography* (London: Collins, 1990), p. 266.

89. Quoted in Forwood's obituary, *The Daily Telegraph*, 27 January 2001.

90. Vitetti (London) to Ciano (Rome), 9 August 1936: *Documenti diplomatici italiani*, 8th Series, Vol. 4, doc. 708.

91. Vitetti (London) to Ciano (Rome), 29 July 1936: ibid., doc. 642.

92. Wysocki (Rome) to Warsaw, 2 August 1936: *Polskie Dokumenty Dyplomatyczne 1936*, ed. S. Żerko (Warsaw: PISM, 2011), doc. 222.

93. Comintern (Moscow) to PCF (Paris), 29 July 1936: UK. London. National Archives, HW 17/14.

94. Comintern (Moscow) to PCF (Paris), 31 July 1936: ibid. Thorez was then in Moscow.

95. Haslam, *Soviet Union and the Struggle*, p. 111. For the instructions: closed letter to regional and district committees and national committees of the Party in the USSR from the CC VKP(b), 2 August 1936: *SSSR i grazhdanskaya voina*, doc. 6.

96. Comintern secretariat (Moscow) to Paris, 7 August 1936: UK. London. National Archives, HW 17/14.

97. Vitetti (London) to Ciano (Rome), 5 August 1936: *Documenti diplomatici italiani*, 8th Series, Vol. 4, doc. 678.

98. Quoted in M. Cowling, *The Impact of Hitler: British Politics and British Policy 1933–1940* (Cambridge: Cambridge University Press, 1975), p. 161.

99. Memorandum by Vansittart, 17 September 1936: *Documents on British Foreign Policy 1919–1939*, 2nd Series, Vol. 17, ed. W. Medlicott et al. (London: HMSO, 1979), doc. 200.

100. Daladier (War) to Delbos (Quai d'Orsay), 13 October 1936: *Documents diplomatiques français*, 2nd Series, Vol. 3, doc. 343.

101. Bossi (Barcelona) to Ciano (Rome), 5 August 1936: *Documenti diplomatici italiani*, 8th Series, Vol. 4, doc. 679.

102. C. Rosselli, *Oggi in Spagna, domani in Italia* (Paris: Edizioni di Giustizia e Libertà, 1938). This contains letters to his wife. Reissued at www.fondazionefeltrinelli.it.

103. L. Longo and C. Salinari, *Dal socialfascismo alla guerra di Spagna. Ricordi e riflessioni di un militante comunista* (Milan: Teti, 1976), pp. 184–185.

104. Longo ran the logistical operation for the formation of the International Brigades based at Albacete: ibid., p. 184.

105. Campaigning "against the reactionaries in France, demonstrating inadequate government action against the [fascist] leagues": "Décisions du Secrétariat du 20 juillet 1936, No. 149": France. Université de Bourgogne, *Fonds de la direction du Parti Communiste Français*: https://pandor.u-bourgogne.fr.

106. Gerő (Paris) to Comintern (Moscow), 3 August 1936: *SSSR i grazhdanskaya voina*, doc. 8.

107. Décisions du Secrétariat, 10 août 1936, No. 152: ibid. On Kol'tsov etc.: Haslam, *Soviet Union and the Struggle*, p. 108.

108. Marty to the PCF Politburo, 4 September 1936: Russia. RGASPI, Arkhiv Kominterna, f. 495, op. 74, d. 510. The behaviour of the French leadership was not that unusual. Pollitt had been treated discourteously by them earlier in the year when he had, perhaps naïvely, expected to be asked to speak at a major Party occasion.

109. "PCF Décisions du Bureau Politique", 21 September and 8 October 1936. France. Université de Bourgogne, *Fonds de la direction du Parti Communiste Français*: https://pandor.u-bourgogne.fr. Nothing was listed with respect to Spain.

110. Procès-verbal du Comité Central, 16 October 1936. France. Université de Bourgogne, *Fonds de la direction du Parti Communiste Français*: https://pandor.u-bourgogne.fr.

111. Díaz (Madrid) to Comintern (Moscow), 5, 7 August 1936: *SSSR i grazhdanskaya voina*, doc. 9.

112. Pedro from Paris, 3–4 August 1936: ibid., doc. 8.

113. PCF (Paris) to Comintern (Moscow), 7 August 1936: UK. London. National Archives, HW 17/14.

114. King (Barcelona) to Foreign Office, 13 October 1936: ibid., FO 371/20543.

115. Firsov, *Sekretnye Kody*, p. 198.

116. Rossi (Barcelona) to Ciano (Rome), 11 August 1936: *Documenti diplomatici italiani*, 8th Series, Vol. 4, doc. 714.

117. Memorandum to Stalin, 9 August 1945: *SSSR i grazhdanskaya voina*, doc. 10.

118. Ibid. docs 12–13.

119. *Arkhiv Kominterna*: USA. Stanford. Hoover Institution, Firsov Papers, Box 37.

120. Entry, 3 July 1936: UK. Cambridge. Churchill College Archives, Cadogan Diary, ACAD 1/4.

121. *Documents on British Foreign Policy 1919–1939*, 2nd Series, Vol. 17, doc. 84.

122. Bingham (London) to Roosevelt (Washington DC), 4 September 1936: USA. Hyde Park. Franklin D. Roosevelt Library and Archive, PSF, Great Britain, Robert W. Bingham, Box 37.

123. "Rezolutsiya sekretariata IKKI", 28 January 1936: Russia. Moscow. RGASPI, Arkhiv Kominterna, f. 495, op. 20, d. 468.

124. Quoted from Hankey's letters to his son: Cowling, *Impact of Hitler*, p. 161.

125. Wysocki (Rome) to Foreign Ministry (Warsaw), 2 August 1936: *Polskie Dokumenty Dyplomatyczne 1936*, doc. 222.

126. Szembek's record of the conversation, 14 August 1936: ibid., doc. 249.

127. "Germany and the Spanish Civil War", 24 August 1936: USA. College Park. National Archives, US Military Intelligence, Germany, 002928-003-0001.

128. Telegram sent on 2 September: quoted in Firsov, *Sekretnye kody*, p. 182.

129. Telegram received in Madrid from Díaz and Duclos, both evidently in Paris, sent on to Kaganovich in Moscow, 4 September 1936: *SSSR i grazhdanskaya voina*, doc. 22.

130. Letter dated 9 July 1942, quoted in extenso: C. Audry, *Léon Blum, ou la politique du Juste* (Paris: Julliard, 1955), pp. 126–127. The letter was written in response to criticism from the American left of Blum's policy during the Spanish Civil War.

131. Rovighi and Stefani, *La partecipazione italiana alla guerra civile spagnola*, Vol. 1, p. 65.

132. This is what Adler told the French Communists: PCF (Paris) to Moscow, 28 July 1936: UK. London. National Archives, HW 17/14.

133. Ehrenburg (Madrid) to Stalin (Moscow), 10 September 1936: *SSSR i grazhdanskaya voina*, doc. 28.

134. Rovighi and Stefani, *La partecipazione italiana alla guerra civile spagnola*, Vol. 1, doc. 6.

135. Mameli (Lisbon) to Ciano (Rome), 26 August 1938: *I documenti diplomatici italiani*, 8th Series, Vol. 9, ed. G Andrè (Rome: Istituto Poligrafico dello Stato, 2001), doc. 437.

136. Tuozzi (Lisbon) to Ciano (Rome), 7 August 1936: ibid., Vol. 4, doc. 694.

137. "Germany and the Spanish Civil War", 24 August 1936: USA. College Park. National Archives, US Military Intelligence, Germany, 002928-003-0001.

138. UK. London. National Archives: record of a conversation between Mounsey and Monteiro, 1 June 1936, "Note on the Portuguese attitude to the proposed Anglo–French–Soviet agreement", 5 June 1939: UK. London. National Archives, CP 131 (39).

139. Dodd (Lisbon) to Foreign Office (London), 14 August 1936: *Documents on British Foreign Policy 1919–1939*, 2nd Series, Vol. 17, doc. 90.

140. Rovighi and Stefani, *La partecipazione italiana alla guerra civile spagnola*, Vol. 1, pp. 81–82.

141. Sánchez (Lisbon) to Barcía (Madrid), 6 August 1936: A. Pedro Vicente, "O cerco à embaixada da República Espanhola em Lisboa (maio a outubro de 1936)", F. Rosas, ed., *Portugal e a Guerra Civil de Espanha* (Lisbon: Colibri, 1998), p. 59 (Apêndice Documental).

142. "Question of aid to the Spanish (poss[ible] organiz[ation] of an internat[ional] corps)." Entry dated 28 August 1936: Dimitrov, *Diary*, p. 27.

143. Winston to Clementine Churchill, 5 September: Gilbert, *Winston S. Churchill*, Vol. 5 *Companion*, p. 338.

144. Morton to Churchill, 16 October 1936: ibid., p. 366.

145. Haslam, *Near and Distant Neighbours*, p. 78.

146. "Protokol zasedaniya prezidiuma IKKI", No. 13, 16–17 September 1936: Russia. Moscow. RGASPI, Arkhiv Kominterna, f. 495, op. 2, d. 248.

147. "Beschluss des Sekretariats des EKKI vom 18. September 1936 betr. Der Kampagne zur Unterstützung des Kampfes de spanischen Volkes": ibid., f. 495, op. 20, d. 262.

148. Uritsky to Molotov, 19 September 1936: *SSSR i grazhdanskaya voina*, doc. 37.

149. Secretary of the Central Committee to Uritsky and Grin'ko, 20 September 1936: ibid., doc. 38.

150. Firsov, *Sekretnye Kody*, p. 199.

151. Haslam, *Near and Distant Neighbours*, p. 78. The original documents are now published: "Zapiski S. Uritskogo L. Kaganovichu i V. Molotovu", 29 September 1936: *SSSR i grazhdanskaya voina*, doc. 54.

152. Haslam, *Soviet Union and the Struggle*, pp. 119–120; Gorev to Voroshilov, 16 October 1936: *SSSR i grazhdanskaya voina*, doc. 91.

153. Haslam, *Soviet Union and the Struggle*, p. 119.

154. This was on 3 October: Firsov, *Sekretnye Kody*, p. 199.

155. Rozenberg (Madrid) to Moscow, 9 October 1936: *SSSR i grazhdanskaya voina*, doc. 71.

156. Krestinsky (Moscow) to Rozenberg, 13 October 1936: ibid., doc. 79.

157. From the archives: *Politburo TsK RKP(b)–VKP(b) i Komintern, 1919–1943*, pp. 342–343.

158. Memorandum from Voroshilov to Stalin, 13 December 1936: *SSSR i grazhdanskaya voina*, doc. 160.

159. Roatta–Franco discussion, 16 October 1936: Rovighi and Stefani, *La partecipazione italiana alla guerra civile spagnola*, Vol. 1, doc. 17.

160. Longo and Salinari, *Dal socialfascismo*, p. 138.

161. Memorandum from Manuilsky to Stalin, Molotov, Voroshilov and Kaganovich, 4 November 1936: *SSSR i grazhdanskaya voina*, doc. 129.

162. Dimitrov and Manuilsky to Stalin and Voroshilov, 13 January 1937: ibid., doc. 192.

163. Memorandum from Litvinov to Stalin, 7 January 1937: ibid., doc. 186. For the decision to send them by sea: ibid., doc. 187.

164. Briefing by Léger: Thomas (Paris) to Vansittart (London), 26 October 1936: *Documents on British Foreign Policy 1919–1939*, 2nd Series, Vol. 17, doc. 333.

165. Record of the meeting, 6 December 1936: Rovighi and Stefani, *La partecipazione italiana alla guerra civile spagnola*, Vol. 1, doc. 21.

166. Corbin (London) to Delbos (Paris), 11 November 1936: *Documents diplomatiques français*, 2nd Series, Vol. 3, doc. 471.

167. Shtein (Rome) to Narkomindel (Moscow), 5 November 1936: *Dokumenty vneshnei politiki SSSR*, Vol. 19, p. 777.

168. Nuncio Francisco Borgongino Duca to Secretary of State Pacelli, 23 November 1936: *L'archivio della nunziatura apostolica*, p. 141.

169. Dimitrov (Moscow) to Thorez (Paris), 5 December 1936: USA. Stanford. Hoover Institution, Firsov Papers, Box 6.

170. Ibid.

171. Mussolini's discussion with Göring and counsellor at the German embassy Schmidt, 23 January 1937: Ciano, ed., *L'Europa verso la catastrofe*, p. 135.

172. "Protokol No. 16 i stenogramma zasedaniya Prezidiuma IKKI ot 3 fevralya 1937": Russia. Moscow. RGASPI, Arkhiv Kominterna, f. 495, op. 2, d. 255.

173. The Seventh Department of Soviet intelligence (GUGB NKVD) had in hand deciphered telegrams to this effect from the US ambassador, Bullitt, to Secretary of State Hull. The first is dated 12 January and the follow up 20 January 1937. Russia. Moscow. Yeltsin Presidential Library. *Vtoraya mirovaya voina v arkhyvnikh dokumentakh, 1937*. ASVR, l. 55–56, photopcopy: prlib.ru.

174. "Stenograficheskii otchet. Zasedanie prezidiuma IKKI ot 20/1X-1937 g.": Russia. Moscow. RGASPI, Arkhiv Kominterna, f. 495, op. 265, d. 20.

175. Biographical record of Codovilla compiled in 1943: USA. Stanford. Hoover Institution, Firsov Papers, Box 37.

176. A. Marty, "Notes sur le PCE", 11 October 1936: Russia. Moscow. RGASPI, Arkhiv Kominterna, f. 495, op. 12, d. 92.

177. "Stenograficheskii otchet. Zasedanie prezidiuma IKKI ot 20/IX-1937 g.": Russia. Moscow. RGASPI, Arkhiv Kominterna, f. 495, op. 265, d. 20.

178. Report, 28 December 1936. Protokol Prezidiuma IKKI No. 15, 19–28 December 1936: Russia. Moscow. RGASPI, Arkhiv Kominterna, f. 495, op. 2, d. 254.

179. *La révolution espagnole*, Vol. 1, No. 3, 17 September 1936.

180. Report, 28 December 1936. Protokol Prezidiuma IKKI No. 15, 19–28 December 1936: Russia. Moscow. RGASPI, Arkhiv Kominterna, f. 495, op. 2, d. 254.

181. "Comando Truppe Volontarie (Il Generale Comandante)" to Ciano, 19 October 1937: A. Rovighi and F. Stefani, *La partecipazione italiana alla guerra civile spagnola*, Vol. 2, (Rome: Stato Maggiore dell'Esercito, Ufficio storico, 1993), doc. 3.

182. "Kampaniya v Zashchitu Ispanskoi Respubliki", 22 November 1936: Russia. Moscow. RGASPI, Arkhiv Kominterna, f. 495, op. 12, d. 92.

183. The original was in French and appears to have been awkwardly translated into Russian, perhaps in too much haste: "Issues for Resolution", 8 September 1937, contained in Dimitrov's memorandum to Stalin, also 8 September 1937: *SSSR i grazhdanskaya voina*, doc. 334.

184. Formerly a minister at the Foreign Office, Hugh Dalton knew Rozenberg as an officer in Soviet foreign intelligence, the InOGPU: H. Dalton, *The Political Diary of Hugh Dalton 1918–40, 1945–60*, ed. B. Pimlott (London: Jonathan Cape, 1986), p. 200.

185. Decision of the Politburo, 21 December 1936: *SSSR i grazhdanskaya voina*, doc. 167 (original emphasis).

186. J. Davies, *Mission to Moscow* (London: Gollancz, 1942), p. 49.

187. Chilston (Moscow) to Eden (London), 14 May 1937: UK. London. National Archives, FO 371/21102.

188. Meeting on 11 December 1936: Casella, ed., *Gli ambasciatori d'Italia presso la Santa Sede*, p. 202.

189. "Protokol No. 20 i stenogramma zasedaniya Prezidiuma IKKI ot 20 sentyabrya 1937 g.": Russia. Moscow. RGASPI, Arkhiv Kominterna, f. 495, op. 2, d. 265.

190. Ibid.

191. Lord Chatfield, *It Might Happen Again*, Vol. 2 (London: Heinemann, 1947), p. 92.

192. "Situazione Forze Rosse Alla Data del 6-1-1938-XVI", Rovighi and Stefani, *La partecipazione italiana alla guerra civile spagnola*, Vol. 2, doc. 2.

193. Mussolini (Rome) to Franco, 2 February 1937: *I documenti diplomatici italiani*, 8th Series, Vol. 8, ed. G. Andrè (Rome: Istituto Poligrafico dello Stato, 1999), doc. 87.

194. O. Harvey, *The Diplomatic Diaries of Oliver Harvey, 1937–1940*, ed. J. Harvey (London: Collins, 1970), pp. 148–149.

195. Quoted in Kershaw, *Making Friends with Hitler*, p. 178.

Chapter 10. A United Front against Japan

1. The minute by "Walker" was dated 20 December 1937: UK. London. National Archives, FO 371/21102. As a section of military intelligence, MI2 focused on the Soviet Union and Scandinavia. "Walker" is not in the diplomatic list.

2. "G-2 Report. Political Parties and Groups. Present Trend of the Chinese Communist Party", 29 January 1936: USA. College Park. National Archives, US Military Intelligence, China, 002825-012-0137.

3. Harriman (Moscow) to Roosevelt (Washington DC), 11 June 1944: *Foreign Relations of the United States: Diplomatic Papers, 1944, China*, Vol. 6, ed. E. R. Perkins et al. (Washington DC: US GPO, 1967), doc. 90.

4. Report of 20 November 1936: USA. College Park. National Archives, US Military Intelligence, China, 002825-012-0137.

5. Report of 29 January 1936: ibid., China, 002825-012-0137.

6. Bartel (Shanghai) to Warsaw, 19 December 1935: InO GUGB NKVD: *Sekrety pol'skoi politiki 1935–1945 gg.*, p. 46.

7. For radio contact: Dimitrov to Stalin, the beginning of July 1936: *VKP(b), Komintern i Kitai*, doc. 374.

8. Tikhvinskii, *Put' Kitaya*, pp. 274–275.

9. Ibid., p. 277.

10. Mi Zanchen, *The Life of General Yang Hucheng* (Hong Kong: Joint, 1981), pp. 90–93.

11. Quoted in Tikhvinskii, *Put' Kitaya*, p. 282.

12. Ibid., pp. 287–290.

13. Report from the director of Soviet military intelligence, Uritsky, to Voroshilov, 23 November 1935: Russia. Moscow. Yeltsin Presidential Library. RGVA, f. 33987, op. za. d. 74, l. 160–

161; and, further to this, on 15 December 1935: RGVA, f. 33987, op. za. d. 740, l. 162, photocopy: prlib.ru. For the impact of the ratification: Zorge (Tokyo) to Uritsky (Moscow), 4 April 1936: *"Delo Zorge"*, p. 99.

14. Haslam, *Soviet Union and the Threat from the East*, pp. 89–90.

15. Ibid., pp. 70–83.

16. Report, 21 July 1937, "Probability of an Outbreak of War. Documents N. Naval Attaché, Tokyo.": USA. Hyde Park. Franklin D. Roosevelt Library and Archive, Box 68.

17. Quoted in Nish, *Japanese Foreign Policy*, p. 214.

18. G-2 Report, "Comments on Current Events, September 2–17 1937", Colonel Joseph Stilwell, military attaché: USA. College Park. National Archives, US Military Intelligence, China, 002825-012-0137.

19. Nish, *Japanese Foreign Policy*, p. 223.

20. Memorandum by Haas, Secretary of the Treasury Henry Morgenthau's secretary, 14 September 1937: USA. Hyde Park. Franklin D. Roosevelt Library and Archive, Morgenthau Diary, Vol. 87, pp. 156–174.

21. Quoted in S. Endicott, *Diplomacy and Enterprise: British China Policy 1933–1937* (Vancouver: University of British Columbia, 1975), p. 114.

22. Quoted in ibid., pp. 104–105.

23. Leith-Ross to Fisher, 3 March 1936: quoted in ibid.

24. "Comments on Currents Events. October 1–18 1937", Joseph Stilwell, 18 October 1937: USA. College Park. National Archives, US Military Intelligence, China, 002825-012-0137.

25. 6 October 1937: UK. London. National Archives, CAB 36 (37).

26. 30 November 1938: UK. London. National Archives, CAB 23 (96)

27. Ibid.

28. The word *ubrat'* is ambiguous. It can mean just 'remove' from a position held, or actually 'take out and kill', depending on the context. For the quotation: V. Nikonov, *Molotov. Nashe delo pravoe*, Vol. 1 (Moscow: Molodaya Gvardiya, 2016), pp. 378–379. Nikonov is Molotov's grandson and appears to believe in the authenticity of the document. An echo of this bizarre finding came to me when meeting one of the leading historians of Comintern at the Institute of Marxism-Leninism in Moscow in 1977. In the course of a long, calm discussion, I dismissed the charges against Trotsky for inciting terrorism, since we had never seen any irrefutable proof. Shirinya almost leapt out of his seat, became extremely agitated and said that he had seen the evidence. He said that we would all see it when Trotsky's personal archive at Harvard was finally opened. We did not, and neither did Isaac Deutscher when he worked in it many years before.

29. "The Class Nature of the Soviet State", 1 October 1933: *Writings of Leon Trotsky 1933–34* (New York: Pathfinder, 1975), p. 118.

30. Lt. Commander H. H. Smith-Hutton, Intelligence Report, US Asiatic Fleet, Shanghai, 6 November 1937: USA. College Park. National Archives, State Department. 761.93/1623.

31. Ibid., p. 91.

32. Quoted in Haslam, *Soviet Union and the Threat from the East*, p. 92.

33. Yurenev (Tokyo) to Narkomindel (Moscow), 17 July 1936: *Dokumenty vneshnei politiki SSSR*, Vol. 19, p. 751.

34. Reported on 19 October 1937: quoted in ibid.

35. I. Ivanov, *Ocherki istorii Ministerstva inostrannykh del Rossii*, (Moscow: Olma-press, 2002), Vol. 2, pp. 245–246.

36. Quoted in Haslam, *Soviet Union and the Threat from the East*, p. 94.

Chapter 11. The Appeasement of Germany, 1937–1939

1. Ciano, ed., *L'Europa verso la catastrofe*, p. 137.

2. The first words uttered by "uncle Albrecht" after he emerged from Chatham House, recorded by the historian Felix Gilbert, in *A European Past: Memoirs 1905–1945* (New York: W. W. Norton, 1988) p. 170.

3. Amery to John Buchan, 29 September 1937: UK. Cambridge. Churchill College Archives, Leo Amery Papers, AMEL 2/1/27.

4. Entry, 13 November 1936: UK. Oxford. Bodleian Library, Dawson Manuscript 40.

5. "The Role of the British Army", a memorandum by the chancellor of the exchequer, 11 December 1936: UK. National Archives, CP 334 (36), also CAB 53/6.

6. R. Rhodes James, ed., *Memoirs of a Conservative: J.C.C. Davidson's Memoirs and Papers 1910–1937* (London: Weidenfeld and Nicolson, 1969), p. 421.

7. Quoted in Thorne, *Approach of War*, p. 29.

8. Entry, 2 October 1938: Bruce Lockhart, *Diaries*, Vol. 1, p. 398.

9. UK. Cambridge. Churchill College Archives, Cadogan Diary, ACAD 1/9.

10. Entry, 12 July 1940: I. Maisky, *Dnevnik diplomata. London, 1934–1943*, ed. A. Chubaryan et al., Vol. 2 (Moscow: Nauka, 2009), Part 1, p. 230.

11. Quoted in M. Gilbert, "Horace Wilson: Man of Munich?", *History Today*, Vol. 32, No. 10, 1982, p. 6.

12. I. Maisky, *Dnevnik diplomata. London, 1934–1943*, Vol. 1 (Moscow: Nauka, 2006), p. 189.

13. Quoted in Gilbert, "Horace Wilson: Man of Munich?", p. 6.

14. Garvin to Amery, 29 November 1933: UK. Cambridge. Churchill College Archives, Leo Amery Papers, AMEL 2/1/26.

15. Bullitt (Paris) to Roosevelt (Washington DC), 10 January 1937: USA. Hyde Park. Franklin D. Roosevelt Library and Archive, PSF, France, William C. Bullitt, 1937, Box 30.

16. Quoted in Haslam, *Soviet Union and the Struggle*, p. 206.

17. Quoted in K. Feiling, *The Life of Neville Chamberlain* (London: Macmillan, 1946), pp. 341–342.

18. Entry, 6 June 1938: H. Nicolson, *The Harold Nicolson Diaries and Letters 1907–1964*, ed. N. Nicolson (London: Weidenfeld and Nicolson, 2004), p. 167.

19. H. Dalton, *The Fateful Years: Memoirs 1931–1945* (London: Muller, 1957), p. 162. Ronald was Barbara Cartland's brother.

20. Entry, 1 October 1936: L. Amery, *The Empire at Bay: The Leo Amery Diaries 1929–1945* (London: Hutchinson, 1988), p. 428.

21. Amery to Neville Chamberlain, 11 and 16 November 1937: UK. Cambridge. Churchill College Archives, Leo Amery Papers, AMEL 2/1/27.

22. Chamberlain to Amery, 15 November 1937: ibid.

23. Amery to Chamberlain, 11 and 16 November 1937: ibid.

24. Amery to Casey, 23 November 1937: ibid.

25. D. Collins, *A Charmed Life: The Phenomenal World of Philip Sassoon* (London: William Collins, 2016), pp. 267–268. Collins mistakenly predates Alba's service to Franco.

26. Entry, 10 December 1938: Bruce Lockhart, *Diaries*, Vol. 1, p. 413.

27. From Alba's unpublished memoir: Spain. Madrid. Archivo de la Fundación Casa de Alba, Palacio de Liria.

28. Churchill to Corbin, 31 July 1936: M. Gilbert, ed., *Winston S. Churchill*, Vol. 5 *Companion*, Part 3, *Documents: The Coming of War, 1936–1939* (London: Heinemann, 1982), p. 297.

29. 8 January 1937: UK. London. National Archives, CAB 23 (37).

30. Quoted in R. Griffiths, *Fellow Travellers of the Right: British Enthusiasts for Nazi Germany 1933–39* (London: Constable, 1980), p. 263.

31. Quoted in ibid.

32. Alba (London) to Fernández Villaverde (Salamanca), 2 July 1937: Spain. Madrid. Archivo General de la Administración, 54/6700, No. 12.

33. Ibid., 28 June 1937: ibid., No. 9.

34. Ibid., 2 July 1937: ibid., No. 11.

35. Ibid., 10 June 1937: ibid., No. 3; ibid., No. 4. Maisky, on hearing Inskip confess to confusion on the subject of identifying the slicing of military divisions, was certainly not impressed with his expertise: entry, 3 November 1938: Maisky, *Dnevnik diplomata*, Vol. 1, p. 309.

36. Ibid., 9 June 1937: Spain. Madrid. Archivo General de la Administración, 54/6700, No. 2.

37. Ibid., 10 June 1937: ibid., No. 3. At the end of World War Two Alba crossed swords with Franco over the latter's rejection of monarchical restoration.

38. Dunant (Paris) to Motta (Bern), 24 June 1937: *Documents diplomatiques suisses, 1848–1945*, Vol. 12, ed. O. Gauye et al. (Bern: Benteli, 1994), doc. 92.

39. Resolution from Comintern's secretariat, 22 July 1937: Russia. Moscow. RGASPI, Arkhiv Kominterna, f. 495, op. 20, d. 574.

40. "Comparison of the Strength of Great Britain with that of Certain Other Nations as at January 1938. Memorandum by the Minister for Co-ordination of defence", 12 November 1937: UK. London. National Archives, CP 296 (37).

41. Russia. Moscow. RGASPI, Arkhiv Kominterna, f. 495, op. 20, d. 82.

42. Referred to by Grandi in a despatch to Ciano, 13 February 1938: Ciano, ed., *L'Europa verso la catastrofe*, p. 251.

43. Entry, 14 October 1937: Bruce Lockhart, *Diaries*, Vol. 1, p. 380.

44. J. Margach, *The Abuse of Power* (London: W. H. Allen, 1978), p. 53.

45. R. Cockett, "Ball, Chamberlain and Truth", *The Historical Journal*, Vol. 33, No. 1, March 1990, pp. 131–142.

46. Diary entry, 10 November 1937: *The Diaries of Chips Channon, Vol. 1: 1918–38*, ed. S. Heffer (London: Hutchinson, 2020), p. 773.

47. Eden (Brussels) to Phipps (Paris), 13 November 1937: *Documents on British Foreign Policy 1919–1939*, Second Series, Vol. 19, ed. W. Medlicott et al. (London: HMSO, 1982), doc. 318.

48. Quoted in M. Gilbert and R. Gott, *The Appeasers*, 2nd edition (London: Weidenfeld and Nicolson, 1967), p. 75.

49. Entry, 5 December 1937: *Diaries of Chips Channon*, p. 786.

50. Quoted in Cowling, *Impact of Hitler*, p. 274.

51. 24 November 1937: UK. London. National Archives, CAB 43 (37).

52. Sargent Minute, 27 October 1937: *Documents on British Foreign Policy 1919–1939*, 2nd series, Vol. 19, doc. 272.

53. 1 December 1937: UK. London. National Archives, CAB 45 (37).

54. "Iz protokola No. 55", 19 November 1937: *Politburo TsK RKP(b)–VKP(b) i Evropa. Resheniya "Osoboi papki" 1923–1939*, doc. 262.

55. "Iz protokola No. 56", 21 December 1937: ibid., doc. 264.

56. Chilston (Moscow) to Collier (London), 24 January 1938: *Documents on British Foreign Policy 1919–1939*, 2nd Series, Vol. 19, doc. 467.

57. "Sir Horace Wilson's power is very great", noted Richard ("Rab") Butler: UK. Cambridge. Trinity College Library, Butler Papers, RAB G10, 30.

58. Vansittart to Amery: entry, 24 January 1940: Amery, *Empire at Bay*, p. 582. For Vansittart's reference to Wilson then usurping his functions: entry, 24 September 1938, Dalton, *Political Diary*, p. 244.

59. Entry, 12 April 1938: Dalton, *Political Diary*, p. 231.

60. Having held his temper as his deputy for too long, Cadogan vented his fury when Vansittart received a Knight Grand Cross of the Order of the Bath. Vansittart's appointment as Privy Counsellor was almost too much to bear: entry, 6 June 1940: UK. Cambridge. Churchill College Archives, Cadogan Diary, ACAD 1/9. On Wilson, Butler wrote that he was "responsible . . . for the removal of senior members of the Diplomatic Service" (since there was only one removed, it must have been Vansittart): UK. Cambridge. Trinity College Library, Butler Papers, RAB G10, 31. For Fisher's attempt to block Cadogan's path: G. Peden, "Sir Warren Fisher and British Rearmament against Germany", *The English Historical Review*, Vol. 94, No. 370, January 1979, p. 42. Fisher, by then a little crazed by ambition, suggested that he might have to take the job!

61. Entry, 15 May 1936: UK. Cambridge. Churchill College Archives, Cadogan Diary, ACAD 1/4.

62. Entry, 18 January 1937: ibid., ACAD 1/6.

63. Clive (Brussels) to Foreign Office (London), 9 November 1937: *Documents on British Foreign Policy 1919–1939*, 2nd Series, Vol. 21, ed. W. Medlicott et al. (London: HMSO, 1984), doc. 343.

64. *Politburo TsK RKP(b)–VKP(b) i Komintern, 1919–1943*, doc. 478; Dimitrov, *Diary*, pp. 65 and 67.

65. *Documents on British Foreign Policy 1919–1939*, 2nd series, Vol. 19, pp. 458–459, note 3.

66. Entry, 20 February 1938: UK. Oxford. Bodleian Library, Dawson Manuscript 42.

67. Quoted in Gilbert, "Horace Wilson: Man of Munich?", p. 6.

68. J.-B. Duroselle, *La Décadence 1932–1939* (Paris: Imprimerie nationale, 1979), p. 327.

69. G. Waterfield, *Professional Diplomat: Sir Percy Loraine of Kirkhale Bt, 1880–1961* (London: Butler and Tanner, 1973), p. 278.

70. Memcon, State Department, 8 March 1938: USA. Hyde Park. Franklin D. Roosevelt Library and Archives, PSF, State Department, Welles, Box 76.

71. Entry, 19 February 1938: Chamberlain's diary, excerpted in *Documents on British Foreign Policy 1919–1939*, 2nd series, Vol. 19, Appendix 1. This reflected the assessment given by the chiefs

of staff on 12 November 1937: Report of the Chiefs of Staff Sub-Committee of the Committee of Imperial Defence: ibid., doc. 316.

72. Entry, 4 December 1940: *Diaries of Sir Alexander Cadogan*, p. 338.

73. Waterfield, *Professional Diplomat*, p. 222.

74. A reference to Stalin's forced collectivisation of agriculture: quoted in G. Gorodetsky, *Stafford Cripps' Mission to Moscow 1940–42* (Cambridge: Cambridge University Press, 1984), p. 57.

75. Maisky (London) to Narkomindel (Moscow), 23 March 1938: Russia. Moscow. AVPRF, f. 059, op. 1, p. 279, d. 1928. The original document, along with an entire collection covering the Czechoslovakian crisis, has been scanned onto www.munich.rusarchive.ru: *Nakanune i posle Myunkhena, arkhivnye dokumenty rasskazyvayut. "Pered litsom germanskoi ekspansii: ustupki ili voina (mart–avgust 1938)"*, doc. 8.

76. Reported in H. de Torrenté (Paris) to Motta (Bern), 13 March 1938: *Documents diplomatiques suisses*, Vol. 12, doc. 228.

77. Quoted in Army Security Agency, "European Axis Signal Intelligence in World War II as Revealed by 'Ticom' Investigations and by Other Prisoner of War Interrogations and Captured Material, Principally German", Vol. 7: "Goering's 'Research' Bureau", 1 May 1946. Ticom, the Target Intelligence Committee, was a joint Anglo–American entity: USA. College Park. National Archives, NSA, European Axis Signals Intelligence in World War II, DOCID 3486670.

78. For confirmation: Duroselle, *La Décadence*, pp. 326–327.

79. Entry, 12 March 1938: J. Reith, *The Reith Diaries*, ed. C. Stuart (London: Collins, 1975), p. 219.

80. Meeting the Italian ambassador, 8 May 1936: Casella, ed., *Gli ambasciatori d'Italia presso la Santa Sede*, p. 197.

81. Grandi (London) to Mussolini (Rome), 3 September 1933: *Documenti diplomatici italiani*, 7th Series, Vol. 14, doc. 142.

82. *History of "The Times"*, Vol. 4, Part 2, p. 901.

83. *Memoirs of Lord Gladwyn*, p. 62.

84. Letter from Litvinov (Moscow) to Aleksandrovsky (Prague), 26 March 1938: Russia. Moscow. AVPRF, f. 3, op. 63, d. 185. Scanned onto www.munich.rusarchive.ru: *Nakanune i posle Myunkhena, "Pered litsom germanskoi ekspansii"*, doc. 13.

85. "Dnevnik S. S. Aleksandrovskogo za vremya prebyvaniya v Bukhareste", 26 April 1938. Alexandrovsky entered these notes into his diary while in Bucharest on Litvinov's instructions: Russia. Moscow. AVPRF, Narkomindel 230, d. 024. Rum. 1938 g. delo No. 3 (173) papka No. 115, 1938.

86. "Protokoly No. 257–258 Zasedanii Sekretariata IKKI Materialy", "Beschluss zu Österreich", 15 March 1938; "Reshenie Sekretariata po Avstrii", 8 April 1938, "Decision of the Sekretariat on Austria, 22 May 1938: Russia. Moscow. RGASPI, Arkhiv Kominterna, f. 495, op. 18, d. 1238.

87. Letter from Litvinov (Moscow) to Aleksandrovsky (Prague), 26 March 1938: Russia. Moscow. AVPRF, f. 3, op. 63, d. 185. Scanned onto www.munich.rusarchive.ru.

88. Gendin, deputy head of the Fourth Directorate, to Voroshilov, 2 April 1938: ibid., doc. 24.

89. Voroshilov to Stalin, 13 May 1938 and Politburo decision, 14 May 1938: ibid., doc. 29.

90. Memorandum from G. Savchenko to Voroshilov, 29 May 1938: Russia. Moscow. RGVA, f. 33987, op. za. d. 1144; ibid., doc. 71.

91. Litvinov to Stalin, 29 May 1938: Russia. Moscow. RGASPI, f. 17, op. 166, d. 590: ibid., doc. 69.

92. "Special communication from the Intelligence Directorate of the Red Army" to Voro-shilov, 28 May 1938: Russia. Moscow. RGVA, f. 33987, op. za. d. 1144: ibid., doc. 68.

93. Thorez (Paris) to Comintern (Moscow), 18 March 1938, also sent to Stalin, 19 March: Russia. Moscow. RGASPI, Arkhiv Kominterna, f. 495, op. 74, d. 517; Firsov Papers, (Hoover Institution), Box 7.

94. Ibid.

95. V. Shavrov, *Istoriya konstruktsii samoletov v SSSR 1938–1950 gg. (Materialy k istorii samole-tostroeniya)*, 3rd edition (Moscow: Mashinostroenie, 1994), pp. 7–8.

96. Buchan to Amery, 20 April 1938: UK. Cambridge. Churchill College Archives, Leo Amery Papers, AMEL 2/1/28.

97. Wilson to Hoare, 26 September 1948: UK. Cambridge. Cambridge University Library, Templewood Papers, XVII, file 1.

98. Bont's record of the meeting, 9 May 1938: Russia. Moscow. RGASPI, Arkhiv Kominterna, f. 495, op. 74, d. 212; Firsov Papers (Hoover Institution), Box 30.

99. Surits (Paris) to Narkomindel (Moscow), 25 May 1938: Russia. Moscow. AVPRF, f. 059, op. 1, p. 279, d. 1943. Scanned onto www.munich.rusarchives.ru, doc. 58.

100. *Memoirs of Lord Gladwyn*, pp. 75–76.

101. "Decision of the Secretariat of the E.C.C.I. Regarding Certain Acute Questions Raised by the Representatives of the C.P.G.B.", 11 May 1938. This was a translation, evidently by an American, of the decision taken on 19 April, "Postanovlenie Sekretariata IKKI po Nekotorym Aktual'nym Voprosam, podnyatym predstavitelyami KP Anglii": Russia. Moscow. RGASPI, Arkhiv Kominterna, f. 495, op. 18, d. 1241.

102. Quoted in Gilbert, "Horace Wilson: Man of Munich?", p. 6.

103. Davies, *Mission to Moscow*, p. 223.

104. Dalton, *Fateful Years*, p. 180.

105. "Beschluss des Sekretariats zur teschechischen Frage", 11 May 1938. Protokol (A) Nr. 279. Sekretariat IKKI, 25 May 1938: Russia. Moscow. RGASPI, Arkhiv Kominterna, f. 495, op. 18, d. 1245.

106. Quoted in Steiner, *Triumph of the Dark*, p. 582.

107. *Memoirs of Lord Gladwyn*, p. 80.

108. Report dated 11 July 1938: Russia. Moscow. RGVA, f. 308, op. 3, d. 437, scanned onto www .munich.rusarchive.ru, doc. 91.

109. Ibid., doc. 103.

110. Ibid., doc. 108.

111. Haslam, *Soviet Union and the Threat from the East*, pp. 113–120.

112. Speech to the military council at the Commissariat, 29 November 1938: quoted in V. Krasnov, *Neizvestnyi Zhukov. Lavry i ternii polkovodtsa. Dokumenty, mneniya, razmyshleniya* (Moscow: Olma-press, 2000), p. 88.

113. N. Yakubovich, *Nasha aviatsiya v 1941 gody. Prichiny katastrofy* (Moscow: Yauza, Eksmo, 2015), p. 16.

114. J. Wheeler-Bennett, *The Nemesis of Power: The German Army in Politics 1918–1945* (London: Macmillan, 1953), pp. 422–432.

115. This has been analysed in convincing detail by W. Murray, *The Change in the European Bal-ance of Power, 1938–1939: The Path to Ruin* (Princeton: Princeton University Press, 1984), ch. 7.

116. USA. Stanford. Hoover Institution, Ivy and Tatyana Litvinov Papers, Box 4, p. 37.

117. From my own interview with Tatyana Litvinova, which took place in 1983; and a subsequent interview that her brother Misha gave to NPR, which was published by A. Garrels, "House on Embankment"; National Public Radio broadcast, 12 June 2005.

118. Davies (Moscow) to Hull (Washington DC), 26 March 1937: Davies, *Mission to Moscow*, p. 80.

119. A. Tooze, *The Wages of Destruction: The Making and Breaking of the Nazi Economy* (London: Penguin, 2008), ch. 8.

120. UK. London. National Archives, CAB 23 (94).

121. Berle to Roosevelt, 31 August 1938: USA. Hyde Park. Franklin D. Roosevelt Library and Archive, PSF, State Department, Box 72.

122. Bullitt (Paris) to State, 31 August 1938: ibid.

123. A French historian sums him up as "opportunist", which is in the circumstances a little generous: Duroselle, *La Décadence*, p. 370. Bonnet's behaviour throughout the September crisis was markedly mendacious in that he was more than once caught out telling outrageous lies about the Soviet position regarding their obligations to the Czechs. His self-serving memoirs confirm this judgement: *Défense de la paix* (Geneva: Cheval Ailé, 1946).

124. Entry, 6 September 1938: UK. Oxford. Bodleian Library, Dawson Manuscript 42.

125. *History of "The Times"*, Vol.4, Part 2, p. 930.

126. "Nuremberg and Aussig", *The Times*, 7 September 1938. The text in the official history shows the words in the original draft by Kennedy and the hardened version by Dawson.

127. Entry, 7 September 1938: UK. Oxford. Bodleian Library, Dawson Manuscript 42.

128. *History of "The Times"*, Vol. 4, Part 2, p. 914.

129. Maisky (London) to Potemkin (Moscow), Stalin, Molotov, Voroshilov, Kaganovich, Yezhov, 8 September 1938: Russia. Moscow. AVPRF, f. 059, op. 1, p. 281, d. 1953: scanned onto www.munich.rusarchive.ru, "Sentyabr'skii krizis in Myunkhenskaya Konferentsiya chetyrekh derzhav (sentyabr' 1938)", doc. 15.

130. Quoted in Haslam, *Soviet Union and the Struggle*, pp. 180–181.

131. J. Wrench, *Geoffrey Dawson and Our Times* (London: Hutchinson, 1955), p. 376.

132. Entry, 26 March 1938: *Diaries of Chips Channon*, p. 846.

133. This is what the Duchess whispered to Channon: entry, 22 June 1938: ibid., p. 893.

134. Quoted in Haslam, *Soviet Union and the Struggle*, p. 182. When Chamberlain reported to the Commons on his return from the Munich conference in late September, the unmistakeable figure of Queen Mary was visible at the back of the visitors' gallery.

135. Quoted in Haslam, *Russia's Cold War*, p. 7.

136. Quoted in K. Smith, "Reassessing Roosevelt's view of Chamberlain after Munich: Ideological Affinity in the Geoffrey Thompson–Claude Bowers Correspondence", *Diplomatic History*, Vol. 33, No. 5, November 2009, p. 855.

137. Quoted in Colvin, *The Chamberlain Cabinet* (London: Gollancz, 1971), p. 270.

138. Jeffery, *MI6*, pp. 305–306. "A noted bon vivant with a stormy private life" and "an astonising flow of forcible language". This was "a man whose expansionist ambitions—matched only by those of Sir Basil Thomson of Scotland Yard—led him to make a distastrous mistake for any intelligence chief: getting too close to politics, and moving from providing intelligence to advising on policy": Stella Rimington, formerly director-general of MI5: *Financial Times*, 1 October 2010.

139. Quoted by Dilks (ed.) in *Diaries of Sir Alexander Cadogan*, p. 93.

140. UK. Birmingham University. Cadbury Archives, Papers of Neville Chamberlain, NC 18/1/1069.

141. Entry, 16 September 1938: *Diaries of Chips Channon*, p. 925.

142. "Iz protokola No. 64", 20 September 1938: *Politburo TsK RKP(b)–VKP(b) i Evropa. Resheniya "Osoboi papki" 1923–1939*, doc. 271.

143. Alexandrovsky (Prague) to Narkomindel (Moscow), 21 September 1938, circulated to Potemkin, Stalin, Molotov, Voroshilov, Kaganovich, Ezhov, Veinshtein: "Sentyabr'skii krizis i Myunkhenskaya Konferentsiya chetyrekh derzhav (Sentyabr' 1938)", doc. 65, www.munich.rusarchives.ru.

144. SÚA, Praha, PMR- Zápisy ze schůzi MR, XVII/41, schůzi 21 září 1938, krab. 4141: translation from the Czech original in *Dokumenty i materialy po istorii Sovetsko–Chekhoslovatskikh otnoshenii*, Vol. 3, ed. C. Amort et al. (Moscow: Nauka, 1978), doc. 346.

145. Alexandrovsky (Prague) to Narkomindel (Moscow), 21 September 1938: "Sentyabr'skii krizis", doc. 68, www.munich.rusarchives.ru.

146. Amery to Smuts, 26 September 1938: UK. Cambridge. Churchill College Archives, Leo Amery Papers, AMEL 2/1/28.

147. Entry, 24 September 1938: *Diaries of Sir Alexander Cadogan*, p. 103.

148. Amery to Chamberlain, 25 September 1938: UK. Cambridge. Churchill College Archives, Leo Amery Papers. AMEL 2/2/28.

149. Quoted in Gilbert, "Horace Wilson: Man of Munich?", p. 7.

150. Sir R. Lindsay (Washington DC) to Halifax (London), 20 September 1938: USA. Hyde Park. Franklin D. Roosevelt Library and Archive, PSF, Great Britain, Box 32.

151. Quoting from Drtina's memoirs, *Československo můj osud* (Toronto: Sixty-Eight Publishers, 1982): Z. Zeman, *The Life of Edvard Beneš 1884–1948. Czechoslovakia in Peace and War* (Oxford: Clarendon Press, 1997), p. 134.

152. Entry, 24 September 1938: *Diaries of Sir Alexander Cadogan*, p. 104.

153. Entry, 8 October 1938: Amery, *Empire at Bay*, p. 529.

154. Quoted in Gilbert, "Horace Wilson: Man of Munich?", p. 6.

155. Quoted in R. Shay, *British Rearmament in the Thirties: Politics and Profits* (Princeton: Princeton University Press, 1977), p. 234.

156. UK. London. National Archives, CAB 51 (38).

157. To Ian Colvin: Colvin, *Chamberlain Cabinet*, p. 267.

158. Ibid., p. 533.

159. Puleston to Morgenthau, 25 March 1940: USA. Hyde Park. Franklin D. Roosevelt Library and Archive, Morgenthau Diary, Vol. 299. Captain W. D. Puleston was formerly head of Naval Intelligence. He assembled from all available sources a regular analysis of the world situation for the treasury secretary.

160. R. Cockett, *Twilight of Truth. Chamberlain, Appeasement and the Manipulation of the Press* (London: Weidenfeld and Nicolson, 1989).

161. Quoted from the Russian military archive: Ken, Rupasov and Samuel'son, *Shvetsiya v politike Moskvy*, p. 204.

162. Alba (London) to Villaverde (Burgos), 26 October 1938: Spain. Madrid. Archivo General de la Administración, 54/7683.

163. Amery to Halifax, 15 November 1938: UK. Cambridge. Churchill College Archives, Leo Amery Papers, AMEL 2/1/28.

164. Amery to Hoare, 27 September 1938: ibid.

165. Amery to Smuts, 20 December 1938: ibid.

166. Letter, 28 January 1939: UK. Cambridge. Trinity College Library, Butler Papers, RAB G10, 3–4.

167. Kondrashov, *Voennye razvedki vo Vtoroi Mirovoi Voine*, p. 132. It looks like this assessment was picked up by Guy Burgess.

168. Entry, 7 March 1939: Channon, *"Chips": The Diaries*, p. 229.

169. Entry, 15 March 1939: Amery, *Empire at Bay*, p. 548.

170. Cockett, *Twilight of Truth*, pp. 104–105.

171. Kaser and Radice, eds, *Economic History of Eastern Europe*, Vol. 2, pp. 85–86.

172. I. McDonald, *The History of "The Times"*, Vol. 5 (London: Times Books, 1984), p. 27.

173. Written some time in June 1939: UK. Cambridge. Trinity College Library, Butler Papers, RAB G10, 29–30.

174. Response to an enquiry from the Polish ambassador to Romania: Arciszewski (Warsaw) to embassy (Bucharest), 14 January 1939: *Polskie Dokumenty Dyplomatyczne 1939*, ed. S. Żerko (Warsaw: PISM, 2005), doc. 21.

175. Entry, 31 March 1939: UK. London School of Economics Archives, Diary of Beatrice Webb, Vol. 53, p. 6,639. Webb heard this complaint from Maisky's wife.

176. Potocki (Washington DC) to Foreign Ministry (Warsaw), 16 January 1939: *Polskie Dokumenty Dyplomatyczne 1939*, doc. 18.

177. Haslam, *Soviet Union and the Struggle*, p. 209.

178. Quoted by Gilbert, "Horace Wilson: Man of Munich?", p. 9.

179. McDonald, *History of "The Times"*, Vol. 5, pp. 22–23. McDonald was the diplomatic correspondent during this period.

180. Ibid., p. 210.

181. Haslam, *Soviet Union and the Struggle*, p. 210.

182. "France would under no condition agree to give the slightest guarantee to the Baltic states", Léger told the German ambassador, Roland Köster, on 24 July 1935: quoted in Lacroix-Riz, *Le choix de la défaite*, p. 234.

183. T. Koblansky, deputy director of the Political Department of the Foreign Ministry to Colonel Pełczyński of the General Staff, 25 March 1938: *Polskie Dokumenty Dyplomatyczne 1938*, ed. M. Kornat (Warsaw: PISM, 2007), doc. 65.

184. Ēķis (Warsaw) to Munters (Riga), 8 March 1939: *Romanian–Latvian Relations*, doc. 142.

185. Record of conversations, 4 April 1939: UK. London. National Archives, CP 88 (39).

186. Litvinov to Stalin, 17 April 1939: *Dokumenty vneshnei politiki 1939 god*, ed. V. Komplektov et al. (Moscow: Mezhdunarodnye Otnosheniya, 1992), Vol. 1, doc. 228; Haslam, *Soviet Union and the Struggle*, pp. 211–212.

187. Quoted in Colvin, *Chamberlain Cabinet*, p. 200.

188. UK. London. National Archives, FO 371/23064.

189. Note by Merekalov, 17 April 1939: ibid., doc. 236. This part of the exchange was too sensitive to go by telegraph. It would have gone by courier. The ciphered telegram despatched the following day contained nothing of this: Merekalov (Berlin) to Narkomindel (Moscow), 18

436 NOTES TO CHAPTER 11

April 1939: *God krizisa: 1938–1939*, Vol. 1, ed. A. Bondarenko et al. (Moscow: Politicheskaya Literatura, 1990), doc. 279. Historians who took the telegram at face value have reason to blush.

190. Quoted in Cockett, *Twilight of Truth*, p. 109.

191. Stalin to Surits (Paris), Maisky (London), Umansky (Washington DC), Merekalov (Berlin), Gel'fand (Rome), Smetanin (Tokyo), Derevyanskii (Helsinki), Nikitin (Tallinn), Zotov (Riga), Listopad (Warsaw), Potemkin (Moscow), Nikitnikov (Ankara), 3 May 1939: *Dokumenty vneshnei politiki 1939*, Vol. 1, doc. 269.

192. Entry, 28 June 1939: Dalton, *Political Diary*, p. 276.

193. Entry, 7 May: ibid., p. 264.

194. Entry, 3 May 1939: ibid., p. 262.

195. "Sekretariat IKKI", 4 May 1939: Russia. Moscow. RGASPI, Arkhiv Kominterna, f. 495, op. 20, d. 573.

196. Record of Terent'ev's conversation with Papen, 5 May 1939: *Dokumenty vneshnei politiki 1939*, Vol. 1, doc. 279. As with Merekalov's conversation, the record would have been despatched via courier. It did not go via telegraph.

197. Letter from Astakhov (Berlin) to Molotov (Moscow), 6 May 1939: ibid., doc. 282.

198. UK. Cambridge. Trinity College Library. Butler Papers, RAB G10, 5–6 and 10–11.

199. UK. London. National Archives, "Military Value of Russia. Report by the Chiefs of Staff Sub-committee", 25 April 1939.

200. "IKKI secretariat", 4 May 1939: Russia. Moscow. RGASPI, Arkhiv Kominterna, f. 495, op. 20, d. 573.

201. UK. London. National Archives, CAB 26 (39).

202. Quoted in Thorne, *Approach of War*, p. 113.

203. Entry, 14 June 1939: Dalton, *Political Diary*, p. 271.

204. Record of the conversation between Molotov and Schulenburg, 20 May 1939: *Dokumenty vneshnei politiki 1939*, Vol. 1, doc. 326.

205. Firebrace to Seeds, 12 May 1939: UK. London. National Archives, FO 371/23678. Litvinov's daughter insisted that her father and Voroshilov had been in agreement about collective security: interview, 1983. It is striking that, with Stalin's suspicions of Britain at their height, on 17 June 1939 Voroshilov asked him whether they could send a Soviet military delegation to attend British manoeuvres scheduled for 17–19 September: Federal'noe arkhivnoe agentstvo, RGVA, *1939 god. Ot 'umirotvoreniya' k voine*, doc. 237.

206. Quoted in Haslam, *Soviet Union and the Struggle*, p. 213.

207. Entry, 28 June 1939: Dalton, *Political Diary*, p. 278.

208. UK. London. National Archives, CP (36), 47th meeting.

209. Entry, 16 May: Harvey, *Diplomatic Diaries*, p. 290.

210. The original briefing is dated 2 May 1939: Panfilov, temporarily deputy head of the First Department, Fifth Directorate RKKA, enclosed in Proskurov to Stalin, 17 May 1939: *Izvestiya TsK KPSS*, 3 (302), March 1990, pp. 217–218.

211. UK. London. National Archives, CAB 28 (39).

212. News contained in telegram from the US embassy in Moscow to the State Department in Washington DC, 20 May 1939: quoted in C. Bohlen, *Witness to History 1929–1969* (New York: Norton, 1973), pp. 70–71. Bohlen received this news from Herwarth at the German embassy in Moscow.

213. Entry, 19 May 1939: *Diaries of Sir Alexander Cadogan*, p. 181.

214. Entry, 19 May 1939: Amery, *Empire at Bay*, p. 553.

215. Entry, 23 May 1939: *Diaries of Sir Alexander Cadogan*, p. 182.

216. Raczyński (London) to Foreign Ministry (Warsaw), 9 June 1939: *Polskie Dokumenty Dyplomatyczne 1939*, doc. 338.

217. Quoted in Smith, "Reassessing Roosevelt's View of Chamberlain", pp. 862–863.

218. UK. London. National Archives, CAB 30 (39)

219. Harvey, *Diplomatic Diaries*, pp. 296–297.

220. "On the question of Universal Military Conscription in Great Britain", 29 July 1939: Russia. Moscow. RGASPI, Arkhiv Kominterna, f. 495, op. 20, d. 40.

221. Entry, 12 June 1939: UK. London. London School of Economics Archives, Diary of Beatrice Webb, Vol. 53, p. 6,665.

222. Quoted in Haslam, *Near and Distant Neighbours*, p. 103.

223. Written some time in June 1939: UK. Cambridge. Trinity College Library, Butler Papers, RAB G10, 30–31.

224. Statement by Karl Heinz Pintsch, 28 February 1948: *SSSR i Germaniya 1932–1941* (Moscow: IstLit, 2019), doc. 261.

225. L. Namier, *Diplomatic Prelude, 1938–1939* (London: Macmillan, 1948), p. 188.

226. Written some time in June 1939: UK. Cambridge. Trinity College Library, Butler Papers, RAB G10, 27–28.

227. In conversation with Juozas Urbšis, Lithuania's foreign minister, and Lithuanian ambassador Natkevičius, 3 October 1939: *SSSR i Litva v gody vtoroi mirovoi voiny*, doc. 48. Those novices who, as a result of the terror, rapidly replaced the diplomats and intelligence officers responsible for briefing Molotov and Stalin may well have misunderstood Foreign Office nomenclature. All senior personnel were officially, following medieval terminology, "clerks".

228. This was what Strange told Lawrence Collier, head of the Northern Department. Pousette (London) to Broder (Stockholm), 15 August 1939: Sweden. Stockholm. Sveriges Riksarkivet, Utrikesdepartementet, 1920 års dossiersystem, HP 516.

229. From Stalin's archive: *SSSR i Germaniya 1932–1941*, doc. 169.

230. Astakhov's record of the conversation with Schulenburg, 17 June 1939: *Dokumenty vneshnei politiki 1939*, Vol. 1, doc. 378.

231. From the KGB archives: quoted in ibid., Vol. 2, p. 559, footnote 136.

232. Entry, 23 June 1939, Maisky's daily record: *Dokumenty vneshnei politiki 1939*, Vol. 1, doc. 388.

233. Federal'noe arkhivnoe agentstvo, RGVA, *1939 god. Ot 'umirotvoreniya' k voine*, doc. 260.

234. Letter from Maisky to Molotov, 10 July 1939; ibid., doc. 422.

235. Quoted in Colvin, *Chamberlain Cabinet*, p. 229.

236. Quoted in N. Gibbs, *Grand Strategy*, Vol. 1 (London: HMSO, 1976), p. 741, note.

237. UK. London. National Archives, CAB 38 (39).

238. Jeffery, *MI6*, p. 312.

239. Letter, 23 July 1939: quoted at length in Gilbert, *Winston S. Churchill*, Vol. 5, p. 1,091.

240. The account of German ambassador Dirksen, 21 July 1939: Federal'noe arkhivnoe agentstvo, RGVA, *1939 god. Ot 'umirotvoreniya' k voine*, doc. 189.

241. Memorandum of the conversation by Dirksen, 3 August 1939: ibid., doc. 219.

242. Buccleugh to Butler, 25 July 1939: UK. Cambridge. Trinity College Library, Butler Papers, RAB G10, 16.

243. *Memoirs of Lord Gladwyn*, p. 76.

244. Ibid., p. 93.

245. Astakhov (Berlin) to Narkomindel, 25 July 1939: *SSSR i Germaniya 1932–1941*, doc. 175.

246. Astakhov (Berlin) to Narkomindel, 27 July 1939: ibid., doc. 176; also excerpt from Astakhov's daily record, 27 July 1939: ibid., doc. 178.

247. 26 July and 2 August 1939: UK. London. National Archives, CAB 39 (39) and 40 (39).

248. R. Plunkett-Ernle-Erle-Drax, "Mission to Moscow, August, 1939", *The Naval Review*, Vol. 40, No. 3, August 1952, p. 251.

249. Ibid., pp. 252–253.

250. *The Naval Review*, Vol. 40, No. 4, November 1952, p. 399.

251. Entry, 5 August 1939: *Dokumenty vneshnei politiki 1939*, Vol. 1, doc. 452.

252. Watt, *How War Came*, p. 406.

253. Rosenberg's Notes, 25 July 1939: 8828/R/Dt. Obtained by Alec Dallin on 27 September 1949: Hoover Institution, Hohenlohe Papers; cited in K. Urbach, *Go-Betweens for Hitler* (Oxford: Oxford University Press, 2015), p. 208.

254. Lord Kemsley's notes of an interview with Hitler: Gilbert, *Winston S. Churchill*, Vol. 5, p. 1,579.

255. Butler to the Duke of Buccleugh, 27 July 1939: UK. Cambridge. Trinity College Library, Butler Papers, RAB G10, 17.

256. Record of Astakhov's conversation with von Ribbentrop and K. Schnurre, 3 August 1939: *SSSR i Germaniya 1932–1941*, doc. 180.

257. The conversation took place on 4 August: Winther (Moscow) to Söderblom (Stockholm), 11 August 1939: Sweden. Stockholm. Sveriges Riksarkivet, Utrikesdepartementet, 1920 års dossiersystem, HP 516.

258. A. Bondarenko, *Fitin* (Moscow: Molodaya Gvardiya, 2015), p. 114.

259. "Memorandum for negotiations with the English and French delegations", 7 August 1939: *SSSR i Germaniya 1932–1941*, doc. 186.

260. *Dokumenty vneshnei politiki 1939*, Vol. 22, Book 2, p. 589.

261. Molotov (Moscow) to Astakhov (Berlin), 12 August 1939: ibid., doc. 189.

262. Quoted in Haslam, *Soviet Union and the Struggle*, p. 226.

263. Ibid.

264. Plunkett-Ernle-Erle-Drax, "Mission to Moscow", pp. 254–256.

265. Revealed by commander of the Soviet air forces Loktionov at the seventh meeting of the negotiations with the British and French military delegations, 17 August 1939: Federal'noe arkhivnoe agentstvo, RGVA, *1939 god. Ot 'umirotvoreniya' k voine*, doc. 21.

266. Entry, 22 August 1939: *The Political Diary of Alfred Rosenberg and the Onset of the Holocaust*, ed. J. Matthäus and F. Bajohr (Lanham, Md.: Rowman and Littlefield, 2015), p. 155.

267. *Dokumenty vneshnei politiki 1939*, Vol. 1, doc. 484 and secret protocol, doc. 485.

268. Entry, 7 September 1939: Dimitrov, *Diary*, p. 116.

269. Entry, 22 August 1939: Harvey, *Diplomatic Diaries*, p. 303.

270. Bohlen, *Witness to History*, pp. 80–83.

271. Kłopotowski (Riga) to Warsaw; record of a conversation with Munters on 18 August, 19 August 1939: *Polskie Dokumenty Dyplomatyczne 1939*, doc. 445.

272. Kondrashov, *Voennye razvedki vo Vtoroi Mirovoi Voine*, p. 134. Once again, Burgess is the most likely source.

273. Reasoning rehearsed from notes made at the time: *Memoirs of Lord Gladwyn*, p. 78.

274. Halifax, "A Record of Events Before the War, 1939": UK. Cambridge. Trinity College Library, Butler Papers, RAB G10, 100. In fact news came in late on the evening of the 21st: Maisky (London) to Stalin (Moscow), 23 August 1939: Russia. Moscow. Federal'noe arkhivnoe agentstvo, RGVA, *1939 god. Ot 'umirotvoreniya' k voine*, doc. 26.

275. Minute on a memorandum by Sargent and Wigram, 1 December 1935: *Documents on British Foreign Policy 1919–1939*, 2nd series, Vol. 15, ed. M. Lambert et al., (London: HMSO, 1976), Appendix 1 (c).

276. Winther (Moscow) to Sandler (Stockholm), 13 September 1939: Sweden. Stockholm. Sveriges Riksarkivet, Utrikesdepartementet, 1920 års dossiersystem, HP 516.

277. Entry, 27 August 1939: Harvey, *Diplomatic Diaries*, p. 307.

278. Halifax, "A Record of Events".

279. Astakhov (Berlin) to Molotov (Moscow), 29 August 1939: *SSSR i Germania 1932–1941*, doc. 201.

280. Entry, 25 August 1939: UK. London. London School of Economics Archives, Diary of Beatrice Webb, Vol. 53, p. 6,710.

281. Entry, 27 August 1939: diary quoted in McDonald, *History of "The Times"*, Vol. 5, p. 25.

282. Entry, 13 October 1939: J. Colville, *The Fringes of Power: 10 Downing Street Diaries, 1939–1955* (New York: Norton, 1985), p. 40.

Chapter 12. War, 1939–1940

1. Quoted in J. Haslam, "Comintern and Soviet Foreign Policy", *The Cambridge History of Russia*, Vol. 3, ed. R. Suny (Cambridge: Cambridge University Press, 2006), p. 655.

2. A sequence of such episodes itemised in various memoirs is listed by Wolfgang Leonhard: V. Leongard, *Shok ot pakta mezhdu Gitlerom i Stalinym* (London: Overseas Publications Interchange, 1989), pp. 58–90. Originally published as *Der Schock des Hitler-Stalin-Paktes* (Freiburg im Breisgau: Herder, 1986). See chapter 2.

3. N. Hooker, ed., *The Moffat Papers* (Cambridge, Mass.: Harvard University Press, 1956), p. 253.

4. "Do 90 let on ezdil v poliklinike na elektrichke", an interview with Molotov's former assistant Mikhail Smirtyukov, *Kommersant' vlast'*, 21 March 2000.

5. "Protokol (B) No. 477, Zasedanie Sekretariata IKKI", 22 August 1939: *Dokumenty vneshnei politiki 1939*, Vol. 1, doc. 479.

6. "Maurice Thorez: notes inédites, novembre 1939. Documents communistes (mai 1939–novembre 1941)", *Cahiers d'histoire de l'Institut de recherches marxistes*, No. 14, 1983, p. 11.

7. Cerreti, *Con Togliatti e Thorez*, p. 254.

8. F. Dahlem, *Am Vorabend des Zweites Weltkrieges 1938 bis August 1939. Erinnerungen*, Vol. 2 (Berlin: Dietz, 1977), p. 356. Dahlem talks about its "formation"—"die Bildung"—though in fact the correct term for it would have been "restoration".

9. In conversation with Lithuania's foreign minister, Urbšis, and its ambassador, Natkevičius, 3 October 1939: *SSSR i Litva v gody vtoroi mirovoi voiny*, doc. 48.

10. Dimitrov, *Diary*, p. 115.

11. Speech to a meeting of the Moscow Party organisation's activists, 5 April 1927: *Problemy dal'nego vostoka*, 1, 2001, p. 154. The preceding introduction describes this as published for the first time: p. 149.

12. Smyth (Beijing) to Secretary of State (Washington DC), 20 June 1940: USA. College Park. National Archives, State Department, 761.94 / 4043.

13. For the most comprehensive account: Duroselle, *La Décadence*, pp. 481–493.

14. Kennedy (London) to Roosevelt (Washington DC), 30 September 1939: USA. Hyde Park. Franklin D. Roosevelt Library and Archive, PSF, Box 10, pp. 325–326.

15. Colvin, *Chamberlain Cabinet*, pp. 218–219.

16. Bullitt (Paris) to Washington, 3 November 1939: USA. Hyde Park. Franklin D. Roosevelt Library and Archive, PSF, France, Book 221.

17. Kennedy (London) to Roosevelt (Washington DC), 30 September 1939: USA. Hyde Park. Franklin D. Roosevelt Library and Archive, PSF, Box 10.

18. UK. Cambridge. Trinity College Library, Butler Papers, RAB G10, 56. As a friend of Chamberlain's: Colvin, *Chamberlain Cabinet*, p. 265. For more on Brocket: Urbach, *Go-Betweens for Hitler*, pp. 294–296. For the butler, see C. Woodhouse, *Something Ventured* (London: Granada, 1982), p. 7. Woodhouse's father, Lord Terrington, was in charge of exemptions for national service, and when he tried to void the exemption he received a visit from MI5.

19. Buccleugh to Butler, 29 September 1939: UK. Cambridge. Trinity College Library, Butler Papers, RAB G10, 18.

20. Address to the Supreme Soviet, 31 October 1939: *Mirovoe khozyaistvo i mirovaya politika*, No. 9, 1939, p. 13.

21. "Minutes of the Soviet Estonian Negotiations for the Mutual Assistance Pact of 1939", *Lituanus*, Vol. 14, No. 2, 1968, p. 92.

22. Conversation with Foreign Minister Urbšis and Ambassador Natkevičius, 3 October 1939: *SSSR i Litva v gody vtoroi mirovoi voiny*, doc. 48.

23. *Komintern i vtoraya mirovaya voina*, Vol. 1, ed. N. Lebedeva and M. Narinskii (Moscow: Pamyatniki istoricheskoi mysli, 1994), p. 10.

24. Russia. Moscow. RGASPI, Arkhiv Kominterna, f. 495, op. 184, d. 4. Also published in "Dokumenty: Depese mezi Prahou a Moskvou 1939–1941", ed. G. Bareš, *Příspěvky k dějinám KSČ*, No. 7, 1967, doc. A14.

25. "The Security Executive. The Communist Party of Great Britain": Note from Lord Swinton, 19 October 1941: UK. London. National Archives, WP (41) 244, CAB 66/19.

26. From Schulenburg's personal archive. Quoted in extenso: *Dokumenty vneshnei politiki 1939*, Vol. 22, Book 2, p. 610.

27. Russia. Moscow. AVPRF, Maisky, *Dnevnik diplomata*, Vol. 2, Part 1, p. 306. In the early nineties the late Lev Bezymensky of *Novoe vremya* lent me his copy of the MS. Gabriel Gorodetsky has since published a translation of the diary in several volumes.

28. Murray (London) to President Roosevelt (Washington DC), 1 October 1939: USA. Hyde Park. Franklin D. Roosevelt Library and Archive, PSF, Great Britain, Box 38. Murray had married Faith Standing, an actress and a cousin of Roosevelt, and had also served as military attaché

in Washington DC in 1917, where he befriended Roosevelt. He subsequently succeeded to the title of Viscount Elibank.

29. "Kommission des Sekretariats zur Frage der KPD, KPOK and KPT sch. Sitzung am 27.xi.39": Russia. RGASPI, Arkhiv Kominterna, f. 495, op. 18. "Nobody in Russia or in the Comintern ever has accused Varga of even a secret rebellious idea": Ypsilon, *Pattern for World Revolution*, p. 159.

30. "SSSR v voine", *Byulleten' Oppozitsii*, No. 79–80, 1939, p. 8.

31. Kazys (Berlin) to Urbšis (Kaunas), 2 October 1939: *SSSR i Litva v gody vtoroi mirovoi voiny*, doc. 46.

32. Russia. Moscow. AVPRF, entry for 24 October 1939, Maisky, *Dnevnik diplomata*, Vol. 2, Part 1, p. 296.

33. Entry, 13 October 1939: Colville, *Fringes of Power*, p. 40.

34. UK. London. National Archives, CAB (57) 39.

35. "Manoeuvres de Russia blanche de septembre 1936", Annexe Rapport du Général Schweitsguth, Chef de la mission française. URSS, enclosed in Daladier (War) to Delbos (Quai d'Orsay), 13 October 1936: *Documents diplomatiques français*, 2nd Series, Vol. 3, doc. 343.

36. U. Salo, "Estimation of Security Threats and Estonian Defence Planning in the 1930s", *Acta Historica Tallinnensia*, Vol. 12, No. 1, 2008, p. 45.

37. "Minutes of the Soviet Estonian Negotiations", p. 65.

38. "Lithuania and the Soviet Union 1939–1940: The Fateful Year—Memoirs by Juozas Urbsys", *Lituanus*, Vol. 35, No. 2, 1989, p. 46.

39. This was 5 October 1939. UK. London. National Archives, FO 371/23678.

40. Quoted in Bondarenko, *Fitin*, p. 116.

41. M. Jakobson, *Finland Survived. An Account of the Finnish–Soviet Winter War 1939–1940* (Helsinki: Otava, 1984), pp. 107–108.

42. J. Paasikivi, *Minnen*, Vol. 1: *1939–1940. Moskva och Finland* (Stockholm: Bonnier, 1958), p. 10.

43. Ibid., p. 39.

44. Ibid., p. 40.

45. Ibid., pp. 49–53.

46. Ibid., pp. 64–65.

47. Quoted in G. Kumanev, "Chto my znaem o 'zimnei voine'", *Sovetskaya Rossiya*, 10 March 1990.

48. From the Baltic fleet, quoted in Ken, Rupasov and Samuel'son, *Shvetsiya v politike Moskvy*, p. 207.

49. Tikhomirov in *Tainy i uroki zimnei voiny 1939–1940. Po dokumentam rassekrechennykh arkhivov*, ed. N. Volkovskii et al. (St Petersburg: Poligon, 2000), p. 74.

50. Sahlin (Helsinki) to Sandler and Ärendena (Stockholm), 20 November 1939: Sweden. Stockholm. Sveriges Riksarkivet, Utrikesdepartementet, 1920 års dossiersystem, HP 101.

51. 18 November 1939: UK. London. National Archives, FO 371/23678.

52. Speaking 17 April 1940, "Soveshchanie pri TsK VKP(b) nachal'stvuyushchego sostava po sboru opyta boevykh deistvii protiv Finlyandii 14–17 aprelya 1940 g.", *Tainy i uroki zimnei voiny*, pp. 504–505.

53. Fred Dearing (Stockholm) to President Roosevelt (Washington DC), 3 September 1937: USA. Hyde Park. Franklin D. Roosevelt Library and Archive, PSF, Box 51. For Kollontai's

epithet, taken from Ivy Litvinova: Carswell, *The Exile*, p. 102. Carswell, once secretary of the British Academy, was a friend of the family.

54. Oral testimony from the late Vladimir Yerofeev, who began his career as a diplomat working under Kollontai before being moved to work directly under Molotov, whom he served for a decade.

55. V. Assarsson, *I skuggan av Stalin* (Stockholm: Bonniers, 1963), p. 26.

56. Entry, 22 November 1939: A. Kollontai, *Diplomaticheskie dnevniki 1922–1940*, Vol. 2 (Moscow: Academia, 2001), pp. 464–466.

57. Sahlin (Helsinki) to cabinet in Stockholm, 1 December 1939; also Swedish military attaché, Helsinki, 3 December 1939: Sweden. Stockholm. Sveriges Riksarkivet, Utrikesdepartementet, 1920 års dossiersystem, HP 101.

58. *Pravda*, 2 December 1939 and *Izvestiya*, 3 December 1939: reprinted in *Tainy i uroki zimnei voiny*, pp. 132–136.

59. *Izvestiya*, 2 December 1939; reprinted in ibid, pp. 139–140.

60. Winther (Moscow) to Stockholm, 4 December 1939; also Söderblom (Stockholm) to Sahlin (Helsinki), 5 December 1939: Sweden. Stockholm. Sveriges Riksarkivet, Utrikesdepartementet, 1920 års dossiersystem, HP 102.

61. Boheman's record of the conversation, 7 December 1939: Sweden. Stockholm. Sveriges Riksarkivet, Utrikesdepartementet, 1920 års dossiersystem, HP 101.

62. Secretary of State for War Hore-Belisha, 4 December 1939: UK. National Archives, War Cabinet 103 (39).

63. Entry, 30 November 1939: Colville, *Fringes of Power*, p. 54.

64. Telegram of 21 October to Halifax (London), cited in UK. London. National Archives, CAB 57 (39).

65. Sargent to Ismay, 22 December 1939: Ibid., FO 371/23678.

66. Bryant to Butler, 18 October 1939: UK. King's College, London. Liddell Hart Centre for Military Archives, Bryant Papers, C69.

67. "Prezidium IKKI Sitzung der Kommission des Sekretariats des EKKI am 29.xi.1939, Protokol Nos. 515–525": Russia. Moscow. RGASPI, Arkhiv Kominterna, f. 495, op. 18, d. 1301.

68. 24 November 1937: UK. London. National Archives, CAB 43 (37).

69. UK. London. National Archives, War Cabinet 99 (39), 30 November 1939.

70. For Bullitt's self-congratulatory account: Bullitt (Paris) to Roosevelt (Washington DC), 19 December 1939: *For the President. Personal and Secret*, ed. O. Bullitt (London: André Deutsch, 1973), pp. 394–396.

71. "P.M.", Östen Undén (Geneva), 10 December 1939: Sweden. Stockholm. Sveriges Riksarkivet, Utrikesdepartementet, 1920 års dossiersystem, HP 102.

72. Aide mémoire, 27 December 1939, and Günther (Stockholm) to Prytz (London), 3 January 1940: ibid.

73. Winther (Moscow) to Günther and Ärendena, 2 January 1940: ibid.

74. The Norwegian foreign minister consulted the minister at the German embassy, Bräver, who, just returned from Berlin, gave the go-ahead: Douglas (Oslo) to Günther and Ärendena (Stockholm), 10 January 1940: ibid.

75. Kollontai to Günther, 6 January 1940: ibid.

76. Quoted in Ken, Rupasov and Samuel'son, *Shvetsiya v politike Moskvy*, p. 214.

77. Hellsted (Tallinn) to Gunther and Ärendena (Stockholm), 15 December 1939: Sweden. Stockholm. Sveriges Riksarkivet, Utrikesdepartementet, 1920 års dossiersystem, HP 458.

78. K. Simonov, *Glazami cheloveka moego pokoleniya* (Moscow: Pravda, 1990), pp. 354–355. Simonov is, however, not always accurate.

79. Marshal G. Zhukov, *Vospominaniya i razmyshleniya* (Moscow: Novosti, 1990), p. 107.

80. Entry, 27 March 1940: Dimitrov, *Diary*, pp. 127–128.

81. UK. London. National Archives, War Cabinet 111 (39).

82. Chamberlain to Joseph Ball, 26 December 1939: UK. Oxford. Bodleian Library, Papers of Sir Joseph Ball, MS Eng.c.6656.

83. Cabinet (Stockholm) to Sahlin (Helsinki), 29 December 1939: Sweden. Stockholm. Sveriges Riksarkivet, Utrikesdepartementet, 1920 års dossiersystem, HP 102. For the Swedish general staff—Mallett's telegram to London, 25 December, intercepted by Beria's special department: *K 70-letiyu Sovetsko–Finlyandskoi Voiny. Zimnyaya Voina 1939–1940 gg. V rassekrechennykh dokumentakh Tsentral'nogo Arkhiva FSB Rossii i arkhivov Finlyandii*, ed. A. Sakharov et al. (Moscow: Akademkniga, 2009)

84. Entry, 5 January 1940: Colville, *Fringes of Power*, p. 67.

85. Beria reporting intelligence from Paris, 13 January 1940: *K 70-letiyu Sovetsko–Finlyandskoie Voiny*, doc. 159. See also J.-B. Duroselle, *L'Abîme 1939–1945* (Paris: 1982, Imprimerie nationale), pp. 87–94.

86. Letter from Maisky (London) to Molotov (Moscow), 26 January 1940: *Dokumenty vneshnei politiki*, Vol. 23, Book 1, ed. G. Mamedov et al. (Moscow: Mezhdunarodnye otnosheniya, 1995), doc. 27.

87. Entry, 31 January 1940: Colville, *Fringes of Power*, p. 77.

88. Entry, 15 February 1940: ibid., p. 84.

89. Haslam, *Near and Distant Neighbours*, pp. 125–126.

90. *Dokumenty vneshnei politiki*, Vol. 23, Book 1, pp. 770–771.

91. Entries, 5 February and 6 February 1940: Kollontai, *Diplomaticheskie dnevniki*, pp. 493–495.

92. Entries, 1 March, 3–5 March: Kollontai, *Diplomaticheskie dnevniki*, pp. 509–515.

93. *Dokumenty vneshnei politiki*, Vol. 23, Book 1, pp. 771–772. Also, entries 7–9 March: Kollontai, *Diplomaticheskie dnevniki*, pp. 516–519.

94. "Mirnyi dogovor mezhdu SSSR i finlyandskoi respubliki", *Pravda*, 13 March 1940.

95. Mallet to Günther, 12 March 1940: Sweden. Stockholm. Sveriges Riksarkivet, Utrikesdepartementet, 1920 års dossiersystem, HP 107; entry, 12 March: Kollontai, *Diplomaticheskie dnevniki*, p. 512.

96. Entry, 3 May 1940: Amery, *Empire at Bay*, p. 592.

97. Ēķis (Bucharest) to Munters (Riga), 22 April 1940: *Romanian–Latvian Relations*, doc. 181.

98. Entry, 7 May 1940: Amery, *Empire at Bay*, pp. 592–593.

99. "Note de la Direction politique. Attitude de l'URSS Représentation diplomatique française à Moscou", 26 May 1940: *Diplomates en guerre. La Seconde Guerre mondiale racontée à travers les archives du Quai d'Orsay*, ed. P.-J. Rémy (Paris: JC Lattès, 2007), p. 271.

100. Assarsson (Moscow) to Ärendena (Stockholm), 30 May 1940: Sweden. Stockholm. Sveriges Riksarkivet, Utrikesdepartementet, 1920 års dossiersystem, HP 516.

101. Molotov's record of his conversation with Hitler, 13 November 1940: *Dokumenty vneshnei politiki*, Vol. 23, Book 2, ed. G. Mamedov et al. (Moscow: Mezhdunarodnye otnosheniya, 1998), Part 1, doc. 511.

102. Quoted in Duroselle, *L'Abîme*, p. 157.

103. M. Gilbert, *Winston S. Churchill*, Vol. 6: *Finest Hour, 1939–1941* (London: Heinemann, 1983), p. 644.

104. Maisky (London) to Narkomindel (Moscow), 3–4 July 1940: *Dokumenty vneshnei politiki*, Vol. 23, Book 1, doc. 244.

105. Kennedy to Welles: *Landis Papers*, p. 547: cited in J. Vieth, "Joseph P. Kennedy: Ambassador to the Court of St. James's, 1938–1940" (Ohio State University, PhD diss., 1975), p. 365.

106. 11 March 1940: Hooker, ed., *Moffat Papers*, p. 299.

107. "The European Situation", 25 March 1940: USA. Hyde Park. Franklin D. Roosevelt Library and Archive, Morgenthau Diaries, Book 299.

108. Entry, 21 March 1940: UK. Cambridge. Churchill College Archives, Cadogan Diary, ACAD 1/9.

109. Comintern executive committee meeting, 17 July 1940: Russia. Moscow. RGASPI, Arkhiv Kominterna, f. 495, op. 18, d. 1322; published in *Komintern i vtoraya mirovaya voina*, doc. 109. The introduction by Natasha Lebedeva and Mikhail Narinsky draw the threads together.

110. Directive dated 19 July 1940: Russia. Moscow. RGASPI, Arkhiv Kominterna, f. 495, op. 74, d. 1322; published in *Komintern i vtoraya mirovaya voina*, doc. 110.

111. "Protokol B, No. 635 (1390)", 5 August 1940: Russia. RGASPI, Arkhiv Kominterna, f. 495, op. 18, d. 1322; published in *Komintern i vtoraya mirovaya voina*, doc. 114.

112. Duclos, Frachon, and Tréand (Paris) to Comintern (Moscow), 21 August 1940: Russia. Moscow. RGASPI, Arkhiv Kominterna, f. 495, op. 74, d. 516; published in *Komintern i vtoraya mirovaya voina*, doc. 116.

113. Butler disingenuously claimed he had by chance encountered the minister in the park and made no record of the conversation. Yet he later produced one for Halifax. His subsequent denials carry no credibility and his private papers have been cleansed of any reference to the affair. Thus the only reliable, contemporaneous record one can rely upon is that of the Swedish minister.

114. Quoted in T. Munch-Petersen, "'Common sense not bravado': the Butler–Prytz interview of 17 June 1940", *Scandia*, Vol. 52, No. 1, 1986, pp. 73–114.

115. Chamberlain to Arnold, 10 January 1940, and Brocket to Bryant, 9 February 1940: UK. King's College, London. Liddell Hart Centre for Military Archives, Bryant Papers, C69.

116. Ibid.

117. Entry, 1 July 1940: Colville, *Fringes of Power*, p. 182.

118. A reference to Charles Edward Stuart (Bonnie Prince Charlie), the Stuart pretender to the throne of the ruling Hanoverians in the eighteenth century.

119. Entry, 10 July 1940: UK. Cambridge. Churchill College Archives, Cadogan Diary ACAD/1/9.

120. Quoted in KGB, "O podgotovke Germanii k napadeniyu na SSSR", *Izvestiya TsK KPSS*, No. 4 (303), April 1990, p. 199.

121. Quoted from Liddell's diary in N. West, *Cold War Spymaster: The Legacy of Guy Liddell, Deputy Director of MI5* (London: Frontline Books, 2018), p. 5.

122. The secret German telegrams relating to this were seized by British intelligence at the end of the war and hidden from the allies to prevent this coming to light, which may well have led to a public outcry that the duke be tried for treachery: ibid., ch. 1.

123. Record of Molotov's conversation with Schulenburg, 17 June 1940: *Dokumenty vneshnei politiki*, Vol. 23, Book 1, doc. 208.

124. Smyth (Beijing) to Secretary of State (Washington DC), 20 June 1940: USA. College Park. National Archives, State Department, 761.94/4043.

125. Cripps (Moscow) to Foreign Office (London), 1 July 1940: UK. London. National Archives, Premier 3, 395/1.

126. "Conversations with Molotov", *Lituanus*, Vol. 12, No. 2, 1965, pp. 16 and 24.

127. Heath (Berlin) to Secretary of State (Washington DC), 17 June 1940: USA. College Park. National Archives, State Department, 740.0011/3884.

128. V. Shamberg, *Lozovskii* (Moscow: Tonchu, 2012), p. 481.

129. The testimony of First Lieutenant Karlheinz Pintsch, 23 February 1948, from Soviet intelligence archives: enclosure in Kruglov to Stalin, 28 February 1948: *SSSR i Germaniya 1932– 1941*, doc. 261.

130. RICHTILINIEN, 21 September 1940: Russia. Moscow. RGASPI, Arkhiv Kominterna, f. 495, op. 18, d. 1324.

131. Tagüeña Lacorte, *Testimonio de dos guerras*, p. 401.

132. Entry, 7 November 1940: Dimitrov, *Diary*, p. 132.

133. Quoting Molotov was Boheman, the senior official at the Swedish Foreign Ministry: Fransoni (Stockholm) to Ciano (Rome), 9 November 1940: *I documenti diplomatici italiani*, 9th Series, Vol. 5, ed. M. Toscano (Rome: Istituto Poligrafico dello Stato, 1965), doc. 210.

134. He repeated this sentiment in January 1941. Admiral Kuznetsov, "At Naval Headquarters", in S. Bialer, ed., *Stalin and his Generals* (New York: Pegasus, 1969), pp. 190–191.

135. Simonov, *Glazami cheloveka moego pokoleniya*, p. 309.

136. Litvinov's daughter overheard him on the telephone more than once berating Molotov in such terms: personal testimony, cited in Haslam, *Soviet Union and the Threat from the East*, p. 16. Tatyana Litvinova, a sculptor latterly living in the apartment her mother, Ivy, rented from historian of Russia Professor Robert Smith, in Hove, England, was totally apolitical and had not shared these memories with anyone before. For this reason I felt she could be trusted. Smith vouched for me.

137. Dated 9 November 1940: *Dokumenty vneshnei politiki*, Vol. 23, Book 2, Part 1, doc. 491.

138. Those at the talks included the young intelligence officer Valentin Berezhkov, who went under the nom de guerre Bogdanov, along with Ambassador Vladimir Dekanozov, the interpreter Vladimir Pavlov and Gustav Hilger from the German embassy in Moscow, who interpreted for Hitler and Ribbentrop. For the detail: Russia. Moscow. AVPRF, Fond Sekretariata Ministra t. V. M. Molotova. op. 2, ind. 160, papka 15; and ibid., op. 2, ind. 161, papka 15.

139. Notes by Pavlov, the interpreter, 12 November 1940: *Dokumenty vneshnei politiki*, Vol. 23, Book 2, Part 1, doc. 497.

140. Bogdanov and Pavlov's record of the conversations, 13 December 1940: ibid., doc. 511.

141. Molotov (Berlin) to Stalin (Moscow), 14 November 1940: ibid., doc. 515.

142. V. Berezhkov, *S diplomaticheskoi missiei v Berline 1940–1941* (Moscow: Novosti, 1966), p. 48.

143. D. Volkogonov, *Triumf i tragediya. Politicheskii portret I. V. Stalina*, Vol. 2, (Moscow: Novosti, 1989), Part 1, p. 54.

144. Steinhardt (Moscow) to Secretary of State (Washington DC), 7 December 1940: USA. College Park. National Archives, State Department, 761.62/825.

145. "Diplomaticheskaya aktivnost' Germanii posle poezdki v Berlin tov. V. M. Molotova (politicheskii obzor za 15–22.xi.40 g.)", Kobulov, chargé d'affaires, and Semyonov (Berlin), 23 November 1940: Russia. Moscow. AVPRF, Fond Sekretariata Molotova, op. 2, por. 146, papka 14, d. 20.

146. Entry, 25 November 1940: Dimitrov, *Diary*, p. 135.

147. Dekanozov (Berlin) to Molotov (Moscow), 14 December 1940: Russia. Moscow. AVPRF, Fond Sekretariata Molotova, op. 2, por. 146, papka 14, d. 20. Also, Dekanozov (Berlin) to Molotov (Moscow), 16 February 1940: ibid. The Swedish military attaché in Berlin was briefing the Soviet naval attaché along these lines.

148. *Komintern i vtoraya mirovaya voina*, p. 455.

149. Ibid., doc. 127.

150. Entry, 28 November 1940: Dimitrov, *Diary*, p. 139.

151. Lavrishchev (Sofia) to Molotov (Moscow), 30 November 1940: *Dokumenty vneshnei politiki*, Vol. 23, Book 2, Part 1, doc. 564.

152. Dimitrov's telephone conversation with Molotov: entry, 20 December 1940: Dimitrov, *Diary*, p. 139.

153. Rosso (Moscow) to Ciano (Rome), 31 December 1940: *I documenti diplomatici italiani*, 9th Series, Vol. 6, ed. P. Pastorelli (Rome: Istituto Polifgrafico dello Stato, 1986), doc. 282.

154. "Po voprusu o perebroske germanskikh voisk v Bolgariyu", Protokol B, No. 684, 1450, 14 January 1941: Russia. Moscow. RGASPI, Arkhiv Kominterna, f. 495, op. 18, d. 1326.

155. Boheman's record of the conversation, 15 February 1941: Sweden. Stockholm. Sveriges Riksarkivet, Utrikesdepartementet, 1920 års dossiersystem HP 517.

156. Assarsson (Moscow) to Söderblom (Stockholm), 19 February 1941: ibid.

157. Vyshinsky's record of the conversation, 22 March 1941: *Dokumenty vneshnei politiki*, Vol. 23, Book 2, Part 2, doc. 730.

158. Jeffery, *MI6*, p. 415.

159. Vyshinsky's daily record, 1 April 1941: Russia. AVPRF, Fond Sekretariata Narkoma V. M. Molotova, op. 3, ind. 375, papka 27. Also, Vyshinsky's record of his conversation with the Yugoslav ambassador, 1 April 1941: *Dokumenty vneshnei politiki*, Vol. 23, Book 2, Part 2, doc. 740.

160. Vyshinsky's record of the conversation, 3 April 1941: *Dokumenty vneshnei politiki*, Vol. 23, Book 2, Part 2, doc. 743.

161. Vyshinsky's record of the conversation, 4 April 1941: ibid., doc. 745.

162. Ibid., doc.747; Vyshinsky's record of the conversation with Simić, 5 April 1941: Russia. AVPRF. Fond Sekretariata Narkoma V. M. Molotova, op. 3, ind. 375, papka 27. The treaty text appeared in *Izvestiya*, 5 April 1941.

Chapter 13. The Invasion of the Soviet Union

1. Record of a conversation between Stalin, Molotov and Eden, 29 March 1935: *Dokumenty vneshnei politiki SSSR*, Vol. 18, doc. 148.

2. F. Chuyev, ed., *Molotov. Poluderzhavnyi vlastelin* (Moscow: Olma-press, 2000), p. 42.

3. Quoted in L. Fischer, *The Life and Death of Stalin* (New York: Harper, 1952), p. 62.

4. "Predlozheniya dlya TsK KP Frantsii", 8 January 1941: Protokoll No. 680–691. Russia. Moscow. RGASPI, Arkhiv Kominterna, f. 495, op. 18, d. 1326.

5. G. Hägglöf, *Diplomat* (London: The Bodley Head, 1972), pp. 161–162.

6. F. Hinsley, *British Intelligence in the Second World War*, Vol. 1 (London: HMSO, 1979), pp. 451–452.

7. Ibid.

8. Gilbert, *Winston S. Churchill*, Vol. 6, pp. 1,050–1,051.

9. Krasnov, *Neizvestnyi Zhukov*, pp. 136–137.

10. 25 June 1941: quoted in Nish, *Japanese Foreign Policy 1869–1942*, p. 242.

11. Hinsley, *British Intelligence*, Vol. 1, p. 429.

12. Minute by Maclean, 10 January, on Kelly (Bern) to London, 6 January 1941: UK. London. National Archives, FO 371/29479. Equally self-assured but ignorant was his comment on Litvinov and Molotov that "both statesmen have no policy of their own but are simply the mouthpieces of Stalin": minute, 11 January 1941, on Craigie (Tokyo) to London, 4 December 1940: ibid.

13. In a minute dated 22 January 1941, Maclean says the War Office agrees with him: UK. London. National Archives, FO 371/29479.

14. Special communication from Golikov, head of military intelligence, to Stalin, Voroshilov, Molotov, Timoshenko, Beria et al., 4 April 1941: *1941 God*, Vol. 2, ed. L. Reshin et al. (Moscow: Mezhdunarodnyi Fond 'Demokratiya', 1998), doc. 367.

15. Cripps (Moscow) to London, 23 April 1941: UK. London. National Archives, FO 371/29480.

16. Signed statement 27 February 1948, in full: *SSSR i Germaniya 1932–1941*, doc. 261.

17. Entry, 13 May 1941: G. Liddell, *The Guy Liddell Diaries*, ed. N. West (London: Routledge, 2005), p. 147.

18. Minute by Sargent, 14 May 1941, on Cripps (Moscow) to London, 13 May 1941: UK. London. National Archives, FO 371/29481.

19. Sargent minute, 30 May 1941, on Cripps (Moscow) to London, 17 May 1941: ibid.

20. Warner (London) to Cripps (Moscow), 10 June 1941: ibid., FO 371/29482.

21. J. Haslam, "Stalin's Fears of a Separate Peace, 1942", *Intelligence and National Security*, Vol. 8, No. 4, October 1993, pp. 97–99.

22. *Izvestiya*, 14 June 1941.

23. Letter from Dekanozov (Berlin) to Molotov (Moscow), 4 June 1941: *Dokumenty vneshnei politiki*, Vol. 23, Book 2, Part 2, doc. 853.

24. Fitin, "Soobshchenie iz Berlina", not later than 16 June 1941: *Izvestiya TsK KPSS*, 4 (303), April 1990, p. 221.

25. Entry, 22 June 1941: Dimitrov, *Diary*, p. 166.

26. Molotov to Ambassador Schulenburg, 22 June 1941: *Nachalo*, Vol. 2, Book 1 (Moscow: 2000).

27. USA. Stanford. Hoover Institution, Ivy and Tatyana Litvinov Papers, Box 9.

28. Quoted in L. Fischer, *The Road to Yalta: Soviet Foreign Relations 1941–1945* (New York: Harper & Row, 1972), pp. 8–9.

29. Cripps (Moscow) to Foreign Office (London), 26 July 1941: UK. London. National Archives, FO 371/29619.

30. Sir R. Clive (Brussels) to Foreign Office (London), 9 November 1937: *Documents on British Foreign Policy 1919–1939*, 2nd Series, Vol. 21, doc. 343.

31. Quoted in H. Boog et al., eds, *Germany and the Second World War*, Vol. 4 (Oxford: Oxford University Press, 1998), p. 520.

32. L. Bezymensky, *Chelovek za spinoi Gitlera: Martin Bormann i ego dnevnik* (Moscow: Veche, 1999), pp. 109–114.

33. General Georg Thomas, in charge of the defence economy and armaments office of the Wehrmacht High Command, quoted in the introduction by W. Birkenfeld, to G. Thomas, *Geschichte der deutschen Wehr- und Rüstungswirtschaft (1918–1943/45)* (Boppard am Rhein: Boldt, 1966), p. 18.

34. UK. London. National Archives, WM (41) 20th Conclusions, 16 June 1941, CAB 65/22.

35. Told to two devotees of the Soviet cause: W. and Z. Coates, *A History of Anglo–Soviet Relations* (London: Laurence and Wishart, 1943), p. 680.

36. A. Werth, *Russia at War, 1941–1945* (London: Pan Books, 1964), p. 149, footnote.

37. "Political Aspects of a German Defeat by Russia", Memorandum from R. Leeper, 7 July 1941. UK. London. National Archives, FO 371/29486.

BIBLIOGRAPHY

Archives

France. Aix-en-Provence. Archives nationales d'outre-mer

France. Fonds de la direction du Parti Communiste Français, Université de Bourgogne, online: https://pandor.u-bourgogne.fr

Italy. Rome. Ministero degli Affari Esteri, Archivio Storico Diplomatico

Russia. Moscow. Arkhiv vneshnei politiki Rossii (AVPRF) at the Russian Foreign Ministry

Russia. Moscow. Rossiiskii gosudarstvennyi arkhiv sotsialno-politicheskoi istorii (RGASPI), Arkhiv Kominterna; sections online at www.sovdoc.ru; see also Firsov Papers, below

Russian Federation. Documentary material from various state and party archives located in the Yeltsin Library (formerly the Presidential Archive), online at munich.rusarchives.ru; Vtoraya mirovaya voina v arkhivnykh dokumentykh (kompleks otsifrovannykh arkhivnykh dokumentov, kino-i fotomaterialov).

Spain. Madrid. Archivo de la Fundación Casa de Alba, Palacio de Liria

Spain. Madrid. Archivo General de la Administración

Sweden. Stockholm. Sveriges Riksarkivet, Utrikesdepartetmentet

UK. Birmingham. University of Birmingham Cadbury Research Library: Neville Chamberlain Papers

UK. Cambridge. Cambridge University Library: Templewood Papers

UK. Cambridge. Churchill College Archives: Leo Amery Papers; Sir Alexander Cadogan Papers; William Strang Papers

UK. Cambridge. King's College, Modern Archives: John Maynard Keynes Papers

UK. Cambridge. Trinity College Library: R. A. Butler Papers

UK. London. King's College London, Liddell Hart Centre for Military Archives: Sir Arthur Bryant Papers

UK. London. London School of Economics Archives: Diary of Beatrice Webb

UK. London. National Archives: FO 371; HW 17; KV; Cabinet Minutes; Cabinet Papers; Committee of Imperial Defence; War Cabinet

UK. Oxford. Bodleian Libraries: Sir Joseph Ball Papers; Geoffrey Dawson Archive

USA. College Park, Md. National Archives, US Military Intelligence

USA. Hyde Park, N.Y. Franklin D. Roosevelt Library and Archive: Roosevelt Presidential Archives

USA. New Haven, Conn. Sterling Library: Henry Lewis Stimson Diaries.

USA. Stanford, Calif. Hoover Institution Archive: Firsov Papers; Hohenloe Papers; Ivy and Tatyana Litvinov Papers

Published Primary Texts and Diaries

Akten zur deutschen auswärtige Politik, 1918–1945, Series A, Vols 3 and 7, ed. W. Bussmann et al.; Series B, Vols 16 and 21 and Series C, Vol. 1, ed. H. Rothfels et al. (Göttingen: Vandenhoeck & Ruprecht, 1971–85)

Akten Kardinal Michael von Faulhabers, Vol. 1, 1917–1934, ed. L. Volk (Mainz: Matthias-Grünewald Verlag, 1975)

Akten der Reichskanzlei: Regierung Hitler 1933–1938, Part 1, Vol. 1, ed. K.-H. Minuth (Boppard am Rhein: Boldt, 1983)

Baron Aloisi, *Journal (25 juillet 1932–14 juin 1936)* (Paris: Plon, 1957)

L. Amery, *The Empire at Bay: The Leo Amery Diaries 1929–1945* (London: Hutchinson, 1988)

Anglo–Vatican Relations, 1914–1939: Confidential Annual Reports of the British Ministers to the Holy See, ed. T. Hachey (Boston, Mass.: G. K. Hall, 1972)

L'archivio della nunziatura apostolica in Italia 1, 1929–1939. Cenni storici e inventario, ed. G. Castaldo and G. Lo Bianco (Vatican City: Archivio Segreto Vaticano, 2010)

G. Berti, *I primi dieci anni di vita del PCI. Documenti inediti dell'archivio Angelo Tasca* (Milan: Feltrinelli, 1967)

R. Bruce Lockhart, *The Diaries of Sir Robert Bruce Lockhart*, Vol. 1, ed. K. Young (London: Macmillan, 1973)

M. Cachin, *Carnets 1906–1947*, ed. D. Peschanski, Vol. 3 (Paris: CNRS, 1998)

M. Casella, ed. *Gli ambasciatori d'Italia presso la Santa Sede dal 1929 al 1943* (Galatina (Lecce): Congedo, 2009)

H. Channon, *"Chips": The Diaries of Sir Henry Channon*, ed. R. Rhodes James (London: Weidenfeld and Nicolson, 1967)

Lord Chatfield, *It Might Happen Again*, Vol. 2 (London: Heinemann, 1947)

The Churchill Documents, Vol. 12, ed. M. Gilbert (London: Heinemann, 1981)

G. Ciano, *Diario 1937–1943*, ed. R. De Felice (Milan: Rizzoli, 1980)

G. Ciano, ed. *L'Europa verso la catastrofe. 184 colloqui con Mussolini, Hitler, Franco, Chamberlain, Sumner Welles, Rustu Aras, Stoiadinovic, Göring, Zog, François-Poncet, ecc. Verbalizzati da Galeazzo Ciano* (Milan: Mondadori, 1948)

J. Colville, *The Fringes of Power: 10 Downing Street Diaries, 1939–1955* (New York: Norton, 1985)

Command 2895 (London: HMSO, 1927)

E. Corradini, *Il nazionalismo italiano* (Milan: Treves, 1914)

N. Crowson, ed., *Fleet Street, Press Barons and Politics. The Journals of Collin Brooks, 1932–1940* (Cambridge: Cambridge University Press, 1998)

H. Dalton, *The Political Diary of Hugh Dalton 1918–40, 1945–60*, ed. B. Pimlott (London: Jonathan Cape, 1986)

"Delo Zorge". Telegrammy i pis'ma (1930–1945), ed. A. Fesyun (Moscow: Serebrannye niti, 2018)

"Depese mezi Prahou a Moskvou 1939–1945", ed. G. Bareš, *Příspěvky k dějinám KSČ*, No. 7, 1967

Deutscher Oktober 1923. Ein Revolutsionsplan un sein Scheitern, ed. B. Bayerlein et al. (Berlin: Aufbau, 2003)

Deutschland, Russland, Komintern. Dokumente 1918–1945, Vol. 1, ed. H. Weber et al. (Berlin: De Gruyter, 2014)

The Diaries of Chips Channon, Vol. 1: *1918–38*, ed. S. Heffer (London: Hutchinson, 2020)

The Diaries of Sir Alexander Cadogan, O.M., 1938–1945, ed. D. Dilks (London: Cassell, 1971)

G. Dimitrov, *The Diary of Georgi Dimitrov, 1933–1939*, ed. I. Banac (New Haven: Yale University Press, 2003)

Diplomates en guerre. La Seconde Guerre mondiale racontée à travers les archives du Quai d'Orsay, ed. P.-J. Rémy (Paris: JC Lattès, 2007)

I documenti diplomatici italiani, 7th Series, ed. R. Moscato and G. Carocci, Vols 3, 4, 10, 12 and 14; 8th Series, ed. R. De Felice et al., Vols 4, 8 and 9; 9th Series, ed. M. Toscano et al., Vols 5 and 6 (Rome: Istituto Poligrafico dello Stato, 1959–2001)

Documents diplomatiques français, 1932–1939, 1st Series, Vols 1 and 2, ed. P. Renouvin et al. (Paris: Imprimerie Nationale, 1964); 2nd Series, Vol. 3, ed. P. Mandoul et al. (Brussels: PIE–Peter Lang, 2005)

Documents diplomatiques suisses, 1848–1945, Vols 8, ed. A Fleury et al.; 10 and 11, ed. J.-C. Favez et al.; 12, ed O. Gauye et al. (Bern: Benteli, 1982–94)

Documents on British Foreign Policy 1919–1939, 1st Series, ed. W. Medlicott et al., Vol. 25; 2nd Series, ed. L. Woodward et al., Vols 6, 10, 12, 15, 17, 19 and 21 (London: HMSO, 1957–84)

Documents on Irish Foreign Policy, Vol. 4, ed. C. Crowe et al. (Dublin: Royal Irish Academy, 2004)

Dokumenty i materialy po istorii Sovetsko–Chekhoslovatskikh otnoshenii, Vol. 3, ed. C. Amort et al. (Moscow: Nauka, 1978)*Dokumenty vneshnei politiki*, Vol. 23, Books 1 and 2, ed. G. Mamedov et al. (Moscow: Mezhdunarodnye otnosheniya, 1995–98)

Dokumenty vneshnei politiki

Dokumenty vneshnei politiki 1939 god, ed. V. Komplektov et al. (Moscow: Mezhdunarodnye Otnosheniya, 1992)

Dokumenty vneshnei politiki SSSR, Vols 6 and 7, ed. A Gromyko et al. (Moscow: Politizdat, 1962); Vol. 14, ed. P. Ershov et al. (Moscow: Politicheskaya Literatura, 1968); Vol. 18, ed. A. Gromyko et al. (Moscow: Politizdat, 1973); Vol. 19, ed. A. Gromyko et al. (Moscow: Politizdat, 1974)

Federal'noe arkhivnoe agentstvo, Arkhiv vneshnei politiki Rossii (AVPRF), *Nakanune i posle Myunkhena, arkhivnye dokumenty rasskazyvayut. "Pered litsom germanskoi ekspansii: ustupki ili voina (mart–avgust 1938)"*

Federal'noe arkhivnoe agentstvo, Arkhiv vneshnei politiki Rossii (AVPRF), "Sentyabr'skii krizis in Myunkhenskaya Konferentsiya chetyrekh derzhav (sentyabr' 1938)"

Federal'noe arkhivnoe agentstvo, Rossiiskii gosudarstvennyi voennyi arkhiv (RGVA), *1939 god. Ot 'umirotvoreniya' k voine.*

For the President. Personal and Secret: Correspondence between Franklin D. Roosevelt and William C. Bullitt, ed. O. Bullitt (London: André Deutsch, 1973)

Foreign Relations of the United States: Diplomatic Papers, 1944, China, Vol. 6, ed. E. R. Perkins et al. (Washington DC: US GPO., 1967)

Glazami razvedki SSSR i Evropa 1919–1938 gody: sbornik dokumentov iz rossiiskikh arkhivov, ed. M. Ul' et al. (Moscow: IstLit, 2015)

God krizisa: 1938–1939, Vol. 1, ed. A. Bondarenko et al. (Moscow: Politicheskaya Literatura, 1990)

S. Gorlov, *Sovershenno Sekretno. Moskva Berlin 1920–1933. Voenno-politischeskie Otnosheniya Mezhdu SSSR i Germaniei* (Moscow: IVI RAN, 1999)

Gouvernement général de l'Indochine, *Contribution à l'histoire des mouvements politiques de l'Indochine française. Documents*, Vol. 5: *La Terreur rouge en Annam, 1930–1931* (Hanoi: GGI, Direction des affaires politiques et de la Sûreté Génerale, 1933)

Hansard. House of Lords, House of Commons. Debates

O. Harvey, *Diplomatic Diaries of Oliver Harvey, 1937–1940*, ed. J. Harvey (London: Collins, 1970)

A. Hitler, *Mein Kampf. Eine kritische Edition*, ed. C. Hartmann, T. Vordermayer, O. O. Plöckinger and R. Toppel (Munich and Berlin: Instituts für Zeitgeschichte, 2016)

N. Hooker, ed., *The Moffat Papers* (Cambridge, Mass.: Harvard University Press, 1956)

T. Jones, *A Diary with Letters 1931–1950* (London: Oxford University Press, 1954)

K 70-letiyu Sovetsko–Finlyandskoi Voiny. Zimnaya Voina 1939–1940 gg. V rassekrechenny dokumentakh Tsentral'nogo Arkhiva FSB Rossii i arkhivov Finlyandii, ed. A. Sakharov et al. (Moscow: Akademkniga, 2009)

KGB, "O podgotovke Germanii k napadeniyu na SSSR", *Izvestiya TsK KPSS*, No. 4 (303), April 1990

A. Kollontai, *Diplomaticheskie dnevniki 1922–1940*, Vol. 2 (Moscow: Akademia, 2001)

Komintern i ideya mirovoi revolyutsii. Dokumenty, ed. K. Anderson et al. (Moscow: Nauka, 1998)

Komintern i vtoraya mirovaya voina, Vols 1–2, ed. N. Lebedeva and M. Narinskii (Moscow: Pamyatniki istoricheskoi mysli, 1994)

Komintern protiv fashizma: dokumenty, ed. V. Dam'e (Moscow: Nauka, 1999)

V. Lenin, *Collected Works*, Vol. 31 (Moscow: Progress, 1966)

V. Lenin, *Pol'noe sobranie sochinenii*, Vols 23 and 42 (Moscow: Gosizdat, 1963)

G. Liddell, *The Guy Liddell Diaries*, ed. Nigel West (London: Routledge, 2005)

I. Maisky, *Dnevnik diplomata. London, 1934–1943*, Vols 1 and 2, ed. A. Chubaryan et al. (Moscow: Nauka, 2006–9)

"Maurice Thorez: notes inédites, novembre 1939. Documents communistes (mai 1939–novembre 1941)", *Cahiers d'Institut Marxiste de la Recherche*, No. 14, 1983

"Minutes of the Soviet Estonian Negotiations for a Military Assistance Pact of 1939", *Lituanus*, Vol. 14, No 2, 1968

Na Prieme u Stalina. Tetradi (zhurnaly) zapisei lits, prinyatykh I. V. Stalinym (1924–1953 gg.), ed. A. Chernobaev et al. (Moscow: Novyi khronograf, 2008)

H. Nicolson. *The Harold Nicolson Diaries and Letters 1907–1964*, ed. N. Nicolson (London: Weidenfeld and Nicolson, 2004)

Nunzio in una terra di frontiera. Achille Ratti, poi Pio XI, in Polonia (1918–1921), ed. P. Bortolato and M. Lenart (Vatican City: Pontificio Comitato di Scienze Storiche, 2017)

Papers Relating to the Foreign Relations of the United States, 1922, Vol. 2, ed. J. Fuller (Washington DC: US GPO, 1938)

La partecipazione italiana alla guerra civile spagnola (1936–1939), Vols 1 and 2, *Documenti e allegati*, ed. A. Rovighi and F. Stefani (Rome: Stato Maggiore dell'Escercito, Ufficio storico, 1992–93)

Peace and War. United States Foreign Policy 1931–1941 (Washington DC: US GPO, 1943)

Perepiska I. V. Stalina i G. V. Chicherina s Polpredom SSSR v Kitae L. M. Karakhanom. Dokumenty, avgust 1923 g.–1926 g., ed. M. Titarenko et al. (Moscow: Natalis, 2008)

Politburo TsK RKP(b)–VKP(b) i Evropa. Resheniya "Osoboi papki" 1923–1929, ed. G. M. Adibekov et al. (Moscow: Rosspen, 2001)

Politburo TsK RKP(b)–VKP(b) i Komintern, 1919–1943. Dokumenty, ed. G. M. Adibekov et al. (Moscow: Rosspen, 2004)

The Political Diary of Alfred Rosenberg and the Onset of the Holocaust, ed. J. Matthäus and F. Bajohr (Lanham, Md.: Rowman and Littlefield, 2015)

Polskie Dokumenty Dyplomatyczne 1936, ed. S. Żerko (Warsaw: PISM, 2011)

Polskie Dokumenty Dyplomatyczne 1938, ed. M. Kornat (Warsaw: PISM, 2007)

Polskie Dokumenty Dyplomatyczne 1939, ed. S. Żerko (Warsaw: PISM, 2005)

Profsoyuzy SSSR: Dokumenty i materialy, Vol. 2, ed. N. Antropov (Moscow: Profizdat, 1963)

A. Ransome, *Russia in 1919* (New York: Huebsch, 1919)

J. Reith, *The Reith Diaries*, ed. C. Stuart (London: Collins, 1975)

The Romanian–Latvian Relations [*sic*]. *Diplomatic Documents (1918–1958)*, ed. S. Miloiu et al. (Târgoviște: Cetatea de Scaun, 2012)

C. Rosselli, *Oggi in Spagna, domani in Italia* (Paris: Edizioni di Giustizia e Libertà, 1938)

La II Républica y la Guerra Civil en el Archivo Secreto Vaticano: Vol. 3: *Documentos de los años 1933 y 1934*; Vol. 4: *Documentos de los años 1935 y 1936*, ed. V. Cárcel Ortí (Madrid: Biblioteca de Autores Cristianos, 2014–16)

Sekrety Pol'skoi Politiki 1935–1945 gg. Rassekrechennye dokumenty sluzhby vneshnei razvedki Rossiiskoi Federatsii, ed. L. Sotskov (Moscow: Ripol, 2010)

G. Sorel, *"Da Proudhon à Lenin" e "L'Europa sotto la tormenta"*, ed. G. De Rosa (Rome: Edizioni di Storia e Letteratura, 1973)

Sovetskoe rukovodstvo. Perepiska 1928–1941, ed. A. Kvashonkin et al. (Moscow: Rosspen, 1999)

SSSR–Germaniya 1932–1941, ed. S. Kudriyashov (Moscow: IstLit, 2019)

SSSR i grazhdanskaya voina v Ispanii: 1926–1939 gody, ed. S. Kudryashov et al. (Moscow: Vestnik Arkhiva Prezidenta Rossiiskoi Federatsii, 2013)

SSSR i Litva v gody vtoroi mirovoi voiny, Vol. 1: *SSSR i Litovskaya respublika (mart 1939–avgust 1940 gg.): Sbornik dokumentov*, ed. A. Kaspavaričius et al. (Vilnius, Leidykla, 2006)

The Stalin–Kaganovich Correspondence 1931–36, ed. R. Davies et al. (New Haven: Yale University Press, 2003)

Stalin's Letters to Molotov 1925–1936, ed. L. Lih et al. (New Haven: Yale University Press, 1995)

Stenogrammy zasedanii Politbuto TsK RKP(b)–VKP(b), 1923–1938, Vol. 3, ed. K. Anderson et al. (Moscow: Rosspen, 2007)

Die Tagebücher von Joseph Goebbels, Part 1, ed. E. Fröhlich (Munich: Saur, 1998–2005)

Tainy i uroki zimnei voiny 1939–1940. Po dokumentam rassekrechennykh arkhivov, ed. N. Volkovskii et al. (St Petersburg: Poligon, 2000)

L. Trotsky, *Arkhiv Trotskogo. Kommunisticheskaya Oppozitsiya v SSSR, 1923–1927*, Vol. 2, (Moscow: Terra, 1990)

United States. *Congressional Record*, 66th Congress, 3rd Session, Vol. 63.

P. Valéry, "Letters from France", *The Athenaeum*, 11 April 1919

VKP(b), Komintern i Kitai. Dokumenty, Vol. 3, ed. M. Titarenko et al. (Moscow: AO "Buklet", 1999)

VKP(b), Komintern i natsional'no-revolyutsionnoe dvizhenie v Kitae. Dokumenty. Vol. 1, Vol. 2, Vol. 3, ed. M. Titarenko et al. (Moscow: AO "Buklet", 1994–1999)

VKP(b), Komintern i Yaponiya. 1917–1941, ed. G. Adibekov and K. Vada (Moscow: Rosspen, 2001)

L. Volk, *Das Reichskonkordat vom 20 Juli 1933. Von den Ansätzen in des Weimarer Republik bis zu Ratifizierung am 10. September 1933* (Mainz: Matthias-Grünewald Verlag, 1972)

Vooruzhennyi konflikt v raione reki Khalkhin-Gol. Mai-sentyabr' 1939 g. Dokumenty i materialy, ed. A. Efimenko et al. (Moscow: Novalis, 2014)

Die Weltpartei aus Moskau. Der Gründungskongress der Kommunistischen Internationale 1919. Protokoll und neue Dokumente, ed. W. Hedeler and A. Vatlin (Berlin: Akademie Verlag, 2008)

Writings of Leon Trotsky 1933–34 (New York: Pathfinder, 1975)

E. Xammar, *El huevo de la serpiente. Crónicas de Alemania (1922–1924)* (Barcelona: Acantilado, 2005)

Die II. Internationale 1918/1919. Protokolle, Memoranden, Berichte und Korrespondenzen, ed. G. Ritter (Berlin: Dietz, 1980) Vol. 1

Periodicals

Acta Historica Tallinnensia
Analecta sacra tarraconensia
The Athenaeum
Byulleten' Oppozitsii
Cahiers de l'Institut Maurice Thorez
Cahiers d'histoire de l'Institut de recherches marxistes
Cahiers du Bolchévisme
Collier's Weekly
Commercial and Financial Chronicle
Communisme
Corriere Diplomatico e Consolare
Daily Worker
Diplomatic History
The Economist
Encounter
The English Historical Review
Financial Times
Hispania Sacra
The Historical Journal
History Today
l'Humanité
Intelligence and National Security
International Press Correspondence (Inprecorr)
Istoricheskii arkhiv
Izvestiya
Izvestiya TsK KPSS
Journal of Contemporary History
Kommunisticheskii Internatsional
Leningradskaya pravda
Lituanus
Mirovoe khozyaistvo i mirovaya politika
Morning Post
The Naval Review

New York Herald Tribune
New York Times
Nezavisimoe voennoe obozrenie
Polen und wir
Il Popolo d'Italia
Le Populaire
Pravda
Príspěvky k dějinám KSČ
Problemy dal'nego vostoka
Review of International Studies
La révolution espagnole
La Révolution prolétarienne
Rivista di Studi Politici Internazionali
Römische Historische Mitteilungen
Die Rote Fahne
Rundschau über Politik, Wirtschaft und Arbeiterbewegung
Scandia
Sotsialisticheskii vestnik
Le Temps
The Times
Twentieth Century British History
La Victoire
Vierteljahrshefte für Zeitgeschichte
La Voix du peuple
Voprosy Istorii
VO SAN (The proletarian)
The Wall Street Journal
Western Daily Press

Memoirs and Personal Reflections

(The items listed here include what look as though they should properly be located under 'Secondary Works' but are in fact almost entirely the product of reminiscences—Borkenau, Carr, Fischer, Thomas, etc.)

J. Beck, *Dernier rapport* (Neuchâtel: La Baconnière, 1951)

V. Berezhkov, *S diplomaticheskoi missiei v Berline 1940–1941* (Moscow: Novosti, 1966)

S. Bialer, ed., *Stalin and his Generals* (New York: Pegasus, 1969)

C. Bohlen, *Witness to History 1929–1969* (New York: Norton, 1973)

G. Bonnet, *Défense de la paix* (Geneva: Cheval Ailé, 1946)

F. Borkenau, *World Communism: A History of the Communist International* (Ann Arbor: University of Michigan Press, 1962)

E. Carr, *International Relations since the Peace Treaties* (London: Macmillan, 1940)

G. Cerreti, *Con Togliatti e Thorez. Quarant'anni di lotte politiche* (Milan: Feltrinelli, 1973)

C. Channon, *The Diaries of Chips Channon*, Vol. 1: 1918–1938, ed. S. Heffer (London: Hutchinson, 2020)

F. Chuyev, ed., *Molotov. Poluderzhavnyi vlastelin*, (Moscow: Olma-press, 2000)

W. Citrine, *Men and Work* (London: Hutchinson, 1964)

F. Dahlem, *Am Vorabend des Zweites Weltkrieges 1938 bis August 1939. Erinnerungen*, Vol. 2 (Berlin: Dietz, 1977)

J. Davies, *Mission to Moscow* (London: Gollancz, 1942)

L. Fischer, *Men and Politics: An Autobiography* (London: Jonathan Cape, 1941)

L. Fischer, *The Road to Yalta: Soviet Foreign Relations 1941–1945* (New York: Harper and Row, 1972)

J. Gil Robles, *No fue posible la paz* (Barcelona: Ediciones Ariel, 1968)

F. Gilbert, *A European Past: Memoirs 1905–1945* (New York: W. W. Norton, 1988)

G. Hägglöf, *Diplomat* (London: The Bodley Head, 1972)

H. von Herwarth, *Against Two Evils* (New York: Rawson, Wade, 1981)

H. Hoover, *The Memoirs of Herbert Hoover, Vol. 2: The Cabinet and the Presidency 1920–1933* (New York: Macmillan, 1952)

D. Livingstone, *Missionary Travels and Researches in South Africa, including a sketch of sixteen years residence in the interior of Africa* (London: John Murray, 1857)

L. Longo, *L'attività degli addetti militari italiani all'estero fra le due guerre mondiali (1919–1939)* (Rome: Stato Maggiore dell'Esercito, Ufficio storico, 1999)

L. Longo and C. Salinari, *Dal socialfascismo alla guerra di Spagna. Ricordi e riflessioni di un militante comunista* (Milan: Teti, 1976)

I. McDonald, *The History of "The Times"*, Vol. 5 (London: Times Books, 1984)

J. Margach, *The Abuse of Power* (London: W. H. Allen, 1978)

The Memoirs of Lord Gladwyn (London: Weidenfeld and Nicolson, 1972)

M. Montagnana, *Ricordi di un operaio torinese* (Rome: Rinascita, 1949)

H. Nicolson, *Curzon: The Last Phase. A Study in Post-War Diplomacy* (London: Constable, 1934)

L. Noël, *Polonia Restituta. La Pologne entre deux mondes* (Paris: La Sorbonne, 1984)

J. Paasikivi, *President J. K. Passikivis Minnen*, Vol. 1: 1939–1940. Moskva och Finland (Stockholm: Bonnier, 1958)

A. Rowse, *Appeasement: A Study in Political Decline 1933–1939* (New York: Norton, 1963)

K. Simonov, *Glazami cheloveka moego pokoleniya* (Moscow: Pravda, 1990)

M. Smirtyukov, "Do 90 let on ezdil v polikliniku na elektrichke", *Kommersant vlast'*, 21 March 2000

E. Snow, *Red Star Over China*, revised and enlarged edition (London: Pelican, 1972)

M. Tagüeña Lacorte, *Testimonio de dos guerras* (Barcelona: Planeta, 1978)

G. Thomas, *Geschichte der deutschen Wehr- und Rüstungswirtschaft (1918–1943/45)*, ed. W. Birkenfeld (Boppard am Rhein: Boldt, 1966)

C. Woodhouse, *Something Ventured* (London: Granada, 1982)

W. Yen, *An Autobiography* (Shanghai, 1946). Republished by St John's University Press of New York in 1974

Ypsilon [nom de plume], *Pattern for World Revolution* (Chicago and New York: Ziff-Davis, 1947)

G. Zhukov, *Vospominaniya i razmyshleniya* (Moscow: Novosti, 1990)

Secondary Works

G. Adibekov et al. *Organizatsionnaya struktura Kominterna 1919–1943* (Moscow: Rosspen, 1997).

Ah Xiang, "Communists and the Japanese invasion of Manchuria": http://republicanchina.org /COMMUNISTS-AND-JAPAN-INVASION-MANCHURIApdf

P. Alatri, "La Fiat dal 1921 al 1926", *Belfagor*, Vol. 29, No. 3, 31 May 1974

M. Alekseev, *Sovetskaya voennaya razvedka v Kitae i khronika "kitaiskoi smuty" (1922–1928)* (Moscow: Kuchkovo pole, 2010)

M. Alekseev, *"Vernyi Vam Ramzai". Rikhard Zorge i sovetskaya voennaya razvedka v Yaponii. 1933–1938 gody* (Moscow: Algoritm, 2017)

M. Álvarez Tardío and R. Villa García, "El impacto de la violencia en la primavera de 1936 y la respuesta de las autoridades", *Hispania Sacra*, Vol. 65, No. 132, July–December 2013

K. Arrow, "Risk Perception in Psychology and Economics", Technical Report No. 351, October 1981. A Report of the Center for Research on Organizational Efficiency, Stanford University

C. Audry, *Léon Blum, ou la politique du Juste* (Paris: Julliard, 1955)

G. Bennett, *The Zinoviev Letter: The Conspiracy That Never Dies.* (Oxford: Oxford University Press, 2018)

P. Bernhard, "Der Beginn eine Faschistischen Interpol? Das deutsch-italienische Polizeiabkommen von 1936 und die Zusammenarbeit der faschistischen Diktaturen im Europa der Zwischenkriegzeit". *Themenportal Europäische Geschichte. Clio-online*, January 2010, https:// www.europa.clio-online.de/essay/id/fdae-1535

L. Bezymensky, *Chelovek za spinoi Gitlera: Martin Bormann i ego dnevnik* (Moscow: Veche, 1999)

E. Bloch, "My Patient, Hitler", *Collier's Weekly*, 15 and 22 March 1941

V. Bogdanor, Review of *The Triumph of the Dark*, *New Statesman*, 18 November 2010

A. Bondarenko, *Fitin* (Moscow: Molodaya Gvardiya, 2015)

H. Boog et al., eds, *Germany and the Second World War*, Vol. 4 (Oxford: Oxford University Press, 1998)

Q. Bortolato and M. Lenart, eds, *Nunzio in una terra di frontiera: Achille Ratti, poi Pio XI, in Polonia* (Vatican City: Pontificio Comitato di Scienze Storiche, 2017)

V. Bovykin, *Frantsuzskie banki v Rossii: konets XIX–nachalo XX v* (Moscow: Rosspen, 1999)

C. Bresciani-Turroni, *Le vicende del marco tedesco*, = *Annali di Economia*, Vol. 7, 1931. Translated into English as *The Economics of Inflation. A Study of Currency Depreciation in Post-War Germany* (London: John Dickens, 1937)

E. Carr, *Twenty Years' Crisis 1919–1939. An Introduction to the Study of International Relations* (London: Macmillan, 1939)

E. Carr, *International Relations between the Two World Wars (1919–1939)* (London: Macmillan, 1947)

E. Carr, *German–Soviet Relations between the Two World Wars, 1919–1939* (Baltimore: The Johns Hopkins University Press, 1951)

E. Carr, *The Bolshevik Revolution 1917–1923*, Vol. 3 (London: Macmillan, 1953)

E. Carr, *A History of Soviet Russia*, Vol. 3: *Socialism in One Country 1924–1926*, (London: Macmillan, 1964)

E. Carr, *A History of Soviet Russia*, Vol. 2: *The Interregnum 1923–1924* (London: Pelican, 1969)

E. Carr, *The October Revolution: Before and After* (New York: Vintage, 1971)

E. Carr, *Twilight of Comintern, 1930–1935* (London: Macmillan, 1982)

E. Carr, *From Napoleon to Stalin and Other Essays*, 2nd edition (London: Macmillan, 2003)

J. Carswell, *The Exile. A Life of Ivy Litvinov* (London: Faber and Faber, 1983)

Central Committee, Japanese Communist Party, *Sixty-Year History of the Japanese Communist Party, 1922–1982* (Tokyo: Japan Press Service, 1984)

P. Coble, *The Shanghai Capitalists and the National Government, 1927–1937* (Cambridge, Mass.: Harvard University Council on East Asian Studies, 1980)

R. Cockett, *Twilight of Truth. Chamberlain, Appeasement and the Manipulation of the Press* (London: Weidenfeld and Nicolson, 1989)

R. Cockett, "Ball, Chamberlain and Truth", *The Historical Journal*, Vol. 33, No. 1, March 1990

D. Collins, *A Charmed Life: The Phenomenal World of Philip Sassoon* (London: William Collins, 2016)

I. Colvin, *The Chamberlain Cabinet* (London: Gollancz, 1971)

Công-Nhân, "Comment conquérir les masses?", *VO SAN* (The proletarian), No. 1, Paris, 31 August 1930

"Conversations with Molotov", *Lituanus*, Vol. 12, No. 2, 1965

M. Cowling, *The Impact of Hitler: British Politics and British Policy 1933–1940* (Cambridge: Cambridge University Press, 1975)

R. De Felice, *Mussolini il fascista. 1. La conquista del potere 1921–1925* (Turin: Einaudi, 1966)

R. De Felice, *Mussolini il duce. 1. Gli anni del consenso 1929–1936* (Turin: Einaudi, 1974)

R. De Felice, *Mussolini il duce. 2. Lo Stato totalitario 1936–1940* (Turin: Einaudi, 1981)

J. Duclos, "Réponses aux questions posés par les journalistes, à la Mutualité", *Cahiers du Bolchévisme*, Nos 8–9, 15 May 1936

J. Duclos, "À la mémoire de mon ami Clément", *Cahiers de l'Institut Maurice Thorez*, No. 13, 1969

J.-B. Duroselle, *La Décadence 1932–1939* (Paris: Imprimérie national, 1979)

J.-B. Duroselle, *L'Abîme, 1939–1945* (Paris: Imprimérie national, 1982)

D. Dutton, "Simon and Eden at the Foreign Office 1931–1935", *Review of International Studies*, Vol. 20, No 1, January 1994

H. Dyck, *Weimar Germany and Soviet Russia* (London: Chatto and Windus, 1966)

S. Endicott, *Diplomacy and Enterprise: British China Policy 1933–1937* (Vancouver: University of British Columbia, 1975)

K. Feiling, *The Life of Neville Chamberlain* (London: Macmillan, 1946)

F. Firsov, *Sekretnye kody istorii Kominterna 1919–1943* (Moscow: AIRO-XXI, 2007)

E. Fischer, *An Opposing Man* (London: Allen Lane, 1974)

L. Fischer, *The Life and Death of Stalin* (New York: Harper, 1952)

L. Fischer, *The Road to Yalta: Soviet Foreign Relations 1941–1945* (New York: Harper and Row, 1972)

M. Franzinelli, *Fascismo Anno Zero. 1919: la nascita dei Fasci italiani di combattimento* (Milan: Mondadori, 1919)

S. Galois [nom de plume], "La vie et la grève des ouvrières métallos?", *La Révolution prolétarienne*, 10 June 1936

H. Gatzke, "Von Rapallo nach Berlin. Stresemann und Die Deutsche Russlandpolitik", *Viertel-jahrshefte für Zeitgeschichte*, No. 4, 1956

D. Gescher, *Die Vereinigten Staaten von Nordamerika und die Reparationen 1920–1924. Eine Un-tersuchung der Reparationsfrage auf der Grundlage Amerikanischer Akten* (Bonn: Röhrscheid, 1966)

N. Gibbs, *Grand Strategy*, Vol. 1 (London: HMSO, 1976)

M. Gilbert, *Winston S. Churchill*, Vol. 5: *Prophet of Truth, 1922–1939* (London: Heinemann, 1976)

M. Gilbert, "Horace Wilson: Man of Munich", *History Today*, Vol. 32, No. 10, 1982

M. Gilbert, *Winston S. Churchill*, Vol. 6: *Finest Hour, 1939–1941* (London: Heinemann, 1983)

M. Gilbert and R. Gott, *The Appeasers*, 2nd edition (London: Weidenfeld and Nicolson, 1967)

A. Gintsberg, "'Politsekretariat IKKI Trebuet': Dokumenty Kominterna i Kompartii Germanii. 1930–1934 gg.", *Istoricheskii arkhiv*, No. 1, 1994

J. Gittings, "Rules of the Game", *New York Review of Books*, 17 May 1973

S. Gorlov, *Sovershenno Sekretno. Moskva-Berlin 1920–1933. Voenno-politicheskie otnosheniya mezhdu SSSR i Germaniei* (Moscow: IVI RAN, 1999)

G. Gorodetsky, *Stafford Cripps' Mission to Moscow 1940–42* (Cambridge: Cambridge University Press, 1984)

R. Griffiths, *Fellow Travellers of the Right: British Enthusiasts for Nazi Germany 1933–39* (London: Constable, 1980)

M. Hàjek, *Storia dell'Interazionale Comunista (1921–1935). La politica del fronte unico* (Rome: Riuniti, 1975)

J. Haslam, "The Comintern and the Origins of the Popular Front 1934–35", *The Historical Journal*, Vol. 22, No. 3, 1979, pp. 673–691.

J. Haslam, *Soviet Foreign Policy, 1930–33: The Impact of the Depression* (London: Macmillan, 1983)

J. Haslam, *The Soviet Union and the Struggle for Collective Security in Europe, 1933–39* (London: Macmillan, 1984)

J. Haslam, "Political Opposition to Stalin and the Origins of the Terror in Russia 1932–36", *The Historical Journal*, Vol. 29, No. 2, 1986, pp. 395–418.

J. Haslam, *The Soviet Union and the Threat From the East, 1933–41* (London: Macmillan, 1992)

J. Haslam, "Stalin's Fears of a Separate Peace, 1942" *Intelligence and National Security*, Vol. 8, No. 4, October 1993

J. Haslam, *The Vices of Integrity: E. H. Carr, 1892–1982* (London and New York: Verso, 1999)

J. Haslam, *No Virtue Like Necessity: Realist Thought in International Relations Since Machiavelli* (New Haven and London: Yale University Press, 2002)

J. Haslam, "Comintern and Soviet Foreign Policy", *The Cambridge History of Russia*, Vol. 3, ed. R. Suny (Cambridge: Cambridge University Press, 2006)

J. Haslam, *Russia's Cold War: From the October Revolution to the Fall of the Wall* (New Haven: Yale University Press, 2011)

J. Haslam, *Near and Distant Neighbours: A New History of Soviet Intelligence* (Oxford: Oxford University Press, 2015)

J. Hernández Figureiredo, "Avances y estado del comunismo en vísperas de la guerra civil espa-ñola, según los informes inéditos del Archivo Secreto Vaticano", *Analecta sacra tarraconensia*, Vol. 83, 2010

F. Hinsley, *British Intelligence in the Second World War. Its Influence on Strategy and Operations*, Vol. 1 (London: HMSO, 1979)

F. Hinsley and C. Simkins, *British Intelligence in the Second World War*, Vol. 4 (London: HMSO, 1990)

The History of "The Times", Vol. 4, Part 2 (London: The Times, 1952)

The History of "The Times", Vol. 5: see McDonald, under Memoirs and Personal Reflections

E. Hobsbawm, *The Age of Extremes: A History of the World, 1914–1991* (New York: Vintage, 1996)

B. Hoppe, *In Stalins Gefolgschaft. Moskau und die KPD 1928–1933* (Munich: Oldenbourg, 2007)

M. Howard, *The Continental Commitment: The Dilemma of British Defence Policy in the Era of the Two World Wars* (London: Martin Temple Smith, 1972)

L. Hunt, *The New Cultural History* (Berkeley: University of California Press, 1989)

A.-A. Inquimbert, *Un officier français dans la guerre d'Espagne. Carrière et écrits d'Henri Morel* (Rennes: Press Universitaires de Rennes, 2009)

I. Ivanov, *Ocherki istorii Ministerstva inostrannykh del Rossii* (Moscow: Olma-press, 2002), Vol. 2

M. Jakobson, *Finland Survived. An Account of the Finnish–Soviet Winter War 1939–1940* (Helsinki: Otava, 1984)

M. Jansen and N. Petrov, *Stalin's Loyal Executioner: People's Commissar Nikolai Ezhov, 1895–1940* (Stanford: Hoover Institution Press, 2002)

K. Jeffery, *MI6. The History of the Secret Intelligence Service, 1909–1949* (London: Bloomsbury, 2010)

M. Kaser and E. Radice, eds, *The Economic History of Eastern Europe 1919–1975*, Vol. 2 (Oxford: Clarendon Press, 1986)

O. Ken, A. Rupasov and L. Samuel'son, *Shvetsiya v politike Moskvy 1930–1950-e gody* (Moscow: Rosspen, 2005)

I. Kershaw, *Making Friends with Hitler: Lord Londonderry and Britain's Road to War* (London: Allen Lane, 2004)

O. Khlevniuk, *Politburo. Mekhanizmy politicheskoi vlasti v 1930-e gody* (Moscow: Rosspen, 1996)

A. Khormach, *SSSR–Italiya, 1924–1939 gg. (Diplomaticheskie i ekonomicheskie otnosheniya)* (Moscow: Institute of Russian History, RAN, 1995)

D. Klieber, "Die moralische und politische Schützenhilfe des Hl. Stuhles für de Staatsumbau Österreichs 1933/34 im Lichte Vatikanischer Quellenbestände", *Römische Historische Mitteilungen*, Vol. 54, 2012

M. Knox, *Common Destiny: Dictatorship, Foreign Policy, and War in Fascist Italy and Nazi Germany* (Cambridge: Cambridge University Press, 2000)

V. Kondrashov, *Voennye razvedki vo Vtoroi Mirovoi Voine* (Moscow: Kuchkovo pole, 2014)

M. Kornat, "Ricordi di Pio XI sul Maresciallo Piłsudski alla luce dei documenti diplomatici polacchi" (in Bortolato and Lenart, eds, *Nunzio in una terra di frontiera*)

S. Kotkin, *Stalin. Waiting for Hitler 1929–1941* (New York: Penguin, 2017)

V. Krasnov, *Neizvestnyi Zhukov. Lavri i ternii polkovodtsa. Dokumenty, mneniya, razmyshleniya* (Moscow: Olma-press, 2000)

A. Lacroix-Riz, *Le Choix de la défaite. Les élites françaises dans les années 1930*, 2nd edition (Paris: Colin, 2010)

A. Lacroix-Riz, "Polen in der aussenpolitischen Strategie Frankreichs (Oktober 1938–August 1939)", *Polen und wir*, No. 3, 2014

B. Leibzon and K. Shirinya, *Povorot v politike Kominterna. Istoricheskoe znachenie VII kongressa Kominterna* (Moscow: Mysl', 1975)

V. Leongard, *Shok ot pakta mezhdu Gitlerom i Stalinym* (London: Overseas Publications Interchange, 1989). Originally published as W. Leonhard, *Der Schock des Hitler-Stalin-Paktes* (Freiburg im Breisgau: Herder, 1986)

G. Leto, *OVRA: fascismo—antifascismo* (Rocca San Casciano: Cappelli, 1952)

W. Link, *Die amerikanische Stabilisierungspolitik in Deutschland 1921–32* (Düsseldorf: Droste, 1970)

"Lithuania and the Soviet Union 1939–1940: The Fateful Year—Memoirs by Juozas Urbsys", *Lituanus*, Vol. 35, No. 2

D. Little, "Red Scare 1936: Anti-Bolshevism and the Origins of British Intervention in the Spanish Civil War", *Journal of Contemporary History*, Vol. 23, No. 2, April 1988

A. Mahouy, "Le conflit Citroën", *La Révolution prolétarienne*, 10 June 1936

A. Mayer, *The Politics and Diplomacy of Peacemaking. Containment and Counterrevolution at Versailles, 1918–1919* (New York: Knopf, 1967)

G. Megaro, *Mussolini in the Making* (London: Allen and Unwin, 1938)

Mi Zanchen, *The Life of General Yang Hucheng* (Hong Kong: Joint, 1981)

L. Michie, *Portrait of an Appeaser: Robert Hadow, First Secretary in the British Foreign Office, 1931–1939* (Westport, Conn: Praeger, 1996)

R. Mirowicz, "Edward Rydz-Śmigły: A Political and Military Biography", MS, trans. and ed. G. Dziekoński (c. 1974)

A. Misyuk, *Spetssluzhby Pol'shi, Sovetskoi Rossii i Germaniei. Organizatsionnaya struktura polskikh spetssluzhb i ikh razvedyvatel'naya kontrrazvedyvatel'naya deyatel'nost' v 1918–1939 godakh* (Moscow: Kraft, 2012)

T. Munch-Petersen, "'Common sense not bravado': the Butler–Prytz interview of 17 June 1940", *Scandia*, Vol. 52, No. 1, 1986

L. Namier, *Diplomatic Prelude, 1938–1939* (London: Macmillan, 1948)

K. Neilson, "Orme Sargent, Appeasement and British Policy in Europe, 1933–39", *Twentieth Century British History*, Vol. 21, No. 1, 2010.

M. Neltyukhov, *Krasnaya armiya i nesostoyavshayasya revolyutsiya v Germanii (1923 g.)* (Moscow: Airo-XXI, 2013)

P. Neville, "A Prophet Scorned? Ralph Wigram, the Foreign Office and the German Threat, 1933–36", *Journal of Contemporary History*, Vol. 40, No. 1, January 2005

H. Nicolson, *Curzon: The Last Phase 1919–1925. A Study in Post-War Diplomacy* (London: Constable, 1934)

G. Niedhart, *Grossbritannien und die Sowjetunion 1934–1939: Studien zur britischen Politik der Friedenssicherung zwischen den beiden Weltkriegen* (Munich: Fink, 1972)

V. Nikonov, *Molotov: Nashe delo pravoe*, Vol. 1 (Moscow: Molodaya Gvardiya, 2016)

I. Nish, *Japanese Foreign Policy 1869–1942: Kasumigaseki to Miyakezaka* (London: Routledge & Kegan Paul, 1977)

E. Nolte, *Der europäische Bürgerkrieg 1917–1945: Nationalsozialismus und Bolschewismus* (Berlin: Propyläen, 1987)

L. Olson, *Troublesome Young Men. The Rebels Who Brought Churchill to Power and Helped Save England* (New York: Farrar, Straus and Giroux, 2007)

G. Peden, "Sir Warren Fisher and British Rearmament against Germany", *The English Historical Review*, Vol. 94, No. 370, January 1979

S. Pelagalli, *Il generale Efisio Marras, addetto militare a Berlino (1936–1943)* (Rome: Stato Maggiore dell'Esercito, Ufficio storico, 1994)

V. Perna, *Galeazzo Ciano, operazione Polonia. Le relazione diplomatiche italo–polacche degli anni Trenta 1936–1939* (Milan: Lunk, 1999)

G. Petracchi, *La Russia rivoluzionaria nella politica italiana: le relazioni italo-sovietiche, 1917–25* (Rome and Bari: Laterza, 1982)

O. Plöckinger, ed., *Quellen und Dokumente zur Geschichte von "Mein Kampf" 1924–1945* (Stuttgart: Franz Steiner, 2016)

R. Plunkett-Ernle-Erle-Drax, "Mission to Moscow, August, 1939", *The Naval Review*, Vol. 40, No. 3, August 1952

N. Pospielov, "Les Conclusions du VIIe Congrès de l'Internationale Communiste. A la lumière de l'experience du Front Populaire en France et le rôle de Georges Dimitrov", *Cahiers de l'Institut Maurice Thorez*, 1966–67, Nos 3–4

G. Procacci, *Il socialismo internazionale e la guerra d'Etiopia* (Rome: Riuniti, 1978)

S. Quinn-Judge, *Ho Chi Minh: The Missing Years 1919–1941* (Berkeley: University of California Press, 2002)

R. Rainero, *L'Italie de Mussolini et le régime fasciste de Métaxas en Grèce (1936–1940)* (Paris: Publisud, 2014)

G. Rochat, *Militari e politici nella Preparazione della campagna d'Etiopia. Studio e documenti 1932–1936* (Milan: Angeli, 1971)

H. Rollin, "Sous le signe de la croix gammée", *Le Temps*, 6 June 1933

F. Rosas, ed., *Portugal e a Guerra Civil de Espanha* (Lisbon: Colibri, 1998)

A. Rovighi and F. Stefani, *La partecipazione italiana alla guerra civile spagnola (1936–1939)*, Vols 1 and 2 (Rome: Stato Maggiore dell'Esercito, Ufficio storico, 1992–93)

T. Ryback, *Hitler's Private Library. The Books that Shaped his Life* (London: Random House, 2010)

U. Salo, "Estimation of Security Threats and Estonian Defence Planning in the 1930s", *Acta Historica Tallinnensia*, Vol. 12, No. 1, 2008

L. Samuelson, *Plans for Stalin's War Machine* (London: Macmillan, 2000)

S. Schirmann, *Crise, coopération économique et financière entre États européens, 1929–1933* (Paris: Comité pour l'histoire économique et financière de la France, 2000)

V. Shamberg, *Lozovskii* (Moscow: Tonchu, 2012)

V. Shavrov, *Istoriya konstruktsii samoletov v SSSR 1938–1945gg. (Materialy k istorii samoletostroeniya)*, 3rd edition (Moscow: Mashinostroenie, 1994)

R. Shay, *British Rearmament in the Thirties: Politics and Profits* (Princeton: Princeton University Press, 1977)

Z. Sheinis, *Maksim Maksimovich Litvinov: Revolutsioner, Diplomat, Chelovek* (Moscow: Politizdat, 1989)

K. Shirinya, *Strategiya i taktika Kominterna v bor'be protiv fashizma i voiny (1934–1939 gg.)* (Moscow: Politizdat, 1979)

K. Smith, "Reassessing Roosevelt's View of Chamberlain after Munich: Ideological Affinity in the Geoffrey Thompson–Claud Bowers Correspondence", *Diplomatic History*, Vol. 33, No. 5, November 2009

G. Spadolini, *Il mondo di Giolitti* (Firenze: Le Monnier, 1970)

P. Spriano, *Storia del partito comunista italiano*, Vol. 1 (Turin: Einaudi, 1967)

C. Stannage, "The East Fulham By-Election, 25 October 1933", *The Historical Journal*, Vol. 14, No. 1, March 1971

Z. Steiner, *The Triumph of the Dark: European International History 1933–1939* (Oxford: Oxford University Press, 2011)

F. Stern, *The Politics of Cultural Despair: A Study in the Rise of the Germanic Ideology* (Berkeley: University of California Press, 1974)

J. Talmon, "The Legacy of Georges Sorel", *Encounter*, Vol. 34, No. 2, February 1970

N. Tarkhova, *Krasnaya armiya i stalinskaya kollektivizatsiya 1928–1933 gg.* (Moscow: Rosspen, 2010)

A. Taylor, *The Struggle for the Mastery of Europe, 1848–1918* (Oxford: Oxford University Press, 1954)

A. Taylor, *The Origins of the Second World War* (London: Hamish Hamilton, 1961)

A. Thimme, *Gustav Stresemann* (Frankfurt am Mein: Goedel, 1957)

K. Thomas, "The Tools and the Job", *Times Literary Supplement*, 7 April 1966

K. Thomas, "History Revisited", *The Times*, 11 October 2006

M. Thorez, "L'organisation du front unique de lutte", *Cahiers du Bolchévisme*, No. 18, 1 July 1934

C. Thorne, *The Approach of War 1938–39* (London: Macmillan, 1967)

C. Thorne, *The Limits of Foreign Policy: The West, the League and the Far Eastern Crisis of 1931–1933* (London: Hamish Hamilton, 1972)

L. Tikhvinskii, *Put' Kitaya k ob"edineniyu i nezavisimosti 1898–1949. Po materialami biografii Chzhou En'lai* (Moscow: 'Vostochnaya Literatura', RAN, 1996)

A. Tooze, *The Wages of Destruction: The Making and Breaking of the Nazi Economy* (London: Penguin, 2008)

V. Ullrich, *Hitler*, Vol. 1: *Ascent 1889–1939* (New York: Knopf, 2016)

K. Urbach, *Go-Betweens for Hitler* (Oxford: Oxford University Press, 2015)

T. de Vergottini, "Fulvio Suvich e la difesa dell'independenza austriaca", *Rivista di Studi Politici Internazionali*, Vol. 60, No. 2 (238), April–June 1993

G. Vidal, "L'institution militaire et la peur d'une insurrection communiste en 1936", *Communisme*, No. 69, 2002

G. Vidal, *La Grande Illusion? Le Parti communiste français et la Défense nationale à l'époque du Front populaire (1934–1939)* (Lyon: Presses Universitaires de Lyon, 2006)

G. Vidal, "L'affaire Fantômas (1932). Le contre-espionnage français et les prémices de la préparation à la guerre", *Vingtième Siècle. Revue d'Histoire*, No. 119, 2013/3, https://www.cairn.info/revue-vingtieme-siecle-revue-d-histoire-2013-3-page-3.htm

G. Vidal, *L'armée française et l'ennemi intérieur 1917–1939. Enjeux stratégique et culture politique* (Rennes: Universitaires de Rennes, 2015)

J. Vieth, "Joseph P. Kennedy: Ambassador to the Court of St. James's, 1938–1940" (Ohio State University, PhD dissertation, 1975)

R. Vivarelli, *Storia delle origini del fascismo*, Vol. 1 (Bologna: Il Mulino, 1991)

D. Volkogonov, *Triumf i tragediya. Politicheskii portret I. V. Stalina*, Vol. 2 (Moscow: Novosti, 1989)

D. Volkogonov, *Lenin: Life and Legacy* (London: HarperCollins, 1994)

G. Waterfield, *Professional Diplomat: Sir Percy Loraine of Kirkhale* (London: Butler and Tanner, 1973)

D. Watt, *How War Came: The Immediate Origins of the Second World War, 1938–1939* (London: Heinemann, 1989)

H. Weber, "Die deutsche kommunistische Emigration in Moskau", *Die Politische Meinung*, No. 443, October 2006

G. Weinberg, *The Foreign Policy of Hitler's Germany: Diplomatic Revolution in Europe, 1933–36* (Chicago: Chicago University Press, 1970)

T. Weingartner, *Stalin und der Aufstieg Hitlers* (Berlin: De Gruyter, 1970)

A. Werth, *Russia at War, 1941–1945* (London: Pan Books, 1964)

N. West, *Cold War Spymaster: The Legacy of Guy Liddell, Deputy Director of MI5* (London: Frontline Books, 2018)

J. Wheeler-Bennett, *The Nemesis of Power: The German Army in Politics 1918–1945* (London: Macmillan, 1953)

R. Wohl, *The Generation of 1914* (Cambridge, Mass.: Harvard University Press, 1979)

J. Wrench, *Geoffrey Dawson and Our Times* (London: Hutchinson, 1955)

N. Yakubovich, *Nasha aviatsiya v 1941 godu. Prichiny katastrofy* (Moscow: Yauza Eksmo, 2015)

Z. Zeman, *The Life of Edvard Beneš 1884–1948. Czechoslovakia in Peace and War* (Oxford: Clarendon Press, 1997)

A. Zhamaletdinova et al., *Zabastovochnaya bor'ba trudyaschikhsya konets XIXv.–70-e gody XXv. (Statistika)* (Moscow: Nauka, 1980)

P. Ziegler, *King Edward VIII. The Official Biography* (London: Collins, 1990)

INDEX

Abetz, Otto, 355

Abyssinia. *See* Ethiopia

Abyssinian war (1935), 167

Afghanistan, 16, 63

Agnelli, Giovanni, 42, 43

Alba (duke of), 265–66, 297–98

Alexander (king, Yugoslavia), 143

Alexandrovsky, 278, 292–93

Alfonso XIII (king, Spain), 206, 216, 275

Aloisi, Pompeo, 139, 170

American Relief Administration, 26

Amery, Leo, 173–74, 421n87; on Chamberlain, 259, 263–64, 294–97, 299, 310, 352; on *Kristallnacht*, 298; on League of Nations, 167; on Spain, 222–23

anarchists: in Catalonian militia, 215; Paris Commune orchestrated by, 16; in Soviet military intelligence, 240; in Spanish trade unions, 16, 215

Anglo–German Naval Agreement (1935), 158, 161

Anti-Comintern Pact (1936), 11

anti-Communism: of Catholic Church, 133–35; of Conservative Party, 264–65; Franco's, 216–20; Hitler's, 151; Mussolini's, 119. *See also* Bolshevism and Bolsheviks

anti-Semitism, 56–57, 59; in France, 203; in Germany, 128–29; in Italy, 172; of *Kristallnacht*, 297–98

Antonov-Ovseenko, Vladimir, 227

Arciszewski, Mirosław, 300–301

Arita Hachirō, 371

Artuzov, Artur, 234

Assarasson, Vilhelm, 342–43

Astakhov, 306, 314, 317, 319, 324

Attlee, Clement, 353

Attolico, Bernardo, 168

Austria, 161; fascism in, 182–84; German dominance over, 171–72; invaded by Germany, 275–76, 278–79

Azaña, Manuel, 209, 210, 212–13

Badoglio, Pietro, 166

Baldwin, Stanley, 65, 77, 160; on British alliance with Germany, 198; on *Front populaire*, 197; on German occupation of Rhineland, 173; replaced as prime minister by Chamberlain, 259; on sanctions against Italy, 165; on Spanish Civil War, 222, 266

Balfour, Arthur, 38

Ball, Joseph, 268, 269

Barnett, Charles, 318

Barrington-Ward, Robin, 276, 277, 325

Bartholdy, Albrecht Mendelssohn, 258

Barthou, Louis, 143, 149

Bauer, Otto, 182

Beck, József, 140, 142, 146–48, 302–3, 326

Belgium, 353

Beneš, Edvard, 278, 292–94, 296, 327

Bennett, Richard, 401n2

Berg, Pavel, 22

Berle, Adolf, 288

Berzin, Jan, 123

Bingham, Robert, 158

Bismarck (prince), 8

Bismarck, Otto von, 31